RENEWALS 458-4574

DATE DUE

MAY 18			
GAYLORD			PRINTED IN U.S.A.

D0962582

The Saudi Arabian Economy:
Policies, Achievements and Challenges

The Saudi Arabian Economy:
Policies, Achievements and Challenges

by

M. A. Ramady. Ph.D, FCIB

 Springer

Library of Congress Cataloging-in-Publication Data

Ramady, M.A. (Mohammed A.)
  The Saudi Arabian economy : policies, achievements and challenges / M.A. Ramady.
    p. cm.
  Includes bibliographical references and index.

  ISBN: 0-387-24833-1   eISBN: 0-387-24935-4
  ISBN: 13: 978-0387-24833-2   eISBN-13: 978-0387-24935-3

  1.   Saudi Arabia--Economic policy. 2. Saudi Arabia--Economic condition. I. Title.

HC415.33.R36   2005
330.9538—dc22   2005042507

Printed in the United States of America.

9 8 7 6 5 4 3   SPIN 1156754

springeronline.com

Dedicated to the memory of my
beloved parents and best teachers
Ali and Mahassen Ramady, to my
wife Fatina and to my children
Ali, Faisal and Layla with thanks
for their patience and support

Contents

KEY CHALLENGES

CONCLUSION

Acknowledgments

This book has been a long time in the making. It draws upon classroom notes from the course I teach on the Saudi Arabian economy at King Fahd University of Petroleum and Minerals (KFUPM), as well as on my experience working in Saudi Arabia and other Gulf countries in banking, finance and business. Some excellent books exist on the Saudi economy but the moment seemed right to bring out a current Saudi economy book, especially given the continuing world-wide interest in the Kingdom.

The characteristics of the Saudi economy have changed beyond recognition since the heady oil boom days of the early 1980s. This book attempts to bring the story forward, analyzing challenges and major issues facing the Kingdom in the modern period. We hope to provide a cohesive picture of what has taken place over the last three decades, and use it to help look forward into the new millennium. At the same time, the book emphasizes aspects of human and social development that have taken place in past periods, and looks at the accelerated pace of change in today's Saudi Arabia.

This helps to identify a unique "Saudi" model and identity on the economy. In this respect, this book differs from others written on the Kingdom, which have tended to examine the economy from the more limited perspective of available data and statistics. They have often neglected to delve deeper into aspects of Saudi human capital development. Saudi Arabia is fully aware that developing its human capital, both male and female, in order to achieve self-sustaining growth, is key to a more prosperous future.

The name Saudi Arabia conjures up different images to different people. These might range from a romantic idealism of the purity of desert life to a place of unchecked commercialization – with all that implies. The truth, as ever, lies somewhere in-between. Saudi society is still imbued with the dignity of traditional desert hospitality, warmth and a noble culture; at the same time, it is part of a fast-moving, consumer-orientated and impersonal world. Society will be truly the poorer if the former is eroded in the face of a relentless march to the latter.

My personal interest in Saudi Arabia goes back to the first "boom and slowdown" period of 1979-1986, when I worked as Vice President with Citibank as well as Assistant General Manager with Saudi American Bank in Jeddah and Riyadh. Some of the material explored in this book, especially concerning the financial and banking sectors, has been augmented by personal experiences, and the direction of research was stimulated and sustained over the past 25 years by a continued interest in the welfare of the people of Saudi Arabia.

The Kingdom, despite its fluctuating fortunes, still attracts an enormous amount of interest worldwide. The Riyadh bombings of May, 2003, and the domestic terrorism that followed propelled Saudi Arabia and its citizens into the limelight – reluctantly and for the wrong reasons. This forced an accelerated internal debate on economic and social reforms that had started prior to these events. This book will attempt to explain how the desert Kingdom's economic systems are opening up and evolving, faster than some would want, slower than others hope for, but evolving and changing, they are Saudi Arabia today is beginning to reflect some of the problems and strains of other developed nations, both in terms of structural adjustments of the economy and of meeting the aspirations of its largely young population. How it handles such issues will be of interest to others facing the same dilemmas, especially those in the Arab world, as well as to the wider international community of nations wishing to see the Arab region make economic, political and social progress.

The Kingdom has left an indelible mark on millions of expatriate workers as well as others who have passed through the country. It has been a good experience for the overwhelming majority. For those who were positively challenged, Saudi Arabia has provided an unique opportunity to assume greater responsibilities, manage mega-scale projects, make substantial financial savings, take bold initiatives, and, in so doing, enrich their professional lives. Few other countries could have afforded them such an encounter. For those experiences, especially the chance to contribute to the development of the current Saudi banking structure, I am grateful.

Any book benefits from the influence and support that others give to its author to help bring it into the public arena.

My grateful thanks go to my colleagues at KFUPM, including Their Excellencies the present and previous Rectors, Drs. Khaled Al Sultan and Abdulaziz Al Dukhhayil, for encouraging me on this book-writing project, and to Professors Mohamed Budair, Abdulaziz Al Swaiyan, Aref Al Ashban, Ibrahim Al Gahtani, Sulaiman Al Sakran, Mohammed Al Sahlawi, Musa Essayad, Zohair Yamani, Usamah Uthman, Mohammed Al O'Hali, Mobarak Al Ghamdi, Abraham Abraham, Fazal Sayyed, Mohsen Al Hijji, Yakubu Umar, Bassam Hamdan, Abdelwahab Al Gahtani, Khaled Al Zamil, and Mohammed Al Homoud. I appreciate their willingness to discuss issues affecting the Saudi economy and society at large and to be a valuable sounding board for ideas, even when we disagreed.

My thanks also go to my many KFUPM undergraduate and postgraduate students of the Econ 306, Econ 305, MBA 501, and Executive MBA 561 classes, for encouraging me on this path and for sharing their thoughts on the aspirations of Saudi youth. In particular, the following students are to be commended for their perceptive class contributions: Mohammed Al Saleh, Nayef Saleh Al Hamdan, Yasser Al Jeraisy, Fahd Khaled Al Saud, Wael Al Gudaihi, Emad Nashar, Ali Al Gafeli, Yousef Al Humaid, Ibrahim Al Nuaim, Mishari Al Assaf, Mohammed Al Aiban, Bader Al Bassam, Mohamed Al Yemni, Bader Al Rajhi, Majed Al Anqari, Ahmad and Akram Sab, Fahad Al Tuwaijri, Turki Al Jammaz, Turki Abdulrahman Al Saud, Ahmad Dawood, Faisal Al Al Sheikh, Mishal Al Huwaish, Alaa Dahlawi, Bader Al Nowaiser, Fawaz Al Jomaih, Sultan Al Sultan, Mohamed Al Bawardi, Saad Al Kroud,Fahd Sulaim Al Zamil, Khaled Bin Abdelrahman Al Faisal Al Saud, Khaled Rubaian, Fawaz Al Tuwaijri, Abdullah Al Ghamdi ,Omar Sulaiman and Mohamed Bin Turki Al Saud. Students such as these inspire confidence in the ability of the Kingdom to meet the challenges of the future.

Over the years I have benefited from various practitioners and experts about the Kingdom and the region in general, and my appreciation is due to Kevin Muehring, John Milne, Michael Field, Sass Ghassanpour, Noel Brehony, Ed O'Sullivan, Guy Gantley, L F T (Tim) Smith, Richard Keck, John Botts, Richard Murphy, Gavin Shreeve, and to many others – too numerous to mention – for their genuine concern about the region, their insightful comments and their sharp wit.

A special word of thanks goes to the Dean of Library Affairs, and to his tireless staff, for meeting my many reference requests. Last, but by no means least, thanks are due to the dedicated efforts of the secretarial and technical staff, Junaid Akhtar and Totty Raborar, and to Sue Katz for the editing. Any shortcomings in the book are entirely my responsibility.

Finally, I would like to acknowledge the financial support provided by KFUPM under Project No. IM/SAUDI ECONOMY/281.

Dr. M.A. Ramady, FCIB
Department of Finance and Economics
King Fahd University of Petroleum and Minerals,

Abbreviations

ACH	Automated Clearing House
AMF	Arab Monetary Fund
Bear market	falling market prices
BIS	Bank for International Settlement, Basle, Switzerland
BOO	Build Operate Own
BOT	Build Operate Transfer
BOOT	Build Operate Own Transfer
Bull market	Rising market prices
CDS	Central Department of Statistics
ceteris paribus	Assuming everything else is equal
CPO	Central Planning Organization
CRR	Cash Reserve Ratio
CSCCI	Council of Saudi Chambers of Commerce and Industry
Downstream	processing of gas and oil for final product delivery
Emir	Ruler
EPCCI	Eastern Province Chamber of Commerce and Industry
ESIS	Electronic Share Information System
EU	European Union
FATF	Financial Action Task Force
Fed (The)	Federal Reserve Bank, USA
FRN's	Floating Rate Notes
GAFTA	Greater Arab Free Trade Area
GCC	Gulf Co-operation Council
GDB's	Government Development Bonds
GDP	Gross Domestic Product
GFCF	Gross Fixed Capital Formation
GNP	Gross National Product
GOSI	General Organization for Social Insurance
Hajj	Annual Muslim Pilgrimage to Makkah
Hallal	permissible in Islam
Haram	forbidden in Islam
IDB	Islamic Development Bank

IMF	International Monetary Fund
IOC	International Oil Companies
IPO	Initial Public Offering
Iqama	Saudi residence permit for foreigners
JIBOR	Jeddah Interbank Offer Rate
KAAU	King Abdulaziz University
Kafeel	Saudi sponsor of foreign labour
KFU	King Faisal University
KFUPM	King Fahd University of Petroleum and Minerals
KSA	Kingdom of Saudi Arabia
KSU	King Saud University
LIBOR	London Interbank Offer Rate
Maaden	Saudi Mining Company
Majls Al-Shoura	National Consultative Assembly or Council
mbd	million barrels per day
MENA	Middle East and North Africa
MMBtu	One million British thermal units
MoF	Ministry of Finance
MoP	Ministry of Planning
NCB	National Commercial Bank
NCCI	National Company for Cooperative Insurance
NEER	Normal Effective Exchange Rate
NGL	Natural Gas Liquids (or sometimes NLG)
OBU	Offshore Banking Unit
OECD	Organization for Economic Cooperation and Development
OIC	Organization of Islamic Conference
OPEC	Organization of Petroleum Exporting Countries
ORR	Official Repurchase Rate
PIF	Public Investment Fund
R&D	Research and Development
Ramadan	Muslim month of fasting
REDEF	Real Estate Development Fund
REER	Real Effective Exchange Rate
Repo	Repurchase Agreement
Reverse Repo	Reverse Repurchase Agreement
Riba	usury interest
RPR	Reverse Repurchase Rate

SAAB	Saudi Arabian Agricultural Bank
SABIC	Saudi Arabian Basic Industries
SAGIA	Saudi Arabia General Investment Authority
SAMA	Saudi Arabian Monetary Agency
SAMBA	Saudi American Bank (until October 2004)
SARIE	Saudi Riyal Interbank Express System
Saudia	Saudi Arabian Airlines
SCB	Saudi Credit Bank
SCCI	Saudi Chambers of Commerce and Industry
SDR	Special Drawing Right
SEC	Security and Exchange Commission
SEP	Saudi Export Program
SFD	Saudi Fund for Development
Sh.	Sheikh
Shariah	Islamic Law
SIBOR	Saudi Interbank Offer Rate
SIDF	Saudi Industrial Development Fund
SIMAH	Saudi Credit Bureau
SIST	Saudi Individual Stock Traders
SLR	Statutory Liquidity Ration
SME's	Small and Medium Sized Enterprises
SPAN	Saudi Payment Network
SPRA	Saudi Pension and Retirement Agency
SR	Saudi Riyal
Status quo	Keeping things unchanged
STC	Saudi Telecom Company
Sunnah	Sayings of the Prophet Muhammad (pbuh)
TADAWUL	Electronic share trading and information system
Takaful Ta'awni	Islamic cooperative life insurance product
TASI	Tadawul All Share Index
T-Bills	Treasury Bills
TCF	Trillion Cubic Feet (of gas)
Upstream	production of oil and gas from wells
Wakeel	Saudi commercial agent of foreign companies
Wasta	connection, favour
WTO	World Trade Organization

Chapter 1

OVERVIEW

> We judge ourselves by what we feel capable of doing, while others judge us by what we have already done.
>
> *Longfellow*

Introduction

Saudi Arabia has changed dramatically over the past three decades – economically, socially and demographically. This would be a short period in the lifespan of many nations; but for the Kingdom, it has been a long time.

This book examines the key factors leading to the fundamental changes that are shaping the future destiny of the Kingdom, often in directions that cannot be predicted with certainty. However, some indicators are emerging in the Saudi economy that point towards possible outcomes and potential solutions.

There are several distinct but overlapping themes in this book. Readers can focus on chapters with common themes or one can use this book to teach a course that blends theory and current policy issues. The choices are yours. Whichever option is followed, it will become apparent that certain overriding issues prevail in all chapters and themes. The key issues relate to diversifying the economy, managing expectations based on a narrow revenue base, coping with the needs of a young and growing population, empowering the private sector to become the engine of growth through job creation and exports and, finally, ensuring this sector's willing cooperation in the process of *Saudization* through replacing foreign workers with Saudis.

The country also has to deal with the consequences of its imminent World Trade Organization (WTO) entry and the challenges and opportunities of globalization. The Kingdom must set up the necessary

regulatory frameworks for an expanded financial and capital market, as well
as overseeing the switch from a public sector-driven delivery base to one
dominated by the private sector, in line with plans to privatize government
corporations.

This hurdle of simultaneous challenges would be a tall order for any
nation to handle. For Saudi Arabia, it also includes reforming the educational
system to be in line with market needs and with a knowledge-based
economy. The country also seeks to meet the aspirations of its female
population through expansion of their participation in the economy and
society at large, but without compromising on basic religious beliefs,
customs, and traditions.

Setting the stage

The first broad themes are covered in Chapters One and Two. Chapter
One addresses how economic planning was introduced and implemented in
Saudi Arabia, and examines its evolution and whether it had managed to
lay the framework for meeting future challenges. The chapter examines the
strategic economic decisions Saudi Arabia made in the early boom era, the
consequences of which are still apparent today. These consequences include
investment in capital-intensive infrastructure and basic industries, reliance
on cheap energy input, the use of subsidies and incentives to promote
economic growth and the import of large numbers of foreign workers.
Planning during this period evolved from being directive to indicative, as the
economy expanded and opened up to international trade. It also focused
more on the private sector and started to set qualitative indicators, rather than
the quantitative indicators of earlier planning periods. Chapter One points to
Saudi Arabia's need for a more strategic and flexible short-term planning
process that is better suited to a faster-evolving global economy.

Chapter Two assesses the Saudi budgetary framework and the urgent
long-term need for a wider revenue base diversification. This will help the
Kingdom move away from an inherent fiscal deficit situation and ballooning
internal debt – currently standing at around 90% of GDP although the
government has signalled its strong intent to reduce this debt in the
2004/2005 budget. The chapter also discusses the possible crowding out of
the private sector, which the government hopes will assume the future
capital project funding needs of the Kingdom, estimated at around $400
billion over the next twenty years. It then examines the centrality of oil
revenue and the lack of government control over nearly 90% of its revenue
sources, pointing towards the need to adopt a new strategy to meet future
fluctuating oil fortunes in order to move away from being a hostage to a
petrolized economy.

The financial sector

We explore our second major theme in Chapters Four, Five and Six, as we examine the evolving, and, in some respects, mature financial sector of Saudi Arabia. Chapter Four also analyzes the evolution of the Saudi *de facto* Central Bank – the Saudi Arabian Monetary Agency (SAMA). It looks at how SAMA has assumed a wide range of responsibilities and supervisory regulatory powers despite being constrained in the use of more traditional central bank policy tools, such as discount and interest rate instruments. However, SAMA has effectively managed the other range of monetary and exchange rate policy tools available to it, as well as ensuring that today the Saudi banking system is one of the most capitalized, liquid and profitable in the world. At the same time, SAMA has supervised the smooth transition of the Kingdom's foreign bank presence to joint partnerships, that is, a *Saudized* banking framework. This has turned out to be an effective partnership tool for transferring technology and management skills to the Saudi financial sector. Chapter Four explores the growing sophistication of the SAMA's use of *repos* and *reverse repos* as proxy monetary instruments, as well as SAMA's management of the national debt. It also considers the rationale of SAMA's fixed exchange rate policy for the Saudi Riyal and the Kingdom's money supply creation process.

Chapter Five further develops this theme and examines the broader financial markets that have evolved in the Kingdom, especially in the commercial banking sector. This sector is comprised of a mix of wholly-owned "pure" Saudi banks, joint-venture Saudi-ized banks, the newly-approved foreign banks and other financial sector players, such as the money exchangers and the specialized government financial institutions. The latter played a crucial role in providing long-term concessionary credit for Saudi economic development when most commercial financial institutions preferred to take short-term risks. Chapter Five examines the core strength and market strategies of these various financial institutions and their financial performance. The emerging insurance sector is also discussed, as well as the growing role of Islamic financing in Saudi Arabia and how the Kingdom's financial sector hopes to cope with globalization threats and opportunities.

The focus on the financial sector concludes with Chapter Six, which analyzes the Saudi Capital Market through a discussion of the evolution of the domestic capital markets, the operating regulatory framework and various obstacles. This is followed by an assessment of the new Capital

Market Law and future prospects for the capital market. We explore the issues of ownership concentration and of the lack of depth of the Saudi Capital market, in contrast to the Kingdom's dominance of the Arab stock markets, in terms of size and performance. This chapter analyzes the sectoral composition of the Saudi stock market and the inherent weaknesses of having a thin market base. We assess investor behaviour, and take an in-depth look at the Saudi mutual fund market, the largest and most diverse in the Arab world. The Saudi government debt market's structure is closely examined, as well as the future evolution of the Saudi Capital Markets in the face of ongoing liberalization and privatization. We provide some estimates for new company listings on the Saudi capital markets; these estimates indicate that an additional entry of 137 new companies would almost double current market capitalization, to take it to around the SR 890 billion levels.

The heart of the Kingdom: The hydrocarbon sector

The third theme of the book revolves around both the private sector and the challenges it faces, and Saudi Arabia's hydrocarbon and mineral sector – truly the heart of the Kingdom's revenue generation, diversification prospects and value-added job generation.

Chapter Seven critically examines the challenges for the Saudi private sector as it shoulders the responsibility of transforming the Saudi economy into a market-driven generator of wealth. It is important to assess whether an appropriate business environment exists in the Kingdom today, one that enables the private sector to take up these challenges. Therefore, we examine the legal, corporate and economic environments under which the private sector has to operate. We look, too, at the issue of foreign labour participation and current Saudi government pressure on the private sector to accelerate the process of *Saudization*. The role of the small- and medium-sized enterprises (SMEs) is examined, as well as the obstacles they face and how the government is trying to overcome these obstacles (given the importance of the SMEs to Saudi Arabia's goal of job generation and regional economic diversification). Chapter Seven also explores the role of the Saudi family businesses and their structures, and advocates for some changes to family businesses to enable them to meet the future challenges of globalization and the situation after Saudi entry to the WTO.

This chapter also considers Saudi women and their growing importance in the national economy; we note the obstacles currently faced by women in managing their own businesses, and investigate how they are overcoming these barriers. During 2004 there has been a greater momentum to generate more female job opportunities, to increase women's participation in economic nation-building and to open up more sectors for them.

The chapter further explores the development over time of the complex and evolving business relationship between the Saudi government and the private sector. We look at the government's role as planner, as financing entity, as buyer and seller, as regulator and as revenue collector. The issue of *Saudization* and how the private sector views it is examined in some detail, showing that the private sector and the government have divergent views. The private sector argues that *Saudization* can only succeed when a supply of skilled labour exists that meets market needs at competitive wage levels, and that the government needs to embark on a more aggressive control mechanism of foreign labour supply to the private sector in order to force Saudi employment.

Chapter Eight discusses the oil and gas sectors and explores the opportunities that lay in the as-yet-relatively untapped non-carbon minerals sector. The importance of oil, its dominant effect on the Saudi economy and the Kingdom's pivotal role in this energy sector is highlighted. This chapter also thoroughly examines Saudi oil policy and its constraints. The record oil prices experienced during 2004, with oil prices exceeding $50 per barrel on fears of supply shortages, underscored the Kingdom's importance as the major excess capacity producer of the world. Saudi gas, a new and important energy sector, is appraised in light of Saudi Arabia's attempts to attract foreign investment and technical partners to this field. Besides having a quarter of the world's proven oil reserves, Saudi Arabia also has the world's fourth largest gas reserves and is the world's largest natural gas liquid (NGL) exporter.

Chapter Eight also looks at the Saudi petrochemical industry, particularly as it could be the major beneficiary of WTO entry. Today the Saudi Arabian Basic Industry (SABIC) is a significant player in the world's petrochemical markets, planning expanded operations both at home and abroad. For some products, SABIC's world share stands at around 18-20%, and it is a credit to the Kingdom that this was achieved in fewer than twenty years' time, literally created out of the desert. Chapter Eight carries on exploring the Kingdom's mining sector and its potential to diversify the economic base and generate an integrated mining industry. If developed, the Kingdom's extensive mining resources could rank Saudi Arabia amongst one of the leading mining countries of the world.

The planned privatization of the Saudi Mining Company (*Maaden*) will involve the restructure of the company into separate units of gold, phosphate, bauxite, aluminium and other minerals. Foreign investors in the mining field will be encouraged to explore under planned new mining law concessions. Chapter Eight presents a new model of mining cooperation with foreign companies that will assist in taking privatization forward. This model could help shield the Kingdom from fluctuations in basic commodity prices, such as oil, resulting in a narrow revenue base, despite the record 21-year high oil prices seen during 2004.

Foreign trade and technology transfer

Chapters Nine and Ten deal with the next theme, Saudi Arabia's foreign trade, along with the issue of technology transfer through the use of economic "offset programmes" used to enhance the economy's base and generate new high technology enterprises.

Saudi Arabia has embraced an open, market-based economy with few restrictions on goods and service, except for those that are in direct conflict with religious beliefs (including the import and consumption of alcohol and pork-related products). This liberal market policy is reflected in the Kingdom's trade relations with the rest of the world. Imports come today from virtually all continents, while Saudi exports flow to all major industrialized and developing countries. Saudi Arabia's major trading partners continue to be the United States, the European Union and the Far East; China is viewed as the major trading partner of the future.

Exports from the Kingdom follow the same import trading patterns, and some effort has recently been made to ensure that Saudi exports become more diversified. Currently some 90% of total exports are made up of oil and energy-related petrochemical products. It is this narrow export base that is worrying those who see potential problems for Saudi non-oil exporters post-WTO entry for the Kingdom. While Saudi Arabia has run relatively consistent trade surpluses, the Kingdom suffers from capital outflows due to large remittances by foreign workers, averaging around SR 60 billion per annum, as well as private sector private capital outflows. Since 2002, Saudi banks have reported some capital repatriation to the Kingdom due to a rising Saudi stock market and a booming real estate sector, in addition to Initial Public Offerings (IPO) and privatization opportunities.

Analysis of Saudi Arabia's trade patterns reveals a shift in the type of products imported over the past three decades: during the earlier boom period, the imports were of capital goods, construction and machinery. Later these imports gave way to spare parts, food and consumer goods. Inter-Gulf Cooperation Council (GCC) trade still plays a small part. Saudi Arabia is a net GCC importer, especially from Dubai and Bahrain which re-export to the larger Saudi market.

The transfer of appropriate technology to the Kingdom has always been of major importance, either through Foreign Direct Investment (FDI), joint ventures or through the Saudi Economic Offset Program. Chapter Ten examines the rationale behind the offset programme. When it was initiated in the mid-1980s, it was the first of its kind in the Middle East. Saudi Arabia sought to obtain benefits from foreign contractors through transferring technology and training local labour. Our analysis reveals mixed success for the current offset programmes, especially in terms of employment generated, but notes that offset companies in general did transfer higher levels of "technology packaging" than did non-offset private sector joint venture companies. Chapter Ten highlights the need for continued reforms of educational institutions in order to produce Saudis with the necessary scientific and technological skills to benefit from such offset ventures. There is also a need to develop a culture of research and development within the private sector.

Meeting future challenges

The final theme involves analyzing some key challenges faced today by the Saudi economy as it goes through painful structural adjustments. These challenges overlap, as they often do, since economic transformation do not occur in compartmentalized isolation, but rather react to one another in a dynamic fashion.

The challenge to the Kingdom's policy makers is to try and identify key positive drivers operating in the economy that will lead the country forward to set objectives while minimizing the negative consequences to society at large.

Under this broad theme, Chapter Eleven examines the Kingdom's hopes and aspirations for Foreign Direct Investment the strategic option for liberalization and privatization, and looks at the potential benefits and costs of globalization and WTO entry. This chapter illustrates that Saudi Arabia's problem is not a lack of good intentions or of proper priorities, but rather that there is no matching consensus as to how much action is needed, and how quickly the Kingdom should act. Some tangible progress has been made through the establishment of the Supreme Economic Council, which has focused on developing the regulatory environment that will allow a successful privatization programme to emerge. Another positive development involves the enhancements of the Foreign Investment Law that offer a number of benefits, including a recent reduction in taxation levels to 20% on foreign companies' profits.

It is the globalization issue that remains unresolved to date. Saudi Arabia's entry to the WTO is only a matter of time, and the Kingdom is using the period before entry to liberalize certain key sectors, especially in finance and insurance, as well as enforcing intellectual property rights. Chapter Eleven closely examines the impact of globalization on Saudi Arabia's financial structure. While it seems clear that this sector of the economy will withstand any negative globalization issues, the rest of the private sector needs to adjust more rapidly, especially in terms of company structure and internal efficiencies.

The critical issues of the moment – employment, *Saudization* and the structure and composition of the Saudi labour market – are dealt with in Chapter Twelve. With nationals accounting for just under 11.5% of the total private sector labour force, or around 640,000 Saudis, the government is making copious attempts to ensure that more jobs are found for nationals, either through creating new jobs or replacing foreigners through an invigorated *Saudization* program.

The government, however, can only push so hard. In the final analysis, Saudis with the appropriate market-driven skills will be employed. Others seeking jobs will realize that is necessary to change their mind-set and to accept positions previously deemed to be either too menial or socially unacceptable. This might be a prime reason why, according to press reports, some 150,000 Saudis failed to complete job application formalities for guaranteed jobs identified through regional employment offices over the past four years.

The mindset *is* changing, and some sections of Saudi youth are beginning to be more realistic in their job expectations as they compete with other new labour entrants, a result of one of the world's highest population growth rates.

Windfall gains arising from one or two years of higher than expected oil revenues, such as those experienced during 2003 and 2004, might produce a short-term "feel good" factor, but cannot solve such long-term demographic realities. This chapter also looks at the issue of female labour participation, since the Kingdom has one of the lowest female labour participation rates in the world. Even within the Middle East, Saudi's rate is about 6% compared with a 17% average for the rest of the Middle East.

Saudi female participation tends to be higher for those in the older age group, forcing younger Saudi women to prolong their entry to the labour market either by pursuing higher education or seeking less qualified jobs. Once again, the Saudi government recognizes these problems and the Saudi Cabinet recently approved a nine-point plan to create more jobs and business opportunities for women, including the restriction of expatriate jobs in areas dealing with women-only services.

In any society, unemployment is not only a cause of social problems and of increased unemployment-related crimes, but also of potential loss to national output and productivity. Chapter Twelve calculates the cost of such a potential Saudi output gap. Using *Okun's Law*, this was estimated at around SR 327 billion for the period 1993-2002, based on fairly high levels of voluntary (or "natural") rate of unemployment for Saudi society. If this natural rate of unemployment were much reduced, then both the output gap and real rate of unemployment would be much higher using *Okun's Law* than those estimated in Chapter Twelve.

Our analysis of earlier themes clearly marks the important role that quality education and the acquisition of market-related skills play in shaping Saudi economic development.

This issue is examined more closely in Chapter Thirteen, which analyses the current Saudi educational structure's achievements and problems. Technological progress and the diffusion of scientific and technical innovations lead to higher productivity and improvement in all sectors of the economy. The ability of any society to produce, select, adapt and commercialize knowledge is critical for sustained economic growth and improved living standards. In relation to its population, size and undoubted quantitative educational investment, Saudi Arabia has produced negligible commercial patents compared with other developing countries such as Malaysia or Singapore.

Quality education output is now a key priority for the Saudi government. The 2004 budget allocation for education showed that the Saudi government is beginning to direct resources towards higher education and vocational training institutions that are graduating students who meet labour market needs. During the 2004 academic year, the government directed Saudi universities to curtail enrolment in some non-job or market-related subjects.

Once again, one must put Saudi Arabia's phenomenal transformation into perspective to assess how far the country has travelled in a short period of time. For the whole period of 1927-1960, the country boasted only seven Ph.D graduates from foreign universities. In 2001-2002 alone, there were 185 Saudi Ph.D graduates from foreign universities, of which 22 were women. The total number of Ph.D graduates from Saudi universities was 154, of which 82 were women. It is a proud achievement for any country, but especially for Saudi Arabia where debate in the late 1950s concerned whether to allow female education *at all*.

Despite massive investment in education over the past three decades, Saudi Arabia's real per capita income has fallen considerably from around SR 62,000 in 1981 to SR 32,000 levels in 2002/2003. The population has grown faster than its oil revenues, and labour productivity has not kept pace with private sector market forces. In order to compensate for this oil drag, both labour productivity and educational standards will have to rise significantly faster in the next decade.

The Kingdom is not an isolated island. Regional developments, whether positive or negative, have profound consequences on internal stability, and on economic and social developments. Chapter Fourteen explores Saudi Arabia's multi-faceted relationship with the other five members of the Gulf

Cooperation Council (GCC), as developments within the GCC could have far-reaching economic consequences for the member states. This chapter examines why the GCC union was established in 1981 and discusses its developments to date.

Chapter Fourteen aims to impart an understanding of the internal economic dynamics of the various GCC member states and of how far similarities and differences could accelerate or impede planned full monetary and customs union by 2010. Economic diversification, generating employment for their young and growing populations, and economic integration is the destiny of the GCC countries. Oil is central to their well-being. Between them, the six GCC countries sit on some 45% of the world's total oil reserves, illustrating the magnitude of the region's importance. Chapter Fourteen shows that some success has been achieved, albeit on a modest scale, in the effort of individual GCC member states to diversify away from a narrow oil and gas revenue base. Dubai and Bahrain are leading the way.

Saudi Arabia's economy, size and market potential continue to dwarf all the other GCC countries. The Kingdom has sometimes pursued policies for the greater good of all other member states rather than for narrow self-interest. The next test of leadership will be GCC's management of the transition towards full monetary union and a single currency by 2010, which requires a greater degree of fiscal and monetary policy harmonization than hitherto.

Integration of various capital markets could be a first step in mobilizing domestic financial resources into large, economically-viable inter-GCC or national projects. Integration would also help facilitate a greater degree of inter-GCC job seeker migration and ease unemployment problems faced by some GCC countries while filling the job openings of other member states. In the long term, it is important to ensure that the GCC becomes open and accessible to its ordinary citizens so that they understand the objectives of the GCC, why it was established and how it affects their lives. It is only by doing this that the viability of the GCC's long-term future can be guaranteed, and that the "GCC family" survival as a stronger political and economic entity in the 21st century can be ensured.

Conclusions

Following these broad themes, Chapter Fifteen concludes by reviewing some key structural issues affecting the Saudi economy and highlighting some of the problems that need to be addressed going forward. There is a new sense of realism in the Kingdom amongst policy markers, the private sector and the population at large. Despite domestic terrorism issues, there is a mood of determination to tackle pressing problems. Reforms and domestic changes are important, but they must not be seen as a competition between external and internal domestic reform agendas. Both need to progress at a comparable pace, without external pressure. Managing both expectations and the pace of reform will be a key challenge as things progress, as will be the management of the *Saudization* process and the maintenance of harmonious relations with expatriate labour.

Reforms, although implemented gradually, can be cumulative in effect. Gradual change may seem slow or less impressive to those outside the Kingdom, but if reforms are to endure and be effective, they have to respond to the needs, customs and mores of all society if they are to succeed. Far too many experts have misjudged and underestimated the resilience of Saudi Arabia, or the adaptability and creativity of Saudi society in meeting future challenges. Consensual change will be the means of change. The key will be a process of evolution and consensus building, the hallmark of Saudi government, thus allowing for longer term economic planning and stability.

Chapter 2

ECONOMIC PLANNING: HISTORY, ROLE AND EFFECTIVENESS

The foundation of every state is the education of its youth.

Diogenes

Learning outcomes

By the end of this section, you should understand:

- *The need for planning*
- *The strategic choices faced*
- *Trends in planning expenditures*
- *Evolution of the Saudi economy*
- *Planning and "engines of growth"*

Gazing into the future

Domestic challenges of change amid transformation are not particular to the oil-producing nations of the Gulf. Neither is the concept of planning new in substance, although the degree of emphasis and the direction can be new. Saudi Arabia is today facing challenges more pressing than at any other time in its recent history; these range from demographic structures to structural economic imbalances, from the absence of key economic drivers for growth and employment to the critical importance of the role of the private sector as the "engine of growth."

According to observers, Saudi Arabia has some of the most sophisticated development planning processes of any nation in the developing world (Cordesman, 2003). However, good intentions and good plans do not, on their own, ensure implementation. As will be discussed, Saudi leaders have indeed set what seemed to be the right priorities for the nation, but sometimes events, both domestic and international, have overtaken their planning exercise, throwing good intentions off-balance. It takes foresight and determination to switch directions and persevere to bring about changes over time.

Why the need to plan?

It is often said that "the best government is the most invisible government." This means that "best" governments are those that establish regulatory and legal frameworks and then allow the competitive pressure of free market forces to determine the optimum allocation of resources needed by society. There are those who would argue that this is a utopian luxury that governments in the modern world aspire to, but few achieve in reality. The real world has witnessed a degree of planning and government control, ranging from central planning to what is termed mixed economies, where the government and private sector work together in partnership. Irrespective of which model of planning is adopted, the central goal seems to be the laying of a broad economic foundation for self-sustaining growth with one or more key factors of production (land, labour, capital or managerial efficiency) creating the precondition for self-sustained growth (Rostow, 1960).

Saudi Arabia's economic development path has sometimes been characterized as one of a classical "rentier" economy (Chaudhry, 1989, 1997, Auty, 2001). In this model, the government seeks to maximize its revenue from a natural resource – oil – and distribute the proceeds amongst various sections of the population. Some distinguish between a "rentier" economy and a re-distributive "welfare state" that derives its income through taxation and other means from one class of society and distributes it to other sections of society (Chaudhry, 1989).

Since Saudi Arabia currently does not impose taxes on its citizens, the term "welfare state" is not technically correct for the Kingdom. The concept of "rentier economy" is a more accurate characterization of the early years of Saudi Arabia's economic development. According to some observers, an alliance developed between the State and certain business groups in the private sector that aimed to promote the national agenda at the expense of some excluded groups (Wilson, 2004, Champion, 2003).

During the early boom period of the Saudi economy in the 1970s and early 1980s, the large inflows of oil "rents" to the State created a momentum of its own, in which it seemed that the State's only function was that of a distributive agent and that the government sector became the exclusive motor of the economy (Chaudhry, 1977). The lack of administrative, educational, managerial and physical infrastructure led to absorbative capacity bottlenecks in those early boom days, with investment decisions being taken that had far-reaching consequences for the future (Mallakh, 1982).

The basic argument against "rentier economies" is that when a state's main source of private revenues is through government expenditures, the society thus supported does not instil a sense of initiative or entrepreneurship amongst its citizens. However, a state that is supported by society through one form of taxation or another will develop a more balanced relationship with its citizens, with both parties responding to the needs of the other (Ehteshami, 2003).

One further effect of the "rentier economy" was the emergence of powerful state bureaucracies which "orchestrated the States' development" (Ehteshami, 2003). The effect was to perpetuate the preference for government jobs in Saudi Arabia, which we shall examine in later chapters, at the expense of the private sector, since bureaucracy viewed the private sector in a subservient relationship instead of as a dominant force. This relationship between the government and private sector affected the "institutional capacity to deliver" (Wilson, 2004). Surveys of attitudes of senior civil servants carried out in Saudi Arabia in the early 1980s showed deficiencies in "psychological drive, flexibility, communication, client relations and impartiality" (Hegelan and Palmer, 1999). According to some observers, there is little evidence that much has changed since those early days (Wilson, 2004).

The above arguments and counter-arguments are easy to discuss in hindsight. The reality of the matter is that Saudi Arabia opted for an operating planning framework to guide the national economy *long before* higher oil prices propelled Saudi Arabia to the forefront of world economic headlines in 1973/1974. The First Plan covered the period 1970 - 1974. By the time the First Plan period had ended, the Saudi economy was fundamentally transformed, as will become evident later in this chapter when we analyze the structure of the national economy.

Strategic choices

In the early 1970s, the Saudi government along with its key planners and consultants grappled with strategic decisions on the direction the economy should be steered. It was not an easy task, given the lack of planning experience, absence of data on the economy and raised expectations of Saudi nationals. Table 2.1 examines some of the strategic development options that were faced by Saudi planners and their potential positive and negative implications.

Each of the options set out in Table 2.1 has appealing positive factors, and these positive factors would have been paramount in the planning discussions – rather than the negative consequences. The country was in a rush to develop rapidly. There were few lengthy discussions or in-depth analysis of potential negative consequences of one strategic development objective or another (Farsy, 1982), although some commentators did raise early concerns (Bashir, 1977).

Table 2.1 Saudi Arabia: economic development options

Development option	Positive Factors	Negative Factors
Large oil production	• Large foreign investments and surplus financial resources • Balance of payment surpluses • No incentive to fund crude oil substitutes	• Economic dependency • International and domestic inflation • Rapid consumption of non-renewable national resources. • Rentier economy
Oil production based on domestic needs	• Moderate investments abroad leading to paced development and equilibrium between domestic development needs and financial resources. • Large oil reserves for future generations	• World oil shortages • High international inflation and world recession • Strong incentive to find crude oil substitute and suppliers
Large scale domestic industrialization and diversification of economic base	• Potential economic independence • Skills acquisition and new working habits. • Exports potential • Technology transfer • Education base widened • Non-oil economic diversification	• Large imports • Need for expatriate labour increased • Balance of payments problems with a large element of exported salaries and profits • Domestic inflation • Institutionalized inefficiency due to subsidy policy (import substitution industry). • Mismatch between domestic labour supply output and market requirements.

From all indications, what has actually transpired from the early 1970s to date is that Saudi Arabia opted for large-scale domestic industrialization and for diversification of the national economic base. The aim was to "transform the economy from overwhelming dependence on the export of crude oil into a diversified industrial economy", while admitting that dependence on oil revenues will continue for a considerable period of time (Farsy, 1982).

Depending on substantial crude oil production alone was not a long-term strategic choice, for it would have magnified the negative consequences of the "rentier economy" system discussed earlier. It would have meant a more rapid consumption of Saudi Arabia's non-renewable natural resource; the only key decision facing the country would simply have been the rate of oil extraction and the price of oil.

Production of oil based merely on Saudi Arabia's domestic needs would have produced oil shortages, international inflation and world recession, along with a strong incentive to find other suppliers as well as crude oil substitutes. As we will explain in later chapters, Saudi Arabia is cognizant of its key role in world oil supply and has pursued moderating policies in its attempt to ease oil supply shortages. The most recent example was the Kingdom's decision in September, 2004, to increase its production from 8.3 million barrels to over 11 million barrels per day – virtually its full capacity – in order to ease soaring prices of over $50 dollar a barrel, compared with a Organization of Petroleum Exporting Countries (OPEC) price band range of $22 to $28 a barrel.

Adopting the large-scale industrialization and diversification option seemed then, on the surface, to have been the most viable option, with significant discernible advantages. The negative factors that have crept into this strategy over time are now causing the most concern. As will be discussed later, issues of mismatch between domestic labour supply and market needs, the continuing strain on balance of payments due to large expatriate labour remittances, institutionalized inefficiencies and, despite diversification, continuing reliance on oil and oil derivative exports are features of the Saudi economy today. Most of these problems are inherited from the earlier development plans. The section that follows discusses the planning process in more depth.

The history of Saudi planning

Saudi Arabia has undergone a substantial and fundamental transformation over the past three decades since planning was first introduced in 1970. The history of development planning has also seen some radical changes, from *directive* to *indicative* planning. Those who were involved in the First Plan admitted that, in essence, the First Plan of 1970 - 1974 was essentially "an exploration, theoretical and empirical", and that the biggest achievement was "the experience gained by Saudis in the field of development planning" (Farsi, 1982). Others are more critical of the whole planning exercise, arguing that the development plans demonstrated good intentions, but did not pave the road to major progress (Cordesman, 2003).

There are those who argue that Saudi Arabian planning has been more "a macroeconomic exercise than a form of detailed microeconomic management" (Wilson, 2004). The argument is that Saudi planning involves designing public expenditure programmes in the light of anticipated revenues and then executing these expenditures. If revenues are actually achieved, then all is well: projects are implemented and delayed projects restarted. Conversely, if anticipated revenues do not materialize, then the opposite happens: ongoing projects are delayed and new ones suspended.

Planning, however, can be carried out under various models and circumstances, ranging from setting targets for the economy as a whole and providing direction on how resources will be invested, to establishing targets for input resources and the desired output. The Saudi model has not established precise *qualitative* output targets, but rather *quantitative* output targets. Planning can also follow an indicative direction on how and where the government wishes the economy to go, providing the necessary rules and regulations to allow the private sector to achieve those directions (Osama,1987).

Planning exercises do not operate in a vacuum and it is important to analyse the administrative structure under which Saudi planning is carried out. The first planning exercises, in the late 1950s and early 1960s, depended heavily on external bodies and consultants such as the Ford Foundation, the United Nations Team for Social and Economic Planning and the World Bank. In 1961 a Planning Board was established in Saudi Arabia and in 1965 it was incorporated into the Central Planning Organization (CPO), which drafted the Kingdom's First Five Year Plan in 1969.

In 1975 the CPO became the Ministry of Planning (MOP), reflecting the importance national planning was being assigned, although some argue that the Ministry of Planning in effect took a back seat to the actual implementation policies undertaken by the more powerful spending Ministries such as Commerce, Industry and Electricity (Wilson, 2004). One factor could have been the lack of interaction between the Ministry of Planning and the Saudi public in initiating and formulating plan objectives. It is most likely that in an attempt to try and overcome this gulf between planners and those whose lives are being most affected, the Ministry of Planning function and role was increased when it was given the extra portfolio of "National Economy." It is now known as the Ministry of Planning and National Economy, following the Saudi Cabinet reshuffle of April, 2003 (Saudi Press Agency, 1 May 2003). The importance of planning had come full circle. The Ministry's added responsibility underscores the importance of some of the urgent economic tasks that need addressing in the new millennium. A new bolder vision is needed in Saudi Arabia today, one which is comparable to some of the early initiatives taken, raising whole industrial infrastructures out of the desert, to become the world's most modern petrochemical complexes, as embodied by today's industrial cities of *Jubail* and *Yanbu*.

To reinforce the importance of involving Saudi Arabia's key decision makers in the planning and implementation process, the Supreme Economic

Council was established in August, 1999, which included Crown Prince Abdullah as Chairman, Second Deputy Premier Prince Sultan as Vice Chairman and the Ministers of Finance, Planning and Economy, Commerce, Labour, Petroleum and Industry as well as the Governor of the Saudi Arabian Monetary Agency (SAMA). The critical role of planning could not have had better support, compared to those earlier days.

Plan achievements

Actual expenditures made by the Saudi government over the whole planning period from 1970 to date have been impressive, standing at around SR 2,613 billion or $697 billion. This is set out in more detail in Table 2.2 for each planning period, organized by broad expenditure categories.

From Table 2.2, it becomes evident how closely government expenditure patterns follow the fortunes of the Kingdom's oil revenues, with the current Seventh Development Plan (2000 - 2004) not reaching the peak "boom years" of the Third Development Plan period (1980 - 1984).

It is even more important to analyse the different emphases placed during each planning period, reflecting national priorities. This is set out in Table 2.3, which captures key "planning indicators" for each plan. It demonstrates that the planning focus has shifted towards allocative efficiency, human skill upgrading and private sector participation in economic diversification. The principal underlying themes of all plans continue to emphasize raising the standard of living of the people, improving general quality of life and enhancing their skill capabilities.

The importance of safeguarding Islamic values, cultural heritage and traditions continues to be emphasized at the outset of each plan. The intension was to promote economic development, but not "Westernization" – something which other traditional societies undergoing rapid development have found difficult to avoid. The Internet revolution makes maintaining a social *status quo* even harder, and Saudi society is no exception (Yamani, 1998, 2000, Rasheed, 2002). The recent advances made by Internet and global communication have broken down barriers; the IT revolution is one that few Saudi planners can ignore in the future. The impact of this flow of information has been researched in other Arab societies with social customs and traditions similar to that of Saudi Arabia; IT access has had a profound societal shaping effect (Masmoudi, 1998, Azzam, 2002).

Table 2.2 Expenditures during the Saudi development plans

Expenditures	Economic Resources Development		Human Resources Development		Social and Health Development		Infrastructure Development		Total	
	SR Billion	(%)	SR Billion	(%)	SR Billion	(%)	SR Billion	(%)	SR Billion	(%)
First Development Plan:										
1970 - 1974 (Actual)	9.5	27.7	7.0	20.6	3.5	10.3	14.1	41.4	34.1	100
Second Development Plan:										
1975 - 1979 (Actual)	97.3	28.0	51.0	14.7	27.6	8.0	171.3	49.3	347.2	100
Third Development Plan:										
1980 - 1984 (Actual)	192.2	30.8	115.0	18.5	61.2	9.9	256.8	40.8	635.2	100
Fourth Development Plan:										
1980 - 1989 (Actual)	71.2	20.4	115.1	33.0	61.9	17.7	100.7	28.9	348.9	100
Fifth Development Plan:										
1990 - 1994 (Actual)	34.1	10.0	164.6	48.0	68.0	20.1	74.2	21.9	340.9	100
Sixth Development Plan:										
1995 - 1999 (Actual)	48.2	11.5	216.6	51.5	87.5	20.8	68.1	16.2	420.4	100
Seventh Development Plan:										
2000 - 2004 (Planned)	41.7	8.5	276.9	56.7	95.8	19.6	73.8	15.2	488.2	100

Source: *Saudi Ministry of Planning*, September, 2002.

Table 2.3 Saudi Arabia's national five year development plans: key indicators

Overall national priorities	First (1970 - 1974)	Second (1975 - 1979)	Third (1980-1984))	Fourth (1985 - 1989)	Fifth (1990 - 1994)	Sixth (1995 - 1999)	Seventh (2000 - 2004)
• Safeguard Islamic values in conformity with Shariah. • Improve standard and quality of life • Develop human resources, increase productivity and replace non-Saudis with qualified Saudis • Realize balanced growth in all regions • Diversify economic base and reduce dependence on production and export of oil • Provide favourable environment for activities of the private sector to encourage it to play a leading role in development	• Focus on provision of modern infrastructure, basic government services • Expansion of human resources and beginning of infrastructure growth.	• Large infrastructure expenditure and economic resources • Large subsidy outlays • Expansion in transport, electricity, water and housing • Starting hydrocarbon industries • Establishment of modern administrative infrastructure	• Expanding Infrastructure, economic resources • Human resources and educational base expansion • Hydrocarbon base expansion • Undertaking regional economic initiatives	• Concentration on operation and maintenance • Reconstructing the economy to allow more private sector participation • Human Resources and health expenditure rose. • Shift from Central planning projects approach to programme planning approach	• Encouraging more private sector participation • Expanding the technology base • Emphasis on human services and Saudization. • Drop in gross fixed Capital formation	• Human resources emphasis as well as social and health. • Aiming for balanced budget. • Reduction in foreign Labour • Private sector expansion • Beginning of partial privatization • Reduction of subsidies.	• Solving human resource problems • Diversify the economy • Increasing gas production • Consolidating efficiency in production, refining and distribution. • Reducing State budget deficit • Increasing Saudization • Preparing for globalization. WTO. • Privatization as strategic option

Source: *Ministry of Planning*, 2002.

As Table 2.3 indicates, one of the primary objectives over the last three plans has been an urgent insistence that the private sector plays a greater role in the diversification of the economy. Saudi Arabia has realized that having rich natural resource endowments does not necessarily bring about sustained economic growth. In fact, other oil rich economies, such as Venezuela and Nigeria, experienced negative rates of per capita income growth between 1965 - 1996 (Gelb et al., 1998, Askari et al., 1997). This is not to underestimate the tremendous social and economic impact that has taken place in Saudi Arabia over the whole planning period, the results of which have been tangible. For example, life expectancy – one measure of economic development – reached 71.6 years in 2001 in Saudi Arabia, up from a modest average of 53.9 years over the period 1970 - 1975.

Over the same period, adult literacy registered 76.3% for those who were fifteen years and older, an impressive increase from 39% in 1970 (Ministry of Planning, 2002). Current historical patterns of plan expenditures have been consistent with the goal of improving the standard and quality of life, with ever-increasing allocation made for human resources, as well as health and social services. It is the erratic nature of government revenues, based on a narrow source of income, that has made the issue of economic diversification and broader private sector involvement more urgent. The next section analyses how this hope has been realized in practice.

The performance of the Saudi economy

The turn of the new century saw Saudi Arabia's economy dominate all other Arab economies in terms of Gross Domestic Product (GDP). Saudi Arabia's GDP, however, was dwarfed by the leading industrialized countries, as illustrated in Figure 2.1 .

The GDP figures for the various countries do not necessarily reflect the quality of life in each country, as only "economic" factors are included in GDP estimates, despite recent attempts to include qualitative measures. What Figure 2.2 illustrates is that, despite massive government spending over the past three decades, the Saudi economy seems insignificant compared to the world's giants, such as the USA or Japan, and is in fact smaller than medium-sized industrialized countries such as Belgium. It is sometimes noted that a GDP the size of the Saudi economy is *added* to that of the USA every 7 - 8 months when the U.S. economy grows at a real rate of 3% p.a.

The basic reason for the lag in Saudi GDP growth is simple: the U.S. economy is diversified while Saudi Arabia's is not. All of Saudi Arabia's economic reform efforts and development plans to date centre around the fact that its economy is essentially oil-driven with the resultant strengths and weaknesses. The performance of the Saudi economy has been heavily influenced by two major factors. First, the level and growth of oil revenues

Figure 2.1 2000 **GDP** comparison (US $ billions)

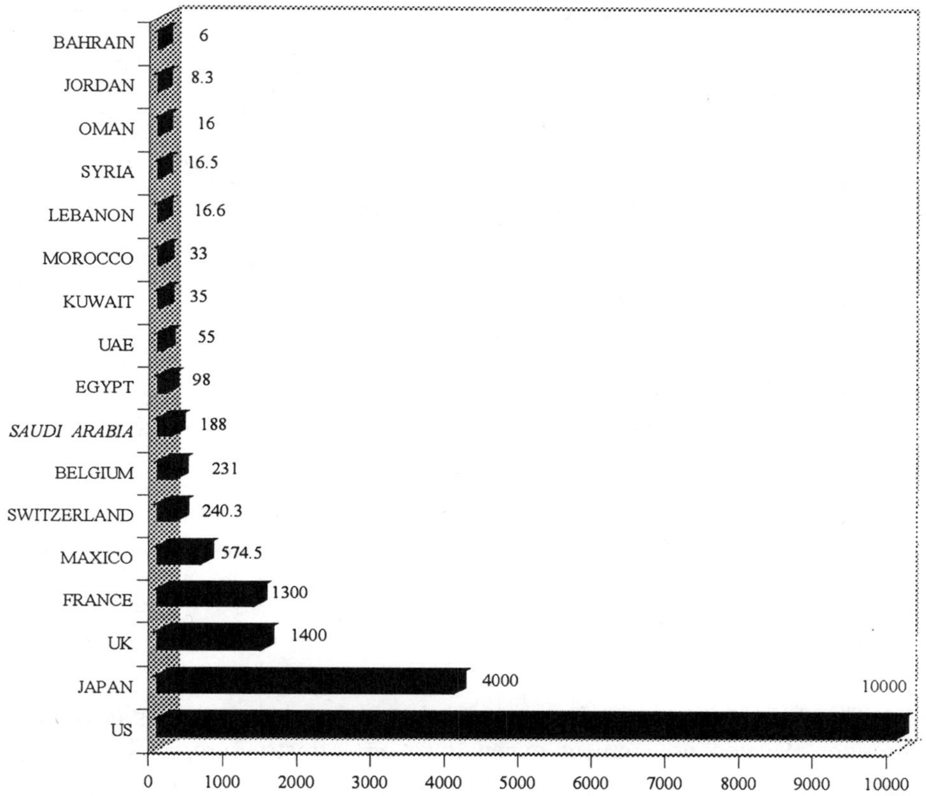

Source: *World Bank*, 2002.

and second, by government budgetary policies. The latter functions as the main link between the oil sector and the rest of the economy on one side, and economic growth in case of reduced or increased oil revenue on the other.

The result has been identifiable major Saudi business cycles, each with its own characteristic, as illustrated in Figure 2.2.

From Figure 2.2 the following major business cycles are identified:

A. *An oil boom cycle from 1970 - 1982*
B. *An oil bust cycle from 1983 - 1987*
C. *A recovery cycle from 1988 - 1992*
D. *A stagnation cycle from 1993 - 1995*
E. *A restructuring cycle from 1996 to date.*

Figure 2.2 Saudi Arabia: major business cycles 1970 - 2003 (SR billions at constant prices. 1999 = 100)

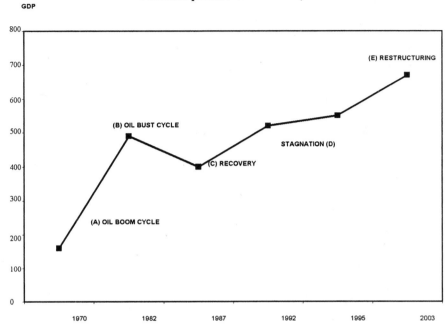

Source: *SAMA*, 2003.

The first cycle was characterized by high oil prices, rapid economic growth, elevated government expenditure on infrastructure, high per capita income and private sector demand. The second cycle – the oil bust era – saw the Saudi economy take a dramatic downturn. Crude oil production declined from an average of 9.81 million barrels per day in 1981/1982 to an average of 3.2 million barrels in 1985. Oil prices dropped from peaks of $34 a barrel in 1981 to $11.5 a barrel in 1986. Government revenues fell drastically to around SR 50 billion in 1986 compared to nearly SR 400 billion in 1981. As a result, imports fell and there was a reduction in investment expenditure by both the government and private sectors. The third phase – or recovery business cycle – showed a reversal of fortunes due to improvement in world oil markets, but was followed by a relatively stagnant business cycle affected by declining oil prices and fiscal constraints.

The period between 1992 and 1995 was characterized by budget cuts across the board, a freeze on capital expenditure and a slow-down in government cash disbursements, which caused some problems to private contractors. From the oil bust cycle, the Saudi government started to draw down on its overseas liquid reserves, resulting in growing budget deficits and debt service payments, as shall be explored in more depth in later chapters.

The fifth or current cycle can be viewed as a critical one, in which economic reforms and major restructuring efforts are taking place, with the government trying to ensure that the private sector becomes the main engine of growth. This cycle saw movement in the field of privatization, liberalization and capital market reforms, in order to attract foreign direct investment and Saudi capital held abroad. This cycle is arguably the most important for the future well being of Saudi Arabia, as a successful outcome will lead to greater national prosperity through a balanced and more self-sustained economic path. As such, it is important to analyze in more depth the effectiveness of previous economic diversification policies to assess the major challenges that might hinder such policies in the future.

Economic diversification: realities

In order to assess the effectiveness of the Saudi economic diversification effort, we must analyze more closely the Saudi national accounts, which provides an insight into the structure of the nation's economy. An examination of these accounts helps one to decide whether the Saudi economy has unique characteristics compared to other economies. The Gross Domestic Product (GDP) is the sum of the value added by the various sectors of the economy – in other words, the market value of the total output of goods and services produced during a year. The Gross National Product (GNP) includes both the results of domestic activity within Saudi Arabia and the results of its economic relationship with the rest of the world. For Saudi Arabia, the government and the foreign sector play important roles as seen in Figure 2.3.

Figure 2.3 highlights three important features of the Saudi Arabian economy. First, as the earlier analysis of the different business cycles showed, the model underlines the crucial role played by the government sector. The importance of oil and oil revenues ensures that the government, through its fiscal budgetary mechanism, is still in a position to influence both the level and the structure of economic activity. These can be transmitted through direct expenditure on consumption and investment, as well as provision of "soft" long-term loans and subsidies.

The second feature of the Saudi model is the degree of interdependence with the rest of the world. This has risen dramatically as oil income increased, with oil exports representing some 54% of GDP in 1979/1980 but falling back to 40% levels in 1999/2000. Imports from the rest of the world were 55% and 30% respectively (SAMA, 2003).

Figure 2.3 Saudi Arabian model of economic flows

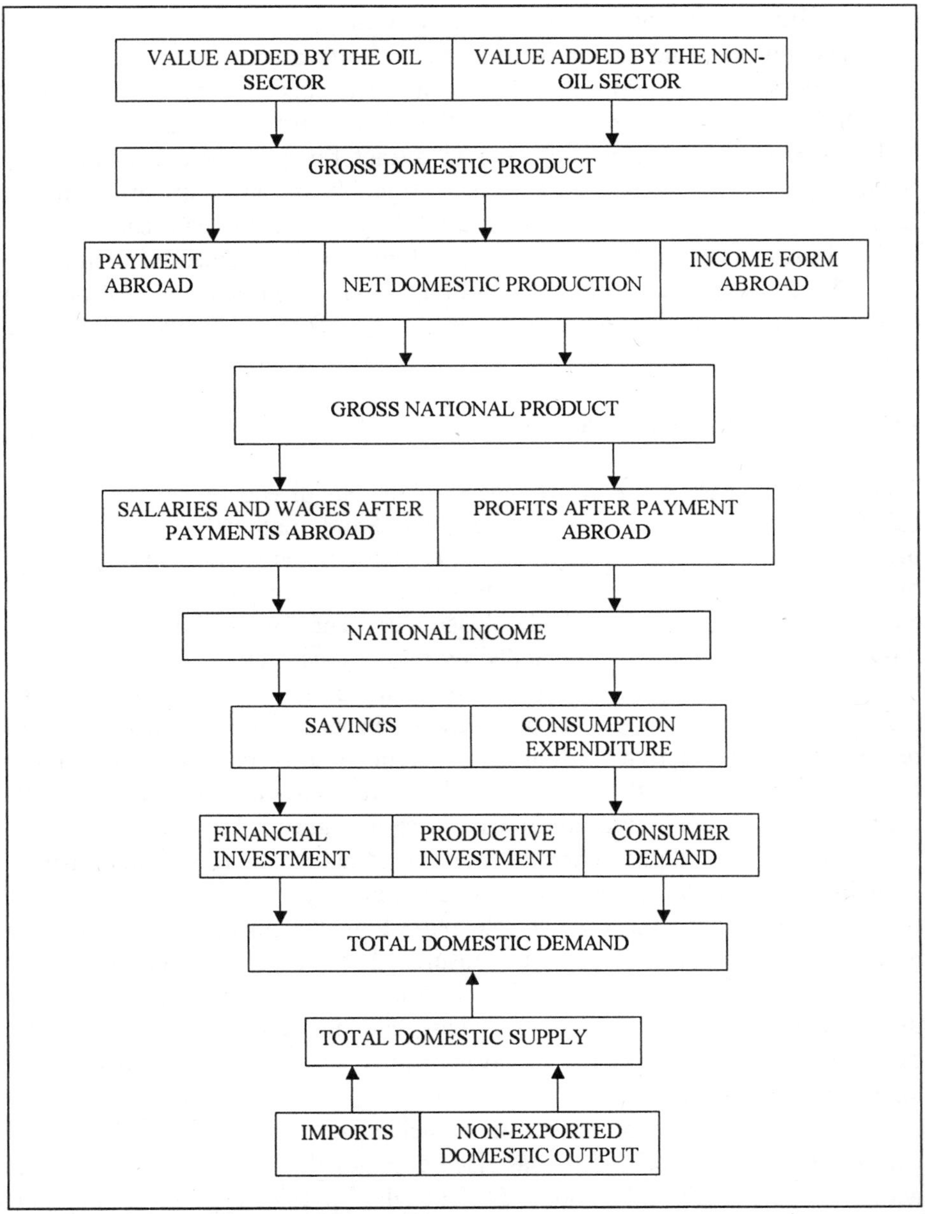

```
┌─────────────────────────────────────────────────────────────────────┐
│   ┌────────────────────────┬────────────────────────┐                │
│   │ VALUE ADDED BY THE OIL  │ VALUE ADDED BY THE NON- │               │
│   │        SECTOR           │        OIL SECTOR       │               │
│   └────────────────────────┴────────────────────────┘                │
│   ┌─────────────────────────────────────────────────┐                │
│   │            GROSS DOMESTIC PRODUCT                │                 │
│   └─────────────────────────────────────────────────┘                │
│   ┌───────────┬──────────────────────────┬──────────┐                │
│   │ PAYMENT   │  NET DOMESTIC PRODUCTION  │ INCOME   │                │
│   │ ABROAD    │                           │ FORM     │                │
│   │           │                           │ ABROAD   │                │
│   └───────────┴──────────────────────────┴──────────┘                │
│        ┌──────────────────────────────────────┐                       │
│        │       GROSS NATIONAL PRODUCT          │                       │
│        └──────────────────────────────────────┘                       │
│   ┌──────────────────────────┬───────────────────────┐               │
│   │ SALARIES AND WAGES AFTER  │ PROFITS AFTER PAYMENT  │               │
│   │    PAYMENTS ABROAD        │        ABROAD          │               │
│   └──────────────────────────┴───────────────────────┘               │
│        ┌──────────────────────────────────────┐                       │
│        │          NATIONAL INCOME             │                        │
│        └──────────────────────────────────────┘                       │
│        ┌──────────────┬───────────────────────┐                       │
│        │   SAVINGS     │     CONSUMPTION       │                       │
│        │               │     EXPENDITURE       │                       │
│        └──────────────┴───────────────────────┘                       │
│      ┌──────────┬──────────────┬──────────────┐                       │
│      │ FINANCIAL │ PRODUCTIVE   │ CONSUMER     │                       │
│      │ INVESTMENT│ INVESTMENT   │ DEMAND       │                       │
│      └──────────┴──────────────┴──────────────┘                       │
│      ┌──────────────────────────────────────┐                         │
│      │        TOTAL DOMESTIC DEMAND          │                         │
│      └──────────────────────────────────────┘                         │
│         ┌──────────────────────────────┐                              │
│         │     TOTAL DOMESTIC SUPPLY     │                              │
│         └──────────────────────────────┘                              │
│         ┌──────────┬───────────────────┐                              │
│         │ IMPORTS  │  NON-EXPORTED      │                             │
│         │          │  DOMESTIC OUTPUT   │                             │
│         └──────────┴───────────────────┘                              │
└─────────────────────────────────────────────────────────────────────┘
```

Adapted from Cleron, 1978, p. 74.

The third striking element is the relatively large portion of the GDP that is paid for the use of foreign owned resources – namely foreign labour working in the Kingdom, as well as foreign-owned oil-related activities. As we will examine later, the campaign to reduce the number of outside workers and the dependency on foreign labour and to replace them with Saudi nationals – the so-called *Saudization* effort – has been partially successful. The size of remittances sent abroad by foreign labour continues to be a significant outflow as illustrated in Table 2.4.

Table *2.4* Remittances from Saudi Arabia (SR billion)

Year	GDP at constant prices (1999=100)	Private transfers	Oil sector payment
1970	148.0	0.81	3.5
1976	416.5	3.5	7.8
1982	480.5	18.0	32.4
1993	552.7	58.8	8.6
1995	557.6	62.2	8.2
1998	608.1	56.0	11.3
2000	632.9	57.7	10.7
2001	641.2	56.9	17.4
2002	647.7	59.4	13.8

Source: *SAMA*, 2003.

According to SAMA, the total amount of private remittances and transfers sent from Saudi Arabia for the period 1970 - 2002 amounted to a staggering SR 979.3 billion ($261.2 billion). Such figures prompt, from time to time, heated debate in the local media about the need to speed up the *Saudization* process or to impose curbs on remittances. Others argue that one way to reduce outflows would be to introduce a more investor-friendly climate in Saudi Arabia so that foreign workers can invest locally. Comparisons are sometimes made with the United States, which has the world's largest immigrant population and yet records lower remittance outflows on a per capita basis compared to Saudi Arabia due to more favourable domestic investment opportunities for U.S. migrant labour. Whatever the arguments, the current level of remittances – amounting to around 10% of GDP – will continue to cause a serious balance of payment problem for Saudi Arabia in the foreseeable future.

Composition of Saudi Gross Domestic Product (GDP)

The next set of tables set out in more detail the composition of Saudi Gross Domestic Product (GDP), from the pre-oil boom period to the "restructuring" era. They provide a closer examination of the "realities" of economic diversification and how far the private sector has taken over from the government in the key areas of consumption expenditure, investment and exports.

Table 2.5 shows the steady progress the non-oil sector has made to stand at around 62% of GDP by 2002, compared with around 22% in 1974 at the beginning of the oil boom era. The private non-oil sector's share of GDP stands at around 40% by 2002, down from 45% to 48% in previous years, indicating that the governmental non-oil sector is still a significant contributor to GDP despite efforts at diversification.

Table 2.5 Gross domestic product sectors and types of economic activity in producers' values

Million Saudi Riyals (in current prices)

	1969	1974	1984	1992	2000	2002
Non-oil sectors	**8,870**	**27,600**	**227,130**	**277,360**	**370,400**	**436,651**
Private sector	7,190	23,310	175,060	202,890	263,700	286,063
Government sector	1,680	4,290	52,070	74,470	106,700	150,588
Oil Sector	**7,740**	**92,800**	**120,300**	**174,940**	**269,320**	**261,822**
Crude oil and natural gas	7,740	92,800	120,300	174,940	269,320	261,822
Gross Domestic Product in producers' values	**16,610**	**120,400**	**347,430**	**452,300**	**639,720**	**681,092**
Import duties	270	440	3,970	9,100	9,620	7,381
Gross Domestic Product in purchasers' value	**16,880**	**120,840**	**351,400**	**461,400**	**649,340**	**698,473**

Source: *Ministry of Planning*, 2002, p. 199.

Table 2.5 also reveals that while the private non-oil GDP has been steadily rising in absolute terms over the years, the oil sector continues to be characterized by volatility, with sharp upswings and downswings, due to fluctuations in both world demand for oil and that commodity's price.

Closer breakdown of the GDP by economic activity reveals the gradual rising value of manufacturing and the services sector in the Saudi economy as illustrated in Table 2.6.

Table 2.6 Gross domestic product by sectors and types of economic activity in producer's values

	1969	1974	1984	1992	2000
Non-oil sectors	**8,870**	**27,600**	**227,130**	**277,360**	**370,400**
Producing sectors	**3,790**	**13,240**	**85,280**	**109,720**	**150,400**
Agriculture, Forestry & Fishing	990	1,350	11,620	28,790	35,570
Non-oil mining	50	210	1,860	1,940	2,520
Manufacturing	**1500**	**6,280**	**27,430**	**39,250**	**58,740**
Petroleum refining	1090	5,130	13,830	18,670	21,590
Petrochemicals			540	3,350	7,080
Other manufacturing	410	1,150	13,060	17,230	30,070
Electricity, gas, & water	260	280	-590	700	970
Construction	990	5,120	44,960	39,040	52,600
Service sectors:	**5,080**	**14,360**	**141,850**	**167,640**	**220,000**
Trade hotels, etc.	990	3,140	30,390	31,240	39,250
Transport, storage & communications	1230	2,610	23,850	28,430	34,780
Finance, insurance, real estate and business services (1/)	950	3,500	25,830	20,900	24,060
Community, social & personal service	230	820	9,710	12,600	15,210
Government services	1680	4,290	52,070	74,470	106,700
Oil product sector:					
Crude oil & natural gas	7740	92,800	120,300	174,940	269,320
Gross domestic product in producer's values	16610	120,400	347,430	452,300	639,720
Import Duties	270	440	3,970	9,100	9,620
Gross domestic product ion purchasers' values	**16,880**	**120,840**	**351,400**	**461,400**	**649,340**

Note:(1/) Net of imputed bank services charges

Source: *CDS National Accounts/MOP, Macroeconomics Calculation, Ministry of Planning,* 2002, p. 201.

As a percentage share of the Saudi GDP, however, manufacturing continues to hover at around 10%, with petroleum refining and petrochemicals representing almost half of the manufacturing contribution to GDP. The service sector accounts for under 20% of the GDP, with finance, insurance and real estate expanding their share, as well as the general trading sector. Construction activity seems to be affected by general business cycle movements, but is still an important segment of the economy at around 8% of GDP. Agriculture, despite massive subsidy support in the early boom period, accounts for around 5% of the GDP with Saudi Arabia a net importer of food products.

The data in Table 2.6 reflects the growing importance of wholesale, retail and restaurant activity. However, this activity consists largely of the marketing of imported goods and growth has been linked to Saudi demographic growth and changing consumer tastes and fashion. The community, social and personal services sectors, and the water and electricity sectors have also grown steadily, but have lagged behind population growth, and are not deemed to be major engines of growth for the Saudi economy.

One area that has potential for the future, as shall be explained in more depth in Chapter 8, is the non-oil mining industry, which has made a slow but gradual contribution to Saudi GDP. This undeveloped aspect of the Kingdom's economic resources is one of the bright hopes of the future.

Saudi Arabian national income data are more difficult to obtain than GDP data. This is due to the high level of data aggregation. National data analysis will help explain who gets what of the national revenue. Intuition would suggest that the government obtains the major component of revenue through oil income. The rest is composed of profits made by business and wages and salaries as well as transfer payments for individuals.

In Saudi Arabia there is also a large element of "transfer payments" through the form of subsidies and subsidized products, especially agricultural products. The Central Department of Statistics is making a commendable effort to overcome this lack of clarity, and has begun to release data on national income. Table 2.7 illustrates these for the years 2000 - 2001. While the level of disaggregation is still not high, Table 2.7 does provide the first level of national income distribution for the Kingdom.

Table 2.7 Saudi Arabia: National disposable income 2000 - 2001 (SR Million)

Disposable income allocation	2000	2001
Compensation of employees	209,446	217,446
Compensation of employees from the rest of the world (net)	(8,657)	(8,505)
Operating surplus gross	476,189	450,446
Property and entrepreneurial income from rest of the world (net)	12,002	18,404
Indirect taxes less subsidies	21,203	18,404
Other current transfers from rest of the world. (net)	(82,157)	(80,032)
Disposable Income	**627,846**	**612,914**

Source: CDS, *National Accounts of Saudi Arabia*, 2001/2002, 2003, pp. 44, 48.

Per capita income, in which Gross National Product is divided by the population, is one measure of national income. Figure 2.4 shows that Saudi GDP per capita reached a peak of SR 52,000 in 1980 ($13,866) before falling to SR 20,000 levels in 1987/1988 ($5,333).

Figure 2.4 GDP per capita (current SR)

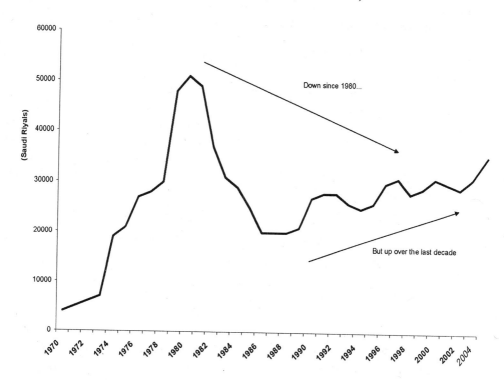

Source: *SAMBA*, 2003.

Stronger oil prices have seen an erratic rise in GDP per capita over the past few years, to take the figure to around SR 32,000 ($8,500) in 2003 and SR38,000 levels in 2004. However, Saudi GDP per capita includes non-Saudis who, according to the latest data, accounted for 6.14 million or 25% of a total population of 24.06 million (SAMA, 2003, p. 298). If one takes into account inflation over the years since 1970, Saudi GDP per capita figures in *real terms* fell sharply to around SR 3,200 ($850), using 1970 as a base year.

In analyzing Saudi Arabia's national income data, the distinction between "stock" and "flow" of income becomes important. Saudi Arabia has what seems to be flows of income, although erratic, from oil and oil based revenues, but seems to be "stock income poor" compared to other developed economies. It takes time to convert "income flows" into "stocks of wealth" which includes infrastructure, capital goods, technical skills and "quality" education output (Chenery, 1979). Social awareness, work ethics and civic participation are also other "intangibles" of a nation's stock of wealth, which, if nurtured, could produce a more sustained growth take-off.

In later chapters we will examine the effects of such tangible and intangible factors on Saudi's economic development prospects, especially on education and employment objectives. While Saudi Arabia has made progress in many areas, the measures the government seems to have taken so far have "lacked the scale and speed" needed to restructure the economy at the rate required (Cordesman, 2003).

This is still evident when one examines the pattern of private and government consumption as well as gross fixed capital formation (GFCF). In more developed economies, the size of private consumption expenditure is higher than government expenditure, as well as a higher rate of GFCF for the private sector (Chenery, 1979, Rostow, 1960). Table 2.8 indicates that the private sector has indeed overtaken the government sector in both consumption expenditure and GFCF since 1986, except for periods of regional crisis, such as the 1990 Gulf crisis during which government expenditure and GFCF rose.

Table 2.8 Expenditure on gross domestic product

Million Saudi Riyals (in current prices)

	1969	1974	1984	1992	2001
Consumption expenditure	**8,910**	**26,870**	**280,290**	**332,890**	**442,354**
Private	5,670	13,920	159,240	183,920	260,898
Government	3,240	12,950	121,050	148,970	181,486
Changes in stock	560	830	19,620	8,500	8,181
Gross fixed capital formation	**2,700**	**12,830**	**92,880**	**93,980**	**126,045**
Private GFCF	1,000	4,300	37,020	54,690	94,347
Government GFCF	1,350	5,350	48,310	32,290	17,508
Oil sector GFCF	350	3,180	9,550	7,000	14,240
Exports of goods & services	9,730	101,470	145,530	207,860	287,850
Less: Imports of goods & services.	**5,020**	**21,160**	**186,920**	**181,830**	162,558
Gross Domestic Product:	**16,880**	**120,840**	**351,400**	**461,400**	**698,473**

Source: *Ministry of Planning*, 2002, p. 210.

However, it is in the area of investment that the private sector has substantially increased its GFCF contribution; it stood at 74% of total GFCF in 2002 compared with 40% in 1984.

Economic theory stipulates the importance of capital accumulation in economic development, with special emphasis on both "capital deepening" and "capital diffusion." The former requires additional input of capital, while the latter involves changes in technology (Bernstein, 1973, Thirwall, 1994, Todaro, 1994). The large oil revenue surpluses Saudi Arabia amassed during earlier boom years allowed it the luxury of investing and expanding its capital stock.

With the rush to modernize and spend the windfall gains, Saudi planners appear to have neglected to take the time to ask essential questions about such concerns as the optimum rates of investment in domestic capital formation (Karl, 1997, Looney, 1989, Askari, 1990). Were these investments to be in tangibles – or intangibles such as quality education – so that a knowledge-based economy built on capital diffusion would become the engine of growth? Given the luxury of earlier capital surpluses, Saudi Arabia could seemingly have chosen both options, as evidenced from the previous analysis of budgetary expenditures on human resource development in the five-year plans. However, expenditures mask qualitative allocations and their economic effectiveness in the long run. The lack of disaggregated data on GFCF makes it difficult to make a judgment, but as Table 2.9 highlights, the major element of GCFC has been in the construction sector.

Table 2.9 Gross domestic fixed capital formation by sectors & type of assets in purchasers values

(Million SR)

	1969	1974	1984	1992	2000	2001
a. By Sector						
Oil Sector	350	3,180	9,550	7,000	9,950	14,240
Non-oil Sectors	2,350	9,650	83,330	86,980	92,740	111,855
Private	1,000	4,300	37,020	54,690	69,630	94,347
Government	1,350	5,350	46,310	32,290	23,110	17,508
Total (GDFCF)	2,700	12,830	92,880	93,980	102,690	126,095
b. By Type of Assets						
Construction	2,100	9,520	67,580	68,190	45,267	57,909
Residential buildings	610	2,320	10,700	14,040	28,052	28,302
Non-residential	1,490	7,200	56,880	54,150	17,215	29,607
Transport equipment	290	1,470	9,690	12,660	19,929	21,004
Machinery & equipment	310	1,840	15,610	13,130	37,494	37,472
Total (GDFCF)	2,700	12,830	92,880	93,980	102,690	126,095

Source: *CDS National Accounts /MOP-Macroeconomic Calculations, Ministry of Planning,* 2002, p. 213.

From Table 2.9, we note that nearly 50% of all gross fixed-capital investment is in residential and non-residential building in 2000, but in 2001 this figure falls to 45%. Investment in this sector has come down substantially from 70 - 75% levels in the earlier boom period, while investment in machinery and equipment has steadily risen and accounted for around 30% of GFCF in 2001, compared with 17% - 20% levels in the earlier periods. Oil sector GFCF has remained steady at around 9 - 10% throughout the period with the exception of a sharp drop in the 1987/1988 period when it reached 2% levels following the collapse in world oil prices discussed earlier.

Given Saudi Arabian intentions to produce oil at nearly full capacity as of August, 2004, as well as plans for expanding the gas sector, investment in these areas will have to involve either greater government expenditures or foreign investment to meet expansion plans. It is not a coincidence that Saudi Arabia has tried to attract international oil companies as partners. The Saudi government has achieved some success in meeting this goal, as will be shown in Chapter 8.

The government data indicate *gross* investments and there are no reliable estimations as to actual *net* investments that the Kingdom is making after taking account of depreciation in the capital stock. The problem of depreciation accounting is well recognized in GDP country estimations, but it is also important to bear in mind that GFCF figures could provide an overly optimistic picture when the true net fixed capital formation figures are much lower. Given that the stock of Saudi capital formation is relatively new, having been built up over the period 1976 - 1986, the rate of depreciation might be lower compared to other countries. This, however, is offset by the relatively harsh environmental conditions under which Saudi projects operate, which could, in theory, accelerate both the rate of depreciation and replacement.

The challenges ahead

While some significant economic achievements have been registered by the Kingdom over the past three decades, meeting the needs of a fast-growing and young population with high expectations poses several challenges to the development process. The planning process that might have served Saudi Arabia in the past needs to be revisited. A more strategic and flexible short-term planning process is probably more suitable in a global economy that is evolving faster. It is worth highlighting that there has been some flexibility in this regard with the current Seventh Five Year Plan, which adopts strategic planning to complement medium-term planning, as well as shorter-term fiscal planning. Most observers of the Saudi economy agree that economic, social and structural reforms are now a necessity and not a luxury (Najem et al., 2003, Wilson, 2004, Champion 2003). However, there are differences of opinion about the pace and scale of reform, as there are many different estimates of trends in the Saudi economy and how these interact with the most pressing issues of the moment, such as population and unemployment levels. In addition, these different estimations disagree about the level of problems that Saudi Arabia will face in the future. Added to this is a debate on the effectiveness of the economic assumptions of "Western" modernization theories that do not take into account non-western cultures and customs (Najem 2003, Abdeen, 1984). Saudi Arabia has made it clear that reforms will come at a pace that is driven by Saudi domestic considerations.

Table 2.10 Saudi Arabia: necessary conditions for growth

Factor　　*Component*	Low	Medium	High
Necessary conditions for growth			
• Macroeconomic stability			
- Government deficits			X
- Inflation	X		
- Exchange rate stability			X
- Solvency of financial system			X
• Deep financial markets			
- Interest rate spreads	X		
- Developed equity markets	X		
- Sophistication of financial system		X	
• Openness to international trade			
- Low import tariffs		X	
- Low hidden import barriers		X	
• Quality of government			
- Public expenditure not wasteful		X	
- Subsidies improve productivity	X		
- Senior management spend little time with government officials			X
- Admin. regulations burdensome			X
• Infrastructure			
- Road quality		X	
- Efficient electrical generation		X	
- High level of competition in provision of basic infrastructure	X		
• Education			
- Years of schooling in population			X
- Perceived quality of education	X		
- Companies invest in training	X		
• Rule of law			
- Independent judiciary		X	
- Ability to successfully litigate against government		X	
• New economy			
- Internet hosts	X		
- Computers per capita	X		
- Development of laws in support of new economy			X

Adapted from *the Arab World Competitiveness Report* 2002 –2 003. pp. 10 – 11.

In the end, there can be no certainties in forecasting data for any country – developed or developing – regardless of the quality of data. Saudi Arabia is a case in point: observers of the economy seem to be either overly optimistic or overly pessimistic about the future, depending on the basic assumptions and trends one picks. The truth of the matter is that the Saudi economy lies somewhere in between despite considerable "developed" country characteristics, which includes overdependence of the GDP and budget on petroleum revenues, lack of economic diversification and a high level of bureaucracy. However, some trends have emerged over the past few years that show Saudi Arabia can still effect meaningful change. These are explored in Table 2.10.

Table 2.10 sets out some necessary preconditions for growth that are sometimes used to assess a country's stage of development. Some of these factors are not based on hard data sources, but instead rely on perceptions. The Table includes eight factors that assist growth without necessarily actively promoting growth (The Arab World Competitiveness Report, 2002 - 2003. p. 12). Poor performance would limit growth. From the table we note that, despite high government budget deficits, the Kingdom has kept inflation low, preserved an open, international trading system, and is beginning to develop a more sophisticated financial system that is fairly solvent. In some areas the economy might seem to be under stress, but overall it is not one that is in crisis. Development of laws in support of a "new" economy is high, but the quality of government services as they relate to interaction with the general public needs to be improved, as does the perceived quality of education.

Table 2.11 Saudi Arabia: Engines of growth

Factor *Component*	Saudi Arabian Setting		
Engines of growth	Low	Medium	High
• Start-ups and entrepreneurship			
- Administrative barriers to start ups			X
- Venture capital availability	X		
- Loans available with low collateral		X	
• Capital accumulation			
- National savings rate		X	
- Investment rate			
(Gross Fixed Capital Formation	X		
• Taxation			
- Low income tax rate		N/A	
- Low corporate tax rate (foreigners only)	X		
- Low value added taxes		N/A	
- Tax system perceived to improve competitiveness		N/A	
• Innovation			
- Highly rated research institute	X		
- Business conducts R+D	X		
- Close collaboration between universities and businesses	X		
- Government supports research			
- High expenditure on R+D	X	X	
• Transfer of technology			
- Foreign direct investment brings new technology		X	
- Licensing pursued to obtain foreign technology			X
• Export diversification			
- Exports other than national resources	X		

Source: Adapted from *Arab World Competitiveness Report* 2002 – 2003.

Table 2.11 includes the more dynamic factors that, in economic development theories, focus on "engines" of economic growth.

The lack of export diversification, of a culture of innovation and of research and development are tied to the perceived weakness from education output, as shown in Table 2.11. As we will note in Chapter 10, the Saudi experience of technology transfer is based on a transfer method that is through licensing operations. This fosters a low level of research and development initiative, despite government support for research.

Administrative barriers to start-ups are high despite loan availability and a non-existent taxation regime for Saudi individuals and corporations. The latter pay a 2.5% *zakat* or religiously ordained levy on total assets, while foreign company corporate taxes were reduced to 20% in 2003. As discussed earlier, Gross Fixed Capital Formation is low despite a fairly high national savings rate, while non-oil related export diversification has not matched national expectations.

Conclusion

Long-awaited structural changes and diversification efforts have not generated the necessary private sector jobs or produced a sustained "knowledge-based" economy. Expansion has been largely in the non-manufacturing services and construction sectors. The Saudi government has, to its credit, recognized a lot of these problems and is seeking ways to overcome them. The planning process has helped to identify key national objectives, but the emphasis going forward must be on *qualitative* rather than *quantitative* outputs. The Kingdom will launch its Eighth Development Plan to cover the period 2005 - 2009. There is hope that the planning exercise this time is more focused on key issues, such as:

- developing a viable educational system through effective education and training strategies to ensure that education output meets market needs
- developing a research and development culture, not just in Academia but amongst Saudi businesses, through incentive schemes
- easing government bureaucracy and red tape by applying e-government policies and instituting new measurable, deliverable policies
- opening the market to international and domestic competition in the telecommunication and IT sectors
- encouraging *Saudization* through a policy of skills enhancement and private sector/government partnership that addresses both sides' concerns
- expanding new productive areas of the economy such as gas and minerals and mining sectors

- realizing the potential importance of women's participation in the economic development of Saudi Arabia

The Saudi government, above all, must not waver in carrying through the necessary, harsh adjustments and reforms, irrespective of temporary oil-related windfalls such as those expected for 2004. Promised reforms in past Saudi Development Plans have been delayed or not fully implemented, particularly at times when the economy seemed to benefit from periods of relatively high world oil prices. It thus becomes easy to delay the economic and social costs of reforms when "windfall" government revenues are available; it takes long-sighted political skill and courage to continue with essential reforms, despite the temptation to ease back.

Summary of the key points

- *Saudi Arabia has put in place a system of sophisticated development planning since 1970 through implementing a series of medium term five year plans,*
- *The process of planning has evolved as the economic structure of the country has undergone transformation with the private sector assuming more importance in both consumption expenditure and gross fixed capital formation,*
- *The strategic choices that early planners made to steer the economy from overwhelming dependence on oil are still being felt today in the area of continued foreign labour dependence, outward remittances and mismatch between domestic labour supply and market requirements,*
- *Planning is now shifting from a "directive" to an "indicative" role as the economy becomes more globalized and interdependent with the rest of the world,*
- *Precondition for growth as well as key "engines of growth" are examined as well as the obstacles that need to be overcome to support the emergence of a private sector led economy.*

Critical thinking

1. "The art of good government is by being invisible". Whey do we then need planning in Saudi Arabia?
2. "Economic planning failed to address the key issues facing Saudi Arabia today". Is this a fair statement? What could the early planners have done better that, in hindsight, you disagree with?

3. Is the Saudi economy ready for "indicative" planning, or should planning be "directive" or both?

4. Which "engines of growth" should Saudi Arabia concentrate on to achieve its (a) short term, and (b) long term goals?

5. How do you foresee Saudi private sector's contribution to GDP in consumption and investment in a decade from now?

Chapter 3

GOVERNMENT FINANCES AND THE SAUDI BUDGETARY SYSTEM

Beware of little expenses; a small leak will sink a great ship.

Franklin

Learning outcomes

By the end of this section, you should understand:

- *The importance of the Saudi budgetary mechanism as a tool for government economic policy*
- *The significant role played by oil revenue in the Kingdom's economic fortunes*
- *Overdependence on oil versus building a diversified private sector for wealth generation*
- *The impact of limited revenue sources on current and capital expenditures*
- *Cyclical and structural budget deficits*
- *Government borrowing, the debt burden and the phenomenon of "crowding out" the private sector*
- *Short and long-term fiscal restructuring solutions*

Overview

The government of Saudi Arabia has made its intentions public on the need for both economic reforms at home and for joining international organizations such as the World Trade Organization (WTO). Economic openness implies a high degree of transparency and accountability to international organizations in which the Kingdom is a member state, such as the World Bank and the International Monetary Fund (IMF). As the Finance Minister of Saudi Arabia sits on the Board of Executive Directors of the IMF, Saudi fiscal policies and budgetary management have been influenced by the methods and practices of such organizations.

By virtue of its economic size in terms of spending, consumption and investment, as well its ownership of the single most valuable economic resource – oil – the fiscal policy of the government of Saudi Arabia directly affects the economic well-being of the country. One key economic policy tool at its disposal is the budgetary mechanism.

The budget – a barometer of the nation's health

Until 1986, the Saudi government scheduled its annual budget on the basis of the *Hejira* calendar, with the financial year beginning on the first day of *Rajab*, the seventh month of the *Hejira* year. In 1987, the budget implementation date was changed to the tenth day of the Capricorn zodiac sign, or January 1 on the Gregorian calendar. Each ministry and government sub-agency prepares its annual budgetary expenditures – and revenues where applicable – according to pre-set guidelines established by the Ministry of Finance. The national budget is then compiled by the Ministry of Finance. Once the budget receives Royal approval, it is published in *Umm al Qura* – the Official Gazette – pursuant to a Royal Decree.

The publication of the Saudi budget for the forthcoming year attracts a lot of attention, both domestically and internationally. The principal reasons for this focus on the budget are that it provides the following:

- a forecast of expenditures to be made for the different economic sectors for the coming year
- signals regarding the intentions of government priorities in expenditures
- the composition of current versus capital expenditure, allowing businessmen to make plans for project bidding
- an indication of the likely forecasted, budgeted deficits or surpluses, thus suggesting whether the government might borrow domestically or internationally, as well as the likely impact on Saudi banking liquidity

The budget also contains quantitative and qualitative assessments of the preceding budget year in terms of actuals versus budgeted figures. In addition, it projects future economic prospects, especially on the expected price level of oil, as this is still the single most important revenue component of the Saudi budget.

By law, the Saudi budget must always be balanced. By accounting definition, the revenues and expenditures must balance on both sides of the balance sheet, but all that really means is that budgeted expenditures must equal budgeted revenues. In reality, the budget has rarely balanced, due to the unpredictable nature of budgeted revenues. However, in the earlier boom years, this concept of "balanced" was accepted as something workable, because of the large reserves built up (Johany et al, 1986).

Previously it worked like this. Suppose that expected oil revenues exceeded planned expenditures. The announced budget would include an item called "shortfall in expenditure," which would be added to general reserves. If expenditures exceeded current year earnings, then there would be a withdrawal from reserves that was entered into the revenue side of the accounts. However, even early Saudi economy watchers noted that this could only last as long as reserves existed, for "…if reserves are too small, then the balanced budget requirement does actually impose a limit on expenditures" (Johany et al., 1986, p. 62). How prophetic these words turned out to be! As we will explain later, with the exceptions of 2000, 2003 and 2004, the Saudi fiscal sector has revealed that Saudi budgets have recorded consecutive deficits since 1983, reaching SR 75.4 billion in 1986 or 28% of GDP. In March 1986, for the first time in modern Saudi history, the government postponed the announcement of its next budget for five months, because the fall in oil prices weighed so heavily on Saudi political and economic decisions.

Primarily because of significant declines and erratic oil revenues, as well as high population growth and the expanded economic base of the country, Saudi Arabia has begun to face both budgetary restraints and financial constraints. The matter of fiscal prudence and budgetary controls is now one of national concern, and this has been emphasized with increasing urgency by no less a person than the Governor of the Saudi Arabian Monetary Agency (SAMA) Hamad Al-Sayyari. Upon presenting the SAMA's 39th Annual Report 2002 – 2003 to King Fahd, Al-Sayyari stated that the government must give priority to "developing an appropriate mechanism to amortize public debts and maintain fiscal balances…(and) stable oil prices and the success of efforts aimed at controlling public expenditures and balancing the budget will help reduce public debt" (Arab News, 4 November 2003). This was the second public announcement by the SAMA Governor on the matter of fiscal restraint and debt amortization.

From oil wealth to oil poverty

As this book will make evident, the Saudi economy grew rapidly in the early 1970s, but the growth was fuelled by a virtual doubling of oil

production. In effect, the Saudi economy became ever more dependent –
like a hostage – to the fortunes of a single commodity: oil (Gehb, 1998,
Looney, 1990). This is illustrated in Table 3.1, which sets out the scale of
Saudi oil production and revenues from 1970 – 2001.

Table 3.1 Saudi Arabian oil production and revenues

	1970 – 1973	1974 – 1978	1979 – 1981	1982 – 1985	1986 – 1991	1992 – 1996	1996 – 2001
Oil Output (million barrels)	8.100	15.202	10.681	6.672	12.292	14.778	14.548
Oil Revenue (SR billion)	69.98	537.6	837.0	540.3	478.3	571.6	742.5
Non-oil GDP (SR billion)	25.1	147.6	224.3	607.8	789.3	808.4	1,522.1

Source: *Ministry of Planning, 2002, SAMA*, 2002 pp. 388, 444, 455.

Oil revenues, while overtaken by non-oil GDP from the mid-1980s, still
account for a large portion of Saudi GDP compared with oil-exporting non-
Middle East countries such as Mexico and Indonesia, as Table 3.2 below
shows.

Table 3.2 Oil and gas rents share in GDP 1970 – 2001
Three countries: (% GDP) Indonesia, Mexico, Saudi Arabia

Country	1970 – 1973	1974 – 1978	1979 – 1981	1982 – 1985	1986 – 1990	1991 – 1994	1995 – 2001
Indonesia	6.70	14.78	27.87	19.45	10.24	6.44	11.60
Mexico	1.77	4.54	15.58	19.51	9.53	4.72	9.45
Saudi Arabia	63.7	68.26	84.63	45.73	37.16	42.93	36.5

Source: *World Bank*, 1999, *SAMA*, 2002, p. 444.

Currently, the Saudi oil sector accounts for around 36% of GDP
compared to levels of nearly two-thirds during the pre-1980 era. However,
this is still far higher than those of Indonesia and Mexico, which are both
under 12% levels.

What Tables 3.1 and 3.2 indicate is that, by the mid-1980s, Saudi Arabia
had moved away from being a "capital surplus" mineral economy that might
evade growth problems through being a "rentier" economy – similar to
smaller, mineral-rich economies such as Brunei, Kuwait and Abu Dhabi
(Johany et al., 1986). The early boom period of Saudi economic history
produced increased oil revenues that permitted the accumulation of financial
reserves with which to lengthen the necessary structural adjustment of the
economy to abrupt contractions of the "rental," or oil, income stream,

compared with capital deficient oil-driven economies such as Indonesia or Mexico who have relied less on oil revenues (Auty, 2001).

Windfall gains...

During the oil "windfall" era, Saudi strategy for deployment of this windfall exhibited a number of characteristics. First, the government captured the bulk of the oil rents through the nationalization of the production of oil and through appropriate taxation levels. It accumulated a substantial part of these oil revenues as reserves overseas, which some sources – IMF and World Bank – calculated as peaking at $170 billion levels in the early 1980s.

The second Saudi strategy seemed to have rejected the "rentier" option adopted in countries such as Kuwait (Auty, 2001) and to have embarked on an extensive diversification of the domestic economy. The result of this change was the overtaking of the oil sector by the non-oil GDP sector as evidenced in Table 3.1.

The third feature of the Saudi windfall strategy was the maintenance of an open economy. The economy was open not only for imported goods and services, but also for foreign workers and international construction companies, in order to ease the boom period bottlenecks. The result of this third feature was to reduce the effect of the so-called "Dutch disease" during a resource boom (Auty, 1999; Balance et al., 2001, Sachs et al., 2001, Gylafson et al., 1999, Gehb et al., 1988). All these studies demonstrated that resource abundance may *reduce growth* by hurting domestic productivity growth. The opening up of the Saudi economy, through increasing the expenditure of foreign exchange on imported goods, helped to "sterilize" the Saudi foreign exchange from appreciating further, while reinforcing the sterilization role of the accumulation of financial reserves overseas. The bulk of imported goods in the early boom period was also primarily for infrastructure and capital-intensive projects. This helped to constrain domestic inflationary pressure in Saudi Arabia from the late 1970s to the mid-1980s, because the import of foreign labour and foreign construction companies helped to eliminate bottlenecks in Saudi absorptive capacity. This was manifested by an annual, average inflation rate of around 22% for the period 1974 – 1979, before declining to around 5% for the period 1979 – 1984 (Ministry of Planning, 2002, p. 246).

... and losses

Due to erratic world oil prices and other factors, which will be explored further below, the Saudi windfall deployment strategies that had seemed to serve it well in the boom years became a liability in the downturn periods that followed. The Saudi economy absorbed a sizeable amount of the windfall gains in current consumption, as opposed to fixed capital formation and domestic savings to sustain it in leaner years. This is illustrated in Figure 3.1 below, which summarizes investment and saving patterns in Saudi Arabia over the period 1970 – 2002, and compares these with the "resource poor" economy of Singapore, which started its independence with little capital surplus in 1965 (Lee Kuan Yew, 1998).

Figure 3.1 Investment and national savings rates (% GDP) for Saudi Arabia and Singapore 1970 – 2002

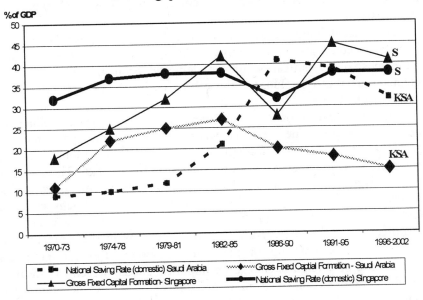

Source: *SAMA*, 2002, pp. 343, 443. *Ministry of Planning*, 2002, 210, 240, *Singapore Department of Statistics, website; www.singstat.gov.sg*

Figure 3.1 shows some remarkable similarities between Singapore and Saudi Arabia during the early period of their economic development. Both countries' gross fixed capital formation (GFCF) and national savings ratios to GDP rose sharply until 1985. The Saudi share of GFCF to GDP then fell sharply to around 18% in 2002, from 26% in the 1982 – 1986 period. The fall in the Saudi GFCF was not matched by a similar fall in national savings, which rose to a peak of 43% in the 1986 – 1990 period, before declining to 36% in the later period.

Unlike Singapore, which continued to sustain its capital investment stock at the 40% level, the Saudi economy seemed to be characterized by declining investment in fixed assets, despite the availability of national savings. This gap became more pronounced following the 1990 – 1991 Gulf War.

A second flaw of the windfall strategy was that Saudi Arabia relaxed market discipline so that the windfall gains did not result in the competitive diversification of the non-oil sector. This was due to subsidy policies in agriculture and manufacturing – which we will examine in more detail in later chapters. Suffice it to say now that the subsidy policy adopted in those early periods of economic boom still linger in some form to date, and continue to have an impact on the Saudi government's fiscal policies, as well as on national productivity and resource allocation.

A third flaw of the windfall strategy was that the Saudi government did not deem it necessary to introduce a wider range of taxation systems to broaden its revenue stream, nor was there an attempt to recover the costs of government services – utilities and others – at more economic rates. The provision of such services at subsidized prices, despite some attempts at recouping part of the charges, is still an inherent drag on Saudi fiscal policy today.

The fourth flaw of the windfall strategy was the sharp increase of employment in the public sector of the Kingdom, with Saudi workers choosing to work in the public sector, thus pushing the private sector to employ foreign workers. The consequence of this early Saudi rental deployment strategy will be more closely examined in the following chapters, but the effects have been to bloat government recurrent expenditures at the expense of capital investment, as well as to spawn an educational system that produces graduates geared for public sector jobs rather than promoting the scientific and technical skills relevant to private sector manufacturing.

This phenomenon of public sector preference is not unique to Saudi Arabia. An earlier study (Chalk et al., 1997) compared capital-surplus oil producers of the Middle East with capital-deficient oil producers and some other OECD countries. It found that the capital-surplus oil producers expended a much higher percentage of their GDP on current expenditures, wages and salaries and subsidies than other countries. The results of the study are set out in Table 3.3 below.

With the exception of Sweden, which has the most liberal subsidy and transfer payment system in Europe, the comparison shows the marked contrast between capital-rich and capital-deficient oil producers in terms of current expenditure levels and wages as a percentage of their GDP. Iran is the only exception, despite having a larger population than the Arab capital-rich oil producers. Later, we will analyze how the Saudi government has been trying to overcome some of this inherent structural deficiency in its fiscal policy.

Table 3.3 Government expenditure, twelve countries (% GDP) 1994

Countries	Current Expenditures	Wages and Salaries	Subsidies and Transfers
Middle East			
Bahrain	27.6	15.8	4.0
Iran	16.2	9.0	2.5
Kuwait	50.3	14.5	16.9
Oman	37.1	10.2	2.7
Qatar	38.1	14.7	0.0
Saudi Arabia	32.7	18.0	1.0
Other oil producers			
Indonesia	8.5	2.7	2.6
Mexico	14.8	4.5	5.4
Nigeria	13.5	2.5	N/A
Venezuela	16.3	4.2	5.3
OECD countries			
Sweden	49.5	3.0	25.6
United States	22.2	2.2	5.9

Source: *Chalk et al.* (1997): 13. *SAMA*, 2002.

Overdependence on oil versus building true wealth

The Saudi Kingdom today is coping with rapid political, demographic and social challenges. A key economic objective is to move away from a state-driven economy that is largely dependent on oil wealth in order to create a more diversified, private sector-led economy. Saudi Arabia can no longer rely on oil wealth alone, and one or two years oil revenues that exceed the forecast, temporarily building up the state's coffers, will not change the long-term need for building true wealth, in place of reliance on a single primary source of revenue.

This dilemma is set out in Figure 3.2, which encapsulates in a simplified manner the main drivers of the Saudi economy during periods of increase and decrease in oil revenues.

With the exception of 2000, 2003 and 2004, the Saudi economy has recently been going through the adjustment phase, seen in the scenario illustrating the decrease in oil revenue, in Figure 3.2. However, despite Crown Prince Abdullah's statements that the oil "boom days" are over, some sections of Saudi society still see the oil boom days from the mid-1970s to the early 1980s, as exemplified by the "increase in oil revenue" section of Figure 3.2, as being the norm rather than the exception. They act as if time and oil wealth will solve all problems in the future. This view postpones the needed hard economic reforms and adjustments to spending patterns, under the misconception that little discipline is needed to restructure the economy. In essence, it is an unsustainable policy of "muddling through," based on the implication that the government will still play a dominant role in the Saudi economy. However, as we will discuss in Chapters Seven and Eleven, the government has already sent out signals about its intentions to disengage through a planned program of privatization and let the private sector assume greater economic responsibility.

Figure 3.2 Saudi oil revenue volatility model

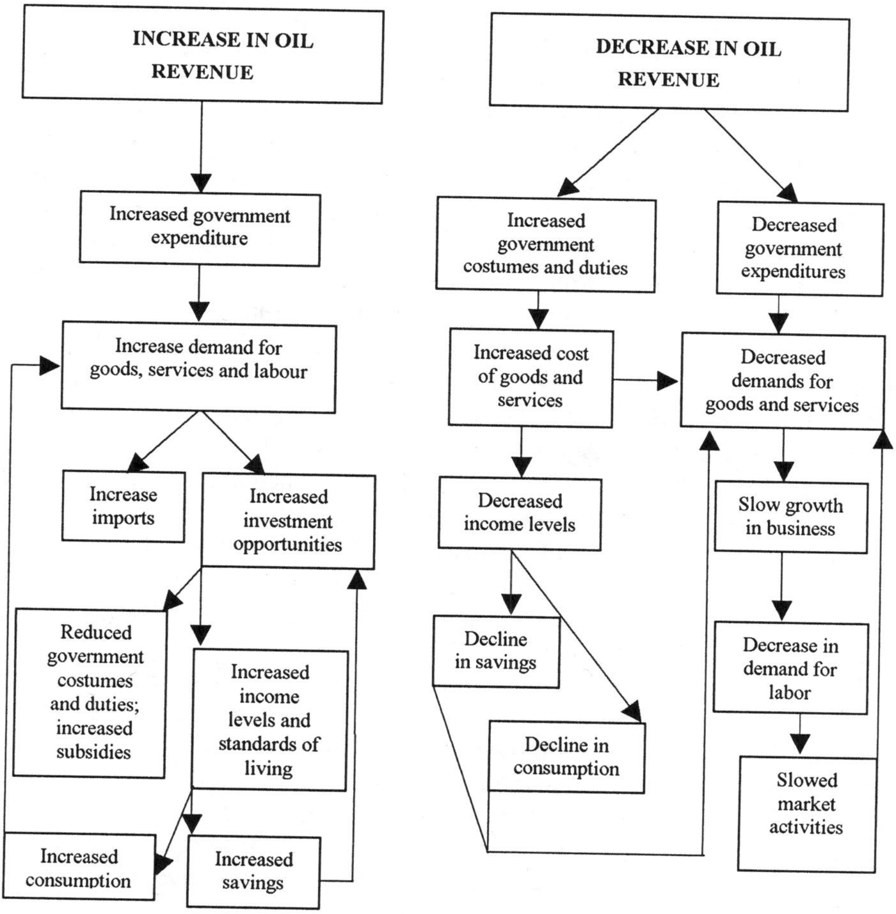

Adopted from Cleron, 1978.

The problem facing many practicing economists in Saudi Arabia is that there is no one way to calculate the precise scale and pace of reform that is needed to build "true wealth," due to differing estimates of the trends for the Saudi economy and how these interact with demographic and social pressures. These different scenarios vary in how they portray the problems that might lay ahead, as well as the pace and direction of economic reform. Such issues increase the challenges that Saudi Arabia faces in managing its national budget. However, the next section explores the general macroeconomic spending trends that indicate that the government was sending out signals as to its long-term spending intentions.

Government intentions are made known

Table 3.4 below sets out the annual planned Saudi budget estimates for revenues and expenditures by broad economic sectoral categories for the year 1982 – a watershed "boom year" – for 1992, and for the years 1998 – 2003, the economic adjustment period.

What the table indicates is that the government's planned (as opposed to actual) expenditures were driven by the need to meet a growing population's health and educational needs. These were offset by reductions in both absolute and relative terms for infrastructure development, economic resource development, government lending institutions and subsidies. Defence expenditure levels varied from 32 to 40%. Given recent internal security issues in Saudi Arabia following the May, 2003, Riyadh bombings, this item will be difficult to reduce in the short run and has, in fact, been increased (Saudi Press Agency, Dec., 2003). Public Administration has accounted for between 15% and 19% of total expenditure, and the Saudi government has been attempting to control this recurrent expenditure item (which is mostly made up of wages and salaries) but without meaningful success, as will be noted later on. Prominent Saudi economists have called for "elimination of waste and switching of expenditures into more productive areas" (Al Sheikh, S. December, 2003).

The government's planned intentions were clear: less for subsidies, infrastructure and capital projects, and more for health and education. The slack in government spending would be made up by the private sector provision of such goods and services. Health and education now accounts for around 40% of total planned expenditures, compared with 30 to 32% levels in the earlier development period. This is the quantitative aspect of government spending, and does not address the qualitative questions of whether such expenditures are yielding an efficient economic and allocative output, especially in education, for meeting Saudi Arabia's future skill needs.

Table 3.4 Saudi Arabia: annual government budget estimates (by sectors)
1982 – 2003

SECTOR	1982	1992	1999	2000	2001	(Million Rls) 2003
A. Revenue						
Oil Revenue	270,579	117,693	75,881	117,895	169,000	122,000
Other Revenues	42,821	33,302	45,119	39,105	46,000	48,000
Total	**313,400**	**151,000**	**121,000**	**157,000**	**215,000**	**170,000**
B. Expenditures:						
Human Resource Development	31,864	31,855	42,792	49,284	53,010	57,475
Transport & Communications	32,535	8,452	5,197	5,534	5,732	6,479
Economic Resource Development	22,045	4,615	4,418	5,955	5,629	3,222
Health & Social Development	17,010	13,534	15,152	16,381	18,089	23,200
Infrastructure Development	11,705	2,090	1,707	2,067	2,532	1,900
Defence & Security	92,889	57,601	68,700	74,866	78,850	68,000 (e)
Public Administration and other Government Spending	44,586	49,176	16,458	19,277	37,372	36,000
Government Lending Institutions	23,382	648	420	436	411	200 (e)
Local Subsidies	11,162	7,107	4,756	5,490	6,151	5,000 (e)
Total	**313,400**	**181,000**	**165,000**	**185,000**	**215,000**	**209,000**

Sources: *SAMA*, 2002 *Ministry of Finance and National Economy*, 2002. *National Commercial Bank, 1ˢᵗ Quarter 2003 Saudi Economic Perspectives.*
(e)Author's estimates.

But in reality, the budgeted plans never materialize

Analyzing projected or planned Saudi budget allocations and revenues might be considered an interesting academic exercise, in the sense that it serves as a guidepost to Saudi government intentions about sectoral allocations. In reality, it is more important to analyze actual, ex-post Saudi budget results. Such an analysis graphically illustrates two fundamental core issues facing Saudi fiscal authorities today: their continued inability to have significant control over a large element of government revenues, and their inability or unwillingness to curb and reallocate expenditures, a problem which may be structurally inherent.

Table 3.5 below sets out planned, as opposed to actual, Saudi budgets for
the years 1996 – 2004.

Table 3.5 Saudi actual vs. budgeted revenues and expenditures
comparison 1996 – 2004

Year	Budgeted Revenue	Actual Revenue	Realized Revenue surplus/ deficit	Budgeted expenditure	Actual expenditure	Realized expenditure deficit/ surplus	Overall Budget Def/ Surplus
1981	340	368	**+28**	298	284.6	**+13.4**	+83.4
1982	313	246	**(67)**	313	245	**-68.0**	+1.0
1987	103	103.8	**+0.8**	159	173	**-14.0**	-69.2
1992	151	169.6	**+18.6**	181	211	**-30.0**	-41.4
1994	120	129	**+9.0**	160	163.7	**-3.7**	-34.7
1996	132	178.8	**+46.8**	150	198.1	**-48.1**	-19.3
1997	164	205.5	**+41.5**	181	221.3	**-40.3**	-15.8
1998	178	143	**(35)**	196	189	**+7**	-46.0
1999	121	147.5	**+26.5**	165	183.8	**-18.8**	-36.3
2000	157	248	**+91**	185	203	**-18**	+45.0
2001	215	230	**+15**	215	255	**-40**	-25.0
2002	157	204	**+47**	202	225	**-23**	-21.0
2003	170	295	**+125**	209	250	**-41**	+45.0
2004[(e)]	200	393	**+193**	230	295	**-65**	+98

Sources: *SAMA, Ministry of Finance.*   *(e) Ministry of Finance, December 2004.*

Table 3.5 reveals that Saudi fiscal planners have, in general, tended to err
on the conservative side when budgeting their revenues. With the exception
of 1982 and 1998, this held true for all the years surveyed. The opposite
seems to hold true when it comes to budgeted expenditures. Saudi planners
tended to underestimate projected needs, with budgeted expenditures lagging
behind actuals in all years with the exceptions of 1981 and 1998. What has
been the reason for this mismatch between planned revenues and
expenditures, and actual revenues and expenditures?

Some argue that the Saudi Ministry of Finance has traditionally tended to
be reactive rather than proactive, cutting current and capital expenditures
after falls in oil prices and increasing them in better times (Wilson, 2003).
According to this argument, no real attempt has been made to date to
anticipate oil price cycles and steer the economy accordingly. Real power is
effectively being held in the Saudi Ministry of Petroleum rather than in the
Ministry of Finance, whose function is therefore relegated to control of
disbursements (Wilson, 2003). Others have supported this argument (Askari
et al., 1997, Gelb, 1998). However, in order to adopt flexible fiscal planning

in the face of changing world economic and political factors that affect the movement and price of oil, Saudi Arabia would need to introduce several "mini budget announcements" during the fiscal year (akin to the UK's "autumn budget") which would take into account changed circumstances and would adjust accordingly for public expenditures.

The years 2003 and 2004 are good benchmarks to illustrate the need for a more proactive budgetary approach, with strikes in Venezuela and Nigeria disrupting oil shipments and with the Iraq war and consequent reduction in Iraq oil supplies also helping to firm prices for those years. The result was that the Saudi government's forecasted oil revenues of SR 122 billion for 2003 (Table 3.3) were grossly underestimated at around $17 per barrel, while local banks were forecasting oil revenues of SR 234 billion (NCB, 2003) to SR 223 billion (SAMBA, 2003) at prices ranging between $25 and $28 per barrel. The Ministry of Finance's 2003/2004 budget statement estimated the 2003 actual revenue at SR 295 billion – some 142% higher than the budgeted SR 170 billion. The 2004 government fiscal projections are now forecasted to be completely underestimated due to stronger oil prices during that year with a surplus of SR 98 billion versus a budgeted SR 30 billion defit.

The 2003 Saudi Cabinet reshuffle and Ministry changes removed the function of Economy from the Ministry of Finance by merging Economy with Planning. Ostensibly, the trimming of the Economy responsibility could free the Ministry of Finance to concentrate on a more effective anticipatory fiscal policy for the Kingdom. The "new-look" Ministry of Finance would no longer be simply seen as a mere disbursing agency, but as an active participant in shaping the direction of the Saudi economy.

Fiscal management to date has been erratic

Implementation of previous fiscal policies have seen little control over major revenue streams and erratic expenditure patterns, especially in terms of ballooning current expenditures over capital expenditures. The next set of figures highlight these inherent unbalances.

Figure 3.3 encapsulates the various phases of Saudi economic development over three decades, with the "boom" era of 1975 to 1981 characterized by a sharp rise in oil revenues, high investment income from abroad, as well as large surpluses in the overall capital account. The sharp fall in oil income starting in 1982, despite some later "spikes" in oil revenue, is generally characterized as belonging to the "economic adjustment" era, with lower foreign investment income, attempts at spending rationalization and a gradual rise in non-oil income (Wilson et al., 2003).

Figure 3.3 Trends of actual oil and non-oil revenues

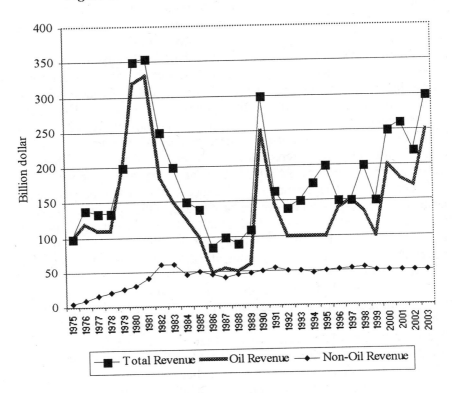

Source: *SAMA*, 2003.

The "economic adjustment" era was also characterized by a low level of capital expenditure, with sharp reductions in this sector during periods of oil revenue falls, as illustrated in Figure 3.4.

Despite a sharp rise to SR 41.6 billion in capital expenditure projects for fiscal 2003, and SR 75.5 billion for 2004, the level of actual capital expenditures as a proportion of total expenditures has remained stagnant at between 12 and 15% for the last decade. This has worrying implications for the future, in the face of the needs of a relatively young population. The disparity between government finances and a fast-growing population is highlighted in Figure 3.5 which shows that, with the exception of the "golden boom" years of 1980 – 1981, the gap between population growth and government financial resources has been consistently widening. Even with the exceptional high revenues forecasted for 2004, a widening gap continues to exist.

Figure 3.4 Developments of capital and current expenditures

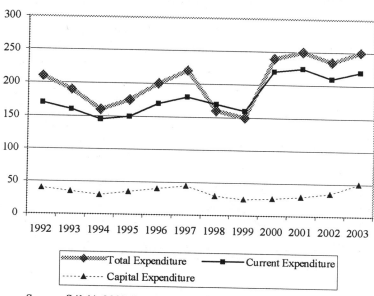

Source: *SAMA,* 2002, *Ministry of Finance,* 2003.

The widening gap between meeting the Kingdom's growing population needs and the revenue shortfall has given an added urgency to speeding up privatization and placed greater emphasis on the private sector in order to build up the nation's capital stock. The Saudi private sector of the 2003 era is a far cry from the private sector of the early development period. The overall effect of the "boom" and "adjustment" economic cycles was that many businesses that entered the market during the economic boom era went bankrupt because of their failure to adjust to new market conditions. They had entered business without due proper planning, experience and cost control. The adjustment period was also one of domestic bank loan crises, which forced Saudi banks to reconsider loan extension and tighten their credit policies (Dukhail, 1995).

On the positive side, however, many of the development strategies put in place towards the end of the boom period provided the basis for growth during the economic adjustment era. The private sector gradually began to emerge as the major contributor to GDP and capital investment, overtaking the government sector by the early 1990s (SAMA, 2002). Of more long-term importance, those private sector companies that did survive the adjustments and downturn did so on a sounder financial, managerial and planning footing, possibly enabling them to take up the challenge in filling the void of government services.

Figure 3.5 Saudi Arabia population and government finances
1970 - 2003 (1980 = 100)

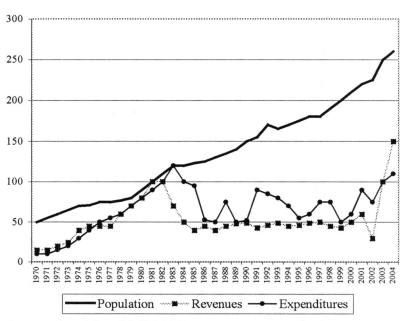

Source: Adapted from *SAMBA*, 2002.
Note: Population and government finances data rebased to an index with the base year
1980 = 100. Lines represent relative change from the base year.

Saudi budgetary planning: an economy dependent on oil

In more economically diversified countries, government revenues are
derived from a variety of sources. In the USA and most Western European
countries, the bulk of government revenues are derived from the private
sector in the form of direct and indirect taxes (IMF, 2002), with governments
applying fiscal and monetary policies to either stimulate or dampen demand
and output, depending on the state of the economy and the business cycle.

In Saudi Arabia, fiscal policy instruments are the chief means of
controlling macroeconomic activity, but in practice this means government
spending as opposed to taxes (Wilson et al., 2003). Oil revenue continues to
be the main driver of the Saudi economy, despite attempts at economic
diversification, and this major source of income is externally rather
internally driven.

In essence, the Saudi economy has been described as having become
"petrolised" (Karl, 1997). The effect of this "petrolisation" is summarized in

Figure 3.6, which sets out actual Saudi budget revenues, expenditures, and surpluses/deficits for the period 1984 to 2004.

Figure 3.6 Saudi Arabia: Budget breakdown 1984 – 2004

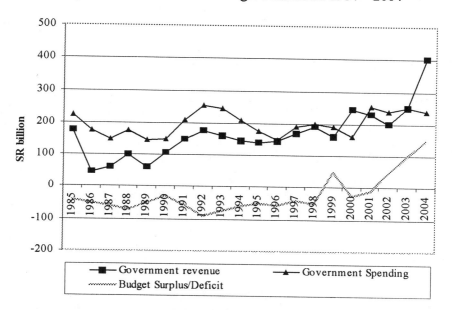

Source: *Finance Ministry, SAMA* 2002, *SAMBA* 2003.
*Budgeted Forecast, 2004, Ministry of Finance.

With the exception of 2000, 2003 and forecasted 2004, the Kingdom has registered a persistent budget deficit.

These pendulum swings in fiscal fortunes are not conducive to sound national management in any sphere of the economy or society. In Saudi Arabia there is no direct income tax on expatriates or Saudis. There was some debate about introducing a flat 10% tax on foreigners during 2003; however, the idea was abandoned (Arab News, 2003). Indirect and sales taxes have also been discussed but not implemented.

Sources of revenue are limited

Besides oil revenue, current Saudi government revenues are mainly derived from corporate and business tax, *zakat*, customs and import duties, charges for government services, other "miscellaneous income" such as investment income, as well as the sale of government assets. Overseas investment income is a hostage to international financial market conditions and to the size of investments held, while import duties do rise and fall in a pro-cyclical manner and could serve, to some extent, as automatic stabilizers (Wilson et al., 2003). Income growth results in a rise in imports and a rise in duties and vice versa, although the Kingdom's desire to join the World Trade Organisation (WTO) and the inter-Gulf Cooperation Council tariff reductions to 5% could diminish receipts from import duties over the long run as import duties could fall with post WTO entry.

Thus, the price of oil remains of crucial importance to Saudi economic planning and, by extension, to the development of social projects such as health and education. Government spending then becomes the main instrument through which the Ministry of Finance exercises control over the economy, trying to restrain spending when oil prices fall, but allowing "budget overruns" when oil prices and, therefore, revenues rise. These Saudi fiscal policies seem to be at odds with traditional Keynesian macroeconomic policies, which call for government revenue injections during periods of economic slowdowns (lower private sector revenues), and higher government revenue collections during economic growth periods (larger private sector revenues).

Saudi expenditure needs seem unlimited

Officially, the Saudi budget classifies expenditures under four "chapters" with Chapters One to Three including recurrent expenditures, and Chapter Four including capital expenditure (Johany, 1986). These chapters are further broken down into operating expenses, other recurring expenditures (subsidies and funds allocated to semi-autonomous government institutions) and salaries. Table 3.4, earlier in this section, set out the broad budgetary sectoral expenditure allocations, but little breakdown is initially provided in the annual Saudi budget announcements.

Table 3.6 sets out budgetary planned authorizations for the period 1996 through 2005 and provides more detailed breakdowns by major expenditure/revenue line items. Table 3.6 also incorporates the 2005 budget projections, which illustrate the lack of initial breakdown of both revenue and expenditure items, with some items being estimated.

What planned expenditures reveal, however, are *government priorities and future trends*. As mentioned earlier, a growing and younger population has ensured that education and health expenditures receive high priority as the government tries to maintain a balance between the other competing sectors. Defence expenditure takes the lion's share, and while the 2004 budget did not provide an actual figure for defence, the budget announcement for the 2003 actuals indicated that there had been a major increase in this line item for 2003 actuals, and, by implication, for the 2004 planned budget. This was due to "the ongoing regional and domestic security situation," as advised by the Ministry of Finance in its 2003/2004 budget statement (Saudi Press Agency, 15 Dec., 2003).

Table 3.6 Saudi Arabian budgetary authorizations: planned 1996 - 2005

	1996	1997	1999	2000	2001	2002	2003	2004	2005
Total Revenue	**132**	**164**	**121**	**157**	**215**	**157**	**170**	**200**	**280**
oil	100	129	66	117	169	97	122	155(e)	n/a
non-oil	32	35	55	39	46	60	48	45(e)	n/a
of which:									
investment income	5	6	8	11	6	n/a	n/a	n/a	n/a
fees & charges	16	22	13	21	21	n/a	n/a	n/a	n/a
Total expenditure	**150**	**181**	**165**	**185**	**215**	**202**	**209**	**230**	**280**
by sector									
education	28	42	43	49	53	47	57.5	63.7	70.1
transport & communication	6	7	5	7	6	5	6.5	7.3	8.95
economic resource development	5	5	4	6	6	5	3.2	5.0(e)	6.0(e)
health & social development	10	14	15	16	18	19	23.2	24.3	27.0
municipal service	5	7	5	6	7	8	7.5	8.6	10.65
Infrastructure	1	2	2	2	3	2.6	1.9	3.0 (e)	17.2
defence & security	50	66	69	75	79	69.3	67.9 (e)	74.0 (e)	85.2(e)
public administration	38	31	16	19	37	39.3	36.0	38.0	40(e)
government lending institutions	0.6	0.3	0.3	0.4	0.3	0.3	0.3	0.5	10.0
local subsidies	7	7	5	6	6	6	5	6.0	5.0(e)
Total expenditure	**150**	**181**	**165**	**185**	**215**	**202**	**209**	**230.**	**280**
By type:									
Current	**128**	**160**	**152**	**176**	**177**	**174**	**187**	**188.4**	**204.5**
of which :									
wage bill	61	91	92	n/a	n/a	n/a	n/a	125(e)	n/a
supplies/services	18	16	12	n/a	n/a	n/a	n/a	n/a	n/a
Subsidies	7	7	5	6	6	6	6	6.0	n/a
Interest	21	26	27	n/a	n/a	n/a	n/a	n/a	n/a
operations & maintenance	18	19	15	n/a	n/a	n/a	n/a	n/a	n/a
Capital (project)	**23**	**21**	**14**	**17**	**38**	**28**	**22.0**	**41.6**	**75.5**
Budget balance	**-19**	**-17**	**-44**	**-28**	**0**	**-45**	**-39**	**-30.0**	**0**
% of GDP (at Current Prices	-3.6	-3.3	-6.5	-2.2	0	-6.1	-5.4	-4.4	0

Source: *SAMA, Ministry of Finance.*
n/a: not available.
(e) estimated.

Another bumper surplus forecast for 2004

The 2004 planned budgetary revenues and expenditures are both underestimated as announced by the government Table 3.6. The actual estimates for both items were set out earlier in Table 3.5 with forecasted revenue at SR 393 billion compared with the SR 200 billion budget, and forecasted expenditures at SR 295 billion compared with a budgeted SR 230 billion. These forecasts predict another budget surplus year of around SR 98 billion for 2004, compared with a government estimated SR 30 billion deficit. Saudi analysts agree that 2004 revenues are underestimated (Al Sheikh, 2003). The estimated higher expenditure forecasted by the market takes into account continued defence-related expenditures as well as marginal adjustments in other recurrent line items. In its 2004/2005 budget statement, the Ministry of Finance put estimated 2004 revenues at SR 393 billion and expenditures at SR 295 billion, giving a surplus of SR 98 billion.

Educational expenditure emphasized

The 2004 budget announced the creation of three new universities (Madinah, Qassim and Taif), taking the total number of Saudi universities to 11. An expansion in vocational training colleges and professional military training courses for 10,000 young Saudis was also planned as a short-term measure to ease youth unemployment (Saudi Press Agency, 15 December 2003). Of more immediate interest for higher-level education allocations were the increased budgeted expenditures for the science-based universities, such as King Fahd University of Petroleum and Minerals and King Faisal University. The stress on manpower development continued in the 2005 budget announcement. This is specified in Table 3.7, which sets out the budget allocations for the semi-autonomous government institutions.

Government intentions were highlighted once again: a drive towards a graduate market that is a more science-based and oriented towards private sector jobs. These budgetary initiatives, if sustained on a qualitative basis, will contribute towards increasing real economic growth and the nation's productivity in the long run.

Table 3.7 Saudi Arabia: budget allocations for semi-autonomous institutions (SR million)

	2001	2002	2003	2004	2005
Saudi Arabian Airlines	10384	10966	11280	12580	13595
General Sea Ports Authority	501	464	1410	1500	465
Grain Silos and Flour Mills Organization.	980	980	1034	1168	1254
Saline Water Conversation Corporation.	3296	2234	2245	2350	2256
Royal Commission for Jubayl and Yanbu	2017	2173	1010	266	2729
General Organization for Military Industries	598	711	716	774	793
King Abdulaziz City for Science and Technology	296	519	504	516	520
Saudi Red Crescent Society	243	249	295	340	418
Government Railroad Organization	217	303	145	143	420
Saudi Arabian Standards Org.	83	81	87	98	105
Telecommunications Authority		70	80	100	185
Saudi Arabian General Investment Authority	60	64	80	80	83.7
Supreme Tourism Council	45	79	125	150	157.4
Saudi Geological Survey	100	120	111	111	117.0
Institute of Public Administration	222	224	203	202	200
General Organization for Technical Education	1396	1509	1540	2880	2488
King Saud University	2257	2268	2403	2420	2608
King Abulaziz University	1433	1456	1538	1500	1620
Imam Muhammed bin Saud University	1255	1257	1250	1170	1223
King Faisal University	700	723	773	867	994
King Khalid University	356	407	422	469	599
King Fahd University of Petroleum and Minerals	547	540	574	622	681
Umm-Al-Qura University	743	711	745	673	754
Islamic University of Madinah	277	281	288	310	317
Taibah University			-	178	257
Qasim University			-	309	378
Taif University			-	122	178

Source: *Ministry of Finance, 2003, 2004.*
     SAMA, 2003.

Actual budget experience: the wake-up calls

As discussed earlier, the Kingdom's economy is still dependent on oil and driven by oil revenue. Although the oil sector contributes only around one third of the total GDP, the importance of oil to the Saudi economy is understated by the GDP figures. It still accounts for approximately 90% of export earnings and between 75% and 85% of budget revenues, depending on oil price fortunes (Wilson and Graham, 1994, O'Sullivan, 1993). Saudi Arabia can be best described as a "low-cost" but "high-needs" oil producer: low cost from the Saudi Aramco perspective of costing around $1.80 to $2.00 per barrel to produce oil (Johany, 1982, Oweiss, 2000), and "high-needs" from the Ministry of Finance perspective of rarely receiving adequate revenues to balance the budget.

Table 3.8 Saudi Arabia budgetary revenues and expenditures: actual outturns 1994 - 2004 (SR billion)

	1994	*1996*	*2000*	*2001*	*2002*	*2003*	*2004*
(A) Total revenue	**129.0**	**178.8**	**248**	**230**	**213**	**295**	**393**
oil	95.5	136.0	198	185	166	247[(e)]	
non-oil	33.5	42.8	50	45	47	48	
Of which:							
investment income	6.0	5.5	5.5	5.0	4.1	4[(e)]	
fees & charges	10.1	18.8	20.8	20.0	23.0	24[(e)]	
income taxes	1.6	1.6	2.2	2.0	2.2	2.3[(e)]	
customs	8.3	8.9	9.7	9.0	8.0	7.7[(e)]	
Others (including zakat)	7.5	8.1	11.8	9.0	9.7	10.0[(e)]	
(B) Total expenditure	**171.1**	**198.1**	**203**	**255**	**233**	**250**	**295**
By type:							
current	**147.1**	**171.3**	**173**	**226**	**203.5**	**215.0**[(e)]	n/a
Of which:							
wage bill	87.4	90.4	104	123.9	117.0	120.5[(e)]	
supplies/services	22.1	26.2	15.0	27.5	22.9	27.0[(e)]	
subsidies	4.4	7.1	5.2	7.9	5.5	6.0	
interest	15.3	23.6	31.3	37.1[(e)]	34.5[(e)]	35.5[(e)]	
operations & maintenance	17.4	23.6	17.5	29.6	23.6	26.0[(e)]	
Capital (project)	**24.0**	**26.9**	**30**	**29**	**30**	**35.0**[(e)]	n/a
Budget balance	**-42.1**	**-19.3**	**45**	**-25**	**-20.5**	**+45**	**+98**
% of GDP (at current prices)	-9.4	-3.6	6.9	-3.8	-2.9	+6.6	+10.5

Sources: *IMF, Staff Report, SAMA, Annual Report*, 2003, *Ministry of Finance*, 2004.
n/a: not applicable, (e): estimates.

Table 3.8 analyses actual budgetary revenue and expenditures for Saudi Arabia over the period 1994 to 2004, broken down by line items for available and estimated data. While overall spending levels have not grown in tandem with demographic needs, the internal structure of the Saudi budget has changed over time.

The actual "outturns" for Saudi revenues reveal the following trends:

There has been a gradual increase in non-oil revenue sources, rising from SR 33 billion in 1994 to around SR 48 billion for 2002/2003, as the government introduced new levies and increased fees on existing services, mostly expatriate fee charges.

Investment income declined in major importance to contribute around SR 4 billion revenues in 2002/2003, with this item affected by lower Saudi international reserves, as well as falling world interest rates and erratic international stock market returns.

The level of income taxes on foreign corporations and local *Zakat* receipts has been relatively stable, with duties coming down in line with Saudi import tariff reductions, due to bilateral and regional tariff-reduction agreements and in preparation for WTO entry.

While there has been some attempt at obtaining a more diversified revenue source for the Kingdom, the dominant problem centres on expenditure out-turns. Table 3.8 reveals that:

A large and growing percentage of expenditure is spent on recurrent, rather than capital, expenditure, of which the wage bill is a significant element. A growing interest rate burdens government finances, with this item estimated at around SR 35 billion for 2003, more than doubling in ten years when compared with SR 15 billion level in 1994. This item was non-existent in Saudi fiscal planning until the 1985/1986 oil price collapse that forced the Saudi government to take the first steps in domestic borrowing to meet its revenue shortfall.

Besides a declining trend for capital expenditure, there is an erratic and low-level expenditure on operations and maintenance, with long-term implications for both the quality and standard of current fixed-assets.

The above issues have not gone unnoticed by Saudi Arabia economic observers, whether foreign or nationals. Structural economic reforms have been called for by Chalk et al., 1996, Looney, 1990, Wilson, 2003, Cordesman, 2003 and Champion, 2003. Local commentators include Abdullateef, 2002, Abalkhail, 2002, and Dukhail, 2003, with the latter estimating Saudi interest payments at nearly 13% of total government expenditures for 2003 (SR 32.5 billion), in line with the author's own estimates (Arab News, 22 Dec., 2003). Salaries constituted 60% or SR 138 billion of total expenditures, according to the same local experts. Such worries about the level of current, as opposed to capital, expenditures are well placed, as Table 3.9 demonstrates.

The implications from Table 3.9 are clear: a seeming runaway wage bill that needs urgent re-examination from the point of economic allocation and productive efficiency. While the quantitative aspect of current expenditure can be assessed, it is the *qualitative* element that is more difficult to gauge. A study carried out in December, 2003, covering 181 government departments in different regions of the Kingdom, revealed that 69% of civil servants stay away from work without good reason and 54% come to work late. The study also showed that the heads of departments rarely check whether the staff keep to their working hours (Abdulghafour, P.K., Arab News, 23 December 2003). In essence, such studies confirm the existence of disguised unemployment within Saudi government bureaucracy.

Table 3.9 Saudi Arabia current expenditures as % of GDP, total government expenditure and oil revenues for the period 1994 - 2003

	Government wage bill as a % of			Investment Expenditure as % of total Gov't Expenditure
Year	GDP	Gov't. Expenditure	Oil Revenues	
1994	18.0%	51.1%	91.5%	14.0%
1995	16.0%	49.5%	81.5%	14.5%
1996	16.0%	45.6%	66.4%	13.5%
1997	24.0%	46.6%	64.5%	10.8%
1998	19.0%	52.8%	101.8%	10.9%
1999	23.0%	56.0%	98.6%	9.0%
2003	17.80%	48.2%	48.8%	14.00%

Source: *SAMA, 2003, Ministry of Finance.*

From cyclical to structural deficits

As previous data demonstrated, Saudi Arabia has registered consecutive budget deficits since 1984, with the exceptions of 2000, 2003 and projected 2004. The fear is that the Kingdom is beginning to exhibit not only cyclical but structural deficit characteristics. These characteristics are illustrated diagrammatically in Figure 3.7.

In the diagram in part (a), potential GDP is Y or 10. When real GDP is less than potential GDP (or 9), the budget is in a cyclical deficit. When real GDP exceeds potential GDP (or 11), the budget is in a cyclical surplus. This has been the mode of Saudi budget cycles to date. However, the situation seems to be approaching a structural deficit situation as illustrated in part(b). Here potential GDP is Y_0 or 9 against real GDP of Y_1 or 10, and there is a structural deficit. But when potential GDP is Y_2 or 11, then there is a

Figure 3.7 Cyclical and structural surpluses and deficits

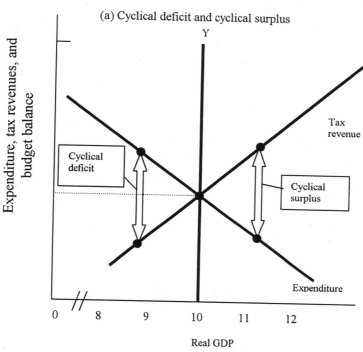

(a) Cyclical deficit and cyclical surplus

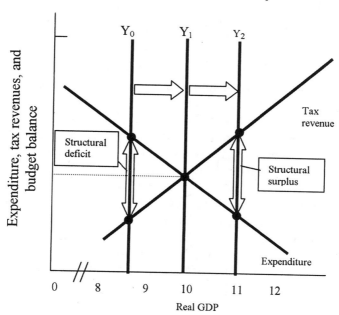

(b) Structural deficit and structural surplus

structural surplus. In theory, the government budget balance fluctuates with the business cycle. A temporary or cyclical surplus or deficit varies when full employment returns. A persistent surplus or deficit requires government action to remove it. Structural deficits are the budget balances that would occur at full employment, and when real GDP was equal to potential GDP. The cyclical deficit is the actual deficit minus the structural deficit; that is, the cyclical deficit is that part of the budget balance that arises purely because real GDP does not equal potential GDP.

"Automatic stabilizers" are the mechanisms that stabilize real GDP without explicit action by the government. These stabilizers operate like shock absorbers. They make the deficits/surpluses less severe, because income taxes and transfer payments (revenues and expenditures) fluctuate with real GDP. If real GDP begins to decrease, tax revenues fall and transfer payments rise, and the government budget deficit changes. To date, Saudi Arabia does not have such a range of fiscal tools and hence there are no automatic stabilizers at work to ease deficit fluctuations.

However, it is not the recurrent expenditures or wage bills that are becoming the major concern, but rather the rise in the level of the national debt.

Debt-led growth and the burden of indebtedness

The release of the Saudi 2003/2004 budget figures sparked a debate among Saudi economists on what was termed a "debt-led growth," and on the threat that the Kingdom would hit a debt-wall in the immediate future if it did not reverse this policy (Taher, N., 22 December 2003). Others pointed out long-term implications; they suggested that within three or four years, without fiscal reforms, lending to government will exceed private lending, which could lead to an internal debt service problem (Wilson et al., 2003).

The Saudi Arabian government has been cognizant of this issue and has tried to maintain some overall fiscal balance in its borrowings. As Figure 3.8 shows, the ratio of fiscal deficit to real GDP has been brought down from the peak levels of 25% in 1985/1986, to under 5%.

While the ratio of fiscal debt to Gross Domestic Product seems to have been brought under control, it is the absolute size of the national debt that is giving cause for some concern. According to latest estimates, the level of outstanding debt varies between 98% to 80% of GDP, but figures depend on whether one uses a real GDP of SR 677 billion (NCB, CCFI 2003), or a nominal GDP of SR 792 billion. (Bourland, December, 2003).

Figure 3.8 Saudi Arabia: Ratio of fiscal deficit to gross domestic product
for the period 1983 – 2004

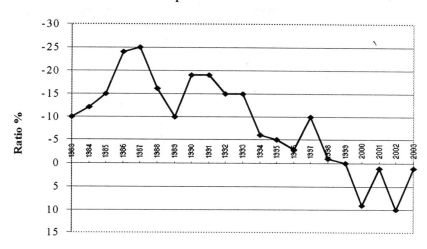

Source: *SAMA*, 2003.

Figure 3.9 examines the level of government domestic debt as a
percentage of real GDP for the period 1993 to 2003.

Figure 3.9 Saudi Arabia: Government domestic debt as a percentage of real
GDP (1993 - 2003)

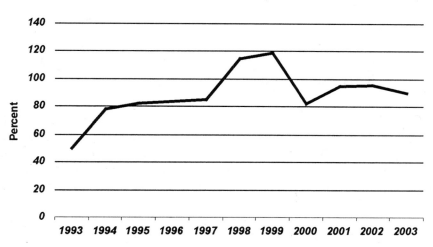

Source: *SAMA*, 2003, *Ministry of Finance*, 2003.

According to SAMA's 2003 annual report, the total level of national debt
stood at SR 685 billion at the end of 2002, compared with SR 643 billion in

the previous year. The Minister of Finance advised that the level of debt stood at SR 660 billion in December, 2003, when asked in a post-budget interview (SPA, December, 2003), and the 2004/2005 budget announcement indicated that the government was aiming to use part of the 2004 budget surplus to reduce the overall debt to SR 614 billion by 2005.

What is the source of borrowing?

Up until 1988, Saudi Arabia financed its deficits through a draw-down on the country's overseas reserves, mostly U.S.-dominated securities, although diversification of holdings in other currencies was held in Sterling, Deutschmarks, Swiss Francs and Yen. According to the IMF, the size of foreign reserves probably peaked at the $170 billion level in 1982/1983. By the end of 2003, the size of SAMA's foreign assets had declined to around $57 billion as set out in Table 3.10.

Table 3.10 Net foreign assets: 1997 - 2003 ($bn)

	1997	1998	2000	2001	2002	2003*
Net foreign assets						
SAMA	56.9	45.4	47.5	48.2	42.0	56.8
Other government agencies	27.8	31.7	32.8	34.0	35.0	35.6
Commercial banks	14.3	11.4	9.8	10.5	14.1	11.6
Total $billion	**99**	**88.5**	**90.2**	**92.7**	**91.1**	**104.0***

Source: *SAMA*, 2003.   (*) *estimate.*

Table 3.10 reveals a gradual erosion of SAMA's foreign assets to $45.4 billion in 1998, before gradually rising to current levels helped by the oil price hikes in 2000 and 2003. However, SAMA's foreign assets include Saudi Riyal foreign currency cover plus gold reserves. When these are deducted, the net free reserves as of October, 2003, stood at $36.5 billion (SAMA, 2003).

What is revealing about the above table is that while SAMA's foreign assets increased in 2003, those for the Saudi commercial banks declined to $11.6 billion for the same year, compared with a high of $14.3 billion in 1997.

Saudi Arabia reports minimal or virtually no direct sovereign state borrowing from the international capital markets, despite a first sovereign credit rating by Standard & Poor's in June, 2003. This rating assigned A+ to local currency long-term, and A-1 for short-term, while foreign currency was A-1 for short-term and A long-term. Moody's followed suit and upgraded the Kingdom to Baa2 from Baa3 in July, 2003 (Reuters, July, 2003). Despite this positive development, the Kingdom's sovereign credit rating was lower than most neighbouring GCC countries (MEED, 2003). While direct sovereign debt was negligible, according to some sources Saudi Arabia had accumulated non-recourse debt of around $25 billion or SR 93 billion in the form of loans from international banks to semi-government institutions (MEED, 2001).

"Crowding out" the private sector

The first budget deficit financing was in 1988 with an SR 42 billion issue of government bonds sold to the Saudi commercial banks and to other government semi-autonomous agencies, such as the General Organization for Social Insurance (GOSI) and the Saudi Pension and Retirement Agency (SPRA) (Dukhail, 1995).

Today, the Saudi national debt, estimated at SR 660 billion in December, 2003, is mostly held by these two government pension organizations, plus some contractors in lieu of delayed payments, as well as the Saudi commercial banks. As of July 2004, the commercial banks held around SR 151 billion or nearly 23% of the total debt (SAMA, August 2004). The composition of the debt among the different borrowers means in effect that the government indirectly owes most of the debt itself. However, the increasing government debt through the Saudi commercial banks implies a competition for financing required by the private sector for business expansion – the so-called "crowding-out" effect highlighted by various commentators on the Saudi economy (Abdullateef, 2002, Taher, 2003, CCFI, 2003, Bourland, 2002). As one commentator put it, "…the effects of fiscal expenditure policy depends on whether the income multiplier effect outweighs confidence and crowding-out effect" (Taher, N., December, 2003). Figure 3.11 illustrates the crowding-out effect on private sector investment demand.

Figure 3.10 shows the direct effect of a government budget deficit. *ID* represents the investment demand curve of the private sector and *PS* is the private sector savings supply curve. It indicates the relationship between private saving and the real interest rate. *SS* shows the sum of private and government saving. At 6% in real interest rates, investment equals saving and the budget is balanced. A government budget deficit is negative government saving (dissaving). The effect of the budget deficit (government dissaving) is to decrease investment from 10 to 9, as interest rates rise from 6% to 7%. However, the higher interest rate level induces an increase in private saving from 10 to 11 as illustrated in the diagram. In reality, the increase in private saving might be small in the short-term, but the increase in the government budget deficit is to decrease investments in the private sector or to "crowd-out" the private sector investment demand.

Figure 3.10 A crowding-out effect

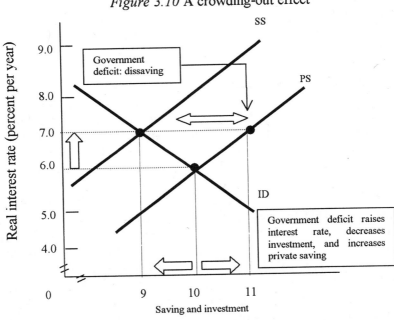

Table 3.11 illustrates the trend of government sales of bonds and securities to the Saudi commercial banks to finance its debt.

Table 3.11 Government and public sectors security holdings by Saudi commercial banks as % of total assets (1996 - 2003)

	1996		2001		2003	
	Million Riyals	In %	Million Riyals	In %	Million Riyals	In %
Government Paper	65,266	18.23	123,833	26.21	148,346	25.13
Private Securities	6,627	1.85	10,261	2.17	8,353	1.41
Total Securities	71,893	20.08	134,094	28.38	156,699	26.2
Total Assets	357,947		472,431		590,532	

Source: *SAMA*, 2003, 2004.

Rising from SR 65.2 billion in 1996, the level of government borrowing from the commercial banks stood at SR 151 billion, or 25% of their total assets as of August 2004 (SAMA, August, 2004). The government has retired part of the debt, at least to the commercial banks, as total borrowing from the banks stood at a peak of SR 159 billion in May 2004 according to SAMA (SAMA, 2004). At the same time, there are encouraging signs that part of the "windfall" oil revenues generated by higher than forecasted oil prices during 2004, will be set aside to retire part of the national debt according to statements made by the Minister of Finance (Saudi Press Agency, 30 August 2004). The projected 2004 surplus will also be used in one time investments of SR 41 billion allocated for development project. This will improve people's daily lives and give greater training and employment opportunities to younger Saudis according to Crown Prince Abdullah (Arab News, 4 September 2004).

Is there any reason to worry?

Some might argue that there are few reasons for concern, as the government debt is translated back into the economy through government expenditure, and thus the working of the income multiplier outweighs the confidence and crowding-out effects. Others might argue that in a resilient and growing economy, debt is not a major concern as government borrowing merely absorbs excess domestic liquidity from the markets which is then put to good use in socially-productive programs instead of creating price inflation and potential stock market bubbles and crashes. These are valid arguments, as the Saudi commercial banks did witness a rise in liquidity since 2001, due to several international and domestic factors (SAMA, 2003), but these arguments presuppose that government bases its borrowing on the golden rule: *that governments borrow to invest rather than for short-term current consumption.* As discussed earlier, this has not often been the case in Saudi Arabia, and changes are required to the current budgetary system.

Based on current population estimates of 24.06 million for mid-2003, of which 17.9 million are Saudis (SAMA, 2003, p. 295), the average debt per Saudi citizen stands at just over SR 35,000 (assuming a national debt level of SR 660 billion). The growth in population, and specifically the young age profile of Saudi nationals, will necessitate continuing expenditures for health, education and basic infrastructure in future years. This has been the prime motivating force behind the Saudi government's drive to privatize the government sector, given the decline in Saudi capital expenditure patterns observed over the past few years.

Some estimated forecasts have examined the revenue needed to sustain a growing population base. Figure 3.11 below sets out fiscal balances and future needs for the period 2004 – 2010 based on certain oil price and oil production scenarios.

Figure 3.11 Saudi Arabia: Fiscal balances and future revenue needs

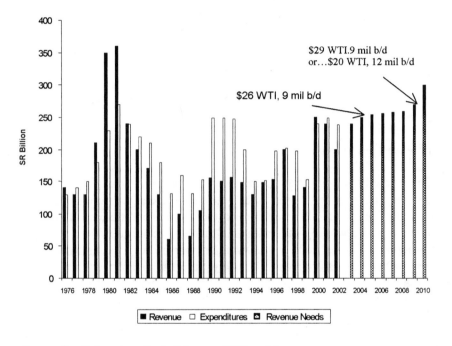

Source: *Saudi American Bank*, February, 2003, p. 14.

According to these Saudi American Bank estimates, assuming no structural changes to spending and a 3.5% overall spending growth per annum, in order to balance the budget Saudi Arabia would require an oil market that needs to accommodate the equivalent of $26 per barrel and an output of 9 million barrels per day in 2006. For 2010, the figures would be $29 per barrel and an output of 9 million barrels per day. These levels of output of production were only reached in late 2004, and not since 1997, when Saudi Arabia produced 9.3 million barrels per day, but at prices of just under $10 per barrel. That forced OPEC to curtail their total daily output from around 30 million barrels per day in 1997 to around 25 million barrels per day in 2002/2003 (Oweiss, 2000, SAMA, 2003).

One must ask if these forecasts are achievable. They presume a sustained production output in current Saudi third quarter 2004 oil production levels of around 9.3 million barrels per day and continuing firm oil prices for the OPEC set price-band of $22 to $28 per barrel for the next six years. As Figure 3.12 also illustrates, future revenue needs can also be met with a lower price of around $20 per barrel and production levels of 12 million barrels per day.

The implication is that in the absence of revenue diversification, the Kingdom's oil policy will be faced with the same two choices it has always faced: either pursuing a larger oil market-share policy at lower prices, or maintaining the current policy of defending firmer prices within a narrow, specified price band, and cutting back on production if the price band comes under pressure through non-OPEC production or changes in economic conditions and aggregate world demand for oil.

Neither option is particularly attractive in the long run. The first means larger government deficits today, and possible reductions in the future as marginal oil producers are driven out due to Saudi Arabia's comparative cost-production advantage. The second option implies facing ongoing deficits of between SR 20 to SR 40 billion per annum for the foreseeable future.

Facing the challenges

Despite the above issues, the Kingdom's future is not all bleak. As many commentators have pointed out, structural budgetary changes are possible. This will require both willpower and a commitment from the government to not be diverted from set goals. Many countries face similar budgetary structural issues as those faced by Saudi Arabia, both in economically developed and developing countries. The Kingdom is no exception and many countries would count themselves fortunate if their problems were only as severe as current Saudi problems. However, solving tomorrow's problems with today's solutions will not work. Saudi Arabia has been encouraged by both its own economists and by the International Monetary Fund (IMF) to rethink its current fiscal strategies.

Solutions: short and long term

The Kingdom is not unaware of what needs to be done and the following steps are clearly spelled out in the Seventh Development Plan:

- Increase non-oil government revenues
- Reduce budget deficits to lowest possible levels

- Finance deficit through the issue of development bonds
- Rationalize and reduce government non-investment expenditures
- Use government surpluses of oil revenues to reduce national debt
- Maintain strict adherence to approved expenditure limits
- Develop an adequate mechanism for attaining long-term fiscal stabilization in order to avoid the adverse effects of fluctuations in government oil revenues

These are all laudable policy objectives, but in reality few, if any, have been consistently followed, as illustrated earlier. Table 3.12 summarizes short and long-term revenue sources and measures that could be implemented to overcome the current structural fiscal imbalances.

Table 3.12 Ideas for improving revenues

Measures	*Major Issues*
Short term	
i) REVENUE ENHANCEMENT	
• Zakat	The 2.5% zakat on companies (Islamic levy on total assets) is earmarked for social welfare purposes. Better collection efforts could generate marginal increases.
• Custom duties	Better collection of duties and tariffs will be offset long-term by inter-GCC tariff reductions and expected WTO entry.
• Fees and charges	Increasing use of this revenue source has provided some fiscal certainty. Expand current base of fees on government service (expatriate and Saudis) as well as more market-based pricing for subsidized services.
ii) MEASURES	
• Budget adherence	Strict adherence to expenditure limits must be applied. Extra budgetary expenditures to be allowed only from other chapter allocations.
• Reallocation of expenditure items to "best" economic use	Reallocation of expenditures to longer-term productive value-added, job generating sectors and gradual reduction in wasteful subsidies. Close examination of defence expenditure while maintaining security needs.
Long term	
iii) REVENUE SOURCES	
• Taxation	Reintroduce personal income taxes on both expatriates and Saudis, after studies on poverty threshold levels.
	Introduce sales tax on luxury goods and value-added tax on range of consumer durable goods.
• Sale of government assets	Speed up sale of key government-owned industries starting with mature ones (banking), Petrochemical (SABIC) and telecommunication (STC). Revenue to be used for debt repayment and capital infrastructure investment.

Table 3.12 (continued)

Measures	Major Issues
iv) MEASURES	
• Civil service reforms	Needed as much as *Saudization* policy. Assess efficiency of current public sector expenditure and allocate according to productivity.
• Privatization at fair market prices	Initiate full privatization of key sectors, but shape these around fair market prices to encourage Saudi private capital repatriation by the private sector.
• Studies on fiscal policies	Establish independent Centre for Fiscal Studies to analyse economic effects of taxation measures on consumers, business and government revenue-generating impact.
• Establish efficiency performance benchmarks	There is a lack of clear overall benchmarks for measuring adequacy of government efforts to meet needs of the public and Saudi economic development. Transparency is growing but more is needed on performance relative to public demand and need. This requires benchmarking through meaningful output measures.
• Stabilisation fund	Establish a "Revenue Stabilisation Fund" to be allocated a specified percentage of annual revenues or surpluses and to be used for budgetary revenue stabilization under strict drawdown guidelines.
• Regional/municipal level economic empowerment	Empower local municipalities and regional economic councils with budgetary allocations and responsibilities. This will result in local prioritization of economic resources and accountability for upcoming municipal elections.
• Introduce "mini" budgets	Current yearly budget announcement and planning is not proactive enough given fluctuating world economic conditions and oil prices. Introduction of bi-annual "mini-budget" announcement will adjust forecast of revenues and expenditures accordingly. Ministry of Finance will become more focused on fiscal stabilization programmes as well as more accurate macro economic production.
• International borrowing	Reinforces financial discipline and obligations. Apply the "golden rule" – borrow to invest and not for the current expenditures. Less burden on domestic banks.

The time for rhetoric is over

As Table 3.12 above indicates, there are no easy options. Above all, no single measure can remedy the situation by itself; but a combination of short and long-term measures can work. Structural reform is measured solely in macroeconomic success and never in intentions, plans, decrees or mere talk.

Some of the measures can be implemented quickly, such as a more efficient collection of *zakat*, which, according to local reports, contributes only a small amount from an estimated *zakat* contribution potential of SR 12 billion on SR 900 billion private-sector wealth in the Kingdom (Al Holayan, E., 20 December 2003). It is estimated that between SR 3 to SR 4 billion is currently collected from this source. Since *zakat* is paid towards charitable and social security transfer payments, some have argued that better collection will help in reducing unemployment-related crimes. A report by the Manpower Council suggested that the crime rate among the unemployed rose by 320% in a six-year period from 1990 to 1996, and was expected to rise by a further 136% by 2005 (Khazindar, A, 30 December 2003).

Taxation has been discussed by the *Majlis Al Shoura* but abandoned, and this was primarily focused on expatriate earnings above SR 5000. The issue of taxation needs to be reintroduced, but for both nationals and expatriates, as the WTO and International Labour Office (ILO) would have deemed it discriminatory and reversed it if it applied only to foreigners. Saudi Arabia did impose a personal income tax before the oil boom era of the early 1970s. The current no-tax situation is an aberration from the norm in most countries, and Saudi economists are debating this option (Taher, 2003, Sheikh, 2003). However, some emphasize value-added and corporate taxes, rather than personal income tax, until a national consensus can be reached for lower income threshold levels and exemptions.

Privatization and proceeds from the sale of government assets would relieve the government from the burden of running state operations in an inefficient manner with a drag on fiscal resources. However, privatization needs to be carefully thought through and the appropriate regulatory and operating framework has to be in place prior to privatization taking place. The issue is divisive in many countries and some, especially Western experts, argue for this option, for the sake of privatization. However, some Saudi government planners tend to promote privatization for the sake of dumping the burden onto the private sector, and this is not an appropriate approach.

A hopeful future

The 2004 State budget confounded critics and provided a glimmer of hope with the announcement of upcoming municipal elections to be held in November 2004, as well as some local accountability. Devolving some economic resources to the regional level will accelerate the positive economic reforms being advocated by the Crown Prince and, at the same time, ensure accountability in how government expenditures are being spent.

As was earlier pointed out, Saudi Arabia is in a more advantaged situation than many countries, but the government must not ease up on the necessary long-term structural reforms, however painful these may be in the short run.

Summary of key points

- *The Saudi budget is a useful barometer of the financial health of the nation as it sets out quantitative and indicative directions as to government intention and priorities in expenditures and revenue forecasts.*
- *Saudi economic development has been fuelled by a rise in oil revenues which was unsustainable due to the inability of the government to control oil prices, white at the same time government expenditures seemed to be consistently overrun. As such budgeted plans never materialized.*
- *Overdependence on oil took place over building a true wealth generating base for the economy, although there are some indications that the government is beginning to shift resources to market required resources.*
- *Sources of revenues are being diversified away from oil dependency, but these are still limited and there are no direct or indirect taxation elements involved. As such, the Saudi budgetary system is evidencing a structural deficit situation, despite occasional bumper revenue years due to higher than forecasted oil prices.*
- *The government has financed its deficits through internal borrowing, including from the domestic banks, which can give rise to "crowding out" the private sector investment demand. Current total national debt level is around 90% of GDP.*
- *The government needs to introduce short and long term measures to diversify its revenue sources, restructure its expenditure patterns and consider taxation.*

Critical thinking

1. "If only the government can control its budgeted expenditures, all will be well with the Saudi budget". Do you agree with this statement? Is this the only factor that needs to be addressed?

2. Why is the Saudi budget important to observers of the national economy? What else is required to be able to assess if government intentions are to be met?

3. "Taxation will solve problems of recurrent deficits in Saudi Arabia". Do you agree? What are the potential positive and negative factors by the introduction of taxation in the Kingdom.

4. "Crowding out the private sector is a theoretical exercise, as Saudi banks prefer to hold government debt while meeting their private sector obligations". Argue the case for and against government domestic borrowing from Saudi banks.

5. "Since not many governments follow the "golden rule" of borrowing i.e. borrowing to invest and not for current expenditure, then Saudi Arabia should not do the same". What do you think the Kingdom should follow and why?

Chapter 4

SAUDI ARABIAN MONETARY AGENCY (SAMA) AND MONETARY POLICY

Money is a good servant but a bad master.

Bacon

Learning outcomes:

By the end of this section, you should understand:

- *The organizational structure and functions of SAMA*
- *SAMA's evolving responsibilities in different financial areas*
- *Saudi monetary policy and instruments*
- *Effectiveness of monetary policy*
- *SAMA and exchange rate policy*
- *Money supply creation*
- *Process of financial deepening in the economy*
- *Inflation in Saudi Arabia*

Introduction

Sitting at the head of Saudi Arabia's financial system is the Saudi Arabian Monetary Agency (SAMA). Established by Royal Decree in 1952, it has now completed 52 years of service to the country. It has been an observer and key player in financial matters, and has seen its role expand with the evolution of the Kingdom's economy and financial system. The history and role of SAMA encapsulates the evolution of Saudi Arabia's banking and financial structures in the gradual institutionalization of the country's financial market. How SAMA operates and the tools and policies it adopts, will have a great impact on all of Saudi society, not merely on the financial sector. This was openly acknowledged by the Saudi Minister of Finance, Dr. Ibrahim Al-Assaf, when he was reported as saying that, despite higher-than-forecasted oil prices during the first half of 2004, the Kingdom's financial sector would be the "driving force" of the economy for the remainder of the year (Arab News, 13 May 2004).

As this chapter will explain, SAMA plays a leading role in the "financial deepening" of the markets, through the creation of new financial instruments and of the regulatory and legal framework within which such developments can occur. At the same time, these changes incorporate evolving public perceptions of monetary assets and increasingly active participation in the market place, while they create a higher level of sophistication leading to economic development (Azzam, 1997). Although the Saudi financial and capital markets still have some way to go to reach the level of well-developed financial markets, SAMA has played a significant role in creating the appropriate conditions for investors to mobilize resources domestically. Erratic oil revenues coupled with the needs of a young and growing population can only accelerate SAMA's effort at financial development, and that in turn could encourage capital inflows for Saudi and foreign investors who seek better opportunities in the Kingdom.

Asserting independence.

The independence of a Central Bank to perform its mission without coming under undue pressure from governments is critical to the success of the Central Bank's policies and public confidence. Over time, SAMA has managed to acquire increased independence, which is a far cry from the original institution that was set up with technical assistance from the United States in 1952 to act as the country's *de facto* Central Bank within the confines of Islamic law.

SAMA is supervised by a Board of Directors that is headed by a Governor and Vice-Governor, both of whom are appointed by Royal Decree by the King for terms of four years. These terms can be extended by Royal Decree for similar periods. SAMA's Board also consists of three other members nominated from the private sector who are also appointed by Royal Decree to serve for periods of five years. The nominations and appointments of members of the Board of Directors, including the Governor and Vice-Governor, rest with the Minister of Finance and the Council of Ministers.

Senior SAMA managers have been in place for many years, providing stability and relative independence in decision-making, although they operate in close coordination with the Ministry of Finance. The current SAMA Governor, Sheikh Hamad Saud Al-Sayari, has been in that position since his appointment in 1983 – making him one of the longest-serving Governors in the world and the longest-serving in the Gulf Cooperation Council (GCC). In 1995, an able technocrat, Dr. Mohammed Al-Jasser, was appointed as Vice-Governor. Mr. Jamaz Al-Suhaimi was promoted to

Deputy Governor in 1989 and was responsible for overseeing the crucial Banking Supervision Department and capital market issues until his appointment as head of the new Capital Markets Authority in 2004.

Previous SAMA Governors served for various periods – George Bowlers (1952 - 1954), Ralph Standish (1954 - 1958), Anwar Ali (1958 - 1974), Abdulaziz Al-Quraishi (1974 - 1983) – and brought with them a blend of different management styles and professional backgrounds, mostly drawing upon Western Central Bank and International Monetary Fund philosophies. Close technical and training cooperation is carried out with leading Western Central Banks and this has resulted in SAMA adopting a basically Western Central Bank approach in terms of bank supervision and risk management (Dukheil, 1995). While this might be true, it does not mean that SAMA does not have different policies from Western Central Banks, but that such differences can be explained by environmental influences based on the nature of the Saudi economy and of public perceptions and acceptance of this sector. The manner in which these particular environmental issues are handled will often determine the choice of organization that evolves. The growth of Islamic banking is one particular point and SAMA, along with the Bahrain Monetary Agency (BMA), have been successful in regulating this fast growing sector and ensuring that it operates under the same "fit and proper" banking supervisory regime that is imposed on conventional banking.

SAMA's stated functions

SAMA's 1952 founding Charter stipulated that it would conform to Islamic law. It could not be a profit-making institution and could neither pay nor receive interest. There were additional prohibitions, including one against extending credit to the government, but this was dropped in 1955 when the government needed funds and SAMA financed about one-half of the governmental debt that accrued in the late 1950s (Abdeen et al., 1984).

The introduction of the Banking Control Law in 1966 was a watershed in SAMA's history, as the new regulation clarified and strengthened SAMA's role in regulating the Saudi banking system (SAMA, 2004, Jasser, 2002). The Banking Control Law vested SAMA with broad supervisory powers and allowed the Monetary Agency to issue regulations, rules and guidelines regarding eight of the international supervisory developments that called for provision of capital adequacy, liquidity, reserve requirements and loan concentration ratios. The Banking Control Law supported the concept of a "universal banking model" that permitted banks to provide a broad range of financial services including banking, investments and securities through their branches.

SAMA sees its main roles as follows:

- issuing the national currency, the Saudi Riyal (SR)
- acting as banker to the government

- supervising commercial banks operating in Saudi Arabia
- advising the government on the public debt
- managing the Kingdom's foreign exchange reserves
- conducting monetary policy for promoting price and exchange rate stability
- promoting economic growth and ensuring the soundness of the Saudi financial system

In addition to the above stated goals, SAMA had also over time acquired for itself several other functions, primarily a direct management role of the conduct of the Saudi Stock Market, as well as the supervision of the non-commercial banking sector, such as the money exchanges. Operationally, SAMA carries out these functions through its head office in the capital Riyadh and in its ten branches located in all the major Saudi cities.

SAMA's evolving responsibilities

In order to better understand SAMA's current roles and responsibilities, one must also understand the historical trajectory of the Monetary Agency in order to better appreciate the significant developments that have taken place in the Kingdom's financial history in comparison with other nations. When analyzing Saudi Arabia's current position, it is sometimes easy to forget just how fast and how far the Kingdom has had to travel in a short period of time, "learning by doing" along the way.

SAMA has had a colourful and unorthodox history since its establishment in 1952, and this has been well documented by others (Abdeen, 2002, Johany, 1986, Dukheil, 1995, SAMA, 2004). When SAMA was established, Saudi Arabia did not have a monetary system exclusively its own. Foreign currencies circulated in the Kingdom as a medium of exchange along with silver riyal coins. Saudi bank notes had not yet been issued and there were no national Saudi banks. Banking was conducted through foreign bank branches and specialized trading houses – the most famous being the Netherlands Trading Company, which later became the Saudi Hollandi (Dutch) Bank.

Major transactions had to be carried out using foreign gold coins, such as the popular "Maria Theresa" dollar, or large quantities of silver riyals. However, expanding oil production from the late 1950s increased national revenues and international payments due to expanded international trade, which necessitated a different financial system. Demand for cash and inter-regional payments grew substantially and the use of coins became almost impossible. An additional motive for financial institutionalization was the absence of a fixed exchange rate between the silver riyal coins and foreign gold coins, so that exchange rates varied widely.

SAMA almost died at birth, as its establishment coincided with acute government financial difficulties due to runaway spending and a near depletion of reserves. The introduction of the paper riyal was abandoned at that time. SAMA, however, assumed responsibility for maintaining the exchange rate of the Saudi silver riyal vis-à-vis the U.S. dollar within a band set by the government. In essence, this was not much different from current SAMA exchange rate policy.

In 1953 SAMA completed the country's indigenous monetary system by issuing Saudi Arabia's own gold coins and by eliminating the circulation of foreign currencies. In 1954 it began issuing so-called "pilgrim receipts" for relieving pilgrims of the burden of carrying heavy metallic currency; these receipts were acceptable for encashment throughout the Kingdom. Again, we can see the genesis of the use of traveller checks by modern pilgrims. The popularity of "pilgrim receipts" and the acceptance of a non-metal form of payment by the public paved the way for the issuance of the Saudi riyal notes in June, 1961. From that date, all gold and silver coins and all pilgrim receipts were de-monetized. It had taken nearly 12 years from the date of SAMA's establishment for a paper currency system to be accepted in Saudi Arabia.

According to SAMA, the last four decades can be classified into four broad eras, each characterized by distinctive features (SAMA, February, 2004):

1960 – 1972: In this era, SAMA focused on establishing the basis for commercial banking regulations against a background of expanding domestic banking business and of Saudi Arabia's acceptance of full convertibility of the Saudi riyal in March, 1961, in accordance with Article VIII of the International Monetary Fund Articles of Agreement.

1973 – 1982: During this period, SAMA was preoccupied with containing the inflationary pressures of a booming Saudi economy fuelled by the massive oil price rises of 1973/1974, and with managing the expansion of the banking system to cover most of the country. SAMA also saw itself catapulted into the international limelight through its management of substantial Saudi foreign exchange reserves, which built up during the boom period. These have been estimated at around $170 – 180 billion by 1984 (IMF, 1999, MEED, 1986). During this period, as the author can testify from his own personal banking experience, SAMA was the magnet to all international bankers hoping to "recycle" some of these "petro-dollars".

1983 - 2004: During this time, SAMA's priorities were to introduce financial market reforms and advise the government in managing the public debt. Both SAMA and Saudi commercial banking came of age with the completion of the so-called "Saudization" of the local branches of foreign banks operating in the Kingdom and the introduction of a wide range of new financial products domestically. The pros and cons of the concept underpinning foreign bank *Saudization* will be dealt with at length in the next chapter, but the issue of advising the government on the level of public debt was certainly of some concern to SAMA. This matter was raised publicly at the highest level when SAMA Governor Sheikh

Hamad Saud Al-Sayari explicitly stated that the government "must restrict its spending to budget allocations and use any surpluses to repay part of the national public debt," upon presenting SAMA's 38th and 39th Annual Reports to King Fahd (Abdul Ghafour, Arab News, 4 November 2003, Arab News, 28 January 2003).

The SAMA Governor's calls are finally being heeded and reduction of the public debt is now a national priority. This was acknowledged in the comments to the press of Dr. Assaf, Minister of Finance, when he stated that forecasted 2004 budget revenue surpluses would be used for "reducing debt... Whatever (Saudis) save will be absorbed by reduction in the stock of debt" (Moody, B. Reuters, 13 May 2004).

During this period, SAMA took the lead in encouraging Saudi banks to invest in and use advanced technologies. Today Saudi banking is at the cutting edge of technology usage with automated cheque clearing systems, electronic fund transfer and "transaction plus zero" days share trading settlement system - probably one of the most advanced in the world.

Further, SAMA is vested with conducting monetary policy, and this includes exchange rate policy within a framework set by the government. How effectively has this been achieved and what are the major issues faced in the pursuit of these policies?

Central bank monetary policy

Generally, monetary policies, in conjunction with fiscal policies, are used to influence economic growth and inflation in an economy within desired limits. Both monetary and fiscal policies are called demand-management policies because they try to influence the economy's output indirectly through increasing or decreasing the economy's aggregate demand for goods and services.

In most countries, the Central Bank acts as the chief monetary authority and lender of last resort to the banking system. By "lender of last resort" we mean lending money to banks on an overnight basis or for longer periods when banks are unable to borrow money elsewhere at market rates. This function of a Central Bank as the last-resort lender provides a certain degree of stability to a banking system.

Central Banks try to influence the economy by changes in interest rate levels and, therefore, the money supply. Various monetary tools are at the disposal of Central Banks to achieve intermediate and long-term goals. One such tool is the *discount rate*. This is the rate the Central Bank charges banks for borrowing funds from it. The Central Bank usually has the power to restrain the commercial banks in their lending by raising or lowering the discount rate as needed, thus restricting or loosening credit conditions. This allows the Central Bank to control bank lending indirectly, and it is a signal to the market of Central Bank intentions. A Central Bank also tries to influence the level of interest rates and hence the pace of a nation's economic growth by adjusting the level of *reserve requirements*. This effectively reduces or increases borrowing rates through increasing and decreasing the level of statutory (obligatory) reserves a commercial bank must keep with the Central Bank, calculated on the basis of its non-borrowed deposit base. Another effective tool is for a Central Bank to increase or decrease bank reserves through *open market operations* – the buying and selling of government securities in the open market. This action decreases or increases the pool of non-borrowed bank deposits, and hence money supply in the system.

Saudi monetary policy in practice

The key objectives of Saudi Arabian monetary policy are to stabilize inflation and the general level of prices, to maintain a fixed exchange rate of the Saudi riyal against the U.S. dollar, and to allow free movement of currency and capital. According to SAMA officials (Al Jasser and Banafe, 2003) there are limitations to current monetary policies in Saudi Arabia "due to the openness of the economy, with the riyal effectively pegged to the U.S. dollar since the suspension of the Special Drawing Right (SDR) riyal link in May, 1981." In practice this has resulted in riyal interest rates closely tracking dollar rates, with a small premium, a phenomenon we will further analyze below,

The Saudi Arabia Monetary Agency relies on four policy instruments in conducting monetary policy: cash reserve ratio/minimum reserve policy, repos and reverse repos, foreign exchange swaps and, finally, placement of public funds. These policy instruments are summarized in Table 4.1, which sets out the rational for using these instruments and their perceived effectiveness.

In line with other Central Banks in the region, SAMA is solely responsible for monetary policy formulation and implementation. It is free to select its operating procedures and to determine the choice of instruments as well as when to apply them. Only in a few cases is prior approval needed from the Ministry of Finance, such as when changing the statutory reserve requirements. To all intents and purposes, SAMA is relatively independent of government pressure.

SAMA applies no direct controls, particularly with respect to the control of interest rates and foreign exchange. The first is due to SAMA's charter, which prohibits the payment and receiving of interest; furthermore, there is no discount rate policy. As such, interest rates play a subsidiary role, as they are predominantly affected by U.S. dollar interest rates. As regards foreign exchange control, SAMA has adopted a regime of free movement of capital for Saudi Arabia. As part of monetary policy implementation, SAMA does not use other direct controls, such as credit ceilings. The Monetary Agency could however, impose credit concentration ceilings on certain economic sectors, as well as overall loans to deposit ratios for Saudi commercial banks, in order to curb or expand bank lending.

Table 4.1 SAMA's monetary policy instruments: comparative analysis

Policy Instrument Tool	Rationale, and Operational Usage	Effectiveness
Cash Reserve Ratio (CRR)	• To ensure banks have adequate liquidity to cover customer deposits • 7% on current accounts and 2% on savings/time deposits since 1980	• Used for implementing structural changes in bank liquidity (credit creation control) and for fine-tuning short-term liquidity • Produces strong signal effects but infrequently used • Not imposed on inter-bank transactions
Statutory Liquidity Ratio (SLR)	• Banks required to maintain minimum amount of specified liquid assets equal to 20% of demand and time deposits	• "Free liquidity" at disposal of banks is reduced and can influence overall bank lending structure (short/long term)
Repos	• SAMA alters liquidity position of banks by dealing directly in the market to make temporary additions to bank reserves through short-dated repurchase agreements (overnight)	• Allows for short-term injection of reserves and automatic withdrawal upon repo maturity • Efficiency depends on SAMA's holding of securities and size and depth of market
Reverse Repos	• Need for banks to place excess liquidity with SAMA through overnight matched sale-purchased operations	• SAMA can absorb rather than provide bank reserves • A definitive purchase of financial assets reversible at short notice not affecting prices in bond market; serves to regulate the money market.
Foreign Exchange Swaps	• Intention to influence capital outflows, avoiding disruptions to monetary policy from foreign exchange markets • Used for liquidity management and currency speculation	• More flexible than repos/reverse repos in terms of their maturity and volume per deal • Affect liquidity but do not generally exercise influence on foreign exchange rate
Placement of Public Funds	• At SAMA's discretion to place governmental institutions' funds with selected banks	• A "rough tuning" instrument providing banks with long-term liquidity support • Can signal crises management and problems in banks

Source: *SAMA, Annual Report*, 2003.

Article 8 of the SAMA Banking Control Law prevents banks from lending more than 25% of their reserves and paid-up capital to any one entity, but at SAMA's discretion, this can be increased to 50%. A significant "secondary" monetary tool at SAMA's disposal is a maximum overall loans-to-deposit ratio that can be extended. While there is some leeway, the current maximum loans-to-deposit ratio stands at a conservative 60% for Saudi banks compared with 85 – 90% ratios for the U.S. banking industry as a whole. Central Banks sometimes use what is termed *moral suasion*, whereby a Central Bank attempts to influence commercial bank lending by *persuasion* rather than by direct means. In Saudi Arabia, this tool had not been particularly effective, especially in the early days of Saudi banking, because, when faced with a decision on lending in a booming era, the Saudi commercial banks chose profit maximization over SAMA "advise." This was compounded in the pre-*Saudization* banking era, when significant out-of-Kingdom forces and pressures were exerted on the foreign bank branches operating in the Kingdom. However, once *Saudization* of the Saudi banking system was completed in the mid-1980s, including the establishment of regular senior-level bank management meetings with SAMA, this policy tool became more effective. It will be interesting to see how SAMA will be able to align the interests of Saudi Arabia with the interests of the "new wave" foreign-owned bank branches that have been licensed to operate in the Kingdom post-2000.

Analyzing the operational usage and effectiveness of the various policy instruments at SAMA's disposal in Table 4.1, we note that Cash Reserve Ratios (CRR) have been infrequently used by SAMA. The last time these were changed was in 1980 when SAMA adjusted the CRR from 12% to 7% on current account liabilities of banks, but left saving and time-deposit CRR at 2%. This provides more of a "signalling" effect than actual fine-tuning of short-term liquidity.

Table 4.2 sets out the current ratios on statutory and other deposits held with SAMA by the Saudi commercial banks over the period 1998 - 2004.

Table 4.2 Reserve position of Saudi banks (end of years)

						SR Million	
	1998	1999	2000	2001	2002	2003	2004(Q1)
Cash in vault	2,657	5,468	5,971	3,453	4,892	4,590	4,018
Current deposits with SAMA	91	572	116	197	1,750	106	277
Statutory deposits with SAMA	9,826	10,504	11,191	12,599	14,270	14,643	16,579
Other deposits with SAMA	---	1	1,605	2,874	7,732	3,023	458
Bank reserves	12,574	16,545	18,883	19,122	28,643	22,361	21,332
Ratios (%) to bank deposits							
Cash in vault	1.1	2.2	2.3	1.2	1.5	1.4	1.1
Current deposits with SAMA	---	0.2	-	0.1	0.5	0.0	0.0
Statutory deposits with SAMA	4.1	4.3	4.2	4.5	4.3	4.4	4.5
Other deposits with SAMA	--	--	0.6	1	2.4	0.9	0.2
Bank reserves	53	6.7	7.2	6.8	8.7	6.7	5.8

Source: *SAMA*, 2003, 1st Quarter, 2004.

The average statutory deposit reserve ratio with SAMA has ranged from 4.1% to 4.5% for the whole period, with a gradual reduction in "other deposits" held with SAMA from the peak of 2.4% in 2002. To put the above in an historical context, the average statutory deposit reserve ratio stood at 6.3% in 1970, 11.5% in 1980 and 4.5% in 1986/87. However, "other" reserve deposits held with SAMA peaked at SR 12 billion or 9.5% in 1986/87 (SAMA, 2003, pp. 324, 333), a reflection of SAMA's occasional requests for such "extra" reserves to be deposited by banks during periods of "extra-ordinary" banking activities. During 1986/87, the Saudi banks, as shall be explored more fully in the next chapters, faced some loan collection difficulties, and SAMA's request for additional reserves was a prudent measure to safeguard the banks' liquidity "safety net". Similarly, in 2002, Saudi banks witnessed private capital repatriation from abroad following the September 11, 2001, events and SAMA encouraged banks to place such funds with it in "other deposits" to avoid overheating certain sectors of the economy.

Inter-bank domestic market transactions are exempted from reserve requirements, but offshore banks' riyal deposits with the domestic banks are subject to CRR.

SAMA has always felt that Saudi banks should not be subject to sudden liquidity pressures due to local or regional uncertainties. As such, a relatively high level of Statutory Liquidity Ratio (SLR) in comparison with banks in more developed economies is imposed on Saudi banks. A minimum amount of specified liquid assets equal to 20% of their demand and time liabilities is set, making Saudi banks fairly liquid, but imposing a "withholding tax" on lost potential earnings by Saudi banks.

Reliance on 'open market' operations

As indicated in Table 4.1, SAMA has several other monetary policy instruments at its disposal, including *foreign exchange swaps, placement of public funds* and *open market operations.* Placement of public funds with banks is entirely at SAMA's discretion and complements its efforts to fine-tune day-to-day liquidity instruments. The placement of public funds is a way of "rough tuning" the money supply; basically the Central Bank is seen to provide long-term liquidity support to a bank. In Saudi Arabia SAMA does this by placing the funds of semi-autonomous government institutions. SAMA has used this in the past to provide support to those banks facing liquidity problems or going through crisis management. The effect, however, is to reduce the returns of those government institutions whose funds are being placed at lower-than-market rates, but, more importantly, it sends a negative signal to the market about the state of health of the recipient bank.

Central bank support, unless it is a temporary measure to be followed by an asset and liability restructuring and by management changes, might induce banks to take more risks, creating a "moral hazard" situation. SAMA has used this type of support infrequently, aware that uncertainty about one bank could easily spread to the rest of the banking sector.

Similarly SAMA has used foreign exchange swaps very sparingly and mostly during periods of external uncertainties and currency speculation, such as the 1991 Gulf War and some speculative pressures in 2003. SAMA uses foreign exchange swaps to provide emergency liquidity to the banking system, and rates up to one year are actively traded. Swaps affect liquidity but do not, under Saudi Arabia's fixed exchange rate system, directly influence the exchange rate (Jasser and Banafe, 2003).

In common with most other developed Central Banks, SAMA has come to rely more on *Repos* and *Reverse-Repos* as the most flexible operating instruments of monetary policy, through the buying and selling of government bonds and securities in so-called "open-market operations." A Central Bank can alter the liquidity position of banks through dealing directly in the market by reducing liquidity (selling securities) or injecting liquidity (buying back securities), but the effectiveness of such operations depends on the size and depth of the capital market, specifically the number of institutional players who are buying and selling securities besides the Central Bank.

The Saudi bond market is still in its early stages, mainly restricted to SAMA, the Saudi banks and a few other institutions. The new Saudi Capital Market Law envisages broadening the range of instruments and players over time. In the short term, open market operations are an effective and more precise tool in changing the money supply of the banking system through the buying and selling of government short and long-term securities. These instruments are deemed to be "gilt-edged" or default-free, with other financial instruments priced above them to reflect liquidity and credit risk.

In 1986 the Saudi Arabian government introduced its first borrowing instrument – the Bankers Special Deposit Account or BSDA as a means of financing growing budget deficits and as an alternative to drawing down on foreign assets to finance the budget deficits. Table 4.3 sets out the main securities that are currently offered by SAMA and it illustrates how far SAMA has come since those pioneering days.

Table 4.3 reveals an extensive "menu" of financial securities that are now on offer, ranging from very short-term liquid instruments such as one-week treasury bills, to long-dated 10-year bonds. The introduction of Floating Rate Notes (FRNs) in 1996 added a new dimension and provided a further rate risk-adjusted option for purchases of Saudi government securities. Pricing is competitive compared to other market instruments, with premiums added to longer-dated securities, especially for Government Development Bonds (GDBs), which in turn are priced at a premium to comparable U.S. bonds. Repo facilities are provided at 35% of total bank holdings of government securities and offered at Market Related Rates or MMR. SAMA's Official Repurchase Rate (ORR) is also available to banks seeking credit, up to the maximum limit of 0.5% of eligible securities. The ORR rate level is determined by SAMA. Given the extremely small amount of credit available to banks at the ORR, this serves more as a signal to the domestic money market in the absence of an official discount rate, than as a transactional influence. "Reverse Repos" allow Saudi banks to deposit surplus funds with SAMA for a short period of time. The rate of investment is called the Reverse Repos Rate (RRR) and is placed at below interbank bid rates.

Table 4.3 SAMA: current securities offerings

Security Issue	Currency Denomination	Tenor	Pricing	Offering	Observation
Treasury Bills (T-Bills)	SR	1, 4, 13, 26 and 52 weeks	Saudi riyal Interbank BID rate	Weekly basis	Replaced the 180 days Bankers Special Deposit Accounts
Floating Rate Notes (FRNs)	SR	5 and 7 year maturities	Saudi Interbank Offer Rate (SIBOR) Plus Margin	Monthly basis	Introduced in 1996 to provide rate risk hedging
Government Development Bonds (GDBs)	SR	2, 3, 5, 7 and 10 year maturities	Priced to reflect relative value in alternative investments (U.S. Bonds) plus 25 - 75 basis points premium	Quarterly basis	Issued on a fortnightly basis until 1996

Source: *SAMA* Annual Reports.

Repos and Reverse Repos are thus automatic mechanisms for regulating the banking system's liquidity. According to SAMA (Annual Report, 2003), Repo and Reverse-Repo agreements entered into with commercial banks averaged SR 1.8 billion and SR 3.2 billion per day respectively during 2002, compared with SR 1.0 billion and SR 2.5 billion in 2001. This demonstrated the relatively higher liquidity position of the Saudi banks in 2002, with reported capital inflows to the Kingdom following the September 11, 2001, events. According to SAMA, this trend continued in the first quarter of 2003, with Repos averaging SR 348 million and Reverse-Repos SR 5.89 billion per day despite an all-time low level of 2% for the ORR and 1.5% for the RRR for the same period.

The centrality of SAMA's exchange rate policy

According to analysts, economic theory suggests that when a country fixes its exchange and interest rate and is subject to high capital mobility, it loses its ability to conduct an independent monetary policy. In terms of economic policy, this means that in Saudi Arabia, fiscal, not monetary, policy is the primary instrument for economic growth management. Fiscal policy – or more precisely government expenditures – can be used to increase or decrease GDP, while monetary policy is focussed on fixing the exchange rate and interest rates (NCB, 2001, Abalkhail, 2002, Jasser and Banafe, 2003). Monetary policy is used to "fine tune" the effects of fiscal policy. With the Saudi riyal effectively pegged to the U.S. dollar since

1981, there have been limitations to Saudi monetary policy on interest rate adjustments. In effect, the Saudi riyal interest rates closely track dollar interest rates, often with a small premium. This is graphically illustrated in Figure 4.1, which sets out U.S. and SR three-month deposit rates for the period 1989 2003. Saudi riyal premiums reflect periods of sharp falls in oil prices, cuts in government expenditures and regional tensions.

Figure 4.1 U.S. and Saudi interest rates 1989 - 2003

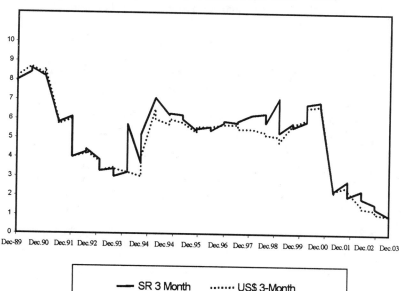

Source: *SAMA, 2003.*

In essence, Saudi interest rates – and by implication, Saudi monetary policy – is closely tied to that of an external Central Bank, specifically that of the United States. What might be prudent and necessary monetary policy in the USA (expanding or dampening the money supply) might not necessarily be the most appropriate interest rate level desirable for Saudi Arabia at the same period of time. A further concern for SAMA is that, under the adopted fixed exchange rate policy, if SR interest rates did not closely track that of the U.S. dollar, an *arbitrage* opportunity would exist for either U.S. or Saudi investors to borrow in the low interest rate currency and invest in the high interest rate currency, making a risk-free profit due to the fixed exchange rate, after allowing for inflation differentials between the two countries.

In Saudi Arabia, the exchange rate is central to monetary policy. SAMA's intervention under the fixed exchange rate regime is influenced by two factors: the level of foreign exchange outflow from the country and the level of dollar/riyal interest rate differentials. As such, SAMA's stated goals centre on internal price stability and balance of payments considerations. Furthermore, the Governor of SAMA has defended its fixed exchange policy for the following reasons (SAMA: Interview Hamad Saud Al-Sayari, 2003). The Monetary Agency believes the fixed dollar/riyal peg has worked well due to the fact that "all of Saudi exports and most of its imports are denominated in dollars; the riyal is fully backed by foreign exchange reserves; such reserves are the result of oil revenues and investment income; the riyal is not a misaligned currency in terms of its nominal and effective exchange rates; and, finally, the stability of the dollar/riyal exchange rate sharply reduces risks for foreign investors." Table 4.4 sets out some of the major arguments for and against fixed exchange rate regimes that are applicable to Saudi Arabia.

Table 4.4 Advantages and disadvantages of fixed and floating exchange-rate regimes

Advantages	*Disadvantages*
Fixed exchange-rate regimes	
• Maintains investors' confidence in the currency, thus encouraging domestic savings and investment and discouraging capital outflows	• Does not allow the implementation of independent monetary policy
• Reduces inflationary pressures associated with devaluation	• Exchange rates cannot be used to adjust for external shocks or imbalances • A fixed peg is also a fixed target for speculators
Floating exchange-rate regimes	
• Allows pursuit of an independent monetary policy; when an economy suffers a downturn, monetary expansion can soften the impact	• Reduces investors' faith in the currency, thus discouraging capital inflows to avoid exchange risk
• Allows a country to adjust to external shocks through exchange rates; that is, lower export prices and higher import prices would help the country regain external equilibrium	• Floating rates can overshoot and become highly unstable, leading to speculation

Source: *Adapted from Azzam*, 2002, p. 98.

Table 4.4 indicates, there are powerful arguments for both fixed and floating exchange rates. As far as Saudi Arabia is concerned, there is certainly some basis for reduction in investor risk due to a fixed rate policy. Saudi Arabia did not experience any of the upheavals seen in other countries during the East Asia and Mexican currency crises of the mid and late-1990s. However, there is some disagreement on the level of imported inflation and nominal and effective Saudi riyal exchange rates, due to the SR being pegged to the U.S. dollar. Disagreements on whether Saudi Arabia should adopt a fixed exchange rate pegged to one currency or to several currencies tend to arise as a result of the short or long-term assumptions being made. Some argue that the fixed peg against the dollar has served Saudi Arabia well and will continue to do so in the long-term with a minimal devaluation risk outlook as long as "there are no excesses ... (and) government overspend, or external deficits surge ..." (Azzam, 2002, pp. 104 - 105).

Other analysts argue for pegging the Saudi riyal to a wider diversification in the basket of currencies, specifically in currencies with which the Kingdom has major trading relations. The erosion in the value of the U.S. currency during 2003 and 2004, coupled with forecasts that a "weak dollar" policy might not be opposed by the USA to try to overcome part of that country's trade deficits, has caused some in the Kingdom to call for a more flexible pegged policy (Dukheil, 2004, Abdul-Lateef, 2002), but others remain neutral on the subject arguing that higher oil prices in 2003 and 2004 more than offset the deterioration in the Saudi import bill (SAMBA, February, 2004).

The sharp fall in the U.S. dollar's value during 2002/2004 has indeed affected Saudi Arabia's import bill, with an estimated 7.2% depreciation in the Saudi riyal for 2003 alone, as Table 4.5 illustrates.

Table 4.5 Trade weighted depreciation on the Saudi riyal (2003)

Currency	% Share of 2002 Saudi imports		2003 Change vs. dollar and riyal		Contribution to total riyal depreciation
Euro	21.0%	x	17.8%	=	3.76%
U.S. Dollar	16.3%	x	0.00%	=	0.00%
Japanese Yen	11.1%	x	10.93%	=	1.21%
GCC currencies	11.1%	x	0.00%	=	0.00%
British Pound	6.0%	x	10.55%	=	0.63%
Chinese Yuan	5.3%	x	0.00%	=	0.00%
Australian Dollar	3.5%	x	23.94%	=	0.83%
S. Korean Won	3.3%	x	-0.51%	=	-0.02%
Indian Rupee	2.7%	x	5.16%	=	0.14%
Brazilian Real	1.7%	x	17.33%	=	0.29%
Swiss Franc	1.7%	x	10.67%	=	0.18%
Swedish Kronor	1.2%	x	17.11%	=	0.21%
Total trade weighted depreciation of riyal				=	7.23%

Source: *SAMBA*, February, 2004, p. 10.

The depreciation of the Saudi riyal could have been larger but for the fact that U.S. imports accounted for around 20% of total imports, and the majority of non-European Union and Japanese imports are still denominated in U.S. currency. From a theoretical viewpoint, the depreciation of the Saudi riyal should have made Saudi exports more competitive, but in reality this is not translated into tangible benefits as the Kingdom's primary exports are oil and hydrocarbon-related products, and additional Saudi oil exports are constrained by Organization of Petroleum Exporting Countries (OPEC) member country quotas.

However, as Figure 4.2 illustrates, both the Real Effective Exchange Rate (REER) and the Nominal Effective Exchange Rate (NEER) for the Saudi currency fell, reflecting the foreign exchange depreciation of the U.S. dollar against other major foreign currencies. This was transmitted to the Saudi NEER, which represents the average of its bilateral rates with currencies of selected countries weighted by the relative importance of Saudi Arabia's trade with them. The NEER depreciated by 2.2% for 2002 according to SAMA, while the REER – representing the NEER index adjusted for inflation in Saudi Arabia and its trading partners – also fell by a significant 3.9% for the same period.

Figure 4.2 Saudi Arabia: Indices of Nominal and Real Effective Exchange Rates 1995 - 2002

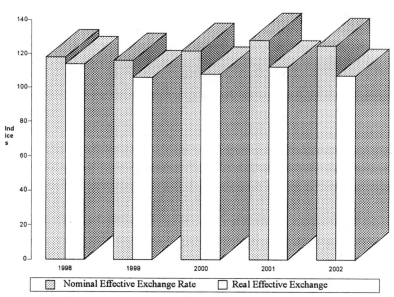

Source: *SAMA*, 2003. p. 87.

Money supply creation and monetary policy

As analyzed above, when exchange rate policy becomes the main plank of Saudi Arabia's monetary policy, it seems difficult to pursue a counter-cyclical monetary policy that is independent of the role of fiscal policy on Saudi GDP growth, money demand/supply and inflation. The major factors influencing monetary aggregates in the Kingdom are the government's fiscal operations and private sector balance-of-payments deficits.

In an oil-based economy like Saudi Arabia, the creation of money typically proceeds as follows. The Government maintains its accounts with

SAMA. The receipt of oil revenues by the government, nearly all in U.S. dollars, directly produces a rise in government deposits held in SAMA's international bank accounts. These foreign oil revenues have no immediate impact on domestic liquidity, since by definition domestic liquidity is held only by the private sector. Only when the government makes payments to contractors is the inflow of foreign exchange translated into domestic liquidity. When expenditures are made, the government draws checks on SAMA, which means SAMA's liabilities are shifted to the banks, thus facilitating credit creation by the banks.

SAMA effectively transforms the dollars held by it on behalf of the government into Saudi riyals, while still holding the dollars as backing for the "created" Saudi riyal money supply. It is the private sector's transactions with the rest of the world that affect domestic liquidity. Given that the Saudi economy is an open economy, and that there are no capital restrictions, a large fraction of the domestic riyals received by households, contractors and foreigners operating in the Kingdom are converted into foreign currencies to pay for imported goods, remittances and investments abroad. This reverses the process of money supply creation, and partially offsets the money creation effects of the government. This is illustrated diagrammatically in Figure 4.3.

Figure 4.3 Saudi Arabia: domestic money creation process

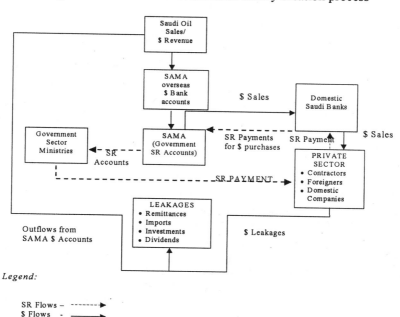

The above diagram is a simplified one, as it assumes that all government SR payments are converted into dollars and are transmitted as leakages out of the system. The net effect in this case is that while SAMA receives back all Saudi riyals through dollar sales to the Saudi banking system, it has in effect "extinguished" the available stock of SR money supply through its draw-down of foreign currency deposits.

In Figure 4.3 the outflows from SAMA's foreign currency accounts exactly match the dollar leakages of the private sector. In reality, the amount of "leakage" is a function of the amount of remittances, the propensity to import, and the amounts retained in the domestic economy by Saudi companies and individuals. The Saudi domestic money creation process seems to set it aside from other economies, where the quantity of money supplied responds to demand for the local currency through the banking system, through the selling of foreign assets or through the "printing of money." In the Saudi model, external government transactions also have no impact on domestic liquidity, as they represent bookkeeping entries in SAMA's foreign currency accounts.

Given the above, it is important to assess the causative factors for changes in Saudi Arabia's broad money supply, or M3, so as to work out the actual net domestic expenditure of the government and the balance of payments deficit of the private sector. This is a set out in Table 4.6 for selected years from 1986 - 2002.

Table 4.6 Factors affecting changes in Saudi M3 (selected years)
SR billion

	1986	1989	1991	1997	2001	2002
Net domestic flows through government spending[1]	71.7	69.1	166.7	145.3	160.4	154.2
Commercial banks claims on the private sector	1.2	2.8	8.3	10.1	14.8	18.8
Net private sector balance of payments	-85.7	-96.0	-106.1	-121.9	-159.0	-161.0
Net other items[2]	23.3	25.9	-41.5	-24.2	1.1	37.1
Change in M3	10.5	1.8	27.4	9.3	17.3	49.1
Annual growth rate of M3 (%)	7.0	1.0	14.5	5.2	5.0	15.2

Note: [1] Including net loans disbursed by government-sponsored credit institutions

[2] Includes payments for goods and services as well as capital outflow

Source: *SAMA*, 2003.

From Table 4.6, we note that the rate of monetary expansion M3 fluctuates over the period in question, reflecting a variety of factors. The positives include government expenditures during periods of regional tensions (such as the 1990/1991 Gulf War) as well as higher oil revenues (2001, 2002). Counteracting these positive developments are net private sector balance of payments outflows, which were consistent for all the years. "Net other items" showed periods of capital outflows (1991 - 1997), but was mostly a net capital inflow in 2002 following uncertainties after 11

September 2001. SAMA's policy of currency stability seemed to have played an important role in capital inflow considerations.

Composition of Saudi Arabia's money supply

Evidence from many countries that have developed their financial markets seems to suggest that people will gradually shift towards savings and other yield-bearing instruments and away from cash and current accounts over time. A shift from a cash-orientated society is taking place in Saudi Arabia, as illustrated in Table 4.7.

Table 4.7 Saudi Arabia monetary ratios (%)

End of Year	Currency/M3	M1/M3	M2/M3
1972	44.4	73.3	88.8
1982	25.5	64.1	86.2
1997	16.8	51.9	80.3
1998	16.0	49.7	79.3
1999	18.3	52.0	80.4
2000	16.2	52.6	81.5
2001	14.9	54.3	82.1
2002	13.7	53.2	81.6
2003	14.2	54.4	81.8
2004 (1Q)	13.2	55.6	81.6

Source: SAMA, 2003, First Quarter, 2004.

While Table 4.7 shows a downward trend in currency held outside banks over time, seasonal fluctuations occur in Saudi Arabia each year around the two (currency/M3), major Muslim calendar events: the *Ramadan* month of fasting and the *Hajj* or pilgrimage season. Demand for cash increases sharply during these periods, as well as to a lesser extent during the summer school vacation, when currency outside banks reaches its peak.

A key factor in the steady rise in demand deposits is the increase in such deposits as bank customers feel more confident about the monetary stability of the country and the soundness of the banking system. The expansion of the use of credit, debit and direct payment cards will also necessitate the use of such accounts to satisfy the *transaction motive* for holding money. The growth in time and saving accounts also indicates that the population's general reluctance and inhibition to receive interest payments due to religious reasons is somewhat diminishing, thereby increasing the *investment motive* for holding money. The increase in time deposits over the years has had a more significant effect on the Saudi banking industry, as this has encouraged Saudi banks to increase the maturity profile of their loans to longer periods and to improve the terms of such longer-term loans, They can more easily match their assets with a longer liability base, further monetizing the Saudi economy.

Financial deepening of the Saudi economy

"Financial deepening" is sometimes difficult to quantify, and different measures have been used for other Arab Gulf countries that can be applied to Saudi Arabia (Eltony, 2000). The measures used are as follows:

K - Currency ratio (cc/M1)
Z - Monetisation ratio (M2/GDP)
KK - Mobilising longer-term assets (M1/GDP)

Table 4.8 and Figure 4.4 show the results of this financial deepening over the period 1971 - 2004, encompassing the pre-boom, boom and adjustment periods of the Saudi Arabian economy.

Table 4.8 Financial deepening in Saudi Arabia (%) 1971 – 2004

Year	K	Z	KK
1971	62.9	13.8	11.3
1973	52.4	13.6	11.7
1979	41.6	21.9	20.2
1986	44.3	39.0	16.1
1990	43.7	36.1	26.1
1997	32.4	35.3	22.8
2000	30.9	36.2	23.4
2001	27.3	38.8	25.6
2002	26.2	39.9	26.9
2003	25.4	42.4	28.2
2004 (1Q)	24.5	43.4	29.1

Legend: K - Currency Ratio (cc/M1)
Z - Monetization Ratio (M2/GDP)
KK - Mobilizing long-term assets (M1/GDP)
Source: *SAMA*, 2004, SAMBA, 2004.

(K) the currency ratio reflects the degree of sophistication of the domestic financial sector. (Z) the monetization ratio reflects the size of the financial market, while (KK) is a measure of the extent of monetization and mobilization of long term assets.

The Saudi data shows that *(K)* the currency ratio followed a decreasing trend, similar to Kuwait data over the same period for the Eltony study. This signifies a high degree of diversification of financial institutions and greater use of non-currency forms of transaction media, such as other bank accounts. The ratio fell from nearly 63% in 1971 to 24% in 2004.

The monetization variable *(Z)* also indicates significant improvements over the data period. This ratio has increased significantly from 14% levels in the early 1970 period to 43% in 2004, indicating further expansion in the financial market relative to non-financial markets. This in turn implies a faster accumulation of a wide range of financial assets, such as savings accounts.The *(KK)*ratio reflects the degree of sophistication of the financial market shown by the level of dependency on cash or liquidity preferences in the Saudi economy. This also has shown significant improvement over the study time period. In summary, the Saudi financial sector is showing substantial improvement in achieving financial deepening.

Figure 4.4 Financial deepening in Saudi Arabia 1971 - 2004

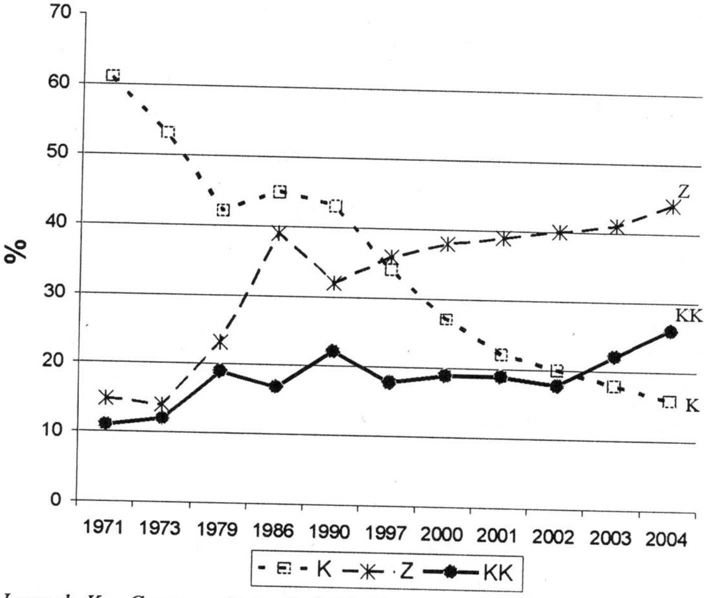

Legend: K - Currency Ratio (cc/M1), Z - Monetization Ratio (M2/GDP), KK - Mobilizing long-term assets (M1/GDP).

SAMA and inflation-control policies

According to SAMA, monetary policy continued to be "geared to the objective of maintaining domestic price and exchange rate stability" (SAMA, 2203, p. 84). The considerable inflation witnessed by Saudi Arabia during the early "boom" years of 1974 - 1976 when inflation reached around 30% p.a. has been effectively tackled (Johany, 1986). According to current SAMA data, inflation continues to fall and, as indicated in Table 4.9, inflation fell by 0.6% for 2002, continuing a five-year trend.

Table 4.9 Annual growth rates of selected indicators, including inflation

	1998	1999	2000	2001	2002
Non-oil GDP deflator (1988 = 100)	0.4	1.2	0.7	0.4	-0.6
Cost of living index (1988 = 100)	-0.2	-1.3	-0.6	-0.8	-0.6
Non-oil GDP (at constant prices)	1.1	1.8	3.9	3.4	3.6
Imports	4.4	-6.6	8.1	3.3	3.5
Money Supply (M3)	3.7	6.8	4.5	5.0	15.2

Source: SAMA, 2003, p. 178.

Table 4.9 also summarizes the main inflation indicators as well as setting out the growth in money supply and Gross Domestic Product (GDP). In order to arrive at a better estimation for changes in the domestic economy and to isolate the impact of oil on the GDP, the non-oil GDP deflator is used. This is a price index that employs the current year's output mix for calculating a price index, using a base year. Because GDP refers to the value added within Saudi Arabia during a year, the non-oil GDP deflator is a measure of domestic inflation. However, it is still an imperfect measurement as much of Saudi Arabia's GDP is produced by foreign-owned factors of production (labour) and the GDP deflator includes this element. What Table 4.9 and Figure 4.5 indicate is that the Saudi Arabian money supply grew by an *inflationless* 15.2% in 2002, more than double the normal rate.

Figure 4.5 Money supply growth and inflation 1994 - 2004

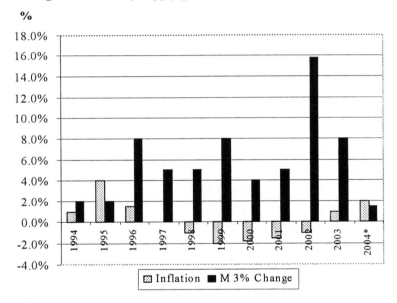

*March 2004
Source: *SAMA*, 2003, 2004.

While Figure 4.5 indicates that the money supply growth had come down to 8.1% levels in 2003, and slowed down further during the first quarter of 2004, the level of inflation as measured by the cost-of-living index fell for each year from 1997 to 2002. Recognizing that the general price index used for measuring the level of inflation in Saudi Arabia was not keeping up with the changing pace of economic development and consumer preferences, the government of Saudi Arabia has instituted an Index Improvement Program through the Central Department of Statistics

(CDS). Since early 2002, CDS has adopted modern techniques in conducting consumer expenditure patterns, has expanded the survey coverage to include all regions of the Kingdom, and has extended the size of the "basket" of goods and services used from 180 to 420 items.

Saudi money supply and inflation: Monetarist or Keynesian?

Table 4.9 and Figure 4.5 indicated that there was no positive correlation between Saudi money supply growth and the level of inflation. As such, the monetarist equation $MV = PY$ does not seem to hold, where (M) is money supply, (V) is velocity of money, (P) is the price index, and (Y) is real income. Table 4.10 sets out the income velocity of money in the non-oil sector.

Table 4.10 Income velocity of money (non-oil sector)

Years	M^1	M^2	M^3
1998	3.82	2.46	1.98
1999	4.12	2.64	2.11
2000	4.42	2.86	2.32
2001	3.94	2.60	2.13
2002	3.66	2.46	2.01

Source: *SAMA*, 2003, p. 84

From Table 4.10 we note that the velocity of money for all categories of money supply (M1, M2, M3) has exhibited relatively small rates of change compared to money supply growth, and has in fact been declining. The general stability of the Saudi price level must be due to other contributing factors. Care must be exercised, however, in applying a simple monetarist explanation to Saudi Arabia's money supply and inflation experience due to the close relationship between money creation and government expenditure examined earlier in the chapter. Increases in government expenditures, without associated increases in money supply, could account for inflation if standard Keynesian assumptions apply. In this case, if money supply were not to change, velocity would fluctuate sufficiently to accommodate price changes caused by increased demand. In Saudi Arabia's case, because money is created as the government spends, velocity need not adjust. Therefore, no firm conclusion can be drawn regarding monetarist versus Keynesian explanations for Saudi Arabian inflation. The contributory factors for Saudi Arabia's apparent decline in inflation over the past few years can be traced to both domestic and external factors.

The moderation of domestic inflationary pressures traces its origin, in large part, to direct government policies, especially ongoing government subsidy programs, as well as price controls for basic goods and services. As explained in previous chapters, such subsidies amount to around SR 6 billion per annum. An effective subsidy policy must see prices maintained at steady levels over a long period of time. Otherwise the government might be faced with the prospect of continually adding to the overall subsidy element to keep pace with inflation, or of allowing the subsidized goods to adjust for the non-subsidized costs to rise over time by increasing their prices in lieu of additional government subsidies. The effect of increased domestic competition amongst merchants might also be a contributing factor in lower prices, as more local manufacturing units start production. According to SAMA, external factors also contributed to the general stability of prices. These were attributed to the stability of both import prices and the Saudi riyal's exchange rates, as set out in Table 4.11.

Table 4.11 Selected indices of international trade

	1999	2000	2001	2002	% change	
					2001	2002
Consumer prices of industrial countries	107.2	109.8	112.1	113.7	2.1	1.4
Export unit values of industrial countries	85.7	83.5	81.7	N/A	-2.2	N/A
Export unit values to the Kingdom (from trading partners)	87.1	80.8	78.6	78.4	-2.7	-0.3
Riyal's nominal effective exchange rate*	116.0	121.7	128.2	125.4	5.3	-2.2
Riyal's real effective exchange rate**	106.4	108.7	111.8	107.4	2.8	-3.9

*Represents the ratio of the period's average exchange rate of the riyal index to a weighted geometric average of exchange rates of the Kingdom's trading partners
**Represents the nominal effective exchange rate adjusted for changes in the relative prices or cost indicators of the Kingdom and its major trading partners

Source: *International Financial Statistics (IFS)*, May 2003 Issue, and *World Economic Outlook, Database, IMF, SAMA*, 2003, p. 179.

While the situation might have reversed slightly during 2003 and 2004 due to the sharp decline in the dollars value as discussed earlier, Table 4.11 indicates that over the past few years there was a rise in both the Saudi riyal's nominal and real exchange rates, as well as a fall in the import unit value to Saudi Arabia. A large proportion of Saudi goods are still imported and one would expect a certain degree of imported price inflation to take place. Table 4.12 illustrates this further.

From Table 4.12 we note that lower medical, transportation and fabrics and clothes indexes contributed to the overall fall in retail import prices. There was a slight rise in the all-food and house furnishings indexes. Further reductions in the transport and communication import index could follow the opening-up of the Saudi communication sector to foreign investment and operators under Saudi economic liberalization plans, as this is now a significant item in the overall retail import index.

Table 4.12 Retail Import Price Index (RIPI) annual averages

			1998 = 100		% change	
	Weights (%)	*2000*	*2001*	*2002*	*2001*	*2002*
General Index	**100.00**	**103.2**	**102.4**	**101.9**	**-0.8**	**-0.49**
All food	46.40	113.5	114.0	115.1	0.4	0.96
Fabrics & apparel	13.82	84.8	83.8	82.9	-1.2	-1.07
House furnishing	13.34	100.3	100.5	99.9	0.2	-0.59
Medical care	0.56	93.2	92.7	90.6	-0.5	-2.26
Transport & communication	12.66	98.6	92.9	86.4	-5.8	-6.99
Entertainment & education	3.80	101.2	101.1	98.1	-0.1	-2.96
Other expenditures	9.39	91.0	89.5	91.3	-1.7	2.0

Source: *Central Department of Statistics, Ministry of Planning,* 2003, p. 105.

Managing the Kingdom's reserves

One important function that SAMA performs is managing Saudi Arabia's external reserve assets. While reserve assets have seen a sharp reduction from peaks in the mid-1980s due to government drawdowns to fund deficits, SAMA still considers this function an important means of diversification in its effort to improve the Kingdom's reserve portfolio.

In line with its evolution of financial instruments and risk management techniques, and in common with other central banks that manage national reserves, SAMA has made a more active use of a broad range of such investment instruments and has developed more performance benchmarks, compared to a mid 1970s investment strategy that was largely confined to bank deposits. Assets allocation then meant deposit allocation among major international banks based on their credit rating.

SAMA's Investment Committee is headed by the Governor and meets regularly to assess market conditions, asset allocation and market performance before deciding on investment decisions. The overall aim is still to preserve principal value with maximum liquidity and returns. As such, safety, liquidity and risk-adjusted returns are the driving goals.

SAMA also emphasizes portfolio benchmarking and performance measurement in order to evaluate internally managed and externally managed discretionary portfolios. In terms of current credit ratings for counterparty institutions, SAMA requires a minimum rating of "C" by the Fitch IBCA rating agency for bank deposits. Sovereign fixed income and supranational and corporate obligations have to be rated at AAA or AA by Moody's and S&P. The U.S. dollar is used as the base currency and it dominates the currency composition of SAMA's portfolios, followed by other major currencies such as the Euro, Sterling and Yen. Currency allocations are not linked to trade flows according to SAMA (SAMA, 2003, p. 9). The benchmarks that SAMA uses reflects the Monetary Agency's diversity of assets and risk tolerance and includes S&P 500 for the U.S. equity markets, JP Morgan Global Bond Index for multi-currency bond portfolios, Morgan Stanley Composite Index for Europe, and Global and TSE for Japan. External fund managers are allocated funds and manage portfolios under SAMA-approved asset guidelines. Portfolio performance is measured on a total return basis with liquidation based on either poor performance or for reasons of asset allocation.

Future development and challenges

The upgrading of Saudi Arabia's sovereign credit rating by both Standard and Poor's and Moody's in the summer of 2003 was a welcome development for the Kingdom, and reflected the positive medium and long-term outlook for the Kingdom based on macroeconomic stability, substantial external liquidity, low inflation, stable exchange rate and a sound banking system. SAMA takes a lot of credit for this development, which saw S&P assign a credit rating of "A+" for long-term local currency and "A" for foreign currency, with both local and foreign short-term currency assigned "A-1". There had been no previous S&P rating for the country. Moody's raised its foreign currency rating to "Baa2" from "Baa3", representing an investment grade rating (Reuters, August, 2003).

While this development was welcome news, SAMA is faced by several domestic and international challenges in the years ahead that could test the Monetary Agency's ability to adapt to new circumstances. Table 4.13 summarizes SAMA's major challenges in the short, medium and long-term.

SAMA has come a long way from those early exotic days of 1952 and, in essence, it is now a fully-fledged Central Bank in all but name. It has tried to overcome the limitations imposed on it through its founding Charter and has successfully introduced a range of innovative capital market instruments to add to the liquidity options of the Saudi commercial banks.

By its own admission, SAMA recognizes that in the years ahead it faces a range of domestic, regional and international challenges. Key objectives set out by SAMA include expediting the issue of regulations and legislations aimed at promoting and expanding the range of financial services in conformity with the "trends towards liberalization of international financial markets and WTO requirements" (SAMA, 2002). This, according to the Monetary Agency, requires the streamlining of the operations of the capital and insurance markets and other financial services. SAMA also advocates changes to the current judicial system as it relates to commercial, financial and banking transactions and contracts, such as insurance and mortgages, as Saudi commercial banks do not currently possess the legal means to mortgage property in their own name.

The list of challenges set out in Table 4.13 seems daunting but SAMA has already started to confront some of the issues. A notable success has been the vigorous implementation of procedures to prevent money laundering and the funding of terrorism. SAMA received a clean bill of health on these matters from the Financial Action Task Force (FATF) in

April, 2004. The Kingdom was commended by FATF for taking several measures including freezing the accounts suspected of illegal dealings and requesting that all Saudi banks complete "know your customer" formalities or close accounts. Under SAMA's recommendations, the Saudi Cabinet endorsed Saudi Arabia's first anti-money laundering law, which stipulated stiff penalties (Arab News, 19 August 2003).

Table 4.13 Challenges faced by SAMA

Short-term	Medium-term	Long-term
• Control of money laundering and terrorism funding	• Establishing guidelines for Islamic banking supervision and regulation	• Effective participation through Islamic Banking Financial Services Board
• E-commerce application and internet banking	• Ensuring Saudi banks comply with new BIS capital adequacy ratios	• Effective participation in Gulf Cooperation Council Monetary Union and proposed single currency for GCC
• Ensure Saudi banks are adequately prepared for Saudi WTO entry	• Supervision and integration of newly licensed foreign banks into Saudi banking system	• Develop corporate bond market
• Overseeing effective Saudization of bank personnel	• Effective participation in international financial supervisory standards	• Supervision and regulation of cross-border Saudi bank mergers and acquisitions
• Establishment of data base and supervision of the insurance sector	• Supervision and regulation of non-bank financial institutions into the markets	• Re-examine SR/U.S. dollar fixed exchange parity policy
• Completion of mergers of local money exchangers into one financial institution	• Develop secondary market instruments for capital market	
• Overseeing partial privatization of government-held bank shares in capital market	• Upgrade SAMA's Banking Training Institute to provide broader financial services expertise	
• Effective participation in new Saudi Capital Market structure		

Saudization of bank personnel is proceeding apace with SAMA insisting that qualified Saudi personnel are appointed to key positions, based on appointment criteria focused on technical proficiency. To help upgrade local banking skills, SAMA's Banking Training Institute is running a wider range of training courses to meet future financial market needs, including for the local insurance markets.

Islamic banking services and operations are becoming more important for SAMA, given the expansion of such services by most Saudi banks and the GCC countries. SAMA became a member of the Islamic Banking Financial Services Board in 2002, which will help in establishing new guidelines and rules to oversee this important market segment. Future development might necessitate a separate Banking Control Law, targeting Islamic financial institutions and subjecting them to proper rules and supervision. This has been successfully achieved in nearby Bahrain, where Islamic banking supervision co-exists side-by-side with "conventional" and investment banking activities.

Other long-term issues that might need to be addressed include revisiting SAMA's 1966 Banking Control Law to allow the Monetary Agency to make more effective use of the full range of monetary policy instruments. In particular, there must be a wider use of the open-market operations, with outright sales and purchases of government securities by the Central Bank itself as a monetary tool, as opposed to the current policy of action initiated by Saudi commercial banks. This will add depth and breadth to the capital market.

The plan of the Gulf Co-operation Council for full monetary union, including the adoption of a single Gulf currency in 2010, is another issue that will have to be addressed by SAMA and by the other Central Banks of the GCC countries. Whether to opt for a unified GCC currency pegged to one currency – the U.S. dollar – or adopt a more flexible multi-currency peg will also be an important issue that SAMA will have to face. This could affect its current fixed parity rate policy.

SAMA will have to coordinate with these Central Banks on economic convergence and on internal harmonization of policies relating to inflation and budget deficit issues. This will require greater macroeconomic discipline by member states as well as Central Bank independence in voicing their concerns should target rates not be adhered to. SAMA acts, for all intents and purposes, as an independent central bank but its independent role must be further clarified to avoid undue influence by short-term economic measures based on political expediency. The recent statements of the SAMA Governor concerning disquiet on the size of the Saudi public debt is a good indication of such independence, but the policy of obtaining prior approval from the Ministry of Finance to change the statutory reserve requirements of local banks needs to be amended to allow SAMA more freedom of action, although this policy instrument has not been frequently used. In the long term, SAMA might face cross-border banking and other financial services mergers and acquisitions, with Saudi banks forming international strategic alliances and foreign banks acquiring interests in the Kingdom. This will test SAMA's cross-border regulatory and supervisory skills. SAMA will also need to supervise foreign-owned financial institutions in the Kingdom whose objectives might be divergent from broader national considerations. This was the case in some instances in the 1970s, before the *Saudization* of foreign banks; it was one of the major factors for the *Saudization* drive to align national interests with those of the "Saudized" banks.

With expected entry into WTO and wholly foreign-owned banking licenses issued during 2002/2003, SAMA feels confident that it has gained sufficient experience from the *Saudization* era to be able to manage the new circumstances, helped by its active participation and membership in leading international multilateral bodies such as such as the International Monetary fund (IMF), the World Bank and the Bank for International Settlements (BIS). The avoidance to date of any major financial crises in Saudi Arabia compared to other economies worldwide, attests to SAMA's regulatory and supervisory policies. The key is to ensure that Saudi Arabia's financial sector remains a vibrant and leading segment of the economy in the future.

Summary of key points

- *SAMA has evolved from being a Monetary Agency with a limited role into a fully fledged central bank with relative independence, a broad range of monetary tools at its disposal and with effective supervisory powers of the financial sector.*
- *Monetary policy is the primary focus of SAMA, whose key objectives are to stabilize inflation and the general level of prices, to maintain a fixed exchange rate policy against the U.S. dollar and to allow free movement of currency and capital.*
- *SAMA uses four main policy instruments in conducting monetary policy: cash reserve ratio/minimum reserve policy, Repos and Reverse-Repos, foreign exchange swaps, and placement of public funds. It has increasingly relied on Repos and Reverse-Repos, the so-called 'open-market' operations.*
- *Today SAMA offers a broad range and mix of securities on behalf of the government, ranging from short term Treasury Bills (under 1 year) to 10 year government development bonds, priced at a premium to similar dated U.S. Treasury and Bonds.*
- *SAMA's monetary policy assigns a high priority to its current fixed exchange policy as a means of controlling inflation, despite recent depreciation of the U.S. dollar against major international currencies.*
- *Domestic money supply creation is a function of dollar reserves held abroad, domestic government spending and the effects of domestic purchases of foreign currencies for trade and remittances.*
- *There is evidence to suggest that the Saudi economy is going through "financial deepening" with a reduction in the level of*

currency ratio, increasing monetization and mobilization of long term assets.

- *SAMA is faced by future challenges including more effective participation in the GCC monetary union and the proposed single currency by 2010, developing a corporate bond market, the supervision and control of cross-border Saudi bank mergers and "new-wave" foreign bank entry to the Saudi market, as well as overseeing the growth of Islamic finance and banking products in the Kingdom.*

Critical thinking

1. Has SAMA been an effective regulator of the Saudi financial markets? What other regulatory powers could help it to manage monetary policies?
2. What have been the major trends in Saudi money supply over the past decades and what does this indicate to you about Saudi societies' preferences in holding money?
3. What have been the guiding principles of SAMA's supervisory policies? Have they been successful? Which should be strengthened?
4. "SAMA is insistent on maintaining its fixed exchange rate policy against the U.S. dollar as an effective tool to combat inflation. The fact that inflation has been at zero or near-zero levels attests to the success of SAMA's policies". Argue the case for and against fixed exchange rate policies for Saudi Arabia.
5. "Remittances from the Kingdom should be controlled as they extinguish a large segment of domestic money supply". Argue the case for and against controlling remittances and dividends by foreigners and their impact on the Saudi economy.

Chapter 5

THE FINANCIAL MARKETS

A father is a banker provided by Nature.

French Proverb

Learning outcomes

By the end of this section, you should understand:

- *The role of the financial sector in Saudi Arabia's economic development*
- *The evolving structure of the Saudi banking sector*
- *SAMA and banking supervision*
- *The challenges faced by Saudi banking today*
- *The performance of Saudi banks*
- *The Saudi insurance sector*
- *Growing importance of Islamic financing*

Introduction

Today, the Saudi financial markets, and the banking sector in particular, are among the financially strongest in the Middle East and, as a group, one of the most profitable in the world. This has been confirmed by independent organizations such as Standard & Poor (Jagannathan, 2002) as well as specialist institutions such as the Middle East Economic Digest (MEED), which have ranked Saudi banks as consistently performing at the highest levels of profitability (MEED, 14 May 1999, 14 March 2000, 22 February 2002). In Chapter 4, we noted that the Saudi banking system is supported and supervised by a well-respected regulatory body, the Saudi Arabian Monetary Agency (SAMA), and that the Saudi banking sector has not been beset by any major financial panic or scandal. As we will see, the Saudi banking and financial systems have derived their characters from American and European institutional developments, with critical underpinning from Islamic economic precepts.

Today, Saudi financial markets stand on the threshold of a new era in their evolution, with the challenges of globalization affecting the sector. How they meet these challenges will be of critical importance, given the increasing significance of the financial sector and its intermediation role vis-à-vis the Saudi Gross Domestic Product, as illustrated in Figure 5.1.

Figure 5.1 Relative % contribution of finance and insurance sectors to non-oil GDP at current prices 1968-2002

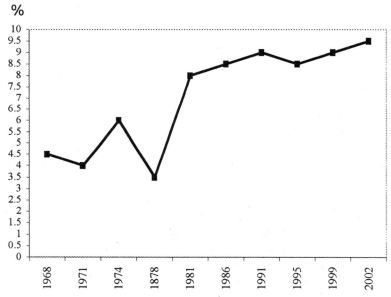

Source: *SAMA*, 2003, pp. 428 - 430, 499.

Today, finance and insurance contribute around 8.5% to the non-oil GDP, compared with 4 – 4.5% in the early 1970s. The finance and insurance sector is expected to grow with the recent decision to allow foreign players in financial services into the Saudi market, a move that will also introduce an element of competition and threat to existing Saudi financial institutions.

The Saudi banking sector

There are currently 12 banks operating in the Kingdom. Table 5.1 shows the status of banks already operating in the Kingdom and those banks that have obtained licences but are not yet operational.

Table 5.1 Status of banks holding licences to operate in Saudi Arabia (2004)

Bank Ownership	Status
Operational	• Wholly-owned Saudi private sector: Al-Rajhi • Saudi private sector and government ownership: Riyadh Bank, NCB, SAMBA • Joint-venture banks: Saudi Fransi, Saudi British, Arab National, Al-Jazira, Saudi Hollandi, Saudi Investment • Foreign Banks: Gulf International Bank, Bahrain, Emirates International Bank, Dubai
Licenced but Non-Operational	• HSBC, UK • Deutsche Bank, Germany • JP Morgan Chase, USA • BNP Paribas, France • National Bank of Kuwait

Table 5.1 shows that of the 12 operational banks, six are joint-venture banks, three have some government ownership, while one is wholly owned by the private sector. These banks operate on the universal banking model, which provides a broad range of products and services, brokerage facilities and derivative transactions, in addition to a variety of other consumer services such as credit cards, Automated Teller Machines (ATMs) and point-of-sale transactions. In addition, as discussed in an earlier chapter, Saudi banks offer and manage an increasing number of mutual funds.

Table 5.1 also highlights a diverse number of foreign banks that have obtained licenses to operate in Saudi Arabia, despite problems related to domestic terrorism. This reflects a sense of optimism in the Kingdom's long-term economic development. SAMA has welcomed these international moves, hoping that they would contribute to "activating competition amongst banks in Saudi Arabia", according to the Vice-Governor of SAMA (Al Watan, 4 June 2004).

Economic theorists on financial development and its impact on economic growth show some disagreement on whether financial institutions grow merely in response to the needs of society as their financial holding patterns evolve, or such financial institutions promote economic development *per se* by instigating changes themselves (Herbert, 1996). There are suggestions in earlier literature on Saudi banking development that Saudi banking followed the passive or "demand-following" approach (Johany et al., 1986, Dukheil, 1995, Abdeen et al., 1984), but that more recently Saudi banks have been following a "supply-leading" approach, especially by introducing electronic banking and investment products (Abdullateef, 2002, Jasser, 2002, Fayez, 2002).

SAMA and bank supervision

The banking system in Saudi Arabia reflects the generally conservative social environment of the country, especially on issues relating to interest and perceptions of *riba* or usury. Under this environment, SAMA applies various rules and policies to regulate the financial markets, as we discussed in the preceding chapter. The main thrust of the supervisory policies of Saudi Arabian banking throughout the evolution of the banking system to date seems to have been guided by certain objectives summarized in Table 5.2.

Table 5.2 Saudi Arabia bank supervisory guiding policies

Guiding Policy	*Observation*
• Maintain open and liberal financial market with minimal restriction on capital flow	• Effectively carried out, including minimal restrictions on capital flow
• Strong and healthy banking sector to maintain sustainable economic growth	• Saudi bank profitability is one of the highest in world and its banking system has grown and adapted as the economy evolved
• Promote fair competition in financial and banking services	• More competition needed due to excessive bank concentration; foreign bank presence could promote more competition
• Benefit from participation of foreign banks and foreign share-holders so as to transfer technology, training of Saudi personnel and improve risk management practices	• Achieved with Saudization of banks in a smooth manner; Saudi banking personnel are in key positions and Saudi banks are positively rated by credit rating agencies
• Ensure Saudi financial markets are at cutting edge of communication and IT	• Achieved, for Saudi banking is one of the most technologically advanced in the world
• Pursue the adoption and implementation of global standards, principles and practices	• Achieved thorough SAMA supervision and the adoption of joint venture best banking practices

While there is general agreement on the relative success of the guiding regulatory principles, there is some debate on the issue of fair competition. Recent bank studies have shown that Saudi banks tend to price their products in an oligopolistic manner (Essayyad, Ramady, Hijji, 2003).

The Saudi banking sector has undergone significant evolutionary phases in a relatively short life span compared to other financial centres around the world. These evolutionary phases were instrumental in preparing the ground for the next evolutionary phases and have been well documented elsewhere (Dukheil, 1995, Jasser, 2002). The main features are recalled below.

The early years (1940s - 1960s): Infancy period

The few financial houses that existed in the pre-1950s era primarily served the pilgrim trade in Jeddah and Makkah, as well as imports and some export finance. The first branch of a foreign commercial bank, the Netherlands Trading Society (today, the Saudi Hollandi Bank), was established in 1927 and concentrated on import and export finance from the city of Jeddah. These foreign banks were initially unpopular, as due to social and religious stigma there was strong resistance to paying and receiving interest. The result was effectively a cash-oriented society until the early 1970s. Money-changers, who carefully avoided the word bank, flourished in those early days, and provided strong competition to foreign banks.

The newfound Saudi oil revenues of the 1950s brought a rise in government expenditure that resulted in an unprecedented escalation in demand for currency, outstripping supply. This oil wealth attracted foreign banks that soon opened branches in Jeddah: Banque Indochine, British Bank of Middle East, National Bank of Pakistan and Egyptian Misr Bank. The late 1950s saw yet more arrivals: Banque du Caire, First National City Bank and Banque Du Liban. In 1937, the Mahfouz and Kaki families successfully petitioned King Abdulaziz to establish the Kingdom's first locally-owned bank, but it was not until 1953 that the Mahfouz-Kaki Company was transformed into what became the National Commercial Bank (NCB). In 1957, a second locally-owned bank, Riyad Bank, was established.

The refusal of many depositors to receive interest meant that profits were sufficiently attractive for commercial banks to operate during this period. Banks were also able to provide loans with "service charges" being applied, without upsetting Islamic sensitivities. However, the bubble soon burst. The lack of available expertise led to incorrect loan processing and bad loan administration and some banks ran into trouble, including Riyad Bank. The government became a shareholder to restore confidence. This required more direct involvement from the *de facto* Central Bank (SAMA), which came of age in the 1960s and enacted the Banking Control Law in 1966.

The 1970s: The adolescence period

This was the beginning of the era of Saudi planned development with the first five-year plan launched in 1970, as discussed in Chapter 2. The 1970s marked the start of the adolescence of the Saudi banking sector, with an increase in direct regulation and supervision.

Complementing the private sector banks, six major government lending institutions were also established during this period: the Saudi Arabian Agricultural Bank, the Saudi Credit Bank, Public Investment Fund, Contractors Fund, Saudi Industrial Development Fund and Real Estate Development Fund. Their aim was to provide medium and long-term loans instead of the short-term loans extended by the commercial banks. Bank assets grew from SR 3 billion in 1971 to SR 93 billion in 1974. Deposits rose from SR 2 billion to SR 68 billion over the same period.

1976 was a watershed year for the Saudi banking sector, as it was the year when the policy of *Saudization* of foreign banks operating in the Kingdom was first introduced, with far-reaching effects to this day. This policy required converting branches of foreign banks into publicly-traded companies with majority Saudi ownership.

A primary reason for *Saudization* was that branches of foreign banks in Saudi Arabia were using policies drawn up by their foreign parent banks. These policies might not always be in harmony with local development plans, for they mostly concentrated on short-term foreign trade, with no priority for long-term loans. Foreign banks were also concentrated in Jeddah and in Riyadh and provided no service in the under-banked rural areas. In addition, they were not reporting to SAMA as their final regulator, and their high profits were repatriated abroad.

Conflicts were bound to intensify as the Saudi economy expanded rapidly starting in the late 1970s, and the Kingdom saw a large part of the financial sector virtually outside its control. Given the enormous profits that foreign bank branches were making in the Kingdom – to which the author can attest from his service in this sector in those early days – there was little choice but to comply with "Saudization", which was made palatable through long-term management contracts and tax breaks.

By 1980, *Saudization* of the major foreign bank branches had been completed. Citibank N.A. of the USA was the final one. The process boosted Saudi banks' capital base and branch expansion in other parts of the Kingdom; it also ensured an opportunity to benefit from foreign expertise and technology transfer.

The total number of bank branches rose to 247 from 145 by 1980. There were several other advantages flowing from the policy of *Saudization* of the foreign-owned bank branches. In competitive terms, the public had a wider choice of banks with which to deal, as well as receiving more competitive services at lower costs. *Saudization* helped to spread the country's new wealth among a wider section of its citizens through dividend payouts and stock ownership. This in effect laid the foundation for share ownership and its acceptance by the Saudi public.

A new and lucrative employment sector opened up for Saudis, with the opportunity to rise through the banks and manage such Saudized banks, as well as "cross-fertilizing" their banking skills with wholly-owned Saudi banks. The increase in capital and reserves of the newly Saudized banks enhanced the banking sector's ability to lend large amounts to individuals and companies. As a result, offshore lending to Saudi Arabia, mostly from Bahrain-based "Offshore Banking Units" or OBUs, was less effective (Bisisu, 1984). Finally, the broader national objectives of the Saudi economy would be harmonized with the banking policies of these Saudized banks. This alignment of interests was quite an improvement on the pre-*Saudization* era when foreign banks' interests were more tightly tied to those of their home countries.

As seen earlier in Table 5.1, the Saudi banking system is today preparing to welcome back foreign banks to the Kingdom. This reflects the domestic banks' self-confidence in their capacity to effectively compete. It also reflects SAMA's ability to regulate these "new-wave" foreign banks. The situation facing the new foreign banks is different this time, with an extensive branch network in place, a sophisticated range of banking products and a cadre of well-trained Saudi banking professionals. It is likely that the new foreign banks will concentrate on niche investment and merchant banking activities such as IPOs and mergers and acquisitions, as well as positioning themselves to provide financing for the large infrastructure project the Saudi government has planned for the years ahead.

Coming of age in the 1980s: Young adulthood

This period proved to be the real test of the strength and resilience of the Saudi banking system and of SAMA's supervisory skills. As discussed in earlier chapters, oil prices fell sharply from the highs of the 1981 boom era; the mid-1980s was a period of sharply reduced government revenues, which fell from SR 368 billion in 1981 to SR 104 billion in 1987.

The decline in government revenues meant significant pressure on the quality of bank assets, and several banks suffered non-performing loans (Dukheil, 1995). A judicial system that seemed to side with defaulters on interest payment issues didn't help either (Wilson, 2004). In 1982, SAMA successfully overcame supervisory and regulatory challenges brought about when irregularities appeared in the operations of Saudi Cairo Bank. These irregularities involved unauthorized trading in bullion with the bank concealing accumulated losses that exceeded its share capital (Suhaimi, 2002). A new share capital was issued which was taken up by the government-owned Public Investment Fund (PIF) and this helped to restore confidence and liquidity to Saudi Cairo. This bank eventually merged with the United Saudi Commercial Bank (USCB) in 1997 to form the United Saudi Bank.

The decade of the 1980s was characterized by bank mergers. USCB itself was born in 1983 of a merger of the branches of foreign banks, namely United Bank of Pakistan, Bank Melli Iran and Banque due Liban et d'Outremer. In 1999, United Saudi Bank merged with Saudi American Bank.

During this period, SAMA came of age and employed a number of measures in reaction to the problems the sector faced (Dukheil, 1995). SAMA required prior approval for declaration of bank dividends, extended the tax holiday period for banks, introduced tax breaks to encourage provisioning of doubtful debts and insisted on improvement in corporate governance. Finally, the Monetary Agency created an unofficial "blacklist" of defaulting clients through the creation of a banking disputes settlements committee.

Other significant policy changes were also introduced in this period, including legislation to control the activities of the money exchangers. Since 1982 SAMA had required that they obtain a licence to operate and that they maintain specified capital and reserves, and that they not take deposits and issue loans. This followed the spectacular collapse of the Al Rajhi Trading Establishment in the Eastern Province in 1984 due to silver speculation.

In addition, the Saudi government, through SAMA, introduced the first public borrowing instrument – the Bankers Security Deposit Account (BSDA), later replaced by bonds and treasury notes. Further, SAMA advised that prior permission was needed for Saudi commercial banks to invite foreign banks to participate in Saudi riyal loan syndication. Finally, equity trading on the Saudi stock market could be conducted only through the local commercial banks.

By the end of the decade, bank branches rose from 247 to 1,036 and employees from 11,000 to 25,000 (Suhaimi, 2002). Total assets rose to SR 253 billion by 1989, a 150% increase over 1979. Saudi banks also ventured onto the international stage, with branches opened in London, Bahrain, Geneva, Beirut and Istanbul.

The 1990s and the period of maturity

This era started traumatically for the whole Gulf. The Iraq-Kuwait crisis of 1990 - 1991 was a severe external shock to the banking system, characterized by outward capital flight. SAMA, however, once again proved adept at crisis management and reacted by providing domestic banks with adequate liquidity in the form of foreign exchange swaps and deposits. Confidence was restored to the financial sector.

Following the resolution of the 1991 Gulf crisis, there was a boom in the Saudi economy. Banking activity picked up, showing its resilience despite the foreign exchange crises sweeping other parts of the world, notably the 1994 Mexican and the 1997 South East Asian currency crises. The 1990s saw Saudi banks begin to reap the benefit of their large investment in technology, which had been introduced in the late 1980s as an antidote to the insufficient number of qualified Saudi banking personnel. The impact of the use of new technology to deliver banking services has been enormous, the most popular being the use of ATMs for cash withdrawal and other consumer transactions such as utility payments, account transfers and general enquiries. Figure 5.2 illustrates the growth of bank branches and ATMs over the period 1994 - 2004, while Figure 5.3 demonstrates the increasing importance and popularity of ATM transactions with Saudi bank clients.

Figure 5.2 Evolution of branches and ATMs
December 1994-March 2004

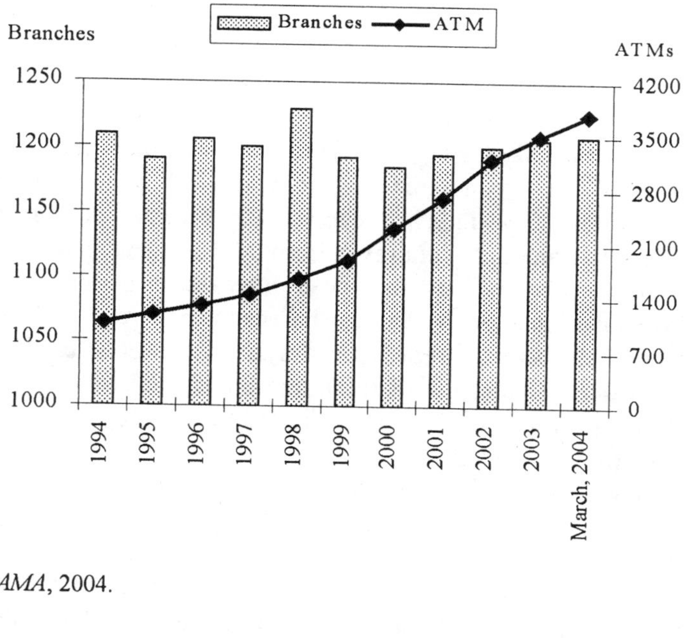

Source: *SAMA*, 2004.

From Figure 5.2 we observe that after reaching a peak of 1,229 bank branches in 1998, the number of branches fell to 1,209 by the first quarter of 2004. The decrease has been attributed to bank branch closures following the mergers of some Saudi banks described earlier. Saudi banks have also found it more cost effective to install ATMs, resulting in a rise in the number of ATMs to 3,789 by first quarter 2004, as compared to 1,080 in 1994.

Figure 5.3 Increasing Saudi Arabia importance of ATM transaction

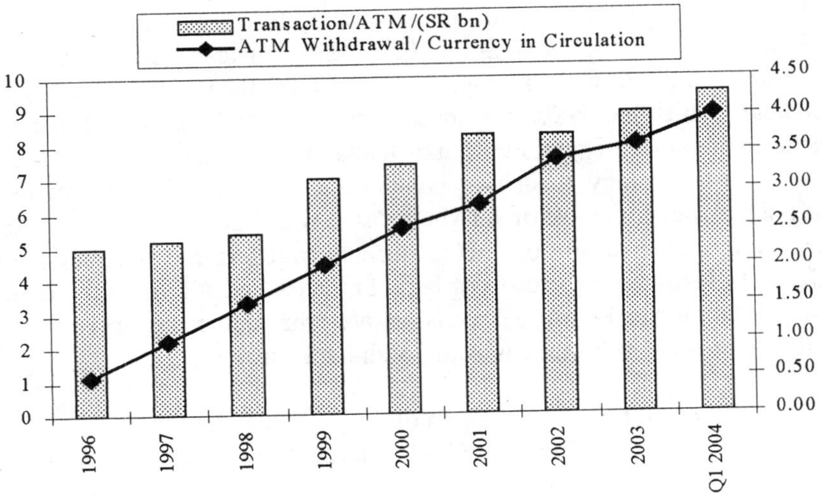

Source: *SAMA*, 2004.

While the numbers of ATMs have increased, so have the number of transactions per ATM (see Figure 5.3) to reach just over SR 10 billion in the first quarter of 2004, compared with around SR 5 billion for the whole of 1996, around a 12% increase every year for the period in question. Furthermore, the amount withdrawn from ATMs relative to the amount of currency in circulation has also been increasing, no doubt encouraging SAMA's elimination of ATM service charges to encourage ATM usage.

This period also saw the rapid spread of the use of debit cards, credit cards and stored value cards (point of sale), and Saudi banks competed fiercely in this new market segment. The cash-oriented society seemed to be gradually changing its transaction habits.

The technological advances made by the Saudi banks have been remarkable compared to the 1950s when the public was reluctant to use anything but silver riyal coins and foreign gold coins. Under the guidance of SAMA, Saudi commercial banks now enjoy a number of sophisticated payment and settlement systems. In 1997, the Saudi Riyal Interbank Express System (SARIE) was introduced, which is a gross settlement electronic fund-transfer system, operating in real-time. It is the backbone of the Saudi payment infrastructure between banks. Other advances included the Automated Clearing House (ACH) and Saudi Payment Network (SPAN), which supported the ATMs and point-of-sales terminal, as well as the Electronic Share Information system (ESIS).

All of these systems have been linked to SARIE, enabling banks to make and receive payments directly from their accounts with SAMA on a real-time basis and to credit beneficiary accounts with transfers of funds on the same day. Another electronic share trading and information system (TADAWUL) has recently been enhanced to provide T+O (transaction plus zero days) settlement capability and to permit the trading of government bonds, treasury bills and mutual funds in addition to corporate shares (Suhaimi, 2002). Few countries in the developing or developed world can boast of such an array of sophisticated payment systems.

Such technological developments have contributed significantly to improving the level and quality of consumer services, reducing costs, enhancing efficiency and strengthening banking control. The Saudi banking sector now has a solid base on which to meet the challenges of information technology in the new millennium. The next section highlights the challenges which still lie ahead and assesses the preparedness of the Saudi financial system to meet them.

The current challenges

The new millennium saw Saudi banks faced with competitive pressures from regional and international banks. While it may take some time before the impact of such competition is felt on the bottom-line profitability of Saudi banks, some of these banks are already trying to reposition themselves in a more focussed manner in the Saudi market.

The international environment of low interest rates affected their margins, as the cost of funds fell faster than lending rates, eroding lending margins. Saudi banks began to search for non-interest investment income and to diversify their product range to reduce dependency on interest income (or commission income, as it is termed in Saudi Arabia). Figure 5.4 illustrates how the Saudi banking industry, as a whole, is still dependent on commission income for around 70% of its total income, although there are some individual bank differences.

The higher investment income ratio for Al Rajhi and Al Jazira banks is due to the fact that these two institutions apply their customer deposits in Islamically-acceptable investments. Al Rajhi's "commission income" is not really a net interest differential, but is based on customer owned investment products, with Al Rajhi acting as a fiduciary agent in managing these investments for a fee. With the foreign licensed banks eyeing the investment income market in Saudi Arabia, the domestic banks realize that they need to develop more expertise and deliver more products if they are to effectively compete in this market segment in the future.

Figure 5.4 Saudi Arabia: Distribution of bank income by various categories
2003

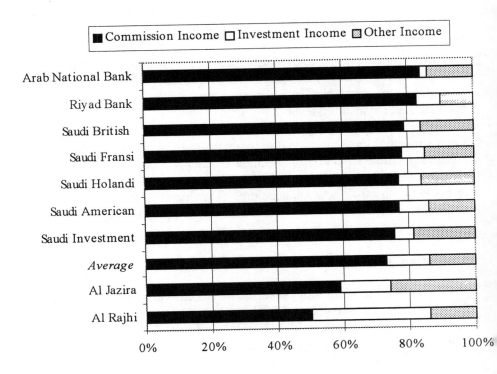

Source: *Bank annual reports.*

The issue of shareholder concentration is one of major concern for the Saudi banking sector, as it is for most other publicly-listed Saudi joint stock companies, which will be examined in Chapter 6 in more detail (Dukheil, 1995, Abdellateef, 2002). From the late 1980s until the present, there has been a significant concentration of shareholders in the banking sector, as shown in Table 5.3.

Table 5.3 Shareholder concentration for selected Saudi banks

Bank	1981	1986	1998	2001
Saudi British bank	8,008	5,100	15,155	11,846
Saudi Hollandi Bank	2,850	2,600	1,033	685
SAMBA	102,594	45,000	15,171	44,600
Saudi Fransi Bank	95,600	73,000	9,668	8,185

Source: *Author's survey* based on bank annual reports and Bank Investor Relations Units.

The increase in the number of shareholders for certain years, such as is seen in the Saudi British Bank in 1998, was tied to capital increases, while for SAMBA in 2001, it followed the merger with United Saudi bank in 1999. The trend towards far fewer shareholders is unmistakable and there are several implications. First, holding a higher concentration of shares in fewer hands might enable some business groups to influence day-to-day operations and bank management through board representation. Second, the concentration of shares in a few hands with block votes "de-democratizes" the role of annual general meetings in joint stock companies. Concentration eliminates transparency and leads to joint stock companies operating like partnerships.

The concentration level shown in Figure 5.4 is also reflected in other "wholly owned" Saudi banks such as Riyad Bank and the National Commercial Bank (NCB), through government major ownership participation in these banks.

Since 1961, the Saudi government has held a 38% stake in Riyad Bank, and 80% of NCB since January 2003. In 1999, the Public Investment Fund (PIF), the Saudi government's domestic investment vehicle, acquired 50% of the privately-owned National Commercial Bank from the Mahfouz and Kaaki families. The PIF went on to sell 10% of its share to the government-owned General Organization for Social Security (GOSI) in 2001.

A survey was carried out by the author on the size of Saudi family ownership of "core" share blocks in the various Saudi banks using available public information from annual reports, as well as share register information and bank sources. This information is displayed in Table 5.4.

Table 5.4 Saudi commercial banks major ownership holdings by number and percentage (2000)

Institution	Private Individuals or Groups				Government or foreign ownership
	Under 2%	3-5%	6-9%	Over 10%	
National Commercial Bank (NCB)	1	1	1	-	80% (Government)
Saudi British	2	2	1	-	40% (HSBC)
SAMBA	2	2	1	2	20% (Government)
Saudi Hollandi	6	3	2	1	40% (ABN-AMRO)
Al Rajhi	-	2	1	2	
Saudi Investment	2	1	3	-	25% (Various foreign institutions)
Saudi Fransi	2	3	1	-	31.5% (Credite Agricole)
Riyadh Bank	-	3	2	-	38% (Government)
Arab National	2	3	-	1	40% (Arab Bank)

Source: *Author's survey.*

Table 5.4 reveals that, of the original Saudized banks, only the Saudi British, Saudi Hollandi and Arab National banks have maintained their original 40% foreign joint venture partner shareholding, with others, such as Saudi Fransi, Saudi Investment and Saudi American, either selling part of their holdings or being diluted through new capital increases.

The year 2003 was also a turning point in the history of Saudi banking, seeing the "complete" *Saudization* of one of the earlier joint venture banks, when Citibank completed the transfer of local management to the renamed SAMBA Financial Group (SAMBA) in October, 2003. The government acquired Citibank's 20% share through the Public Investment Fund (PIF). According to its 2003 Annual Report, SAMBA decided to liquidate its overseas branch holdings in the UK and Luxemburg, but retained a wholly-owned subsidiary specializing in mutual funds operating in Guernsey (SAMBA Annual Report, 2003. p. 26). From all accounts, the transfer of management to Saudi citizens went smoothly, and it demonstrated the faith the government and SAMA in particular had in the *Saudization* process and management "technology transfer."

Table 5.4 indicates that major shareholder concentration is more pronounced within Saudi Hollandi, SAMBA and Al Rajhi banks, with Saudi British the least concentrated of the three. Historical reasons explain the high level of Saudi bank concentration, especially for the joint-venture banks. These banks usually started life through a founding group of investors who were granted a certain percentage of the founding share capital, with remaining shares distributed between the foreign joint-venture partner and the general public. Because there were few shares distributed to the smaller investors, over time they sold out to the larger investors and founding shareholders.

The Saudi government is aware of these issues, and is encouraging wider share ownership by planning a partial privatization of its own bank holdings, especially in the Kingdom's largest bank, the National Commercial Bank. According to press reports in 2003, the government is planning to sell up to 50% of its current holding in NCB sometime in 2004/5, which, if it happens, would give a large boost to the newly-formed Saudi capital market authority discussed in Chapter 6 (Abdul Ghafour, 12 May 2003).

This partial privatization sale would provide both short and long-term benefits to the government, which would still retains a major stake in NCB. In the short run, the flotation proceeds could be used to repay part of the government's outstanding debt, while in the long run the government would see its share value appreciate on the capital markets once NCB shares are listed, while continuing to receive future dividends from NCB. No plans have been announced for selling part of the government's holdings in Riyad

Bank, and it will be interesting to see what the government wants to do with its newly acquired 20% share holding in the profitable SAMBA.

Performance of the Saudi banks

Despite the impressive growth registered over the past thirty years, the level of banking penetration in the economy is still not as large as other countries at different levels of economic development. This is illustrated in Figure 5.5, which compares the ratio of deposits/GDP of Saudi Arabia with several other countries, including South Korea and a newly-emerging Eastern European country, Poland.

Figure 5.5 Saudi Arabia and selected countries: deposits/GDP and loans/GDP (2002)

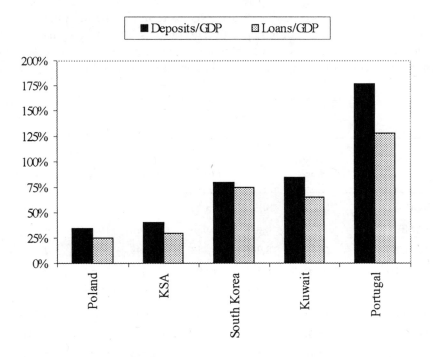

Source: EFG-Hermes, Cairo, August, 2003.

According to EFG-Hermes, which carried out the comparative study, the reasons for the lower banking penetration level for Saudi Arabia were diverse (EFG-Hermes, August, 2003). They include the following:

- the large role of the government in GDP,
- the fact that the largest companies in Saudi Arabia are state-controlled and still borrow at preferential rates from government-owned funding institutions,
- the fact that banking conducted under Islamic transactions is excluded from the overall calculation of "loans;" such transactions are classified as investments rather than loans.

All these will understate the loans/GDP ratio.

These are valid arguments, but in the long run the Saudi banking penetration ratios will rise due to several factors. First, the government has signalled its intentions to sell a large portion of state assets under the privatization programme. Such privatized companies will no longer automatically be able to borrow at preferential rates from the government. Second, Islamic funding will grow and will be re-classified to take account of the venture capital risk-taking characteristics found in Islamic financing.

Though the private sector deposit/GDP ratio is low in comparison with the surveyed countries, the Saudi banking sector continues to enjoy sizeable profits and healthy returns on equity and assets, as illustrated in Table 5.5.

Table 5.5 Saudi banks at a glance 2003

| | | | | | Million SR | |
Banks	Total Assets	Equity	Net Income	Total Deposits	Return on Equity (%)	Return on Assets (%)
NCB	117,432	10,332	3,013	90,447	31.3%	2.6%
SAMBA	79,037	8,878	1,436	61,768	16.2%	1.8 %
Al Rajhi	70,438	8,386	1,413	45,449	20.7%	2.4%
Riyad Bank	71,507	8,547	1,592	45,879	18.6%	2.2%
Saudi Fransi	53,502	5,050	1,185	42,634	23.5%	2.2%
Saudi British	46,061	4,746	1,257	36,089	26.5%	2.7%
Arab National	49,200	3,977	767	33,700	19.3%	1.6%
Saudi Hollandi	27,965	2,551	601	21,583	23.6%	2.1%
Saudi Investment	21,078	2,160	462	14,404	21.4%	2.2%
Al Jazira	8,988	885	93	7,535	11.4%	1.3%
Total	545,202	55,815	11,819	399,535		

Source: *Saudi banks annual reports*, 2003.

With the exception of SAMBA and Al Jazira, the return on equity for 2003 averaged out at between 18 - 23%, with NCB putting in a star performance at 31% following its management restructuring and government shareholding support.

SAMBA's poor showing in 2003 was connected to loan loss reserves being taken, as well as some fear that the termination of the Citibank technical agreement might affect the bank's future. Positive first quarter results in 2004 for SAMBA proved that such fears were unfounded, with a net income of SR 581 million being recorded, the highest ever in SAMBA's history.

An analysis of Saudi bank performance must also address the issue of competition. Such competition has not been significant in the past, primarily because Saudi banks have experienced high profit ratios in terms of net return on assets and equity compared to other banks worldwide. Barriers to entry – at least before the new foreign bank licences were granted in 2004 – and the low cost of funds due to the large element of current/non-interest-bearing accounts both help to explain this. The lack of external entry and competition has led to a high banking industry concentration level in Saudi Arabia compared to other countries. Table 5.6 summarizes the level of Saudi bank concentration and notes that three banking groups – NCB, SAMBA and Al Rajhi – have around 50% of the banking market. Kuwait banking also evidences high concentration levels.

Table 5.6 Comparison of Saudi Arabian and selected countries' concentration levels in the banking sector (2001)

Country	Number of banks	Concentration
Saudi	9 commercial, 1 Islamic	3 groups have 54% of loans, 51% of deposits, 49% of assets and 58% of branches
Kuwait	7 commercial, 1 Islamic, 2 specialized	3 groups have 70% of loans, 69% of deposits, 62% of assets and 62% of branches
South Korea	11 nationwide com., 6 local, 5 specialized 43 branches of foreign banks	11 Nationwide banks have 45% of loans, 66% of deposits, 84% of assets and > 80% of branches
Poland	64 commercial	5 groups have 50.6% of loans, 60.4% of deposits and 53% of assets; 10 groups have 75.3% of loans, 80.7% of deposits and 77.6% of assets
Portugal	57 commercial	5 groups have 80% of loans, 79% of deposits, 80% of assets and 69% of branches

Source: *EFG-Hermes*, August, 2003.

The effects of such concentration levels have been researched for the Saudi market (Essayyed et al., 2003). From the 2003 data set out earlier in Table 5.5, it appears that the three-bank concentration ratio still accounts for less than 50% of customer deposits compared to the 2001 level. Studies conducted in the area of bank concentration and economic efficiency indicate that a high concentration ratio may induce banks to charge borrowers with higher interest rates than when there is a low banking concentration.

According to Saudi studies, the non-interventionist policy of SAMA in this area of bank regulation could hamper the growth of companies, particularly small and medium-sized industries, due to more restrictive credit conditions by the banks within a system of imperfect competition (Essayyed, Ramady, Hijji, 2003). The scope of the problems faced by Small and Medium Sized Enterprises (SMEs) in Saudi Arabia, discussed later in Chapter 7, confirmed this finding.

While the percentage of current accounts to total deposits has dropped from 78% in the 1977/1978 period, this type of account still represents a significant element. According to SAMA's 2004 first quarter reports, these stood at 49% of total deposits (SAMA, 2004, First Quarter, 2004, p. 25). However, there are individual bank variations within this total industry average, as illustrated in Figure 5.6.

Figure 5.6 Non-interest bearing deposits Saudi banks 2002

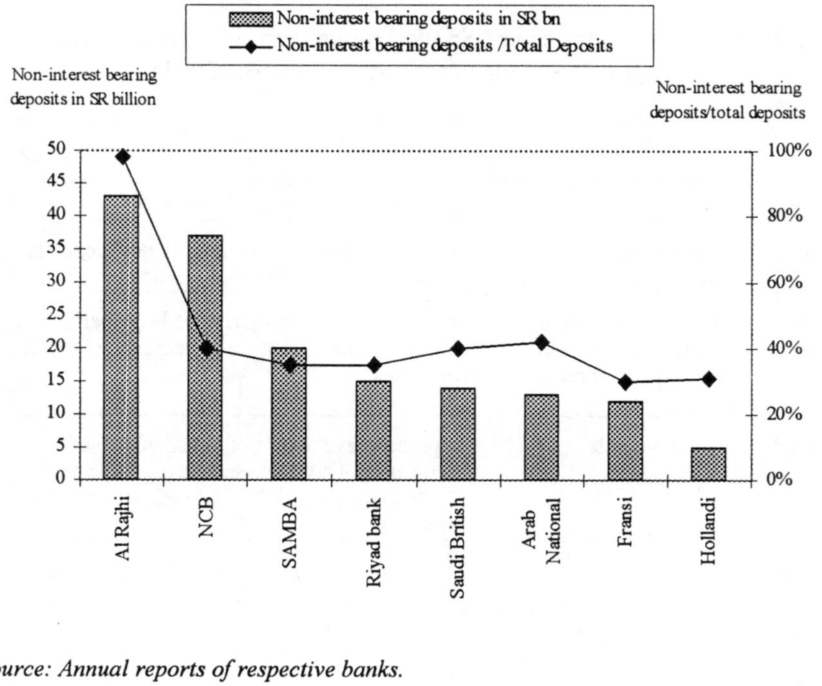

Source: Annual reports of respective banks.

Figure 5.6 shows that Al Rajhi's special position amongst the Saudi banks in terms of non-interest deposits is notable at the 100% level, followed by NCB and Arab National banks at around 42%, but with all banks registering higher than 25%. Al Rajhi Banking and Investment Corporation (its full official name) stands out, for even though SAMA did not grant it the word "Islamic" in its banking licence in 1988, it operates to all intents and purposes with the public as if it were an Islamic bank. Based upon this principle, Al Rajhi became Saudi Arabia's most profitable bank by 2000, and by 2004 had the largest domestic branch and ATM network in the country, at 394 and 1,090 respectively. Al Rajhi ATMs represented nearly one-third of the national total (SAMA, 2004).

While the social prohibition against taking interest was gradually easing, as evidenced by the incremental rise in time and savings deposits when compared to the early 1970s, Al Rajhi's success seems to highlight the fact that Islamic banking still has an important role to play in Saudi Arabia in the future, which we will discuss later.

The rush to segmentation

Competition in Saudi Arabia amongst banks is along various segmentation lines, and each of these is further segmented by gender. Segmentation by gender means that "ladies only" banking operations were developed as a niche market, either in separate branches or in sections within the same branch. This has proved to be both successful and profitable, and all Saudi banks today operate "ladies only" branches. For example, nearly 90, or 23%, of Al Rajhi's branches mentioned above are "ladies only" branches.

In Saudi Arabia, segmentation also seems to follow asset size and class, like the various prestige-level card awards of hotels or airlines (blue, silver, gold, platinum). Saudi banks seemed to realize that traditional "old wealth" private banking clients (with their emphasis on wealth preservation), are not as numerous as the larger affluent segments, for which wealth creation is the main objective. The former clients seem to be the domain of international private banking financial institutions, while the latter are those who created wealth in the Saudi stock and real estate markets.

The author's personal experience of working in the banking sector in the Kingdom is reinforced by market surveys indicating that consumer preferences are determined not by individual bank strengths, but rather by the national origin of the bank. Important too is the family tradition in dealing with "Islamic"-oriented banks or "conventional" banks, even though each Saudi bank has used the media to portray different strengths, reputations and allegiances.

While it is difficult to generalize, Table 5.7 attempts to capture the main marketing strengths and public perceptions of the different Saudi banks, which could partly explain their varying performances in separate market segments.

Table 5.7 Saudi commercial banks: perception of key strengths

Institution	Perception - Strengths
• Saudi British Bank	• Electronic banking, investments, treasury products, international links, medium term facilities to Saudi corporate
• SAMBA	• Corporate banking, treasury and investment products, electronic banking, high net worth clients, international links, syndications
• Riyad Bank	• Consumer loans, trading activities, investments, government accounts, oil and agricultural sector, syndications, small business
• Al Rajhi	• Islamic investments, foreign exchange, trading activities
• Arab National	• Electronic banking, mutual funds, consumer banking, small business, treasury products
• Saudi Fransi	• Corporate banking, investments, treasury products, loan syndication
• Saudi Hollandi	• International trade, medium corporate loans, international capital markets, off balance sheet products
• Saudi Investment Bank	• Corporate finance medium to long term loans, international trade, treasury products, syndications
• National Commercial Bank	• Consumer banking, small businesses, Islamic products, Corporate and government lending, foreign exchange and treasury

These perceived strengths in each bank's niche markets are also partly reflections of the different management styles, philosophies and orientation of the pure "Saudi" banks, such as NCB and Riyad bank with their "domestic roots" on the one hand, and those with foreign affiliation and management control on the other. The concentration of the joint venture banks, such as Saudi Fransi, Saudi Hollandi, Saudi British and SAMBA, on core corporate business, investment and treasury products meant that they left the consumer loan mass-market and small business lending to the "pure" Saudi banks, in order to concentrate on "big-ticket" corporate loans. Figure 5.7 analyzes the obvious and clear differences between national and joint venture assets per branch.

Figure 5.7 Saudi Arabia: comparison between National Saudi Banks(NB) and Joint Venture Banks (JV) by branches and assets per branch 2002

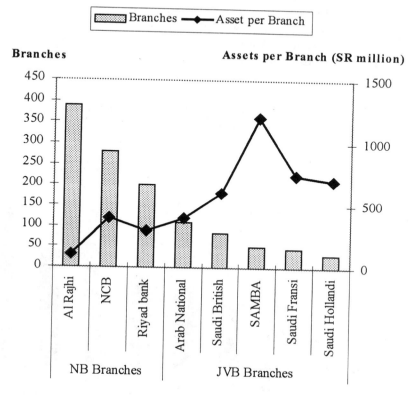

Source: *Bank annual reports*, 2002.

The differences between joint venture banks (JV's) and the national banks go deeper than their origins and ownership structures. Their underlying banking philosophies differ, with the joint ventures targeting the upper wealth segment, both corporate and individual, and the national banks targeting the lower segments, although each national bank also has a segment for its high net worth clients.

Because of these differences, the national banks operate a larger branch network, as seen in Figure 5.7, but joint ventures enjoy a higher asset-to-branch ratio. However, in analyzing costs, especially wage-related expenses per employee, the national banks enjoy lower costs than joint ventures, thus allowing them to open more branches at a lower cost than the joint ventures, and so to enjoy greater geographical coverage. This is demonstrated in Figure 5.8.

The entry of the "new wave" foreign banks into Saudi Arabia is not expected to change this structure; the new foreign banks will probably operate out of key Saudi cities or even through a specialized head office branch in the capital Riyadh, concentrating on the upper-level corporate and individual markets, although the Emirates Bank of the UAE which opened for business in Riyadh in August 2004, stated that it would open 15 branches in the Kingdom and would be a full service bank in retail, corporate and investment banking (Arab News, 26 August 2004).

Figure 5.8 Salaries and employee related expenses per branch in SR million for Saudi joint venture and national banks 2002

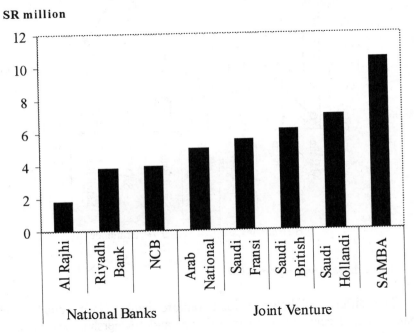

Source: *Annual reports of respective banks.*

While the costs per branch of the joint venture banks are significantly higher than those of the national banks, so too is their operating income per employee, signifying greater productivity per employee for the joint venture banks, as shown in Table 5.8 for the year 2002.

Table 5.8 Saudi banks at a glance: 2003

Banks	Gross Operating Income (000)	Salaries & Employee Related Expenses (000)	No. of Employees	Employee Cost (000)	Operating Income/ Employee (000)
Saudi American (SAMBA)	2,995,919	689,862	2,171	318	1,388
Saudi Investment	469,454	81,195	355	229	1,323
Saudi Fransi	1,322,255	291,419	1,329	219	995
Saudi Hollandi	856,758	236,773	1,048	226	818
Saudi British	1,557,435	417,931	1,994	210	781
Arab National	1,390,389	374,923	1,815	207	766
Riyadh	2,519,755	669,578	3,461	193	728
Al Rajhi Banking	3,189,113	539,667	5,403	100	590
Al Jazira	164,942	60,626	318	191	519
Average	*1,607,336*	*373,553*	*1,988*	*210*	*878*

Source: *Annual reports*, 2002.

With just under 40,000 employees in the whole financial market (banking and insurance), this sector continues to attract calibre expatriates and Saudi nationals alike, drawn by the relatively high level of compensation in this sector. Table 5.9 sets out the number of employees in the financial sector by Saudis and non-Saudis, as well as total employee compensation and revenue and expenditure.

Table 5.9 Economic indicators for banking and insurance sector
1997 - 2001

Index	1997	1998	1999	2000	2001
Total Employee	**31,401**	**32,713**	**33,735**	**36,812**	**38,659**
- Saudi	15,475	16,297	16,858	18,358	20,782
- Non-Saudi	15,926	16,416	16,877	18,455	17,877
Employee Compensation (million SR)	6,405	6,262	6,761	7,259	7,569
Revenues (million SR)	39,499	41,008	44,437	51,769	55,609
Expenditures (million SR)	28,858	31,006	31,898	35,148	37,305
Fixed Assets (million SR)	1,996	2,089	1,514	1,721	1,819

Source: *CDS, Annual yearbook*, 2002, p. 465.

According to Table 5.9, the average total compensation per employee – Saudi and non-Saudi – was around SR 204,000 in 1997, but then dropped to

SR 195,000 per employee by 2001. This occurred despite a rise in net revenue per employee to SR 473,000 in 2001, compared with SR 338,000 in 1997. The trend for lower average compensation packages was to be expected, given that the financial sector in 2001 had a larger pool of skilled labour than a decade or so earlier and competitive pressures were driving compensation packages down.

Despite these trends, employment in the financial sector is much sought after in the Kingdom, for both male and female employees, and "average" compensation packages can encompass wide variations. Table 5.10 breaks down banking and insurance sector average monthly earnings by Saudis and non-Saudis, as well as by gender.

Table 5.10 Banking and insurance sector average monthly earnings Saudi and non-Saudi employees and by gender 2000

Earning Category	Saudi Male	Saudi Female	Non-Saudi Male	Non-Saudi Female
SR < 801	0	0	19	0
801 –1500	0	0	100	0
1501 - 3000	88	0	406	0
3001 - 6000	2,805	71	2,843	3
6001 - 10,000	7,157	536	3,068	0
10,001 - 15,000	3,385	164	2495	0
15,001 - 25,000	2,020	47	1,602	3
25,001 - 50,000	1,140	0	1,076	0
50,000 plus	282	3	276	0
Total	16,877	821	11,885	6
Total all economic sector employees	223,024	10,760	1,180,413	29,098

Source: *CDS. 2002 Annual Yearbook.* pp. 16, 17. Riyadh 2003.

It is interesting to note the fairly senior level of Saudi female employment in this sector. This was due to the availability in the financial sector of the "ladies only" working environment discussed earlier. Table 5.10 also illustrates the continuing dependence on senior-level expatriate labour in the financial sector, despite rapid progress of *Saudization* in terms of the total number of Saudis employed.

There were rumours that some expatriate senior level management might prematurely depart from Saudi Arabia due to the domestic terrorism campaign witnessed during 2003 and 2004 in the Kingdom, but Saudi banks did not report any significant departures. The Saudi financial industry seems to have a sufficiently capable pool of skilled employees to be able to withstand any large departure of foreign labour from this sector.

Saudi banks' current lending policies

Saudi banks generally have a low loan-to-deposit ratio, and thus more liquidity compared to other western or U.S. financial institutions (Azzam, 2002, NCB, 2002). SAMA maintains a 65% loan-to-deposit ratio level due to its requirement that commercial banks maintain liquid reserves of at least 20% of their deposit liabilities in the form of cash, gold, Saudi government bonds or qualifying assets that can be converted into cash within a period of no less than 30 days (SAMA, 2003, EFG-Homes, 2003, p. 19). As Table 5.11 indicates, most Saudi banks maintain the recommended SAMA ratio level.

Table 5.11 Saudi banks' loans/customers deposit ratios

Banks	1998	1999	2000	2001	2002	Average
Saudi Investment	75%	74%	72%	69%	63%	70%
Saudi Hollandi	70%	66%	64%	66%	66%	66%
Al Rajhi Banking	61%	65%	52%	60%	85%	66%
Al Jazira	56%	62%	59%	58%	57%	58%
Saudi American	60%	61%	56%	56%	58%	58%
Saudi British	57%	61%	56%	51%	58%	56%
Saudi Fransi	56%	57%	55%	50%	58%	55%
Riyad	59%	51%	53%	53%	55%	54%
Arab National	44%	53%	56%	53%	57%	53%
Total	**59%**	**59%**	**56%**	**56%**	**63%**	**59%**

Source: *Bank annual reports.*

Once again it must be noted that the figures for Al Rajhi Bank should be treated with caution, as loans here are not strictly "loans" in the traditional sense, but investment accounts. Saudi Investment Bank's ratio is consistently higher than other Saudi banks, as this bank provides medium to long-term loans for industrial projects, which are not matched by short-term customers' deposits, but rather through inter-bank funding.

While this high liquidity cushion of Saudi banks, ranging from 35 - 45%, might be looked upon favourably from the regulatory aspect of a central bank, it raises some other issues. First, the low ratio imposes a restriction on domestic lending opportunities, and excess liquidity is absorbed through the acquisition of foreign deposits or local investments. This could be profitable when foreign interest rates are higher than domestic rates, and if domestic investment opportunities are positive. The downturn in international interest rates, specifically U.S. dollar interest rates, as well as uncertainties in the international stock markets (to be examined in the next chapter) has prompted some repositioning of lending to the domestic markets, which rose from SR 151 billion in 1999 to SR 233 billion by first quarter of 2004 (SAMA, First Quarter, 2004, p. 31). However, the majority of bank lending, SR 153 billion or 59%, was of less than one year's duration, with SR 66 billion or 25% being longer term at an average maturity rate of three years.

This type of lending structure is not conducive to long-term industrial investment and planning. Filling a need for long-term investment capital was the prime reason for the Saudi government's establishment of its own lending agencies. It will be interesting to see if some of the newly-licensed foreign banks spot a market niche and establish long-term credit relationships with Saudi corporations.

Consumer lending takes off

An analysis of the sectoral allocation of bank lending reveals the growing importance of consumer lending. It dominates all other lending activities. This can be seen from Table 5.12 and Figure 5.9.

Table 5.12 Bank credit to private sector by economic activity

			SR billion	
Sector	*1999*	*2001*	*2003*	*2004*
Agriculture/Fishing	1,458	2,138	2,549	2,638
Manufacturing	23,753	24,659	26,604	26,149
Mining/Quarrying	1,799	1,206	650	614
Electricity/Water	1,454	1,220	1,837	2,038
Building/Construction	19,373	16,746	21,955	21,647
Commerce	38,966	40,167	51,886	50,811
Transport/Communication	6,858	9,917	12,803	11,491
Finance	6,469	6,703	11,877	17,128
Services	9,891	9,514	8,839	9,627
Miscellaneous	41,955	64,534	82,124	91,550
Total	151,976	176,803	221,123	233,692

Source: *SAMA, First Quarter*, 2004, p. 32.

Figure 5.9 Saudi Arabia: Evolution of consumer loans 1998-2004

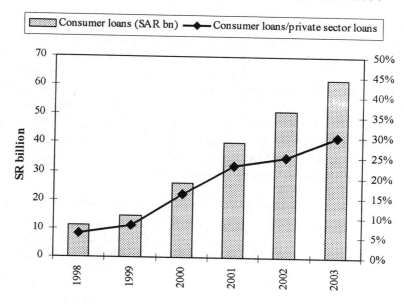

Source: *SAMA*, 2004.

Consumer loans represented around 29% of all private sector loans, or nearly SR 63 billion in 2003, compared with 12% in 1998. According to SAMA, the majority were for financing motor vehicles and "other" unspecified personal loans; real estate and credit card financing remained steady. This situation is unlikely to change in the foreseeable future, at least not until Saudi banks feel they have more legal certainty over extending real estate loans. At present they cannot hold mortgages. Credit-card facilities are normally backed up by appropriate cash collateral – mostly time deposits. Given such uncertainties, foreign banks are not likely to be competing in this market segment in Saudi Arabia.

What is more worrying for Saudi manufacturing growth is the relative decline in the share of lending to this sector, which has seen a drop from around 15% in 1999 to 11%, for current years, as set out in Table 5.12. This fall, combined with the short-term nature of lending in Saudi Arabia, is a matter of concern if the Saudi private sector is to be able to meet the challenges of diversifying the economic base of the country.

While consumer lending has risen sharply, so has commercial bank lending to the government through the purchase of development bonds and short-dated treasury notes. The introduction of these instruments and their supervision by SAMA has been dealt with at length in Chapter Four.

Saudi banks' capital adequacy

Saudi banks are subject to a capital adequacy ratio similar to the Basel-based Bank for International Settlements (BIS) requirement set at 8% of risk-weighted assets. Saudi Arabia, through SAMA, has been actively participating in all international groups concerned with the safety and soundness of the global financial markets. As such, SAMA has ensured that all Saudi banks not only comply with the BIS minimum requirements, but exceed them. According to SAMA, the year-end 2003 Saudi banks' capital and reserves stood at SR 49.2 billion, representing an 18.8% risk-weighted capital to assets ratio (SAMA, 2003, p. 106). As Table 5.13 indicates, some Saudi banks surpass this level by a wide margin.

Table 5.13 Saudi banks loans/customers deposit ratios

Bank	2002	
	Core Capital	Core Backup Capital
Al Rajhi Banking	25.9%	25.9%
Riyad Bank	20.0%	25.0%
Saudi Investment	19.0%	24.0%
Al Jazira	24.0%	24.0%
Arab National	19.0%	19.0%
Saudi American	16.5%	17.8%
Saudi Fransi	17.1%	17.1%
Saudi British	16.3%	16.3%
Saudi Hollandi	13.0%	14.0%

Source: *Annual reports*, 2002.

One implication of this high capital adequacy ratio is that all Saudi banks operate with capital in excess of what is required, and that return on equity is lower than would have been if banks had operated at a lower capital adequacy ratio. However, both the banks and SAMA think it more prudent to sacrifice incremental returns in favour of a sound banking system.

Paradoxically, while Saudi banks' capitalization might be one of the highest in the world, they are under-capitalized domestically when it comes to participating in large-scale loan projects on an individual basis. The current SAMA banking control law does not permit any bank to grant a loan or extend a credit facility and give a guarantee that exceeds 25% of a bank's capital to any single person or any related group. This can be increased to 50% only with the prior approval of SAMA.

Although this increase approval is technically available, in reality the 25% ratio acts as a constraint, especially on the smaller capitalized banks, such as Arab National, Saudi Hollandi, Saudi Investment and Al Jazira, as noted earlier in Table 5.5. They might not be able to attract lending business from the larger corporations without entering into "loan syndications" with larger banks, or consolidating and merging with other banks to improve their competitive position in this market segment. This was the route taken by the Saudi bank mergers of the 1980s and 1990s, as was mentioned earlier.

However, mergers might reduce competition and encourage monopolistic pricing. That would hinder economic growth in the long run (Gupta, 1984, IMF, 1999). Saudi Arabia seemed to have adopted a non-interventionist free-market approach, but the approval of new foreign bank licences implies that the government is also encouraging more competition in the domestic market. Table 5.14 summarizes the emphasis of SAMA's overall regulations concerning Saudi commercial banks.

Table 5.14 Saudi banking regulatory checklist.

Category	Availability	Non-Availability	Observations
• *Government safety net*		• Not available	• No formal deposit insurance scheme exists
• *Restriction on bank holdings*		• Not available	• No restrictions, large concentration in few hands
• *Capital adequacy requirement*	• Available		• Basle BIS capital adequacy ratios exceeded
• *Disclosure requirements*	• Available		• Large loans need SAMA approval
• *Chartering and bank examination*	• Available		• SAMA makes onsite and off-site audits and approves new bank licences
• *Consumer protection*	• Available		• Maximum SAMA-imposed commissions and charges
• *Restriction on competition*		• Not available	• No formal regulatory restrictions exist as to branch network numbers or to type of banking activities to be carried out.

Source: *Essayyed, Ramady and Hijji*, 2003.

Table 5.14 points to the lack of a formal government safety net for bank depositors, such as that of the U.S. Federal Insurance Deposit scheme, which guarantees the first $100,000 of bank deposits. However, SAMA has shown that despite no formal guarantee, it acted as a bank of "last resort" when it intervened to avert banking crises from developing, such as those with Riyad bank in the 1960s and Saudi Cairo and NCB in the 1980s and 1990s. A major regulatory deficiency seems to be in the area of restrictions on bank holdings, as reviewed earlier in this chapter.

Facing future challenges

On the face of it, Saudi banks seem well positioned to meet future challenges, supported by a well-developed technology base, lucrative low-interest deposits, domestic liquidity and profitable market segmentation, especially in consumer banking. However, several challenges need to be addressed, for they might become both threats and opportunities.

First, given the rapid pace of technological advancement sweeping the world, the Saudi banking industry must continue to advance its capabilities. New technology will not only alter, enhance and add to the mix of financial products, but it will also change the face of competition. Technological changes and innovations increase competition among financial institutions, while introducing new banking products that can be accessed more widely using electronic means.

As we explained in our earlier discussion of Saudi banks' perceived strengths, some Saudi banks are clearly putting some thought and energy into long-term strategic planning to ensure that they maintain a competitive advantage in electronic banking.

The entry of foreign banks into the Saudi financial marketplace will bring about a greater reliance on technology as compensation for their more limited physical presence in the Kingdom. This will challenge the domestic banks further. The current level of Internet penetration in Saudi Arabia is not as high as other Arab countries, as illustrated in Figure 5.10, but the level of Internet usage is expected to rise with reductions in telecommunication rates, when foreign companies are allowed into the lucrative Saudi telecommunications sector.

Figure 5.10 indicates that while Saudi Arabia had the lowest level of Internet penetration at 2.6% of the population, actual Internet usage at 16% was the second highest of the Arab world, and Saudi PC sales far outstripped the other Arab countries, including Egypt with almost three times the population size of Saudi Arabia. On the surface, the future of e-commerce and delivery of financial services using this new technology seems to be assured, and the public's acceptance of new delivery methods was demonstrated by the growth in ATM usage over a short period of time.

Figure 5.10 Internet penetration, usage and PC sales in the Arab world 2002

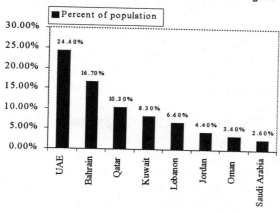

(A) Internet penetration rates in the region

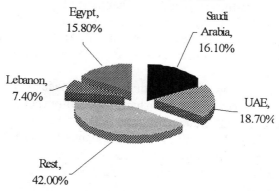

(B) Internet users in the Arab world

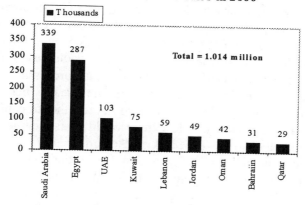

(C) Arab countries PC sales in 2000

Source: *NCB, The Economist, First Quarter,* 2001, p. 12.

However, the reduced costs to use technology mean that other players can enter the Saudi financial markets and compete with Saudi banks, such as insurance companies, brokers, hire purchase and consumer finance companies. These "low-cost" entrants could pose a challenge to Saudi banks with larger branch networks and overhead costs, despite the fact that the majority of such branches are in smaller cities and villages where Internet usage and penetration might not yet be widespread. To remain abreast of technology development in the financial delivery area, Saudi banks might form both domestic and international strategic linkages and associations, thus leveraging on their IT strengths.

Once again, as was noted from the earlier analysis of individual Saudi banks' perceived strengths, it was apparent that some of the joint venture banks did indeed leverage off their foreign partners' perceived strengths in information technology and "modern" financial product delivery. As long-term foreign joint-venture management contracts expire or are not renewed, or as the foreign partner sells out – as happened between Citibank and Saudi American Bank (SAMBA) – current Saudi joint venture banks need to be aware of this issue and need to ensure that either separate technology agreements are agreed upon or new strategic alliances with other institutions are established.

A second means by which Saudi banks can face future challenges is by pooling their resources and establishing "special-purpose" vehicles or banks that are owned by all Saudi financial institutions and which can deliver specialized services. This will allow Saudi banks to concentrate on their core businesses. A promising start was made in 2004 when it was announced that Saudi banks had agreed to establish a new bank to collect utility payments with an estimated capital of SR 500 million. SAMA will supervise the operation of the new banks. According to the reports, the Saudi commercial banks currently handle around 180 million utility bills per annum, mostly for electricity, water and telephone, despite the facility to pay these utilities through ATM machines (Saudi Commerce and Economic Review, February, 2004, p. 14). A successful launch of this bank could ensure cooperation in establishing joint credit card operations and data processing centres, which would create Saudi employment opportunities in these new fields.

The Saudi commercial banks have also got together to confront problems of commercial fraud and how to extend credit loan facilities to small and medium sized industries (SME's). According to press reports, the Kingdom's commercial banks have established the Saudi Credit Bureau (SIMAH), the only monitoring agency of its kind in the Middle East (Zawya, 18 September 2004). According to the reports, the Saudi banks have an estimated 140,000 defaulters owing SR 1.3 billion annually.

Concerning the SME's sector, SIMAH would in future provide commercial credit reports on SME's and evolve a system of credit scoring as SME's were finding it difficult to obtain bank loans in the absence of financial guarantees. In a move to promote a degree of transparency into its operations, SIMAH will be able to inform applicants whose loans have been neglected, with full details of the records held about them. Again, this is another first in the Middle East.

Expanding the financial sector base

As mentioned earlier, the Saudi banking sector is concentrated in the hands of a few players. The government's plan to sell part of its shareholding in NCB, the country's largest bank, is a welcome development, but there is room for additional specialist financial institutions to enter the market.

Previous chapters examined the role of the Saudi money exchanges. The year 2004 saw yet another exotic chapter of Saudi financial history coming to an end, with the announcement that the government had agreed to the merger of the country's leading money exchanges into a new bank (Abdul Ghafour, 8 June 2004). Apparently the new bank would be capitalized at SR 3 billion, with the founding money exchanges keeping half and selling the remaining fifty percent of SR 1.5 billion through 30 million shares to the public at a per value of SR 50 per share. If the massive response to the Sahara Petrochemical Company IPO is anything to go by, the new bank flotation is bound to be another record success. As we will learn in Chapter 6, the Sahara IPO was oversubscribed by 125 times for the SR 300 million on offer.

The money exchangers are the oldest known financial institutions in Saudi Arabia, originating in the effort to serve pilgrims who came to *Makkah* with different currencies from all over the world. As the Saudi economy developed in the 1950s, more money exchanges sprung up, such as Al-Mukairn, Al Subaeii, Kaaki, Bamaoda, Baghlaf, Amoudi, Al Roumaizan and Al Omary. The most prominent exchangers are the Al Rajhi family. Different members of the family established money exchange businesses: Al Rajhi Commercial Establishment, Al Rajhi Exchange and Commerce and Al Rajhi Trading. Of these, only Al Rajhi Commercial remained as a money exchanger, while Al Rajhi Exchange became the Al Rajhi Bank and Al Rajhi Trading ceased to exist following its entanglement in the silver trading debacle of 1984, which involved international names such as the Hunt Brothers of Texas and Banque Brussel Lambert of Belgium. In 1981, SAMA divested the money exchangers of all banking activities, except for foreign exchange remittances, and that limited their growth. Their reputation for integrity, honesty and reliability, however, made them popular for the mass of expatriates and Saudis, who appreciated their more flexible opening hours, network of branches and competitive exchange rates.

The founding bank to be called Al Bilad will involve eight exchange companies including Al Rajhi Commercial for Exchange, Al Subaeii, Saleh Sairafi, Injaz Money Exchange, Hazza, Al Amri, Al Mukairn and another Al Rajhi exchange company called Al Rajhi Trading Establishment in Dammam, not to be confused with the similarly-named company that ceased to exist in 1984. Al Bilad is expected to launch its operations in 2005 (Saudi Press Agency, 9 September 2004). Although moves for mergers, consolidation and rationalization are always welcome, as well as prudent supervision of financial institutions, thousands will mourn the demise of these customer-friendly money exchangers. The public's expectation is that the new merged bank will continue to focus on the area that the founding members do best – money exchanging. The new bank owners have already announced that Al Bilad will operate on the basis of Islamic banking principles, no doubt following in the profitable footsteps of Al Rajhi Investment and Banking Corporation.

The Insurance sector's importance

One of Saudi Arabia's hopes for deepening the financial market lies in the insurance sector. The insurance industry in Saudi Arabia is relatively new, as the country's insurance activities in the past were mainly focused on imports and there were only foreign players or their agents in the market. Social and religious reluctance to engage in insurance activities also played a role, due to perceived restrictions imposed by Islam. In 1983, the Saudi market saw the emergence of an insurance concept called "Co-operative Insurance" which was Islamically acceptable.

The concept of cooperative insurance was based on the principle of joint and several liabilities among the insured persons who participated in compensating any of the insured individuals, and thus, the insured persons within this cooperative system are the participants or owners of the insurance operations. They have a right to receive surpluses after allocations are made for reserves.

This concept is different from commercial insurance where policy-holders do not share profit; it is more akin to the Lloyds of London "Names." The cooperative insurance concept was implemented by the Saudi government in 1996 through the establishment of a publicly-owned joint stock company called the National Company for Co-operative Insurance (NCCI). The insurance market in Saudi Arabia is at its infancy stage compared to other more mature markets worldwide. Table 5.15 illustrates how insignificant this market is in relation to total world insurance premiums of nearly $1,521,253 million. Total Saudi insurance premiums amounted to $757 million (SR 2.84 billion) but represented less than 0.09% of the world's total.

Table 5.15 Saudi and world insurance market 2000

Index	Saudi Arabia	World Market Share
Life Insurance		
• Premium (million $)	13	1,521,253
• %	0.00%	100%
Non-Life		
• Premium (Million $	744	992,420
• %	0.08%	100%

Source: *Swiss Reinsurance, Sigma*, No. 6, 2001.

Gross premiums paid in Saudi Arabia were also insignificant in relation to GDP and amounted to under 0.5% for 2000, one of the lowest in the world as illustrated in Table 5.16, which also shows that other Muslim countries had a higher level of insurance to their GDP compared with Saudi Arabia.

Table 5.16 Insurance premium comparisons 2000

Country	Premiums ($ million)	Share of world market (%)	Premiums as % of GDP	Premiums per capita ($)
Canada	46,587	1.91	6.56	1,516
Cyprus	524	0.02	5.67	680
Germany	123,722	5.06	6.54	1,491
Japan	504,005	20.62	10.92	3,973
Lebanon	498	0.02	2.63	151
Kuwait	198	0.01	0.52	104
Malaysia	3,474	0.14	3.72	150
Qatar	158	0.01	1.09	263
UK	236,960	9.7	15.78	3,759
USA	865,327	35.41	8.76	3,152
Saudi Arabia	*757*	*0.03*	*0.44*	*36.9*

Source: *Swiss Reinsurance, Sigma*, No. 6, 2001.

A mere 1% increase in the ratio of premiums to GDP would unleash an insurance market in excess of SR 7 billion in Saudi Arabia. According to latest NCCI data, the insurance market in the Kingdom in 2002 totalled around SR 15 billion with gross insurance premiums of SR 4.324 billion being paid, as can be seen in Table 5.17.

Table 5.17 Saudi insurance market subscriptions by foreign companies and NCCI market share 1991 - 2002

SR million

SECTOR	1991	1993	1995	1997	1999	2002
Total subscription	1,743	2,205	2,568	2,852	2,861	4,324
- Foreign	1,282	1,586	1,773	2,180	2,232	3,243*
- NCCI	461	619	795	672	629	1,081

Source: *NCCI, Life and Fidelity*, 2002 .
*Estimated.

Table 5.17 also highlights the relative importance of the foreign insurance companies and brokers in the Saudi market, capturing around 75% of the business. However, both NCCI and foreign companies have increased their respective market shares. In term of market segments, life insurance continues to lag behind other segments, and, as illustrated in Figure 5.11 and Table 5.18, the major Saudi insurance market is in the medical and motor vehicle field.

Figure 5.11 Saudi insurance market's premiums by type of insurance

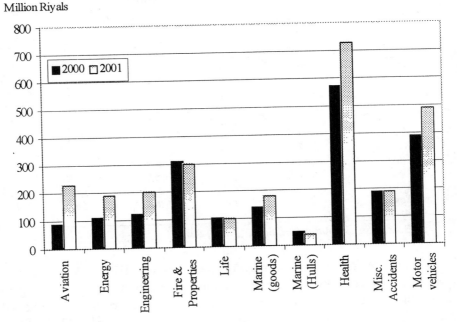

Source: *NCCI, SAMA*, 2003.

Table 5.18 Subscriptions to NCCI by market segment

Type of Insurance	1995	1997	2000	SR million 2001	2002
Fire	70	53	58	68	189
Engineering	139	91	55	92	85
Motor vehicle	68	93	111	148	270
Miscellaneous accidents	18	19	25	25	18
Medical	42	49	251	285	237
Marine	103	102	38	47	54
Aviation	78	53	63	209	150
Energy	269	212	112	145	77
Joint liabilities	-	-	900	1	1
Total	795	672	1613	1020	1081

Source: *NCCI, SAMA*, 2003.

Table 5.18 shows that from 2002, motor vehicle insurance overtook medical insurance, but the market expects both these sectors to increase sharply over the coming years due to two 2002 landmark rulings made by the Saudi government concerning these sectors. In effect, these decisions made third-party car insurance compulsory for all motorists from 20 November 2002 (Qedaihy, 31 October 2001). According to press reports from NCCI, there are more than four million cars registered in Saudi Arabia and demand for motor insurance has been increasing due to the country suffering one of the highest traffic accident rates of the world. According to the Saudi Ministry of Interior, there were 2.2 million accidents in the Kingdom over a ten year period, with nearly 40,000 people losing their lives. In terms of economic loss to the country, the Ministry studies indicate that accidents, loss of life and property as well as cost of treatment costs Saudi Arabia around SR 21 billion annually (Arab News, 20 September 2004). The insurance market has estimated that this mandatory policy will increase car insurance premiums to SR 2 billion and that the overall insurance market will reach over SR 6 billion by 2004 (Qedaihy, 2001, Parker, 17 June 2002).

In order to ensure that only financially-fit companies operate in this sector in Saudi Arabia, the *Majlis Al Shoura* passed legislation in September, 2002, specifying that insurance companies intending to provide cooperative insurance services should have a minimum capital level of SR 100 million (Qedaihy, 23 September 2002). This amount was raised to SR 200 million for companies providing re-insurance.

The second major significant insurance event concerned a mandatory scheme of medical insurance for some seven million expatriates and their families working and living in Saudi Arabia (Parker, 17 June 2002). According to reports, the Saudi Ministry of Health was giving employers up to 3 years to introduce this scheme, depending upon the number of employees. Because the impact of these decisions on the Saudi private sector would be to make the cost of hiring expatriate labour more expensive, there were attempts to postpone their implementation for smaller Saudi companies. The Kingdom is planning to introduce private sector health insurance scheme for Saudis 3 years after the completion of health sector insurance for expatriates. This could boost the Saudi insurance sector to around SR 18 billion within the next 5 years.

The implication for the Saudi economy is much wider. First, the medical insurance law will help to ease pressure on the Kingdom's budgetary outlays in the medical sector, as the Saudi government provides free medical services for all citizens and non-citizens alike, and this budgetary item had been increasing each year, as we pointed out in Chapter 2.

Second, the boost in insurance services has encouraged the introduction in December, 2001 of an interest-free Islamic insurance system, with some of the local banks such as Al Jazira Bank pioneering the launch of Islamic Insurance or *Takaful*, and introducing *Takaful Ta'awni* or an Islamically-acceptable Islamic life insurance product. This product is the only *Shariah*-compliant insurance product approved by SAMA to data (SAMA, 2003). Recognizing the importance of this Islamic insurance market, the Saudi government endorsed a new Islamic insurance law in July, 2003, and it is expected to boost the market's turnover according to reports.

*Table 5.*19 Insurance indicators from NCCI 1998 – 2002

Insurance indicators (Million SR)	1998	1999	2000	2001	2002
Total subscribed insurance premiums	683.8	628.7	717.0	1,023.2	1,081.2
Total claims paid	440.8	357.4	355.2	724.8	456.7
Net surplus of insurance operations	45.0	6.8	58.1	63.1	34.2
Technical reserves	267.2	333.8	331.2	340.7	798.0
Total assets	1,190.2	1,252.1	1,381.7	1,534.9	1,698.9
Net profit	45.0	6.8	85.1	63.1	56.5
Liquid assets (investments)	779.4	852.8	940.9	933.4	1,021.4

Source: *NCCI, SAMA* 2003.

The third important factor is the ability of the insurance sector to provide long-term investment funding to Saudi capital market projects. Table 5.19 illustrates the gradual rise in liquid assets available for investments, and the important intermediation role that this financial sector can play in mobilizing additional financing outside the banking sector.

While the liquid assets in Table 5.19 might seem modest in comparison with the size of the banking sector, this actually represents NCCI investments alone. Foreign company investments are not included. However, until the Saudi capital market allows direct foreign investment to take place, the presumption is that foreign company "liquid assets" are transferred abroad.

Given the growing importance of this sector to the national economy and in preparation for the Kingdom's expected entry into the WTO, the government of Saudi Arabia passed an Insurance Law in July, 2003, which allowed the Saudi Arabian Monetary Agency to become the licensing and regulatory authority for this sector. All existing market participants are to be licensed and a regulatory infrastructure is being developed by SAMA to ensure a competitive and transparent market. (SAMA, February, 2004). According to press reports, SAMA has created an "Insurance Control Department" within the agency to maintain its role as a monitor and licensor of this sector (Shaikh, 9 June 2004). As part of economic liberalization measures, the Saudi government also took a decision in May, 2004, to sell the government's stake in NCCI (Reuters, 24 May 2004). Given the emerging importance of this sector, the Saudi government has announced that NCCI would sell 70% of its shares to the public through an IPO, with the government owned General Organization for Social Insurance and Pension Corporation also retaining 15% in NCCI.

These recent rapid developments in the Saudi insurance sector are one of the more promising features of the domestic financial market. Some commentators estimate that this liberalized and invigorated sector could create as many as 10,000 jobs, mostly for Saudis, and reach an annual turnover of SR 50 billion in another five years (AFP, 15 July 2003).

Islamic finance in the Kingdom

Islamic financing, and a rapid increase in both Islamic and "conventional" institutions offering Islamic products and services, attests to the growing popularity of this market segment (Archer et al., 2002, Faroqui, 2002, Abdeen et al., 1984). The Saudi market is no exception, as evidenced by the remarkable market share that Al Rajhi Banking and Investment Corporation currently enjoys, and the conversion of a large number of the branches of the National Commercial Bank to "Islamic branches".

Despite the lack of the word "Islamic" in the title of any financial institution, there is widespread support and encouragement for Islamic financing in the Kingdom. This support is manifested in the establishment of the Jeddah-based Islamic Development Bank (IDB), with the Kingdom contributing 25% of the $8 billion capital of the largest Islamic financial institution owned by all the members of the Organization of Islamic Conference (OIC). In addition, the Islamic Investment Company (IIC), a subsidiary of the Geneva-based *Dar Al Mall* Group has nearly 20 branches in the major cities of Saudi Arabia, operating under a "quasi-legal" status through the personal sponsorship of HRH Prince Mohammed Al Faisal Al Saud, the late King Faisal's son. As we saw in Chapter 4, SAMA has been closely monitoring the experience of other GCC Central Banks in relation to controlling and supervising Islamic financial institutions.

The Bahrain Monetary Agency seems to have been the most successful one, as it served as a model of "co-existence" of conventional and Islamic banks under one regulator. SAMA's increased confidence about regulating this sector has been mirrored by the granting of more product licenses and approvals for the launch of Islamically-complaint mutual funds. NCB's experience in this sector reflects this, for its traditional funds were overtaken by Islamic funds, reaching SR 14 billion in 2001 compared with SR 3 billion in 1997.

It is in the area of project finance that Islamic-oriented institutions such as Al Rajhi could play a developmental role in the economy. Currently, because of interest considerations, unlike the other Saudi banks, Al Rajhi does not purchase government bonds or treasury notes to finance government budget deficits. However, Al Rajhi has successfully funded government projects on Islamic financing principles (lease financing, buy and sell, or buy, operate and lease) such as school construction and electricity projects. They are considering other government-related project financing. The success of such Islamically-acceptable financing will open up a large market segment for the Saudi government, using Al Rajhi and other Islamic financing entities to fund the large capital projects the Kingdom needs over the next few decades. During 2004, one of the world's largest Islamic financing transactions was announced when a consortium of Saudi and Gulf banks (Al Rajhi, NCB, Abu Dhabi Islamic House, Emirates Bank, Citi group and SAMBA acting as arranger bank) concluded a $ 2.35 billion *murabaha* financing for Ettihad Etisalat Company which had been awarded the second GSM licence in Saudi Arabia (Ghazanfar, 27 September 2004).

Market reports indicate that Al Rajhi is going one step further in identifying new Islamic financing instruments and is considering underwriting a multi-billion riyal Saudi government Islamic bond program. This would represent Saudi Arabia's first Islamic bond, and would follow on the footsteps of Bahrain's successful issue of similar Islamic leasing bonds of $450 million. They were heavily over-subscribed (Parker, 19 May 2003). Such Islamic instruments would undoubtedly add breadth to the new Saudi capital market and provide Saudi investors with the choice of participating in Islamically-acceptable products, and, in the process, further deepen the Saudi financial system.

Conclusion

The Saudi banking sector's recent performance attests to its financial strength and efficiency. Management, risk control and cost efficiency have greatly improved which to some extent explains the milder impact of lower oil prices on the Kingdom's financial institutions compared to previous periods of oil price downturns.

A main challenge facing the financial sector is the country's commitment to joining the WTO, which requires that the domestic financial market open up to outside competition. This will be examined in more detail in later chapters, but suffice it to say that while the ten domestic banks currently meet most domestic banking needs, international pressure might create problems for those with less capital, not as much innovation, and fewer international linkages and alliances than others. With the process of financial globalization accelerating, there could be pressure for consolidation between local banks and for cross-border alliances. Banks could pursue regional expansion in other parts of the GCC or the Arab world.

The re-entry of foreign-owned banks into Saudi Arabia could force more intensive competition than currently exists amongst Saudi banks. The foreign banks might well concentrate on certain profitable "niche" market segments and allow the Saudi banks to concentrate on other areas where their local knowledge and risk assessment gives them an advantage. As the Saudi government disengages from the financial markets by reducing the amount of lending it provides through its specialized credit institutions, the local banks will have to come up with a more innovative approach to tap domestic and international resources in order to meet future capital investment needs. They will be helped by exciting new developments in insurance, Islamic and capital market instruments. The long-term prospect looks bright; Saudi banks have indeed come a long way since those early days in the 1950s when some sections of the population did not wish to deal with banks at all. The reaffirmation by Standard & Poor of Saudi Arabia's sovereign credit rating in April, 2004, reflects a positive view of the Kingdom's long-term outlook. The stability and maturity of the Saudi financial sector has played a large part in this perception.

Summary of the key points

- *The Saudi banking sector is one of the financially strongest and profitable in the world, with high capitalization in excess of international required levels, advanced automation and a diversified range of banking services delivered to well defined target market segments.*
- *Banking supervision is through SAMA control. The transformation of previously wholly owned foreign bank branches into "Saudized"*

banks, passing on technology and management skills, has been of benefit to the banking sector.

- *The Saudi financial markets passed through several phases of evolution, each laying the foundation for the next phase. Currently the banking sector is going through a phase of consolidation, mergers, and preparing to face globalization threats in face of imminent WTO accession, as well as the granting of banking licences for wholly owned foreign banks to enter the Saudi market.*
- *Saudi banks are characterized by a high degree of shareholder concentration levels, which could be counterbalanced by partial privatization of government held shares in some Saudi banks.*
- *Saudi banks lending policies are still limited by their small capital base as well as SAMA mandated loan to deposit ratios, but consumer lending has become a major growth sector.*
- *The amalgamation of all remaining money exchangers into a new bank will add some future depth to the financial market, as well the expansion of the insurance sector due to foreign entry and government mandated insurance laws in health and vehicle insurance.*
- *Islamic finance has acquired more importance, and both Islamic and non-Islamic banks have entered this market segment to finance some large scale projects.*

Critical thinking

1. Why was the policy of *Saudization* of the foreign banks operating in the Kingdom initiated? Do you think that SAMA should Saudize the "new-wave" foreign banks too?
2. "International competition will be good for Saudi banks and the economy in general". Do you agree? How will Saudi banks compete with globalization?
3. "The Internet revolution will make banking as we know it today redundant". Do you agree? How do you see Saudi banking evolve over the next two decades in the face of Internet and technology advances?
4. "Niche market segmentation is the key for survival for Saudi banks in the face of foreign competition". In what areas can Saudi banks maintain a competitive advantage over foreign rivals?
5. "There are too many banks in Saudi Arabia. Mergers will ensure that Saudi banking can effectively compete". Discuss the pros and cons of more Saudi bank concentration.

Chapter 6

THE SAUDI CAPITAL MARKET

Better know nothing, than half know many things.

Neitzsche

Learning Outcomes:

By the end of this section, you would understand:

- *Role of capital markets in economic development*
- *The historical development of the Saudi capital market*
- *Previous and current operations of the capital market*
- *The importance of the new Capital Market Law*
- *Performance of the Saudi capital market and its international comparisons*
- *Sectoral performance of the Saudi capital market*
- *Analysis of Saudi investor behaviour*
- *The Saudi mutual fund industry*
- *The government debt market*

Introduction

The role of capital markets in economic development has increasingly been emphasized as an important tool of financial intermediation. Saudi Arabia has been endowed with enormous wealth, gained in a short period of time. An efficient capital market structure could help in recycling capital surpluses, especially those held by the private sector. There is no doubt that Saudi Arabia possesses such capital surplus. We can take the examples of the Sahara Petrochemical Company and Ettihad Etisalat's Initial Public Offerings (IPO's) during 2004. The SR 300 million ($80 million) IPO offered six million shares at a par value of SR 50 per share. It was oversubscribed by 125 times and raised a staggering, world-breaking sum of SR 37.5 billion ($10 billion) (Arab News, 5 June 2004). Apparently, 552,000 individuals subscribed to the shares. This was followed, in the same year, by the 1 billion Saudi Riyal issue for the Ettihad Etisalat IPO, with 4.2 million applications and raising a world record of SR 51 billion (Hanware, 1 November 2004).

The Sahara IPO marked another first for Saudi Arabia, for the flotation process was highly transparent, with automated data subscription details made available to potential investors to track each day's transactions. The IPO reinforced the arguments of those who were calling for a faster development of the Saudi and Gulf Arab capital markets (Azzam, 1988, 1997, Bakheet, 1999, Bolbol et al., 2004, Dukheil, 2002).

At the same time, the record-breaking IPO seemed to underline the acute shortage of investment channels facing Saudi Arabia and indicated that the Saudi public was now more ready to effectively participate in capital market developments than it had been in the past. In 2003, the Saudi Orix Leasing Company made history by issuing the Kingdom's first private sector debt instrument; it was medium-term with a value of SR 50 million.

The three-year paper was guaranteed by the company's principal shareholders, the Saudi Investment Bank and the International Finance Corporation, which is the private-sector lending arm of the World Bank (MEED, 7 March 2003). These debuts of equity and fixed income instruments are an important development for Saudi Arabia, as they will provide the capital market with added depth and versatility in the coming few years, especially as the need increases for long-term capital for projects. They also will allow the private sector to play a leading financing role.

The development of a broader and deeper capital market will lead to other benefits, encouraging the creation of new risk-management instruments (such as interest rate hedging, futures and options) while widening the scope of Central Banks to allow them to conduct monetary policy through open market operations (Azzam, 2003). It is also recognized that a well-developed capital market, especially a stock market, performs at least three other functions. It is a signalling mechanism to managers regarding investment, a source of finance and a catalyst for corporate governance.

A key question is whether stock market prices affect investment, independent of fundamentals of the economy and the financial health of companies, causing a misallocation of capital, which can lead to considerable damage at the sectoral level (Bolbol et al., 2004). As will be discussed later in this chapter, the 2003/2004 sharp price movements in the Saudi stock market were one sign of the need for a speedier implementation of the Saudi Capital Market Law.

Saudi capital market developments: An historical perspective

Plans for establishing a formal Saudi stock market have been in the making since the early 1980s (Abdeen et al., 1984). It is interesting to note some of the major concerns raised then regarding elements that might be a hindrance to the smooth functioning of a Saudi stock market, and then assess whether the same "problems" continue to exist in the new millennium. According to earlier observers (Dukheil, 1995, Abdeen, 1984), the first problem related to the lack of an "organized legal framework for a stock exchange", with three sources of official directives controlling the stock market. A second problem concerned the "non-specialist" offices that emerged to deal with shares. A third difficulty was the "ownership of a large percentage of shares by board members and founders." A fourth challenge was that "most Saudi citizens have little understanding of stock market operations and transactions." Such transactions were based on rumours, because of a lack of analysis of companies' financial positions, profitability or other financial considerations. Another problem, according to the early market observers, was that citizens from "other Gulf countries invested in Saudi stocks via Saudi agents."

Even in those early days, there were recommendations for overcoming such problems. These included the "assigning of one government body responsible for share companies; establishment of an effective set of regulations for the organization of stock operations and transactions", and the imposing of limits on individual stock ownership. A final plea was made for increasing the number of publicly-held companies in the Kingdom in order to "increase the potential number of issues and shares." In 1983, Saudi Arabia could only boast 38 publicly-listed companies, while Kuwait had 48 (Abdeen, 1984, Nashashibi, 1983).

We will see that some of the issues raised many years ago still persist in the Saudi stock market of 2004. Until the Saudi Capital Market Law (CML) was passed in 2003, the Kingdom was slow to restructure its stock market to encourage private domestic investment. The Saudi stock market remained more a "government-controlled banking consortium" than a real stock market (Cordesman, 2003).

Others have commented that the growth of the Saudi stock market has been hindered by family business groupings and "mentalities" which are still prevalent in Saudi Arabia today, despite attempts to widen the entrepreneurial class base (Seznec, 1987, 1995, Field, 1985).

The Sahara IPO and Etisalat subscriptions mentioned earlier, which were so unexpectedly large, showed that, although the Saudi stock market has great potential, its structure needs to be addressed. The benefits from such a determined reform can contribute to the economic development of the

Kingdom, fuelled by the provision of risk capital. Transparent, efficient and well-regulated markets can add to the general level of investor confidence and can reverse capital flight. During the period 2001- 2004, conditions were right for Saudi capital repatriation, due to the fear of being invested in western assets and concern about the collapse of the U.S. and some European stock markets.

A new capital market law, although essential to market reform, has dragged on for many years. The new Capital Market Law, which was approved by the Cabinet and passed into law in November, 2003, was only implemented in July, 2004. The pace of change has more to do with the conservative regulatory approach adopted by the Saudi Arabian Monetary Agency (SAMA), the financial market supervising authority. Reforms to date mostly seem to be designed to avoid undue speculation and stock market panics, such as the famous collapse of the Kuwait *Souk Al-Manakh* unofficial stock market in the early 1980s. However, the intentions for reform seem to address most of the issues and problems highlighted by observers of the early stock market. The next section considers these proposed reforms.

Saudi capital market operation

Before analyzing the new Capital Market Law, it would be useful to examine the stock market structure that this new law replaced. By examining the deficiencies in the previous system, we can assess whether the new law has rectified outstanding operating concerns. Figure 6.1 illustrates the workings of the "old" stock market structure.

As noted from Figure 6.1, the "old" Saudi stock market structure operated under three masters. The Ministry of Commerce was directly responsible for the formation of new companies, the conversion of firms to joint stock companies and IPOs. In essence, it was the primary market function. The second regulator was the Ministry of Finance, which set the overall policy directives and objectives of the stock market. Finally, SAMA controlled the operational and functional management of the Saudi stock market. This was the secondary market function. Share trading activity was executed through Saudi commercial banks that were responsible for the settlement of transactions between buyers and sellers against a maximum 1% commission. Figure 6.1 highlights the absence of an exchange bourse and of independent market makers. Under the old regulations, forward trading of shares and acceptance of post-dated checks to settle transactions were prohibited, no doubt influenced by what happened during the Kuwaiti *Souk Al-Manakh* 1982 stock market crash.

Figure 6.1 "Old" Saudi stock market

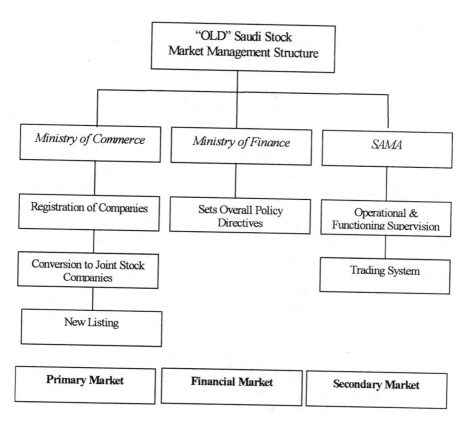

In 1985, SAMA introduced certain operational improvements in the share-dealing process. First, it established the Saudi Shares Registration Company (SSRC) and limited its shareholding to banks. However, share ownership was based on a physical documentation exchange. In 1990, SAMA introduced an electronic trading system called Electronics Securities Information System (ESIS), through which all the buy and sell orders placed at individual banks are transferred from bank computers to a central system at SAMA for matching. This fostered market liquidity and increased trading volume. The overall price movement in the Saudi stock market was tracked by the *Bakheet* and CCFI Stock Market Indexes, which were the most widely quoted Saudi indexes, similar to the Dow Jones index for the USA.

In 2001, an automated trading system called *Tadawul* was launched which enabled trading to be carried out through the Internet. By virtue of its ease, transparency and speed in processing, *Tadawul* gave yet another boost in trading volumes for the Saudi stock market. It is no exaggeration to state that as of 2004, the Saudi stock market trading system became one of the most technologically advanced in the world, with *T + Zero* delivery – transaction plus zero days.

Participation in the Saudi stock market is currently restricted to Saudi citizens, Saudi corporations and Gulf Cooperation Council (GCC) citizens. Foreign participation was initially allowed only in the banks' mutual funds, with the first closed Saudi Mutual Fund (SAIF) introduced by Saudi American Bank in 1997. In 1999, the stock market was opened for foreign investment through a wider range of Saudi banks' mutual funds.

The establishment of *Tadawul* enabled a new stock market index to emerge called TASI or Tadawul All Share Index and it is currently quoted as the official Saudi stock market index.

One of the major drawbacks of the Saudi stock market is the small number of listed companies in relation to the size of the Saudi economy. In 2003, there were 69 listed companies with share capital of SR 38 billion compared to 121 registered joint stock companies, with SR 81.3 billion share capital (SAMA, 2003). There were another 6,000 limited-liability Saudi companies operating in the Kingdom and 1,400 joint venture companies (Saudi and non-Saudi), with a combined SR 85.5 billion of share capital. There was a potential market for IPOs and for the expansion of the stock market base. However, according to analysts, current listing requirements have been onerous (Naggar, 1994, Dukhail, 2002, Azzam, 2002, Cordesman, 2003).

According to the Saudi Ministry of Commerce regulations, the procedure to convert into a joint stock company involves several necessary conditions. The major requirements are listed in Table 6.1, which sets out both the old listing requirements and those that were introduced in 1999 by the Ministry.

Table 6.1 Rules for company conversion into a Saudi joint stock company

Parameters	Pre-1999	Post-1999
• Net assets	• SR 75 million	• SR 50 million
• Return on shareholders equity	• 10% for the last five years to be maintained for next five years	• 7% for the last three years to be maintained for next three years
• Public subscription	• 51%	• 40%
• Company age	• ten years	• five years

Source: *Ministry of Commerce*, Riyadh, 2002.

Besides the requirements listed in Table 6.1, there was another, rather unspecified condition relating to the management of a joint stock company. That provision set that the company was to have "able administrative and efficient internal controls."

Even with all these regulations, the standard of corporate disclosure is somewhat poor in Saudi Arabia (Dukhail, 2002). Quarterly results are required from listed companies, but these often lack detailed analysis and compliance is poor, with no penalties imposed on those companies that do not publish financial results on time. The Saudi stock market thus suffers from "asymmetrical information" – where one party has information that is not known to the rest of the market.

However, the reduction in the Saudi shareholder base over time is of more concern. In stock markets around the world, the number of shareholders expands over time with new IPOs, despite mergers and acquisitions and shareholder exit. In Saudi Arabia, the static number of listed companies has meant that, in term of shareholder numbers, the Saudi stock market is characterized by a very high degree of concentration in a few hands. Table 6.2 reflects a pattern across all industries listed in the Saudi stock market.

Table 6.2 Saudi companies with significant reduction in number of shareholders

Company	1996	1998	2001	Change
Livestock	134,000	5,439	NA	-96%
Mubarrad	45,658	12,500	36,921	-19%
Al-Bank Al-Saudi Al-Fransi	12,883	9,919	6,370	-51%
Tabuk Cement	12,402	9,668	8,185	-34%
Saudi American Bank*	19,968	16,171	44,600	123%
Jazira Bank	33,737	27,459	24,056	-29%
Makkah	88,194	72,168	61,077	-31%
Riyad Bank	107,260	90,340	57,480	-46%
Al-Ahsa	6,673	5,703	5,038	-25%
British Bank	17,590	15,155	11,846	-33%
Saudi Hollandi Bank	1,168	1,033	685	-41%
Medical Appliances	112,703	101,063	92,964	-18%

*The increase in the number of shareholders is attributed to SAMBA's merger with United Saudi Bank.

Source: *CCFI Database*, 2002.

Besides some of the concentration levels given in Table 6.2, there are other listed companies that have as few as seven shareholders (Saudi Chemicals), and some with fewer than 100 shareholders.

Such concentrated ownership levels enables business or family groups to influence the day-to-day management of these companies through board representation and "de-democratizes" the role of joint stock companies and its General Assembly. Together with the lack of transparency, this leads to joint stock companies operating like partnership firms. This undermines confidence in the stock market and has been highlighted by others (Wilson, 2004, Dukheil, 2002, Azzam, 1997).

The new capital market law

After deliberation by the *Majlis Al-Shoura* or Consultative Council of Saudi Arabia in December, 2002, a new Capital Market Law composed of 67 Articles was passed by the Council of Ministers in June, 2003, with the law taking effect from November, 2003, after publication in the Official Gazette (Saudi Press Agency, 17 June 2003). The new law was not implemented until July, 2004, which added some uncertainty in the market.

Figure 6.2 The new Saudi capital market regulatory structure

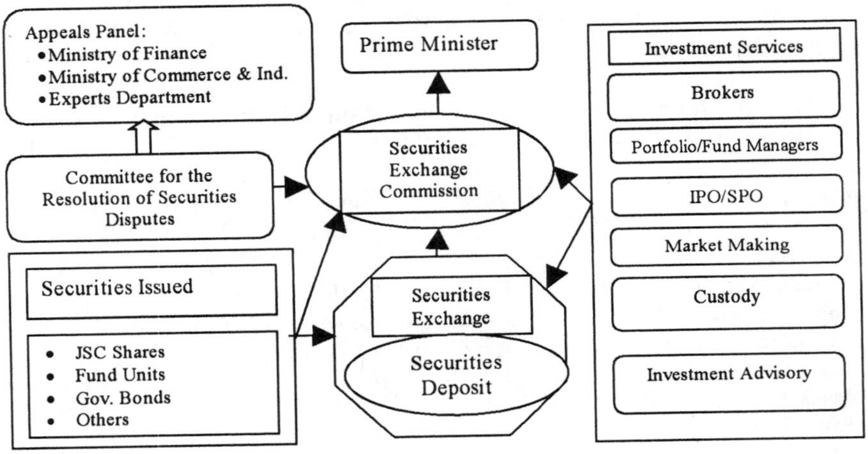

At first glance, the new law seems to address some of the more glaring shortfalls of the "old" stock market structure, which had no independent brokerage firms, no investment advisory and custodial services and little or no market-making capabilities. Above all, the "old" law lacked an independent financial market regulator. The "new" law establishes an independent Saudi Arabian Securities and Exchange Commission (SEC), with the objective of protecting investor interests, ensuring orderly and equitable dealing in securities and promoting and developing the capital markets. The SEC will have the power to license non-bank financial intermediaries and to authorize the offering of securities to the public.

It will also establish the first-ever national Securities Depository Centre. In terms of management, the SEC will be governed by five Commissioners to be appointed by Royal Decree, one of whom will be nominated as Chairman and another as Vice Chairman. In July, 2004, a Royal Decree was issued naming Jammaz Al Suhaimi as Chairman with Ministerial rank, and Mohammed Al Rumaih as Vice Chairman, as well as the other three members of the Commission (Saudi Press Agency, 3 July

2004). The appointment of the Chairman was widely welcomed because of the continuity it brought. Mr Suhaimi was the Deputy Governor of the Banking Control Department at SAMA and had been closely involved in the "old" Saudi stock market operations.

Figure 6.2 also highlights the "Committee for the Resolution of Securities Disputes," which can use the services of an appeals panel composed of members from the Ministry of Finance, Ministry of Commerce and the Experts Department.

A novel feature of the Capital Market Law is the establishment of a Securities Exchange or "bourse" which will incorporate the National Securities Depository. The Exchange will be a private sector company, with a board of nine members, three from the government (Ministries of Finance and Commerce, as well as SAMA), and six from shareholders of the Exchange. It will be the only stock exchange operating in the Kingdom, and its wide powers will include:

- Ensuring fairness and transparency of the market
- Admitting members (broking and clearing)
- Listing new companies
- Promoting high ethical standards amongst members, employees and market participants
- Promoting high standards of corporate governance
- Ensuring timely and accurate dissemination of market information
- Establishing and operating a nationwide system for securities trading, settlement clearing and depository service

The above seems laudable and could reduce deficiencies in corporate disclosure under the old law. The new Capital Market Law also sets out in some detail (Articles 35 to 64) the type of penalties and punishment for wrongdoing, which could be an important deterrent.

However, some could argue that the imposition of a maximum fine of SR 100,000 for each violation committed (Article 59(b)) is too lenient, given that no jail sentences are specified in the new law, especially for "insider information" trading, which has been a flaw in even more developed and regulated capital markets.

What then are the remaining areas of weakness in the new Capital Market Law? Figure 6.3 identifies several areas that are still in need of improvement.

Figure 6.3 points to strengths in independence, technology, transparency, size, independent brokers and researchers, and liquidity. Weaknesses however, remain in the areas of the number of companies currently listed, the lack of direct foreign investment (outside of mutual funds), and the low level of floating stock available for investment due to the high level of shareholder concentration discussed earlier. Overall, the new capital market law is a measurable improvement over the old system, and the Saudi financial markets are poised for a challenging era.

Figure 6.3 Critique of the new Saudi Capital Market Law

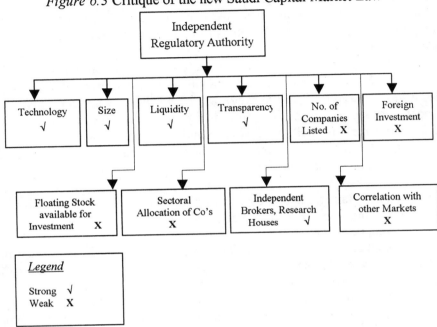

Potential benefits of the new Capital Market Law

The passing of the new Saudi Capital Market Law will go some way in convincing the Saudi private sector and the international community at large that policy makers in the Kingdom are serious about implementing reform strategies aimed at economic liberalization, competition and market efficiency. Time and time again, commentators have said that while the intentions of the Saudi government and policy makers were sound and well-meaning, the problem has been the speed of implementation. The case of the new Capital Market Law is one example of divergence between intention and implementation.

The Saudi authorities have sent robust signals that the way forward for the economy lies in decentralized, private-market based activities, and the proposed new capital market would play a vital role in the following areas. First, Saudi Arabia can attract back Saudi capital resources held abroad. A deeper and more dynamic Saudi capital market has the potential to draw back Saudi resources invested abroad, which could contribute towards the financing of the non-oil sector.

In the past, liquidity, safety and dependable market infrastructure of overseas markets have attracted private Saudi wealth. There are varying estimates as to the size of this overseas investment, ranging from a conservative $480 billion to a generous $900 billion according to various bank sources (NCB, 2002, SAMBA, 2003). Whatever the actual figures, these are substantial sums and the response to the latest IPO's shows that the public is ready to invest locally. However, for this capital repatriation to be sustained, the new Saudi Capital Market must build solid investor confidence.

Second, the development of the domestic Saudi Capital Market will contribute directly to the growth of the non-oil sector by promoting the financial services industry. A market-based expansion of contractual savings to service pensions, insurance and diversification needs will create a demand for institutional investors, such as pension funds, insurance companies and mutual funds. They will be in a better position to satisfy the economy's demand for long-term resources and to assume the role now played by specialized government credit agencies. From the early "boom" days of the mid-1970s and early 1980s, government financing was made available for manufacturing enterprises at zero interest rates. This encouraged reliance on the state, it institutionalized operating inefficiencies and it promoted a business culture of relying on commercial bank debt financing and soft loans from the government, rather than equity financing.

Third, a well-developed Capital Market will improve risk management practices. In previous chapters, we showed that the volatility of oil prices leads to volatility and unpredictability in Saudi government revenues, resulting in a magnified effect on other sectors of the economy. Financial market developments can contribute to better risk management in the economy; for example, the introduction of derivative instruments (hedging) can help domestic market participants manage the effects of oil price volatility on their activities. This can lead to greater macro-economic stability, thus improving the investment climate and growth in the non-oil sectors.

Fourth, a well-developed local Capital Market can respond to the demand of infrastructure services. With the Saudi government signalling its disengagement from public investment and announcing its ambitious privatization program, infrastructure finance will be at risk if international capital markets lose their appetites for taking risks on emerging countries. Furthermore, international capital is more likely to flow when there is evidence of private domestic capital in the projects they are called to finance. As such, limited recourse finance needs a diversified menu of financing instruments that can expand without relying on government guarantees. Only a capital market that is liquid, transparent and diversified could help in this process.

Performance of the Saudi capital markets

Figure 6.4 shows that the Saudi stock market has great potential, but that, while its performance and market capitalization may be very good by Middle East standards, it remains underdeveloped by the standards of other regions.

Figure 6.4 Percent shares of Arab Capital Markets in the composition of the Arab Monetary Fund's Index at the end of 2002

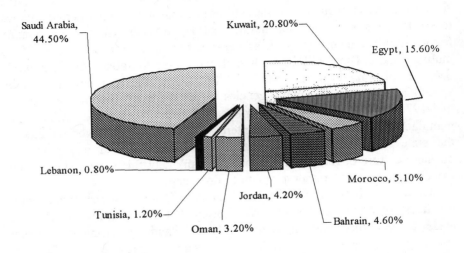

Source: *SAMA,* 2003, p. 144.

Egypt, with almost triple the population of Saudi Arabia, had the second-largest stock market with a 15.6% share of the total Arab stock market index, while Lebanon's was the smallest at under 1%. In terms of performance, the Saudi stock market was the only Arab stock market to deliver a sustained growth over the period 1999-2001 as illustrated in Figure 6.5.

The Tunisian market was the second-most consistent performer; the Egyptian market gave the most volatile performance for the period 1999-2001. However, by emerging market standards, the combined Arab stock markets are small, accounting for some 6.5% of total market capitalization of the 38 emerging markets in Asia, Latin America, Africa and Eastern

Europe and for 0.6% of the world's total stock market capitalization of $32,000 billion in 2000 (Azzam, 2002, p. 65).

Figure 6.5 Performance of Arab stock markets, 1999-2001

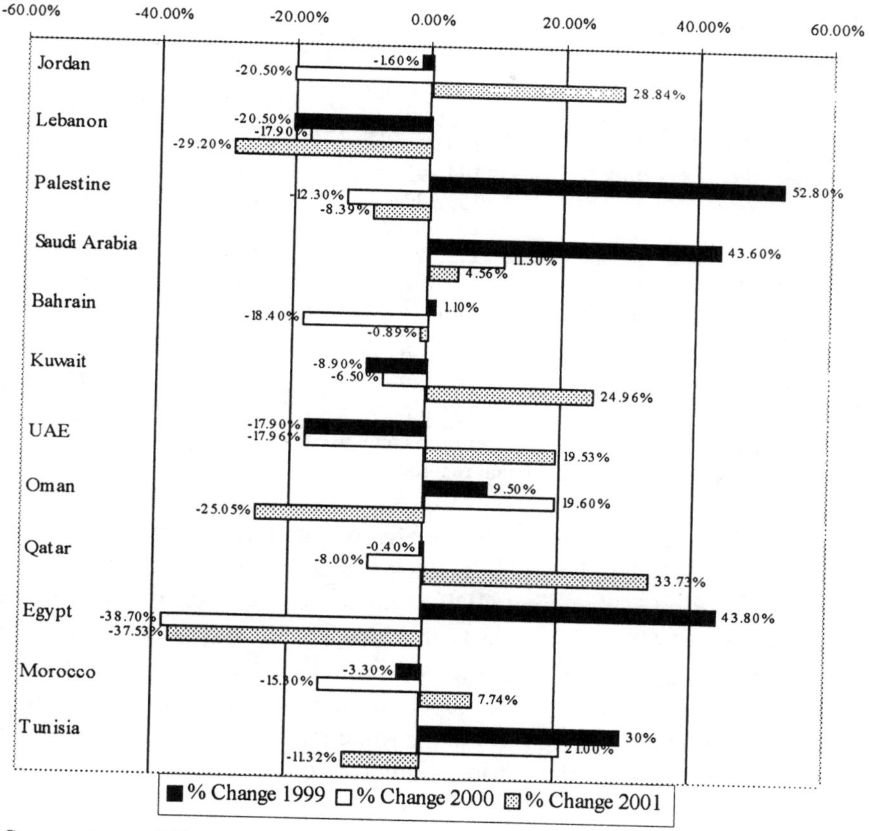

Source: *Azzam*, 2002, p. 69.

This has not stopped some of the Arab stock markets from extending both their share market depth and their turnover. Kuwait, despite poor performance, was the Arab stock market leader in these two measures. With a GDP of $35 billion at the end of 2003, the Kuwaiti share market depth (measured by market capitalization to GDP) stood at 101% and share turnover (value of shares traded to market capitalization) was 63%. For the same period, Saudi Arabia's share market was just under 40% and turnover ratio at 47.6% (SAMA, 2003, p. 143).

In most developed countries, the turnover ratio generally exceeds total market capitalization. Despite recent improvements, trading in the Saudi market is still relatively "thin", with nearly 48% of the total 1.96 billion supply of shares available tradable at the end of 2002, as illustrated in Table 6.3.

Table 6.3 Value of Saudi Arabian shares traded as % of market capitalization 1993-2003

Year	Value of shares traded (SR Million)	Market capitalization (SR Million)	Turnover ratio (%)	Market capitalization as % of GDP
1993	17,360	197,900	8.8%	44.6%
1994	24,871	144,892	17.2%	32.2%
1995	23,230	153,390	15.1%	32.0%
1996	25,397	171,982	14.8%	29.1%
1997	62,060	222,698	27.9%	36.0%
1998	51,509	159,907	32.2%	29.3%
1999	56,579	228,592	24.8%	37.9%
2000	65,293	255,000	25.6%	36.1%
2001	83,601	275,000	30.4%	39.4%
2002	133,500	280,487	47.6%	40.4%
2003*	44,100	367,100	48.0%	48.9%

* First quarter, 2003 (2003 turnover ratio annualized)
Source: *SAMA*, 2002, 2003, annual reports.

The Saudi stock market is also relatively small compared to the size of the GDP. In 2002, Saudi Arabia's stock market capitalization amounted to 40.4% of the country's nominal GDP as illustrated by Table 6.3. In 1993, the ratio stood at 44.6%; this suggests that despite the recent movements seen during 2003 and 2004, the Saudi stock market has been less active in fostering economic growth. The level of liquidity (measured in terms of value of shares traded as a % of GDP), while rising from around 4% in 1993 to 20% in 2002, is regarded as less liquid in comparison to other developed exchanges.

Again, one of the key reasons seems to be the almost static number of companies listed on the Saudi stock market. Between 1991 and 2003, only 14 new companies were listed, while 11 companies disappeared because of mergers, thus providing a net new addition of just one company to the existing 69 listed companies.

The Saudi Telecom Company (STC) share flotation in December, 2002, has given a tremendous boost to the Saudi stock market and we will look at how beneficial this new share market segment has been in terms of turnover and liquidity ratios. Despite the entry of STC, the amount of "free float" shares in the Saudi stock market is very low as illustrated in Table 6.4.

Table 6.4 shows that nearly half of all outstanding shares are outside market trading, despite a gradual improvement in the free-float compared to 1995, when it was estimated that the free-float was 47.7% (Azzam, 1997, p. 154). The Saudi Telecom Company flotation did indeed give a boost to the

Saudi stock market, for without this sector the free-float would have fallen to 48.8% in 2003.

Table 6.4 Total Saudi Arabian shares outstanding and those held by the public 2003

Sector	Total shares outstanding (Million)	Shares held by general public (Free-float) (Million)	Free-float as of % of total shares outstanding
Banking	378.9	226.8	60%
Industry	455.7	186.8	41%
Cement	118.9	80.8	68%
Services	177.5	127.8	72%
Electricity	765.7	290.9	38%
Agriculture	36.0	30.6	85%
Telecommunications	300.0	249.0	83%
Total	*2,232.7*	*1,192.7*	*53.4%*

Source: *SAMBA*, August, 2003, p. 21-22; NCCFI, 2003.

International comparisons

The Saudi market has out-performed all other major western markets over one-year, three-year and five-year periods ending in 2002, with the exception of the German (DAX) and French (CAC 40) markets in the five-year period. The last two turned in returns of 78.5% and 98.6% respectively (CCFI, 2003).

Figure 6.6 Correlation between S&P 500 Index and Saudi Arabia TASI (Tadawul All Share Index) 1994-2004

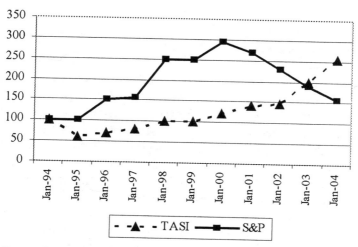

Source: *SAMBA*, 2003, *CCFI*, 2004.

Compared to the USA, the Saudi stock market has steadily risen and now out-performs the S&P 500 Index, as demonstrated in Figure 6.6, which correlates the S&P Index and the Saudi TASI or Tadawul All Share Index for the period 1994-2004.

To put the Saudi stock market performance in perspective, we must compare it with other emerging and developed world stock markets and analyze its correlation with international markets. This can highlight the differences and suggest the likely policy direction for improvement.

In 1998, the International Finance Corp (IFC) added Saudi stocks to its IFCC Composite Indexes for Emerging Markets (later merged with Standard and Poor). However, the inclusion is more a theoretical exercise than a practical one, as the Saudi market is closed to foreigners. Table 6.5 shows that the Saudi share of the index stood at 3.13%, with Taiwan at 13.38% and India at 6.51%. The whole Middle East is a mere 16% of the index.

Table 6.5 Market Weights in Standard & Poor International Finance Corporation Composite Index (IFCC) 2000

Markets	No. of stocks	Market capital ($Million)	Weight in IFCC composite (%)
Saudi Arabia	21	35,115	3.13
Taiwan	117	150,244	13.38
China	246	146,376	12.68
Brazil	88	103,837	9.25
Korea	160	92,881	8.27
Mexico	56	91,914	8.18
India	131	73,082	6.51
Middle East and Africa	357	178,282	15.88

Source: *IFCC Handbook*, 2000.

Table 6.6 compares the Saudi stock market with others in the emerging markets and developed countries in terms of relative performance. While Saudi Arabia might be one of the largest markets from a regional (Gulf or Arab) perspective, when compared with some of the emerging markets of the world or the developed markets, its significance diminishes in terms of the number of listed companies and market capitalization. The table shows that most markets have free access to foreign investors, although some have restrictions (such as China, India and Malaysia).

The comparative Table 6.6 shows that more developed countries had higher price/earning (P/E) ratios than Saudi Arabia, with Malaysian and Indian P/E ratios also on the high side. In terms of price to book value (P/B), the developed markets tended to be higher than the emerging markets.

Table 6.6 International stock market comparisons and Saudi Arabia 2000

Country	No. of listed companies	Market cap ($ Million)	Value traded ($ Million)	P/E	P/B	Dividend yield	Entry to foreigners
Saudi Arabia	*71*	*67,171*	*17,313*	*17.17*	*2.41*	*3.15*	*Closed*
Emerging:							
Brazil	459	226,152	101,282	11.53	1.42	3.67	Free
Mexico	179	125,204	45,340	13.0	1.68	1.42	Free
China	1086	580,991	721,538	49.9	3.62	0.46	Restricted
India	5937	148,064	509,812	16.8	2.6	1.52	Restricted
Malaysia	795	116,935	58,500	91.4	1.48	3.0	Restricted
South Africa	616	204,952	77,494	10.7	2.08	3.74	Free
Developed:							
USA	7525	1,510,4037	31,862,485	24.3	5.4	1.2	Free
Japan	2561	3,157,222	2,693,856	55.3	2.4	0.8	Free
UK	1904	2576992	1835278	19.1	3.7	2.2	Free
France	808	1446634	1083268	27.6	4.6	NA	Free
Germany	1022	1270243	1069120	19.5	4.0	NA	Free

Source: *Emerging Market Fact Book*, 2001.

In terms of dividend yield, Saudi Arabia scores well against others, especially in the developed markets, although Brazil and South Africa score higher than Saudi Arabia. Again, this is a theoretical exercise as the Saudi market is closed to foreign investors.

Sectoral performance of the Saudi market

Like any other stock market in the world, the Saudi composite stock market index (TASI) masks sectoral differences. Figure 6.7 sets out the market capitalization of the Saudi stock market as of September 2004 showing it had reached SR 889 billion – a staggering 142% rise over the market capitalization figure of SR 367 billion, seen earlier in Table 6.3.

The current sectoral composition of the stock market does not accurately reflect the composition of the overall economy. Between them, the banking sector and telecommunications (STC) accounted for slightly under 50% of total market capitalization. The service sector, which accounted for around 8% of GDP in 2002, accounted for 5% of stock market capitalization, while agriculture with 5.5% of GDP contributed less than one percent to Saudi stock market capitalization (SAMA, 2003, p. 134). The sectoral allocation becomes even more concentrated when we note that six Saudi companies – Riyad Bank, SAMBA, Al-Rajhi Bank, SABIC, Saudi Electric Company and Saudi Telecom Company – accounted for nearly 70% of the total market capitalization. Share price movements for these key players will undoubtedly influence the rest of the market. Table 6.7 sets out the main sector indicators in terms of outstanding shares, market capitalization and market weighing as of August, 2003.

Figure 6.7 Market capitalization by sector, as of September 2004
SR 889 billion

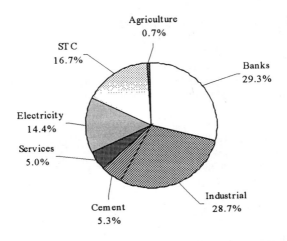

Source: *NCB*, October 2004. p.17.

Table 6.7 Saudi stock market sectoral analysis (August, 2003)

Sector	Outstanding shares (Millions)	Capitalization (SR Billions)	Marketing weighting (%)
Banking	378.9	152.8	32.29%
Industrial	455.7	87.05	18.39%
Cement	118.9	40.15	8.48%
Services	177.5	15.84	3.35%
Agriculture	36.0	1.59	0.34%
Electricity	765.7	58.77	12.42%
Telecoms	300.0	117.08	24.74%
Total	2,232.0	473.27	100.0%

Source: *SAMBA*, August, 2003, p. 21-22.

The banking and the telecommunications sectors accounted for 30% of outstanding shares and, at the same time, for 57% of market capitalization, again attesting to the narrow shareholder and company base of the current Saudi stock market.

According to analysts, 2003 was a record year for the Saudi stock market, which surged by 76.2%, helped by a combination of such strong macroeconomic fundamentals as a sizeable fiscal surplus and high profitability growth by the listed Saudi company market leaders.

Figure 6.8 below illustrates the dramatic rise in the TASI index for the year 2003, in which the 4000 level was broken in August followed by a record high of 6,455 points in May, 2004 (Arab News, 19 August 2003, 28 May 2004). Despite some profit taking sales, the TASI Index continued strong during 2004 and reached a new height of 7,000 in October 2004 and 8,000 in November 2004. This represented an 82% gain for 2004.

Figure 6.8 Saudi stock market 1999-2004 (TASI-Tadawul All Share Index)

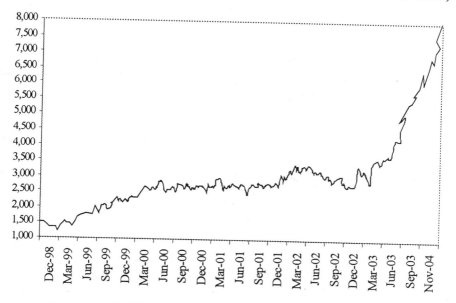

Source: *SAMBA*, 2003, *TASI*, 2004.

However, these were signs that the Saudi market was "overheating", and during May and June of 2004, the TASI index had daily and weekly falls of between 10% and 15%, causing some panic selling of even "star" performers. The Saudi Electricity Company's share price, which accounted for 12% of market capitalization, fell by a massive 37% to SR 101 in a one-week period in May, 2004, compared with a record high of SR 196 earlier the same month (Arab News, 28 May 2004). By all accounts, investors who have been in the Saudi stock market since 1999 have done extremely well, seeing their investments grow by 250% since 1 January 1999, especially in a period of falling domestic and international interest rates.

New listings such as SEC, together with the sharp rise in share prices, have created a "wealth effect" in the Saudi economy, adding a considerable amount of additional wealth, especially during 2003 and 2004. Some have calculated this additional wealth effect to be as high as 32.3% of nominal 2003 GDP (NCB, 2004, p. 9). However, it still remains to be seen whether this newfound "wealth effect" will start to penetrate into the local economy by way of the creation of real businesses and jobs, or if it will continue to be used in speculative share purchases.

The danger of share-holding concentration is that if institutional investors trigger selling sprees to realize profits, they could leave the small investors exposed to nominal and real losses and reduced wealth positions. Smaller investors would be discouraged from participating further in the Saudi stock market and seek "safer" investments, such as traditional real estate markets.

Investor behaviour

While extensive analysis has been performed on the actual mechanics of stock market price movements in Saudi Arabia, little research has been carried out on Saudi investor behaviour. According to the limited research carried out in this area, results obtained have interesting implications for the new Saudi Capital Market Law. The survey shows that the number of male and female investors reached 250,000 in 2004, compared with 50,000 in 2002 (Khoshhal, 2004). The investor behaviour research surveyed Saudis of both sexes who had actively traded in the local markets for one day or more. The data was analyzed using the statistical package for social sciences (SPSS). The results were as follows for "Saudi Individual Stock Traders" or SIST:

- The levels of financial and technical knowledge among the SISTs were below average; 80% had no formal training in stock trading
- The majority of SISTs were risk takers who believed that they would continue to make high profits on the Saudi stock market, despite falls
- Bank brokerage services were perceived to be below average,
- In picking stocks, some 40% of SISTs depended on technical analysis, some 32% depended on financial analysis, while 25% depended on other people's opinions and Internet forums. Only 3% went with their personal "feelings"
- The 25-35 age groups seemed to make the most profit on the Saudi stock market, which the research survey correlated to higher levels of education and formal course training
- The lowest level of profits were found amongst those who depended on others' opinions, while the highest was achieved by those who depended on technical analysis
- Respondents with the highest education levels (masters and doctorates) depended on financial analysis and made medium-to-high profits. Those with lower levels of education depended on others' opinions and made the lowest profits

- Respondents with lower risk aversion depended solely on financial information in their decision-making and realized medium profits

The Saudi research seemed to corroborate similar research results for developed markets (Ackert et al., 2003). This Saudi Individual Stock Traders Survey has important implications for the future development of the Saudi stock market. We have already seen that there is dissatisfaction with current Saudi commercial banks' brokerage services, due to high commission charges and lack of competition (Wilson, 2004, p. 70).

The New Capital Market removes commercial bank monopoly privileges by introducing independent brokerage dealers. This could force Saudi banks to establish separate companies to deal with the stock market in order to remain in this line of business. The need for more specialized technical training for investment in general, and for stock market trading in particular, is apparent from the research survey. The use of Internet forums to obtain feedback and tips was interesting, as the new Capital Market authority could use the Internet to provide investors with information and technical analysis on individual stocks.

Figure 6.9 Regional and domestic contributory factors on the Saudi stock market

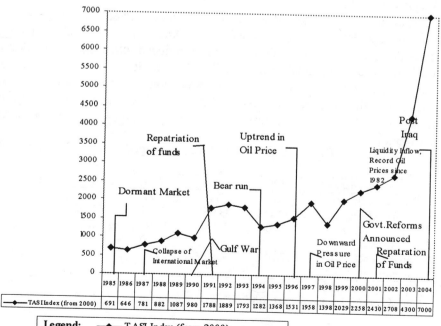

	1985	1986	1987	1988	1989	1990	1991	1992	1993	1994	1995	1996	1997	1998	1999	2000	2001	2002	2003	2004
TASI Index (from 2000)	691	646	781	882	1087	980	1788	1889	1793	1282	1368	1531	1958	1398	2029	2258	2430	2708	4300	7000

Legend: —◆— TASI Index (from 2000)

However, it is not just technical or financial analysis, let alone personal feelings, that influence market prices, but rather external uncontrolled events that can and do influence market conditions.

Figure 6.9 sets out major regional and domestic factors that seemed to have a direct influence on Saudi stock market prices.

Figure 6.9 shows the relative positive correlation between oil prices and Saudi market prices, as well as regional tensions, although the 2003 Iraq war and continuing violence in that country during 2004 did not have the anticipated degree of negative impact on Saudi stock prices. The announcement of domestic economic reforms in the Kingdom seems to have also contributed to both the recent "bull" run in the local market, and the beginning of some Saudi capital repatriation from 1991.

Saudi mutual fund market

The mutual fund market has exploded in size and diversity of products all over the world and now constitutes a large and important segment of the financial and capital markets. The U.S. market, the largest in the world, saw the market share for mutual funds reach $5.8 trillion in 2000 from $371 billion in 1984, according to the number one U.S. fund manager, Fidelity, which handled around $550 billion in its institutional retirement group alone (Fidelity, 2002).

The history of the Saudi mutual funds market has been equally impressive and today Saudi Arabia has the largest mutual funds industry in the Arab world. Mutual funds were first introduced into the Saudi market by the National Commercial Bank (NCB) through its "open-ended" *Al Ahli Short-Term Dollar Fund* in 1979. It was aimed at the smaller investor, particularly the expatriate worker, and it quickly became a success with this market segment due to the fund's low service charges, ease of entry and redemption.

Table 6.8 Growth in Saudi managed funds

Characteristics	1992	1995	1998	2002	2004 [1]
Number of funds	52	71	121	143	170
Number of subscribers	33,162	33,051	69,543	165,044	172,197
Domestic assets (SR Million)	5,300	5,800	12,001	32,827	37,695
Foreign assets (SR Million)	7,100	7,200	13,008	15,999	16,650

[1] First Quarter, 2004
Source: *SAMA*, Annual Report, 2003, 1st *Quarter Statistical Bulletin*, 2004.

Over the years, public interest and demand for this financial product has risen sharply, as the figures in Table 6.8 show, with assets under management in all mutual funds standing at SR 54.2 billion by end of first quarter, 2004.

The growth in fund assets took off in 1998 after a flat growth rate in the early 1990s, when total assets were around SR 12-13 billion. Similar increases were registered in both the number of funds managed by banks and the number of subscribers. These stood at 170 and 172,000 respectively by the first quarter of 2004. The outstanding feature of Saudi mutual funds has been the shift towards domestic investment of fund assets, as illustrated in Figure 6.10.

Figure *6.10* Assets of investment funds at domestic banks

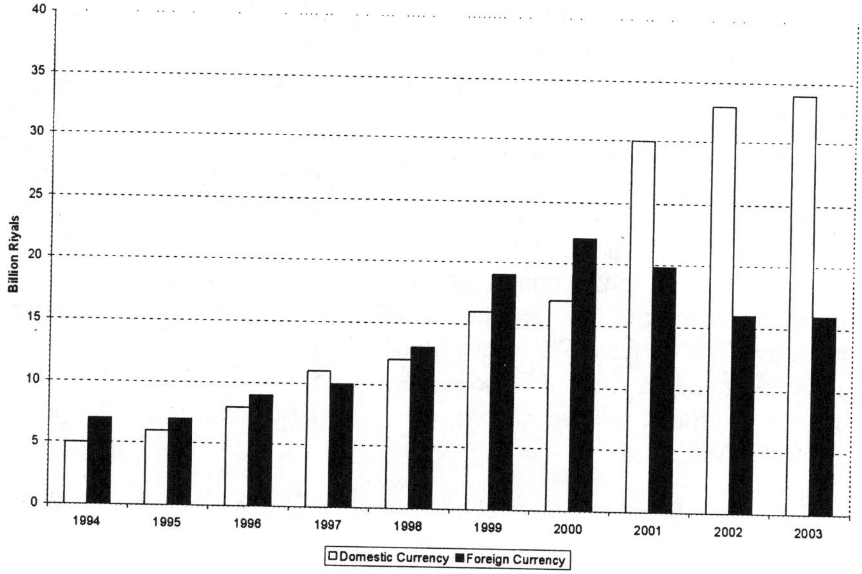

Source: *SAMA*, 2003.

The causes of the switch towards domestic assets are many, including the sharp rise in Saudi share prices compared to international equity markets, the growth of Islamic mutual funds, and the growing expertise over time amongst Saudi banks in managing such funds by themselves.

The reasons for investing in Saudi mutual funds are also varied. Only a decade ago, most Saudis looked to their employers – whether in the government or private sector – to provide them with a pension, but an increasing number of Saudis (and expatriates living in the Kingdom) have now invested in these funds as a form of retirement hedging. The attraction of holding mutual funds is apparent: pooling the resources of small investors and sharing risk in many diversified stock/bond portfolios while minimizing transaction costs and information costs. Mutual funds also provide greater liquidity, meeting investors' need for cash.

As mentioned earlier, the growth of mutual funds in Saudi Arabia has been impressive over such a short period of time. Initially, the focus was on select high net worth or "private bank" clients, but all Saudi banks have now expanded their target market to include the professional middle income and top-tier expatriates. Competition has been fierce amongst banks and some have developed in-house expertise to manage their funds, while others have established strategic alliances with international fund managers to design funds exclusively for their Saudi clients. Those Saudi banks with foreign affiliation and part-ownership such as Saudi British Bank, SAMBA, Saudi Fransi and others had a head-start over the "pure" Saudi banks such as NCB and Riyad Bank. However, as evidenced from recent individual banks' fund performances, all Saudi banks seem to have developed domestic expertise and international alliances, with the "pure" local banks doing as well, if not better, than the "Saudized" banks.

SAMA has been a benevolent supervisor and regulator of mutual funds; 1997 modifications of rules and regulations around mutual funds have made it easier for banks to issue new mutual funds. A Saudi equity fund can now be fully invested in local equities, provided they have sufficient liquidity for redemption. Since the new regulations of 1997, a single investor can now hold up to 10% (up from 5%) of net assets of a particular Saudi Riyal mutual fund. Within such a fund, a bank is allowed to own up to 5% of the issued equity of any Saudi joint stock company, instead of less than 1% under the previous SAMA rules.

Table 6.9 Saudi commercial banks mutual fund market share 2002

Bank	Closed funds	Open-ended funds	Fund assets (SR billion)	% Share	Number of subscribers ('000)	% Share
Riyad Bank	-	22	7.2	13.9%	70.3	42.6%
Arab National Bank	1	19	3.4	6.6%	5.8	3.5%
SAMBA	-	20	3.2	6.3%	6.9	4.2%
NCB	1	17	23.2	45.0	51.0	30.9%
Saudi Fransi	1	16	1.5	2.9%	4.8	2.9%
Saudi British	1	15	7.4	14.4%	12.4	7.5%
Saudi Hollandi	-	13	1.4	2.7%	3.0	1.8%
Al Rajhi	-	12	4.0	7.8%	10.5	6.4%
Al Jazira	-	5	0.2	0.4%	0.3	0.2%
TOTAL	*4*	*139*	*51.5*	*100%*	*165.0*	*100%*

Source: *SAMA*, 2003, Annual Report, p. 150.

Table 6.9 highlights Saudi banks' market share in the local mutual fund sector. National Commercial Bank (NCB) took the largest share of assets with 45% of the market, while Riyad Bank headed the market share of subscribers. Bank Al Jazira, the smallest of the Saudi banks, had 0.2% of both markets.

Table 6.9 masks differences in the types of mutual funds managed by the Saudi banks. According to current SAMA data, the largest share of funds were those in equity investments, non-interest or *hallal* and short-term cash/money markets. These accounted for 36%, 20% and 15% respectively of the 135 open-ended mutual funds.

In Saudi Arabia, the largest Saudi bank, NCB dominates the market in terms of "Islamic" or non-interest *Shariah*-compliant trade finance or equity funds.

Figure 6.11 illustrates the phenomenal growth in NCB's Islamic Mutual Funds, which had overtaken its 'traditional" funds by 1999.

Figure 6.11 Asset growth of NCB's Islamic vs. conventional funds

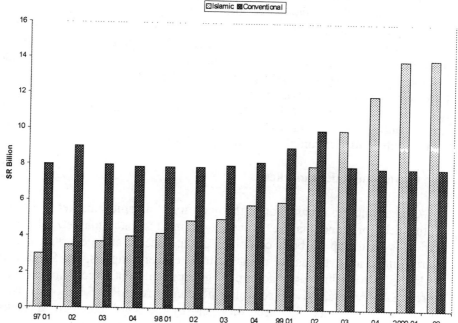

Source: *NCB, Second Quarter*, 2000, *NCB, Economist*, p. 10.

According to NCB, there is a growing desire among Saudi investors to participate in Islamic-based mutual funds that are *Shariah*-compliant and are consistent with the principle of equity participation and risk-sharing. For the Saudi economy, this type of funds not only improves market liquidity, but also provides risk diversification opportunities in medium to long-term maturity structures, although most of the Islamic mutual funds started through low-risk and modest-return instruments such as *Murabaha* (short-term secured commodity trade finance) and *Ijara* (structured medium-term leasing).

According to a bank survey carried out by NCB, most participants in mutual funds are Saudi males, the majority of whom have college degrees. Nearly half of the female investors were in the 18-25 age group. According to the survey, the most important objective for investing in the mutual funds was to secure a comfortable retirement. About 38% of those surveyed said they would not tolerate any risk, while 40% were prepared to take some risk, suggesting that a very small proportion of Saudi mutual fund investors are ready for higher risk (NCB, 2000).

The risk profile seems to be different from those investing directly in the equity markets, which we examined earlier, but given that a large number are investing in the mutual funds for long-term retirement pension objectives, this risk aversion is not surprising.

Based on the 2002 data in Table 6.9, the average investment per person is around SR 312,000, reinforcing the fact that mutual funds are mostly investment instruments for the upper income groups, while lower to middle income groups depend mainly on bank deposits or individual share purchases to grow their savings.

In conclusion, the outlook for the Saudi mutual market looks bright, with growth anticipated in total assets, the number of funds and the number of participants. *Shariah*-compliant funds have the most potential.

The Government debt market

Another important indicator of the maturity of a capital market is the size of the debt or bond market structure. In most capital markets, the debt market is made up of both corporate private sector and government debt instruments. However, as we pointed out in earlier chapters, the Saudi debt market is overwhelmingly made up of government debt. According to most current SAMA data, private securities accounted for SR 7.6 billion or 4.7% out of the total outstanding securities held by the Saudi commercial banks, SR 160.9 billion (SAMA, April, 2004). Government debt to the banks amounted to 26.6% of the Saudi commercial banks' consolidated balance sheet as of April, 2004. Total government commercial bank debt reached SR 153.3 billion in the same month, down from a peak of SR 159.5 billion the previous month. This was the first serious sign of government repayment of the national debt due to high world oil prices in late 2003 and early 2004. However, the size of the domestic government debt is estimated to be around SR 660 billion or 95% of GDP as of the end of 2003.

The Saudi government debt is almost entirely domestically owed, and in addition to the local banks, it is also owed to the major Saudi government pension organizations. There are no precise breakdowns of the nature of the government debt holdings by various institutions, but according to SAMBA, some indication of the breakdown of the debt was revealed by an article written by a member of the *Majlis Al Shoura,* which provided the first glimpse of these breakdowns (SAMBA, February, 2003, p. 16).

According to SAMBA, the breakdown was as follows, with no time period indicated for the figures provided.

Amount of debt	% of total debt	Sector holding debt
• SR 235.7 billion	36.1%	• Special government bondholders – contractors in lieu of late payments
• SR 37 billion	5.7%	• Farmers
• SR 137.9 billion	21.0%	• Saudi Pension and Retirement Agency (SPRA)
• SR 68.4 billion	10.5%	• General Organization for Social Insurance (GOSI)
• SR 120 billion	18.3%	• Saudi commercial banks
• SR 54.8 billion	8.4%	• Other establishments and unspecified funds

Total government debt amounted to SR 653.8 billion, according to the source. From the level of debt owed to the Saudi commercial banks (SR 120 billion), one can only deduce that the estimated breakdowns were for the period 2001, given that, as of December 2001, government bank debt stood at SR 121.8 billion (SAMA, April, 2004, p. 23).

The above information points out that the government sector holds about 40% of the public debt itself, with 60% held by banks, contractors and farmers. According to the International Monetary Fund (IMF), very little of this debt is short-term in nature; the average maturity of outstanding government debt is seven years. This reduces the risk of rollover of the debt. According to the IMF, the amount due in less than one year is 7%, and between 1 to 5 years is 35% (IMF, 1997).

At present, there is a very limited two-way bond market in Saudi Arabia. SAMA, as discussed earlier, is the only market maker for the bonds, with *Repos* and *Reverse-Repos* introduced over the past few years to add liquidity to the system. Bank-guaranteed commercial paper was first issued in 2000 and such corporate debt is a mere $500 million for a few prime names, although other family businesses are in discussion with local banks about issuing commercial paper. While the primary market has grown in size, diversity of maturities and instruments issued, the market organization and distribution processes has not progressed correspondingly. The primary market development, in which the government bond issues are the most important part, appears largely to be supported by the existence of captive sources of bank funding and by government organizations. The secondary market remains weak and is one of the areas slated for reform in the new Capital Market Law.

Conclusion

While significant strides have been made in the development of the Saudi Capital Market over recent years, some further changes are needed to make the Saudi market even more attractive to both domestic and international investors. Countries are competing for investment capital; either they constantly try to improve or they will be left behind. Saudi Arabia, while blessed with a national private sector capital surplus, needs as well to attract international investments in order to establish a better investment, financial and regulatory environment that will maximize their potential to attract investment. Table 6.10 summarizes the changing pace and face of the Saudi capital market.

Table 6.10 The changing face of the Saudi capital market

1970s	1980s	1990s	2000 onwards
• No disclosure	• Regulatory regimes improving	• Technology utilization	• Commercial paper and bonds
• External funding on selective basis	• External funding	• Specialized funds	• Family businesses going public
• Poor regulatory and legal structure	• Government soft loans	• Government debt increasing	• Mergers and acquisitions
• Commercial bank funding on secured basis	• Syndicated loans	• Islamic financing	• More disclosure and transparency
• Dominance of family companies	• Some disclosure available	• Foreign ownership on joint venture basis	• Securities and Exchange Commissions
		• Non-recourse finance	• Foreign Inward Investment
			• Privatization
			• IPOs
			• Securitization
			• Islamic financing

The Saudi capital market took off during the 1990s, with the beginning of domestic economic reforms in the field of privatization and liberalization, especially when the country opened up to the outside world for inward investments. The post-2000 era requires an even bolder capital market reform program to address several key issues highlighted in this chapter.

First, the government should vigorously encourage and support listings of new companies on the Saudi stock market. The Ministry of Commerce can re-examine some of its stringent guidelines, procedures for listing and the laborious documentation that accompanies conversion to joint stock companies. The current number of listed companies and their narrow sectoral basis cannot be sustained. Research carried out amongst the top 1,000 Saudi non-listed companies revealed that around 137 new companies could be listed in the Saudi bourse using current Ministry of Commerce joint stock company "benchmarks", as set out earlier in Table 6.2. The study indicated that for year-end 2003 this would raise the total number of listed companies to 205 from the current 69, increase market capitalization by SR 472 billion, thereby taking Saudi market capitalization to around SR 900 billion from levels of SR 450-500 billion (Rofali, 2003). However, as noted earlier in this chapter, Saudi stock market capitalization had already reached SR 890 billion levels by September 2004, without the additional impact of the new IPO listings from Ettihad Ettisalat. An additional net capitalization of around SR 500 billion from new listed companies would take Saudi market capitalization to SR 1,390 billion levels, making the Saudi stock market the largest in the Islamic world.

Table 6.11 summarizes the estimated benefits to the Saudi capital market through the projected additional new company listings.

Given limited public data for major Saudi private companies, the research on potential new listings has certain limitations, as the major variable used in calculating the potential increase in market capitalization was the current average sector price-earning ratios, along with the earnings for those sectors. Of more interest was the wider sectoral allocation of the proposed new company listings, especially in the industrial and services sectors. According to Table 6.11 the service sector would add another 112 new companies, with a market capitalization of around SR 440 billion – nearly 90% of the existing Saudi capital market capitalization. This would break the cycle of sharp share-price fluctuations currently dominated by a few companies in a few sectors as we discussed earlier. The study projects a virtual doubling of limited companies in the industrial sector, with an additional 20 companies joining the stock market. Given the government's objective for economic diversification and emphasis for the private sector to expand the economic base of the country, such an increase in the number of listed companies could help with stated government objectives. Based on the research results in Table 6.11, Saudi market depth would rise significantly, taking the market capitalization of GDP ratio to 128% from current levels below 50% for 2002/2003, as laid out earlier in Table 6.3.

Table 6.11 Estimated increase in current Saudi stock market through new listings by sectors and capitalization

Sector	New company listing turnover (SR Million)	Earnings ratio (%)	Earnings (SR Million)	Sector average P/E ratio	Expected new company listings	2003 listed companies	Expected combined company listings	Expected additional market capitalization (SR Million)	2003 market capitalization (SR Million)	Expected total market capitalization (SR Million)
Banks	5,111	6%	307	15.9	1	9	10	4,907	145,696	150,603
Industry	12,221	12%	1,467	17.2	20	23	43	25,224	80,588	105,812
Cement	-	-	-	-	-	8	8	-	38,497	38,497
Services	156,048	10%	15,605	28.2	112	17	129	440,055	15,121	455,176
Electricity	-	-	-	-	-	1	1	-	47,285	47,285
Agriculture	3,359	4%	134	18.02	4	10	14	2,415	1,499	3,914
Telecommunication	-	-	-	-	-	1	1	-	87,000	87,000
Total	176,739				137	69	206	472,601	415,687	888,288

Source: Rofali, 2003, KFUPM.

Second, besides encouraging increased listings, the government needs to explore how to broaden the shareholding base. The closed, family-owned nature of many companies in the region and in Saudi Arabia seems to have been transplanted to the publicly-quoted Saudi joint stock companies through share ownership concentration. The government should examine the extent to which a family or an "affiliated" family grouping can own a particular company, in order to provide more investor confidence. Insufficient transparency and insider trading engender vulnerability, and the government must ensure that the required quarterly and annual audited accounts are released on time, along with enforcement of legal action against insider trading. A stock market that is not properly regulated becomes a speculative paradise, resulting in price manipulation and market inefficiencies (Azzam, 2002).

A third policy shift that can help in deepening the Saudi capital market is the privatization of government holdings in public-owned corporations. A significant start has been made with the partial sale of government-owned shares in the Saudi Telecommunications Company (STC). This reinvigorated the Saudi stock market in 2003 and added an extra 300 million shares to the market. The planned partial and full privatization of several key sectors in 2004 and early 2005 should keep the reform momentum going, creating the additional employment and growth opportunities that Saudi Arabia is seeking.

It is anticipated that the newly passed Capital Market Law will also help in providing the sort of corporate finance structure that has never existed in Saudi Arabia, which will enable a transfer of financial knowledge to Saudi corporate finance professionals. Tasks that were once performed offshore by "suitcase bankers" will now be done onshore in Saudi Arabia. The empowered capital market could also be the catalyst in developing the Islamic financial market and in expanding the existing demand for Islamic securitization of asset financing. Mergers and acquisitions for the Saudi family businesses could be an important service provided by the Capital Market Law.

Above all – and this must be emphasized continuously – the new Saudi Capital Market Authority must carry out its regulatory responsibilities vigorously. Capital markets that function well offer their investors the twin virtues of transparency and protection. Through transparency, investors will be able to see exactly what is going on inside the listed companies; they will feel protected if they see that their money is safeguarded from intermediaries. Such changes in attitude and regulatory frameworks take decades to achieve. The omens are good. In fact, the Finance Minister has publicly stated that, "The key goal of the new regulatory body is ensuring transparency and encouraging investor confidence" (Saudi Press Agency, July 2004). The road that Saudi Arabia has taken could be a long one, but the Kingdom has achieved much in the development work already. If this is now put into practice, the new Capital Market Regulatory Authority in Saudi Arabia will become one of the leading regulators in the world, and the Saudi capital markets will become one of the most productive developments that Saudi Arabia has witnessed.

Summary of the key points:

- *Efficient capital markets can play an effective role in recycling capital surpluses and promoting economic growth. The Saudi private sector has demonstrated that it has the liquidity to participate in any deepening of the current capital market.*
- *The Saudi capital market has evolved from the formal establishment of a stock market in the 1980's to the passing of the Capital Market Law in 2004 which created an independent Securities Exchange Commission (SEC) to oversee the stock market.*
- *The establishment of the new SEC cold help to overcome some of the previous obstacles in expanding the capital market, namely an increase in the number of listed companies, increase in the number of shareholders, expansion of brokerage and investment advisory services and licencing of non-bank financial institutions.*
- *The benefits of the new Capital Market Law could be felt in several areas: potential to draw back Saudi resources invested abroad, growth of non-oil financial services sector, improve risk management practices, and respond to the demand of infrastructure services.*
- *In terms of performance, the Saudi capital market dominates the rest of the Arab world in size and has registered impressive performances, especially during 2003-2004 when it outperformed most international market indices. However, the Saudi market still lags in term of turnover ratio, and market capitalization as % of GDP.*
- *The total "free float" shares for trading is around 50% of all listed shares. This could benefit from additional planned government privatization sales and private sector IPO's.*
- *The capital market is characterized by a high degree of sectoral concentration and the dominance of banking, electricity and telecommunications, with 6 companies accounting for nearly 70% of the total market capitalization.*

- *Investor behavior in the capital market is characterized by a mixture of sophisticated technical analysis and those with no formal training in stock trading who depend on opinion and make the lowest profits.*
- *The Saudi mutual fund market is now relatively mature with a broad range of investment vehicles catering to middle income Saudi investors. A discernible growth in demand for Islamic investments has been noted.*
- *The government debt market is an important element in the capital market, but government paper is not yet publically traded. Opening this market to the public could add liquidity and depth, as well as the further privatization of state assets.*

Critical thinking

1. "The new Capital Market Law has overcome all previous problems that restricted an efficient market operation". Do you think this is a fair assessment? What future measures could improve the new Capital Market Law?

2. "Without transparency no markets can function effectively". How transparent is the Saudi capital market today compared with twenty years ago?

3. "Investing in the Saudi stock market guarantees profits as demonstrated by its recent performance compared with other markets". How comfortable are you in making such a recommendation? What have been the main driving forces that have led to the Saudi market's recent performance? Can they be sustained?

4. What are the effects of introducing new listed companies to the Saudi stock market on (a) current listed companies, (b) market performance, and (c) investor behavior?

5. What have been the benefits from the growth of the Saudi mutual funds industry? Why do people invest in them?

Chapter 7

THE PRIVATE SECTOR: CHALLENGES AND OPPORTUNITIES

It is not the crook in modern business that we fear, but the honest man who does not know what he is doing.

Owen D. Young

Learning outcomes

By the end of this section, you should understand:

- *The growing responsibility placed on the private sector to diversify the economic base*
- *The operating framework under which the private sector works (legal, corporate, economic)*
- *Foreign participation in the private sector*
- *The importance of Small and Medium sized (SME's) industries*
- *Saudi family business structures*
- *Saudi women and the national economy*
- *Government and business relations in Saudi Arabia*
- *Promotion private sector growth*

Introduction

In spite of tangible past accomplishments, Saudi Arabia faces future challenges that, if not addressed, will be difficult to overcome. One key objective is for the private sector to take the lead in reducing its reliance on oil revenues and in diversifying its economy. As we will explain in the chapters that follow, the Kingdom has not yet created a sufficient number of jobs for its Saudi population, nor has it adequately diversified its economy.

The Saudi government signalled its intent to gradually "disengage" from the economy and let the private sector assume a greater share of the economic transformation of the economy when it announced in mid-November, 2002, its massive privatization plans to open up 20 sectors to the private sector (Saravia, 2002). To assume this responsibility, the private sector faces both a unique historical challenge as well as potential opportunities. It must come of age in order to transform itself into the dominant economic sector and to provide self-sustaining, steady economic growth. A viable state-private sector relationship is essential to attaining this objective. How these two sectors co-operate is vital to the private sector's success in taking the lead economic role.

The aim of this chapter is to assess the inherent strengths and weaknesses of the private sector in meeting the challenges and responsibilities that the Saudi government is devolving to it. An important aspect of the present study will be to assess whether an appropriate business environment exists in the Kingdom to enable the private sector take up these challenges.

The operating framework

Modern commercially-oriented societies operate under certain frameworks that enable the private sector to carry out its function with a degree of certainty. A successful government-private sector partnership depends on some key services being provided by the state to enable the private sector to flourish. These are: an effective bureaucratic framework, a clear legal regulatory system and the appropriate infrastructure to deliver the necessary goods and services. The overall aim is for the private sector to be able to produce desired goods and services in the most efficient and cost-effective manner, compared to the public sector, thus freeing the government to concentrate on providing the most suitable operating environment for the private sector (Awaji, 1989).

The legal setting

As in other Islamic nations, the fundamental source of law in Saudi Arabia is Islamic law or *Sharia'h*. The *Sharia'h* consists of the Holy Koran, the teachings of the Prophet Mohammad (*Pbuh*), called the *Sunnah*, and the writings of renowned Islamic legal scholars. Several other sources of law elaborate on the *Sharia'h* and govern commercial relations. Decrees are adopted by the Saudi Council of Ministers and provide broad rules for particular areas, such as commercial law, labour law and taxation. These laws are published in the Saudi Official Gazette, *Umm Al Qura*.

In the past, potential new laws covering commercial activities, not generally open for discussion, were considered by ad-hoc ministerial committees and legal experts before being promulgated by Royal Decree. Other, less important regulations were developed within relevant ministries.

Interpretations and enforcement of these regulations were executed at ministerial levels, as were elaborations and provision of more specific requirements. Such interpretations could vary, which is not conducive to long-term private sector business planning.

If a dispute arises, a company may sue – or be sued – in Saudi court. As such, both Saudi and non-Saudi businessmen should be aware of how potential disputes are settled in the Kingdom. This issue becomes more important with Saudi Arabia's imminent entry into the World Trade Organization (WTO) and the encouragement of Foreign Direct Investment (FDI) as part of the ongoing liberalization initiatives. If a dispute arises between a foreign company and a Saudi party, the case can be heard in Saudi Arabia, unless specified otherwise by both parties. Saudi law prohibits government agencies from disputing a contract in another country. Table 7.1 sets out the main legal and commercial systems for settling disputes operating in Saudi Arabia.

Table 7.1 Saudi Arabia: Legal, commercial and dispute settlement system

Legal System	*Observations*
• Judicial System	• Consists of both general courts and specialized tribunals. Courts may consist of a combination of judges and non-judges. Decisions can be quick or lengthy. Decisions may be appealed.
• Jurisdiction	• *Sharia'h* courts are courts of general jurisdiction. *Sharia'h* judges preside over almost any disputes, unless Saudi law provides otherwise. *Sharia'h* judges apply Islamic law to decide a case. Decisions may be appealed.
• Board of Grievance	• Has exclusive power to decide disputes over Saudi government contracts and may decide some types of commercial disputes. Unlike *Sharia'h,* the board observes a system of *precedent.* Decisions may be appealed.
• Civil Rights Directorate	• Responsible for enforcing judgement of Saudi courts or tribunals.
• Negotiable Instruments Committee	• Decides on cases involving bills of exchange, promissory notes and checks.
• The SAMA Committee	• Resolves disputes between banks and clients
• Conciliation Committee	• At the Saudi Chambers of Commerce, assisting in problems between foreign partners and Saudi companies, especially in agency matters.
• Preliminary Committee for Settlement of Labour Disputes	• Hears all matters related to labour and employee relations.

One issue that the Saudi government is addressing is *precedence* in commercial disputes and judgements in *Sharia'h* courts. Unlike the Board of Grievance, which observes a system of precedence in reaching a judgement, the *Sharia'h* system allows individual judges to pass down judgements based on their personal interpretations, rather than precedence for similar cases. As such, under the current Saudi judicial system, it becomes hard for specialized *Sharia'h* courts and judges to evolve into ones that can handle more complex commercial cases, especially involving multinationals from different countries.

Saudi Arabia has ratified several international legal agreements, the most important being the Convention on the Settlement of Investment Disputes between States and Nationals, and the Convention on Foreign Arbitral Awards. In July, 1995, an agreement on legal protection for guaranteed foreign investment between the Multilateral Investment Guarantee Agency (MIGA) and Saudi Arabia was signed (Sheikh and Abdelrahman, 2003).

The corporate setting

Saudi law recognizes nine different forms of business organization structures. Three involve limited liability structures, while the others do not. Firms that are owned entirely by Saudi citizens may either be limited partnerships or joint-stock companies; in addition, more than one such company may enter joint venture agreements or form co-operative societies. Table 7.2 below sets out by legal structure the cumulative number of companies operating in Saudi Arabia as of 2002.

Table 7.2 Companies operating in Saudi Arabia by legal structure (2002)

Type of companies	Number	Capital SR Million
1. Joint-stock companies	121	81,305.6
2. Limited liability partnerships	7,816	83,567.3
Saudi	6,159	52,238.6
Joint venture	1,421	29,896.9
Non-Saudi	236	1,431.8
3. Joint-liability partnership	2,630	3,747.6
Saudi	2,593	3,714.8
Joint venture	19	15.7
Non-Saudi	18	17.1
4. Mixed liability partnerships	1,054	2,747.1
Saudi	1,043	2,709.7
Joint venture	8	21.9
Non-Saudi	3	15.5
5. Mixed liability partnerships by shares	1	0.5
Total	11, 622	171,368.1

Source: *SAMA*, 2003, p. 251.

Establishment of joint stock companies in the Kingdom requires ministerial, or sometimes even a Royal Decree. The formation of the other types of companies is less complicated, involving registration of partnership deeds with a notary public. The creation and registration of the new company must be advertised in the Companies Register at the Ministry of Commerce.

Foreign firms wishing to carry out business in Saudi Arabia have a number of options, ranging from the appointment of local agents, or *wakeels,* to the formation of partnerships with Saudis. Table 7.2 indicates that this was the favourite route of local companies, as 1,421 joint venture limited liability companies were operating with a combined capital investment of SR 29.9 billion as of 2002. Since 2001, when the Kingdom started to encourage FDI, wholly-owned foreign companies began to operate legally under their own name without a local *wakeel* or partner (SAGIA, 2002). Table 7.2 shows that between them, joint stock companies and limited liability partnerships account for almost 96% of company capital. However, joint stock companies represent 1% of companies and 47% of total capital. It is from amongst these 121 registered joint stock companies that the 68 listed Saudi companies operating on the Saudi stock market are derived.

The economic setting

We have to analyze the structure of the operating companies by economic activity in terms of employment, efforts towards Saudization and contribution to the national economy to better understand whether the private sector has achieved some of the diversification objectives the government set for it. Table 7.3 sets out the key economic indicators by major productive sectors for 2001.

Table 7.3 Economic indicators for major economic sectors (2001)

Index	Petroleum and Minerals	Wholesale and Retail	Electricity, Water, Gas	Construction	Manufacturing	Real Estate	Restaurant, Hotels.
Total employees	65,139	1,048,749	57,347	461,106	549,207	32,014	163,412
- Saudi	52,618	258,100	38,087	46,928	99,136	16,117	25,831
- Non Saudi	12,521	790,649	19,260	414,178	450,071	15,937	137,581
Employee Compensation (Million SR)	13,200	21,588	5,450	11,470	17,036	457	2,747
Revenues (Million SR)	259,045	245,898	21,289	55,570	169,018	2,638	15,216
Expenditure (Million SR)	29,189	211,543	19,799	46,981	129,787	1,608	11,671
Fixed Assets (Million SR)	18,637	N/A	7,043	3,795	14,892	1,658	373

Source: *CDS, 2003 Annual Statistical Yearbook*, 2003.
N/A not available.

Table 7.3 highlights several important characteristics of present-day Saudi economic sector activities. Clearly the bulk of employees – Saudi and non-Saudi – is concentrated in the wholesale and retail sectors. This includes the single-owner proprietorships and smaller partnerships that are at the heart of the so-called Small and Medium-sized Enterprises, or SMEs, which we will discuss in greater detail later in this chapter. Except for the petroleum and minerals, the electricity and gas, and the real estate sector, Saudis are in the minority in the other economic sectors. The Saudi Aramco oil company dominates the petroleum sector and the 80% level of Saudization in this sector demonstrates the commitment of the Saudi government to implement such a policy, at least in sectors that it controls. This is also evident in the other government-owned sectors, such as electricity, water and gas, where the Saudization level is around 67%. The overall Saudization level for all sectors stood at 22% as of 2001. The lowest levels of Saudization are found in the wholesale and retail, construction and manufacturing sectors, with construction at the bottom at around 10%. Table 7.3 also sheds some interesting light on why government jobs seem to be preferred by most Saudis over employment in the private sector. Table 7.4 sets out the average compensation level per employee for each of the economic sectors, as well as the gross and net return per employee in these sectors for the year 2001.

Table 7.4 Saudi Arabia: average compensation, gross and net return per employee by major economic sectors (2001)

Sector	Average Compensation/ Employee(SR)	Gross Return	Net Return
Petroleum/Minerals	202,000	3,970,000	3,528,000
Wholesale/Retail	20,500	234,000	32,700
Electricity/Water/Gas	95,000	371,000	25,900
Construction	24,800	120,000	18,600
Manufacturing	31,000	307,000	71,400
Real Estate	14,200	82,300	32,100
Restaurant	16,800	93,000	21,000

Source: *Table 7.3, CDS, Annual Statistical Yearbook*, 2003.

The average compensation package per employee in the petroleum sector towers over all others at SR 202,000 per annum, with the lowest in real estate at SR 14,000 levels. The other government sectors (electricity, water and gas) show the second highest level of compensation per employee at SR 95,000 while manufacturing compensation is around SR 31,000. However, with the exception of the oil sector, the net return per employee changes, with the private sector return being higher than those for the government sector. This is a worrying implication for future privatization plans of such sectors as water, gas and electricity, because private sector operators looking for cost reductions to improve net margins might target the labour force in such industries for reduction. The spectre of increased unemployment in Saudi Arabia would not be politically acceptable and this could be one reason for the delay in implementing the Kingdom's privatization plans.

Table 7.4 also highlights the relative inefficiency of the wholesale and retail sector that registered the sharpest drop between gross and net return per employee. However, the average compensation levels per employee mark wide differences between Saudi and non-Saudi employees. The average monthly earnings of Saudis are higher for most industries, with the exception of high skill sectors, such as banking and insurance (CDS, 2000).

These salary differentials are illustrated in Figure 7.1.

Figure 7.1 Saudi and non-Saudis: average monthly wages (Riyals) by economic activity

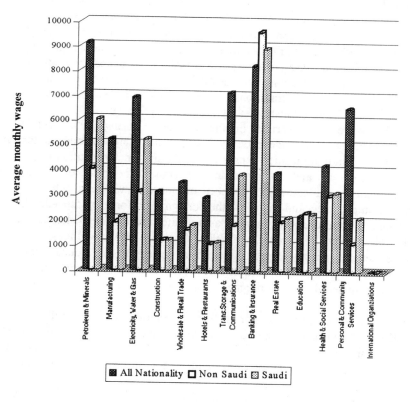

Source: *Central Department of Statistics Employment and Wages*, 2000, p. 32.

The largest salary differentials, as shown in Table 7.4, were in those industries that registered the sharpest drop in net return per employee over gross return. The implication is clear: increasing the level of higher-cost Saudi manpower, without a commensurate increase in return per Saudi employee, will lead to further erosion of net return per employee for the private sector. Private sector growth over the past decades seems to have been built on cheap imported labour. The objections to current Saudization policies will be examined in more detail from the private sector perspective in a later chapter dealing with the structure of the labour market in the Kingdom. Leading Saudi companies emphasize the principle of employing productive Saudi employees at a reasonable cost for the job categories in which they are hired. They stress that Saudization is not about raising a company's Saudi employee head count (Zamil, 2003).

Foreign participation

Ever since the beginning of Saudi Arabia's development process, the Kingdom has welcomed foreign participation in the transformation of the country's economic structure. The relationship with the outside world has been ambivalent at times. On one hand the Kingdom welcomed the transfer of technology, skills and know-how, but on the other hand it sought to shield itself from "cultural pollution" out of fear of impacting deep-rooted cultural traditions and customs. The transition to a society with all the trappings of a modern state has been difficult at times, with pressure being exerted on those same traditions and customs (Abir, 1988, Khalaf, 2003, 2004, Yamani, 2000, Qusti, 16 July 2003, 9 July 2003).

The wave of terrorism in the Kingdom during 2003 and 2004 highlighted the mutual dependency between the Kingdom and its foreign labourers. Saudi authorities expressed their utmost determination to protect foreign workers and to maintain the continued presence of foreign investments in the country. A franker and more sympathetic public debate on the importance and value of the foreign workforce to the Kingdom's economy began to emerge, as well as a greater respect for the human rights of such workers (Sulaiman, Al. 2004, Rashid, 2004). At the same time, these debates acknowledged the need to speed up the educational and economic reforms that would enable Saudi citizens to assume the tasks currently undertaken by foreigners. These issues will be addressed in later chapters.

The most popular or preferred form of Saudi and foreign collaboration at the corporate level seems to be the appointment by a foreign distributor of a local Saudi commercial agent or *wakeel*. Table 7.5 sets out the total number of outstanding agencies in Saudi Arabia in 2002 by agency country of origin.

According to Table 7.5, nearly 76% of all agencies granted to Saudi representatives were from developed countries, with Egypt and China showing a strong presence. The apparent bias towards agencies from the developed countries could be attributed to the desire of Saudi consumers, with their new-found "oil boom" wealth and subsequent conspicuous consumption, to obtain western goods and services, especially after they had become familiar with them while studying in these countries, as well as making contacts on behalf of their families. Some of the agencies might only involve a distributorship on behalf of the foreign company against agreed-upon commission on sales.

Table 7.5 Trade agencies granted by country of origin (up to 2002)

Country of Origin	Number of Agencies held
Total outstanding	**7,903**
Saudi Arabia	48
UK	1,001
Danish	123
French	503
German	764
Italian	493
Japanese	331
South Korean	141
Spanish	160
Swedish	113
Swiss	353
USA	1,564
Egyptian	263
Chinese	137
Subtotal	5,994
% of subtotal to total agencies	75.8%

Source: *CDS*, 2002, p. 451-452.

Franchising became popular in Saudi Arabia as a form of doing business. Most Saudi cities and towns today boast an array of world-famous franchise brand names, with the USA accounting for around 35-40% of the current franchise market in Saudi Arabia. This began with the introduction of a Saudi franchise law in 1992 (U.S.-Saudi Arabian Business Council, 2003).

Table 7.6 Saudi Arabia: Establishments by economic activity and nationality of ownership (2002)

Sector	Saudi	Joint Ownership	Foreign Ownership	Total
Agriculture, Fishing	240	1	6	247
Mining, Petroleum	155	22	27	201
Manufacturing	6,652	65	191	3,908
Electricity	204	15	28	247
Construction	10,419	75	101	10,595
Trade, Hotel	15,480	54	85	15,619
Transport & Communication	910	49	28	987
Financing & Real Estate	599	60	53	712
Community & Social Services	3,364	17	33	3,414
Total	35,020	358	552	35,930

Source: *CDS, Statistical Yearbook*, 2003, p. 305.

Examination of joint venture and wholly-owned foreign enterprises operating in Saudi Arabia reveals that while they are to be found in all major sectors of the economy, the main concentration is in manufacturing, with construction coming second as set out in Table 7.6.

A primary aim of such foreign investments is the transfer of appropriate technology and skills. Chapter Ten will analyse the effectiveness of such technology transfer by comparing the Saudi private sector joint venture with "offset" investment programs in the Kingdom. Our preliminary results seemed to indicate that the level of technology transfer, or "packaging", was relatively higher for the offset companies. The private sector joint venture technology transfers were mostly in the form of franchises and other less comprehensive technology transfer mechanisms, with the exception of some joint venture investments in the petroleum and finance sectors.

In terms of their employment profile, the joint venture and foreign companies operating in Saudi Arabia seem to be located in both extremes of the employment scale, as Table 7.7 illustrates.

Table 7.7 Saudi Arabia: Establishments by classes of insured employment size and by nationality of ownership (2002)

Class of Insured Employment	Saudi	Joint Ownership	Foreign Ownership	Total
Less than 20	20,834	186	195	21,215
21-39	6,800	46	80	6,926
40-59	2,382	31	52	2,465
60-79	1,217	19	36	1,272
80-99	770	17	23	810
100-199	1,517	23	70	1,610
200-299	509	8	26	543
300-399	290	6	27	323
400-499	175	5	15	195
500 plus	526	17	28	571
Total	**35,020**	**358**	**552**	**35,930**

Source: CDS, Statistical Yearbook, 2003, p. 310.

Table 7.7 seems to indicate that around 51% of the joint venture companies and 35% of the wholly foreign-owned companies had less than 20 insured employees, with both groups representing less than 2% of total establishments in this employment category band. However, the share of joint venture and foreign establishments in the higher insured employment band of over 400 employees, reached 8.5% of total establishments. The preponderance of such foreign-affiliated companies in manufacturing, oil-related and construction sectors accounts for the higher employee bands, while the lower bands reflect activities in the personal services, financial and trade sectors.

What Table 7.7 reveals is that the vast majority of Saudi establishments seem to employ a small number of employees and that despite massive expenditures on the past development plans, the backbone of Saudi employment still lies with so-called Small and Medium Enterprises or SMEs.

The Small and Medium Enterprises

The figures for total establishments in Table 7.7 do not give us a complete picture on the status of small and medium-sized enterprises operating in the Kingdom today, as the data in Table 7.7 only relates to establishments employing insured employees. Single owners and joint proprietorships are not included in the figures. According to SAMA, there are currently around 540,000 individual proprietorships in Saudi Arabia, spread throughout the country, with the majority located in the major cities as illustrated in Figure 7.2.

Figure 7.2 Individual proprietorships in Saudi Arabia by location

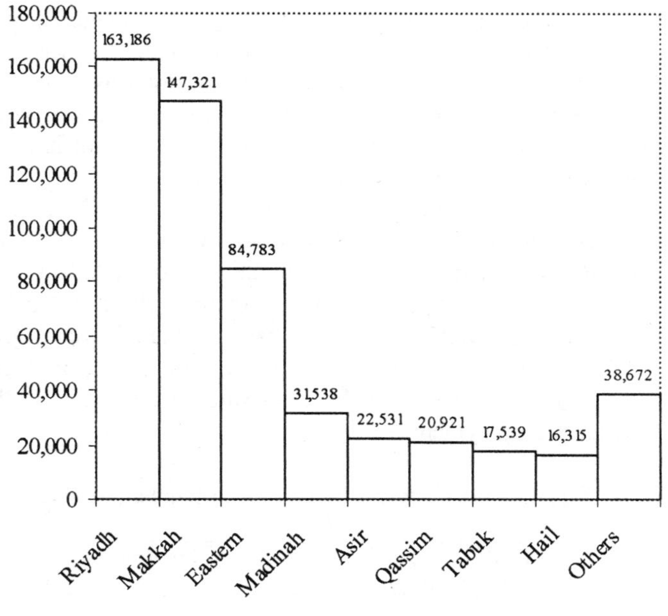

Source: *SAMA*, 2003, p. 252.

Figure 7.2 shows that the Riyadh, Makkah/Jeddah and Eastern Regions accounted for nearly 75% of the SMEs. Some estimates claim that around five million people depend on them for their livelihood. As such, this sector has come to assume a major socio-economic importance in Saudi planning (Radwan, 2002, Sugair, 2002, Malik, 2004).

What these figures for proprietorship do not tell us, however, is how many enterprises survive and how many close their business for different reasons. It is important that Saudi authorities collect such information so as to assess the obstacles faced by SMEs and the efficiency of these enterprises in meeting national goals. From such studies one can then draw appropriate conclusions about the necessary private sector adaptations to new economic conditions that are facing them, following the Saudi government's retrenchment from its dominant role in the economy.

Saudi businesses of all sizes face issues or problems particular to their sector, and SMEs are no exception (Sugair, 2002, Sajini, 2004, Estimo, 2004). Part of the problem lies in the development path that Saudi Arabia chose in the early days, as we have already discussed. The modern Saudi economy took off in the oil boom of the 1970s with massive investment in both infrastructure and capital-intensive industries, such as petrochemical and basic industries. The establishment of large-scale manufacturing enterprises, whether Saudi-owned or joint venture, received substantial preferential treatment in the form of subsidised financial assistance from the Saudi state and input subsidies. In the rush to industrialize, the SMEs were neglected, not because of any ill-will towards them by the bureaucracy, but because they were not "glamorous enough" or organized managerially, and state bureaucrats preferred to handle the needs of larger corporations. The past lack of attention to this sector was compounded by the feeling that SMEs were not a priority segment in the "oil boom" era, that SMEs relied on non-Saudi labour and that they did not have a role to play in the wider economy (Sugair, 2002). This perception is gradually changing, with studies indicating that for every one million Saudi riyal invested in large companies, one additional job was created, while a similar amount invested with SMEs created around 28 new jobs (Radwan, 2002).

SMEs can also offer political and economic diversification, which encourages a more sustainable consumer base for the Kingdom, given their diversified spread in the Kingdom which we saw earlier in Figure 7.2. Table 7.8 demonstrates that the Saudi private sector today *is* the SME sector in terms of employment.

Table 7.8 Economic sectors by employee segmentation (2001)

Sector	Wholesale and Retail	Real Estate	Restaurant & Hotels	Construction	Electricity, Gas, Water
Employee Segment					
1-9	548,245	19,478	69,835	8,150	1,595
10-49	196,672	10,151	55,963	88,256	921
50-99	83,442	1,059	4,372	31,855	1,644
100+	220,390	1,366	33,242	332,845	53,187
Total	1,048,749	32,054	163,412	416,106	57,187

Source: *CDS, Statistical Yearbook*, 2003.

Based on the definition of SMEs used by the Saudi Chambers of Commerce, they employ 64% of the total workforce. This identifies SMEs according to employee and asset size. "Micro" companies have fewer than 10 employees and less than SR 200,000 in assets; "small" companies have 10-25 employees and SR one million in assets; "medium" companies employ 25-100 workers and have assets of SR five million. It is obvious from Table 7.8 that SMEs are concentrated in the wholesale and retail sector, and that they make up the bulk of the real estate and restaurant and hotel business. Given the prominence of growing youth unemployment in Saudi Arabia, the government is paying close attention to SMEs and is assisting them to overcome perceived obstacles, with the Seventh Five Year Plan addressing SME concerns. According to observers, SMEs seem to suffer in their access to finance (short and long-term), from an inappropriate business environment, lack of development service and managerial inadequacies, as well as an underdeveloped IT structure and insufficient market data (Kurdi, 2002). A position paper on SMEs prepared by the Saudi Arabian General Investment Authority (SAGIA) pointed to the sector's "low quality, high prices and inadequate marketing skills... compounded by lack of modern technology, experience and constant problems with cost and raw material purchases..." (SAGIA, 2004).

It would not be surprising, then, to see a significant number of SMEs shut down due to a combination of any of the above problems. According to the Ministry of Commerce, there were a total of 44,893 SME permits non-renewed or cancelled in 1988 and 88,808 in 1999 by the different Saudi municipalities (Ministry of Commerce, 2001). This represents a serious waste of productive capacity in the economy, with unused resources, especially employment. In the same years, the number of renewed and new permits granted to SMEs by the municipalities was 183,712 and 155,352 respectively, indicating the attraction of this sector of first time businesses. Table 7.9 sets out the trend for net company registrations in Saudi Arabia for selected years.

Table 7.9 Company registrations granted and not renewed by economic sectors (net additions)

Sector	1993	1997	1999	2002
Agriculture	739	(25)	(14)	(9)
Petroleum, Mining	573	39	28	27
Industry	2,563	52	(209)	(29)
Electricity and Water Extraction	94	14	402	2
Building and Construction	67,157	830	(2,659)	2,303
Wholesale/Retail	144,824	(463)	(843)	26,119
Business and Financial Services	615	9	64	(29)
Transportation, Storage	15,470	644	797	(313)
Personal and Social Services	(599)	(1)	(0)	(0)
Total	231,463	1,149	(2,434)	28,069

Source: *Ministry of Commerce, CDS*, 2003, p. 455.

Table 7.9 illustrates the uneven pattern of net additions of new companies in the various economic sectors; this seems to follow business cycles. Net company additions stood at a staggering 231,000 establishments in 1993, driven by the positive factors following the end of the 1991 Gulf War. In 1999, due to sharp falls in world oil prices in the preceding few years, there was a net reduction of 2,400 establishments, which was eventually reversed in 2002. Once again the wholesale and retail trade – the backbone of the SMEs – was the dominant swing factor. The expected entry of the Kingdom into the WTO will add further pressure on the SME sector according to some observers (Sajini, 2004). The argument is that SMEs will be swamped by the entry of cheaper and higher quality imports, with technology transfer through foreign-owned companies adding more pressure. Others argue that competition will force those SMEs that are particularly inefficient out of the market, so that in the long run the sector will be better off in terms of competition and high quality products. This is a big "if" and a lot needs to be done to ensure that the SME sector flourishes in the face of expected WTO entry. To its credit, the Council of Saudi Chambers of Commerce and Industry (CSCCI) have started to take some concrete measures to help the SME sector. According to CSCCI, and following detailed studies conducted with the help of financial institutions with experience in this field such as the UK's HSBC, the following measures have been recommended:

- Creation of an office for the development of SMEs called Saudi Small Business Agency (SSBA) that is a single umbrella organization sponsored by the government for the small firms, but with autonomous private management
- Establishment of a loan guarantee fund for the SMEs
- Establishment of business incubation centres for SMEs in the various regional Chambers of Commerce and Industry
- Establishment of training and advice centres at the Chambers for SMEs through Business Support Centres (BSCs)
- Provision to the SME sector of the full support and attention of the government by giving the Director of the SSBA access to different ministers

The studies of the CSCCI indicated that for the SME sector as a whole, fewer than 20% of the firms set up conducted feasibility studies, fewer than 33% kept financial records, fewer than 20% prepared annual budgets, and 33% had no separate bank accounts. To reinforce the need for intensive management training for this sector, the CSCCI noted that "typical" SMEs could not correctly assess assets and liabilities, insolvency, profitability and how finance was to be raised or used.

Besides the above initiatives, the SME sector needs a clear source of financing, unencumbered by bureaucracy and burden of collateral and excessive guarantees. According to the Minister of Finance Dr. Ibrahim Al

Assaf, a special programme to finance SMEs through Saudi banks and the State would be set up with an equal contribution of SR 100 million, to be disbursed through the Saudi Industrial Development Fund (SIDF) (Abdul Ghafour, May 7, 2003). In a further development, the Saudi Credit Bank was to expand the scope of SME lending, and raise the current lending ceiling to SR 200,000 (Sugair, 2002).

SME model for growth

In line with other country experiences that have successfully focused on the SME sector as a vital engine of growth, the Saudi government needs to realign its traditional approach, not just for the SMEs, but also for the private sector as a whole, along the following lines:

Traditional Approach	*New Path*
• Public sector is the main economic driver	• Private sector delivery of goods and services
• Subsidized inputs	• Market based pricing
• Supply driven	• Market-demand driven, commercially viable
• Unsustainable allocation of resources	• Long term sustainability

The above approach will help to enhance the survivability of the SMEs and the private sector by focusing on their areas of weaknesses and enhancing their areas of strength, as illustrated in Figure 7.3.

Figure 7.3 Enhancement of SME survival and growth in the Saudi economy

Legend: ━━━━ *Actual achieved*
———— Target

Figure 7.3 sets out an "optimum" path for SME enhancement in Saudi Arabia in light of the current strengths of each of the identified "enhancements". Some will take longer to achieve, especially in the area of management training, IT skills and quality control. Others can be established sooner and produce more immediate results, including establishing and fostering SME "clusters", improving access to finance, networking alliances and, above all, encouraging the larger Saudi companies to source local tenders for goods and services from SMEs. This has worked elsewhere, notably in the Far East and Japan; and they could be a model for cooperation in Saudi Arabia. Above all, because the Saudi government also recognizes that SMEs constitute an important economic segment, it is adapting some of its lending and regulatory policies to help this sector to survive, flourish and grow in a more dynamic environment (Radwan, 2002).

Saudi family businesses

Much has been written about the role of family businesses in the Arabian Gulf and Saudi Arabia, with most writers highlighting the significant economic impact of such family businesses on domestic economies in terms of investment, employment, international agency alliances and capital flows (Field, 1985, Fahim, 1995, Holder et al, 1981, Wright et al, 1996, Carter, 1984). More recent writers have stressed the problems faced by such family businesses, and the need to transform them into joint stock companies to enable them to survive global competitive pressures and liberalization moves by national governments (Azzam, 2002, Speakman, 2002).

In Saudi Arabia, family businesses are estimated to hold around SR 250 billion in domestic investments, with 200 family companies dominating commercial life in all sectors of the economy (Daghsh, 2004). An examination of any of Saudi Arabia's trade directories will reveal that the majority of franchises and agencies highlighted earlier in Table 7.5 are owned by no more than 100 of the top Saudi family businesses.

Given this prominent impact on the nation's economy, the Saudi government has encouraged family businesses to examine their current structure and to try to address the potential problems that might affect both the family business and the national economy. Several high-profile forums have been held to discuss issues of concern, such as the need to separate business and family loyalties, hiring only the most competent family members as managers in the business, and giving serious consideration to taking family businesses public (Arab News, 25 May 2004). The issue of succession, or more precisely of *competent* succession, in the Kingdom's family businesses has been brought into the public discourse following some high-profile cases of family business break-ups due to succession problems. The key is either to agree a succession plan or to separate management from ownership (Malik, 2004).

Mergers and acquisitions are other options for like-minded family businesses, but these have been rare in Saudi Arabia. They have mostly been concentrated in the banking sector and some allied food industries led by Prince Waleed bin Tallal bin Abdulaziz, such as the *Savola* and *Panda* Groups. In a society where mergers and acquisitions imply social and managerial failures, there is reluctance to sell to "outsiders", leading some family businesses to continue to operate despite significant financial losses. The preferred option in the Arabian Gulf seems to be "informal" family-related alliances through marriage or blood-line (Field, 1985, Wright, 1996).

To an outsider, it would be difficult to discern who is related to whom by marriage or blood affiliation, but for those operating in the Kingdom this is more transparent and it influences how business is carried out.

Such alliances could influence the efficient management of family businesses, whereby decision-making could be constrained by ethical considerations of whether to act independently or in line with external socially-driven factors. This is illustrated in Figure 7.4, which sets out the social and ethical environments in which Saudi Arabian family businesses operate.

Figure 7.4 Decision-making and ethical dilemmas in family-run businesses

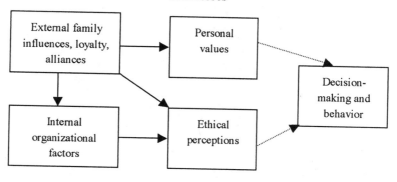

Adapted from *Marris et al*, 1996.

Figure 7.4 describes the external environmental factors that affect internal organizational factors, which in turn impact upon ethical considerations and decision-making. If moral conduct and ethical behaviour conflicts with the larger interests of the country, then increased government regulation will result (Ostapski et al, 1996).

In Saudi Arabia, the government has not yet reached the stage of imposing regulations on family-run businesses, preferring instead internal reforms of such family groupings.

To face future challenges, the Saudi family business management structure has to change . A centralized decision-making "power culture", in which tasks are assigned downward by the chief executive or owner and strict hierarchy is tempered by heavy doses of paternalism – this is not the way forward (Azzam, 2002). Under these conditions, family companies are more likely to provide clients with the kind of goods that are already available, rather than customized goods that meet clients' needs. Obsession with balance sheet size, rather than size and growth of market share, becomes a feature, which explains the enormous interest shown by Saudi family businesses in being included in the *Saudi Top 100 Companies* surveys published by local media (Al Sharq Al Awsat and Arab News, 2002). While some companies provide data on assets, turnover, and sales, as well as capital and employee numbers, they give little information on the profitability and market share of these companies (Fadhel, 2004)

Table 7.10 outlines areas of changing management structure to which some family businesses are adapting. Others will need to address such structural issues.

Table 7.10 Family businesses: changing management operating structures

Characteristic	Current Structure	New Structure
• Organization	• Pyramid, strict hierarchy	• Horizontal, delegation
• Focus	• Balance sheet growth, agencies and franchises	• Profitability, maximizing shareholder value, production
• Ownership	• Family, affiliated groups	• Publicly listed joint stocks
• Financial structure	• Internal raising of capital	• External funding, IPOs
• Resources	• Physical assets	• Human capital
• Competition	• Between family groups	• Between brands, services and products
• Expansion	• Using influence, family alliances and *"Wasta"*	• Productivity and achievement
• Financials	• Internal, annual, not audited	• Quarterly, audited
• Leadership style	• Top down, paternalistic, dogmatic	• Bottom up, inspirational
• Worker	• Mere employees	• Shareholders, participatory, critical
• Job expectation	• Look for security, obedience	• Personal growth, satisfaction.

Adapted from *Azzam*, 2002, p. 18.

Table 7.10 reveals how fundamental a shift in mind-set the Saudi family businesses need in order to proceed into the next "new structure" age. Above all, the paternalistic leadership style from top-down has to change to a bottom-up, inspirational leadership approach, which might still remain in the hands of the younger, educated and technically-proficient family members, aided by independent professional managers with a stake in the family business (Yamani, 2000). Instead of having employees with a civil-service attitude, only mindful of rank and title and rewarded for obedience to the family hierarchy, true empowerment of professional talent would be emphasized.

Saudi Women and the National Economy

During 2003 and 2004, women-related issues moved to the forefront in Saudi Arabia. Social customs and traditions came under passionate social debate and many old taboos were broken. As we will discuss in a later chapter, the Kingdom has made a great effort to provide Saudi females with all levels of education. It may surprise many to learn that females outnumber males in higher education. However, some have argued that while such education is valuable as an end in itself, the returns are lowered by minimal participation of Saudi women in the formal workforce (Wilson, 2004). Higher education, international travel, access to the Internet and gender developments in nearby Gulf Cooperation Council (GCC) countries have all ensured that the subject of more effective participation of Saudi women in society at large will continue to be an important issue. Over 85% of the estimated 272,000 working women in Saudi Arabia are employed in the public sector in education, healthcare and government work (Doumato, 2001). The private sector is expected to be the major employer of female Saudi job seekers, theoretically putting pressure on male jobs seekers. In reality, Saudi social custom preludes women from entering employment where they can openly mix with men. Ways have to be found, therefore, to employ Saudi women in an environment that respects local customs and traditions, but which allows them to contribute more fully to the country's economic development.

However, as we already mentioned, social taboos and stereotypical perceptions about Saudi women are being broken. A female Saudi television presenter – Buthaina Al Nasr – made history by becoming the first Saudi woman to read the opening news bulletin of the Kingdom's all-news satellite channel, launched in January, 2004 (Arab News, 13 January 2004). Despite criticism from some quarters, the TV presenter is now accepted as a feature of the new channel. Another landmark was achieved when Hanadi Hindi become the Kingdom's first commercial female pilot. Some female Saudi commentators lament the fact that while the oil boom era brought great changes to the GCC societies in material terms, it did little to alter "fundamental attitudes towards women" (Hafni, 2003).

Officially the Saudi government has been sympathetic to women's issues, and, while the Crown Prince Abdullah advised patience, the leadership has encouraged continued national dialogue on women's issues under the forum of the King Abdulaziz National Dialogue Centre, set up by the Crown Prince (Abdel Ghafour, 6 June 2004). Several such dialogue forums were held in *Makkah* and *Madinah* during 2004, and by all accounts there were some heated debates and disagreements on the direction of change (Akeel, 15 June 2004). Some social commentators were disheartened by the outcome, stating that what happened at the dialogue forum "yet again illustrated our incapability to solve our own differences and problems" (Qusti, 16 June 2004).

Saudi women's issues have been addressed not only in domestic forums, but also in international forums such as the 2004 Jeddah Economic Forum. This was attended by international dignitaries such as Queen Rania of Jordan, Lebanese Premier Hariri, and former Presidents Bill Clinton (USA) and Ernesto Zedillo (Mexico), as well as the Prime Minister of Turkey, Mr. Erdogan, and Malaysia's ex-premier, Dr. Mahathir. The Chairperson of the 19-member women's business committee at the Jeddah Chamber of Commerce and Industry was no less than Crown Prince Abdullah's daughter Princess Adela bint Abdullah. She stated that it was important to support qualified Saudi women by giving them the opportunity to actively participate in key social and economic activities (SAGIA, 18 January 2004).

Because of their need to help support the family by working, Saudi Arabian women are motivated to change facts on the ground. They have become a formidable presence in the economy. They are not afraid to take on jobs that were previously considered "menial", such as factory work. There was astonishment when 1,500 women applied for 400 positions at a major dairy factory outside Riyadh in 2003, proving that the search for jobs was not limited to university graduates alone (Abdul Ghafour, 23 March 2003, Ahmad, 2004). Unfortunately, the pioneering dairy farm decided not to proceed with the hiring, but other Saudi businesswomen have initiated women-only assembly line employment.

The demand for this type of female labour has encouraged Saudi businesswomen to petition for "women-only" industrial cities and, according to the Saudi Arabian General Investment Authority (SAGIA), such women-only industrial cities are being planned for Riyadh and Jeddah (SAGIA , June 3, June 13, 2004). Apparently a 600,000 square metres site has been allocated for this purpose in Riyadh and a site of similar size has been allocated in Jeddah, which would accommodate 83 factories. It is said that, "two foreign firms will operate the city and train 10,000 women for two years" (SAGIA, June 3, 2004).

Estimating the size of Saudi women's investments

Data on the economic status of women in Saudi Arabia is somewhat sketchy, with varying estimates given, but all point to substantial economic involvement in the country. According to a study carried out by King Abdulaziz University in Jeddah, Saudi women hold nearly 70% of the bank accounts in the Kingdom with deposits worth SR 62 billion, hold 20% of corporate shares and own 15% of the private companies and 10% of the real estate sector (Abdul Ghafour, 4 June 2004). The same study states that women have a 34% stake in private businesses in Riyadh, 25% in Jeddah and 6% in Makkah, and that there are an estimated 5,000 businesswomen in Riyadh and 4,000 in Jeddah. Not to be outdone, the Eastern Province Chamber of Commerce and Industry (EPCCI) set up a joint committee of Saudi businesswomen at the chamber with the aim of encouraging women to participate and invest in different projects. This was followed by a "women-only wing" of the Riyadh Chamber of Commerce and Industry. Other chambers will no doubt follow suit.

Other studies report that Saudi women own 40% of private wealth (which might have been passively acquired due to Islamic inheritance laws), and approximately 15,000 commercial establishments or 10% of private businesses in Saudi Arabia (Doumato, 2003). To better service this lucrative market segment, all Saudi banks have opened women-only branches, and one of them, the Saudi British Bank, went one step further and inaugurated a women-only centre for financial and investment consultancy for lady clients (Nasir, 01 May 2003). Even SAGIA decided to offer its services to Saudi businesswomen and to establish a "one-stop" service centre for women only, staffed by professional female experts who will be able to provide fully-fledged services to both Saudi and foreign businesswomen intending to invest in the Kingdom, while ensuring their privacy. SAGIA was encouraged by the response of Saudi women, for apparently a large number have applied for investment licenses (Arab News, 25 May 2003).

When it comes to types of businesses set up by women, Saudi businesswomen certainly seem quite innovative (Akeel, 2003, Doumato, 2001). Besides the usual tailoring shops, beauty and hair salons, jewellery and clothing, Saudi women are now running businesses in marketing, public relations, event management, Web design, programming and recruitment consultation. In addition, Saudi businesswomen have invested in industries such as iron and steel, furniture, plastic products and solar cell technology (Doumato, 2003). Women now work as architects and journalists and there is great interest in nursing, after this sector was previously frowned upon by society as being a less-than-acceptable job. Many jobs available for women continue to be filled by foreigners in Saudi Arabia. Some 600,000 foreign women work as nannies, secretaries and housemaids. This huge foreign work force holds jobs that Saudi women cannot fill either because they are not qualified or because they reject the job as low prestige or unsuitable for women, such as secretarial work in a mixed-sex environment. However, some companies are now using segregated female secretarial pools.

Some analysts who follow the issues of Arab and Gulf women have noted, however, that there is a danger that current reform moves are being headed by "elite" female groups – women who are not representative of society at large (Hijab, 1988, Khoury et al, 1995, Sanabary, 1994, Doumato, 2003). When one notes the distinguished academic credentials of most Saudi women participants at such forums, one sees the validity of this argument. At the same time, one is convinced by their claim that they are more in tune and can better articulate what Saudi women in general wish to achieve than can men. However, informal contact following the most recent national forum with a wide range of Saudi females of all ages, revealed some disappointment amongst younger Saudi females. Some felt that superficial issues were discussed, and others had not heard of the forum discussions at all (Meccawy, 22 June 2004). Saudi businesswomen have come a long way in a short period, and it is only a matter of time before some of the more onerous bureaucratic impediments before them are removed so that they can play a more effective role in the Saudi economy. Table 7.11 lays out the status of some of the current issues facing Saudi businesswomen.

Table 7.11 Saudi businesswomen's operating barriers

Barriers	*Status*
• Difficulty for businesswomen to accomplish official business in person without using male intermediary	• Government is studying allowing women to submit applications directly without intermediary
• Lack of training organizations and specialist women-related business programmes	• Chamber of Commerce establishing training programmes
• Difficulty of obtaining required market information	• Special sections of Chamber of Commerce set up to provide data
• Difficulty in qualifying for loans	• Government lending institutions instructed to handle female loan applicants on equal basis
• Limited allowable investment sectors	• Industrial zones planned and special investment advisory service from SAGIA set up
• Unavailability of women's sections in major government ministries	• Some progress in this field and some ministries have established women-only sections
• Clarification of legal rights of businesswomen with government agencies	• Steps are being taken to ensure that women can correspond direct in their own legal capacity without intermediaries
• Limited networking groups for businesswomen	• Businesswomen's associations established to facilitate networking

Table 7.11 indicates that both the government and the various Chambers of Commerce and Industry are trying to facilitate the operating needs of Saudi businesswomen. The key is to pursue this momentum while ensuring that society at large is willingly accepting the changes taking place, without affecting basic Islamic beliefs and traditions.

Government and business relations in Saudi Arabia

The centrality of governmental interaction with the private sector in Saudi Arabia has been undeniably demonstrated throughout the preceding chapters. A successful public-private sector dialogue and ongoing cooperation will bring about a business environment that will allow the private sector to flourish, while the government continues to play a supportive role.

Figure 7.5 Saudi Arabia: Evolving government-private sector relationships

1970s-1980s

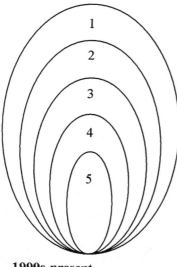

1. *Government as planner*

2. *Government as financing entity*

3. *Government as buyer and seller*

4. *Government as regulator*

5. *Government as revenue collector*

1990s-present

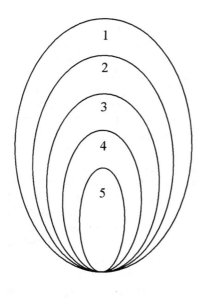

1. *Government as regulator*

2. *Government as seller and buyer*

3. *Government as planner*

4. *Government as financing entity*

5. *Government as revenue collector*

In the Kingdom, as in many other developing nations, governments assume the responsibility of setting goals and guiding the discharge of both public and private resources to achieve the objectives of development. Previously, we examined the various development processes adopted by the Kingdom and what the government had hoped to achieve over the past three decades. In the section that follows, we will analyze the development process from the private sector's perspective, before assessing a suitable model for public-private sector cooperation. We will look at the roles of the government in relation to the private sector in five key areas and how these have evolved over time. Within each of these five roles, there are different mechanisms that the government might use to influence the degree of participation of the private sector in the national economic development process. Figure 7.5 is based on the five relationships between the public and private sector throughout the 1970s and 1980s, and then from the 1990s to date. The five areas of public-private sector cooperation and mutual dependency are:

- Government as planner
- Government as financing entity
- Government as buyer and seller
- Government as regulator
- Government as revenue collector

As Figure 7.5 illustrates, there has been a noticeable shift in emphasis over the two periods in question, with the first ranking indicating the most important emphasis, and the fifth ranking indicating the lowest emphasis. The rankings in between show other levels of emphasis and priorities for the different periods.

One: The government as a planner. The crucial fact of economic development since 1970 has been the Saudi government's comprehensive planning for the short and long-term activities of the public and private sectors. Over time, there was less emphasis on direct planning and indicative planning was introduced in order to promote the state's objectives of economic diversification and greater private sector, value-added industrial investment. The government had used earlier oil revenue surpluses to build up capital and energy intensive industries. The private sector in general knows that it is assuming this new national economic responsibility, but it is also arguing for a more effective government-business relationship to implement it. Research indicated that despite some praise for the government on what it has done to date, the private sector was still critical of the business environment, which the private sector felt did not yet meet their needs (Malik, 2004). The government needs to involve the private sector in a closer dialogue from the outset, before committing itself to far-reaching decisions. The proposed entry of the Kingdom into the WTO is one case in point where the private sector feels that there was not enough preparation and consultation between the government and the private sector on the economic ramifications of entry.

Two: the government as a revenue collector. The significant increase in oil revenues in the 1970s eliminated the need for Saudi Arabia to introduce direct or indirect taxes. The government hoped that the resultant limited fiscal collection role would promote a stimulating climate for Saudi industrial and business activities, with the 2.5% *Zakat* or religious prescribed levy being the only one imposed on Saudi companies. This rate is considered low by international corporate tax standards and it is doubtful that the government will raise Saudi corporate taxes. What might be introduced are indirect taxes that could be placed on luxury consumer goods in line with some other GCC countries. However, as a result of this low tax environment, the business sector in Saudi Arabia took the situation for granted, and government attempts to remove subsidies on certain basic utilities such as electricity met with such resistance that they were cancelled. This reinforces the Saudi business sector's perception of the government's role as being a *provider* rather than a *partner,* although the inevitability of the introduction of some form of taxation is accepted by some businesses, probably under the guise of WTO equalization regulations. Foreign companies operating in the Kingdom, whether wholly-owned or in partnership, pay a corporate income tax of 20%, following a reduction from a top tier of 45% in order to attract foreign direct investment. How Saudi Arabia will be able to maintain this dual tax policy towards foreigners and nationals after WTO entry will be of major interest to both parties.

Three: government as a buyer and seller. As both buyer and seller, the Saudi government is a key economic player in a Keynesian macroeconomic sense of managing aggregate demand. The government is a *de facto* seller through its use of subsidies. In the early 1970s the Saudi government became the provider of a wide range of free and subsidized goods and services. These actions had long-term negative effects on economic development efforts, by underestimating the true cost of production and thereby encouraging some resources to be over-utilized (Nazir, 2002, Saravia, 2002, Trivedi, 2002). Subsidies currently stand at around SR 5-6 billion per annum or 3% of total expenditures, down substantially over early periods, when subsidies were at SR 10-11 billion levels in 1981/1982 or 4% of total expenditures (SAMA, 2003, p. 377). The Saudi government is aware of the cost of this support and has, over the years, taken some steps to rationalize its subsidy policies by cancelling some, such as the wheat subsidy in 1995. Of more long-term significance for the private sector is the government's strategic decision to rationalize its use of resources by selling part of its share in the huge industrial projects in *Jubail* and *Yanbu,* including its holdings in the Saudi Arabian Basic Industries or SABIC. This trend will accelerate with the implementation of the government's multifaceted privatization programme (Nazir, 2002, Speakman, 2002). Figure 7.5 demonstrates how the role of the government as a buyer and seller will increase in the current period due to this privatization strategy.

In most countries, the government is the private sector's major purchaser of goods and services, and the degree to which the government is effective in using this tool often determines the size and growth of existing private sector industries and future private sector investments. The private sector–government experience of buying and selling in Saudi Arabia has been mixed. The Saudi government has gradually passed numerous decrees insisting that government contracts stipulate a domestic input of goods and services, but these are not always adhered to and foreign goods are imported instead. The government complains of the lack of response from the private sector to government tenders and its lack of professionalism in meeting tender specifications, while the private sector complains in turn that government agencies lack an understanding of what is currently available in the market and impose unrealistic specifications (Nazir, 2002, Wright, 1996). Others argue that the system can sometimes lack transparency, with government tenders linked to favours and whom you know or *wasta*, especially for large government tenders (Malik, 2004).

Some progress has been made in Saudi Arabia in this regard, with a more transparent bidding system and discussions on the required specifications. More effort, however, is required in order to better understand each sector's needs, including resolving the issues of late government payments and late private sector delivery. How long the Saudi private sector can obtain favoured supplier status from the Saudi government for its contracts remains to be seen following entry into WTO, but Saudi companies who have established themselves on such contracts will need either to diversify or to become even more competitive, should foreign companies be allowed to bid openly for government contracts.

Table 7.12 Outstanding loans of the Saudi specialized credit institutions (Million riyals)

Institution	1987	1992	1996	1999	2002
Saudi Agriculture Bank	11,784	9,043	7,712	8,195	9,414
Saudi Credit Bank	562	610	675	762	819
Public Investment Fund	43,011	34,204	25,802	21,852	25,567
Saudi Industrial Development Fund	42,380	4,797	8,372	10,353	9,280
Real Estate Development Fund	69,430	66,547	70,438	69,892	68,711
Total	167,167	153,087	150,884	148,939	151,676

Source: *SAMA*, 2003, p. 369.

Four: government as a financing entity. One of the key foci in developing the state's ability to finance industrial enterprises has been the creation of specialized loan institutions to make funds available to industry on terms more favourable than those offered by commercial banks. As Figure 7.5 indicates, this was an important function in the 1970s and 1980s, but has been relegated to a lower level from the 1990s. To meet its development objectives, the Saudi government established several funding institutions and Table 7.12 sets out the amounts of outstanding loans for each institution.

Each of these government financing institutions filled a niche in its respective area, with the Saudi Industrial Development Fund (SIDF) concentrating on medium to long-term loans for industrial investment, the Saudi Agricultural Bank providing loans for agricultural farm projects and mechanization, and the Real Estate Development Fund (REDEF) granting personal as well as commercial housing loans. The Saudi Credit Bank (SCB) filled a gap by lending to the smaller businesses and artisans, as was noted elsewhere in this chapter, and today SCB is the vehicle for SME funding along with the SIDF. Table 7.12 shows the declining amount of outstanding loans, especially for the PIF and SIDF, in contrast with the Saudi Credit Bank, where it is increasing. The message is clear: the government has moved away from long-term infrastructure financing and looks to the private sector to fill any future gap in financing. One consequence of such government financing was the ample funding opportunity of the Saudi private sector to expand during the "boom years". However, during the adjustment periods that followed, many of these companies did not survive the downturn for they were not able to sustain their repayments to the government credit institutions despite extremely low funding rates. As a result, the government lending institutions had to depend more and more on government funding to expand any new lending operations in times of declining government revenues, while at the same time see their loan collections suffered due to delayed payment or non-payment by the private sector.

Five: the government as a regulator. Notwithstanding the free-market ideology stated in all Saudi development plans, the Saudi government regulates the market place to some extent, and in Figure 7.5 we have assumed that this role will receive the highest priority going forward. On the financial side, the government controls currency prices by fixing the price of the Saudi Riyal against the dollar. The government also intervenes to regulate both safety in the workplace and the environmental effects of production. The government is still the major supplier and regulator of the education sector, and is now encouraging more private sector universities and colleges to ensure that the private sector will have the skilled manpower they require. The government is still the regulator in terms of establishing the overall commercial and legal regime within which the private sector can operate, although according to a sample survey of Saudi businessmen, there was some dissatisfaction with the status of the legal system (Malik, 2004).

The Saudi government, to its credit, has gone to great lengths to meet some of the challenges and issues raised by the private sector, including its requests for a less burdensome bureaucracy, more predictability of regulations, and a legal system conducive to business, which adapts to deal with the realities of modern international business. E-commerce and e-government is being seriously studied, and according to the most recent survey carried out by the Economist Intelligence Unit (EIU) and IBM, Saudi Arabia was ranked 45th in terms of "e-readiness" amongst the world's 60 largest economies (EIU/IBM Survey, June, 2004).

Promoting private sector self-sustained growth

This chapter has already established that fostering diversification and competitiveness in the Saudi private sector in order to enable it to meet future challenges requires a multi-program and long-term process of adjustment. It will entail measures that private firms, industries, regions, the labour force and the government will consciously have to adopt, promote, maintain and increase, despite any short-term set-backs or disagreements between the government and the private sector. This was illustrated during 2004 when the Kingdom decided to establish a separate Ministry of Labour, after having split off the Ministry of Social Affairs from it, as well as abolishing the Manpower Council (Saudi Press Agency, 23 March 2004). A veteran Saudi Minister, Dr. Ghazi Al Gosaibi, was appointed to head the Labour Ministry. The Manpower Council was absorbed into this new Ministry, which was charged with dealing with labour disputes, employment in the private sector and visa issues. The Ministry of Labour issued bans on recruiting workers from overseas and stopped issuing visas for small Saudi companies, some of which they accused of "trading in visas" and helping to compound the domestic unemployment situation. Debate on this action raged in the press, and in the end there were compromises on the ban deadline, but the minister made it clear that tackling unemployment would now be a "national policy" rather than a government "concern" (Bashir, 4 June 2004). During 2004, the Ministry of Labour took more drastic steps to stem foreign worker mobility in the Kingdom. It banned the transfer between employers of visa sponsorship for low-skilled workers, limiting such transfers to professionals with university and technical degrees. At the same time, the SME sector with fewer than 20 employees, which had previously been exempted from certain Saudization quotas, are now required to apply the same Saudization regulations. To sweeten the pill to the private sector, the Minister of Labour promised to review the situation of settling labour disputes by introducing a new labour law, which has been discussed in the *Shoura Council*.

In the past, the Saudi private sector has shown it can adapt itself to the changed economic fortunes of the country. However, with greater globalization and international competition, the private sector needs to be even more resilient. Table 7.13 summarizes some of the challenges to be faced.

In Table 7.13, we find the first steps that the private sector ought to take if it wishes to continue conducting an effective partnership with the government in the years to come. The beginnings of a fruitful dialogue already exist. The government cannot afford to see the private sector fail, given the Kingdom's free mobility of capital and the fact that nearby GCC countries are an attractive alternative location for any sections of the Saudi private sector that feel pressured by unacceptable demands or are frustrated by bureaucracy and outdated regulation (Abdulaziz, Al Waleed bin Tallal, 9 July 2003).

Table 7.13 Private sector challenges and solutions

Challenges	Opportunities and Solutions
• Promoting government-business dialogue and collaboration	• The private sector has to engage the government in a dialogue on competitiveness and impediments to improving productivity
• Internal business environment and international competitive comparisons	• Up-to-date information on local and international market opportunities made available as well as comparing relative costs and efficiency with international standards
• Expansion of the privatization policy	• Private sector must engage in dialogue to ensure that transfer is done on a transparent basis with no "hidden" costs and commitment;; flexibility in hiring and firing
• Paying attention to scientific research that might serve the production sector	• Poor communication between the productive sectors and research centres must be overcome through R + D funding, and developing science park/incubator concepts
• Increasing investment locally	• Better coordination with SAGIA and Chambers of Commerce to create business and investor friendly environment; update and harmonize business regulations; create a demand driven economy
• Reduce national unemployment	• Short term "fix" through expatriate labour reduction vs. long-term solution of employing productive Saudis; ensure that the market knows of the skill needs of the private sector

Looking ahead: A model for cooperation

Despite some element of mistrust on both sides, there is a genuine desire to see the private sector succeed. Figure 7.6 sets out a business relationship model between Saudi Arabia's private and governmental sectors that captures the main relationship flows between the parties in the context of external forces, such as the World Trade Organization.

By its own admission, the quality of the civil service in Saudi Arabia needs improvement and lags behind the private sector by as much as a decade, according to some (Janoubi, 2002, Khemani, 2002, Nazir, 2002). This is the "glass ceiling" under which the private sector has to operate, but fortunately both the private and government sectors are seeking solutions.

Figure 7.6 Saudi Arabia: A government-private sector business model of cooperation

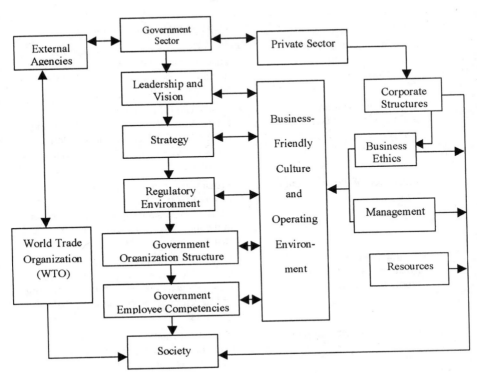

In summary, the private sector has to learn to take charge of its own economic life and move forward, requesting that the government provides the necessary business-friendly environment under which the private sector has to operate. The lower the "glass ceiling", the less effective the private sector will be. All indications are that the government is happy to improve the business environment although the speed at which this is being done has caused some concern.

Summary of the key points:

- *The private sector is being urged to assume a greater degree of responsibility in national developing in the areas of job creation, economic diversification and international competitiveness.*
- *The Saudi private sector is currently having to operate under multiple legal settings, corporate structures, as well as government pressure to accelerate the pace of Saudization of the labour force.*
- *Foreign participation is still important to the Saudi economy whether through the provision of labour and key management, or though foreign joint ventures. Franchising and agency distribution was the preferred method of cooperation but with globalization, the*

Saudi private sector has to find new ways of foreign participation and cooperation.

- *The Small and Medium Sized Enterprises (SME's) dominate private sector economic activity but face particular problems which need addressing, particularly in the field of financing, training, advisory and dedicated business centers in the chamber of commerce and industry.*

- *Saudi family businesses play a prominent role in the nation's economy. With globalization and international competition, it becomes urgent that they adapt internally to meet these challenges. Such adaptation can take the form of publicly listing family businesses, hiring of external professional management and delegation of authority.*

- *Saudi women are beginning to play a more visible role in society at large, and in the economy in particular. Estimates as to the size of their investments and corporate ownership varies but it is substantial. To take account of their effective participation, initiatives have been taken by the various chambers of commerce and industry to meet their concerns and try to overcome some of the operating obstacles facing them. The government has been sympathetic to their issues and has encouraged an open dialogue on women's role in society, bearing in mind Islamic principles and social customs.*

- *The relationship between the government and the private sector and how it has evolved over time in the areas of planning, financing, regulation and revenue collector is examined, as well as the important role of the government as a purchaser and seller to the private sector. The relationship is still evolving. It is expected that regulatory issues will predominate in the foreseeable future as the government "disengages" from the economy and allows the private sector to assume greater responsibilities. A model of government-private sector cooperation is examined.*

Critical thinking

1. "SME's are a waste of time and money. Giving them funding will not help the economy". Is this a fair assessment of the importance of SME's to the Saudi economy? Why have they been neglected?

2. "Family businesses are important to Saudi Arabia as they have built up the modern economic structure we know of today. As such, there is no need to restructure them". Do you agree? What are the pros and cons of the current Saudi family business infrastructure? How can they survive in the 21st century in the face of globalization?

3.   "Women's participation in the national economy needs to be managed carefully, given social customs and traditions. As such, priority must be given to solving male unemployment first". What are the merits of expanding Saudi women's economic participation and in which fields? Do you agree with the statement?

4.   "Government as a planner will still be important in the next decade. There is still a long way to go for regulations". Do you agree? Is planning still the prime responsibility of the government?

5.   "The private sector will always look after its self-interest irrespective what the government asks of it. As such, the government is right to introduce curbs on foreign employment and introduce penalties on the private sector who do not comply with Saudization". How successful do you think these measures will be? Are the private sector's concerns being adequately taken into account?

Chapter 8

THE KINGDOM'S HEART: THE HYDROCARBON AND MINERALS SECTOR

Business is like oil. It won't mix with anything but business.

J. Graham

Learning outcomes:

By the end of this section, you should understand:

- *The important role energy plays in Saudi economic development*
- *The centrality of Saudi Arabian petroleum sector to world output and demand*
- *Saudi oil policy and constraints*
- *Saudi oil and GDP contribution*
- *The growing importance of the Saudi gas sector*
- *Foreign participation in the gas projects*
- *Saudi petrochemicals and their role in economic diversification*
- *The Saudi mining sector and its future development*

Introduction

Energy is a necessary and vital input to economic activity throughout the world. Oil plays a key role in this regard; crude oil is today one of the most highly-valued commodities in international trade. While some might consider oil as a homogeneous commodity that should carry the same price worldwide, in reality price differentials among regions of the world exist due to market conditions, shipping distance and political factors. The sharp oil price increases to over $50 per barrel during 2004, as well as Saudi Arabia's decision – along with its fellow Organization of Petroleum Countries (OPEC) member states – to raise oil production levels, vividly illustrates that the future of the Kingdom's petroleum sector will be as important to the world as it is to Saudi Arabia for many years to come. While the hydrocarbon sector has brought about undoubted material benefits to the Kingdom over the past thirty years, it has also brought great responsibilities and limitations on how far Saudi Arabia can act in pursuing its own energy interests, unlike marginal oil producers that wish to optimize on current revenues, knowing that their reserves will run out in the short run. According to Saudi Aramco, the Kingdom sits on 260 billion barrels of oil, or a *quarter* of the world's total known reserves (Saudi Aramco, 2002). If one adds the little-known fact that the Kingdom also has the world's *fourth* largest gas reserves at 230 trillion cubic feet (TCF), one can more fully comprehend the strategic importance of the Kingdom in meeting the world's energy needs.

The government's recent emphasis on economic diversification encompasses energy-based manufacturing and the exploitation of gas and mineral resources, both for domestic consumption and for the establishment of a new export market. However, despite efforts at diversification away from oil, the hydrocarbon sector will continue to be at the heart of the Kingdom's economic well being for some time. Given the Kingdom's low-cost production, which gives it a comparative advantage estimated at between $1-3 per barrel for extraction compared to other high cost energy producers, it is not unreasonable to assume that future private-sector-led economic diversification will somehow be associated with energy-related products.

The petroleum sector

The history of oil, specifically that relating to the formation of the so-called "oil cartel", the Organization of Oil Producing Countries (OPEC), in 1960, has been extensively reviewed elsewhere and falls outside the scope of this book (Johany, 1982, Newberry, 1981, Parra, 2004, Kuwaiz, 1986, Farsi, 1982). However, it is relevant to examine the negotiating strength of the oil cartel and assess whether OPEC contributes to oil price stability in the world markets. Based on basic economic principles of demand and supply, if OPEC is to affect the price of oil, it must affect the quantity. Figures 8.1 and 8.2 illustrate the latest world demand and supply for oil.

Figure 8.1 reveals that world demand for oil in 2002 was just under 80 million barrels per day (b/d), with the Organization for Economic Cooperation and Development (OECD) countries consuming around 50 million b/d or over 63%.

Figure 8.1 World demand for oil

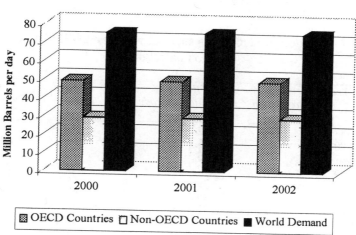

Source: *SAMA*, 2003.

Figure 8.2 World crude oil production

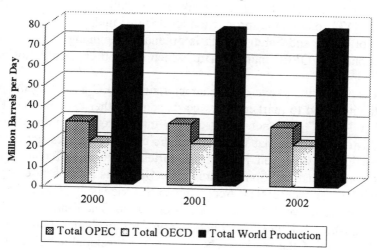

Source: *SAMA*, 2003.

In 2004, the International Energy Agency (IEA) raised its estimates of world oil demand to 82.2 million barrels per day and was forecasting 84 million barrels per day for 2005 (IEA, 10 October 2004). According to Figure 8.2, OPEC's share of world supply is around 30 million b/d or 37%. The share of OPEC in world production has fluctuated around the 36-39% levels since 1987, coming down substantially from the 60% levels seen in the mid and late 1970s (Parra, 2004). The later years are shown in Table

8.1, which also sets out Saudi Arabia's production as a percentage of world and OPEC output.

Table 8.1 Saudi oil production as share of world and OPEC oil production (Million barrel/day)

Year	World Production	OPEC Production	Saudi Production	Saudi Share of World	Saudi Share of OPEC
1987	62.4	19.7	4.1	6.6%	20.9%
1990	66.9	25.1	8.1	12.1%	32.4%
1992	67.2	26.5	8.3	12.4%	31.5%
1994	68.6	27.4	8.1	11.7%	29.4%
1997	74.3	29.9	8.0	10.8%	26.8%
1999	74.1	29.4	7.6	10.2%	25.7%
2000	76.7	30.8	8.1	10.5%	26.3%
2001	76.8	30.1	7.9	10.2%	26.2%
2002	76.6	28.5	7.1	9.7%	24.9%
2003(2Q)	77.9	29.9	8.2	10.5%	27.4%
2004(F)*	82.1	31.5	8.9	10.8%	28.3%

Source: *SAMA*, 2003, *Petroleum Intelligence Weekly, EIU.*   *2004 Forecast.

After reaching a production peak of 9.9 million b/d in 1980 (SAMA 2003, p. 447), today Saudi production level is just under 11 million b/d (third quarter of 2004) and Saudi Arabia is gradually beginning to regain both its international and OPEC market share, which it had been steadily losing since 1990.

According to the above data, characterizing OPEC as setting the price of oil without regard to market forces needs some further explanation. To label OPEC a "cartel" does not really convey much economic information. The world "cartel" implies that OPEC members co-operate to restrict output and generate higher world oil prices. But cartels come in different forms and change form over time. Some characterize OPEC as a "loosely co-operating oligopoly" (Adelman, 1995). According to this viewpoint, OPEC has tended to move between two different modes of operation. The first is a "full cartel" mode, in which all members operate together to change output so as to control a share of the market. The second is a "residual supplier" mode, in which only certain key producers take responsibility for controlling the market price by playing a "balance wheel role".

The history of OPEC from 2000 to 2004 seems to confirm both modes of operation. The period 2000-2003 was characterized by OPEC's greater determination to stick to agreed-upon production quotas, while in 2004 Saudi Arabia acted as the price "balancing wheel" by producing more oil to counteract higher oil prices, which touched over $50 per barrel in the second half of 2004. This accounts for the increasing Saudi share of world and OPEC output in Table 8.1.

For OPEC to operate like a cartel and control prices, a number of conditions must be met (Johany, 1982). These are summarized in Table 8.2 where it is clear that OPEC does not meet a "full cartel" characterization.

Table 8.2 Cartel characteristics and OPEC: A score sheet

Characteristic	OPEC Reality	Comment
• Small number of members	• Meets the condition	• Members vary from smaller producers (Qatar 500,000 b/d to Saudi Arabia 11 million b/d)
• Secret price cuts observable	• Does not meet	• Difficult to monitor "discounts"
• Offending members subject to punishment	• Does not meet	• Voluntary membership in OPEC
• Entry barriers must exist	• Does not meet	• Other oil producers enter the market outside OPEC
• Market demand and cost conditions stable	• Does not meet	• Cost conditions change with technological advances outside OPEC's control

If OPEC wished to expand its market share, theoretically it should not have any problem based on its oil reserves. While OPEC's share of the world's output is under 40% as seen earlier, this becomes less significant when compared with the size of the reserves of OPEC member countries in relation to the rest of the world. Table 8.3 examines this further.

Table 8.3 Proven world oil reserves (billion barrels) 2002

Country	Barrels (billion)	% World Share	Reserves/Production (Years)
Saudi Arabia*	261	25.0%	82
Iraq*	112	10.8%	Over 100
UAE*	97.8	9.3%	Over 100
Kuwait*	96.5	9.2%	Over 100
Iran*	87.7	8.6%	65.7
Venezuela*	76.9	7.3%	66.4
Mexico	28.3	2.7%	23.5
Russia	48.6	4.6%	20.6
Libya*	29.5	1.4%	57.4
USA	29.7	2.8%	10.4
China	24.0	2.3%	20.2

Source: *BP Statistical Review of World Energy*, 2003.
* OPEC members. OPEC members not included are Nigeria, Indonesia, Qatar and Gabon.

Table 8.3 indicates that the larger OPEC members account for around 72% of the world's proven reserves, or slightly more, at 75%, if the additional smaller OPEC producing members are included in world reserves. Clearly, OPEC nations in general are using their proven reserves much less intensively than other countries that are producing the 60% of world output from 25% world reserves. Some suggest that these OPEC output restraints are meant to maintain "cartel-like" high oil prices, rather than reflect a lack of "need" for revenue or a conservationist concern about future energy supplies (Mettale, 1987, Gelb et al., 1998). However, this is another generalization, for different OPEC members have different needs and some smaller members, such as Gabon, exhibit higher production to reserve ratios than others. With the Middle East accounting for around 64% of total world oil reserves, Table 8.3 highlights the continuing strategic importance of the Middle East region in general and the oil producers in particular to the rest of the oil-consuming world.

Saudi oil policy

The Kingdom has never expressed a single unified policy statement regarding its crude oil. This is probably wise, given the complex and changing external issues affecting world oil markets (Ali Sheikh, 1976, Mettale, 1987).

Table 8.4 Implicit and explicit Saudi oil policy objectives

Policy Objectives	Observations
• Reasonable oil prices which gives producer sufficient income	(a) OPEC price band of $22-28 per barrel has been maintained but in 2003/2004 it overshot the range due to political factors and strikes in some oil producing countries (b) In real terms, the price of oil exports per barrel has fallen sharply.
• Sufficient supplies to satisfy market needs at all times, including maintenance of excess capacity	(a) Achieved to a large extent; Saudi Arabia planned to increase output to 11 million b/d in 2004 to meet world demand.
• High level of cooperation among oil producers	(a) Achieved to a large extent during the period 2000-2004, including non-OPEC members such as Russia, Norway and Mexico
• Close communication with oil consuming nations	(a) Achieved to a large extent with dialogue at highest national levels
• Recognition that oil is important to the health of the world economy	(a) High oil prices can cause rise in inflation, restrict economic growth and cause political damage in oil consuming nations (b) Saudi Arabia argues for conciliatory approach in OPEC
• Commitment to protect the environment	(a) Kingdom applying latest world environment protection standards
• Maintaining a robust oil industry ready and able to supply future energy needs	(a) Saudi Aramco investing in future capacity and new energy fields such as *Shuaibah*

However, by examining various public statements made recently by senior officials in the oil industry, notably by the oil minister, Ali Al Naemi, and other Saudi Aramco executives, it is possible to identify some of their broader objectives (Harrison, 21 January 2004, Agence France Presse). Table 8.4 summarizes these and assesses how far they are being met.

The information in Table 8.4 confirms that, overall, Saudi oil policy has been a relative success. The primary concern, however, has been to ensure oil prices which provide the Kingdom with "sufficient" income to meet its revenue needs. As discussed in earlier chapters, with the exception of a few years during which oil prices were driven higher than budgeted, the Kingdom ran persistent budget deficits. Of greater concern is the fact that, despite record oil prices of $45-50 per barrel during 2004, in *real terms*, the purchasing power of the Kingdom's oil prices has fallen due to inflation and depreciation of the dollar's value. The historical decline in the real value of Saudi oil export prices have not been fully compensated by recent higher world oil prices, as illustrated in Figure 8.3.

Figure 8.3 Real oil prices (Base year: 1970)

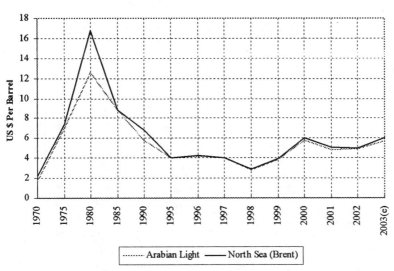

Source: *SAMA*, 2003.

Non-OPEC oil producers

There has been tangible progress in the level of cooperation between OPEC and non-OPEC oil producers, as exemplified by the visit to non-OPEC Russia by Saudi Arabia's Crown Prince Abdullah bin Abdulaziz in September, 2003, to cement the relationship between the world's two largest oil producers (Saudi Press Agency, 2 September 2003). The Russian

Federation's net exports were averaging 5.4 million barrels per day in 2003 and oil experts expected this to rise, driven by 2004's stronger oil prices. Russia accepted the offer to attend OPEC meetings on an observer status, as Mexico does.

However, higher oil prices creates a dilemma for Saudi and OPEC oil pricing policy: should they defend current higher oil prices with no growth in production volumes or revenues year after year, or should they let prices drop to discourage non-OPEC oil production in order to capture a larger market share for future years.

Both options have negative revenue implications for Saudi Arabia. Defending current higher oil prices means gradually increasing government deficits, while non-OPEC producers benefit from higher prices and continue to produce more oil, potentially causing a market share loss for the Kingdom. The second option might bring substantial short-term revenue shortfalls and growing deficits, in the hope of capturing a higher market share and greater future revenues. This dilemma is illustrated in Figure 8.4, which shows clear increases in non-OPEC oil production during oil price rises and vice-versa.

Figure. 8.4 Non-OPEC oil supply and oil prices

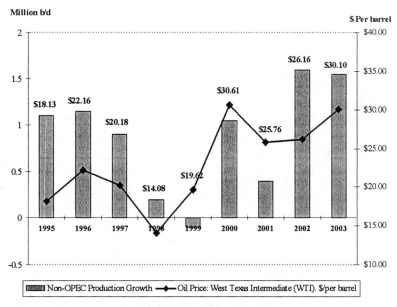

Source: *IEA Forecast for non-OPEC supply growth*, 2003.

Figure 8.4 shows that when oil prices touch the upper limits of the OPEC price band range of $28 per barrel, there is a perceptible increase in non-

OPEC oil supply. Major non-OPEC oil supply currently comes from Russia, Kazakhstan, Mexico, Brazil, the North Sea (UK and Norway), offshore USA, non-OPEC Africa and Canada. While the situation in Iraq following the 2003 Gulf War remains unclear (as of 2004), with erratic oil shipments of around 1.5-2.1 million barrels per day, larger Iraq oil supplies could be a major destabilizing factor if Iraq is forced to operate outside its OPEC set quotas due to reconstruction needs.

In the face of new production realities, OPEC decided to shift its strategy from strict price fixing, which could not be defended without massive "balancing wheel" scarifies by countries such as Saudi Arabia, to an OPEC strategy of quantity fixing and trying to defend a wider price band (Oweiss, 1996, Parra, 2004, Cordesman, 2003). OPEC members have bitterly complained that 2004's high oil prices were the result of forces other than supply and demand, and of new players in the oil market that had not been a factor only a decade earlier. The developing countries' nationalization of oil resources at the upstream stage – the production or recovery stage – meant that the "oil majors" who had controlled such upstream production no longer controlled large volumes of petroleum within vertically integrated channels, from production to refining to distribution. The oil majors were transformed into major buyers of oil, and an active spot and forward commodities market was developed by oil brokers.

By the 1990s, the spot and futures oil market accounted for over 60% of oil sales, compared with less than 5% in the 1960s (Parra, 2004, Oweiss, 1996). These new market players were reactive to day-to-day variations in demand and supply, supported or exaggerated by real events or rumours in the market. OPEC officials complained that the higher prices seen during 2004 had a 10-15% "rumour premium" added to world prices. In the long run, fundamentals such as the cost of exploiting reserves, consumer demand for current or new markets like China, and the availability of other energy substitutes will be the dominant factors affecting oil prices. This is the prime reason why Saudi Arabia would like to diversify its revenue source, beyond crude oil sales.

Looking forward, it is more than likely that Saudi Arabia will continue with its current oil pricing strategy within OPEC, while at the same time trying to ensure that new production capacity is added to the oil industry, through using the latest technology and lowering costs. Saudi Arabia unquestionably has always had very low recovery costs, at $0.30 per barrel in the 1960s to between $1.80-$2.80 a barrel in the 1990s (Johany, 1986, Cordesman, 2003). This gives the Kingdom a comparatively large advantage over other high-cost oil producers. Industry experts attribute this advantage to the high pressure of the oil wells in Saudi Arabia, which eliminates the need for pumps to bring oil to the surface, as well as to the high production "flow" rate of these wells. By way of comparison, fewer than 1,500 wells in Saudi Arabia yield current production levels of 9 million barrels per day, in contrast to a U.S. production of 6.4 million barrels per day from around 590,000 wells (IEA, 2003).

Oil and GDP contribution

The oil sector currently contributes around 35-37% of the Saudi GDP; this is down from 60% in the early 1970s, as we can see in Figure 8.5, covering 1968-2002.

Figure 8.5 Oil and non-oil GDP

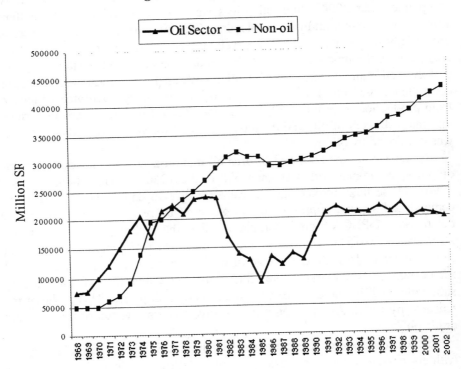

Source: *SAMA*, 2002, 2003.

Non-oil GDP growth has been on a steady increase since 1982/1983 and the Saudi government is encouraging this trend, but oil revenue and oil related products continue to be the major source of government revenue. Table 8.5 highlights the growing importance of the export of refined oil products.

Table: 8.5 Saudi Arabia: Hydrocarbon sector indicators (1962-2002)

Index	1962	1972	1982	1992	2002
• Oil production (Million barrels)	599	2,201	2,366	3,049	2,588
• Oil exports (Million barrels)	501	1,992	2,058	2,408	1,928
• World export market share	0.6%	2.6%	4.7%	3.25%	2.57%
• Refined production (Million barrels)	94	222	310	541	582
• Refined export (Million barrels)	81	208	195	473	362
• Natural gas liquids (Million barrels)	1.06	19.8	156.7	227.7	292.4
• Nominal oil prices ($/barrel)	N/A	3.61	33.42	19.33	25.03
• Real oil prices (at 1970 prices $/barrel)	N/A	3.28	12.19	4.79	4.93
• GDP at current prices (SR billion)	N/A	38.3	524.2	510.4	705.8
• Oil sector GDP at current prices (SR billion)	N/A	22.4	254.7	199.8	261.8

Source: *SAMA, Annual Report*, 2003.

N/A: Not available.

While the composition of the Saudi GDP was changing over time, so too were the trading links of Saudi Arabia's petroleum and other energy export sectors. Today, the Far East, South East Asia and emerging economies of Africa are the prime customers of Saudi petroleum products, as Figure 8.6 demonstrates.

Figure 8.6. Saudi petroleum and other hydrocarbon exports by destination (2002)

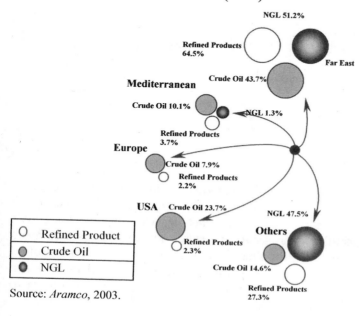

Source: *Aramco*, 2003.

It is interesting to note from Figure 8.6 how few refined products are imported by European and U.S. markets from Saudi Arabia, with around 6% of total exports in this category. The existence of domestic petrochemical refining industries in Europe and the USA coupled with accusations of "unfair" or low-priced Saudi feedstock inputs has ensured that Saudi Arabia seeks alternative markets in the Far East. China is fast becoming a major trading partner for Saudi Arabia. As Figure 8.7 shows, China today is the third largest importer of oil, after the USA and Japan. Chinese economic growth rates of around 7-9% p.a. over the past few years have kept commodity prices – including oil – relatively high in the face of weaker European and U.S. economic growth rates during 2003 and 2004.

Figure 8.7 Top ten oil-consuming countries
(Million barrels/day), 2001

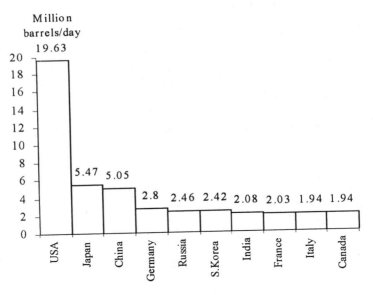

Source: *Saudi Aramco*, 2003.

The disproportionate energy consumption of the USA, relative to its population size, together with the expected depletion of domestic oil reserves in around 11 years at current production levels, explains the USA's future problem. Identifying and securing a stable source of oil is paramount for the USA, as is the search for alternative fuel sources. Saudi exports of oil to the USA account for around a quarter of all daily US oil imports and underlie the close economic and strategic relationship between the two countries in terms of energy policies.

Maintaining the Far East pricing premium

It is not generally known that different regions of the world have different pricing formulas for the same crude oil exports. Saudi Arabia adopted "formula pricing" since the late 1980s, which involves the use of three indices for sales of Saudi and other Middle East oil to various regions around the world. These indices or "markers" are as follows:

- West Texas Intermediate (WTI) as a benchmark for sales to the North American markets
- IPE Brent crude prices for sales to Europe
- Dubai and Oman averages for sale to the Asian markets

The selling price formula is then calculated applying a discount or premium to the price of the "marker" indexes. The cost of freight is an essential element in the calculation of the final pricing. Currently the Saudi market prices the different regions through the following formulas:

European market = IPE Brent – Discount
American market = WTI – Discount
Asian market = Average Oman/Dubai + Premium

This explains the steady growth in sales of Saudi crude to the Far East as it enjoys a premium, while sales to the European and US markets suffer a discount to the "marker price". Further, Russia's proximity to the European market has ensured that Russian oil export strategy in the short-term will concentrate on obtaining a greater European market share at the expense of Middle East producers. In the long term, Russia could also pose a potential competitive threat to Saudi's Far East oil exports, as Russian oil companies are planning to commission different pipeline systems through Central Asian and Far East countries to reach the main Chinese and Japanese markets. Should this be successfully completed, the current Saudi Arabian premium on Far East sales could be eroded. Given the logistics of building these pipelines, crossing many different nations, it could take the Russians some time. The main worry for Saudi Arabia in the short term is further loss in the already-discounted European market.

Oil sector capital investments: public or private?

When it surveys the future of the oil market, Saudi Arabia can claim many favourable factors, including massive reserves, low production costs, high production capacity and a well skilled labour force that has one of the highest "Saudization" ratios in the entire Kingdom. According to Saudi

Aramco, the total number of the petroleum sector employees stood at just under 55,000, 86% of which were Saudis. This is illustrated in Figure 8.8, which also gives the break-down of expatriate labour by nationality.

Figure 8.8 Saudi Aramco: Numbers of employees year-end 2002

(a) Saudi and expatriate employees

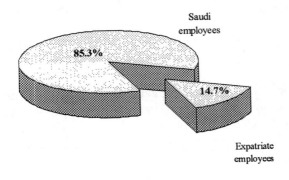

(b) Expatriates by major global regions

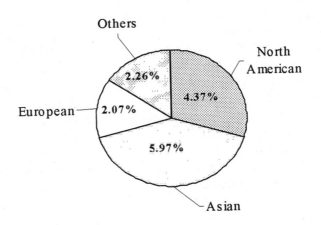

Source: *Saudi Aramco*, 2003.

There is an historical explanation for the relatively high number of North American expatriates working for Aramco in comparison with other nationalities. The Saudi company enjoyed a close relationship with the founding U.S. oil companies which had formed the Arabian American Oil Company (Aramco) that was later renamed Saudi Aramco when it was nationalized by the Saudi government.   This high percentage of skilled technical and administrative Saudi staff in the most economically critical and sensitive of Saudi industries is reassuring, especially if some foreign workers decide not to renew their contracts with Saudi Aramco due to the wave of domestic terrorism in Saudi Arabia which particularly targeted western expatriates (Saudi Press Agency, 6, 12 June 2004).

In the long run, Saudi Arabia must determine the amount and origin of investment needed for maintaining and expanding its oil industry capacity, if it is to continue playing its dominant and strategic role as a world producer. As Table 8.6 indicates, the amount of oil sector Gross Fixed Capital Formation (GFCF) declined over the years, only to pick up from 2001.

Table 8.6 Gross fixed capital formation: Oil and non-oil private sectors (billion SR)

Sector	1969	1972	1982	1989	1992	2001
Oil Sector	0.327	2.04	14.881	1.53	7.00	14.24
Non-Oil Private Sector	1.056	1.66	34.16	35.59	54.69	94.35

Source: *SAMA*, 2003, p. 438.

According to Table 8.6, while non-oil private sector GFCF had risen steadily to around SR 95 billion in 2001, the oil sector's investment in this vital area had almost ceased in 1989 when oil prices collapsed, and investment only began to achieve the higher levels of 1982 when Saudi Arabia was producing as much oil in 2004 as it was in 1982.

The opening up of the new Saudi capital market can provide the means for Saudi Aramco to tap into the domestic capital markets to finance its long-term capital projects, without having to readmit foreign companies into the lucrative upstream industry. The enthusiasm shown for IPOs in the energy-related sector by Saudi investors could provide the means to maintain Saudi control of both wealth generation and of this strategic sector altogether. Unlike other start-up or less competitive industries, Saudi Arabia's oil industry is well known and profitable, so investment will not be made based on theory but on demonstrated profitability.

A new energy star: The gas sector

The Kingdom's gas sector made the headlines during 2003 and 2004, first for the announcement of the cancellation of major gas projects and then for the signing of replacements with new partners of choice. As noted

earlier, Saudi Arabia has the world's fourth largest gas reserves and is the
world's largest exporter of Natural Gas Liquids (NGL), but this fact does not
make the headlines like oil does (Saudi Aramco, Master Gas System, 2003,
p. 2). Saudi Arabia's position amongst the world's ten largest gas reserve
countries is set out in Figure 8.9.

Figure 8.9 Estimated gas reserves: Ten largest country reserves
Trillion cubic feet (year-end 2002)

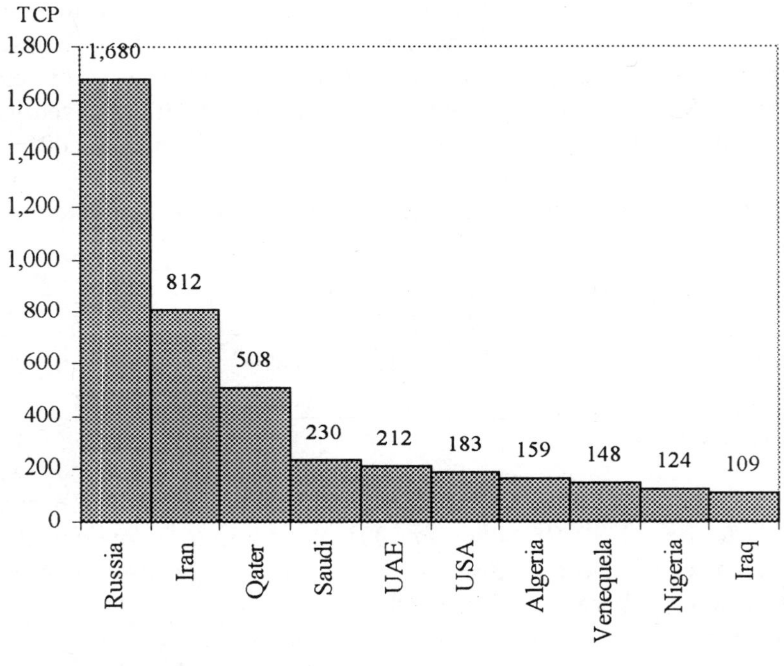

Source: *Saudi Aramco, Master Gas System*, 2003.

Unlike nearby Qatar, whose gas is mostly "non-associated" – extracted
without producing oil – roughly two-thirds of Saudi Arabia's proven gas
reserves consist of "associated" gas, mainly from the onshore *Ghawar* field
and offshore *Safaniya* and *Zuluf* fields. Most of Saudi Arabia's natural gas
was flared or burned off when oil was produced prior to the start-up of the
Kingdom's master gas system, which was completed in 1982. This system
cost some $13 billion and was created to meet domestic demand and to
provide most of the 0.7 million barrels per day of NGL. By all accounts, gas
production has done much to meet domestic energy needs and to reduce
domestic demand for oil, which is easier and more economical to export than
liquefied natural gas. Gas requires large onshore investments for gas
liquefaction and then it requires transportation in specialized container

vessels. Domestic oil consumption is not insignificant, and accounted for around 25% of total Saudi oil production in 2002 as seen earlier in Table 8.5.

Foreign interest in gas projects

Unlike crude oil production, the Kingdom of Saudi Arabia signalled its intention early on to invite foreign companies to participate in the development of its large gas sector. In 2000, ten International Oil Companies (IOCs) noted their interest in participating in the ambitious plan to develop upstream gas and processing facilities. Plans for three integrated gas projects were submitted by the Saudi government: the *Haradh* gas development project, the *Rabigh* integrated refinery and petrochemical projects, and the *Kidan* and *Shaybah* gas development projects. Saudi Aramco was to be a partner in all three projects. In May 2001, Saudi Arabia selected a mix of eight IOCs to participate in the huge $25 billion "Saudi gas initiative", as it was to be called. This Saudi gas initiative was to develop an *integrated* gas sector comprising upstream gas development (production), with "downstream" (processing) petrochemicals, power generation and desalination plants. The IOCs involved in the bidding were the elite of the energy industry, including Exxon Mobil, Royal Dutch Shell, BP and Conoco Phillips. And yet, by June 2003, the discussions with these IOCs were halted (Financial Times, 7 June 2003, AFP, 14 July 2003), despite some initial confusing claims and counter-claims that the gas deals were still on track. According to public press reports, the collapse centred on the acceptable rate of return on the IOCs' investments in the projects. The Kingdom argued that investors' return was double the commercial borrowing rates that big international oil companies with good debt ratings could secure. The IOCs, however, insisted that the returns were well below the 12-15% target ranges, and they sought a larger share of gas off-take through increased exploration acreage (Financial Times, 7 June 2003). It is useful to closely examine the major factors that drove the great gas initiative, as well as the reasons for the breakdown of discussions with the initial round of IOCs.

First, the initiative was launched during a time when oil prices were falling, sharply reducing Saudi oil revenues. The need for outside investment was probably felt more severely than during a period of higher oil prices, such as the years 2003 and 2004. The IOCs probably sensed this earlier Saudi need and held out for more concessions in terms of a larger gas acreage.

Second, it is not always true that foreign investors will bring a cheaper source of capital to Saudi Arabia. Saudi Arabia can still borrow on relatively good terms in its own name, as the reaffirmation of its long-term credit rating by Standard & Poor's in June, 2004 confirms. Moreover, there is no guarantee that a foreign IOC will pass on the full benefit of such cheaper international borrowing to Saudi Arabia; in fact, it might add an additional country risk premium for carrying out Saudi projects.

Third, some argued that foreign companies would transfer appropriate technology to Saudi Arabia. This is not a convincing argument (Mabro, 2002, Cordesman, 2003). There is no technology for upstream development that Saudi Aramco does not possess or is unable to acquire from sources other than IOCs. The irony is that, by their own admission, IOCs are *not* specialists in power generation or water desalination plants, which were one of the key components of the "Great Gas Initiative".

Fourth, the management aspects of these large integrated projects were put forward as justification for IOC participation. There is some merit to this argument, if an IOC itself was to handle all the integrated components through upstream development and transmission infrastructure, as well as constructing and running plants of different sizes for final users of gas. As it stands, this challenge can probably not be met with the present resources of Saudi Aramco. However, the alternative is to break the project into smaller parts and subcontract to industry specialists, with Saudi Aramco retaining overall project management control.

In the final analysis, what the IOCs were really seeking was an involvement in Saudi Arabia's upstream *oil* industry and this clashed with Saudi Aramco's desire to remain in total control of this strategic sector (Mabro, 2002).

In short, the oil companies wanted an involvement in a sector that Saudi Arabia does not really want to grant, even if it agreed on some concessions, while Saudi Arabia wanted IOC investment in sectors which were not of real interest to the oil companies, even when they had expressed a conditional interest to do the job. There was no commonality of interest, so it was no surprise the talks broke down.

New partners step in

Given Saudi Arabia's energy position in the world, it was not surprising that other international oil companies would step in to replace the consortiums that withdrew. In March, 2004, Saudi Oil Minister Ali Al Naimi announced the signing of gas exploration contracts with companies from Russia (Lukoil), China (China Petrochemical Company Sinopec), Italy (ENI), and Spain (Repsol YPF) (Hassan, 6 March 2003). Under the agreements, nearly 122,000 sq. km. of land was assigned for gas exploration to these foreign companies. Saudi Aramco maintained a partnership in all the ventures planned, and held 20% of the stake in each of the three projects.

According to press reports, the contracts will run for a maximum of 40 years and are expected to generate around 35,000 additional high-value jobs for Saudis in this new energy sector. The entry of the Chinese into the Saudi hydrocarbon sector attracted much positive interest and seemed to further cement growing trade relations between the Kingdom and China. The Russian participation was also significant, as it may herald a closer relationship between the world's two largest oil producers, raising the possibility of joint ventures inside and outside the Kingdom. This was discussed during the historic visit of Crown Prince Abdullah to Russia mentioned earlier, when the two countries signed a five-year oil and natural gas agreement, which Russian officials said could lead to deals worth up to $25 billion (Saudi Press Agency, Reuters, 27 January 2004).

These developments in the Saudi gas sector auger well for the Kingdom, as not only does it allow for energy diversification so as to compete with other gas producers, but also is able to enter the more environmentally friendly energy sector which gas represents.

Petrochemicals: adding value

Only a couple of decades ago, Saudi Arabia seemed a most unlikely location for a major industrialization drive. The great "oil shocks" of the mid-1970s opened up vast new opportunities for the Kingdom's planners to deploy large revenue sources for industrial and economic diversification and to move away from being a primary energy supplier. Industrialization, especially in hydrocarbon energy-related industries where Saudi Arabia enjoys comparative cost advantages, remains at the heart of Saudi development plans and strategies. The earlier emphasis on state ownership and expenditure might be giving way, in the new millennium, to public-private partnerships or pure private sector initiatives, but the petrochemical sector remains one of the more promising for the future.

Petrochemicals are certainly making their impact felt worldwide. The scope of products manufactured from petrochemicals is broad, ranging from insulators, cable wraps, sockets, tires, plastic and rubber parts, to everyday items such as home furnishings, bed sheets, typewriters, ribbons, book covers, clothes, soap and detergents. The modern world's mass consumption of goods would be greatly hindered without the final output of the petrochemical industries.

Today, Saudi Arabia is home to twenty-one large, modern petrochemical complexes located in the two industrial cities of *Jubail* (on the eastern coast of Saudi Arabia) and *Yanbu* (on the western coast). Eighteen of these complexes are owned by affiliates of the Saudi Basic Industries Corporation (SABIC). The remaining three are private sector joint ventures with international companies such as Shell. Of the eighteen SABIC petrochemical affiliates, two are wholly owned by SABIC, five are SABIC partnership with Saudi private investors, and the remaining eleven complexes are joint ventures with international companies. *Jubail* hosts 14 of the SABIC owned complexes, 3 are in *Yanbu* and 1 is in *Dammam* in the Eastern Province. The engineering projects to transform the desert to their current status have been on a monumental scale. As an illustration, some 270 million cubic meters of earth was moved to prepare the *Jubail* site alone, which is enough to build a road around the world at the equator one meter deep by seven meters wide (Royal Commission for Jubail and Yanbu, 2004)

In 2002, Crown Prince Abdullah bin Abdulaziz inaugurated the cornerstone for further expansion of a second industrial city at *Jubail* at a cost of SR 131 billion. It is forecasted to employ an additional 55,000, mostly Saudi, workers.

Generating secondary industries

Of more long-term importance to the Kingdom is SABIC's ability to promote a second-generation industrial linkage with the rest of the Saudi private sector. To some extent this has been successful, for there are currently 12 secondary industries and 115 light and supporting industries serving the SABIC complexes. Some have argued for more labour-intensive industries, such as textiles and clothing, besides traditional plastics (Wilson, 2004). The emphasis on secondary industries will grow with the completion of the second *Jubail* industrial city, where plans for smaller, more labour intensive projects are being developed. However, given Saudi labour costs, which tend to be higher than foreign labour, enterprises that might be established must try to achieve comparative cost competitiveness in the international market. This is due to the close proximity and competitively priced feedstock of gas and oil products to Saudi industries. It is no coincidence that the *Jubail* industrial city is located very close to its primary source of energy input in the Eastern Province of the Kingdom, thus reducing the cost of transportation of its feedstock. It is this availability of low-cost feedstock, along with excellent infrastructure support and low utility costs in the industrial cities of *Jubail* and *Yanbu*, that has attracted international joint-venture partners to Saudi Arabia's petrochemical industries. The Saudi government has also extended attractive financing facilities through the Saudi Industrial Development Fund (SIDF) to joint venture operations at low rates. The degree of interest, both Saudi and international, in developing the industrial sector is a far cry from the earlier days of basic industry infrastructure, when it was observed that "no private investors are financially capable of undertaking such basic industries" (Johany et al., 1986). There were also doubts about the profitability of the hydrocarbon-related basic industries.

Today, petrochemicals make a sizeable contribution to the Saudi GDP. To put this in perspective, SABIC generates around nine to ten billion dollars worth of sales annually, with net profits of 2.6 billion dollars for the third quarter of 2004, by transforming 10 billion cubic meters of natural gas into 32 million tonnes of petrochemicals. The net effect was 60% of non-oil Saudi exports for 2002 (SAMA, 2003), and forecasted 80% for 2004.

Table 8.7 summarizes SABIC's main product groups, demonstrating the growing importance of exports.

Table 8.7 SABIC's production and exports by product group
1998-2002 ('000 tons)

Product group	1998	2000	2002
(A) Production Total	**25,293**	**27,979**	**40.619**
• Basic chemicals	10,954	12,523	15,845
• Metals	2,499	2,864	3,489
• Intermediates	4,778	4,816	7,227
• Fertilizer	4,339	5,115	5,259
• Polymers	2,633	2,661	4,608
• SEPC*	0	0	3,958
(B) Export Total	**13,413**	**14,188**	**20,232**
• Basic chemicals	5,593	6,484	7,315
• Metals	625	498	480
• Intermediates	2,764	2,588	3,699
• Fertilizer	2,341	2,670	2,784
• Polymers	2,090	1,948	3,831
• SEPC*	0	0	2,123

Source: SABIC Central Department of Statistics, Statistical Yearbook, 2002, p. 350.
* SEPC = Saudi European Petrochemical Company (Holland).

It is interesting to note from Table 8.7 that SABIC has now branched out overseas. They have acquired petrochemical companies to complement its domestic operations through the acquisition of the Saudi European Petrochemical Company (SEPC) in Holland. SPEC contributed around 10% of total export sales during 2002. This international trend might continue, with SABIC locating nearer to its primary markets in Europe, and (of even more importance), in Asia. In July 2004, SABIC and the Iranian Marun Petrochemical Company finalized a joint venture agreement to establish an equally owned company to produce 1.1 million tons of ethylene as intermediate product, as well as 1.35 million tons of polymers (Arab News, 28 July 2004). The Saudi company may well evolve into a truly international player (Zamil, 2002). Table 8.8 indicates that SABIC is already a significant player in the world's petrochemical market, accounting for around 18% of the world market share for some product lines (Nojaidi, 2002).

Table 8.8 **SABIC share of world markets for selected petrochemicals, 2001**

Product	Global capacity (million t/y)	SABIC capacity (million t/y)	SABIC share (%)
Ethylene Glycol	12	2.1	18
Methanol	27	3.8	14
MIBE	21	2.7	13
Polyethylenes	50	3.5	7
Styrene	20	1.0	5
Polypropylene	27	0.9	3

Source: *Nojaidi*, 2002.

Table 8.9 Major private sector petrochemical companies: Saudi and joint venture (2002)

Company		Products
(A) Saudi Private Sector		
National Petrochemical Industrialization Co. (NPIC)		Propylene, PP
Saudi International Petrochemical Co. (SPIC)		Methanol, Acetic Acid, VAM, BDO
Arabian Industrial Dev. Com. (NAMA)		Epoxy, ECH, Caustic, Chlorine
Saudi Chevron Petrochemicals		Benzene, Cyclohexane
Arabian Chemical Latex-Dow		Latex Products
Alujain Teldene-Montell		PP
(B) Foreign Joint Venture Partnerships		
Chevron Chemical	Saudi Chevron Petrochemicals	Benzene, cyclohexane
Dow Chemical	Arabian Chemical Latex	Polystyrene, Latex products
Ecofuel	Saudi European Ibn Zahr	MTBE, PP
Exxon Mobile Chemicals	Yanbu Petrochemicals Yanpet	PE, EG, PP
Exxon Mobile Chemicals	Jubail Petrochemicals, Kemya	Polystyrene
Mitsubishi + partners	Saudi Methanol Ar-Razi	Methanol
Mitsubishi + partners	Eastern Petrochemical Sharq	PE, EG
Montell	Xenel Teldene	PP
Panhandle, Hoechst	National Methanol Ibn Sina	Methanol
Shell Oil Co.	Saudi Petrochemical Sadaf	Styrene, EDC, MTBE/ETBE
Taiwan Fertilizers Co.	Jubail Fertilizers Samad	Urea, Ammonia, DOP

(C) Major Planned Joint Venture Projects			
Company	Estimated Investment	Products	Startup
National Petrochemical Industrialization Co. (NPIC)	$500 million	Propylene, PP	2002
Saudi International Petrochemical Co. (SPIC)	$500 million	Methanol, Acetic Acid, VAM, BDO	2004
Arabian Industrial Dev. Com. (NAMA)	$284 million	ECH	2003

Source: *Nojaidi*, 2002.

The results of the Saudi petrochemical industries have been impressive over such a short period of time; today they account for around 5% of the world's total petrochemical output and about 8% of global exports. In composition, about 52% of Saudi petrochemicals are in basic products, 26% in intermediates and 22% in final products. Saudi Arabia is aware that it needs to diversify its production line into a broader mix, preferably in intermediate and final products. In a later chapter, we will look at how Saudi Arabia imports a large quantity of final petrochemical products and note the irony that some of these imports contain a large element of Saudi basic petrochemical exports. However, Table 8.9 shows us that the major new plants being established by the private sector, either wholly Saudi owned or through joint ventures, will concentrate on final product lines.

Future challenges

SABIC's success has made it a natural target for domestic and international investment, and the commercial track record could make any further government sales of its share in SABIC an assured success. The Saudi government has already announced that it plans to reduce its current ownership in SABIC from 75% to 25% through sales to the Saudi public. The initial government sale of 25% to the public in 1987 was a success in terms of investor confidence and of market acceptance of such partial privatization moves. However, there are several challenges facing SABIC in the future.

First, SABIC, and all those entering the petrochemical sector, have to ensure that their future feedstock demand is met. The availability of cheap feedstock derived from gas and NGL will be a main preoccupation for Saudi Aramco, which might have difficulty in meeting supply commitments for the upcoming new projects. Increased production of gas, particularly non-associated gas, is crucial for the petrochemical industry's future prospects and puts into perspective the recent international gas deals signed by the Kingdom. The two go together.

Further, Saudi Arabia has to prepare itself for WTO entry and strategize around how that affects the petrochemical sector. While it is argued that WTO accession for Saudi Arabia could provide greater market access and improved trade security, some members of the WTO, particularly in the European Union (EU), are likely to resist Saudi petrochemical exports to the EU, arguing that Saudi Arabia affords an unfair competitive advantage to its petrochemical industries through cheap or subsidized feedstock. The Kingdom is aware of these issues and is committed to removing subsidies on its feedstock prices. During 2002, the price of feedstock was raised from $0.5 one million British thermal units MMTBU to $0.75 MMTBU; that brought Saudi domestic prices into line with others in the Gulf Cooperation

Council. However, the problem lies in the domestic market, where there is a large differential in Liquefied Petroleum Gas (LPG), sold at a nearly 30% discount on international prices. This appears to be in conflict with WTO rules, although Saudi Arabia has now successfully concluded its bilateral trade agreement with the EU.

Another factor is the relative inefficiency of the system for marketing SABIC products. Despite great advances made in this regard over the years, the primary approach seems to have been built around the hope that SABIC's foreign joint venture partners would assure market access to the joint venture products in their home countries. Unfortunately, with the exception of the Japanese and Taiwanese markets, this approach has been disappointing. To address the situation, SABIC is now pursing a policy of direct sales and of establishing a manufacturing presence in its primary markets.

In order to sustain the long-term success of the petrochemical industries, SABIC must remain at the cutting edge of petrochemical research. To achieve this, there needs to be growth in the internal dynamics of SABIC, especially in regards to qualified human resources and to building the internal research and development capability. The establishment of advanced R&D facilities in the Kingdom and in SABIC's Houston-based operations, along with associations with the Kingdom's leading science-based universities, is a step in the right direction.

The Mining sector: A hidden gem

After being assigned a low priority in both government planning and public expenditure in the 1970s and 1980s compared with the hydrocarbon sector, the Saudi mining industry now has a more prominent place in the Kingdom's strategy to diversify its economic base, as evidenced in the most recent announcement of the plan to privatize the state-owned mining company *Maaden* (Reuters, 24 May 2004). According to press reports, *Maaden* will be restructured into separate units of gold, phosphate, bauxite, aluminium and minerals.

Table 8.10 The Saudi Arabian Mining Company (Maaden) production

Year	Gold (thousand ounces)	Silver (thousand ounces)	Copper (tons)	Zinc (tons)
1988	163.0	445.1	782	3,550
1999	147.2	336.7	821	3,161
2000	116.7	279.7	804	2,520
2001	139.2	321.1	839	1,911
2002	135.3	384.5	587	1,209

Source: *The Saudi Arabian Mining Company (Maaden), SAMA,* 2003, p. 248.

It may come as a surprise that Saudi Arabia is home to a wide and rich resource base of mineral deposits – the largest in the Gulf region. This base includes gold, copper, zinc, phosphate, iron ore and bauxite. Table 8.10 summarizes *Maaden's* production of these minerals.

The Saudi Arabian government, through its privatization announcement for *Maaden*, is moving away from the old policy of mere mineral extraction to a policy aimed at creating a well-integrated mining industry over the next two decades. Some of the Saudi mining industry's current operating framework needs to be reassessed, however, to bring industry policies in line with international practices (Marboli, 2002; Dabbagh, 2002).

The legal framework needs to be addressed. The current framework under which the Saudi mining industry operates was established more than 30 years ago with comparatively little expenditure in the mining sector – a total of around SR 9 billion over all these years. Expenditures were mostly for basic surveys, exploration activities, laboratories and basic infrastructure support. The level of government attention did not encourage either domestic or international mining company investment in the mining sector, with local Saudi company participation confined to providing building material, crushers and quarry supplies.

The government concluded that, in order to open up the mining sector, it needed to carry out the following steps:

- Modernize the mining code
- Formulate a Saudi geological survey
- Formulate a comprehensive strategy for the mining sector
- Construct a railway network

During 2001, the Ministry of Petroleum and Minerals started discussions with the Ministry of Finance about reviewing the mining code. It forwarded the code to the Council of Ministers for ratification. The Saudi Cabinet approved the new mineral investment law in September 2004 (Saudi Press Agency, 14 September 2004). The key point of the mining code ratification was ensuring that the Kingdom was competitive with other international mining investment regimes. According to Article 14 of the Saudi Basic Governing Law, all resources that lay under or over the ground within the perimeter of the land or offshore of the Kingdom belong to the State. The problem for the mining industry in Saudi Arabia is how to reconcile this with the international practice of "licensing concessions" to the private sector. The amendments before the Council of Ministers will allow for such licenses to be issued by the Ministry of Petroleum and Minerals.

In a speech, the Minister of Petroleum outlined the other major changes to be introduced by the new mining law (Saudi Commerce and Economic Review, May 2004). They include:

- All permits, licenses and leases classified as "licenses"
- Principle of "first come – first served" introduced
- Removal of requirements for technical and financial qualifications of exploration licenses
- No limit to number of licenses applied
- Introduction of the right to explore all minerals in the licensed area
- Requirement for advance payment removed
- Bank guarantees for exploration licenses removed,
- Exploration work program replaced by mining exploration expenditure
- Investment incentives introduced
- Total tax liability not to exceed 25% of profits

The above, once fully implemented, will supply a major boost to the Saudi mining industry, so that the government can achieve one of its desired objectives: to broaden the economic base of the country and create new employment opportunities through high-value jobs. It has been estimated from mining countries' experiences that for every dollar spent on mining, the net return is $8 to the national economy (Marboli, 2002). The establishment of a viable and integrated Saudi mining industry will also ease Saudi Arabia's balance of payments, as today the Kingdom imports around 5 million tonnes of raw minerals every year. Import substitution of these minerals could be effective if it is conducted on an economic, cost-efficient and scientific basis. These imports cost Saudi Arabia around SR 8-9 billion per annum (CDS, 2003). One key area that needs addressing, whether by the government or through a public-private partnership, is the construction of an integrated railway network to service the diverse mineral-producing regions. It has been estimated that such a network will cost around $1.5 billion over a five-year period and bids from international companies, mostly Japanese, were submitted during 2002 and 2003.

Establishing a model for mining cooperation

Foreign participation in the Saudi mining sector is considered essential due to the relative lack of experience in this field, in contrast to the petroleum sector where Saudi technical skills exist in all work areas. However, in order to attract foreign investment and concession sales, certain issues will need to be clarified. While the proposed new mineral code law addresses many problems faced by the industry, there are other questions about the timing and process of obtaining mineral concessions, the Saudi government's right to a specified percentage of net profits, the states rights to participate in private mines management, and clarification of the exact role of joint venture equity policies.

Figure 8.10 sets out a model of mining cooperation between the private sector and the government and it incorporates many of the mining law's proposed changes.

Figure 8.10 Model for mining cooperation

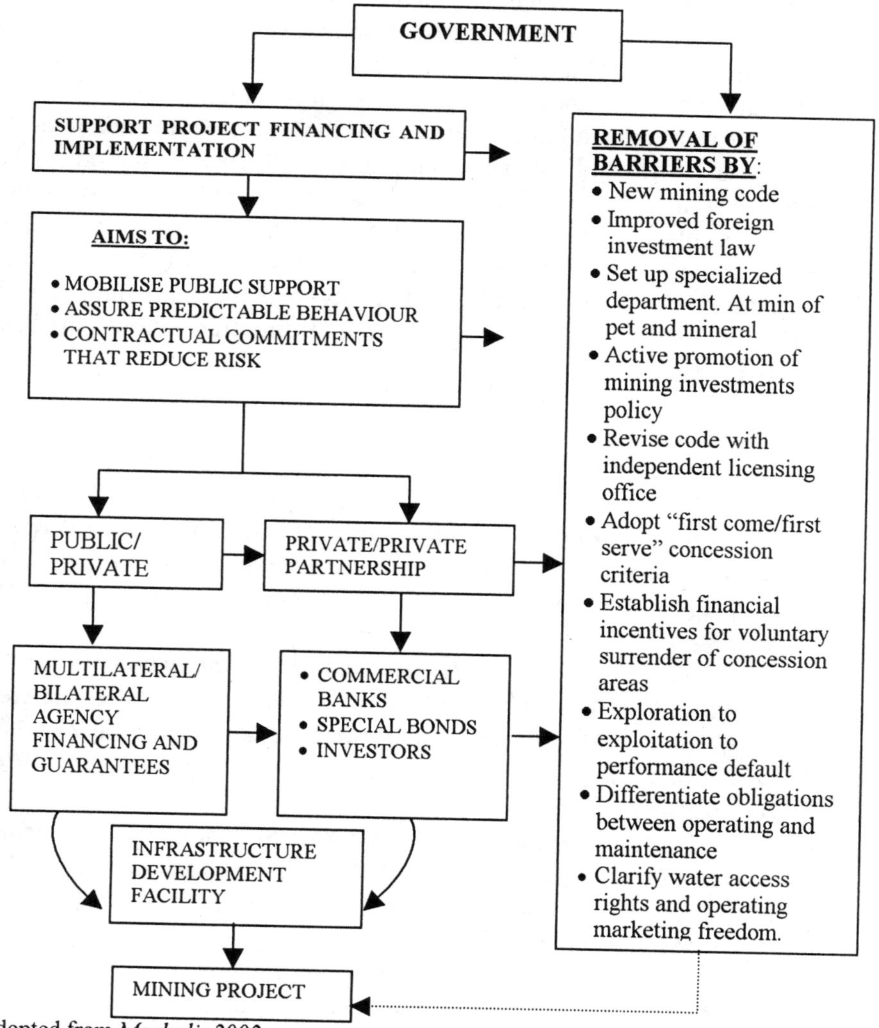

Adopted from *Marboli, 2002.*

Figure 8.10 sets out a vision for the future of mining in Saudi Arabia. There are already expressions of interest from countries with rich mining experience, such as Canada, Australia and South Africa, to become involved with Saudi Arabia's "hidden" treasures. In a couple of decades, mining could be playing a role in the Saudi economy like the one oil played two decades ago.

Conclusion

The hydrocarbon and mineral industries will remain at the heart of the Saudi economy for a long time to come, despite diversification attempts into non-hydrocarbon areas. Saudi Arabia is blessed by an abundance of oil, gas and mineral resources and, with luck and far-sighted planning, it can position itself to become a major player in all three sectors. Economic cycles will mean that as demand for one diminishes, it will rise for the other. The Kingdom must also continue to pursue its current policy to add value, whenever possible, to its exploration of these raw resources, rather than settling with mere extraction and sale. It is only through this economic approach that economic integration, diversity and skill building can be achieved in order to shield the Kingdom from fluctuations in basic commodity prices.

Summary of key points

- *The petroleum sector has played a significant role in Saudi Arabia's economic development. Rising world oil prices and Saudi Arabia's response to meet world demand by increasing its output levels have once again demonstrated the Kingdom's importance as the world's leading oil supplier.*
- *Saudi oil policy attempts to meet national goals while taking into consideration consumers and environmental interests. At the same time, Saudi Arabia plays an important moderating influence within OPEC and tries to establish working relationships with non-OPEC oil producers.*
- *The oil sector currently contributes around 35% of GDP compared with 60% levels in the early 1970's. The majority of oil and oil products are currently exported to the Far East, with the North American and European markets next in importance.*
- *Saudi Arabia has the world's fourth largest gas reserves and is the world's largest exporter of Natural Gas Liquids (NGL). Most Saudi gas is "associated" (gas-produced when oil is produced), but new*

"non-associated" gas fields are being developed with foreign partners.

- The petrochemical industries are located in the industrial cities of Jubail and Yanbu and Saudi Arabia is a major petrochemical producer accounting for around 8% of world output. Plans are underway to expand the petrochemical production base through international acquisitions by SABIC and the establishment of secondary and support industries in Jubail and Yanbu. These are expected to be carried out by the private sector, be more labour intensive and create value added products and jobs for the Saudi market.
- The mining industry has a lot of future potential, as Saudi Arabia holds large quantities of mineral resources which have not yet been exploited. The passing of new mining laws, opening this sector to domestic and international investments, should enable further economic diversification to the economy.

Critical thinking

1. "Oil has been a blessing and a curse to Saudi Arabia". Discuss. In the long term, which factor could turn out to be more valid?

2. "Saudi oil policy has always played a moderating influence on world markets, to the detriment of Saudi Arabia's interest". Is this a fair statement? What other options could Saudi Arabia have followed and what are the consequences of your proposed action?

3. "Saudi Arabia should concentrate on value added petrochemical products and rely less on oil exports". Discuss the pros and cons of following such a policy in the short and long term.

4. "The gas sector should be developed over the oil sector, given world demand for clean energy sources. Saudi Arabia should export more gas and less oil". What are the flaws in this argument for Saudi Arabia?

5. "Mining will be the future of sustainable economic diversification for Saudi Arabia, in terms of employment, integrated industrial projects and foreign investments". Discuss

Chapter 9

FOREIGN TRADE

Commerce is the equalizer of the wealth of nations.

Gladstone

Learning Outcomes:

By the end of this section, you should understand:

- *The need to trade for Saudi Arabia*
- *The composition and evolving patterns of imports*
- *The changing origins of imports*
- *The importance of the export sector*
- *The dominance of the oil sector*
- *The need for efficiency and competitiveness in the export market*
- *Saudi Arabia's trade and balance of payments*
- *Saudi foreign aid*
- *The need to establish export sector trade competitiveness best practices.*

Introduction

Saudi Arabia leads the Arab world in exports and imports, and ranks among the top five in the Islamic world, along with Malaysia, Turkey, Indonesia and the UAE (Wilson, 2003). This chapter discusses the various aspects of foreign commerce, principally imports and exports; we will look at how the composition has changed over time as well as their impact on the Kingdom's balance of payments. We will closely examine Saudi exports to assess the success of the economic diversification program to date, as well as to analyze Saudi product export competitiveness. The final section of the chapter sets out model guidelines for a more effective export promotion program to help the private sector achieve the country's economic diversification goal.

Figure 9.1 Change in real trade ratios

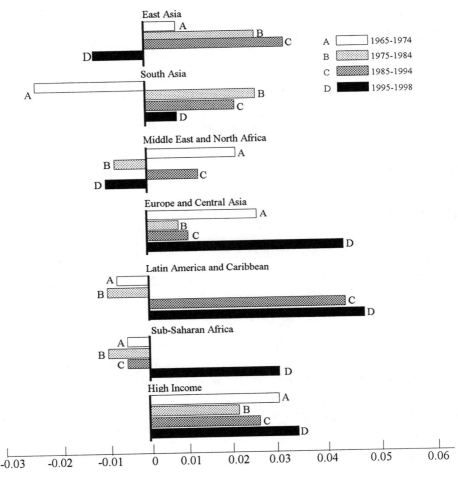

Source: *World Bank, Global Development Indicators*, 2001, *Araba World Competitiveness Report*, 2003.

Why does Saudi Arabia need to trade? Economic theory postulates that countries trade with each other based on either absolute or comparative advantage. In trade, countries specialize in exporting commodities where specialization gives them cost-of-production advantage. Saudi Arabia, with large, homogenous and low-cost oil fields, undoubtedly has a comparative advantage over other high-cost oil producers. But it does not have an absolute advantage, for the Kingdom never had to make the choice of producing non-oil products, and as such, there was no opportunity cost or alternatives forgone (Wilson, 2003). There was no trade-off between oil and non-oil production, but rather a positive relationship between oil exports and revenues and imports, with imports rising during oil booms and remaining static or declining in oil depressions. The next major challenge for the Kingdom is the expansion of Saudi Arabia's export base into other finished and semi-finished products not directly related to oil. It will be based on production efficiency and specialization, in competition with similar products produced worldwide. This will not be easy. According to the *Arab World Competitiveness Report 2003* (World Economic Forum, 2003), Saudi Arabia and the Middle East and North African countries have seen their share of global trade diminish since the mid-1980s compared with other world regions. This is illustrated in Figure 9.1.

According to the *Report*, the Middle East and North Africa (MENA) region reduced their trading integration with the rest of the world, with the lion's share of growth in world trade occuring in the economies of East Asia, Eastern Europe, Central Asia and Latin America. Growth of real trade ratios for the MENA region has been weak, only fortified by oil-related volatility for oil producing countries in times of oil booms. High-income, industrialized economies have led the growth in real trade ratios since the mid-1970s. According to the Word Trade Organization (WTO), in 1980, Saudi Arabia accounted for 5.36% of global exports, but this fell to 1.1% by 2001. Imports also fell from a global share of 1.45% in 1980 to half of one percent by 2001 (WTO, 2002).

Merchandise trade – Imports

An observation of the Kingdom's past three decades' merchandise trade reveals an astonishing transformation taking place since 1970 for both imports and exports during the period 1970-2002, as illustrated in Figure 9.2.

While exports rose significantly following the oil price rises of 1974, these tended to fluctuate erratically due to word oil price levels. Imports saw the largest sustained rises, with this sector growing at an annual compounded rate of over 33% during the first boom period of 1974-1982 (Johany, 1986). From a peak of SR 124 billion in 1992 following the end of the second Gulf War, imports have stabilized at around the SR 120 billion levels. Even more striking are the marked changes in the composition of imports and their points of origin, along with the relative changes in sectoral demand. Table 9.1 illustrates the evolution of the composition of imports for the period 1970-2002. Imports of goods and services are virtually unrestricted to the Kingdom, with the exception of those goods and services that are deemed *haram* or forbidden by Islam (such as pork and alcohol products), as well as immoral or security-related commodities. Goods from countries that the Kingdom is still boycotting, such as Israel, are also forbidden.

Figure 9.2 Saudi Arabia: merchandise trade 1970-2002

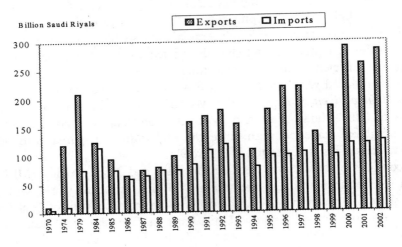

Source: *Central Department of Statistics*, 2002, *SAMA*, 2003.

Table 9.1 Saudi Arabia: Imports by major commodity group
1970-2002

SR Million

	1970	1979	1984	1989	1992	1996	2000	2002
Foodstuff, etc.	1,011	10,432	18,739	12,564	13,225	17,956	20,258	19,563
Mineral & chemical products, plastic materials, rubber	355	6,917	11,625	8,944	13,280	13,318	14,716	15,330
Hides & skins, wood & articles, paper, carboard & articles	116	3,533	4,185	2,811	4,416	4,113	4,194	4,160
Textile garments, footwear	157	5,321	9,675	8,729	10,886	8,709	7,573	7,881
Ceramic products, glass & glassware, articles of stone, plaster	42	2,666	3,669	1,666	2,313	1,749	1,931	N/A
Precious metals, gems, pearls & articles	90	1,297	3,605	3,848	5,910	4,399	4,575	3,964
Base meta;s & articles	300	12,709	14,183	6,475	11,179	10,396	8,895	N/A
Machinery, mecanical & electrical equipment, appliances	590	22,539	28,410	14,556	26,285	21,848	24,982	N/A
Transport equipment	428	10,297	15,916	14,640	29,910	15,903	19,996	N/A
Optical, precision & surgical instruments, watches, sound records & reproducers	66	2,888	5,014	2,927	3,423	2,897	3,048	N/A
Misc. manufactured articles, works of art	42	2,925	3,716	2,059	3,710	2,692	3,072	3,159
Total	3,197	81,524	118,737	79,219	124,537	103,980	113,240	121,089

Source: *Foreign Trade Statistics and Import Statistics, Central Department of Statistics*, 2003.

In 1970, the import of foodstuffs accounted for around 31% of total imports, but the oil-led boom of the mid-1970s changed the composition of imports, with machinery, transport equipment, and mineral and chemical products becoming nearly 60% of imports until the mid-1980s. With the decline in government capital expenditure, discussed in earlier chapters, the private sector increasingly drove import demand. Today, in addition to foodstuffs that account for around 15-16% of total imports, textiles, machinery and vehicle imports account for a signifcant portion of imports that meet domestic and expatriate consumer needs.

For the year 2002, fixed assets made up around 18% of total imports, with final and intermediate consumption goods at 39% and 43% respectively, as illustrated in Figure 9.3 (A).

Figure 9.3 **(A)** Import by utilization of items, 2002 (SR billion)

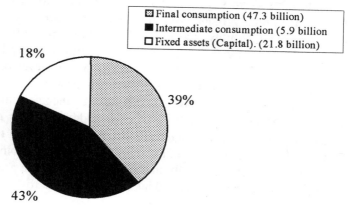

(B) Imports by nature of items, 2002 (SR billion)

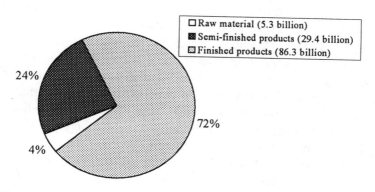

Source: *Central Department of Statistics,* 2003.

Figure 9.3 (B) illustrates that raw material imports average around 5%, while the bulk of imports (72%) are composed of finished products in value terms. Semi-finished products stood at around 24% of total import value for 2002. This high proportion of finished product imports for the Kingdom is a function of the open economy. It also reflects the degree to which consumer demand has been influenced by international consumption habits. Relatively sophisticated local advertising and marketing compaigns have also developed brand awareness, especially for high-value luxury items.

Saudi Arabia now has large, flourishing shopping malls, catering to a younger generation. Figure 9.2 showed the level of imports to be fairly steady, despite fluctuations in exports. The same is true of national income, for oil accounts for the overwhelming portion of exports, as we will soon discuss. This implies that the economy's aggregate import level does not seem to respond to variences in the (oil) aggregate income, but to non-oil income and to other factors. In previous chapters, we have seen that non-oil GDP has been gradually rising over the past few decades, contributing to some import demand stability. Earlier studies carried out on the level of the Saudi marginal propensity to import (MPM) indicated a fairly high level of MPM, almost 75% (Bashir, 1977), as well as a high level of correlation between imports and non-oil GDP. By marginal propensity to import, we mean the fraction of each increment or addition to income that is spent on imports. In the earlier research, 0.75 of each addditional one riyal income was spent on imports. It will be interesting to note whether, in the long run, this high level MPM will continue in the face of domestic Saudi manufacturing expansion, especially in the food sector where Saudi products have established brand recognition and international standards.

Origins of imports are changing

It is not just the composition of imports that has changed over time for Saudi Arabia, but also the origins of these imports. This reflects an interesting mixture of economic relations, consumer tastes and political realities. Table 9.2 sets out the share of total imports by value, accounted for by the top five exporting nations to Saudi Arabia over the period 1972-2002.

On the whole, the Kingdom's trade direction is largely determined by the private sector; it is based on commercial relations, the agencies held, and the level of comfort in dealing with their international counterparts, rather than being based on political considerations. While some government-to-government lobbying does certainly exist to obtain government-related contracts, such contracts have become less important over time as the Saudi government has emphasised the role of the private sector in economic decisions.

Table 9.2 Saudi imports by origin: Top five country positions by % of total import value 1972-2002

Ranking	1972		1982		1998		2000	
	Country	%	Country	%	Country	%	Country	%
1	USA	19.4	USA	20.1	USA	21.3	USA	16.3
2	Japan	14.3	Japan	19.1	Japan	8.6	Japan	11.1
3	Lebanon	12.2	Germany	10.9	U.K	8.5	Germany	8.4
4	U.K	7.3	U.K	6.6	Germany	6.3	U.K	6.0
5	West Germany	6.2	Italy	6.0	China	3.2	China	5.3
Top 5 country % of total import value	59.4%		62.7%		47.9%		47.1%	

Source: *SAMA*, 2003, *Central Department of Statistics*, 2002.

Table 9.2 shows the pre-eminent position of the USA as the Kingdom's major import trading partner. This is not surprising considering that the USA is, in turn, the largest importer of Saudi oil. Following the 11 September 2001 events, the premier position of the USA has been eroded to around 15-16% in 2002, down from 20-21%. Political sensitivities and travel problems to the USA for Saudi citizens have also been issues. What the table further demonstrates is that Saudi Arabia's import relations are mainly carried out with non-Arab and non-Muslim countries. This supports our earlier observations that Saudi buyers are generally knowledgable of and sensitive to market conditions, especially when it comes to the import of "quality" or "brand name" items that are lacking in the wider Arab or Muslim world (Johany, 1986).

Currently imports from all the Arab and Muslim countries account for around 11% of total imports. The presence of Lebanon in 1972 amongst the top five exporting countries to the Kingdom is an interesting historical aside. It came about because of Lebanon's position as a trans-shipment centre in the early 1970s for Saudi goods; Saudi Arabia used Lebanese ports because of its own limited port facilities in that early boom era. In 1970, the handling capacity of the combined Saudi ports stood at around 2000 tons, rising to 3700 in 1974. By 2000, Saudi port capacity had risen to 252,000 tons. It is interesting to note the rising market share from China, with imports accounting for around 5.3% of total imports in 2002 and rising fast. Figure 9.4 illustrates the sharp increase in both imports and exports to China over the period 1991-2002.

The almost doubling of Chinese exports to Saudi Arabia in a decade is a reflection of the sharp increase in Saudi oil exports to that country, raising China's importance to the Kingdom as a major trading partner for the future. As noted from Chapter Eight, 2004's strong oil prices have been largely underpinned by strong demand from China. This is expected to remain robust over the next few years according to oil industry analysts. Over the next decade, the origin of Saudi imports could continue to shift towards the Asian markets, given that Japan has also been the second most consistent exporter to Saudi Arabia, while imports from the USA could see further volatility, despite competitive U.S. product prices, due to the fall in the value of the U.S. dollar during 2002-2004.

Figure 9.4 Saudi-China trade trends, 1991-2002

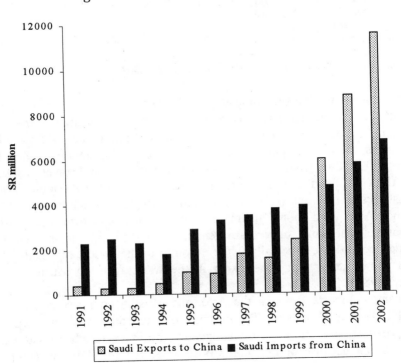

Source: *Central Department of Statistics.*

Most Saudi imports are financed by Saudi commercial banks through letters of credit opened in favour of overseas beneficiaries. The major financing is applied to motor vehicles and foodstuffs, followed by textile and clothing, as iillustrated in Table 9.3.

Overall, around 65-70% of total imports are financed through banks. The remaining imports use different forms of direct payments or suppplier credit arrangements. With the growth of local Saudi industries and a wider manufacturing base, the level and compositon of future imports to Saudi Arabia could yet undergo fundamental change. There could be more machinery, spare parts and raw material imports, and fewer imports in foodstuffs, appliances, construction material and textiles.

Table 9.3 Private sector imports financed through Saudi commercial banks (SR million)

	2000	2001	2002	2003	2004*
Foodstuffs	9,072	9,848	10,080	12,636	5,866
Motor vehicles	8,923	11,792	13,717	13,929	6,391
Textiles & clothing	3,995	4,944	5,096	4,485	1,708
Machinery	3,903	5,240	3,458	3,494	1,683
Constructon materials	3,502	4,514	4,282	3,889	1,927
Appliances	3,342	3,754	3,244	3,074	1,879
Other goods	38,614	40,933	39,4878	44,669	26,524
Total	71,351	81,026	79,755	86,175	45,980
Ratio of total to imports (cif)	63.0	69.3	65.9	N/A	N/A

Source: *SAMA*, 2004.   *2nd Quarter 2004.

The export sector

Despite efforts to diversify the country's production base, and specifically its export base, oil exports continue to dominate the Kingdom's foreign export trade. As such, any overview of Saudi Arabia's exports is much simpler than that of its imports.

Figure 9.5 Arab world exports relative to total world exports, 1980-2001 (in US$ million)

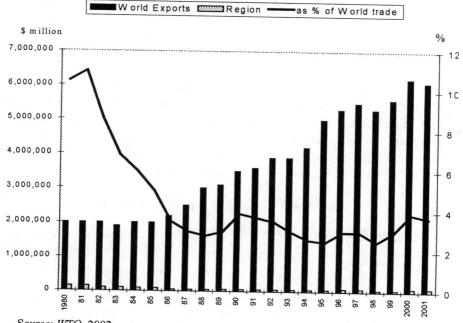

Source: *WTO*, 2002.

The lack of meaningful export diversification could have implications for the Kingdom following entry into the World Trade Organization (Azzam, 2002, Husseini, 2002). According to the WTO, the Arab world in general has fallen behind in the export race relative to world growth in exports; one key reason is the lack of diversification of export products. Figure 9.5 illustrates the relative decline in Arab world exports over the period 1980-2001.

From a peak of around 12% of total world exports in 1980, the Arab world's share is now fluctuating between 3-4%, despite a 200% increase in world export value over the period 1980-2001.

Significantly, the expansion of exports in the Arab world has not kept pace with world export growth, but rather it has mostly correlated with changes in oil prices. The year 2004 will no doubt see a marked improvement in the Arab world's exports relative to world exports, due to the highest oil prices in twenty years of nearly $50 a barrel. Saudi Arabia lags behind its fellow Gulf Cooperation Council (GCC) member states in terms of *per capita* merchandise trade (exports and imports). According to the WTO, Saudi *per capita* merchandise trade stood at $5,000 for 2001, while it was $24,000 for Qatar, $13,000 for Bahrain, $7,000 for Oman and just under $30,000 for the United Arab Emirates. The latter country is helped by the fact that Dubai, Saudi Arabia's main trading partner in the UAE, serves as a major re-export centre for the Kingdom. We will explore this in more depth in Chapter Fourteen.

Oil is still king of exports

Crude oil exports currently account for around 70-80% of total Saudi exports, down from 95-98% during the period 1974-1980, but still giving a one-dimensional emphasis on a single commodity. If one adds petroleum-related finished and semi-finished products, exports from this sector accounted for around 87% of the total in 2002 and they are forecasted to rise to 90% levels for the year 2004, as illustrated in Table 9.4.

Table 9.4 Merchandise exports by main sections

-Million Saudi Riyals	(fob values in current prices)						
	1970	1979	1984	1992	2000	2002	2004[e]
Crude petroleum	9,080	200,225	114,568	148,312	219,470	200,600	322,500
Petroleum products	1,799	11,019	13,292	25,932	51,480	38,800	55,000
Other	28	1,939	4,439	14,081	24,805	32,300	35,000
Total	10,907	213,183	132,299	188,325	295,755	271,741	412,500

Source: *Central Department of Statistics*, 2003, *Ministry of Planning*.

[e] Estimate, SAMBA Financial Group, Report 2004.

Saudi Arabia's other petroleum-related product exports are important sources of revenue especially refined oil products, including bunker fuel. Included under the "other" export category in Table 9.4 are petrochemicals, construction material, agriculture and foodstuffs and miscellaneous items, such as re-exports. These "other" exports currently account for 10-11% of total exports, nearly half of which are still derived from petrochemical exports, as illustrated in Table 9.5.

Table 9.5 Saudi non-oil exports
(SR billion)

Item	1984	1989	1995	1999	2002
Foodstuff	0.166	1.442	1.589	1.768	1.845
Chemical products	1.460	5.616	10.166	9.189	13.681
Plastic products and construction material	0.029	4.160	5.455	3.529	6.115
Base metals	0.185	0.995	2.631	2.175	2.537
Electrical, mechanical, equipment	0.008	0.200	0.851	0.873	1.138
Other exports	0.079	0.692	1.866	1.953	2.907
Re-exports	2.5.5	2.349	1.762	1.869	4.077
Total	4.432	15.454	24.320	21.356	32.300

Source: *SAMA*, 2003, *Central Department of Statistics.*

Analysis of Table 9.5 reveals that the Saudi manufacturing and processing industry is slowly coming of age, with steady export rises in foodstuffs, equipment and base metals, in addition to plastic and construction materials. The Saudi government aims to ensure faster growth of such exports so that they will constitute a larger share of overall Saudi exports, achieving diversification within a non-oil based economic structure (Zarouk, 2002, Khemani, 2002). This will be a long-term task. In the meantime, the Kingdom will continue to be primarily a raw material, intermediate consumption good exporter (goods which still need value added input), as illustrated in Figure 9.6 (A) and (B).

In 2002, according to Figure 9.6, some 78% of Saudi exports were composed of raw materials, with finished products accounting for 13% and semi-finished for 9%. It is the second category that needs to be encouraged to grow, as it is a high-value export category. Similarly, Figure 9.6 (B) points out that only 1% of total exports were in fixed assets and 4% in final consumption goods. An increase in finished product exports will assist in the growth of exports in the value of final consumption goods , that is goods that have final use. Developing these export sectors will reduce the instability of export earnings that result from oil dependency.

Figure 9.6 (A) Export by nature of items, 2002
(SR billion)

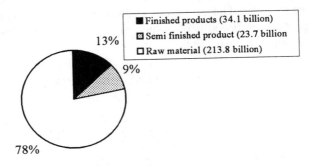

(B) Export by utilization of items (2002)
(SR billion)

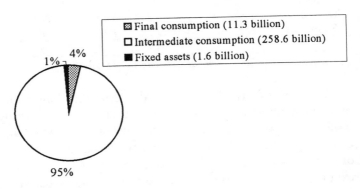

Source: *Central Department of Statistics*, 2003.

Asian exports predominate

Saudi Arabia's main export market is Asia, which accounted for some 35% on average during 1994-2000, as illustrated in Figure 9.7.

These were followed by North America and Western Europe, each with around 20-21%, while the GCC states took 8% of exports. The Saudi exports to other Arab countries were a meagre 3%, and the non-Arab Islamic States took 6%. Once again, it was the predominantly industrialized western and Asian economies that received the bulk of Saudi oil exports and petroleum-related products.

Figure 9.7 Geographic distribution of average Saudi exports, 1994-2000

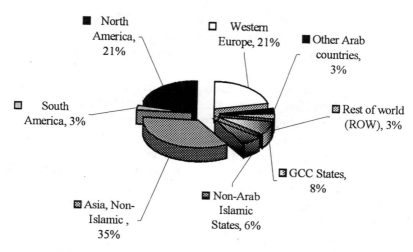

Source: *Central Department of Statistics*, 2002.

As discussed earlier, oil exports to China and to South East Asian economies are forecasted to rise at the expense of the Western Europe and the North American markets, as these regions are hoping to diversify their energy imports from sources nearer home, such as Russia and Canada respectively. This trend is clearly identifiable in Table 9.6, which illustrates Saudi crude oil exports by destination to the major regions.

Table 9.6 Saudi crude oil exports by destination
(Million barrels)

Destination	1974	1996	1998	1999	2000	2002
Asia and Far East	957.4	1,031.5	974.4	921.7	1,044	942
Western Europe	601.8	530.6	645.7	454.3	483.8	343
North America	521.4	490.7	544.2	534.2	577.2	488
Middle East	81.5	83.6	76.5	68.9	60.4	49.6
Africa	35.2	35.0	49.6	73.6	79.4	68.3
Latin America	60.4	47.2	31.4	26.7	22.5	22.8
Oceania	17.7	17.2	13.6	7.8	14.4	5.51

Source: *SAMA*, 2003.

The fall in Saudi crude oil exports to virtually all the regions in 2002 is partly in response to the economic slowdown experienced in many countries following the September 11, 2001 events in the USA. However, it was the

Chinese and South East Asian economies that recovered faster during 2003-2004, and they fuelled the rise in oil prices in that period.

Saudi Arabia's relatively narrow export base is also a reflection of the government's development strategy during the first planning periods, discussed in Chapter 2. This strategy emphasized import substitution as an explicit goal, as well as investment in petrochemical-related industries. The result of import substitution policies was the creation of protected domestic manufacturing industries that looked to the lucrative domestic consumer market as their first choice for expansion and sales (Jalal, 1985). An export-oriented, non-oil manufacturing base was not emphasized, and Saudi Arabia is now trying to find its niche in this competitive sector to create some stability in exports, as compared with oil. This could take several decades, but is not impossible given the financial resources that are available to the private sector as evidenced from earlier chapters. This leads us to a discussion on the required change in the operational environment of the non-oil export sector.

Focusing on efficiency

Saudi Arabia needs to adopt a new export promotion strategy that focuses on efficiency and competitiveness and which encompasses both oil and non-oil related products (Nojaidi, 2002, Richard, 2002). Broad macro-economic data such as export volumes or values do not reflect individual sectors' export performance based on competitive efficiencies. The *Arab World Competitiveness Report, 2002-2003* has conducted intensive studies in this area and has ranked 16 countries of the Arab world amongst 100 exporting countries based on their Trade Performance Index (TPI). The composite rankings of the TPI were supposed to capture many dimensions of export performance for various commodities based on competitiveness and efficiency. Trade Performance Indexes were classified as current TPI and *change TPI* and countries were ranked from 1 (the most efficient and competitive), to 100 (the least efficient and competitive). Table 9.7 sets out the results for Saudi Arabia for the five-year period 1995-2000.

Table 9.7 establishes that the Kingdom has five sectors in which it competes with mixed results on the international level. Surprisingly, this list excludes fresh and processed food, an area where some positive strides have taken place in terms of export growth, as noted earlier. Analysis of Saudi Arabian ranking by current TPI seems to be reversed when analyzed by change TPI rankings. Simply defined, current TPI assesses export competitiveness and performance based on *current* conditions, while change TPI is a more dynamic concept focusing on *changes* in export performance and on the extent to which countries are gaining or losing market share. Table 9.8 explores the TPI indicators and the basic concepts further.

Table 9.7 Saudi Arabia: current and change Trade Performance Index (TPI) by world ranking 1995-2000

Sector	Current TPI	Change TPI
Minerals	7	53
Chemicals	16	52
Clothing	-	-
Textile	-	-
Fresh food	-	-
Processed food	-	-
Basic manufacturing	62	42
Misc. manufacturing	87	74
Non-electrical machinery	75	24
Electronic component	-	-
Consumer electronics	-	-
Transport equipment	-	-
Leather products	-	-
Wood products	-	-

Source: *The Arab World Competitiveness Report*, 2002-2003, pp. 128, 129.

Not surprisingly, Saudi Arabia ranks high (at seven) in the current trade performance index for minerals and at 16 for chemicals. Outside the minerals sector, the results are disappointing, including manufacturing, whether basic, miscellaneous or non-electrical.

However, the situation is reversed when analyzing change trade performance index. The manufacturing sector then ranks higher for Saudi Arabia, but both minerals (oil) and chemicals fall back dramatically in world ranking, denoting a deterioration in export performance in the mineral sector compared to other mineral producers for 1995-2000, the five-year period of the study. Saudi Arabia's ability to adjust production capacity to meet higher world demand in 2004, from around eight million bpd to over 9.2 million bpd, will undeniably raise the country's change and current TPI indexes, but the inescapable conclusion of the international survey is that there is a striking lack of diversification in the overall export structure of the Kingdom.

This is not to underestimate or diminish the role of resource-based exports such as oil. While resource-rich countries like Saudi Arabia have been served well by basing their export trading advantage solely on natural resources, such a strategy is not conducive to long-term sustainable development.

Table 9.8 Trade Performance Index (TPI) indicators

Type	Indicator	Basis
* Current TPI	Value of net exports	• Importance of the trade balance in the sector considered
	1. Per capita exports	• Extent to which the labour force produces for the world market
	2. Share in world market	• Success on the world market
	3. Product diversification, measured by:	• Number and weight of relative contribution of exported products
	(a) Equivalent number of products	• Number of export products of equal size that would lead to the observed concentration of exports
	(b) Product spread	• Spread of export markets for products
	4. Market diversification, measured by:	• Number and weight of partner countries
	(a) Equivalent number of markets	• Number of markets of equal size that would lead to the observed concentration of exports
	(b) Market spread	• Spread of destination markets
* Change TPI	Percentage annual change in world market share explained by: 1. Change in competitiveness	• Change in global performance • Gain (loss) in market share due to increased (worsened) competitiveness
	2. Initial geographic specialization	• Benefits associated with the initial specialization of domestic exporters on dynamic markets
	3. Initial product specialization	• Benefits associated with the initial export specialization on products characterized by dynamic demand
	4. Adaptation to changes in world demand	• Ability to adjust export supply to changes in world demand

Source: *The Arab World Competitiveness Report*, 2002-2003.

Trading based on advantages in resources will lead to depletion of such resources in the long run, and makes a country hostage to fluctuations in world commodity prices. What should the strategy be then? In practice, it is not necessary to move away from resource-based exports completely, but it is important to build alternatives, especially high-value added export alternatives. In order to achieve a higher level of sustainable growth, Saudi Arabia needs to shift from trading on resource-based advantages towards trades based on products, skills, processes, quality and innovation. This requires improved productivity, upgrading existing technology and increasing the efficiency of the use and allocation of resources. It is only in this manner that countries like Saudi Arabia can meet the challenges of gaining an increasing share of a growing world export market.

Identifying export champions

Countries often try to identify both specific industries and clusters of industries that have the potential of being export-led "champions" and sectors that are underachievers or in decline. The reason is simple: to allocate resources to support the champions, while at the same time to try to turn around the underachievers through efficiency and productivity restructuring. Once again, the *Arab Competitiveness Report 2002-2003* has carried out individual country studies to identify the various achievers and non-achievers in the export sector for the period 1996-2000. Figure 9.8 sets out Saudi Arabia's key export profile, while Table 9.9 identifies the sectors affected.

The chart in Figure 9.8 shows the export value of the product group and compares the national increase in world market share (on the horizontal axis) to the growth of international demand (on the vertical axis). Exports are grouped into champions, underachievers, declining sectors and achievers in adversity. As Table 9.9 summarizes, "champions" are those sectors that win in growth markets and in which Saudi Arabia has performed well enough to increase its share of world exports.

In the case of Saudi Arabia these champions constitute eleven products, but only three of them – cyclic hydrocarbons (6), crude oils (1), and ethers and their derivatives (4) – outperformed world growth levels, with the remaining seven products growing at levels below world trade growth ranges, thus confirming the Saudi Trade Performance Indexes discussed earlier. Similarly there are six products which are "underachievers" and would profit from the implementation of internal restructuring, productivity and export support: paper (13), non-crude petroleum oils (2), acyclic hydrocarbons (8), insulated wire or cable (10), polymers of ethylene (5) and structures and part structures (19).

Underachievers represent particular challenges for trade promotion efforts, as they indicate that while international demand has been growing at above average rates, the country has been falling behind in these products. The issue then is not demand, but rather internal supply-driven constraints and efficiencies. As a result, Saudi Arabia has been losing market share in these six products, due to internal inefficiencies.

Figure 9.8 Saudi Arabia: Export profile chart for selected key products (1996-2000)

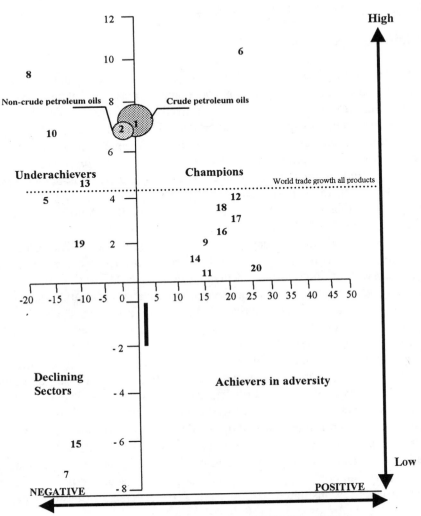

Source: *Arab World Competitiveness Report*, 2002-2003, p. 303.

The export profile chart indicates two declining sectors, mineral or chemical fertilizers (7) and sodium hydroxide/potassium hydroxide (15). Here some major structural production and efficiency changes have to occur to either turn these sectors around or to seek alternative solutions that might involve international strategic alliances. The export prospect for these declining sectors is bleak, however, as world demand has been falling and the Saudi market share has fallen in turn. Trade promotion efforts will be time consuming for such sectors and could result in marginal gains, since bottlenecks are both internal (industry inefficiencies) and external (demand shifts).

Table 9.9 Export performance: Saudi Arabia

Category	Export Sector
1. **Champions** Features: - Growing World Market - Country is increasing its share of the world market	1. Crude oil 4. Ethers and their derivatives 6. Cyclic hydrocarbons 9. Halogenated derivative of hydrocarbon 11. Portland, alum and slag cement 12. Polymers of vinyl chloride 14. Stainless steel 16. Polymers of propylene 17. Organic surface-active agents (not soap) 18 Polymers of styrene
2. **Underachievers** - Growing World Market - Exports are losing their market share	2. Non-crude petroleum oils 5. Polymers of ethylene 8. Acyclic hydrocarbons 10. Insulated wire or cable 19. Structures and part structures 13. Paper and similar products
3. **Declining Sectors** - World market stagnating or declining - Country losing its market share	7. Mineral or chemical fertilizers, nitrogenous 15. Sodium hydroxide, potassium hydroxide
4. **Achievers in Adversity** - World market stagnating - Country increasing its market share	- None

Source: Figure 9.8 (numbers relate to the specific export sectors).

The Kingdom evidenced no achievers in adversity sectors. Such sectors are characterized as being winners in declining markets, that is, that countries gain market share in world import markets that are declining. In essence, Saudi's export promotion strategy should aim to move these industry sectors from their declining quadrant to the achievers in adversity quadrants over the long term. It is encouraging to note that industry analysts are thinking along the same lines for those petrochemical industries currently in operation (Zamil, 2002, Nojaidi, 2002).

Trade and balance of payments

Thanks to extraordinarily high world oil prices in 2004, Saudi Arabia's trade position is forecasted to achieve a 20-year high for its current account surplus, surpassing the record SR 142 billion seen in 1980. Table 9.10 summarizes the Kingdom's balance of payments over the past three decades. This reveals that, on the whole, Saudi Arabia consistently registers surplus balances on its visible trade, while registering payment deficits on its overall capital accounts, particularly in periods of erratic oil revenues and regional uncertainties.

Table 9.10 Saudi Arabia: Balance of payment summary (SR billions)

Item	1970	1974	1980	1984	1992	2002	2004[e]
Merchandise trade	6.1	106.7	250.0	31.2	74.5	156.7	300.0
Services and transfers	(5.6)	(24.7)	(107.8)	(96.0)	(140.9)	(112.9)	(97.0)
Private transfers	(0.8)	(1.8)	(13.6)	(18.6)	(50.2)	(59.4)	(50.0)
Capital movements and reserves (1)	(0.5)	(81.9)	(142.2)	64.8	66.4	(43.8)	(153.4)

Source: *SAMA*, 2003.

Note: (1) Negative balances denote outflows in capital movements
      [e] Estimated, SAMBA Group, 2004.

Visible merchandise imports and exports are only one measure of the balance of payments; the current account is a broader measure than merchandise trade. The current account for Saudi Arabia includes services and transfers, workers remittances and the private transfer of money abroad by Saudis. It also includes private and government purchases of services and military equipment from abroad. These payments and transfers can offset much of the merchandise trade surpluses. Figure 9.9 shows us that since 1979, Saudi Arabia suffered a persistent current account deficit until 2000, when the trend was reversed.

In essence, the country was disbursing more then it was receiving, making up the shortfall through an inward transfer of accumulated capital surpluses, and in later years, through capital transfers and deficit financing. This was discussed in Chapter 3. Table 9.10 also highlights the importance of outward remittances and private transfers from Saudi Arabia since 1970. As long as the Kingdom continues to rely on imported foreign labour and places no barriers on overseas remittances, these outflows, currently running at between SR 50-56 billion per annum, will represent a major source of outflow for the foreseeable future.

Figure 9.9 Balance of payments

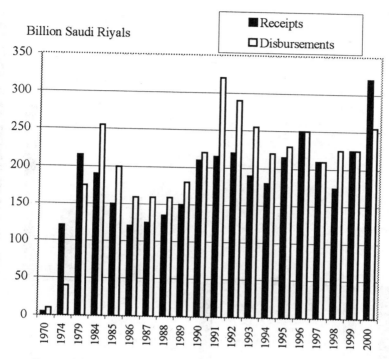

Source: *Ministry of Planning*, 2002.

As explained above, Saudi Arabia is set to register its biggest current account surplus in 2004. This will represent the fifth consecutive year when sizeable current account surpluses have been registered, reversing a twenty year trend. This is illustrated in Figure 9.10.

The surpluses of the period 2000-2004 can be attributed to a mixture of unexpectedly high world oil prices, and, according to banking sources, to an inflow of private Saudi capital following the September 11, 2001 events. Another factor was the poor international equity market returns compared to the domestic markets, which we explored in Chapter 6.

The forecasted current surplus of around SR 193 billion for 2004 compared with SR 105 billion in 2003 has provided a certain degree of official and private sector optimism, but few predict that such surpluses will recur on a consistent basis over the coming years, given the extraordinary turbulence that had affected the world oil market during 2004.

Figure 9.10 Saudi Arabia balance of payments current account
(1993-2004) SR billions

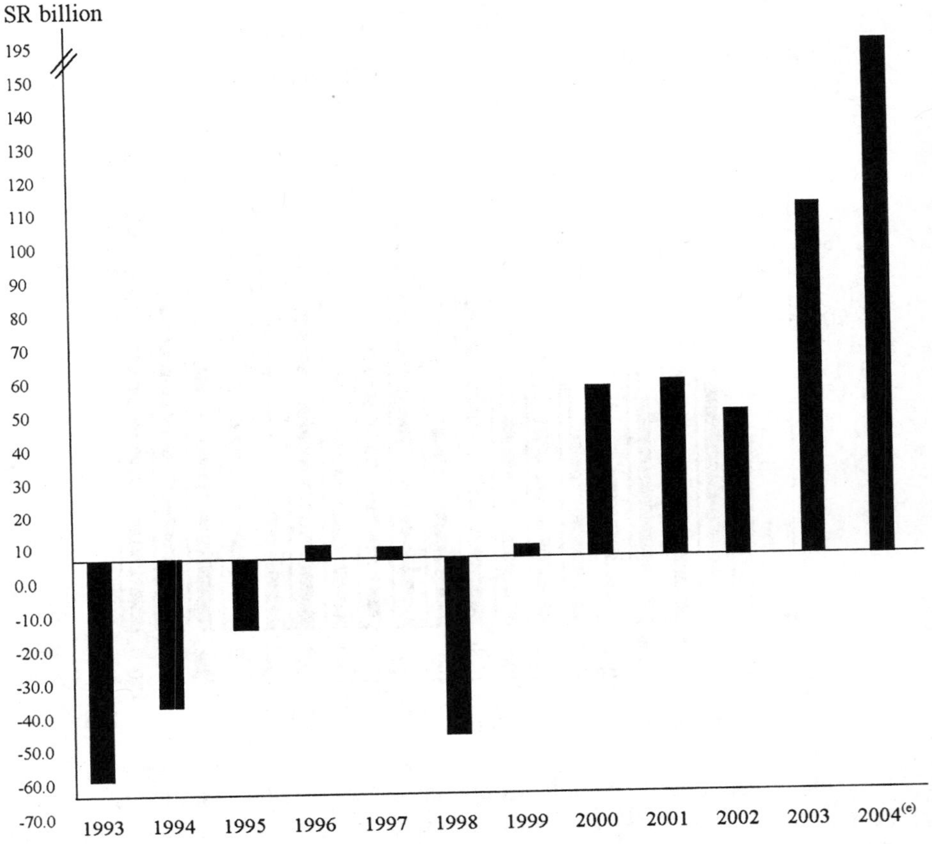

Source: *SAMA* Reports, 2003,   (e) *Ministry of Finance*, December 2004.

Foreign aid and trade

Saudi Arabia has traditionally been a large and generous contributor of foreign aid, both on a direct bilateral basis and on a multilateral basis through international organizations such as the World Bank, the International Monetary Fund (IMF), and the Saudi-based Islamic Development Bank (IDB). Most Saudi bilateral project and development aid has been channelled through the Saudi Fund for Development (SFD). The trend over time was for direct project assistance as the SFD built up disbursement and project monitoring capabilities. Table 9.11 sets out Saudi Arabia's subscriptions to the various international multilateral development aid organizations, for a total of approximately $21 billion.

Table 9.11 Saudi Arabia's subscriptions to multilateral development institutions

Name	Capital in US $ million	Saudi subscription U.S.$ million	Saudi %
Arab Fund for Social and Economic Development	2,151	516	24.00
Arab Monetary Fund	1,244	184	14.80
Arab Bank for Economic Development in Africa	1,500	367	24.50
Arab Corporation for Investment Guarantee	81	12	14.80
Arab Association for Agriculture and Development Investment	325	73	23.00
Islamic Development Bank	5,100	1,267	25.00
OPEC Fund for International Development	3,435	1,033	30.10
African Development Bank	22,403	36	0.16
African Development Fund	11,476	336	2.28
World Bank	188,606	4,504	2.87
IMF	271,360	8,941	2.29
International Development Association	106,646	3,133	2.00
International Finance Corporation	2,358	30	1.28
Multilateral Investment Guarantee Agency	1,952	47	2.40

Source: *Saudi Commerce and Economic Review*, No. 97, May, 2002.

Since its establishment in 1975, the SFD has signed 369 loan agreements totalling SR 24.3 billion, by the end of 2003. The majority of loans, 39, went to African countries, while Asia came in second with 24 loans. There were five given to other countries. Some SR 8 billion was disbursed for transport and communication projects, followed by SR 5 billion in power sectors (SFD, 2004). Unlike other aid donors, Saudi Arabia does not "tie" its aid; that is, the Kingdom does not expect the majority of its loans to be recycled back to its own economy. This action sets Saudi Arabia apart from other major donors. In effect, the Kingdom subsidizes third country exports to developing countries, since Saudi aid recipient countries are free to import goods and services from the countries of their choice (Farsy, 1986).

There are no official Saudi government data on direct aid payment breakdowns, but these items are included under "other government services" in the balance of payments account, which also includes contributions and capital subscriptions to international and regional development agencies. As such, data under this general item has be treated with caution, but Figure 9.11 sets out payments made under "other government services" for the period 1970-2000, and they seem to mirror the volatility experienced in Saudi Arabia's revenue flows.

Figure 9.11 Saudi Arabia: Other government services payments,
1970-2002

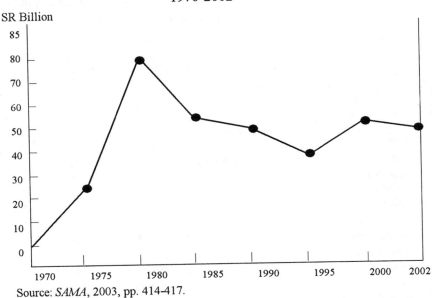

Source: *SAMA*, 2003, pp. 414-417.

Although faced with its own pressing domestic needs, the Kingdom has continued to shoulder its international aid responsibilities. Despite reduced aid payments compared to the early boom days, Saudi Arabia is still a significant aid donor, especially to African and other Middle East countries.

According to the United Nations, the annual target for aid donors for the richest countries of the Organization for Economic Cooperation and Development (OECD) was set at 0.7% of their GDP. With the exception of some Nordic countries, such as Norway, Sweden, Denmark and the Netherlands, nearly all other countries' aid donations fall short of the 0.7% target.

In contrast, according to the Saudi embassy in London, the Kingdom has extended a total of $48.56 billion (SR 182 billion) in direct, multilateral and bi-lateral aid to 70 countries over the past 17 years. These include $27.73 billion to members of the Organization of Islamic Conference (OIC), $14.66 billion to developing countries through regional international aid organizations, and $6.17 billion through the Saudi Fund for Development mentioned earlier (The Embassy of the Kingdom of Saudi Arabia, London, 2004). Assuming an average of $2.8 billion (SR 10.5 billion) per annum in aid donation over the past 17 years, this would represent around an average of 1.2% to 1.3% p.a. of Saudi GDP in aid donation. According to SAMA, this had fallen to just under 0.9% for the period 1990-2002, but still significantly higher than the 0.7% United Nations target (SAMA, 2003).

Given the domestic growth of Saudi manufacturing industries, the Kingdom will eventually be forced to "tie" some of its aid to purchases of Saudi products. This became evident when a portion of Saudi Arabia's economic reconstruction aid pledges to Iraq following the 2003 war was in the form of 'tied' aid for Saudi industries and services (12 July 2004, Saudi Press Agency). Some Saudi industries have come of age internationally, and it is important that the Kingdom try to maintain a competitive edge in exports of key commodities and manufacturing, as well as establishing mechanisms for a sustained export program.

Foreign sector trade development

The Kingdom is conscious of the wealth-generating effect of export promotion; the world has observed the remarkable growth in the GDP of the so-called "Asian Tiger" economies, as well as that of China in more recent years. Studies have indicated that the traditional development strategies of import substitution that were adopted by many developing countries in the post-Second World War period have been ineffective for long-term sustained economic growth (World Bank, 1993, Solow, 1970, Romer, 1994). A shift towards export-led growth has taken place, with many developing countries seeking to establish supremacy over competitors in niche areas, based on productivity and efficiency. Saudi exporters face both opportunities and challenges, evidence of which is the broad range of products exported by the Saudi Arabian Basic Industries Corporation (SABIC).

However, there are some areas of institutional support that are needed to make Saudi exports more competitive, as in the final analysis it is firms that compete and not nations and the focus of the Kingdom should be to assist individual exporters as they tackle concrete problems of market entry, while protecting them from unfair competition and dumping practices. This support can take different forms:

- *Direct assistance for exporting firms*

As exporting is generally new to the Saudi Arabian private sector, exporters might require assistance at each stage of the export process, including customer and market identification, product development and client adaptation, pilot testing in the target market and finally developing a detailed marketing strategy. Further stages involve process development, productivity and quality improvement, production launch and sales. There needs to be follow-up performance analysis and modification of the marketing strategy.

Very few Saudi private sector companies have carried out all or some of the above processes. Instead, they have concentrated on the domestic market, securing sales through "net-back" discounts and special offers. It was left to the government-owned and joint venture companies in the petrochemical sector, along with well-established and managed Saudi private sector companies to enter the export market. There have been some notable private sector successes in this field. Table 9.12 lists some selected private sector companies operating in the export sector that have also established an international presence.

Table 9.12 Selected prime Saudi private sector exporting companies

Group	Product range	International presence
Al Babtain	Household appliances	No
Amiantit	Pipes, storage tanks	*Yes*
Halawani	Food products	No
Al-Qahtani Pipes	Coated pipes, equipment	*Yes*
Savola Snack Food Co.	Snacks, general confectionary	No
Abdulateef Jameel	Car accessories	*Yes*
Al Zamil	Air conditioners, steel fabrication, aluminium, plastics	*Yes*
Arasco	Fertilizers, feedstock	No
Abdulhadi Qahtani Co.	Oil field equipments, machinery	No.
Al Marai	Dairy products	No
Al Rajhi	Foodstuffs, juices, shrimps	No
Bahrawi	Cosmetics, perfumes, food	No.
Al Jomaih	Beverages, cans	No
Nissah	Bottled water	No
Jeraisy	Smart cards, PC equipment	*Yes*
Fakieh	Poultry, fast food	*Yes*
Hail Agriculture Dev. Co.	Food product	No
Saudi Cement Co.	Cement	No
Saudi Cable Co.	Cables, electrical wires	*Yes*
Fitaihi	Jewellery, perfumes	*Yes*
Savola Group	Ghee, edible oils, foodstuff	*Yes*

Source: *Top 1000 Saudi Companies, 6ᵗʰ Edition*, 2000-2001, *IIT, Publishing*, Khobar.

Table 9.12 highlights the major emphasis on food products by Saudi exporters, with the majority of companies concentrating on the nearby Gulf Cooperation Council (GCC) markets due to shorter communication routes, logistics and GCC trade harmonization policies. A few companies such as Al Zamil, Amiantit and Fakieh have ventured into Europe, Asia and North

America. On the whole, Saudi exporting experience has been confined to tried and well-tested regional markets.

- *Assist all sizes of firms to export*

Most of the Saudi company names listed in Table 9.12 belong to the top-tier family businesses, often in the top 100 companies of the Kingdom. For exports to succeed at the national level, neither size nor ownership should be criteria. The Saudi government should be able to assist those smaller companies that are willing to help themselves enter the export market, if they are willing to take the associated risks. Resources of like-minded smaller companies could be pooled to share export risks and the government could be more generous in providing financial support in the form of larger export guarantee insurance to this sector.

- *Establish institutional development programs*

Coordinate exports through an export development agency that will be able to develop strategy and coordinate amongst members, besides having a powerful "lobbying" voice to discuss specific export issues of concern with the government.

- *Develop international trade in services*

During the past two decades, the provision of services has become the major economic activity of many countries in the world. Within the region, the economies of Bahrain and of Dubai in the United Arab Emirate have shifted towards international and domestic services, whether in the transportation of goods and people, banking and insurance services, communications, leisure industry or in entertainment. Other economies have established expertise in legal services, education and health. For Saudi Arabia, the service sector accounted for around 45% of GDP in 2002, compared with 28% in 1980 (SAMA, 2003). The Saudi government has begun to make some serious plans to expand its domestic tourism industry so as to attract year round visitors to the holy Muslim sites of *Makkah* and *Madinah* and to other tourist areas of interest. While the overall Saudi GDP percentage of services is lower than that of the USA, which stood at around 75% in 2001, in Saudi Arabia the service sector accounted for 78% of the labour force compared to 71% for the USA If in the future, the provision of services becomes a more "knowledge based" activity, with information and ideas as the most precious resources, the Kingdom would have to adapt accordingly if it is not to be left behind in this sector (Zarouk, 2002).

- *Adopt best practices*

Nations do not need to "reinvent the wheel" as there are many best practice models available around the world to draw upon and to adapt to domestic conditions. Saudi Arabia can benefit from the experiences of those countries that have transformed themselves to outward-looking, export-oriented economies, and can choose models that best suit the Kingdom's current human, technological and capital resources. The aim is to give Saudi exporters some comparative advantage over competitors by adapting selected "best practices". Table 9.13 outlines a best practice export promotion program for Saudi Arabia that draws upon the experiences and practices adopted by countries such as Malaysia, Ireland, Singapore, India and Tunisia (Khemani, 2002). Table 9.13 also highlights the current Saudi status in implementing such a proposed program. In some areas the government has taken some action, especially in funding and lead agency assistance, but so far the assistance has not been wide enough to make a significant impact.

Table 9.13 Saudi Arabia: An export promotion program model

Program	Required Action	Current status
Marketing	Market promotion, strategies, internet marketing, market development	Internet marketing is still not fully developed; market research tends to be product driven rather than customer driven.
Technological	Quality assurance, product and technology development, skills development, information technology, tooling, productivity	Uneven quality assurance and internal R+D development, productivity low
Investment and working capital	Export credits and guarantees, bonded warehouses, marketing finance, seed capital, R+D finance/incentives, export insurance cover	Available but limited in amount and only recently extended to non-oil exports. Limited bonded warehouses, limited R+D finance from commercial banks and government
Collective promotion programs	Research, marketing and trade missions, group promotional programs, comprehensive system of marketing, information collection, global sourcing	Effected through the regional chambers of commerce and industry, some national trade missions; comprehensive data base at national level not yet developed, global sourcing on a pooled basis
Funding and cost sharing	Government funds, 50% cost sharing	Saudi Export credit program exists, using the Saudi Fund for Development (SFD)
Lead agencies	Export promotion authority; export centres, industry associations, and insurance corporation	Export non-payment risk coverage exists through SFD using the French COFACE as partner; amounts are limited; no national insurance corporation

The Saudi Export Program (SEP) was established in 1999 under the auspices of the Saudi Fund for Development, with the SEP providing loans and guarantee services to both domestic and foreign entities. The SEP also provided insurance products to support the needs of non-oil Saudi exporters. To some extent, the SEP has filled a vacuum in the absence of a specialized Saudi agency for export credit and insurance. In terms of operations, the SEP extends support for goods and services that contain at least 25% Saudi domestic value added, and the minimum transaction value must exceed SR 100,000. The maximum financing facility is based on both country credit assessment and on "country exposures and availability of funds at time of request" (SFD, 2004). Repayments are based on the type of goods exported, with consumer goods like foodstuffs repayable up to 360 days, consumer disposables up to three years, and capital goods contracts and projects up to seven years.

In 2002, the SEP extended around SR 508 million in export finance and insurance, up from SR 350 million in 2001 (SFD, 2003). By comparison, private sector exports financed through the Saudi commercial banks totalled SR 10.951 billion in 2002, down from SR 13.1 billion in 2000 and SR 11.6 billion in 2001. Again, the September 11, 2001 events and the subsequent world economic recession were contributory factors to the fall in export financing registered in 2002 (SAMA, 2003). Establishing an independent export promotion authority to oversee regional export centres could be a key driver for Saudi's export promotion program. This idea has already been discussed in Saudi Arabia and a ministerial committee has proposed the allocation of SR 200 million to run the proposed authority.

According to reports, the government believes that the cost of establishment will be far outweighed by the advantages gained from employment generation. It estimates that every SR 1 billion of new exports will generate some 25,000 new jobs (Saudi Commerce and Economic Review, February 2003). In the final analysis, however, government support is needed not only to ensure market access and market development, but also to create an integrated trade support program that deals with the central issue of export *competitiveness*. Export promotion should not be conceived in isolation. The creation of new supervisory institutions, however good, cannot alone bring about needed institutional change in an export climate that involves all organizational sectors of society: universities, research institutes and government departments. There is a need for dedicated and qualified personnel, data-bases and an entrepreneurial spirit to venture into new markets.

Conclusion

Saudi Arabia is a country with an unusually large foreign sector and a, particular reliance on exports from a narrow commodity base to fund its developments needs. The composition and origins of its international trade have changed over the past three decades and Saudi Arabia today stands on the eve of new trade relationships. The impending accession to the World Trade Organization by Saudi Arabia, preceded by bilateral trade agreements with WTO member states, has created a new set of internal dynamics. There is a greater sense of urgency to position the Kingdom's trading relations on more competitive terms than ever before.

WTO entry is expected to benefit the Saudi petrochemical industry whose exports to western European markets in particular have been hit by an imposition of tariffs against Saudi petrochemical products. WTO entry would ensure a fair and level playing field for Saudi exports in this market. Similarly the private sector is also beginning to position itself for greater competition after Saudi accession, despite some reservations from vested interests that see WTO entry as a threat to their domestic markets.

It is not that Saudi Arabia has limited experience in establishing multilateral trade partnerships. As we will demonstrate in Chapter Fourteen, the Gulf Cooperation Council (GCC) has achieved some success in harmonizing the six member countries' trading policies with a reduction in tariffs to 5% in January, 2003, and with duty-free access to products originating in the GCC, if 40% of value added is from the GCC region.

It is no wonder that Saudi exporters have tended to concentrate on the GCC market, as we explained earlier; but the size of the GCC market is small compared to the potential economies of scale for Saudi exports to larger non-GCC markets. The Kingdom is also a member of the Greater Arab Free Trade Area (GAFTA), which extends from the Gulf to North Africa and includes 18 member states. It was established in 1997 with the objective of eliminating all tariffs, taxes, and other barriers by 2007, but with specific items exempt from tariff reduction in health, security and religious areas. Given the list of national exemptions, especially by North African countries, it is doubtful that the target date set for elimination will be met, but the trade negotiations and the experience gained has helped Saudi Arabia in its own bi-lateral negotiations with the WTO. Saudi Arabia's impending entry promises to be one of the most significant economic events in the history of the Kingdom.

Summary of key points

- *Saudi Arabia is the Arab world's leading exporter and importer and trade plays a vital role in the economic development of the country, despite the gradual erosion of the Kingdom's overall world trading share.*

- *Imports have risen in quantitative terms since the early 1970's, fueled by oil revenues but the composition of imports has changed over the past decades. Imports are now more diversified towards consumer goods orientated compared to equipment, machinery and infrastructural demand of the earlier period. Import origins has also began to change, with China becoming a major trading partner.*

- *Exports are still dominated by oil and oil related products which account for around 90% of total exports despite attempts at export diversification. Foodstuffs and chemical products are the major non-oil exports followed by base metals and electrical equipment.*

- *Saudi Arabia, in common with other exporting nations, is focusing on efficiency and competitive advantage for its exported products. Analysis of Saudi Arabia's "Trade Performance Indexes" (TPI) reveals a mixed picture with "export champions" dominating a wide variety of products (including oil), but with "underachievers" identified in several petrochemical related exports.*

- *Saudi Arabia runs a consistent positive trade balance (difference between exports and imports). Until 2000, it registered an overall balance of payment deficits due to private transfers and inward capital movements to fund government deficits.*

- *Saudi Arabia is a significant multi-lateral and bi-lateral aid contributor to developing countries, with the Kingdom's aid contribution surpassing the United Nation's set target of 0.7% of GDP. Most Saudi aid has been "untied", and totaled around SR 182 billion over the period 1986-2004.*

- *Foreign sector trade development could benefit from several institutional programs. These include: direct assistance for exporting firms, establish institutional development programs through an export development agency, develop international trade in services, and adopt best practices.*

Critical thinking

1. Why does Saudi Arabia need to trade?

2. "Imports of certain manufactured goods and foodstuffs should be banned as Saudi industry can produce these". Do you agree? What are the economic arguments for and against adopting such a policy?

3. "Despite all efforts at diversifying the Kingdom's export base, then non-oil exports account for only 10%. The government should not waste its time and concentrate only on oil exports". Is this a practical solution in the long-term? How will WTO entry affect current Saudi exports?

4. Should Saudi Arabia focus on a few export products where they have competitive advantage and ranked high in the global Trade Performance Index (TPI) and discontinue exports in those products identified as "underachievers"?

5. "Saudi foreign aid should be "tied" from now on". Discuss the pros and cons from donor and recipient country perspectives.

Chapter 10

THE SAUDI ECONOMIC OFFSET PROGRAM: A TOOL FOR TECHNOLOGY TRANSFER

> **Steam is no stronger now than it was a hundred years ago, but it is put to better use.**
>
> *Emerson*

Learning Objectives:

By the end of this section you should understand

- *The concept of offset programs as one of foreign direct investment*
- *The rationale for implementing the Saudi Economic Offset program*
- *Types of offset programs and their benefits*
- *Offset obligations and their results to date*
- *Economic impact of the Saudi offset program*
- *Motives of the foreign partners for their participation in the offset program*
- *Investment structure of non-offset Saudi private sector projects*
- *Comparison of the economic aspects of the offset and non-offset programs*
- *Methods and components of technology transfer*
- *Evaluation of the components of technology transfer for offset and non-offset projects in Saudi Arabia*

Introduction

A wide range of literature exists on the economic and political effects of Foreign Direct Investment (FDI) between countries. In essence, FDI exists because of market imperfections arising from impediments to the free flow of products between nations, as well as impediments to the sale and transfer of "know-how".

Offset programs might be considered a special type of foreign direct investment and transfer of technology. Offset is one form of counter-trade, in which the importing country's requirements for their purchase price is to be offset in some way by the selling nation (Hammond, 1990). The exporter/seller may be required to source some of the production locally, to increase imports from the importing country or to transfer technology. Saudi Arabian offset programs have concentrated on the latter requirements.

An overview of Saudi Arabia's offset program

The Economic Offset Program (EOP), as it became known, is an innovative investment program launched by Saudi Arabia in 1984, requesting that international contractors re-invest in the Kingdom a percentage of the value of (mostly) defence-related contracts awarded to them.

In 1984, Saudi Arabia was the first country of the Gulf Co-operation Council (GCC) to establish an offset program. This was followed by the United Arab Emirates in 1991 and Kuwait in 1994 (Al-Ibrahim, 1996). As we already mentioned, offset programs are used by developing countries in an effort to reduce the economic burden created by an underlying import contract.

Types of offsets

Offset programs can be classified as *direct* and *indirect*. Simply defined, direct offsets are those by which the purchasing country joins the selling country to supply elements of the underlying purchased product through co-production, technology licenses and other supply arrangements. Indirect offset means the seller agrees to assist the importing country in its development or investment plans, unrelated to the principal import contract. The two methods are summarized below.

Saudi Arabia and the other GCC states that later implemented offset programs adopted the indirect offset approach. The focus of this type of program is to take advantage of the expertise and experience of foreign contractors with the aim of supporting the development efforts of their economies towards non-oil industrial diversification (Al-Ibrahim, 1996, UAE Offset Group, 1994). The hope is that these offset programs help countries like Saudi Arabia to obtain benefits from foreign contractors through transfer of technology and training of local labor (Evans, 1996, Sandusky, 1996).

Table10.1 Direct and indirect offsets

Direct Offsets	Activity
• Co-production	• Oversees production based on government–to-government or producer agreements that permit a foreign government to acquire the technical information and tooling to manufacture all or part of a defence contract
• Direct sub-contracting	• Procurement of domestic-made components for incorporation or installation in items sold to that same nation under direct commercial contracts
• Concessions	• Commercial compensation practices whereby capabilities and items are given free to the buyer
• Technology transfers/licensed production	• Assistance in establishing defence industry capabilities by providing valuable technology and manufacturing know-how
• Investments in defence firms	• Capital invested to establish or expand a company in the purchasing country
Indirect Offsets	*Description*
• Procurements	• Purchases of parts/components from the purchasing country that are unrelated to the military system being purchased
• Investments in non-defence firms	• Establishing corporations in the purchasing countries to invest capital in the nation's companies
• Trading of commodities	• Using brokers to link buyers with commodities sellers in the purchasing country.
• Foreign defence-related projects	• Assisting the recipient country's military services

According to Saudi Arabia's National Development Plans, some of the key economic objectives of the state are the promotion of industrial development, technology transfer, economic diversification and national training and employment (Ministry of Planning, 2001).

Table 10.2 Saudi offset program: stated benefits and fields of investments

A. Benefits	i. Generation of advanced technical training and high-value employment for Saudi nationals ii. Boosting foreign investment in productive services and activities iii. Imports substitution as well as products for exports iv. Development of local technical, professional and managerial expertise in high technology industries v. Transfer of technologies know-how through research, development and manufacturing processes vi. Making use of the Kingdom's raw materials
B. Field of Investments	i. Industry, specifically non-oil related, high technical content ii. Defence iii. Services iv. Agriculture

Source: *Economic Offset Office*, Riyadh, 2003.

According to the Economic Offset Office (EOO), the Saudi offset program complements the national objectives in several areas. The EOO has articulated the benefits and areas of investments under the offset, and these are summarized in Table 10.2 (Sugair, H. 2003).

While the terms and conditions set by the Saudi Economic Offset administrators varied from one offset to another, depending both on the size and nature of the contract on which the offset was based and on the relative negotiating strength of the parties, the overall implied benefits and the fields of investment remained the same. To date, the Kingdom of Saudi Arabia has had offset programs comprising of contractors from three nations: the USA, the UK and France.

Investment structure of the Saudi offset program

Table 10.3 summarizes the Saudi Economic Offset program and main foreign contractors. With the exception of the AT&T Offset contract, which was the first and, to date, the only civilian-related offset program, all the other offset programs were military-related.

Table 10.3 Saudi Arabia - economic offset programs and contractors

Offset Program	Prime Contractor	Year Signed	Associated Contract Description	(US$ Million)
Peace Shield I	The Boeing Co.	1984	AWACS Platform Command Control and Communication Systems for the RSAF	5,600
Al-Yamamah	British Aerospace (BAe)	1986 (I) 1988 (II)	Tactical fighter aircraft, associated equipment and services, and airbase construction for the RSAF	7,600
Peace Shield II	Hughes Aircraft Co.	1991	Extension of the Peace Shield Program	837
General Dynamics Economic Balance Program	General Dynamics Corp.	1992	Supply of M1 A2 Abrams Main Battle Tanks and associated equipment and systems for the Royal Saudi Land Forces (RSLF)	N/A
McDonnell Douglas Peace Sun IX	McDonnell Douglas Corp.	1993	Supply of F-15 fighter aircraft and associated equipment and systems for the RSAF	N/A
Al-Sawari	Thomson – CSF	1994	Supply of frigates and associated weapons systems for the Royal Saudi Naval Forces	3,500
AT&T Offset	AT&T International	1994	Sixth Telecom Expansion Project (TEP-6) for 1.5 million new telephone lines and 200,000 GSM lines	6,000
Total				**$25,537**

Source: *Economic Offset Office*, Riyadh.

Obtaining precise and up-to-date information on the Saudi Economic Offset program is difficult, due to confidentiality reasons and the sensitive nature of some of the offset operations. Publicly disclosed data was obtained directly from the Saudi Offset Office in Riyadh, as well as from the individual offset operating companies.

The operating guidelines

The follow offset structure guidelines as advised by the Economic Offset Office, reflect the best advice for the operating mechanism of the Saudi Offset program.

Table 10.4 Saudi offset structure guidelines

Structure	Implementation
1. Administration	Economic Offset Committee (EOC)
2. Focus	Defence and civilian projects
3. Amount of obligation	35% of value of (technical) component
4. Earning Offset Credit	- Investment in import substitution joint ventures
	- Equity contribution to joint ventures
	- Medium to long-term debt financing
	- Retained earnings
	- Investment in expansions
	- Investment in Research & Development
	- Training costs of local labour
	- Project commissioning costs
5. Timeframe of obligation	10 years
6. Non-performance penalty	None
7. Others	- Emphasis on high technology projects
	- 60% of investment must be in industry
	- Cash equity contribution must equal at least 20% of total obligation
	- "In-kind" equity contribution to joint venture allowed (these include technical know-how, license agreement, assignment of scientists, engineers and technicians to the offset).

Source: *Saudi Economic Offset Secretariat*, Riyadh, 2003.

Table 10.4 implies that the most desirable type of investment projects for gaining offset credit are manufacturing and services projects that (i) involve a significant degree of high technology; (ii) contribute to the training of Saudi Arabian nationals in management and high technology; or (iii) increase import substitution or provide export potential.

The offset guidelines state that at least 60% of a contractor's offset commitment should consist of manufacturing activities, although the EOO has shown flexibility with this requirement. They argue that the large number of defence projects that have been subject to offset may have depleted the pool of substantial offset opportunities in manufacturing. Investments may be made through establishing new joint ventures, expanding or diversifying already existing joint ventures, through jointly executed research and development programs which substantively contribute to the Kingdom's capabilities, or through contractor-funded training of Saudi Arabian nationals (Pike, 1989, Sandusky, 1996).

The guidelines also provided that high technology transfer may be accomplished through in-kind contribution of technical know-how as equity investments in joint venture companies, through license agreements or through the assignment of scientists, engineers and technicians to the joint ventures. The guidelines mandate that cash contributions to equity in the aggregate must equal at least 20% of the contractor's overall offset commitment.

Offset operating mechanism

Although Saudi Arabia Company Law allows in-kind equity contributions, including technology transfer, the mechanisms which generally apply to determining the value of such direct contributions dictate that, in practice, such contributions are not made by foreign investors.

The guidelines require that the contractor's offset commitment must be fulfilled within ten years, and further sets forth the manner in which credit for fulfilling such commitment will be granted.

The guidelines do not state when the credits will be granted, but this is often addressed in an Economic Offset Commitment Agreement, which records the parties' obligations with respect to the offset program, including the timeframe for submitting such proposals.

It is interesting to note that whilst the Saudi Economic Offset program does not specify a non-performance penalty clause, the economic offset programs that were adopted in Kuwait and the UAE imposed penalty clauses of about 8.5%, with Kuwait's program also including a partial fulfillment clause (Al-Ibrahim, 1996, Kuwait Ministry of Finance, 1995).

Some have argued that this indicated a more serious commitment and impetus for the offset partners of UAE and Kuwait to perform, unlike their counterparts in Saudi Arabia. The amount of Saudi offset obligation is also somewhat blurred, as sometimes it refers to 35% of the contract value, and sometimes it refers to 35% of the technical content of the project. This results in varying estimates of the expected local offset investment content.

This is particularly true for the first offset program – the U.S. *Peace Shield I* with the Boeing Company. In that program the technical content was put at $2,000 million and the total project value at $5,600 million. For the purpose of our study, we have assumed the total value of the project, in line with other Gulf offset programs.

Offset implementation: obligation vs. compliance

From available data, the total value of contracts liable under the offset was $25.5 billion. Under the 35% rule, that means that $8.925 billion ought to have been "offset" locally. According to a recent study, the rate of compliance was 10% for all the offset partners, as indicated in Table 10.5.

Table10.5 Saudi economic offset program offset obligations and rates of compliance

Nationality	Offset Obligation (\$ Million)	Rate of Compliance
USA	1,700	16%
U.K.	2,00	8%
France	700	6%
Total	**4,400**	**10%**

Source: *The Economic Bureau*, 1998.

The Author believes that this rate of compliance is an underestimation. The above offset obligation of $4.4 billion is far below the level of around $9 billion estimated earlier, which was based on the more conservative figure of $25.5 billion offset contracts signed. Official Saudi Ministry of Defence data indicates commitments of SR 13 billion or $3.46 billion from all the offset programs as of 2002 (Economic Offset Office, 2002).

The offset projects: few in number

Table 10.6 summarizes offset projects by country of contract origin. It provides detailed information on the joint venture partners, the business line of the local offset project, the investment made and its operational status.

The percentage share of the foreign and local partners is also indicated. From this one can derive the actual offset capital contribution of the foreign partners in order to arrive at a more precise rate of offset compliance.

Analysis of the offset projects in Table 10.6 reveals a wide diversity of objectives of the joint venture offset partners.

Table10.6 Saudi Arabia Economic Offset projects

Name of Project/ Venture Entity	Joint Venture Partners (Share In Equity)	Line of Business	Project Location	Project Cost ($ million)	Status	Foreign Partner Share (%) and Investment
A.) U.S. PROJECTS : PEACE SHIELD-I OFFSET PROGRAM						
Advanced Electronics Co. (AEC)	Boeing Industrial Technology Group (BITG) – 10% Arabic Computer Systems – 10%; Gulf Investment Corp. (GIC) – 10%; National Commercial Bank (NCB) – 10%; National Industrialization Co. (NIC) – 10%; Saudi Arabian Airlines (Saudia) – 10%	Manufacture and repair of advanced electronics equipment	Riyadh	$125 Million	Operational	10% ($12.5 Million)
Alsalam Aircraft Co. Ltd.	BITG 50%, Saudia 25%, GIC 10%, NIC 10%, and Saudi Advanced Industries Co. (SAID) – 5%	Modification, manufacture, remanufacture assembly, repair, maintenance and overhaul of military, commercial and civil rotary and fixed hydraulics	Riyadh	$190 Million	Operational	50% ($95 Million)
Aircraft Accessories and Components Co. (AACC)	BITG and British Aerospace (BAe) – 50%; Arabian Aircraft Services Col. (Arasco) – 30%; Saudia – 10%; and SAIC 10%	Repair and overhaul of critical aircraft systems: in-flight control, pneumatics, life support, fuel and hydraulics	Riyadh	$24 Million	Operational	50% ($12 Million)
International Systems Engineering (ISE)	BITG and Hughes Aircraft Co. 50%; United Systems Engineering 50% – consortium of 6 Saudi software companies.	Computing system projects in the military, government and commercial sectors	Riyadh	$20 Million	Operational	50% ($10 Million)
Middle East Propulsion Co. (MEPC)	Foreign Partners 50% General Electric (GE), Pratt & Whitney and Rolls Royce (RR); Saudi Partners GIC, NIC, SAIC and Saudi	Maintenance, repair, and overhaul of gas turbine engines and their companies	Riyadh	$52 Million	Operational	50% ($26 Million)
: PEACE SHIELD-II OFFSET PROGRAM						
Middle East Battery Co.	Raytheon and General Motors (GM) – 49% and 6 Saudi companies holding the remaining 51%	Automotive battery manufacturing	Dammam	$59 Million	Operational	49% ($28.9 Million)
B.) U.K. PROJECTS: AL-YAMAMAH OFFSET PROGRAM						
United Sugar Co. (USC)	Tate & Lyle 15%; Savola Co. 51 %; and Saudi Imports Co. (SIC) 15 %	500,000 tpy sugar refinery plant	Jeddah	$150 Million	Operational	15% ($22.5 Million)
Glaxo Saudi Arabia Ltd. (GSAL)	Glaxo Wellcome (UK) 30% and Saudi Imports Co. (SIC) 70 %	Manufacture of pharmaceutical products.	Jeddah	$26 Million	Operational	30% ($7.8 Million)
Cyclar Project	Licensing agreement between Saudi Basic Industries Corp. (SABIC) and technology suppliers UOP and BP 25%	Supply of technology for the Cyclar Plant at SABIC and training packages	Yanbu	$365 Million	Operational	25% ($91.25 Million)
Cumene Manufacturing Project	Universal Petrochemical Co. Ltd. (Unichem), Phenochemie (Germany), and Herdilla (India) 50%	Cumene manufacturing facility	Yanbu	$60 Million	Negotiation Stage	50% ($30 Million)

Table 10.6 (Continued)

Name of Project/ Venture Entity	Joint Venture Partners (Share In Equity)	Line of Business	Project Location	Project Cost ($ million)	Status	Foreign Partner Share (%) and Investment
Dhahran Harco Chemical Inds. Ltd.	Harlow Chemical Co. Ltd. (30%) (Harco) and Dhahran Chemical Industries Ltd. (DCI)	Manufacture of a range of dispersion products used in the paint and adhesive industries	Dammam	$2 Million	Operational	30% ($0.600 Million)
Rezayat Flover Co. Ltd.	Flover Ltd. 50% and Rezayat Trading Company	Repair or remanufacture of instrumentation equipment across the range of Saudi industry	Eastern Province	$2 Million	Operational	50% ($1 Million)
Saudi Development and Training Co.	BAe Systems 50% Al Gosaibi 50%	Development of local manpower, technical training	Riyadh	$3 Million	Operational	50% ($1 5 Million)
Electronics Training Organization	BAe Systems 50% Al Gosaibi 50%	Advanced electronic training, aircraft engineers training	Riyadh	$28 Million	Operational	50% (14 Million)
Waste Oil Recycling	Enprotech (ME) Ltd. 30%, various Saudi investors 70%	Waste oil recycling plant	Eastern Province	$53 Million	Operational	30% ($15.9 Million)
Saudi Polyolephins Co. (SPC)	Basell (Shell/BASF) 25% and National Petrochemical Industry Company (NPIC)	Polypropylene, 450,000 tonnes p.a. propane dehydrogenation plant	Jubail	$530 Million	Under Construction	25% ($132.5 Million)
Gulf Advanced Chemical Co.	Hunstman (USA), Davy Process Technology (UK) – 10% each, and Saudi International Petrochemical Co. (SPIC) GCC Investors	Maleic Anhydride and Butanediol production, 50,000 tonnes p.a. for export (Textile use Lycra)	Jubail	$220 Million	Under Construction	20% ($44 Million)
C.) FRENCH PROJECTS: SAWARI OFFSET PROGRAM						
Dhabab Co. Ltd.	Thomson CSF 49% and Saudi Investors 51%	110 tpy gold refinery	Jeddah	$53 Million	Operational	49% ($25.6 Million)
Al Bilad Catalysts Co. Ltd.	European Catalyst (Eurocat) 35%, Al Bilad Trading & Econ. Est. 20%, and National Contracting Co. 20%	Regeneration of hydro-treating used in oil refineries and petrochemical units	Jubail	$10 Million	Operational	35% ($3.5 Million)
Arabian Meter Co.	Market Trading Co. Schlumberger 30%	Manufacture of electric meters (90,000 units/year)	Dammam	$3.2 Million	Operational	30% ($0.96 Million)
Saudi French Chemical Co.	Atiq of France 35% and Sawa of Gassim	Chemical products	Riyadh	$10.6 Million	Operational	35% (3.71 Million)
D.) AT & T OFFSET PROGRAM						
AT & T Offset Program	AT & T 35% AEC Saudi 65%	Manufacture of PCBs for assembling switch and transmission systems	Riyadh	$252 Million	Operational	35% ($88.2 Million)

Notes: BITG comprises of Boeing, Westinghouse, the Saudi Amoudi Group. ITT and United Support & Service (a joint venture of the US' Frank E Basil and Saudi Operations & Maintenance Co., Inc.) Investment by BAe and Rolls Royce in two Peace Shield Offset companies (i.e. AACC and MEPC respectively) are under the Al-Yamamah offset commitment.

Sources: *Ministry of Defence, Riyadh. Economic Offset Secretariat*, 2003, *The Economic Bureau Riyadh*, 1998.

Analysis of the offset projects in Table 10.6 reveals a wide diversity of objectives of the joint venture offset partners. Table 10.7 summarizes the key offset emphases of the projects, both operational or under construction, in order to assess whether they met the stated preferred objectives of the offset program.

Table 10.7 Saudi Offset projects: actual areas of project implementation vs. preferred areas of project investments

Preferred Offset Investment Objective Areas	Actual Number of Projects Implemented/Under Construction	Size of Offset Projects ($ Million)	Foreign Share Ownership ($ Million)
1. Generating advanced technical training and high value employment for Saudis	1	3	1.5
2. Boosting foreign investment in productive services and activities	4	119.2	45.96
3. Import substitution and products for exports.	4	455.0	103.2
4. Development of local technical, professional and managerial expertise in high technology industries	6	316.0	158.0
5. Transfer of technological know-how through research, development and manufacturing processes	3	742.0	191.95
6. Making use of the Kingdom's raw materials	4	602.6	166.81
Total ($ million)	**22**	**2,237.8**	**667.42**

Source: *Table-10.6.*

While there is some overlap between objectives number 1 and 4 in Table 10.7 (as advanced technical training can be obtained through both formal training methods and on-the-job professional and technical training), it is interesting to note that the bulk of projects in relative value terms were based on the transfer of technological know-how in manufacturing processes, and on the utilization of the Kingdom's raw material base in petrochemical feedstock. While total investment in the offset projects amounted to $2.237 billion, committed investments by the foreign partners totalled $667.42 million or 30%. However, the foreign participation commitment, as a total percentage of the overall contracts, becomes drastically lower as noted in Table 10.8.

Table 10.8 Actual foreign investment participation rate in total Saudi offset

Country	Total Offset Contract Value ($ Million)	Offset Projects Undertaken ($ Million)	Foreign Offset Investment Participation Value ($ Million)	Foreign Participation Rate in Total Offset Contract (%)
USA	6,437	470.0	184.0	2.9%
UK	7,600	1,439.0	361.1	4.8%
France	3,500	76.8	33.8	0.9%
Other				
- AT & T	6,000	252.0	88.2	1.5%
Total	**25,537**	**2,237.8**	**667.5**	**2.6%**

Source: *Table 10.6.*

The breakdown by actual foreign offset investment participation and commitment shows a 2.6% rate of compliance for all offset participants, a much lower figure than the 10% compliance rate mentioned earlier. When we look at individual countries, the UK does better at 4.8%, with the USA coming in at just under 3%, while France comes at under a 1% compliance rate. The above table emphasizes the importance of separating the foreign offset investment component from the overall offset project investment, so as to exclude the Saudi contribution and arrive at a more meaningful level of foreign offset participation.

Employment objectives not met

The low financial foreign offset participation level seems to be matched by an additional low level of participation rate in a key policy objective area of the Saudi offset program: Saudi employment.

An expanding industrial base translates into employment opportunities for Saudi nationals in the private sector, whether that expansion is wholly Saudi-owned or through joint ventures such as those envisaged under the Offset Economic Program. According to the Saudi Ministry of Defence Economic Offset Secretariat Office, the number of Saudis employed in the 15 offset companies totalled 967 out of 2,251 employees, or 43% as of year end 2001. This is illustrated in Table 10.9, which shows a *Saudization* level ranging from a high of 82% to a low of 11% for different offset companies. The total number of Saudis employed in the offset program is very small in relation to official expectations and to the investment made to date.

The number of Saudis who might eventually be employed in all the fully-operational offset-related projects could be much higher when current plants under construction – especially the petrochemical projects under the British *Al-Yamamah* program – come on-stream. However, given the capital-intensive nature of such projects, the eventual employment numbers might not be sufficiently significant to make any meaningful contribution to reducing current Saudi unemployment levels.

Table 10.9 Actual foreign investment participation rate in total Saudi offset by project value – 2003

Company Name	Total Employees	Saudi Employees	% Saudis
International Systems Engineering	111	91	82%
Advanced Electronic Company	402	300	75%
Arabian Meter Company	12	7	85%
Aircraft Access and Component	94	39	42%
Middle East Batteries	187	73	41%
Al-Salaam Aircraft	717	261	36%
Electronic Training Organization	125	45	36%
Middle East Propulsion Company	29	10	35%
Al-Bilad Catalyst	23	8	35%
Middle East Energy	72	22	31%
Saudi French Chemical Company	18	5	28%
United Sugar Company	296	74	25%
Saudi Development and Training	67	14	21%
Dhahran HARCO Company	80	15	19%
Rezayat Flover	27	3	11%
GLAXCO	N/A		
Waste Oil Recycling	N/A		
Dhabab Company Limited	N/A		
Cyclar Project	N/A		
Total	**2,251**	**967**	**100%**

Source: Economic Offset Secretariat, Riyadh. 2003.

Evaluation of the Saudi offset program

It has been stated elsewhere that the various offset programs undertaken in Saudi Arabia, Kuwait and the UAE serve as a catalyst in transforming the economies of the Gulf countries (Gutierrez, 1996). The programs are helping to break a traditional vicious cycle in the Gulf business environment and to generate a forward-moving one. According to Gutierrez, with offset programs, the vicious cycle is being gradually replaced by a virtuous one, in which multinational corporations have a vested interest in the future of the Gulf economies so that they ensure that their offset programs remain profitable. However, he admits that as the offset concept is relatively new to the region, the pace of new investment under the program has generally been slow, with the result that "achievements on the ground have been minimal when measured against the magnitude of the resources employed" (Gutierrez, 1996).

The official reasons put forward for this seemingly slow pace, as evidenced from the number of operational offset projects in Saudi Arabia to date, has been the difficulty of identifying "good" investment opportunities. Foreign contractors have been unable to obtain reliable local market data or information on potential local partners. The long gestation period of 3-4 years on average before offset ventures start to do business is another obstacle. In addition, some complain about the multiple levels of foreign, corporate and government administration they must deal with.

This argument might have had some merit in the earlier days of the offset program. However, since 2000, the Saudi Arabian government has come a long way towards establishing a foreign investment-friendly organization to smooth bureaucratic hurdles, by providing services through a "one-stop" office run by the Saudi Arabian General Investment Authority (SAGIA).

Furthermore, defence contractors could turn out to be the wrong kind of investors to develop a civilian industrial base, with doubts about the future viability of a project in terms of market prospect, managerial capability, technology transfer and new product development, once the project's underlying military contract is finished (Evans, 1996). We will assess the validity of such impediments in greater detail when we compare the performance of the non-offset industrial investments that took place in the Kingdom over the same period to the offset programs.

Offset project benefits

Table 10.10 summarizes the major economic benefits that we believe have accrued to Saudi Arabia under the various offset program projects implemented to date.

As stated earlier, Saudi Arabia was the first country of the Gulf Cooperation Council (GCC) to introduce the offset program, emphasizing high technology investment as part of the initial U.S. Peace Shield military project. This emphasis seems to have paid off in terms of both industrial diversification and human resource skills development as summarized in Table 10.10.

Table 10.10 Perceived economic benefits of offset programs

Area of Benefit	Observations and Comments
1. Industrial Development & Diversification	• Inflow of new technologies has spurred development of new industries, including aviation engineering, electronic engineering, computer and information technology, sugar, precious metal refining. These could be the launching pad for other industries.
2. Strategic Self-Sufficiency	• Offset program components have provided KSA with high technical capabilities in crucial military sector areas, such as defence systems, aircraft repair and modification, components and electronic manufacturing and repair. In defence and security areas the Kingdom now produces aircraft parts, tactical radios, cockpit control units, electronic warfare systems and flight data recorder systems.
3. Import Substitution and Export Development	• Export potential for many products, e.g. batteries, gold ingots, sugar, catalysts, pharmaceutical, as well as avionics equipment and specialized military components. Providing aircraft maintenance for other GCC Airlines.
4. Employment and Human Resource Development	• High-tech training has lessened the Kingdom's dependence on imported systems, engineering support contractors, and has produced high-tech specialists in computer, IT, electronic engineering, aircraft maintenance and aerospace support.
5. Promotion of new Business Opportunities	• The current offset program can act as a drawing power for other projects, for example British Offset's cumene manufacturing project, which represents a downstream integration of the Kingdom's aromatic projects. Joint offset company projects (e.g. between AEC and AACC).
6. Drawing power of the Offset Companies	• Presence of offset companies, especially high-tech and those that use the Kingdom's raw material resources (gas/oil) can enhance KSA's comparative advantage and strengthen its attractiveness as an investment destination.

As an example of the spin-off effect of such high-tech offset programs, it was announced in June, 2003, that Advanced Electronic Company (AEC) has manufactured Saudi Arabia's first satellite-based Automatic Vehicle Location System (AVLS) that makes it possible to track the movement of a vehicle on a bilingual Arabic-English digital map, the speed at which the vehicle is travelling and the route it is following (Arab News, 12 June 2003). Whilst the number of projects and the level of employment generation to date have been modest, given the potential size of available offset credits from foreign contractors, still the "qualitative" human capital aspect of the offset program should not be underestimated. Saudi Arabia had none of the skills associated with these high technology ventures prior to the offset programs. This issue should be borne in mind when one compares the relative contribution of offset and non-offset investment in Saudi Arabia.

Foreign offset partners: low equity stake

The relatively small equity contribution of the foreign offset partners, seen earlier in Table 10.7, might actually be due to the generous financing terms available for offset projects. We would have expected that foreign offset partners contribute anywhere between 35% to 50% equity ownership levels. However, the data in Table 10.6 indicated that the participation rate ranged from 10% to 30%, especially for the earlier offset projects. While there is no public information on concessionary financing available to the U.S. and French offset contracts, the United Kingdom seems to have taken the initiative in this regard, and current BAE financial assistance is summarized below. This might be due to the fact that the UK's *Al-Yamamah* offset contract was the largest, and that the British government had a more energetic involvement. The financing program is generous by world standards: in effect, a UK offset partner could end up being a 50% local Saudi joint venture owner with only a 6.5% equity participation. It operates in the following manner and is supported through BAE System PLC.

According to BAE (British Offset, 2002), it has established a fully supported bank facility aimed at reducing the initial investment risk and enhancing the level of return from any joint venture. Figure 10.1 provides an illustration.

According to this enhanced financing structure, which was introduced in 2001, a typical UK offset investment will benefit from a 50% Saudi Industrial Development Fund (SIDF) loan to the joint venture, up to SR 400 million or $106.7 million. The joint venture could then generally seek a further 25% loan from Saudi commercial banks, leaving 25% equity to be funded equally by the Saudi and foreign partner. The 12.5% foreign equity funding can be further reduced, using the "BAE System Project Finance Initiative", as it is called, which offers a low-interest, non-recourse loan for up to 50% of the 12.5% stake, i.e. 6.25%. This means in effect that a foreign partner has all the benefits of a 50% share-holding in a joint venture for just

6.25% of the total project funding. The joint venture company should have a minimum capitalized value of $16 million.

Figure 10.1 BAE financing structure: Saudi offset program

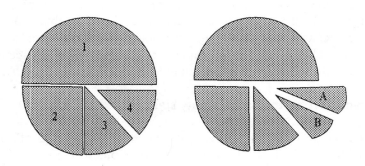

Funding structure for a joint venture
1.   50% Saudi Industrial Development Fund
2.   25% Local banks
3.   12.5% Saudi Partner
4.   12.5% Technology Partner
Technology Partner
A.   6.25% British Aerospace soft financing loan
B.   6.25% to be funded by the Technology Partner
Source: *BAE Systems*, 2002.

As a further measure to help reduce UK companies' risk, the loan repayment schedule is based on the dividend payments made by the joint venture company. To cap this, should a Saudi bank require a parent company loan guarantee from the UK offset partner, then BAE systems would contribute a share of the guarantee on a dollar for dollar basis, up to a maximum amount of $10 million. This can be used for equity loan or loan guarantee or be split between them. With such seemingly-generous financial support from participating governments, at least from the UK, why were the results not forthcoming in terms of the number of offset projects? We will explore this issue by analyzing the principal motives of the foreign offset contractors in participating in the Saudi program to date below.

Foreign offset partners: motives for investment

Foreign contractors may gain some strategic benefit from offset arrangements, as such programs potentially provide an opportunity to establish a local base from which to diversify into both the host market and nearby countries. From this point of view, offset is not an obligation, but rather an opportunity to invest in the purchasing country's economy.

Information was sought to ascertain foreign offset partners' motives for participating in the offset program, and to assess how the program was currently viewed. All 22 existing and planned joint venture offset companies were approached at a senior management level.

Table 10.11 summarizes the questionnaire responses received from the various economic offset companies, grouped by their primary offset contracts.

Table 10.11 Saudi Economic Offset program: questionnaire survey response

Nature of Offset Joint Venture Project	Number of Existing Companies	Numbers of Responses	
		Saudi Partner	Foreign Partner
1. High Tech Defence Related	3	0	0
2. High Tech Non-Defence Related	3	2	3
3. Manufacturing/Chemicals	13	4	11
4. Training/Human Resources	2	2	2
5. Mining Extraction	1	1	0
Total	**22**	**9**	**16**
Percentage Response		**41%**	**73%**

Source: *Author's Survey*, 2003.

Table 10.11 shows that both Saudi and foreign joint venture partners were reluctant to divulge information for high-tech defence-related projects. This was not an issue for the other projects. The overall Saudi response was 41% while 73%of the foreign joint venture offset partners targeted responded. Given that the aim was to analyze the motives of the foreign equity offset partners, the analysis below concentrates on the foreign segment only. The results of the questionnaires are set out in Table 10.12

Table 10.12 Offset foreign partners: Offset participation objectives

	Increased Market Share in KSA	Export Potential	Sourcing Local Raw Material	Profitable Venture	Marketing Tool to Win Bid	Total
Number of Respondents	4	3	4	4	1	16
%	25%	18.7%	25%	25%	6.3%	100%

The respondents indicated that the original aim of their joint ventures was primarily to increase market share, source raw material and export potential. Only one respondent indicated that the offset project was used as a marketing tool to win a bid. As for their perception of Saudi Arabia's political and economic considerations, more than half of the respondents did not comment, but 75% rated government–to-government relations as good to excellent. Future Saudi economic prospects were generally rated positively, as were natural resources and high *per capita* income.

Investment structure of non-offset program in Saudi Arabia

The necessity for economic diversification of the Saudi Arabian economy away from an overwhelming dependence on erratic oil revenues is now of paramount importance and is repeatedly stressed in all official policy statements as mentioned in earlier chapters. Policy documents stress the prominent role of the Saudi private sector in contributing to economic growth and employment. This latter issue is now of utmost urgency in the country, in light of one of the highest population growth rates in the world at 3.5-3.7% per annum and with nearly 70% of the population under the age of 30 (SAMA, 2002).

Table 10.13 offers a snapshot views of the progress of Saudi industry over the period 1982-2000, by setting out the number of operational industrial units by sectors. Major concentrations are seen in engineering machinery and equipment, chemicals and chemical by-products, construction and food beverages.

Table10.13 Summary: Factories under production 2000

Industrial Sector and Code	(Nos.)					
	1982	*1985*	*1990*	*1995*	*1999*	*2000*
Food and beverages	187	235	308	391	529	539
Textile, wearing apparel and leather industries	22	28	55	108	156	167
Wood and wood products, including furniture	38	53	81	109	155	174
Paper products, printing and publishing	86	109	131	163	205	211
Chemicals & petroleum, coal, rubber & plastic	150	220	311	463	670	693
Construction materials, chinaware, ceramic & glass	261	314	387	464	560	570
Basic metal industries	5	6	9	15	11	12
Manufacture of fabricated products, machinery and equipment	294	388	545	685	915	948
Other manufacturing industries	16	29	51	59	79	83
Transportation & storage	19	19	19	19	20	21
Total	**1,078**	**1,401**	**1,897**	**2,476**	**3,300**	**3,418**

Source: *Ministry of Industry & Electricity, Industrial Statistics Bulletin*, 2001.

A feature of Saudi industrial development has been the active participation of foreign companies in the process, with the number of joint ventures increasing from 344 in 1995 to 475 in 2000 (see Table 10.14). These joint ventures, which exclude the offset-related projects, were undertaken through the initiative of Saudi and foreign private sectors based on their own commercial interests. The revision of the foreign investment regulations (especially the reduction in the top rate of taxation to 20% on foreign companies in 2003), along with other institutional reforms, is expected to contribute towards more such joint ventures.

Table 10.14 Summary of industrial joint ventures in Saudi Arabia

				(SR Million)
	1995		2000	
Admin. Area	*No. of units*	*Investment*	*No. of units*	*Investment*
Riyadh	116	4,388	168	6,718
Qassim	4	15	1	3
Makkah	95	14,448	139	17,023
Madinah	11	15,505	20	36,780
Eastern Province	116	54,452	144	71,777
Assir	2	2	2	2
Tabouk	-	-	1	175
Total	**344**	**88,810**	**475**	**132,478**

Source: *Ministry of Industry & Electricity, Industrial Statistics Bulletin,* 2001.

According to Table 10.14, total investment in the joint ventures rose to SR 132.14 billion in 2000, compared with SR 88.8 billion in 1995. They averaged a 6.6% growth per annum over the 5-year period 1995-2000. Notably, the majority of investments were in the Eastern Province of Saudi Arabia. They were attracted to its oil and petrochemical base, even though it has a smaller population base than the other regions. This reinforces the predominance of the chemical and engineering units seen earlier in Table 10.13.

The growth of manpower in these joint ventures has also risen steadily over the period 1990-2000, as illustrated in Figure 10.2.

Figure 10.2 Growth of manpower in joint venture factories 1990-2000

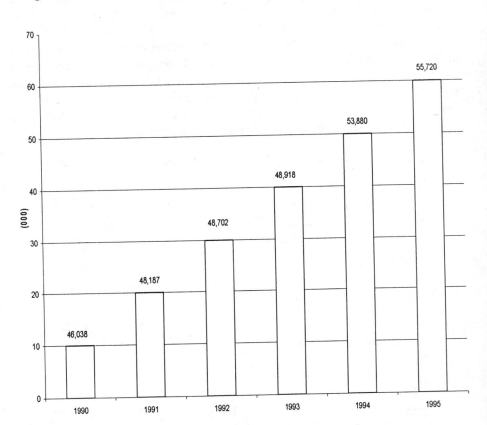

Source: *Ministry of Industry & Electricity, Industrial Statistics Bulletin* , 2001.

Non-offset projects seem to meet national objectives

In comparison with offset-related projects over the same period, the Saudi joint venture non-offset investments have been much more of a success in terms of economic indicators, as analyzed in Table 10.15.

Table 10.15 Comparison of offset and non-offset Saudi joint venture projects (2000)

	Total Investment	Total Employment	Investment Per Employee	Total Projects	Employees Per Project
Offset Joint Venture Projects	SR 8.388 billion	2,251	SR 3,723,000	22	102
Non-Offset Joint Venture Projects	SR132.479 billion	55,720	SR 2,373,000	475	117

Source: *Tables 10.8, 10. 9, 10.14 and Figure10. 2.*

At a first glance, Table 10.15 seems to indicate that the role of large industries in creating job opportunities has certain limitations, especially those which are high-tech and capital-intensive. For offset projects, the investment per employee was nearly SR 3.7 million or $1 million, while for joint venture non-offset companies it stood at around SR 2.4 million or $650,000 per employee. Both offset and non-offset projects have, in general, opted for capital-intensive industries where the process of production can be more controlled. This is evidenced through Table 10.16, which breaks down Saudi industrial joint ventures into their appropriate industry sector classification.

Table 10.16 Saudi industrial joint ventures and their capital investment 1995-2000

	YEAR	Food & Beverages		Textiles & leather industries.		Wood & wood prod., including furniture		Paper products., printing & publishing		Chemicals & petroleum, coal, rubber & plastics		Construction materials, chinaware, ceramic & glass		Basic metal inds. & fabricated metal products, machinery & equipment		Other manufacturing industries, including transport & storage		TOTAL	
		units	SR Million	units	SR Million	units	SR Million	units	SR Million	units	SR Million	units	SR Million	units	SR Million	units	SR Million	units	SR Million
TOTAL	1995	32	1,582	7	199	15	148	18	1,370	93	75,448	44	6,052	129	3,739	6	249	344	88,787
TOTAL	2000	37	3,057	19	463	19	325	20	1,542	133	113,416	58	6,488	181	6,755	8	433	475	132,479

Source: *Industrial Statistics Bulletin, 2001, Ministry of Industry & Electricity.*

The preponderance of investment in chemicals, petroleum and other associated products is evident and explains the high capital-labour ratio.

The total number of employees rose to 318,542 in 2000 compared with 224,877 in 1995, or a growth rate of 5.9% per annum for the five-year period 1995-2000. Table 10.18 breaks down employment by sectors.

Table 10.17 Total number of employees by sector, 1995-2000 (non-offset projects)

Industrial Sector	Total Manpower	
	1995	2000
Food & beverages	31,405	45,696
Textile, wearing apparel & leather	12,905	19,775
Wood & wood products including furniture	9,241	14,928
Paper products, printing and publishing	12,242	17,312
Chemicals, petroleum, coal, rubber & plastics	51,937	74,191
Construction materials & chinaware, ceramic & glass	40,758	50,602
Basic metal industries	3,727	3,037
Fabricated metal products, machinery & equipment	56,251	85,282
Other manufacturing industries	4,455	7,056
Transport & storage	1,956	663
Total	**224,877**	**318,542**

Source: *Table 10.18.*

The growth rate in private sector employment is patently not keeping pace with labour market entrants, estimated at around 150,000 per annum and rising, given the young population age structure of the Kingdom (Saudi American Bank, 2003). What is also evident is that the capital-labour ratio is still relatively high at SR 754,000 per employee ($201,000) for all industries in 2000, as set out in Table 10.18.

Table 10.18 Average capital investment per employee in Saudi industry 1995-2000

Industrial Sector	Number of units		No. of units started during the five year period	Investment (SR Million)		Capital invested during the five year period (SR Million)	Number of employees		No. of people employed during the five year period	Investment per employee 2000 (SR)
	1995	2000		1995	2000		1995	2000		
Food & beverages	391	539	148	11,294	17,457	6,163	31,405	45,696	14,291	382,024
Textile, wearing apparel & leather	108	167	59	2,592	4,103	1,511	12,905	19,775	6,870	207,484
Wood & wood prods. Including furniture	109	174	65	1,496	2,697	1,201	9,241	14,928	5,687	180,667
Paper prods, printing & publishing	163	211	48	4,599	6,700	2,101	12,242	17,312	5,070	387,000
Chemicals, petroleum, coal, rubber & plastics	463	693	230	100,875	151,686	50,811	51,937	74,191	22,254	2,044,533
Construction mat'l's. & chinaware, ceramic & glass	464	570	106	21,169	26,572	5,403	40,758	50,602	9,844	106,774
Basic metal industries & fabricated metal prods., machinery & equipment	700	960	260	19,830	29,233	9,403	59,978	88,319	28,341	106,466
Other mfg. Industries, transport & storage	78	104	26	1,325	1,631	306	6,411	7,719	1,308	211,296
Total	2,476	3,418	942	163,180	240,900	76,900	224,877	318,542	93,665	753,683

Source: Ministry of Industry and Electricity, 2001, Saudi Commerce and Economic Review, 2002.

The relatively high level of investment per employee is due largely to the capital intensive nature of the chemical and petrochemical industries, where SR 2.044 million ($545,000) was invested per employee as noted in Table 10.18, while other industry investments ranged between SR 105,000 (construction) to SR 378,000 for the food and beverage industry. The choice for Saudi Arabian non-offset companies seems to have been either to opt for low-tech industries to promote employment opportunities, or for high-tech industries, which are capital-intensive, to add value to the economy through a more diversified export orientation and import substitution base. Breaking into established export markets takes time, and Saudi Arabia could be accused of unfair trading practices and dumping by competitors due to the low cost of its hydrocarbon feedstock for its petrochemical industries. The alternative is to opt for import substitution industries and employment generation.

Table 10.19 summarizes offset program projects with all non-offset industrial projects with respect to investments and employment.

Table 10.19 Comparison of offset and total private sector non-offset industrial projects 2000

	Total Investment	Total Employment	Investment per employee	Total Project	Employees per project
Offset Projects	SR 8.388 billion	2,251	SR 3.723 million	22	102
Total Private Sector Non-Offset Projects	SR 240 billion	318,542	SR 750,000	3,418	93

Source: *Tables 10.15, 10.18.*

The data for 2000 would indicate that, in absolute terms, between 1990-2000, the non-offset private sector invested nearly 29 times, employed 141 times and identified and operated 155 times more projects than the offset program. This was carried out with minimal government direction or guidance. This is the quantitative aspect. In qualitative terms, one has to estimate the value-added component of technology transfer in the offset projects in order to establish a fairer comparison with non-offset investments, which we will now examine.

Components of technology transfer

Technology is transferred between countries through a variety of methods and channels, ranging from the relatively simple, such as equipment purchase and direct recruitment of foreign experts, to the more complex, such as total project contracting or complete "packaging" of technology transfer.

This notion of comprehensiveness refers to the totality of the transfer package, including such elements as training, provision of equipment and plant services. It is thus possible to categorize the packaging of technology transfer into various levels, according to the respective degree of comprehensiveness, or totality, of the transaction.

Methods of technology transfer

Various methods of technology transfer have been proposed. Patel (1974, p. 5) outlined eight types of channels through which transfers might be completed to developing countries. These range from flow of books to direct foreign investment and operation. The United Nations Conference on Trade and Development (UNCTAD) presents another classification (UNCTAD, 1978, p. 6). They classify transactions involving international flows of technology into three main types: (i) simple direct transactions in which the purchaser attempts to buy each technology transfer element at the best possible price and terms, resulting, in essence, in "package-free" deals; (ii) process package transactions through which supplying firms market "systems" along with managerial and technical skills; and (iii) project package transactions in which the supplier undertakes to set up the complete project with the technology embodied in it.

From the above literature, it is possible to establish the classification of transfer methods for technology transfer, as set out in Table 10.20.

Table10.20 Methods of technology transfer

Complexity	Methods
Most Complex	1. Total project contracting
	2. Total process contracting
	3. Major process contracting
	4. Know-how contracts
	5. Patent contracts
	6. Trademark agreements
	7. Franchise agreement
	8. Engineering services contracts
	9. Technical consultancy contracts
	10. Machinery supplies
	11. Employment of experts
	12. Technical publications
Least complex	13. Personal contacts

Adapted from Patel, 1974, UNCTAD, 1978, Shubber, 2003.

Table 10.20 sets out methods ranging from the most complex to the least complex in the order of their perceived level of "comprehensiveness" (Shubber, 2003). The more an economy lags behind in terms of technical skills, diverse manufacturing and a scientific base, the more complex or comprehensive will be the method of technology transfer.

Packaging the technology transfer

Based on the channels for technology transfer, it is now possible to define the degree of packaging of technology transfer. By packaging, we refer here to the degree of comprehensiveness in the provision of technology transfer by the principal technology supplier. On this basis, five main packaging levels can be identified (Shubber, 2003), along with associated transfer methods, as follows:

A. *Ultra-packaged Transfer:* This corresponds to total project contracting

B. *Highly-packaged Transfer:* This corresponds to total process contracting

C. *Medium-packaged Transfer:* This corresponds to the methods of major process contracting, know-how and patent contracts

D. *Low-packaged Transfer:* This corresponds to patent-contracting, trade-mark contracts, and franchising

E. *Package-free Transfer:* The methods here are engineering services contracts, supplies of equipment, employment of experts, technical publication, technical consultancy, personal contacts.

The five levels of packaging are summarized in Table 10.21.

Table 10. 21 Components of technological transfer: Packaging levels

Component Element		Basic	Ancillary
		1. Industrial Property Rights (patents, trademarks)	1. Building Design/Construction
		2. Hardware	2. Energy Provision
		3. Software (Computer programs, blueprints, instruction manuals)	3. Maintenance and/or Provision of Spare Parts
		4. Training of Personnel	4. Supply of Materials
		5. Technological Services (Product design, engineering)	5. Operational Management
Most Advanced Component			
	A.	All 5 basic elements present	*Plus*: At least 3 ancillary elements exist.
	B.	All 5 basic elements present	*Plus*: Up to 3 ancillary elements exist.
	C.	3 to 4 basic elements present	*Plus:* Up to 3 ancillary elements exist.
	D.	2 to 3 of basic elements present	*Plus*: 1 to 3 ancillary elements exist.
	E.	1 to 2 basic elements present	*Plus*: 1 to 2 ancillary elements exist.
Least Advanced Component			

Note: A = Ultra Packaged Transfer, B = Highly Packaged Transfer,
C = Medium Packaged Transfer, D = Low Packaged Transfer,
E = Package Free Transfer.

How did the various Saudi economic offset projects fare in terms of the listed technology component transfer packaging levels? We examine this next.

Saudi offset technology transfer

Having developed a framework of packaging levels in international technology transfer transactions, along with associated methods, the challenge is to apply these criteria to the Saudi Economic Offset projects that have either been implemented or are under construction in the Kingdom. As discussed earlier in this chapter, the total number of offset projects was 22. They were evaluated, using publicly-available information about their operations, as to the level of technology packaging applicable for each project. Supplemental management information was sought wherever possible. The assessment focused on major variables, such as the relevant industrial sector, technological and managerial complexity, and patents and trademarks, as set out in Table 10.21.

The results summarized in Table 10.22 must be treated with a certain degree of caution due to the imprecise nature of evaluating technological comprehensiveness, as well as the sensitivity of some of the offset projects, especially those that are defence-related. However, we believe that Table 10.22 captures the overall essence of the nature of operations of the offset projects.

Table 10.22 Saudi Arabian level of technology "packaging" for economic offset companies

Industrial Sector	*Level of Packaging*				
	A	B	C	D	E
1. Advanced Electronics	4	2	1		
2. Oil, Petrochemicals			2		
3. Chemicals, Pharmaceuticals			4	1	
4. Consumer products, Food			1		
5. Metal products, Mining			1		
6. Training, Human Resources		1	1		
7. Manufacturing			2	2	

Note:
A = Ultra Packaged Transfer, B = Highly Packaged Transfer,
C = Medium Packaged Transfer, D = Low Packaged Transfer,
E = Package Free Transfer

Source: *Table 10.6.*

The results for the offset companies, in terms of transfer technology packaging, were quite positive. Nineteen projects or 86% of the total fell in the "A-C" category of technology packaging, and only three projects or 14% were in the "D" low technology packaged transfer range. There were no offset companies in the "E" or package-free transfer category. Even more encouraging, seven projects or 31% of the total belonged to the "A/B" or ultra-packaged/high-technology packaged categories. This was one of the principal objectives of the original economic offset program. In terms of industry, the advanced electronic sector and specialized technical training stood out as being in the 'A' or ultra-packaged technological transfer category, as they scored the highest level of pre- and post-operational technological complexity. The majority of the remaining offset projects fell into the 'C' or medium packaged technology transfer, including projects in the oil, petrochemicals and chemical industries.

The reason was self-evident: Saudi Arabia had an already-established track record in the oil, petrochemical and chemical industry sectors *prior* to the offset programs. The level of packaging was not significant. However, there were no advanced electronic industries or expertise in the Kingdom in these sectors *prior* to the offset projects. The level of technology transfer packaging was significant in these "new industries".

Offset vs. non-offset technology packaging

Earlier in the chapter we observed that, in general, the non-offset joint venture projects achieved better results in relation to employment and general investment levels than did offset projects. Table 10.23 sets out the level of technology packaging for the private sector non-offset joint venture projects using the same packaging component schedule as Table 10.21. Fortunately there was more information available on the non-offset companies, but again the results should be treated with caution.

Table 10.23 Saudi Arabian level of technology "packaging" for private sector non-offset joint venture companies 2000

Industrial Sector	Level of Packaging				
	A	B	C	D	E
a. Chemicals, petroleum, rubber and plastics		4	32	63	34
b. Food & Beverages			6	14	17
c. Textiles and leather industry				5	14
d. Wood and wood products and furniture				2	17
e. Paper products, printing and publishing			4	6	10
f. Construction material, chinaware, ceramic and glass			1	19	38
g. Basic metal industries, fabricated metal products, machines and equipment			3	107	71
h. Other manufacturing industries, transport and storage				3	5

Note:
A = Ultra Packaged Transfer, B = Highly Packaged Transfer
C = Medium Packaged Transfer, D = Low Packaged Transfer
E = Package Free Transfer
Source: *Adopted by Author from Industrial Statistics Bulletin, 2001, Ministry of Industry and Electricity, Table 66.17, "Top 1000 Saudi Companies", 6th Edition, 2000, IIT, Al-Khobar, Saudi Arabia, 2001.*

The results of the survey of the 475 non-offset private sector joint venture companies, displayed in Table 10.23, indicate that there is some reason for supposing that the level of transfer technology packaging for the non-offset projects was considerably less significant that those for the offset projects. Some 50 non-offset companies, or 10% of the total, were in the "B-

C" highly packaged/medium packaged range, with 219 projects, or 47%, in the "D" low packaged range and the remaining 206 projects (43%) in the "E", or package free transfer range.

Those that operated in the relatively greater technology packaged ranges were similar to the offset projects. They also operated in the chemical, petroleum and metal industries, as well as in the advanced food and beverages sectors.

The majority of non-offset joint venture projects seemed to operate on franchise agreements, engineering services contracts, technical consultancies, general machinery supplies and *ad hoc* employment of experts. Those operating in the more "technologically comprehensive" packaging areas, such as chemicals, did so using the know-how contract, patent contract or through a major process contracting basis with their foreign partners.

Conclusion: offset score sheet

The Saudi economic offset program can be viewed as one special case of economic management in which certain policies were devised to overcome perceived internal constraints in the Saudi economy, specifically the lack of an advanced technology skills base. While both the objective and the strategy were laudable, the actual results to date have not been commensurate with the size of investments made. Further, the offset program has not achieved the expected direction and sustained economic impact on other industrial sectors, nor has it created a "virtuous cycle" of interdependencies.

With the exception of a few key family industrial groupings and offset partnerships, the majority of Saudi businessmen who could benefit from participation in the offset program are either unfamiliar with or unaware of the programs' existence (Ramady, 2004). The fact that the Economic Offset Office operates as part of the Saudi Ministry of Defence seems to create a psychological barrier to potential investors and the Ministry might well consider locating some of its operational advisory functions in a more "civilian-friendly" environment.

The shortcomings to date of the offset program are due more to institutional, human and marketing constraints than to physical or technological restrictions, as evidenced by the growth of non-defence related offset ventures pursued by the UK offset program, which opted for that route. The Saudi Chambers of Commerce and Industry need to be more involved than they have been to date in identifying absorptive capacity for new and existing offset projects.

The current constraints are in identifying investment opportunities, the size of local market demand, the potential export market and provision of labour with appropriate technical skills. These should be addressed by these chambers, for they are able to draw upon a wider number of potential partners to participate in the program, either singly or through "pooled" ownership with common industrial interests. One success of the current offset program has been the provision of advanced electronic and technological skills to Saudis. This could be the pattern for future expansion of the offset program, instead of identifying new projects, which, as we have seen earlier, the private sector can successfully undertake outside the offset framework. However, in order to benefit from a wider range of technology transfer, the Saudi government must also undertake a structural educational reform program that provides scientific and technological skills to Saudis, as well as encouraging a culture of research and development in the private sector. Only through such a well-endowed human capital base will the Kingdom benefit from a true technology transfer.

Summary of key points

- *Offset programs are considered to be a special type of foreign direct investment and transfer of technology. Offset is a form of counter trade.*
- *Saudi Arabia was the first country of the GCC to introduce offset in 1984 requiring international contractors from the USA, UK and France to re-invest in the Kingdom a percentage of the value of the awarded foreign contracts.*
- *Offsets can be classified as "direct" or "indirect". By direct the purchasing country joins the selling in supplying some components of the underlying contract. By indirect, the seller country agrees to assist the buyer country in its development and investment goals. Saudi offset has been in the indirect field.*
- *Saudi offset guidelines specify amounts of obligation (35%), timeframe (10 years) and areas of investments (industry, defence, services, and agriculture). There are no penalty clauses for non-compliance.*
- *Currently there are 22 operational and planned offset projects in a wide variety of sectors ranging from training, to making use of the Kingdom's raw materials. Total foreign equity stake, participation levels and employment of Saudis in offset programs have been low.*
- *Saudi Arabia also benefits from technology transfer brought through private sector non-offset joint ventures. The number of units in such joint ventures are much larger than offset projects in terms of*

      operating units, investment, and employees. Both however, tend to be capital intensive due to concentration in the petrochemical areas.
- *Methods of technology transfer are discussed. These range from the most complex (total project contracting) to the least complex (personal contacts and technical publications). A model of "packaging technology transfer" is examined which sets out 5 levels of technology transfer packages.*
- *Examination of the technology transfer packaging levels for offset and non-offset private sector joint ventures reveals that the offset companies do provide a higher level of technology transfer compared to non-offset companies. These were more pronounced in the advanced electronics and technical training areas, expertise that Saudi Arabia did not possess prior to offset.*

Critical thinking

1. "Offset programs can be a valuable means of transferring appropriate technology to developing countries". Discuss how offset was handled in Saudi Arabia.
2. Which type of offset – direct or indirect – is more beneficial to Saudi Arabia in the long run and why?
3. "Saudi Arabia should concentrate on technical training as part of offset, as the rest can be acquired but technical training is the most important". Do you agree? Should there be more insistence on this aspect of offset? What are the pros and cons of following this route to both buying and selling countries?
4. "The private sector knows best the type of industries to be established under offset". Do you agree, based on the type of joint ventures established in non-offset projects by the private sector in Saudi Arabia?
5. "Offset cannot really succeed until Saudi education is directed towards a science based system and the private sector spends more on research and development". Discuss.

Chapter 11

ECONOMIC LIBERALIZATION : GLOBALIZATION, PRIVATIZATION AND FOREIGN DIRECT INVESTMENT

> The world is like a board with holes in it, and the square men have got into round holes, and the round into the square.
>
> *Bishop Barkeley*

Learning outcomes

By the end of this section, you should understand:

- *The key challenges facing Saudi Arabia's economy*
- *The approaches adopted to bring about economic reforms*
- *The WTO option and the opportunities and threats to Saudi Arabia*
- *Financial globalization as a test case for world economic integration*
- *Privatization as a strategic goal of the state and its consequences*
- *Foreign Direct Investment as a principal tool of economic reform*

Key challenges

In the new millennium, the Kingdom of Saudi Arabia has set itself the objective of reducing the economy's vulnerability and heavy dependence on oil market fortunes, and has opted for decentralized, private market-based economic activities (Auty, 2001). The Kingdom aims to achieve this through a three-pronged approach. First, Saudi Arabia will join the World Trade Organization (WTO) to enable a bigger Saudi world market share. Second, it will initiate a domestic programme of the privatization of core Government services. Finally, Saudi Arabia will use Foreign Direct Investment (FDI) to foster technology transfer and domestic economic stimulus (Najem, 2003).

This chapter aims to examine the role of each of those objectives and assess their interdependence. Some have argued that implementing some or all of the objectives can no longer be postponed (Cordesman, 2003), due to a multitude of challenges faced by the Kingdom. Amongst these are a wide range of external forces that shape the value of the Kingdom's petroleum revenues in ways it cannot control. These forces include serious problems in planning budgets and five-year plans, because of an inability to predict cash flow. There also has been low productivity in many subsidized and sheltered sectors. In addition, the pace of structural change has been slow, so that despite all the measures of diversification away from oil, the private sector still only accounts for a base of around 35% of the GDP. Diversification efforts have also had a limited productive impact and the economy has neither generated sufficient number of jobs for Saudis nor induced a "knowledge based" society.

The choices ahead

There is a consensus amongst Saudi economic observers and practitioners that the Kingdom truly needs to make economic reform work, and it can only do so by strengthening the private sector, finding other sources of investment and encouraging repatriation of Saudi capital in viable domestic projects. What then are the obstacles? It's not that Saudi Arabia lacks good intentions or hasn't set the proper priorities. Rather, there is *no matching consensus* as to how much action is needed and how quickly itshould act. While different economists and government planners might assign different priorities and values to the urgency of the effort needed, most would agree that success will depend on far more progress being made in the following areas:

- Privatizing key public assets
- Attracting more effective Foreign Direct Investment (FDI)
- Strengthening the private sector in a meaningful manner
- Repatriating Saudi capital into domestic projects
- Creating meaningful and value-added jobs for the Saudi economy

Taking the first steps

Until it announced its wide-scale privatization program in late 2002, the Saudi government had run core services itself or through the private sector via operation contract methods. The decision to privatize government services and transfer them wholly to the private sector is an implicit acknowledgement that both the operation contract method and the use of direct government services have failed. This failure can be traced back to the government's inability to deliver on its commitments in the face of increased domestic demand, and to the inherent conflict of interest created by the fact that the government was judging its *own* performance.

Countries worldwide are redefining the roles of government and of the private sector. As they rely more on the private sector for the provision of infrastructure and public utility services, which in many cases are exposed in the short and medium-term to little or no competition, there is also a need for economic regulation.

Economic regulation is required to protect consumers from monopoly or from the abuses of limited competition and, at the same time, to give the private sector the necessary incentives for short and long-term efficiency. On the other hand, there is some evidence to indicate that, in their zeal to regulate, this could have an adverse effect on economic growth (Speakman, 2002).

Regulators must therefore play the important role of an independent and impartial referee who balances the interests of government, consumers and private-sector providers of infrastructure and services. For most countries that do not have a regulatory tradition, the establishment of entities that are responsible for economic regulation poses major challenges, as is the case for Saudi Arabia.

Until recently, the economic regulation of infrastructure and utility services was not an issue in the Kingdom, as most of these services were provided directly by government entities (Al Bazai, 2002, Khemani, 2002). As such, issues related to policy, ownership and operation of assets for the provision of the services were interconnected and any regulation that existed was primarily in the form of self-regulation. To date, the government of Saudi Arabia has not (with the exception of the Postal Services) totally privatized – and therefore economically regulated – any major sector of services or industry. It has only sold part of its shareholding to the public in companies such as the Saudi Arabian Basic Industries (SABIC) and Saudi Telecom Company (STC).

Recognizing the need for such a regulatory framework, the Saudi government had approved the Telecommunications Regulations in 2001 and, in the same year, established the Saudi Telecommunications Authority. This built upon the experience of the Electricity Services Regulation Authority set up in 1998 (SAMA, 2003).

While there are some disagreements on approaches to be taken, most experts would agree that "good" economic regulation should aim to maximize the overall welfare of societies, otherwise changes will only add to confusion and lack of direction (Saravia, 2002). The key tasks are the design of regulatory institutions and of processes that are seen to be independent and accountable, as well as transparent and consistent.

To its credit, the Saudi Arabian government is aware of all these issues. Despite Crown Prince Abdullah's declaration in 2000 that privatization is a strategic choice for the Saudi economy, the Supreme Economic Council, which has been mandated to implement economic policies, has attributed the slow progress on privatization to the nature of structural changes that are required (Saudi Press Agency, 2002). The council has focused its efforts on developing the regulatory environment, without which the outcome and direction of the new economic liberalization will be beneficial in terms of sustained structural economic diversification.

Globalization: the WTO route

Saudi Arabia is expected to join the World Trade Organization (WTO) sometime during 2005; it formally requested accession in 1995. This is another important step towards economic reform (Sassanpour, 1996). Saudi Arabia has run trade surpluses virtually every year, as seen in an earlier chapter; and over the past five years, it has run a current account surplus. However, the overall volume of trade has not grown much over the past decade. One cannot ignore the fact that the globalization of finance and financial practices has been more rapid than the globalization of trade. The Saudi government's aim is that by promoting growth in trade, the WTO accession will make a strong contribution to GDP growth, increase business productivity and encourage an efficient allocation of resources (Wilson, 1997).

There are concerns amongst Saudi businesses and in some intellectual circles about globalization and its impact on the Saudi economy (Salah, 2002). They point to the worldwide disquiet that is widely expressed during WTO meetings in world capitals. Some seem to share in the belief that trade liberalization and open markets will widen the gap in income between the developed and underdeveloped countries of the world. The sudden collapse of the WTO talks in Cancun, Mexico in September 2003 due to unbridgeable differences between the more advanced and less developed countries only added to some scepticism (Reuter, 15 September 2003). Saudi businessmen assert that the consequences of joining will be harmful to a large sector of Saudi industry. The reasons for their fear are not entirely erroneous.

Globalization means taking some fundamental decisions about changes that are necessary in order to be part of this so-called "global family". If Saudi Arabia does enter the WTO, it should, in theory, help increase Saudi Arabia's volume of trade; but it also presents several negotiating, cultural/religious and economic problems. WTO accession will require that

Saudi Arabia remove protectionist barriers, place ceilings on tariffs, open further key service sectors to foreign participation (such as banking, finance and the upstream oil sector), and improve protection for intellectual property rights. It will have to endeavour to build an open, transparent and rules-based regime with tribunals on trade disputes and new legislation on technical trade barriers, customs evaluation and food health regulation. Additionally, WTO calls for tariff limitation, several sectoral initiatives (including an Information Technology Agreement), a government procurement agreement, and agreements on pharmaceuticals, medical and construction equipment, in addition to all publishing services.

Membership will entitle Saudi Arabia to all the benefits that have been exchanged among WTO members, especially protecting Saudi Arabia from arbitrary exclusion of its exports to other WTO members: petrochemicals are a key example. However, it is not clear so far from the talks whether the Kingdom will join WTO on stricter "richest country" terms or on the looser rules and exemptions normally granted to developing nations. In a country such as Saudi Arabia, where change does not happen speedily, these requirements can engender hesitancy and self-doubt, even when there is a more favourable political commitment.

What specifically is requested from the Kingdom?

In accession talks the WTO requested that the Kingdom introduce further liberalization reforms in the following key areas:

- Reducing import tariffs from around 15% to 7%, with further decreases in the future, with a few exceptions
- "Binding" tariff levels on individual products to a guaranteed ceiling beyond which they cannot be increased
- Phasing out government subsidies to the private sector and agriculture
- Applying non-discriminatory treatment to the goods and services of other WTO members
- Enforcing intellectual property rights
- Guaranteeing "predictable and growing access" to the Kingdom's markets
- Allowing majority foreign ownership of investment projects
- Treating foreign and local investors equally, which means equal tax treatment, removing the requirement that trade must be conducted through commercial or sponsorship agents (*Wakeels*) and allowing foreigners to own real estate
- Opening up service sectors such as banking, legal, insurance and capital markets to greater foreign participation

What has the Saudi government response been?

In turn, the Saudi government has indicated that it will take a *phased* approach to the following issues:

- Establishing new trademark and intellectual property laws
- Removing technical barriers to trade by easing travel visa requirements
- Signing the Information Technology Agreement and phasing in tariff-free trade in information technology equipment
- Phasing in the Basic Telecommunications Agreement to allow competition in telecommunications services
- Changing competition laws to provide anti-trust protection and consumer protection in accordance with WTO rules (Salah, 2002)

Saudi Arabia has also insisted that its cultural and religious requirements be respected by its trading partners, particularly with regard to the treatment of goods such as pork and alcohol, the import and sale of which are forbidden in Saudi Arabia. Despite seemingly slow progress, real concrete steps have been taken. In addition to the EU trade agreement of August, 2003, Saudi Arabia has already signed 13 bilateral trade agreements with other major trading countries and hopes to sign an additional 16 bilateral agreements in the second phase of negotiations, according to Fawaz Al Alami, chairman of the Saudi negotiating delegation (Arab News, July 2003). A major negotiating goal is to sign a bilateral trade agreement with the USA, which would ease Saudi Arabia's entry into the WTO. In the meantime, other concrete steps have been taken.

First, in May, 2001, Saudi Arabia took steps to liberalize trade, independent of their WTO accession process, and tariffs on most items were reduced from 12% to 5%.

Second, tariffs between the Gulf Cooperation Council (GCC) countries were also lowered to 5% in December, 2002, laying the groundwork for a full customs union for the GCC by 2003.

Third, the Foreign Investment Law, a package of legal measures aimed at encouraging foreign investment in the Kingdom, was passed in 2000. The Saudi Arabian General Investment Authority (SAGIA) was formed in the same year to oversee Foreign Direct Investment (FDI) into Saudi Arabia. These measures will be explained more fully in the next section of this chapter, but it is important to note that the new economic liberalization trend has been positively greeted by most outside observers (World Economic Forum, 2003, Auty, 2001, Bourland, 2002, Cordesman, 2003).

Impact of globalization

The impact of globalization can be viewed from short and long-term perspectives. Table 11.1 sets out a brief summary of the potential impact of globalization on the Saudi economy, based on field research for different Saudi business sectors carried out by the author.

Table 11.1   Impact of globalization on Saudi Arabian economy

Impact	Short-Term Impact	Long-Term Impact
Negative	• Encouraging more imports to Saudi Arabia, with balance of payment implications	• Questions about the ability of some Saudi industries to meet modernization challenges and adjustment costs.
	• Weaker local producers under competitive strain	• Potential structural unemployment
	• Govt. procurement policy giving local priority will be scrapped, making some local firms unable to effectively compete against foreign competition	• Exit of some industries due to reduction of subsidies, subsidized loans and tariff protection
	• Export sales may not go up due to quality considerations	• Foreign ownership of certain strategically deemed sectors (e.g. Communications)
	• Growth in some sectors could slow down, with unemployment consideration	
	• Implementation of international patent laws will have impact on certain sectors, such as pharmaceuticals and chemicals	
	• Less efficient service providers in Insurance, banking and telecommunications will be negatively affected by competition	
Positive	• Lower priced imported inputs	• Shift from exporting primary products to exporting value-added industrial products
	• Higher multinational investment in local industry with implementation of international patent laws	• Local firms restructuring
		• Formation of international strategic alliances with brand name manufacturers
		• Development of specialized expertise in range of products
		• Higher multinational investment in local industry with implementation of international patent laws
		• Wider variety of technology transfers

Source: Authors *survey, Eastern Province Chamber of Commerce.* 2003.

Table 11.1 indicates a mixed score sheet of positives and negatives. As far as the private sector was concerned, their major worries centred on the loss of export markets. Of even greater significance was the loss of the lucrative and discriminatory government contracts, for which only Saudi companies could bid, resulting in the institutionalization of local industrial inefficiencies. Some Saudi service and manufacturing enterprises were designed and set up to function in a secure environment protected by high tariffs and monopoly agency agreements.

Having to operate under WTO rules might put them out of business, as opening up the economy to foreign multinationals and imports will threaten profit margins and the monopoly of commercial agencies. The insistence of the industrialized countries on fully implementing these changes was one of the prime causes for the failure of the Cancun 2003 WTO talks.

The concerns of some sections of Saudi business about the potential negative impact of globalization on their sectors is not misplaced. Table 11.2 examines the potential impact of globalization on selected key Saudi industries. The analysis indicates that few Saudi industries would be able to withstand international competitive pressures following the Kingdom's WTO accession.

There is also an understandable reluctance on the part of the Saudi government to rush forward without a careful study of potential negative impact. It fears the creation of more unemployment in the Saudi economy, an issue that is now of paramount political importance as will be seen in a later chapter. The Saudi government, however, has made a very public commitment to join the WTO. Furthermore, the rules under which Saudi Arabia is applying for accession are somewhat different than those under which other Arab countries joined the WTO.

Seven Arab countries – Bahrain, Kuwait, Qatar, UAE, Egypt, Morocco and Tunisia – have already joined the WTO under what was termed an "accelerated process". The level of WTO scrutiny was significantly less than that now being applied to Saudi Arabia's entry, but this increased scrutiny is also being applied to Jordan and Oman. However, even those who entered the WTO on the "fast track" have been given until 2005 to comply with some requirements, at which point their membership will be revisited (World Economic Forum, 2003).

Table 11.2 Globalization impact on selected Saudi industries

Sector	Major features	Potential globalization impact
Poultry	• SR 6 billion industry, with 2 companies having 50% of the market. 450 companies operating in the sector. • Subsidized (30% cash subsidy on poultry equipment, plus SR 160 per tone on imported feedstock). 20% custom duties.	• Industry will face major competitive forces after WTO entry with smaller companies at risk
Edible oils	• 9 operating units with capacity of around 360,000 tones. Current domestic demand 290,000 tones. Industry investment around SR 490 million.	• Fairly competitive industry with exports to Gulf countries, and some joint ventures abroad
Furniture	• SR5 billion market size with 65% imported. 125 large units operating, with another 7000 small units. • Low cost funding provided (50%) by SIDF. Tariffs set at 12% on imports plus 20% on protected items.	• Not a competitive industry as has no cost advantage. Raw material imported.
Refrigeration	• 24 local manufacturing units. Joint ventures exist with world brand names. Capital investment around SR900 million, employing around 5000. Production capacity 320,000 units p.a. • SIDF low cost funding (50%)	• Will face some competition after WTO entry but industry is mature with joint venture partners in-Kingdom and appropriate technology transfer having been made.
Paints	• 27 industrial units, capacity around 600,000 tones, domestic demand around 360,000 tones p.a. 8 units operate as joint ventures, total capital investment SR 850 million, employing around 3000.	• Competitive industry, mature and can cope with WTO entry due to rising world demand and paint prices.
Steel and base metals	• Capital investment around SR 8 billion employing 31,000 in 357 projects in GCC. Saudi share 60% of GCC. Annual demand 2.5 million tones. 16 Saudi projects are FDI joint ventures • Protection exists for 116 items out of 740 lines, with 20% custom duty on imports.	• Export diversification taking place. Around 9,500 tones p.a. exported compared with domestic demand of 22,000 tones p.a. • Will face tough competition post WTO entry
Dairy	• SR 10 billion industry with domestic demand around 1.25 million tones p.a., 61 operating units, capital investment of SR 2.6 billion and employing 6,000 workers. 16 large units have capacity of 320,000 tones p.a. • Heavily subsidized up to 30% of total costs. SIDF loans.	• Will face major WTO competition with smaller operators at risk.
Cement	• 8 cement companies produce around 16 million tones p.a. Industry is mature and will organized domestically following restructuring.	• Export momentum continuing with around 18% for exports. Mostly regional markets leveraging on Saudi comparative advantages.
Aluminum	• 26 units operating with capacity of 110,000 tones with 4 units producing 95,000 tones. Domestic consumption of around 120,000 tones. • No aluminum smelters exist in Saudi Arabia – reliant on imported aluminum ingots • Shielded from competition – 20% custom duties	• Will face competitive pressures post WTO accession, especially for smaller units.
Pharmaceuticals	• SR 6 billion market. Dominated by few companies, mostly with foreign joint ventures. 80% of consumption imported (40% government, 60% private sector)	• Very open to WTO trade. Liberalization and joint ventures will assure smooth transition.

Source: *Industry annual reports, NCB Economist various editions* 2000-2004.

The financial sector of Saudi Arabia, a vital segment of the Saudi economy, will face both challenges and opportunities from WTO and globalization. It is worthwhile exploring the issues in more detail, using as a test case one vital modernizing sector. We shall discuss the impact of globalization on broad stylized trends that appear to characterize the evolution of financial markets worldwide, namely *modernization, disintermediation and institutionalization,* and assess their impact on the Saudi financial sector.

Financial globalization

As mentioned earlier, WTO's membership requirements regarding financial markets (Grais, 2002) impact on financial sector globalization in the following ways:

- Full access to the domestic market for International Financial Services companies
- Access to underdeveloped financial sectors, such as brokerage firms, insurance and pensions for international service firms
- Full access to domestic markets for portfolio investors

There are also international standards and codes that aim at facilitating global financial flows. In addition to WTO rules, various segments of financial markets have organized across countries to produce global standards for niche areas. Two examples are the Accounting and Auditing Organizations for Islamic Financial Institutions (AAOIFI) based in Bahrain, and the Islamic Finance Supervisory Board (IFSB) based in Malaysia. Both deal with regulatory and corporate governance for the Islamic finance sector. The Islamic finance industry, operating in 75 countries, is estimated to be growing at 15% p.a. and it accounts for $200 billion (Faroqui, 2002).

The continued globalization of the Islamic finance sector poses similar challenges to those raised by conventional finance, but sometimes has its own peculiarities, such as national differences in *Shariah* interpretation, in legal systems and in different financial instruments. Saudi Arabia has to keep abreast of developments in these niche accounting standards if it is not to be left behind in supervising and regulating emerging Islamic financial institutions in the country (Abdullatif, 2002). The Saudi Arabian Monetary Agency, SAMA, is now moving forward on the issue of Islamic financial institutions approval. The local Bank Al Jazira is expected to be converted to an Islamic Bank (MEED, 2002). However, SAMA needs to revisit its 1961 Banking Control Law and make amendments to enable it to supervise and regulate Islamic banks in the Kingdom (Abdeen, 1984). Since Kuwait passed its Islamic Banking Law in May, 2003, Saudi Arabia and Oman are the only remaining members of the Gulf Cooperation Council not to have an Islamic Banking Law in place (Arab News, 2003).

As globalization brings more mega-institution competition to local markets, Saudi Banks will also need to keep up with global trends of mergers and strategic alliances; but this could pose competitive problems, as previously explained.

Financial modernization

Modernization encompasses advancement in systems and practice as well as technology. The aim is to reduce the costs of transaction, to expand the affordability of financial investments and to contribute to economic growth (Fayez, 2002).

Saudi Arabia has advanced further in the technological area of financial market modernization than it has in terms of its regulatory framework and rules (Dukheil, 1995).

As discussed in a preceding chapter, stock market regulation in the Kingdom was dispersed across several ministries, organizations and committees, including the Ministry of Finance, the Ministry of Commerce and SAMA. The distinction between regulator, supervisor and market manager therefore needed clarification. The fact that SAMA assumed multiple functions was not conducive to a perception of clarity and transparency within the regulatory framework. The new Saudi Capital Market Law, which was finally approved and passed into Law in June, 2003, aims to address this issue (Arab News, 17June 2003).

Saudi banks may be required after a transition period to separate commercial banking from investment, brokerage and advisory activities. The SAMA Banking Control Law needs to be revised. Besides the above services, Saudi banks have recently been permitted to offer insurance products and invest in specialized leasing companies. This monopolistic advantage will be challenged by foreign competition and new market players entering these sectors (Dukheil, 1995).

Financial disintermediation

In its broadest sense, "disintermediation" means eliminating the middleman. In this case, banks lose their market share as investments go directly to the investment market. The rationale for banks fulfilling the role of intermediaries is their ability to reduce *information asymmetries.* However, technological and information flows have now provided market participants with relevant market knowledge, as we can conclude by looking at the sharp rise in Internet usage and communication lines per head of population (World Economic Forum, 2003, World Bank, 2001).

Disintermediation in Saudi Arabia's financial markets is progressing. Stock market capitalization has risen more rapidly than bank assets. For the years 1996 and 2002, market capitalization was SR 172 billion and SR 308 billion respectively. Bank assets were SR 360 billion and SR 495 billion respectively. These numbers reflect the growing weight of capital markets and the progress of disintermediation, as the ratio of market capitalization to banking assets increased from 48% in 1996 to 62.3% in 2002 (SAMA, 2003).

However, as our analysis in Chapter 6 indicated, disintermediation in Saudi Arabia's financial systems is limited to the stock market and the large holding of government bonds of nearly SR 650 billion. Bank-guaranteed commercial paper was under SR 2 billion. The secondary market remains weak, despite the wide interest generated by IPO's launched during 2004.

Obtaining an international credit rating would help build up investor confidence. Saudi Arabia had no S&P rating until July, 2003, when the rating agency assigned "A+" for Saudi long-term local currency and "A" for long-term foreign currency (Reuters, 14 July 2003). S&P reconfirmed this rating in 2004 despite domestic terrorism issues.

Institutionalization

Institutionalization represents the gradual domination of financial markets by institutions as opposed to individual investors, and was the worldwide trend in the nineties (World Economic Forum, 2003).

Different institutions have, at one stage or another, assumed the role of market players. Pension funds, mutual funds, insurance companies, venture capital funds and leasing companies have each contributed and shown leadership in their way. For Saudi Arabia, this has predominantly been driven by the mutual fund industry, and, to a lesser extent, by the insurance sector, as discussed in Chapters 5 and 6.

However, pension resources are not playing their full role in promoting institutionalization. Pension assets held by the two Saudi government pension organizations, the General Organization for Social Insurance (GOSI) and the Saudi Pension and Retirement Agency (SPRA), are SR 315.9 billion or 46% of GDP as of June, 2003 (SAMA, 2003). The composition of assets has undergone a change from 89% foreign securities and 14% public sector bonds in 1996, to 38% foreign securities and 62% public sector bonds in 2002, as these pension organizations purchased bonds to finance government budget deficits.

The large pool of End-of-Service Benefits (ESBS) remains untapped or unfunded, especially from smaller establishments, due to the lack of a regulatory framework. ESBS can play a major role if funded, so that a pool of long-term investment funds would be made available to the bond markets, similar to the trends seen in more mature capital markets.

The insurance sector remains small, as noted in Chapter 5, and represents around 1% of GDP, the lowest of all emerging markets. However, it has one of the strongest potentials for growth, with the enactment of compulsory insurance regulation and the agreement to foreign insurance company participation (Arab News, 3 February 2003).

Figure 11.1 plots the four stages of financial development as outlined above and compares Saudi Arabia's progress against a more developed ideal economy that has achieved expansion on all fronts. The model is adapted from one used by the World Bank.

Figure 11.1 notes significant progress in technological modernization, mixed progress in globalization and institutionalization, but somewhat better progress on disintermediation where new investment vehicles seem to be appearing on the Saudi capital markets.

Figure 11.1 Saudi Arabia and financial expansion

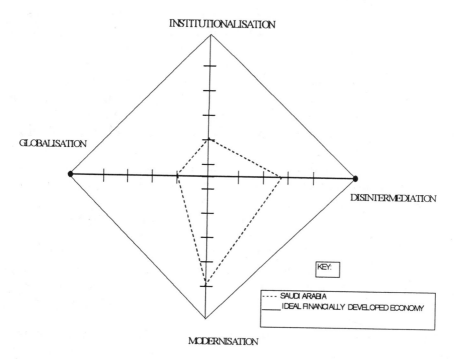

Adapted from *Batley, Grais and Semaan, World Bank*, 2003.

Privatization

Since its first appearance in England in the late 1970s under Prime Minister Thatcher, privatization has been, by far, the most controversial instrument of economic policy of the past two decades. Economics, politics and ideology have punctuated the debate on privatization and have polarized opinion, but do not diminish the importance of privatization as a policy instrument and as a process shaping the economics of the twenty-first century. As we highlighted earlier, the rulers of Saudi Arabia have publicly stated that privatization is a strategic goal of the state.

What is privatization?

Privatization is an instrument of economic policy through which there is a transfer of property or control of assets, usually owned by the state, to the private sector. Thus, in its purest form, privatization encompasses the privatization of management and ownership.

A broader definition describes privatization as the abolition of barriers to private sector provision of services or to the infrastructure necessary for their delivery. This broad definition usually applies to privatization of a sector (telecommunications, electricity, gas, water, etc.) and it often requires a restructuring of the whole sector rather than just one firm. It also requires legal and regulatory mechanisms to ensure that private providers do not overlook the public dimensions and responsibilities of the services they are licensed to deliver, and to ensure they meet the pre-agreed targets and policy objectives, such as coverage to certain areas and access for the public. It is this issue – the regulatory framework – that has kept the Saudi privatization process from advancing more rapidly than hoped for, given the political statements of support.

Different economies and countries have adopted privatization for different ends. Thus, for example, the former Socialist economies of Eastern Europe used privatization to increase the role of the private sector in the economy. Some Arab economies going through transition and change, like Egypt and Algeria, are striving to move from a state-controlled and dominated economy to a market-based economy where the private sector plays a much greater role.

The oil-rich countries of the Gulf Cooperation Council (GCC) have used privatization as a means of diversifying their economic base, moving away from a heavy reliance on the oil sector (Al Bazai, 2002, Seznec, 2002). It is also fortunate that the earlier adoption of privatization in many countries will make it possible for Saudi Arabia and others in the GCC to learn from these experiences and to draw important lessons that are relevant to their own economic structures.

Figure 11.2 Privatization pattern – industry ownership in selected OECD countries and Saudi Arabia (1998)

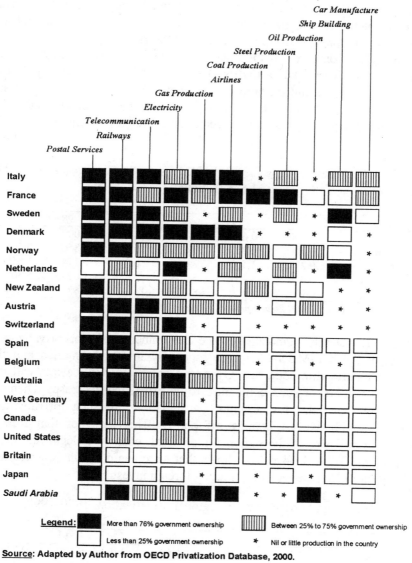

Source: Adapted by Author from OECD Privatization Database, 2000.

Figure 11.2 compares the status of Saudi privatization with those of selected Organization for Economic Cooperation and Development (OECD) countries in 1998. It is interesting to note that, with the exception of Britain,

Japan and the USA, the majority of OECD countries have yet to privatize many state industries. It is worthwhile noting that Saudi Arabia's nascent car manufacturing industry is entirely in private sector hands, like all other OECD countries (with the exception of Italy and France). Saudi car production, though, is more of an assembly line operation for trucks, buses and other specialized cargo vehicles carried out through a Saudi-German partnership of the Jeddah based *Juffali* Group with Mercedes Benz and the Riyadh-based *Al Jomaih* Group with General Motors.

To date, as compared with other world regions, privatization in the Middle East and North Africa (MENA) region has been more of a political wish rather than a sustained reality, a fact that is highlighted in the next set of tables which demonstrate how far MENA lags behind other regions in terms of both privatization revenue receipts and foreign participation in such programmes.

Table 11.3 Privatization revenues: MENA versus other regions, 1990-1999
US $ Billions

Region	90	92	94	96	98	99
MENA	0.200	0.690	0.782	1.478	1.000	2.074
Sub Sahara	0.740	0.307	0.605	0.745	1.356	0.694
South Asia	0.290	1.557	2.666	0.889	0.174	1.859
E Asia/Pacific	0.376	5.161	5.508	2.680	1.091	5.500
Latin America	10.915	15.560	8.199	14.142	37.685	23.614

Source: *World Bank, Global Development Finance*, 2001, pp. 180-189.

Table 11.3 clearly demonstrates the determined push for privatization occurring in the non-MENA regions, especially in Latin America and the East Asian/Pacific Rim countries. Over time, such revenue receipts will fall back as the number of state companies to be privatized decreases. Of more interest are the data for foreign participation in such privatization programmes, with MENA coming off poorly. This indicates that foreign investors are still shy of the region for political, economic, legal and other considerations. Table 11.4 below shows that once again, Latin America and East Asia/Pacific led the way in attracting foreign investors.

Table 11.4 Foreign participation in regional privatization, 1990-1999, US$ billions

Region	90	92	94	96	98	99
MENA	0	0.190	0.246	0.126	0.430	0.747
Sub Sahara	0.380	0.660	0.453	0.299	0.694	0.418
South Asia	0.110	0.440	0.997	0.528	0.110	0.104
E Asia/Pacific	0.100	1.556	4.036	1.990	1.082	4.982
Latin America	6.358	4.037	5.058	6.448	21.535	19.567

Source: *World Bank, Global Development Finance, 2001.*

Latin America seems to have taken the lion's share of foreign investment flows, despite economic upheavals in several countries in that region. Investors, it would appear, were taking a longer-term structural view of economic reforms, rather than following shorter-term economic movements.

Routes to privatization

Privatization follows many different routes, from a minimal or low level of private ownership to total private ownership, as Figure 11.3 illustrates.

Figure 11.3 Privatization scales

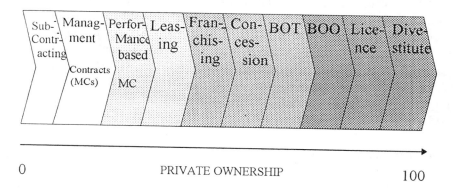

0   PRIVATE OWNERSHIP   100

Each public-private partnership noted here entails a different set of agreed commercial and operational elements, as well as a specified period for the privatization. The subcontracting and management contracts (MCs) are of shorter duration than the leasing contracts, franchising, etc., until total divestiture (sale) of the public asset. As discussed in earlier chapters, the MCs and subcontracting have been the main method of operation of the Saudi government to date in involving the private sector. Other countries in the region, especially Turkey, pioneered the concepts of Build-Operate-Transfer (B-O-T) and Build-Own-Operate (B-O-O) as part of their privatization strategy.

The political push for privatization as a strategic choice is necessitated by the forecasted capital expenditure needs of the Kingdom in key areas. Current estimates of such capital expenditures over the next 20 years are around $540 billion or SR 2,025 billion for education, electricity, oil, gas, mining, water and agricultural projects (National Commercial Bank, 2003). The government cannot meet these needs, so it must either borrow or turn over key sectors to the private sector to operate on a profitable and cost-efficient basis.

In November, 2002, the Saudi Arabian government announced plans to privatize 20 economic sectors, including telecommunications, civil aviation, desalination, highway management, railways, sports clubs, health services, municipality services, water and sewage, highway construction, airport services, postal services, grain and flour silos, hotels, seaport services and industrial city services. Privatization would also cover state share sales in the Saudi Electricity Company (SEC) and the Saudi Arabian Mineral Company (*Maaden*), as well as local petroleum refineries.

It was a staggering list in both size and diversity, and one of the most ambitious privatization announcements of any country in the world over the past few decades.

Experiences of privatization elsewhere, including pioneering Britain, showed that government revenue maximization through privatization is not necessarily the best option. It is the method and quality of privatization that is of more importance, specifically the management and technical capabilities of those new operating owners who will be answerable to shareholders. The checks and balances through independent industry regulators are also important, especially for utilities such as water, electricity and gas.

Basic privatization objectives

In June, 2002, the Supreme Economic Council (SEC), under the Chairmanship of Crown Prince Abdullah bin Abdulaziz, approved the privatization strategy for Saudi Arabia (Saudi Press Agency, June, 2002). The strategy consists of eight basic objectives, each of which requires the adoption of a number of policies. These are set out in detail below:

Objective 1 Improving the capacity of the national economy and enhancing its ability to meet the challenges of regional and international competition

Objective 2 Encouraging private sector investment and effective participation in the national economy and increasing its share of domestic production to achieve growth in the national economy

Objective 3 Expanding the ownership of productive assets by Saudi citizens

Objective 4 Encouraging local investments of domestic and foreign capital

Objective 5 Increasing employment opportunities, optimizing the use of the national work force and thus ensuring the equitable increase of individual income

Objective 6 Providing services to citizens and investors in a timely and cost efficient manner.

Objective 7 Rationalizing public expenditure and reducing the burden of the government budget by giving the private sector opportunities to finance, operate and maintain certain services that it is able to provide

Objective 8 Increasing government revenues from returns on the sale of assets to be transferred to the private sector.

While these are laudable objectives for any government to pursue, the Supreme Economic Council also recognized when setting these objectives that, in order for them to be successful, a regulatory framework had to be in place for the privatized industries. In addition, they needed to prepare and restructure the sectors and public enterprises to be privatized. They also indicated that one option was to pursue foreign strategic partners to provide capital, risk sharing, advanced technical and management expertise, and to assist in creating a suitable climate for a successful privatization programme. What have been the accomplishments to date?

Privatization efforts by sector: mixed results

The Saudi government's actions to date have been partly characterized as market-driven and partly as an effort to shift current and future investment burden away from the government. They do not seem like a serious effort to privatize functions now operated by the state sector on a commercial basis. The eight broad privatization objectives set out so clearly by the Supreme Economic Council seem to intuitively recognize that privatization, in the Saudi Arabian context, can only have the required impact on growth and reform if it means conversion of state-held functions to truly competitive private enterprises. These enterprises can charge market prices, and by extension, reduce labour and overhead costs so as to become more productive and profitable. Below is a summary of the major initiatives undertaken or planned (SAMA, Annual Report, 2002).

The Saudi Basic Industries Corporation (SABIC). SABIC is one of the pillars of Saudi industrialization policies and represents the Middle East's largest non-oil hydrocarbon-based industrial company. The government currently owns 70% of SABIC and 30% is owned by the private sector.

SABIC shares are actively traded on the Saudi Stock Market. To date, there has been no sign of further government sales of SABIC shares to the public, despite a cabinet approval in principle to sell three-quarters of its 70% share. What has occurred in the interim is that SABIC has been soliciting additional foreign and local Saudi investment in private petrochemical projects to ease the burden on public funding. One such case is the Saudi International Petrochemical Company (SIPC), capitalized at SR 500 million, and 15% owned by the *Al Zamil* Group, with the rest of shareholders drawn from both Saudi and GCC-based investors.

The Saudi Electricity Company (SEC). SEC is the merger of the previous four separate Saudi Electricity Companies (SCECO) in the East, West, Central and South. These supplied around 85% of Saudi power supplies and in 2000 the various SCECOs and ten private power companies were all merged into the SEC. The government share in SEC is 74.15% and the private sector holds the remainder. The restructuring of the SCECO system was intended to lead to a more efficient streamlining of the Saudi power sector base, with the expectation that SEC would develop three separate sector companies for generation, transmission and distribution. The government has established an Electricity Services Regulation Authority to assist with the privatization programme and is considering alternative forms of private sector participation in this sector through BOO, BOT and even BOOT (Build-Own-Operate-Transfer) schemes. According to SAMA, the financial requirement for the power sector through 2023 is estimated at SR 341 billion or $90.9 billion (SAMA, 2003).

Saudi Telecommunication Company (STC). A 30% stake of STC was sold to the private sector in December, 2002, in one of the largest government sales of shares; it raised around SR 15 billion or $4 billion. Following the sale, the STC became the Saudi stock market's second largest listed company in terms of capitalization, after SABIC (Arab News, 16 December 2002). Work is currently underway to create a specialized body with the administrative and financial autonomy to organize the telecommunications sector and provide rules and regulations to ensure fair competition amongst private firms.

Saudi Arabian Airlines (SAUDIA). The first pronouncements on privatizing the national airline SAUDIA were mooted as early as 1994. In 2000, SAUDIA's board of directors invited investment banks to prepare bids for the privatization of the company, although the scale of such privatization (full-scale or partial, domestic or international components) was not made clear. These studies are still underway.

General Railway Organization (GRO). Currently, the GRO operates a railway system connecting the Eastern Province with Riyadh. Saudi Arabia has always sought to expand this railway network by linking Riyadh to *Makkah, Madiina and Jeddah.* Other plans call for establishing a rail network to link the mining regions in the northwest of the Kingdom to Riyadh, and to continue on to the *Jubail* industrial port. The World Bank was asked to make detailed studies, the results of which were submitted to the Supreme Economic Council, and, according to SAMA, "the project of expanding the railway network will be put out for execution by floating a tender to specialized companies on the basis of BOT."

Saudi Post Corporation. This sector is one of the most advanced in terms of privatization, with just under 90 private sector operating agencies providing a full range of postal delivery services by the end of 2002. The government has also privatized the maintenance of postal buildings, including 137 construction projects at a cost of SR 1.2 billion (SAMA, 2003).

General Port Authority. The Saudi government started to involve the private sector by granting 10-year lease contracts to operate general port services on an income-sharing basis, through which the state owns the port assets, but they are operated by the private sector. Besides the shorter term contracts, some 20-year contracts were also awarded. All eight Saudi ports have such private sector involvement ranging from general goods to containers, bulk grain, roll-on cargo, chilled and frozen food.

We can see that some progress has taken place and that there is the political will to pursue a meaningful privatization programme. This political will is made doubly urgent by the forecasted estimates of future investment costs and capital needs if privatization is ignored or delayed.

According to Saudi American Bank estimates (Saudi American Bank, 2001), the required government capital expenditures would total about SR 56 billion or $15 billion a year, or up to 10% of GDP. This could translate into increased domestic and foreign bank borrowing by the government, as well as domestic and foreign investments under FDI schemes. As we saw earlier in Figure 11.3, the track record of foreign investment into MENA was not very encouraging.

Obstacles to privatization

Within the Saudi Arabian context, there has been some debate amongst economists on the various problems and impediments that might arise out of the current desire to privatize (Arab News, 16 February 2003, CCFI, November, 2002), explored in Table 11.5.

Table 11.5 Saudi privatization: possible obstacles

Obstacles	Rationale
1. Fair book value for public assets	• A wide gap could arise between the fair book value and the market price. There could be limited availability of information concerning government operations and future risk factors, thus affecting the valuation method.
2. Rigid pay structure	• Government employee pay scales are higher than in the private sector, and sometimes are not related to productivity. There is the problem of adjusting wages and reducing employment numbers, and of allowing the private sector to strike a balance between wages and productivity expectations.
3. Government Subsidies	• The removal of government subsidies on basic services such as utilities or healthcare could cause social problems. At the same time, artificially imposing low price levels will affect the most efficient allocation of private sector resources. Other forms of income support for those who are less well-off can be found.
4. Lack of Regulatory Framework	• The government needs to address this major concern to ensure consumer protection and a degree of competition after privatization.
5. Updating public sector accounting standards	• These need to be updated so as to allow prospective investors to evaluate the true worth of these privatized public corporations.
6. Financial Resources	• There is a lack of depth in current Capital Market structure that will make it more difficult to transfer public to private ownership. • Domestic banks have an aversion to long-term risk capital and there is an uncertain commercial /legal framework.
7. Employment	• Potential unemployment becomes an issue, as the government faces pressure to reduce current unemployment levels.

The list of possible obstacles to privatization in Saudi Arabia highlights one fundamental point: that structural reform should precede privatization, and that the benefits accruing from privatization are most sustainable when competition is free, the economy stable and the regulatory sector strong. Privatization remains more of a politically-driven goal, albeit driven by a fear of the unknowable consequences of selling strategic state companies that have been supported for years by government assistance and protection. For those countries that have embarked on this unknown journey, the results have, in general, been more positive for industries and services after privatization than before. Studies for both industrialized and developing countries (Bourbaki, 1997, D'Souza, 1998) have indicated that, on average, there are improvements on all counts of productivity and efficiency measures as set out in Table 11.6 below.

Table 11.6 Consequences of privatization

Concept	Measure	Countries		Source	Median 3 Yrs. before Sale	Median 3 Years After Sale
Profitability	Net Income/ Sales	(IC)	=	MNR	5.5%	8.0%
		(DC)	=	BC	4.3%	11.0%
		(IC)	=	DM	14.0%	17.0%
Efficiency	Sales/number of employees*	(IC)	=	MNR	0.96*	1.06*
		(DC)	=	BC	0.92*	1.17*
		(IC)	=	DM	1.02*	1.23*
Investment	Capital Expenditure/ Sales	(IC)	=	MNR	12.0%	17.0%
		(DC)	=	BC	11.0%	24.0%
		(IC)	=	DM	18%	17.0%
Output	Sales adjusted by CPI	(IC)	=	MNR	0.90*	1.14*
		(DC)	=	BC	0.97*	1.22*
		(IC)	=	DM	0.93*	2.70*
Employment	Number of Employees	(IC)	=	MNR	40,850	43,200
		(DC)	=	BC	10,672	10,811
		(IC)	=	DM	22,941	22,136
Leverage	Debt/assets	(IC)	=	MNR	66%	64%
		(DC)	=	BC	55%	50%
		(IC)	=	DM	29%	23%
Dividends	Dividends/sales	(IC)	=	MNR	1.3%	3.0%
		(DC)	=	BC	2.8%	5.3%
		(IC)		DM	1.5%	4.0%

Notes: *Ratio in year of sale set to 1.00 to avoid large differences among industries
    IC   = *Industrialized Countries, DC = Developing Countries.*
    MNR-   *Source: Megginson, Nash and Van Randerborgh (1994)*
    BC-- *Source: Bourbaki and Cosset (1998)*
    DM-   *Source: D'Souza and Megginson (1999).*

What is interesting to note from the empirical studies carried out and documented above is that employment considerations post-privatization were not as bad as feared by some opponents of privatization. They worried that the policies would contribute to a greater level of unemployment in the long run, as highlighted in Table 11.5.

Foreign Direct Investment (FDI)

Saudi Arabia contributed nearly 25% to the GDP of the whole Arab Middle East in 2002. Net private capital inflows into the Middle East were $8.5 billion in contrast with Asia ($59.4 billion), European Transition Countries ($31.9 billion) and Latin America ($46.3 billion) (SAMA, 2002, p. 25).

Saudi Arabia has *not* been successful in attracting FDI levels to match the size of its economy. For example, between 1984 and 1997, FDI to Saudi Arabia was $4.32 billion, compared with Singapore ($51.4 billion), Malaysia ($36 billion) and South Korea ($14.6 billion).

Table11.7 Net flows of FDI into Saudi Arabia from major countries, June 1999

Rank	Country	Number of Projects	Paid-Up Capital (US$ Million)	As % of Total
1.	United States	267	2,252.5	45.3
2.	Japan	35	576.8	11.6
3.	Bermuda	18	312.3	6.3
4.	Netherlands	51	219.9	4.4
5.	Jordan	114	214.7	4.3
6.	France	67	198.3	4.0
7.	United Kingdom	146	147.1	3.0
8.	Panama	24	107.6	2.2
9.	Italy	54	100.7	2.0
10.	Switzerland	58	97.1	2.0
11.	Lebanon	149	90.1	1.8
12.	Egypt	30	84.1	1.7
13.	Cayman Islands	30	79.6	1.6
14.	Kuwait	36	77.6	1.6
15.	Finland	15	74.5	1.5
16.	Germany	77	58.1	1.2
17.	Bahrain	11	57.0	1.1
18.	Korea	38	49.3	1.0
19.	Iran	11	39.7	0.8
20.	Taiwan	5	39.0	0.8
	Sub-Total	*1,236*	*4,875.9*	*98.0*
	Other Countries	373	9737.0	2.0
	Total	**1,609**	**4,973.6**	**100.0**

Source: *National Centre for Economic and Financial Information*, June, 1999.

Table 11.7 sets out the net flows of FDI into Saudi Arabia from all major countries as of 1999. The overall picture has not changed much since 1997, with Saudi Arabia attracting about $5 billion of private foreign investments through 1,609 joint venture projects from 64 countries.

The USA is the largest equity partner in terms of number of projects (267) and paid-up capital ($2.25 billion), which is equivalent to 45% of all FDI. Japan follows with 11.6%. Jordan was the largest source of Arab capital with $215 million, followed by Lebanon and Egypt. The country of ownership origin for those listed under the tax havens of Bermuda, The Netherlands Antilles and Cayman Islands are not known, but they represent around 10% of all FDI and, according to unofficial Saudi Chamber of Commerce sources, the majority of countries of ownership are from the USA, UK and Lebanon.

Sometimes the driving force behind FDI is not new projects or joint venture projects, such as those envisaged under the Saudi Economic Offset Programme, which we discussed in Chapter 10, but rather through cross-border mergers and acquisitions of existing companies. In the developed world, mergers and acquisitions (M&As) have become the primary mode of entry of FDI, while in the developing world their importance is small but growing. In the developed countries, one regularly hears of megadeals such as the acquisition of Mannesmann of Germany by Vodafone (UK) for $200 billion in 2000 and of Voice Stream (USA) by Deutsche Telecom (Germany) for $24.6 billion in 2001 (Financial Times, 2001).

Cross-border M&As in the Arab countries are very small in comparison. Tables 11.8 and 11.9 set out the value of such M&A sales during the period 1987-2000 in Arab states, as well as the ten largest deals during the same period. In terms of value, we note the erratic fluctuation from year to year, with 2000 showing deals worth $1.744 billion, compared with total developing country sales of $69.6 billion during the same year, or 2.4% for the Arab world.

Table 11.8 Cross-border M&A sales in the country members of the league of Arab states, 1987-2000 (US$ million)

Region/ Economy	1987	1988	1989	1990	1991	1992	1993	1994	1995	1996	1997	1998	1999	2000
Algeria	-	-	-	-	1	-	-	-	-	-	-	-	42	127
Bahrain	-	-	-	-	-	-	4	-	-	-	-	-	36	161
Egypt	143	-	24	-	-	131	177	17	10	171	102	48	738	528
Jordan	-	-	-	-	-	-	-	-	26	-	-	-	-	567
Kuwait	-	-	-	-	-	-	6	-	-	-	-	11	-	-
Lebanon	-	-	-	-	-	-	-	83	-	-	168	-	-	54
Morocco	-	-	-	-	-	-	64	-	-	40	578	5	123	-
Oman	-	-	-	-	78	-	15	-	-	7	-	-	28	-
Qatar	-	-	2	-	43	24	12	-	8	26	-	-	-	2
Saudi Arabia	-	-	-	-	-	8	-	-	-	-	-	-	-	-
Sudan	-	-	-	-	-	-	-	-	-	-	-	-	3	-
Syrian Arab Republic	-	-	-	-	-	-	-	-	-	-	-	403	11	301
Tunisia	-	-	-	-	-	58	-	-	-	-	56	-	200	4
United Arab Emirates	-	-	-	-	-	5	-	-	-	-	-	-	-	-
Yemen	-	-	-	-	-	-	-	-	-	-	-	-	-	-
Total	143	-	26	-	122	226	278	100	44	244	904	467	1,181	1,744

Memorandum:

	1987	1988	1989	1990	1991	1992	1993	1994	1995	1996	1997	1998	1999	2000
Developing Economies	1,704	2,875	5,057	16,052	5,838	8,119	12,782	14,928	15,966	34,700	64,573	80,775	73,601	69,664

Source: *UNCTAD, Cross-border data-base, 2002.*

Table11.9 The ten largest cross-border M&A deals in the League of Arab States, 1987-2000

Acquired Company	Target Country	Acquiring Company	Acquiring Country	Year	Value in Million Dollars
Telecommunication Corporation of Jordan	Jordan	Investor Group	France	2000	508.0
Assiut Cement	Egypt	Cemex	Mexico	1999	373.0
Societe Marocaine de L'Industrie	Morocco	Corral Petroleum Holding AB	Sweden	1997	372.5
Societe des Cimens de Gabes	Tunisia	Secil (Semapa – Sociedade)	Portugal	2000	251.0
Al Ameriya Cement Corporation	Egypt	Lafrge Titan	France	2000	249.0
Societes des Ciments de Jbel	Tunisia	Cimpor – Cimentos de Portugal EP	Portugal	1998	229.9
Alexandria Portland Cement (EG)	Egypt	Blue Circle Industries PLC	United Kingdom	2000	196.0
Al-Sharif Group	Egypt	Investor Group	Saudi Arabia	1993	177.3
Societes des Ciments d'Enfidha	Tunisia	Uniland Cementera SA	Spain	1998	169.1
Credit Libanais (Lebanon)	Lebanon	Investor	Saudi Arabia	1997	163.0

Source: *UNCTAD, Cross-border M&A Database*, 2002.

This low level of activity could be due to several factors. One factor is the types of company structures in the Arab world, which often tend to be closed, family groupings with no intention of selling to outsiders. Another factor is the lack of suitable publicly-listed corporations that meet foreign investors' criteria in terms of market share, profitability and management structure (Field, 1985, Fahim, 1995, Wright, 1996).

Table 11.9 shows the ten largest M&A Arab deals and highlights the fact that the majority of such large deals are carried out by *non-Arab investors*. Unspecified Saudi investors participated in two deals in Lebanon and Egypt. The largest deal was $508 million, with French investor interests acquiring Telecom Corporation of Jordan in 2000. The table also illustrates that those Arab countries with the longest experience of privatization, such as Egypt, Tunisia and Morocco, have led the way in cross-border M&A deals. However, the key implication of this table is that Arab capital, by and large, *prefers to migrate to non-Arab opportunities*. The exception to this is the international Saudi investor, Prince Al Waleed Bin Tallal Bin Abdulaziz, who has diversified his holdings in both western and Arab countries, particularly in Egypt, Jordan, Lebanon and Syria (Abdulaziz, Al Waleed Bin Tallal, 2003).

How this situation will continue to play out following the post-September 11 events is difficult to judge, but reports indicate a perceptible shift in investment preferences away from the USA and some other European countries, towards Asia and selective Arab countries.

Continuing investor perception of a lack of development in the Arab world's general legal framework governing foreign investment, such as labour laws, company laws, bankruptcy laws and intellectual property laws, is a contributory factor to this negligible Arab cross-border activity. Knowing that they are being left behind in the FDI race, most Arab countries are taking steps to amend existing legislation and laws and to introduce new ones that are more foreign investor-friendly. These changes are still not enough for international Arab investors like Prince Al Waleed who is scathing about "mindless bureaucracy being rife in the region" (Abdulaziz, Al Waleed, 2003).

Figure 11.4 FDI flows to the League of Arab States

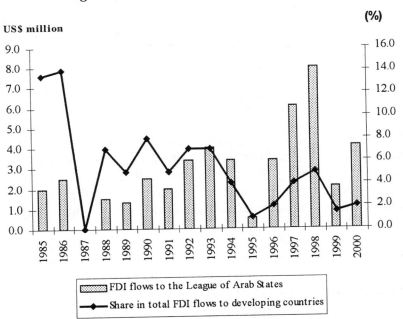

Compared with FDI, privatization is more politically sensitive, as a government has to decide to whom it should and should not sell. In Saudi

Arabia, the sale of state-owned companies has been restricted to Saudi nationals and the companies of GCC citizens. Other Arab countries have allowed Arab and foreign investors to participate. This cautiousness in opening the market to FDI foreign investment has resulted in an FDI inflow into the Arab world that represents around 2% of the total developing country FDI inflow in 2000, as seen in the next set of tables and figures.

We note from Figure 11.4 and Table 11.10 of FDI inflows of the League of Arab States for 1985-2000 that, with the exception of Bahrain, Egypt, Tunisia and Sudan, there was hardly any significant inflow. On the contrary, Saudi Arabia, Yemen and Libya experienced outflows for some years. According to the figures, Saudi Arabia had added an extra $1.5 billion to its FDI portfolio by 2000, compared to the figure of $5 billion for 1999 – mentioned earlier in the chapter – to stand at $6.5 billion.

Table 11.10 FDI inflows in the League of Arab States, 1987-2000

Country	Annual Average					
	1985-2000	*1996*	*1997*	*1998*	*1999*	*2000*
League of Arab States	2,187.2	3,320.7	6,930.8	7,866.9	2,653.4	4,990.5
Algeria	8.8	4.0	7.0	5.0	7.0	6.3
Bahrain	191.4	2,048.1	329.3	179.5	447.6	500.0
Comoros	1.9	2.0	2.0	2.0	1.0	1.7
Djibouti	1.0	5.0	5.0	6.0	5.0	5.3
Egypt	870.5	636.4	891.0	1.1	1,065.3	1,235.4
Iraq	2.4	-	1.1	7.1	-6.9	0.4
Jordan	14.4	15.5	360.9	310.0	158.0	300
Kuwait	-1.2	347.4	19.8	59.1	72.3	16.3
Lebanon	10.1	80.0	150.0	200.0	250.0	180.0
Libyan Arab Jamahiriya	25.2	-134.9	-82.0	-151.9	-128.1	-
Mauritania	5.5	5.0	3.0	0.1	2.0	1.7
Morocco	-237.6	357.4	1.079.3	329.0	847.0	201.3
Oman	106.3	59.8	65.0	101.4	20.8	62.4
Territories under the Palestinian National Authority	-	4.2	-	-	1.3	0.4
Qatar	33.3	338.9	418.3	347.3	144.3	303.3
Saudi Arabia	98.8	-1,129.0	3,043.5	4,289.2	-782.1	1,000.0
Somalia	-0.8	-	-	-	60.9	20.3
Sudan	-2.3	0.4	97.9	370.7	370.8	392.2
Syrian Arab Republic	83.1	89.0	80.0	80.0	91.0	83.7
Tunisia	258.9	351.1	365.7	670.2	367.6	780.6
United Arab Emirates	96.9	30.5	232.4	252.7	-12.6	100.0
Yemen	145.7	-60.1	-138.5	-266.1	-328.7	-200.9
Memorandum:						
Developing Countries and Economies	50,744.9	152,492.9	187,351.8	188,371.4	222,009.6	240,167.4

Source: *UNCTAD, FDI/TNC Database*, 2002.

Figure 11.5's diagram, showing the volatility of capital flows, highlights the important fact that FDI is more stable than other forms of financing. Typically, FDI is based on a long-term view of the market, along with growth potential and structural characteristics of the recipient countries. It is thus unlikely to respond more negatively to news and adverse situations than bank lending and portfolio investment.

Figure 11.5 Volatility of capital flows in developing countries

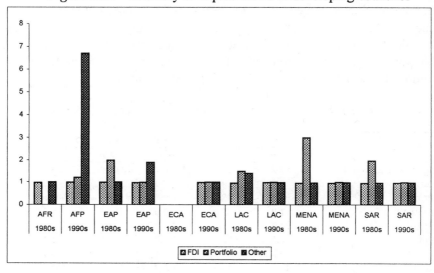

Source: *World Bank, Global Development Finance,* 2002.

The volatility of portfolio investment is one factor that explains why there has been a reluctance to date by the Saudi government to open up the Saudi stock market to foreigners other than through mutual funds. This viewpoint is shared by some local economists who point to the crises in the Mexican and East Asian currency and stock markets in the late 1980s and '90s as vindication of current Saudi policies. However, one can also argue that such crises are self-correcting in the long-term, and are usually accompanied by further structural reforms of the affected economies that make them more resilient and economically efficient than before the crisis. Once again, the central issue of meaningful and *actual*, as opposed to *announced*, structural reform arises. As one long-time observer of Saudi Arabia puts it, "will words finally begin to translate into action?" (Montague, 2003).

One such concrete action has been the Saudi Foreign Investment Law.

Before looking at the new Foreign Investment Law in some detail, let us briefly examine the pros and cons of FDI and see how they relate to Saudi Arabia, as set out in Table 11.11.

Table 11.11 Foreign direct investment: Saudi Arabia stock sheet

FDI Factor	Analysis	Saudi Arabia Applicability
POSITIVE FACTORS 1. *Capital Formation*	• This is more stable than other forms of investments. Essentially it is an equity investment – profits are repatriated when projects yield returns and part of the profits are reinvested in the host country. • Risks are borne by foreign shareholders. • FDI will not lead to debt crises (like bank lending) that require bailouts.	• Applicable: In Saudi Arabia investments are in either Saudi majority-owned companies, or, now, in 100% foreign-owned companies.
2. *Productivity Growth*	• A new understanding of the growth process treats technological changes as endogenous growth. This also involves the "soft" side of technological advances (organizational structure, managerial practices, etc.) that contribute to productivity growth. Rather than re-invent technological advances, developing countries can benefit from best practices in standards, embodied technology and markets of parent company.	• Applicable: This is the main reason why SABIC established international joint venture affiliates as examples.
3. *Economic Linkages*	• The impact of FDI on domestic economic growth depends on spreading out best practices through backward linkages with local producers and distributors, horizontal linkages with local competitors, and linkages with local institutions such as Universities and research institutes.	• Applicable: Local sourcing is an important stimulant to domestic companies. Linkages to Universities are also important (e.g. Science park, Institute of Research at KFUPM). • More is needed on backward linkages with local suppliers, but this varies with the industry.
4. *Employment and Labour Standards*	• Employment can be created via 3 areas: (a) direct employment in operations, (b) backward and forward linkages in enterprises that are suppliers, subcontractors and service providers, and (c) employment in sectors not directly related to FDI project. • Quality of labour standards is improved in the domestic economy, through good labour practices, superior working conditions and positive career prospects. • Adopting international global management-labour practices that are different from host country and ensuring that practices are of international standards	• Applicable: The quality of labour employment and the creation of best employment practice has been more important to date than the quantitative aspect of employment.

Continued Table 11.11

5. *Environmental Standards*	* FDI can lead to higher environmental controls and procedures.	* Applicable: Saudi Arabia insists on the latest environmental-friendly technology.
NEGATIVE FACTORS		
1. *"Crowding Out" effect*	• FDI may remove investment opportunities of the domestic firms and drive them out of business (e.g. in financial markets). • If FDI borrows locally, interest rates could rise if there are scarce resources, making borrowing for local firms uncompetitive. • FDI could pre-empt entry into the market of some types of production, especially if the foreign company employs aggressive marketing practices.	• There is not yet any evidence of this in Saudi Arabia, as most FDI has been capital intensive and the joint venture majority is Saudi owned.
2. *Balance of Payments Problem*	• FDI profits could be repatriated, constituting financial outflows to be set against net annual FDI inflow. This is important for countries with exchange controls.	• This is not an issue for Saudi Arabia as no exchange control regime exists.
3. *"Enclave Economies"*	• FDI investments could be narrowly based with a limited overall impact on domestic economy and benefiting only a small group of population. Examples are in mining natural resource extraction or "Export Processing Zones whereas if mining is only for exports, then it will not generate secondary industry employment. Neither would repackaging of goods in a duty free "export processing zone."	• Not applicable as oil sector in state hands and no foreign owned exclusive zones exist.

The above analysis shows that FDI is a critical ingredient to *long-term* sustainable growth, and presents Saudi Arabia with an effective way to enhance productivity and develop an internationally-competitive private sector. How has the Saudi government reacted to FDI?

Saudi Arabia's foreign investment law

In 2000, the Government of Saudi Arabia enacted the Foreign Investment Law and approved the formation of the Saudi Arabian General Investment Authority (SAGIA). It was headed by Prince Abdullah bin Faisal bin Turki, former Secretary General of the Royal Commission for *Jubail and Yanbu* to oversee FDI activities. In 2004, Prince Abdullah was succeeded by Amr Dabbagh as head of SAGIA. The SAGIA's aim was to be a one-stop-shop authorized to issue licenses and incorporate new foreign and joint venture companies, and to cut through the legendary red tape of Saudi bureaucracy.

To this end, SAGIA energetically acted to establish an operating framework totally different from customary Saudi governmental departments. SAGIA sought to have representatives from sixteen government agencies at its disposal to speed up decisions and approvals. Such approvals would be forthcoming in thirty days if all the paperwork was in order. Such speed was unheard-of when dealing with Saudi bureaucracy. It would also provide information to foreign companies and investors and create service centres at the Saudi Chambers of Commerce and Industry in the three major cities.

Table 11.12 summarizes the main changes in the 2000 Foreign Investment Law. In essence, the new law gives foreign investors the same level of benefits, incentives and guarantees offered to Saudi Arabian individuals and companies, with the exception of the rate of taxation on profits. However, as will be discussed below, even this issue is being addressed.

As can be seen in Table 11.12, the new legislation regarding FDI benefits provides for a lower taxation threshold, no limitation on the number of years to carry forward financial losses, the ability to obtain full concessionary Saudi financing from Saudi Industrial Development Fund (SIDF) and 100% foreign ownership and self-sponsoring of company staff. These measures, it seems, were not enough to attract foreign investment to the Kingdom, and, in April, 2003, the *Shoura* Council decided to cut taxes on foreign companies' profits to 20% from the previous maximum of 30%. The new legislation offers certain tax exemptions, especially for spending on research, development and geological surveys, and allows losses to be carried over from one year to the next.

Various sectors of the Saudi government reacted quite differently to this decision. SAGIA publicly welcomed the move and called for further reductions in the tax rate on the grounds that this reduction still discriminated between foreign investors and Saudi businesses, which only pay 2.5% *zakat* tax (Arab News, 30 April, 2003); but Finance Minister

Ibrahim Al Assaf just as publicly ruled out further tax cuts, on the grounds that doing so "will be a waste of public money without any legitimate reason" (Arab News, 08 May, 2003).

Table 11.12 Comparing the main features of the old and new laws - Saudi Arabian foreign investment law

Feature	New Law	Previous Law
Tax-holiday	• No reference is made to tax holidays and dividends taxes. This and many other details need to be clarified.	•If the Saudi share in the company is greater or equal to 25%, foreign investors will not pay taxes during the first ten years for industrial projects, or five years for services and agricultural projects.
Taxing Scheme	• If the corporate profits of a company are: • less than SR 10,000; they are taxed at the rate of 20%; the rate rises to 30% if corporate profits are more than SR 100,000. The new law reduced the tax brackets from four to just two.	• If the corporate profits of a joint venture company are: - less than SR 100,000, the tax rate is 25%; - more that SR 100,000, but less than SR500,000, the tax rate is 35%; - more than SR 500,000, but less than SR 1,000,000, the tax rate is 40%.; - more than SR 1,000,000, the tax rate is 45%.
Financial Losses	• There is no limitation on the number of future years that financial losses can be allocated to	•Financial losses can only be allocated to next year's operations.
Loans from the Saudi Industrial Developme nt Funds (SIDF)	• Companies fully or partially owned by foreigners can apply for subsidized loans from SIDF.	•For company to apply for SIDF loans, the Saudi share in equity has to be at least 25%.
Ownership	• Full ownership of the project is granted to the licensed firm (including land, buildings, and housing for employees).	•There must be a Saudi partner/sponsor who would own the land.
Sponsorship	• No Saudi sponsor is needed for the foreign investor. The licensed company will be the sponsor for the expatriate workers.	•The Saudi partner will be the sponsor for the foreign investor and for expatriates working in the joint venture company.

Source: *SAGIA*, 2002.

Removing more restrictions

While the new investment law was encouraging, the Supreme Economic Council did retain a long list of areas where foreign investors could not invest in the Kingdom. This so-called "negative list" was a cause of complaints by potential investors and SAGIA took these criticisms on board.

Since 2000, the number of activities prohibited to foreign investors has been reduced to exploration, the drilling and production of petroleum, the manufacturing of military equipment and uniforms and civilian explosives. In the service sector, foreigners are not allowed to invest in military catering, security or real estate in *Makkah* and *Madina* nor can they invest in real estate brokers television and radio stations, advertising and public relations (SAMA, 2003).

Excluding the negative list, all sectors are now open to foreign investment in Saudi Arabia. The latest area to be removed from the negative list was the insurance sector in 2003 (Arab News, 03 Feb 2003).

Following the formal ending of the third Iraq Gulf War in April, 2003, the Saudi Arabian government has attempted to make FDI even more attractive. A "full and frank" review of all obstacles blocking FDI has been undertaken, and SAGIA continues its efforts to further reduce unnecessary red tape and bureaucracy (A. Smith, 2003, Fehaid, 2003).

Some observers of the Saudi economy believe that, despite enhancements that make foreign direct investment more attractive, such a route is not in the final analysis an attractive option for foreign companies (Wilson, 2003, p. 95). We have touched on the reason before: government contracts.

It is wholly-owned or majority-owned Saudi companies that can benefit from existing regulations enabling them to qualify for government contract awards and automatic ten-year tax holidays on profit. This discriminatory purchasing bias might have to be scrapped when Saudi Arabia eventually joins the WTO, as it hopes to do by 2005, according to Saudi chief WTO negotiator Fawaz Al Alami (Al Khereiji, 2003).

Another area that the Kingdom has to address prior to joining the WTO, in order to make FDI attractive, is the creation and implementation of an effective uniform commercial code and a working legal system for steps such as debt collection and contract enforcement (Cordesman, 2003).

Conclusion

Most neutral observers commend the Kingdom's recent economic reforms, including the adoption of the new Foreign Investment Law allowing foreigners to own land, and the introduction of a comprehensive and inspiring privatization strategy. But most observers also agree that the pace of reform has to be much more urgent and that reforms need to be transparent, realistically-budgeted, and, above all, professionally implemented.

It is refreshing to see more openness expressed by public figures concerning the problems facing the Saudi economy, not least of which is the gap in policy making and the need for changes to meet the challenges of a rapidly growing population, of which some 70% are under 30 years old.

If the government is to succeed in its globalization, FDI and privatization drive, an area for urgent reform is that of statistics and information. This issue has recently been brought up publicly by Dr. Ibrahim Al Awaji, ex-Deputy Minister of Interior, when in March, 2003, he called for the creation of a national data centre, as "a lack of correct information was hampering government efforts to solve problems" (Arab News, 7 March 2003). Very often information is inadequate, non-transparent in terms of collation and methodology, too optimistic and very poorly presented. An open statistical culture is still lacking in both the public and private sector, and it is important to emphasize the importance of these to policy, strategy, performance and direction for investment.

A beginning has been made, but the pace has to be picked up.

Summary of key points

- *Saudi Arabia has opted for a decentralized, market based economy to be achieved through joining the WTO, perusing a program of domestic privatization, and encouraging foreign direct investment (FDI)*
- *The Kingdom has committed to joining the WTO and has taken the necessary steps to fulfill certain accession requirements, especially in tariff reduction, phasing out subsidies, enforcing intellectual property rights and allowing majority foreign ownership of investment projects and services, including the banking and insurance sectors.*
- *The potential impact of WTO accession and globalization on the Saudi economy is not yet certain. In the short term the negatives could outweigh the positive factors before long term structural adjustments bring about desired benefits.*
- *Financial globalization is more advanced in the Kingdom. The Saudi financial system is well integrated into the global network in terms of modernization and disintermediation, but lagging behind in terms of institutionalization.*
- *Privatization was officially launched in 2002, and planned to encompass all spheres of economic activities in the Kingdom. First*

steps have already been taken through the establishment of various regulatory agencies under which the privatized entities would operate.

- *Privatization is an instrument of economic policy whereby there is a transfer of property or control of assets owned by the state to the private sector – both management and ownership. To date, Saudi Arabia has carried out "partial privatization" through the sale of shares of government held corporations, such as SABIC and SCECO, SEC. More are being planned.*
- *Certain obstacles need to be overcome before privatization could become effective. These relate to assessing the fair book value of public assets, overcoming rigid pay structures of the privatized labor force, reduction of government subsidies and updating public sector accounting standards.*
- *Saudi Arabia has not been successful in attracting sizeable FDI to the Kingdom despite the size of its economy, market depth and more recent enhancements to the Foreign Investment Law such as a reduction to 20% in foreign corporate profit tax. Cross-border mergers and acquisitions are still not common in the Middle East. Investor perception is that more is needed to enhance the legal and operating frameworks such as labour, company and bankruptcy laws.*

Critical thinking

1. "Joining the WTO will hurt both big and small companies. Why join?" . Do you agree with this statement? What long term benefits might arise to Saudi Arabia from joining the WTO?
2. "The benefits of FDI are limited. There will be limited additional employment, technology transfer or value added to the economy. Saudi Arabia should instead concentrate on encouraging domestic enterprises". What are the benefits of FDI to a country in the long run?
3. Discuss the main obstacles and potential outcomes in implementing a full scale range of privatization in Saudi Arabia.
4. "Governments should not privatize. They only sell state assets at below market prices and lose out in future dividends." Why then do governments privatize? Should Saudi Arabia continue with the privatization program?
5. 5. Discuss why Saudi Arabia has decided to take the globalization route as a strategic option for the future of the country.

Chapter 12

POPULATION AND DEMOGRAPHICS: SAUDIZATION AND THE LABOR MARKET

After all there is but one race – humanity.

George Moore

Learning outcomes

By the end of this section you should understand:

- *The issue of rising Saudi youth unemployment*
- *Saudi demographic trends and their economic impact*
- *Government Saudization policies and results to date*
- *Private sector and Saudization*
- *Expatriate labor in the Saudi economy and its impact*
- *Trends in the Saudi labor market*
- *A model for Saudi labor participation*
- *Measurement of potential GDP losses due to unemployment*
- *An examination of current and planned structures of the Saudi labor market*
- *Duality of Saudi and foreign labor market structure*

Overview

There are a multitude of reasons – economic, social and political – for the Saudi Arabian government's serious approach to the current state of the labor market and to Saudi unemployment issues. Unemployment means less output, a lower standard of living and a high and worrying dependency rate. Some studies have put the number of Saudi dependents as high as 56 per 100

Saudi workers, some 2.4 times the world average (Al Sheikh, 2003). Thus, any major decline in income per worker, or a total lack of work, could have a dangerous effect on living standards and social cohesion. A worrying rise in juvenile crime rates connected with unemployed youth has now been widely reported in the local Saudi press and this adds further pressure on the government (Arab News, 5 March 2003).

But, as we will soon see, the Saudi government's effort is hampered by two factors. First, Saudi Arabia has a relatively young population age structure, with increasing numbers of new labor market entrants; this is coupled with one of the highest birth rates in the world. Second, there is a continuous flow of foreign workers into the Kingdom. However, the system does not seem to match available jobs with the skills of existing foreign workers, but merely compounds the problem by bringing in additional foreign workers under the Saudi private companies' sponsorship scheme, known as the *Kafeel* system.

The Saudi government has adopted a program of "Saudization" directed at gradually replacing expatriate workers with Saudi employees. The private sector is being steered towards increasing the proportion of nationals in employment through a policy of inducements and punishments, with charges for work permits or *Iqamas* and exit/re-entry visas raised substantially. This makes it more expensive to hire expatriate workers. Foreign labor visa issuance is also being more vigorously enforced. However, as we will discuss, the process of Saudization should not take place at the expense of efficiency and productivity in the national economy. The government is emphasizing improved education and training to provide Saudi graduates with the skills and the quality of education demanded by the private sector.

Population and demographics

An evaluation of a country's labor market and its characteristics would be somewhat meaningless without an understanding of the underlying demographic trends and composition of the population. Such an analysis will provide an insight into the potential problems that might arise in the future, based on current government labor policies. By its own admission, Saudi Arabia is amongst the fastest growing nations in the world in terms of population growth (SAMA, 2003). The Kingdom's population grew three-fold from 7.3 million in 1975 to 22.67 million in 2003. The high growth rate of the Kingdom's population, currently put at between 3.4-3.8% p.a., is due to a number of demographic transformations in the structure of Saudi society. These changes resulted from great improvements in living, health and social conditions over the past three decades. Some analysts have argued that there is no way to be sure of the true size of the Kingdom's demographic challenge, as no comprehensive census has been taken recently

(Cordesman, 2003). Despite this, there is some agreement that the population data used by the Saudi Ministry of Planning to forecast current and future population trends probably errs on the conservative side (U.S. Census Bureau, 23 March 2003).

The age composition of the population is a major worrying point for future labor market entrants. Countries can be characterized as either having an "ageing" or "young" population structure, with most countries of Western Europe falling in the first category and Saudi Arabia in the second. This is illustrated in Figure 12.1 which show that, as of 2002, the age groups below 30 years account for 72.6% or 11.3 million of the population.

Figure 12.1 Breakdown of the Kingdom of Saudi Arabia's population by age group in 2000

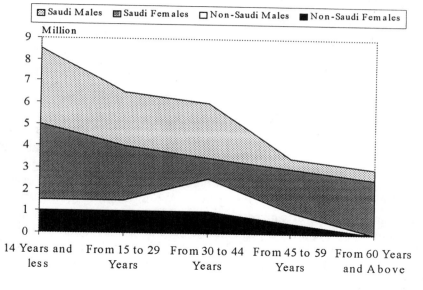

Source: *SAMA*, 2002.

The Saudi population under 15 years constitutes 7.1 million or 45% of the total population. This reinforces the dependency ratio explained earlier, without adding those over 65 to the ratio.

Table 12.1 sets out demographic trends for Saudi Arabia compared with other Arab countries, as well as the developing countries, the Organization for Economic Cooperation and Development (OECD) and the rest of the world. It immediately highlights the high Saudi population growth rate, young population profile and high fertility rate compared to the other blocs mentioned.

Table 12.1 Demographic trends: A comparison of Saudi Arabia and the
world

Description	Year (Period)	Saudi Arabia	Arab Countries	Developing Countries	OECD	The World
Total Population	1975	7.3	126.4	2,898.3	924.4	3,987.4
(Million)	1999	21.3	240.7	4,609.8	1,122.0	5,862.7
	2015	31.7	332.7	5,759.1	1,209.2	7,048.2
Annual Growth Rate of Population (%)	1975-1999	4.2	2.7	1.9	0.8	1.6
	1999-2000	3.0	2.0	1.4	0.5	1.2
Urban Population	1975	58.4	40.4	25.9	70.4	37.8
(Ratio to Total)	1999	85.1	54.0	38.9	77.2	46.5
	2015	89.7	61.9	47.6	81.3	53.1
Population below 15 years (Ratio to Total Population)	1999	40.8	40.8	33.1	20.6	30.2
	2015	28.1	28.1	28.1	17.3	25.8
Fertility Rate (Infants Per Woman)	1970-1975	7.3	6.5	5.4	2.5	4.5
	1995-2000	6.2	4.1	3.1	1.8	2.8
Life Expectancy (years)	1970-1975	53.9	51.9	55.5	70.4	59.9
	1995-2000	70.9	65.9	64.1	76.4	66.4

Source:*Central Department of Statistics, Ministry of Planning*, 2003, and *Human Resources Development Report of* 2001, *UN Development Program*, 2002.

Regardless of whether Saudi or non-Saudi estimates are absolutely correct, it is extremely clear that rapid population growth is taking place in Saudi Arabia. What was largely a rural society fifty years ago has become a relatively urbanized one. According to the World Bank, roughly 49% of the total population was urbanized as early as 1970, and 12% of the population were living in cities with a population of one million or more (World Bank, World Development Indicators, 2002). By 2000, the percentage living in cities was 86%, with 25% of the population living in cities of one million or more.

This urbanization trend will undoubtedly affect the numbers of Saudis seeking jobs in cities as opposed to agricultural work, with the percentage of those employed in agriculture dropping from 45% in 1970 to fewer than 7% in 1998 (World Bank, 2002).

The Saudi population was not only one of the fastest growing, but also one of the most fertile; the proportion of infants per woman was considerably higher than in other regions of the world.

These current population growth trends have sharply widened the gap between the population and Saudi government finances over the years, especially from the end of the 1980s "boom years". The erratic revenue pattern over the past decades and sharp population growth reinforce the government's determination to diversify the base of the Saudi economy in order to create more private sector jobs. As countries economically develop and urbanize, the demographics shift towards a lower birth rate, as seen earlier in Table 12.1, especially as women enter the labor force and economic pressures lead to smaller families. According to a recent study conducted amongst Saudi females, 22% of Saudi mothers wanted "a maximum of six children". Only one in 10 women wanted fewer than four children (Arab News, 24 April 2003). The study revealed some changing social customs. Younger women between 20-29 felt freer to discuss this subject than those older than 29, and 35% of married women discussed family size with their husbands.

So far the impact of such shifts in social attitudes on Saudi Arabia's population growth has been limited. Saudi population figures provide an insight into future trends. The Seventh Development Plan (2000-2004) estimates that the Saudi population will increase from 16.2 million in 2000 to 29.7 million in 2020, a rise of 89.2% and an average annual growth rate of 3% (Ministry of Planning, 2000). According to SAMA, (SAMA, Thirty Seventh Annual Report, 2001), the total population (Saudi and non-Saudi) could rise to 33.4 million by 2020, assuming an average annual growth rate of 2.1%.

These estimates show the extent of the impact Saudi population growth will have on internal social cohesion, economic wealth and development (Kanovsky, 1994, Abdelkarim, 1999). In turn, population growth will determine the size of the labor force and the degree to which a policy of *Saudization* will ease unemployment. It will also indicate the level of investment needed for infrastructure and education.

There are no figures on the distribution of income within Saudi Arabia. As such, Saudi per capita income data are not of much value in providing a meaningful analysis of real wealth. The published official figures seem to indicate, however, that due to higher population growth and declining revenues, Saudis are getting poorer in relative terms. SAMA data (SAMA, 2004, p. 4619) shows that GNP per capita rose from SR 4,588 in 1972, to a peak of SR 51,178 in 1981, only to gradually fall back to around SR 35,000 in 2003. These are at current prices, so if the calculations were made at constant prices, the per capita figures would be even lower.

Saudization: A viable solution?

Saudi Arabia recognized very early the necessity to *Saudize* the workforce . In 1970, the government decreed that 75% of workers in all businesses operating in the country should be Saudi, and that they should receive at least 51% of the company's total salary payment (Wright, 1996). However, as Figure 12.2 shows, the number of foreign workers steadily increased, reaching a peak of 4.5 million in 1995, and was estimated at 3.7 million for 2003 in both the public and private sectors.

Figure 12.2 GDP and expatriate workforce in Saudi Arabia 1975-2000 (at market prices)

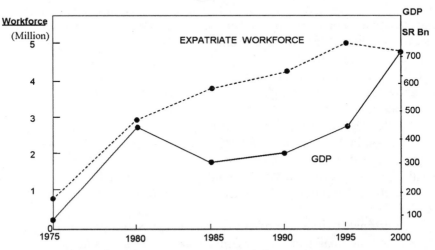

Source: Adapted from *SAMA*, 2002, *Ministry of Planning*, 2002.

One clarification is needed: sometimes data on "foreign workers" adds together actual workers and their dependents in the Kingdom. Thus, when figures of 6 million expatriates or higher are mentioned, they would include 2.3 million dependents in Saudi Arabia under the age of 18 (Al Najjar, 1998). Past that age, they cease being dependents and are not granted residence visas.

Figure 12.2 shows that the number of expatriates rose despite the erratic fluctuation in GDP over the same period.

The Government of Saudi Arabia hopes that manpower demand and supply projections, resulting from various schemes and administrative policies that we will describe later, will reverse the trend and ensure a majority Saudi labor force by 2005. This is set out in Figure 12.3, while Table 12.2 displays the government's own projections for the Seventh Plan period (2000-2004) and its long-term perspective to 2020. By that year, the number of non-Saudi workers will have been reduced by 2.25 million, to stabilize around 1.25 million. The assumption is that no new foreign labor will enter the market. The aggressive foreign labor visa approval policy adopted in 2004 by the new Minister of Labor, Dr Ghazi Al Gosaibi, seems to be precisely aimed at bringing forward the government's *Saudization* plan.

Figure 12.3 Evolution of total jobs

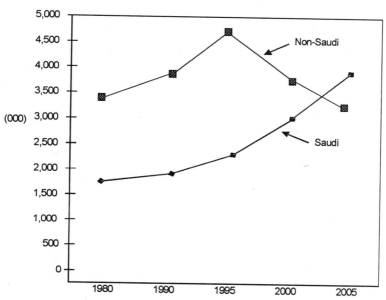

Source: *Ministry of Planning*, 2002.

However, official statements on long-term plans for replacing foreign labor with Saudis seem to conflict with each other. For example, the Saudi Ministry of Labor issued an announcement in May, 2001, that it intended to cut foreign jobs by 85% over the next thirty years, from 7.2 million to 1 million.

Table12.2 Manpower demand and supply projections (1999-2020)

Description	Thousands			Average Annual Growth Rate %	
	1999	2004	2020	7th Plan (2000- 2004)	Long Term Perspective (2000 – 2020)
1. Demand					
Government Services	916.2	923.3	984.0	0.35	0.34
Crude Oil & Gas	98.9	100.4	127.0	0.30	1.20
Private Sector	6,161.2	6,472.2	9,635.0	0.99	2.15
Total Demand	7,176.3	7,504.9	10,746.0	0.90	1.94
2. Supply					
Saudi Population	15,658.4	18,520.3	29,717.0	3.41	3.10
Saudi Labor Force	3,172.9	3,990.2	8,263.0	4.69	4.66
3. Demand/Supply Balance					
Non-Saudi Labor Force	4,003.4	3,514.7	2,483.0	(2.57)	(2.25)

Source: *Ministry of Planning*, 2002.   (Figures in brackets denote negative values)

At the same time, it still projected that foreigners would make up 10 million out of a projected 39 million people in 2030 (Associated Press, May 9, 2001).

Some have argued that *Saudization* can be both a blessing and a curse for Saudi Arabia (Chadhury, K. 1989, Kapiszewski, A. 2001, Cordesman, 2003). The "blessing" is that inherent in Saudi Arabia's present dependence on legal (and illegal) foreign workers lies one solution: to create Saudi employment, theoretically, by expelling most of the foreign workers. The "curse" of the present dependence on foreign labor is that most of the non-Saudi jobs are the type, due to social values, that many young Saudis do not want.

Figure 12.4 Saudization program 1983-1999

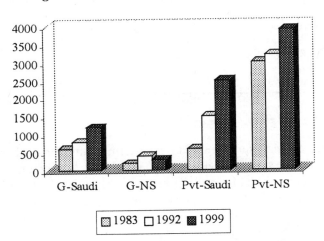

Source: *Manpower Council*, 2002.

To some extent, the *Saudization* program has been successful in replacing foreign workers with Saudi employees, but this has been primarily in the government sector where there is much more hiring control than in the private sector. Figure 12.4 illustrates the success of this government policy, which ensured that by 1999, the majority of employees in the government sector were Saudis.

Fortunately for Saudi Arabia, according to official data, there is a large pool of highly skilled and educated foreign workers who occupy jobs that many Saudis may well accept once they have more realistic job expectations. SAMA reports (SAMA, 2002, p. 309) that there are 1,341,000 foreign workers – 31% of the total foreign labor force – who are educated to University, pre-University diploma and secondary certificate levels. Why then have they not been replaced?

Mixed results in the private sector

In contrast to the public sector, the private sector, which generates the majority of jobs in the country, employed around 10% of Saudis by the mid-1990s although the situation had improved by 1999 (see Figure 12.4). According to the latest government reports, this rose to around 11.5 % by 2003. The employment pattern of Saudis in the private sector, however, varied between industries. Sectors such as public utilities, banking and insurance, transportation and real estate employed a larger percentage of Saudis than others. In April, 2003, the Government announced that a further 10,000 banking positions were to be *Saudized* and banking employment data revealed that Saudis accounted for 66% of the work force. The *Saudisation* level fluctuated between 58% and 75% amongst the different banks (Arab News, 9 April 2003). The National Commercial Bank had the highest Saudi level at 75%, and Al Rajhi and the Saudi Investment Bank the lowest at 60%. Table 12.3 reveals the distribution of workers in the private sector by nationality and economic activity during the period 1996-1997. Oil and mining, manufacturing, construction, hotels, restaurants, education and health services were predominantly run by foreigners.

Why is there reluctance on the part of the private sector to hire Saudis to replace foreigners, despite government directives, encouragement, and now threats? In 2000, the Saudi Government set up the Human Resources Development Fund (HRDF), headed by Dr. Mohammad Sahlawi, to help Saudis obtain employment in the private sector. HRDF agreed to pay private sector companies 75% of the salaries of young Saudis for their first two years of employment, up to a maximum of SR 2,000 per month, to encourage their employment.

Table 12.3 Distribution of workers by nationality and economic activity 1996-1997 (excluding the government and agricultural sector)

	Sector's share in total employment	% of Saudi participation	% of Non-Saudi participation
Oil & Mining	4.19%	9.3%	90.7%
Manufacturing	19.70	11.5%	88.5%
Public Utilities	0.70%	55.7%	44.3%
Construction	17.07%	9.8%	90.2%
Wholesale & Retail	31.66%	13.4%	86.6%
Hotels & Restaurants	5.55%	4.7%	95.3%
Transportation & Storage	6.59%	28.8%	71.2%
Banking & Insurance	1.64%	52.4%	47.6%
Real Estate & Business	7.14%	25.4%	74.6%
Education	1.36%	16.9%	83.1%
Health	2.05%	9.8%	90.2%
Community & Personal Service	2.36	13.1%	86.9%

Source: *National Commercial Bank*, 2002, *SAMA*, 2002.

According to reports, HRDF targeted the IT, construction and health sectors as part of a new strategy to create 20,000 jobs for Saudis in 2003 (Arab News, 27 May 2003). The fund is financed by a levy of SR 100 per expatriate worker in the Kingdom. While HRDF succeeded in collecting SR 400 million in the first 10 months of its establishment, there has not yet been a noticeable improvement on the job front, although most recent official data seems to suggest that the percentage of Saudis employed in the private sector has risen to around 53.2% in 2004 compared with 39% in 1999 (SAMA, 2004, p. 313). Hence, the question again arises: why the seeming reluctance to employ Saudis by the private sector?

Culture and work ethics

Some ascribe the obstruction to cultural attitudes towards work inherent in Saudi society. The fact is that due to negative attitudes about certain types of work among Saudis, there are many expatriates in the Kingdom, even though it is the only country in the GCC with a large enough population to carry out the country's development on its own (Looney, 1992, Nur Uthman, 1995). Additionally, the combination of importing foreign workers while offering generous state welfare benefits to nationals has reinforced this negative attitude towards work and created a vicious cycle that encourages Saudis to stay out of a large part of the job market. It is certainly hard to explain the staggering statistic from the Ministry of Labor that some 150,000 Saudis did not bother to return and complete formalities for guaranteed private sector jobs they had been assigned through the various labor offices over the past four years (Abdul Ghafour, Arab News, 3 August 2004). The issue of work ethics has attracted some debate both from within and outside Saudi Arabia (Shatkin, 2002, Cordesman, 2003, Niblock, 1980, Binzagr, 2003).

That said, certain changes for the better have taken place. The younger generation has indicated its willingness to accept positions that have been traditionally rejected by their fathers, such as jobs at hotels, restaurants, barber-shops and other direct services to customers.

However, there are several reasons for the private sector's resistance to *Saudization*. These are summarized in Table 12.4 and are based on the author's own observations and interviews with leading Saudi businessmen, in addition to comments raised in the media by several Saudi industrial leaders.

As the private sector sees it, market forces drive at least part of the solution to these problems. Over time, Saudi nationals will need to be more realistic in their demands around wages and employment conditions.

Table12.4 Private sector Saudization issues

Issues	Private Sector Justifications
1. Labor cost	• The relatively high cost of Saudi manpower, compared to foreign manpower, results in private sector reliance on imported cheap manual labor, deployed in labor-intensive occupations. This helps private sector profitability despite government attempts to increase expatriate costs (Residency or *Iqama*, Visa renewals, etc.).
2. Social and cultural perceptions	• Saudis are reluctant to take up and seriously pursue certain types of jobs, despite *Saudization* directives. For example, the forced *Saudization* of employees in the vegetable markets has failed. *Social Status is* still important for young Saudis as it affects marriage and other social relations.
3. Control over process of production	• Expatriate workers are easier to control and more disciplined than Saudis. Control is exercised through short-term employment contracts. In some cases, there are few legal obligations towards expatriates, who are prohibited from changing jobs without their sponsor's permission.
4. Lack of social integration in multi-cultural work environment	• Local populations are reluctant to integrate into multi-cultural work environments, fearing that it might degrade their existing status.
5. Job tenure	• It is more difficult to fire Saudi workers than foreign workers.
6. Inadequate qualifications	• Saudi employees may have inadequate qualifications, a lack of good English or a non-technical background.
7. Mobility	• Saudi workers are less mobile than foreigner workers; they are reluctant to change job locations.

Saudi government policy has largely focused on preventing, through quotas and higher fees, the employment of expatriates. This might not be the most appropriate policy at this stage of Saudi economic development, given the relative lack of skills in the Saudi labor force. However, the foreign workforce at the lower skill levels might never be completely *Saudized*, possibly because they add very little to overall national productivity. For example, in 1999 there were some 1.7 million foreign females in the Kingdom, with a large number working as housemaids. Most of these jobs are unlikely to be replaced by Saudi men or women, for cultural and social reasons, although it is interesting to note that some Saudi women are now being placed in household day jobs with Saudi families (Author's personal interviews with employment and social agencies).

Similarly, there are about 800,000 foreign males who work in extremely menial, low-status jobs that will be hard to *Saudize* (SAMA, Thirty Sixth Annual Report, 2000, p. 258). Turning *Saudization* theory into practice means restructuring much of the present Saudi labor market in order to create new types of knowledge-based, high value jobs for young Saudis. Restructuring might help avoid fiascos such as the imposition of *Saudization* on complete sectors, like the markets of the vegetable sellers, travel agencies and gold sellers, only to see results flounder later on when foreign labor was rehired back to these sectors due to lack of interest from Saudi labor (Arab News, June, 2003). The seeming inability of the private sector to hire large numbers of new Saudi employees or to replace foreign workers with Saudis has attracted adverse comments. Some advocate even tougher government action, since, "... if the government did not force *Saudization*, we would never see a Saudi working in the private sector" (Al Quaiefer, M. *Al Jazirah*, 17 Sept 2003). They dismiss such issues as the inability to speak English or not getting the "right Saudi in the right place".

The private sector is responding vigorously to these charges. According to Khalid Al Zamil, past Chairman of the Eastern Province Chamber of Commerce and Industry, and President of one of Saudi Arabia's renowned group of industrial companies, the matter was one of appropriate skills and education, for "no matter what the *(Saudization)* policies are, if we don't combine that with the tools, training and education required, we cannot implement *Saudization* in its entirety" (Arab News, 13 July 2003).

It is not that the private sector is doing little about this issue. The Jeddah Chamber of Commerce and Industry (JCCI), for example, is currently examining the possibility of setting up a training program for Saudis interested in making printing their career. They are shifting away from "overnight *Saudization*" of entire sectors, to the training of young Saudis for a range of jobs. This will allow reliance on expatriate workers to be phased out organically (Arab News, 18 Sept 2003).

To this end, the Saudi government needs to concentrate on two key areas:

One – focusing on education and the skill base. Many now admit that the Kingdom's education and training system has failed to meet the needs of the economy (Al Dosary, 2002, Diwan and Girgis, 2002). Half of the Kingdom's eight Universities focus on religious studies and only 12% of Saudi students graduate in engineering and sciences, while 42.2% graduate in social and religious studies (Arab News, 8 January 2003). The technical institutes are under-subscribed, with negligible links to the private sector.

The Saudi education system is not expanding quickly on a number of levels and needs to improve its quality and focus. This does *not* mean that education should not be Islamic; rather, Islamic education must do a far better job of training the young men and women of Saudi Arabia to be truly competitive in the real world.

Two -- focusing on sector specific employment. To date, the various government development plans have been vague, neglecting to specify priority areas of employment and thereby neglecting to send a signal about educational focus and resource allocation. The Saudi cabinet reshuffle decreed by King Fahd bin Abdulaziz in April, 2003, saw the amalgamation of the functions of planning and economy under a new Ministry of Planning and National Economy (Arab News, 1 May 2003). Hopefully, this would ensure that planning would better align with sector-specific objectives and not broad macro-economic directives.

Expatriate labor: needed but not wanted?

As we said earlier, opening up the Saudi economy to globalization and making it attractive to Foreign Direct Investment (FDI) could cause conflict for the twin objectives of *Saudization* and liberalization. The Kingdom's aggressive *Saudization* policy could be seen as too negative for foreign companies that prefer to operate in an open labor market, one that is dictated by experience, qualifications and the needs of market supply and demand. These foreign companies might refuse to comply with imposed *Saudization* quotas.

In February, 2003, the Saudi Government decided to take an even more drastic step to reduce foreign workers in the Kingdom. Prince Naif bin Abdulaziz, the Interior Minister and Head of the Manpower Council, announced that 3 million expatriates were to be phased out from Saudi Arabia within a decade, and that the total number of expatriates must not exceed 20% of the Saudi population by 2013 (Arab News, 3 February 2003). This brings forward from 2020 to 2013 the "optimum" number of expatriates of 1.25 million that is the government's preferred foreign labor target.

The surprise decision also stipulated a quota system for foreign nationalities in which no single nationality must exceed 10% of total expatriates (Arab News, 5 February 2003).

This system will hit the Asian communities in Saudi Arabia particularly hard, as they represent the largest component of the work force (see Table 12.5). The Egyptians, Filipinos and Yemenis will also be affected, since they too represent a large percentage of the current work force, especially when their dependents are included. Those least affected are the small numbers of highly paid and professional expatriates from the USA and Europe. It is interesting to note the absence of the large numbers of Korean and Thai workers seen during the early 1980s construction boom (Moon, Chung In, 1996).

Only time will tell how rigorously this announced quota system for nationality groups will be implemented, but it is more than likely that citizens of Arab states such as Egypt and Yemen will be granted some form of extension. This is due to inter-Arab governmental sensitivities about the relatively high unemployment in the wider Arab world.

*Table 12.*5 Major expatriate communities in the GCC countries, 1997
(estimates in thousands)

Expatriate Communities	Bahrain	Kuwait	Oman	Qatar	Saudi Arabia	UAE
Indians	110	262	300	90	1,250	1,000
Egyptians		271	35	29	1,200	100
Pakistanis	70	100	70	60	800	400
Filipinos	25	60		40	500	100
Yemenis					500	
Sri Lankans		167	25	30	150	125
Jordanians/ Palestinians				40	270	100
Syrians		95			170	
Indonesians					250	
Sudanese					250	
Kuwaitis					120	
Turks					95	
Iranians		69		20		
Total Expatriate Population	242	1,409	614	365	6,000	2,038

Source: *Various estimates, Gulf Organization for Industrial Consulting*, 2002, *ESCWA, Statistical Abstract of the ESCWA Region*, 1998.

Foreign workers in Saudi Arabia bring both positive and negative economic and social consequences to the Kingdom.

Expatriates contribute both as consumers and producers to the Saudi economy. While expatriate workers -- especially those who are single -- have a high propensity to save (Sinclair, 1988), and thus to transfer funds outside the Kingdom in remittances, the expatriate population as a whole spends a considerable amount of money within the Kingdom. They are a major source of income to Saudi-owned establishments, such as travel, luxury items, supermarkets and hotels. A drastic reduction in expatriate numbers will cause dislocation to some local businesses, unless increased Saudi spending patterns provide compensation.

A recent GCC study called for encouraging expatriate workers in the Kingdom to bring their families in order to increase their spending within the country and to cut down overseas remittances. The study was prepared by the GCC Secretariat based in Riyadh (Arab News, 2 June 2003). Another view is that government actions to *Saudize* interfere in business affairs and pose challenges, such as a loss of competitiveness in those labor-intensive industries which employ cheap labor.

These issues are especially pertinent in the face of WTO trade liberalization moves (Jasim Ali, *Gulf News*, 9 June 2003). The WTO accession talks are certainly impacting on Saudi labor law policies. According to *Shoura* Council member Saleh al Humaidan, "...among the requirements for joining the WTO is streamlining of the human resources sector". As such, the Saudi *Shoura* Council is currently studying the draft of a revised Saudi labor law to replace the current law, which was passed nearly 35 years ago. The new law will be "conforming to the new business environment and broadening its scope to cover many new areas" (Saeed Haidar, Gulf Bureau, Arab News, 26 June 2003). The council of Ministers approved the new labor law in 2004.

The bombings in Riyadh on 12 May 2003 brought a sharp focus to the relationship with and the presence of expatriates in Saudi Arabia. In its official announcements, the government made it extremely clear that both Saudis and foreigners would be protected and that expatriates were welcome guests who contributed positively to the Kingdom's development (Saudi Press Agency, 13, 18 May 2003). In addition to the purely economic ramifications, the presence of other diverse nationalities amongst an indigenous population often creates an intangible two-way benefit to both sides.

On the Saudi side, getting to know and working with many different national groups could enable Saudis to encounter and perhaps adopt the best possible work ethics and practices from amongst them, increasing their own productivity without changing basic Saudi social norms or customs. Outside visitors to the Eastern Province of the Kingdom often comment on how similar the attitudes of Saudis in that region are to American working attitudes. This is a function of the long-term involvement of American companies in the Eastern Province.

The Saudi labor market: separating fact from fiction

In March, 2003, local newspapers reported that the unemployment rate had reached 31.7% in Saudi Arabia, according to a study entitled "Unemployment: Causes and Remedies" conducted by SAMA (Arab News, 5 March 2003). If this is true, then it is an alarming jump in the previously announced government unemployment levels, which ranged from 8% to 14% according to the Manpower Council. Prior to this announcement, the only comprehensive labor and unemployment data had been released by the Central Department of Statistics of the Ministry of Planning in September, 2002, putting unemployment for 1999 at 8.1% (Saudi American Bank, 2002).

The truth of the matter is that there is no precise way to measure the rate of Saudi unemployment; there is no "signing-up benefit" system similar to other countries that registers those who are involuntarily unemployed, that is, able and willing to take up jobs.

The way in which unemployment data are shrouded in secrecy has triggered some lively debate, mostly critical, amongst Saudi commentators. More precise research is needed on both the regional and national levels in order to arm the Saudi government with the appropriate unemployment data to enable it to implement a realistic job creation and job replacement program.

In an effort to alleviate the suffering of thousands of jobless Saudi youths, the Secretary General of the Manpower Council, Abdul Hamid Al Humaid, following a study, announced in January, 2003, that they were considering the possibility of implementing a "dole" – that is, an unemployment benefit program for the unemployed (Arab News, 8 January 2003). This initiative breaks yet another social taboo in the Kingdom. There used to be a social stigma attached to accepting such unemployment benefits, and this complicated matters when trying to establish precise data on voluntary and involuntary unemployed. While unemployment rates may vary with each announcement, the greatest challenge remains the same: the labor force is increasing faster than the available jobs, based on the demographic structure of the Kingdom.

However, we must avoid confusing two issues: the number of jobseekers not working, and the overall number of people of working age who are not working. The number of jobseekers, as a percentage of the overall population, is called the *labor participation rate*, and this is expected to be low for Saudi Arabia, given its very youthful demographic profile and low participation rate of females.

Table 12.6, based on Central Department of Statistics data for 1999, does indeed show that Saudi Arabia has a lower male and female participation rate than the rest of the Middle East and other parts of the world.

Table 12.6 Select labor participation rates*

	Male	*Female*	*Total*
Saudi Arabia	32%	6%	19%
Middle East	49%	17%	33%
Sub-Saharan Africa	51%	37%	44%
Latin America	55%	27%	41%
East Asia	61%	51%	56%
Europe	72%	18%	45%
United States	77%	23%	50%

*Labor force as percentage of the total population
Source: *Saudi Central Department of Statistic for Saudi Arabia*, 2001,
        World Bank "Social Indicators of Development" for all others,
        2001.

Female participation in the labor force

The low Saudi female participation rate is confirmed in Figure 12.5, which shows that the highest female participation levels are in the 25-34 age groups, followed by the 20-24 age group. With parental and family commitments, participation rate for the older age groups falls off or is completely negligible.

This could be due to the fact that there were few job openings for females several decades ago, when it was not socially accepted that women seek jobs.

Figure12.5 Participation rates by gender and age group, 1999

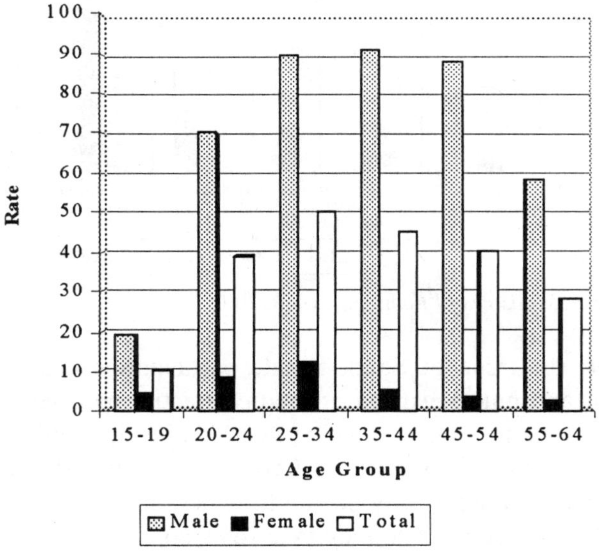

Source: Ministry of Planning, Riyadh, 2002.

Even other countries of the socially conservative Gulf Cooperation Council (GCC) had higher female participation rates than Saudi Arabia; the World Bank's data for 2000 puts Oman at 17%, Kuwait at 31%, UAE at 19%, Bahrain at 35% and the MENA region as a whole at 28% (World Bank, World Development Indicators, 2000, pp. 46-48).

Figure 12.6 shows 1999 participation rates by gender and educational levels, according to the Central Department of Statistics. Females with higher levels of education, both undergraduate and postgraduate, had the highest level of job participation, compared with those with secondary or primary schooling. Most female employment tended to be concentrated in the government sectors of education and health/social services. Very few worked in the private sector due to social sensitivities around direct interaction with males. Earlier we closely examined the economic and social issues hindering a greater participation level for Saudi females, and noted the wider range of economic activities in which they are now engaged.

Figure 12.6 Participation rates by gender and educational level 1999

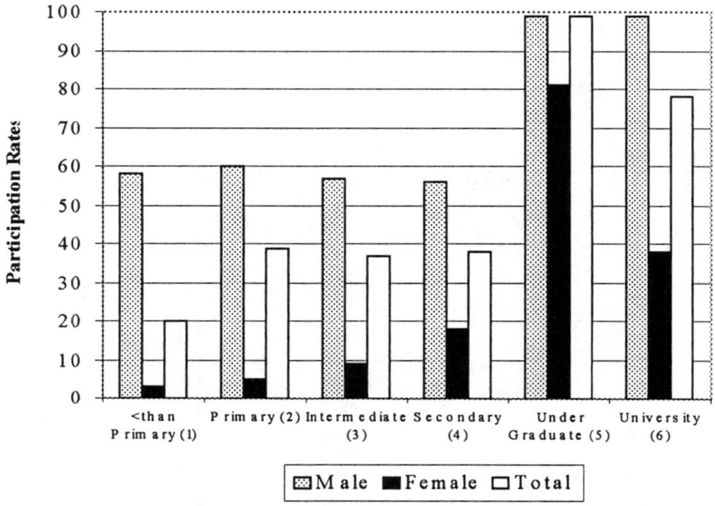

Source: *Ministry of Planning, Riyadh*, 2002.

However, the issue of Saudi female participation cannot be effectively tackled until and unless women are more directly involved in Saudi nation-building. This matter is commanding attention inside Saudi Arabia. Indeed, no less a person than Crown Prince Abdullah himself stated as early as 1999 that, "…we will not allow any person to undermine the role of Saudi women or marginalize the active role they take for their religion or country… Saudi women have proven their ability to handle responsibilities with great success, whether through their principal duties as mothers or professionals. We look forward to women playing a major role in a way that will promote the interest of this nation on the basis of *Shariah* (Islamic law)" (Arab News, 12 September 2003).

Statements of encouragement and support like those of the Crown Prince have galvanized women's groups to demand better treatment on the economic front. Saudi businesswomen have petitioned the *Majlis Al Shoura* for ways to facilitate their investment activities, so that they can play a greater role in the country's economic development.

Why then can't Saudi women participate more in the national economy? The barrier stems from procedural and operational problems in conducting their business. Despite the obstacles discussed in Chapter 7, Saudi businesswomen continue their battle to remove these obstacles.

Women's economic issues and the speed of women's integration within Saudi society also meet strong resistance in the name of tradition and values. Despite the Saudi government's desire for change and reform on women's issues, some sources of resistance cannot be ignored. According to one of the Kingdom's well-known modernist officials, Prince Khaled Al Faisal, "...Saudi Arabia is probably the only country in the world where the government is pushing for reforms and the people are pulling back..." (Raid Qusti, Arab News, 18 June 2003).

Labour participation – a model for new entrants

Analysis of Saudi Arabia's future labor market is particularly difficult given the lack of precise data on the constitution of the current labor force. As such, researchers have to come up with a model that realistically captures labor entrant flow. This is important for planning an effective *Saudization*, and for economic and educational planning.

The total number of the nation's labor force is illustrated below. This does not take account of expatriate labor entrants, as the entry and exit of the Kingdom's foreign (legal) workers can be controlled.

Figure12.7 Sources of new entrants into Saudi labor market (Saudis only)

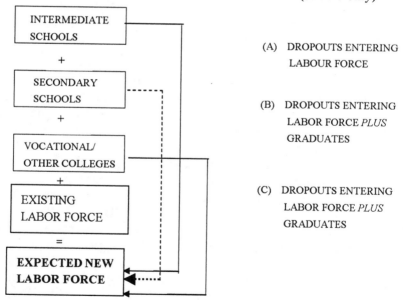

Figure 12.7 concentrates on the educational sector and its impact through providing new labor entrants. Like other societies, some Saudi youth drop out of the educational system at various stages while others continue until graduation. Again, Saudi education data focuses only on current school or

higher education enrolment numbers and does not provide figures for dropouts.

From this, one can extrapolate the current level of labor force or
jobseekers, and the level of unemployment focusing primarily on Saudi
males for whom some government data exists. We shall use the base data
extrapolated by the Saudi American Bank (SAMBA) from the Central
Department of Statistics data, as well as our own estimates for Saudi student
graduates and dropout rates. SAMBA arrived at an unemployment level of
around 12% for 2002, based on the following analysis:

Table 12.7 Saudi male unemployment calculation, 2002 (Saudi American
Bank and author's estimation)

Employment Base Data 1999 (CDS)		
- Saudi Male Labor Force 1999 of which:		2,411,006
• Employed	2,247,720	
• Unemployed	163,286	
Employment Developments 2000 – 2002		
	SAMBA	*Author's Estimation*
Male Entrants to Labor Force	340,000	450,000
Jobs Created	175,000	170,000
2002 Male Labor Force of which:	2,751,006	3,031,006
• Employed	2,422,720	2,417,720
• Unemployed	328,286	443,286
Saudi Male Unemployment	**11.93%**	**14.6%**

Source: *SAMBA*, 2001, author's estimation.

The difference between SAMBA and the author's unemployment rate
estimations can be explained by the approximately 450,000 new male
graduates for the years 1999/2000 coming in from the intermediate,
secondary and higher education systems (Ministry of Planning, 2001). If one
adds an additional 110,000 dropouts, about 5% of the total of 2,214,000
male students enrolled in 1999/2000 in all the three educational sectors, the
unemployment level will reach around 18%. This is still lower than the 31%
Saudi unemployment levels highlighted at the beginning of this chapter, but
closer to it than SAMBA's estimates of around 12%. In 2002, SAMBA
adjusted the figure upwards to 15.25% (SAMBA, 2002, p. 22). The total
unemployment figure will rise further if female entrants are added to male
jobseekers, which might possibly explain the higher unemployment figures
recently mentioned in the local press.

The next table forecasts employment changes for Saudi males, for the
period 2003-2013, based on the model of labor entrants developed in Figure
12.7. We must emphasize at the outset that the approach taken to arrive at
new job entrants, new job creation and estimated unemployment levels is
based on several assumptions and data that is possibly incomplete.
Therefore, the estimates are liable to a wide margin of error. However, this is

a first attempt to understand the dynamics of all these factors over the next decade.

Table12.8 Employment developments from 2003-2013: Saudi Arabia (males only)

	*2003	2006	2008	2011	2013
Male Entrants to Market Labor Force	450,000	497,478	531,882	587,999	628,663
Private Sector GDP Growth		4%	4%	5%	3%
Jobs Created – New	150,000	167,107	182,481	207,221	224,130
Total Male Labor Force	2,861,006	4,304,904	5,351,179	7,057,809	8,294,463
Employed*	2,417,720	2,900,007	3,257,951	3,854,130	4,293,770
Unemployed*	443,286	1,404,897	2,093,228	3,203,679	4,000,693
Employment Rate	84.51%	87.37%	60.88%	54.61%	51.77%
Unemployment Rate	15.49%	13.63%	39.12%	45.39%	48.23%
Total	100.00%	100.00%	100.00%	100.00%	100.00%

Source: *2003 as base year from Table 12.7, Ministry of Planning, 19th Issue, Achievements of the Development Plans, 2002, pp. 300-301.*

Starting with the employment base level from Table 12.7, we used male education data from the Ministry of Planning statistics for the year 2002. Students currently at the elementary school age 11 mark our starting point. We projected forward to 2013 for all these students in the education system, assuming a 5% dropout rate for intermediate schools, 10% for secondary education and 10% for higher education. The results appear as the male entrants to the market labor force in Table 12.8. We have also assumed that the private sector will be the major source of new job creation for the Saudi economy and that it will grow at levels of 3%-5% p.a. over the next ten years. The latest economic forecasts indicate that this was a reasonable estimation (Saudi British Bank, 2003, SAMBA, 2003, Riyadh bank, 2003).

Based on an ever-increasing number of new male entrants into the labor force due to the demographic trends explained earlier, Table 12.8 highlights the possibility that Saudi male unemployment levels could reach 48% within a decade.

In summary, Saudi Arabia needs job creation and skills creation to ensure job growth. As discussed earlier, the job creation need will eventually be somewhat alleviated by the ability of the current *Saudization* program to replace foreigners and employ some Saudis. However, since the data analyses only male labor entrants, the employment picture becomes even gloomier if female labor entrants are added. Currently there are 2,351,000 female students at all levels of education compared with 2,473,000 males (Ministry of Planning, 2002, pp. 300-303). If one assumes one fifth of females wish to enter the labor market, then the forecasted combined unemployment levels for both sexes would be much higher.

The "oil boom baby boomers"

While there are no official data on the level of dropout rates in the Saudi education system, we believe that the average level of 5% that we used in our earlier analysis erred on the conservative side. Dropout rates calculated for the early 1980s averaged around 25% for all three educational sectors (Johany, 1986). Plentiful and easier job opportunities in those early "boom years" may well have contributed towards higher dropout and labor participation rates.

The situation will become more difficult as growth in the labor force exceeds population growth. There is likely to be a natural increase over time in the labor participation rate due to the demographic bulge of the "oil boom baby boomers" coming into the job market in greater numbers, as indicated in the following figures.

*Figure12.*8 Saudi population and employed 1999
(male and female expatriates excluded)

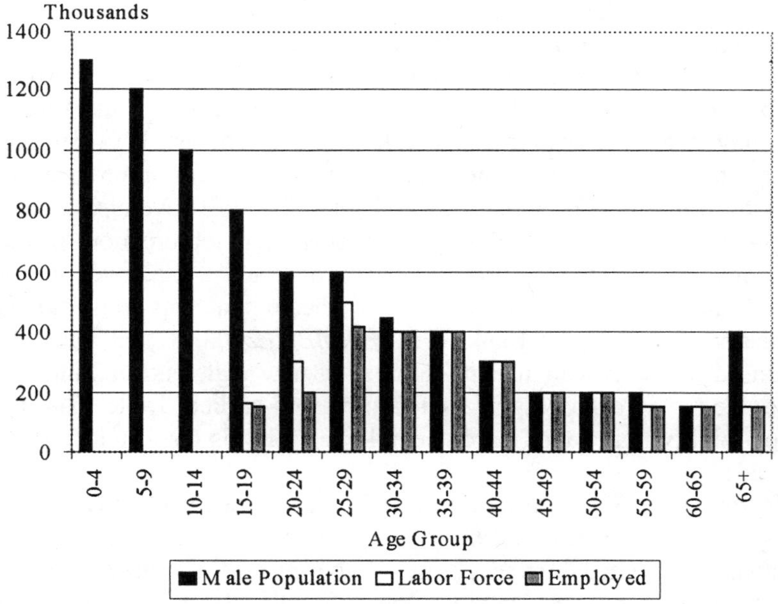

Source: *SAMA, 2002.*

Figure 12.8 shows that as of 1999, the labor force comprised 2.82 million Saudis (19% of the total population of 14.87 million), representing 35% of working age Saudis.

What is striking is that both male and female unemployment was closely correlated with age groups: the younger age groups have the highest unemployment rates. Thus, unemployment was 28% for Saudis who are 20-24 years old, but only 9.8% for Saudis between 25-39. According to 1999 government data, the unemployment level for all Saudis over the age of 30 was almost non-existent at 0.9%. Again, this is a function of those who found employment more readily during the earlier "boom" period and held onto those jobs.

Figure 12.9 Non-Saudi population and employed, 1999

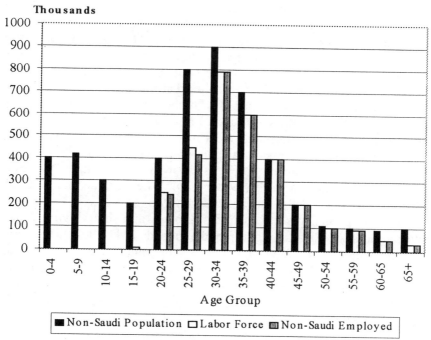

Source: *SAMA*, 2002.

The employment pattern of the non-Saudi expatriate population in Figure 12.9 shows that there is greater unemployment amongst the younger expatriates in the 20-24 and 25-29 age groups; employment rates rise the older the expatriates. Expatriates under the age of 19 are the dependents of foreign workers and are not expected to join the Saudi labor market. The younger expatriate workers tend to be unskilled, with low educational levels. In times of economic downturn, they are the vulnerable ones, more likely to be dismissed than the older, professional/technical fixed-contract term expatriates. Non-Saudi population data and employment patterns only cover those who are officially registered, and therefore do not include large numbers of illegal migrants, such as *Hajj* pilgrims who do not return to their countries, despite intensive efforts by the authorities each year to repatriate them. In economic terms, the illegal expatriates only manage to drive down the wage levels of low-paid legal workers. Government efforts to remove such illegal workers every year does not help *Saudization* much, as most Saudis would not take on their low- paid and menial jobs.

Counting the cost of unemployment

Besides the social cost of unemployment, to which the government now openly admits, unemployment also gives rise to economic waste. The economic loss in output to society is known as "the potential output gap", and has been statistically measured in more developed economies. One such measure is *Okun's Law*, pioneered by the U.S. economist, Arthur Okun using data for the U.S.A. This Law states that each extra percentage point of cyclical unemployment is associated with about a two percent point increase or decrease in the output gap, measured in relation to potential output. Thus, for example, if cyclical unemployment increases from one to two percent of the labor force, the recessionary gap will increase from 2% to 4% of potential GDP. When actual output is below potential output, the resultant output gap is called a *recessionary gap*. When actual output is above potential output, it is called an *expansionary gap*.

Table 12.9 attempts to quantify, through applying *Okun's Law*, the potential loss of Saudi output for the period 1993-2002. There are no detailed statistics available on two major inputs: the actual rate of unemployed (signified as U), and the natural rate of unemployed (signified as U^*). The base year of 1993 was chosen as it coincided with the first official pronouncements on the existence of some level of Saudi unemployment.

Further, non-oil GDP at producer prices was used for the period. This was felt to provide a better estimation for GDP, given the oil sector's volatility and the uncontrolled external factors determining this component. The Saudi Arabian "natural rate of unemployment" (U^*) is based on the author's own estimation, taking into consideration Saudi extended family structures, where the kinship system looked after those who did not have a job or did not wish to enter the labor market, as well as the lower female participation rate examined earlier. As such, compared with other countries, the higher Saudi "natural rate of unemployment" cushions the impact of the actual rate of unemployment.

Table 12.9 Saudi unemployment and potential GDP losses 1993-2002

	(1)	(2)	(3)	(4)	(5)	(6)
Year	Non-Oil GDP at Producer Prices (SR bn)	Unemploy-ment Rate %	% Natural Rate of Unemploy-ment %	Output Gap (%)	Value of Output Gap (SR Bn)	Potential Output (SR Bn)
	(Y)	*(U)*	*(U*)*			*(Y*)*
1993	296.8	7%	5%	4%	11.9	308.6
1994	304.1	8%	6%	4%	12.2	316.3
1995	314.9	9%	6%	6%	18.9	333.8
1996	328.9	9%	7%	4%	13.2	342.1
1997	347.5	11%	8%	6%	20.8	368.3
1998	351.8	12%	9%	6%	21.1	372.9
1999	361.9	13%	9%	8%	28.9	390.8
2000	379.6	15%	10%	10%	37.9	417.5
2001	390.9	18%	11%	14%	54.7	445.6
2002	402.6	20%	12%	16%	64.4	467.0

Legend: Y = Real Output; Y^* = Potential Output
               U = Unemployment Rate U^* = Natural Rate of Unemployment
Sources: Author's own forecasts for (U^*)
               Central Department of Statistics, Media Reports, SAMA, 2002
<u>Footnotes</u>: "Output Gap" is measured by subtracting (3) from (2) and multiplying by a factor
   of 2 as per Okun's formula. The resultant % is multiplied to actual GDP (1) to arrive at
   value of output gap in (5). Potential output (6) is derived from adding (1) plus (5).

The results show a virtual doubling of the Saudi unemployment rate every five to seven years, but at an accelerating pace, with sizeable losses in potential output in GDP. The GDP "losses" increase virtually every year. Our estimate for an unemployment level of 20% for 2002 is below the government's estimate of 31.7%, as reported in the media. If we were to err on the higher side, then the rate of unemployment increases, and potential output losses would be much higher for these years. However, more studies are needed that examine both the natural and real rate of unemployment in the Kingdom.

Saudi labor model: unique to Saudi Arabia?

In this section we argue that the Saudi labor model sets it apart from conventional labor models, by introducing "Saudi specific" interconnected socio-economic preconditions. These are:

Continuous high economic growth: High and sustained economic growth rates were once thought to make it possible for the country to achieve full employment and at the same time to provide sufficient scope for the redistribution of oil wealth. This feeling of "well being" permeated Saudi society at all levels and contributed to the high population growth rates we now witness.

High oil prices: The oil export-led growth model was dependent on a high oil income compatible with the Saudi government's welfare spending and investment. Until the oil shocks of the mid 1980s, the country seemed to believe that oil prices could rise forever and that OPEC was in control of market supply. Today, the government does not publicize the effects of high oil prices, arguing that they are temporary and could be harmful to Saudi interest in the long run. One aim of such a low-key public policy is to avoid building up higher expenditure expectations, based on "windfall gains" from higher oil prices that exceed forecasted revenues at lower oil price levels. The Saudi government's silence on what to do with the higher price oil windfall gains for fiscal 2003 is an illustration of this more subtle policy.

Availability of highly paid jobs in the public sector: In Saudi Arabia, private sector compensation is generally lower than compensation in the government sector. There is a widespread view that the government has better pay and benefits for Saudis than in the private sector. This has been borne out by government data on wage and compensation published by the Central Department of Statistics for 2000. This differs from most developed economies, where private sector pay generally outstrips the public sector, and is more in tune with economic productivity and measurable performance.

Controlling the public sector "free ride"

The figures below show the bias towards public – as opposed to private – sector employment. Figure 12.10 shows that despite a small decrease in the growth rate of public sector employment during 1992 from 1983 levels, by 1999 the public sector still employed over 80% of the total Saudi labor force.

Figure 12.10 % of Saudis in Government and private sector 1983, 1992, 1999

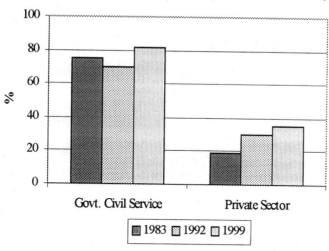

Source: *CDS*, 2002.

The disparity between public and private sector pay is illustrated below in Figure 12.11. It shows that public sector pay and benefits are higher than the private sector at education levels one through eight, according to the government's civil service grades.

Figure 12.11 Saudi Civil Service and private sector monthly wages by educational grade levels 1999.

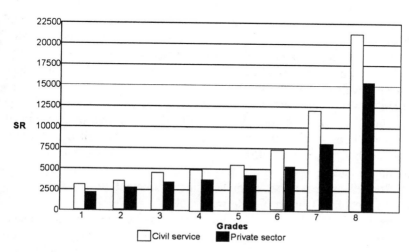

Source: *CDS*, 2001.

The preponderance of employees in the government sector has come at a heavy price. Table 12.10 shows that the wage bill for 1999 stood at 56% of total government expenditures, as opposed to 9% for capital/investment spending during the same year.

Table 12.10 Government wage bill as % of government expenditure and oil revenue 1994-1999

Year	Government wage bill as of percentage of:			Investment expenditure as % of total Gov't. expenditure
	GDP	government expenditure	oil revenue	
1994	18.0%	51.1%	91.5%	14.0%
1995	16.0%	49.5%	81.5%	14.5%
1996	16.0%	45.6%	66.4%	13.5%
1997	24.0%	46.6%	64.5%	10.8%
1998	19.0%	52.8%	101.8%	10.9%
1999	23.0%	56.0%	98.6%	9.0%

Source: IMF, SAMA, Ministry of Planning, National Accounts of Saudi Arabia.

The wage bill has sometimes equalled or exceeded oil revenues, especially during times of falling oil prices. The Saudi government is attempting to rationalise this expenditure and has frozen hiring for certain government positions in a bid to direct more employment to the private sector. However, until the trend is significantly reversed, Saudi Arabia will continue to exhibit one of the world's highest government employment ratios to labor force and population, with 770,000 Saudis employed in the public sector in 1999 compared with 300,000 in 1983 (Abdelgader, 2002). The high wage policy for Saudis in the public sector has had some important economic implications. The successful policy of *Saudization* in the government sector has been accompanied by a financial cost, a function of the wage differential between Saudis and non-Saudis. Studies have shown that had the Saudi government maintained the same ratio of expatriates to Saudis in 1999 as in 1983, the national wage bill would have been 30% less than at current levels (Kapiszewski, 2001).

The large Saudi public sector wage bill is not necessarily reflected in the level of public sector performance. Some studies indicate that an overhaul of this sector's methods and procedures is necessary to improved productivity (AlJannoubi, 2002, Sharway, 2002). The level of *disguised unemployed* hidden in unproductive jobs within the public sector is high in the GCC countries. Studies estimate that disguised unemployment ranges from 40% for Kuwait to 14% for Bahrain (Cordesman, 2003).

Since the late 1980s the Saudi labor model has come under increasing strain, as the set of socio-economic conditions listed earlier began to erode due to the volatility of oil prices. The drastic reduction in oil export revenues after 1986 led to a reduction in economic growth, followed by the appearance of unemployment for the first time. This signalled that the period of financial prosperity and of the welfare state after the oil boom had come to an end. This period was officially pronounced dead by Crown Prince Abdullah bin Abdulaziz during the GCC Summit held in Abu Dhabi in December, 2001, when he announced that citizens had to get used to more austere times, and that the generous government welfare support system was over (Arab News, 31 December 2001).

The historical turning point of the Saudi socio-economic system was also the beginning of a more earnest debate on economic structural adjustment and on the future of the Saudi labor market model.

Structure of the Saudi labor market

Table 12.11 sets out the national employment structure during the Seventh Development Plan period (2000-2004), and Table 12.12 highlights the government's aim to ensure that the main growth of the labor market comes through the private non-oil sector. This is forecasted to grow to 6.472 million by 2004 from 6.161 million in 1999. Some 328,000 new jobs are to be created, of which 16,000 will be in the government sector. The non-oil sector, non-oil mining, utilities and manufacturing are slated to grow the fastest, with the rest of the sectors showing minor increases.

According to Table 12.12, the composition of the labor force is forecasted to change over the period 1999-2004. The Saudi private sector should increase their share of jobs from around 39% in 1999 to 48% in 2004. This would take the national average (including the government sector) to over 53.2% by 2002, compared with 44.2% in 1999. The overwhelming majority of government jobs will be in Saudi hands by 2004, with the Saudi government's employment share rising to 86.5% by 2004 from 78.2% in 1999.

Table 12.11 Structure of the labor market in the Kingdom by sector during the period 1999-2004

(Thousand)

	1999		2004	
	No. of Workers	% Distribution	No. of Workers	% Distribution
Total Labor Force	7,176.3	100.0	7,504.9	100.0
Saudis	3,172.9	44.2	3990.2	53.2
Non-Saudis	4,003.4	55.8	3,514.7	46.8
Total Labor at Government Sector	916.2	12.8	923.3	12.4
Saudis	716.5	78.2	806.1	86.5
Non-Saudis	199.7	21.8	126.2	13.5
Total Labor at Private Sector	6,260.1	87.2	6,572.6	87.6
Saudis	2,422.7	38.7	3,184.1	48.4
Non-Saudis	3,837.4	61.3	3,388.5	51.6

Source: *Ministry of Planning*, 2001, *SAMA*, 2002, pp. 313.

Table 12.12 Employment structure during the Seventh Development Plan
(2000-2004)

Description	Employment (Thousands)		Share (%)		Thousands	Change (%)	Average Annual Growth (%)
	1999	2004	1999	2004			
1. Private Non-Oil Sector:	6161.2	6,472.2	85.9	86.2	311.0	94.6	1.0
1.1 Private Producing Sectors:	2273.3	2460.6	31.7	32.8	187.3	57.0	1.6
Agriculture	557.9	582.3	7.8	7.8	24.4	7.4	0.9
Non-Oil Mining	13.2	14.7	0.2	0.2	1.5	0.5	2.2
Manufacturing	589.0	661.0	8.2	8.8	72.0	21.9	2.3
*Oil Refining	21.5	21.8	0.3	0.3	0.3	0.1	0.3
*Petrochemical	9.4	10.1	0.1	0.1	0.7	0.2	1.4
*Other Industries	558.1	629.1	7.8	8.4	71.0	21.6	2.4
Electricity, Gas and Water	93.5	101.5	1.3	1.4	8.0	2.4	1.7
Construction	1019.7	1101.1	14.2	14.7	81.4	24.8	1.5
1.2 Private Services Sectors:	3887.9	4011.6	54.2	53.5	123.7	37.6	0.6
Trade	1036.6	1071.2	14.4	14.3	34.6	10.5	0.7
Transport and Communication	299.2	310.1	4.2	4.1	10.9	3.3	0.7
Finance and Real Estate	334.9	375.2	4.7	5.0	40.3	12.3	2.3
Community and Personal Services	2217.2	2255.1	30.9	30.0	37.9	11.5	0.3
2. Government Services	916.2	932.3	12.8	12.4	16.1	4.9	0.3
3. Non-Oil Sectors	7077.4	7404.5	98.6	98.7	327.1	99.5	0.9
4. Crude Oil and Natural Gas	98.9	100.4	1.4	1.3	1.5	0.5	0.3
Total Sectoral	7176.3	7504.9	100.0	100.0	328.6	100.0	0.9

Source: *Ministry of Planning, Seventh Development Plan*, 2000.

The Ministry of Planning data is not explicit on how these forecasts meet the needs of the private sector, and there is no breakdown between male and female labor entrants. All that the data confirm is a freeze on government jobs and that any meaningful Saudization and job creation in the plan must come from the private sector. This government assumption was the basis of our earlier crude estimates of labor market entrants' and our forecasted unemployment levels until 2013.

Professional structure of the Saudi labor force

Analyzing the labor force by professional classification, Figure 12.12 show that around 62% of the total Saudi and non-Saudi workforce is concentrated in the services, production/construction and transport sectors. Another 15% are in scientific and technical jobs, while clerical/sales jobs make up around 15% of the professions. Those who were classified as "administrative and business directors" were about 2% of the workforce. Agriculture and fishing has remained around 8% of the work force for the past few years, despite the pressure of urbanization.

Figure 12.12 Professional structure of labor force in the Kingdom of Saudi Arabia in 2002

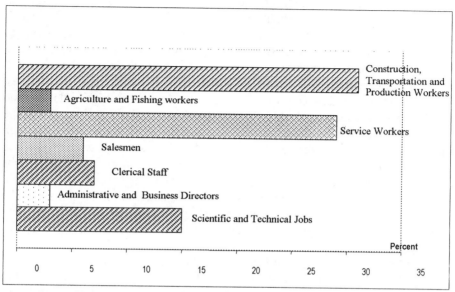

Source: *SAMA*, 2002.

The "duality" of the Saudi wage market

There has been a long-term erosion in the average wage levels of Saudis and non-Saudis, both male and female. Table 12.13 illustrates the gradual decline in wage levels from 1995 to 2001; non-Saudis (male and female) have been most affected. The average wage of Saudi males has also consistently fallen since 1996 to reach SR 6,684 in 2001 from SR 7,298 in 1994. There has also been a large difference between the Saudi and the non-Saudi average wage levels.

Table 12.13 Average wage in Saudi Arabia during the period 1994-2001

	Saudis		Non-Saudis	
	Males	**Females**	**Males**	**Females**
1994	7,298	3,660	2,153	3,133
1995	7,896	3,864	2,142	3,016
1996	7,711	4,090	2,103	2,966
1997	7,570	4,144	2,046	2,716
1998	7,473	3,812	1,934	2,740
1999	7,124	3,489	1,858	2,505
2000	6,877	3,217	1,763	2,391
2001	6,684	3,151	1,710	2,403
2002	5,984	2,703	1,543	2,221

Source: *Council of Labor Force, SAMA*, 2004, p. 314.

The average wage level for a non-Saudi male fell to SR 1,543 by 2002 from SR 2,153 in 1994. This is due to the fact that a large number of non-Saudi labor have low-level skills and work in wage professions. Again, such low wage levels are a problem for potential *Saudization* and for Saudi entrants. There is anecdotal evidence that some Saudis are beginning to accept lower salaries in areas that were once deemed to be "beneath" them, such as restaurants, barbershops, porter services and others, but these are still rare. Wide variations are found in actual salaries: the banking, services, insurance, legal and accounting professions command high salaries and benefits that are comparable to, if not better than, similar positions in Europe or the USA. Similarly, the expatriate wage levels mask some extremely high salary levels for professionals and technical experts, whose tax-free compensation packages provide superior levels of earnings than similar jobs in their home countries. Overall though, decreased economic growth, volatile oil prices and government expenditures, competition for jobs and the private sector's desire to control labor costs have together tended to create a downward push on wage levels in the Kingdom. This is set to continue for the foreseeable future.

The "duality" of wages between Saudis and non-Saudis can be explained in terms of two distinct labor markets. This case was made by a Saudi economist, and it seems applicable to the wider GCC labor market (Al Sheikh, 2003).

Figure 12.13 Duality of GCC labour markets

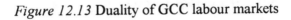
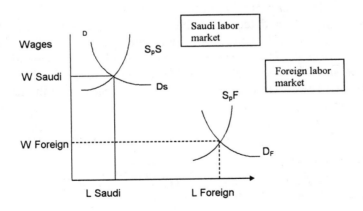

Figure 12.13 sets out the concept in terms of differentiated demand and supply for Saudi and non-Saudi labor markets. In the Figure, Ds and SpS stand for demand and supply for Saudi labor, while D_F and S_pF stand for demand and supply for foreign labor.

As pointed out earlier, there are wide differences in wage levels not only between Saudis and expatriates, but also between different skill groups of expatriates. As such, the demand and supply for foreign labor in Saudi Arabia exhibits a greater degree of market segmentation and supply elasticity, leading to different wage levels amongst foreign workers. By supply elasticity we mean the responsiveness of the supply of labor to changes in the wage level. This is illustrated in Figure 12.14.

Figure 12.14 Demand supply for expatriate labor in Saudi Arabia by market segmentation

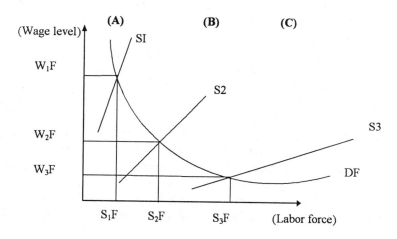

Figure 12.14 shows that in segment **(A)**, the supply of expatriate labor is relatively inelastic due to specialized technical or managerial skills, and as such, these foreign workers enjoy higher wages at W1F levels. Segment **(B)** shows a relatively more elastic supply curve for foreign workers, including middle management, accountants, salesmen and others who command a lower salary level at W2F, for Saudis are more competitive over these positions in terms of similar skills and training. Segment **(C)** shows the wage level paid in the almost wholly elastic supply curve of manual and menial foreign labor at W3F. A small adjustment in the supply of labor causes sharp movements to salary levels. Effective short-term *Saudization* policies should aim for job creation in segment **(B)** and eventual knowledge-based, high-value job migration to segment **(A)**.

Conclusion: expectations, realism and adaptation

The labor market in Saudi Arabia has changed due to internal population dynamics, as well as a breakdown of the old Saudi labor model. The policy of creating special privileges for nationals in the labor market has had additional adverse, long-term effects. For the younger nationals, it has meant growing up with the assumption that a standard of living higher than that of non-nationals is an inalienable right, irrespective of any personal contribution to the wealth and well-being of society as a whole. By guaranteeing positions in the public sector for their citizens, the authorities unintentionally engendered the notion that they were the universal benefactors of their citizens. Strong public signals are now being sent out that this will have to change, and that employment will be based on skill, education and productivity. The private sector has been arguing for this, rather than the arbitrary policies of *Saudization* of economic sectors. According to press reports in mid-2003, some Saudi industrialists threatened to move their factories to Dubai in response to what they described as increasing pressure on them to accelerate *Saudization*.

While Saudi Arabia somewhat lags behind other GCC states, such as Bahrain, Kuwait, Oman and UAE, the increased employment of Saudi women is expected to continue in the near future. Among Saudi women there is a strong interest in working and in attaining an improved education. The government has also been willing to openly address this issue.

Increased participation of women in the labor market should be possible due to the spread of modern technology that allows employees to be productively engaged electronically, while remaining in protected places (for example, banking call centres). However, as we know from the low participation rate for women in the Saudi labor force, there is still some social pressure on them to accept the traditional housewife role and not to go out and work.

Current government policies to reduce foreign labor and encourage *Saudization* have had mixed results. It has been difficult to introduce and effectively manage the regulations restricting the number of expatriates, because the importation of foreign labor enjoys strong support from the powerful lobbies of trading and merchant families. Their fortunes have been built to a large extent on cheap expatriate labor. The sponsorship system of foreign workers or *kefalaa* artificially hinders market demand and supply forces, creating rigidities in certain sectors with surplus labor and supply shortages in others. This results in further importation of foreign labor under the sponsorship system. The government should consider a policy of gradually scrapping the sponsorship system after compensating those employers for the costs of sponsorship. These costs can be recouped from workers' wages on a pro-rata basis. In the short-run, the Saudi government has decided to limit the number of new work visas they grant in order to curb new foreign labor entrants to the market and to create a Saudi "labor supply" pool. This has caused friction among some parts of the private sector, but the Saudi Minister of Labor has made this restrictive policy a central plank in his effort to direct Saudi labor to available jobs.

The liberalization of labor policies could become an issue during the process of gaining WTO membership, with WTO provisions demanding that member states allow free movement of labor. This could involve scrapping local sponsorship laws. Furthermore, the International Labor Organization (ILO), of which Saudi Arabia is a member, may challenge the continuation of existing polices towards foreign workforces. The ILO has been urging Saudi Arabia, as well as other GCC countries, to accept basic International Labor Standards and to ratify relevant conventions relating to workers rights.

Summary of key points

- *The current state of the Saudi labour market and unemployment is becoming a major issue of concern to the Saudi government. Underlying causes are the relatively young age profile of the population, high fertility rates, and a mismatch between Saudi labour entrants and market needs in terms of required skills*
- *Saudization has become one tool by which the government aims to replace foreigners with Saudis, using a dual program of incentives and visa restrictions for foreign workers.*
- *The private sector would be the main source of Saudi employment generation as government jobs become frozen at current levels for the next decade. Saudi employment in the private sector indicates that the Saudization policy has had mixed results, with only public utilities, and finance achieving majority Saudi employment.*
- *Changing perceptions about culture and work ethics is important. Indications are that Saudi youth are beginning to be more realistic about their job expectations and adapt their skills to meet market needs. The private sector continues to raise issues of concern that need addressing before they increase the level of Saudization: labor costs, control over the process of production (with expatriate labor easier to control), Saudi job tenure, inadequate qualifications, mobility, and lack of integration in a multicultural work environment.*
- *Both the private sector and the government are focusing on improving the education and skill base of job entrants. Saudi planning is becoming more focused on sector specific employment goals.*
- *The issue of foreign labor needs to be addressed carefully and sympathetically, as the Kingdom is still in need of large numbers of skilled expatriates for the foreseeable future. The presence of other diverse nationalities amongst a local population can sometimes create a two way intangible benefit to both sides.*

- *It is difficult to quantify precisely the current level of the Saudi labour force as not everyone registers for employment. As such, it is also difficult to calculate the precise number of unemployed Saudis. This is doubly difficult for Saudi female labour, where it is estimated that Saudi female labour participation levels are among the lowest in the world.*
- *Unemployment not only causes social problems and a rise in unemployment related crimes, but has an economic cost to society. It is estimated that around SR 280 billion was lost in GDP "output gap" between 1993-2002 due to Saudi unemployment levels, using a simplified "Okun's Law" calculation for the output gap.*
- *The Saudi labor market is characterized by its "dual" nature for Saudis and non-Saudis in terms of differentiated demand and supply of labor for these two labor segments, as well as different supply and demand elasticities..*

Critical thinking

1. "Saudi Arabia has 4 million foreigners. As such, Saudi Arabia has no unemployment problems. Saudis can take over foreigners jobs". Discuss this statement. Is this the correct means to solve Saudi unemployment?
2. How do you calculate the effects and consequences of unemployment on a society such as Saudi Arabia?
3. "Controlling foreign visas would solve the issue of employing more Saudis in Saudi companies". Discuss the pros and cons of adopting such a policy.
4. "In the end, free market forces will determine supply and demand for labor and the majority of Saudis will be employed". Do you agree that this approach is the best? Can the private sector be trusted to employ Saudis even under these scenarios without government intervention?
5. "Time and education will bring down the high population growth rates seen today. As such, the labor market will balance itself in the future". Discuss.

Chapter 13

EDUCATION AND KNOWLEDGE FOR DEVELOPMENT

If a man empties his purse into his head no one can take it from him.

Longfellow

Learning outcomes:

By the end of this section, you should understand:

- *The growth in education expenditure to meet population needs*
- *Facing up to the globalization challenges*
- *The Saudi educational structure*
- *Moves to restructure the educational system*
- *Saudi education and market needs*
- *Options for change in the education structure*

Introduction

Saudi Arabia has been able to build a large educational infrastructure within a short time because of the financial resources they derive from oil revenues. The growth in Saudi expenditure on human resource development accounted for SR 53 billion or 24% of 2002's budget allocation, the second highest category after defence. The 2004 budget raised this allocation to SR 61.7 billion or 28% of total expenditure. As a result of this consistent expenditure pattern, literacy rates and enrolment ratios at all levels have been increasing (Ministry of Planning, 2002, Arab News, 16 December 2003).

There are a number of reasons why education plays such a crucial role in Saudi Arabia: its smaller population, the influx of expatriate labour, the lack of natural resources besides exhaustible oil and a relatively new educational system. The major issue, however, is not the amount of expansion, but rather the orientation of the educational system. A major problem with this system is that it attributes high social prestige to university education, while underestimating the significance of technological and vocational education. It is widely, if unfairly, believed that only school dropouts and academically poor students enter technical training (Kibbi, 2002). This belief is further strengthened by employment policies which, until recently, encouraged an educational structure that offered priority employment opportunities in the government sector to university graduates, thus making technical and vocational education even less attractive and less socially desirable (The Economist, 1997).

In development literature, the role of education in building "human capital" has been consistently highlighted. The positive role of higher education in the construction of knowledge-based economies and democratic societies is highly promoted by international organizations such as the World Bank (Larocque, 2002). These groups stress that higher education exercises a direct influence on national productivity, which in turn largely determines living standards and a country's ability to compete in the global economy. Investment in quality training and higher education generates major external benefits that are crucial for knowledge-driven economic and social development (World Bank, 2001).

Technological progress and the "diffusion" of scientific and technical innovations lead to higher productivity. That encourages improvement in all sectors of the economy. Higher skill levels in the labour force – an outcome of increased educational levels – and improved education permits workers to use new technology and boosts productivity. As such, the ability of any society to produce, select, adapt and commercialize knowledge is critical for sustained economic growth and improved living standards. In relation to its population, size, and educational investment, Saudi Arabia has produced a negligible number of commercial patents, compared to other countries. Singapore, Malaysia and Korea have invested smaller amounts per capita in higher education than Saudi Arabia, but seem to have used it better to generate sustained economic growth. As Saudi Arabia continues with its accession talks to join the World Trade Organization (WTO), it faces both opportunities and threats stemming from changes in the global environment, and specifically in the educational sector.

Meeting the globalization challenges

Developing economies face significant new trends in the global environment, the most critical of which is the increasing importance of knowledge, the main driver of growth within this information and communication revolution (Salmi, 2002).

Today, economic growth is as much a process of knowledge accumulation as of capital accumulation. Firms in developed countries devote more and more of their investment to knowledge-based intangibles such as training, research and development, patents, licensing and design. The aim is to gain a competitive edge over others in the global economy.

The same applies to countries as well as to companies; information and communication technologies (ICT) speed up the flow of knowledge across boundaries.

However, joining the global knowledge-based economy brings with it both opportunities and threats. Some of these issues are highlighted in Table 13.1.

Table 13.1 Opportunities and threats stemming from changes in the global environment

Change factor	Opportunities	Threats
Growing role of knowledge	• Possibility of leapfrogging in selected areas of economic growth • Resolution of social problems (food, security, health, water supply, energy, environment)	• Increasing knowledge gap among nations.
ICT revolution	• Easier access to knowledge and information	• Growing digital divide among and within nations
Global labour market	• Easier access to the expertise, skills and knowledge of professionals	• Growing brain drain and loss of advanced human capital
Political and social change	• Positive environment for reform • Spread of democracy	• Growing brain drain and political instability • Loss of human resources

On the positive side, the role of higher education in the construction of knowledge-based economies and of democratic societies is more influential than ever. On the negative side, the technological transformation of knowledge-based societies carries the real danger of a growing digital, and by implication, economic divide between nations.

Figure 13.1 demonstrates how, according to World Bank studies, two countries – South Korea and Ghana – that had almost identical per capita GDP in 1957/1958, diverged in their economic growth paths by the late 1990s, due to the place of knowledge in their development.

Figure 13.1 illustrates the significant difference a knowledge-based development strategy makes to economic growth. Such knowledge-based development exercises a direct influence on national productivity, which largely determines living standards, as the per capita divergence between Ghana and South Korea confirms. This development approach supports knowledge-driven economic growth strategies and poverty reduction by (a) training a qualified and adaptable labour force, including scientists, professionals, technicians, teachers, and business leaders; (b) generating new knowledge; and (c) building the capacity to access existing stores of global knowledge and to adapt that knowledge to local use (Salmi, 2002, Dukhayil, 2002, Larocque, 2002).

Figure 13.1 Knowledge as a factor in income differences between
countries: Ghana and the Republic of South Korea 1956 –90

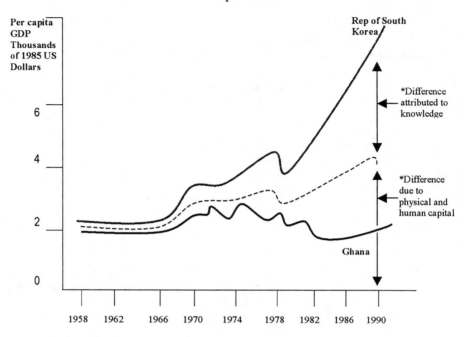

Source: *World Bank* (1999).

Education in Saudi Arabia

Education has been an important unifying and nation-building
facilitator from the proclamation of the modern Kingdom of Saudi Arabia
in 1932 to date (Al-Rasheed, 2002, Champion, 2003). Education advances
nation-building by promoting greater social cohesion, trust in social
institutions, national participation and appreciation of diversity in social
class. These are the *positive externalities* of applying a national educational
programme. Saudi Arabia's wealth in oil resources has provided the means
for broader economic and national infrastructural development, including
education. This natural desire to develop the nation's human resources has
been undertaken with enthusiasm by successive rulers of the Kingdom who
have taken a great personal interest in this area (Al-Rasheed, 2002).

However, the information and communication revolution that is
sweeping the globe is having a profound effect on Saudi Arabian society in
the social, educational and economic spheres. It has not been lost upon the
Saudi government that new communication technologies have had a
positive economic impact on many developing countries, such as China,
India, Malaysia and the nearby GCC countries, particularly Dubai and
Bahrain. With the help of a relatively effective educational system, these
countries have all successfully created information technology that allows

them to compete in the global market. Dubai's "Internet City" is indeed a powerful model for Saudi Arabia. However, as the figures below show, there is still a wide divide between the distribution of Internet access and the world's population. The USA and Canada, with 5.1% of the world's population, account for 65% of Internet host sites , compared to around 6% of Internet sites for the developing countries, which have 80% of the world's population (World Bank, 2002).

Figure 13.2 Distribution of Internet hosts and of world population, by region 1999

(i) Distribution of Internet hosts

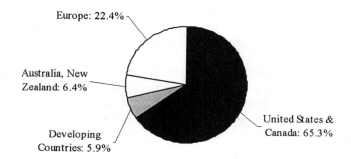

(ii) Distribution of world population

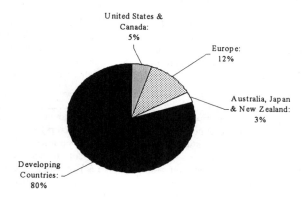

Source: Data from *International Telecommunications Union and the United Nations Populations Fund, World Bank,* 2002.

According to a recent World Bank report (Salmi, 2002), the spread of technology and information communication is still not widespread amongst the Saudi population. The study revealed that for the year 2000, there were 1.58 Internet hosts per 10,000 people in Saudi Arabia against 2,419 for the USA, 129 telephone main lines per 1000 people for Saudi Arabia against 640 for the USA, and 57.4 personal computers per 1000 people for Saudi Arabia against 511.6 for the USA. Saudi Arabia has still a long way to go to bridge this digital divide.

Globalization, declining communication and transportation costs, and the opening of borders combine to facilitate increased movement of skilled people, leading to a global market place for advanced human capital. In the 21st century market place, richer countries try in many ways to attract and retain the world's best-trained minds. For example, according to the World Bank, nearly 25% of the science and engineering students in U.S. graduate schools come from other countries, and in 2000 the USA made available 600,000 new visas for immigrant scientists and engineers (World Bank, 2002).

With its relatively high population growth of 3.8% p.a. and its fluctuating economic wealth due to erratic oil revenues, Saudi Arabia faces challenges in the educational field that have wider implications for human development and economic growth (Looney, 1989). These challenges are summarized in Table 13.2.

Table 13.2 Summary of challenges facing Saudi Arabian education

Economic	*Access*
• Education spending comprises 26 percent of the national budget	• Population growth of 3.8 percent per annum
• 96 percent of the national budget goes on wages and salaries.	• 50 percent of the population is under 18 years of age
• Budget deficit is 7.6 percent of GDP	• The higher education sector cannot accommodate over 30 percent of the high school graduates
• High percent of Saudi males are unemployed while only 6 percent of Saudi females are in employment	• An estimated 300,000 students in higher education by 2010
Relevance	*Quality*
• New teaching methodology, materials and syllabi needed to meet the needs of the knowledge economy.	• High, though reducing, drop-out and repetition rates
• There is a mismatch between skill development and labour market requirements	• Wide variation in the ability of entrants at each education level
• English language instruction from primary school level is important	• Lack of national capacity to assess educational quality and trends against comparable international data.
	• Adaptability to worldwide information base

The summary table highlights the issues of relevance and quality facing the Saudi educational system today. Current educational norms affect work ethic perceptions.

A survey of Saudi and U.S. male undergraduate students showed that Saudi students in higher education placed greater emphasis on social, non-economic issues in their perception of potential benefits resulting from their studies. U.S. students gave a lower priority to issues of status. The results are set out in Table 13.3.

Table 13.3 Potential benefits from higher education: Saudi Arabian and U.S. college students' perceptions

Benefits	*Private issues*	*Public spill-over*	*Saudi students*	*U.S. students*
Economic	• Higher salaries	Greater productivity	M	H
	• Employment security	National and regional development	H	H
	• Higher savings	Reduced reliance on government financial support	L	H
	• Improved working conditions	Increased consumption	M	H
	• Personal and professional mobility and advancement	Increased potential for transformation from low-skill industrial to knowledge-based economy	M	H
	• Leadership	Nation-building and development of leadership	H	L
	• Being a decision - maker	Affecting society's future	H	L
	• Improved personal status	Public standing and status	H	L
Social	• Conventionality	Rigid social customs	M	L
	• Healthier lifestyle and higher life expectancy	Improved health	M	H
	• Autonomy	Initiative culture	L	H
	• Working by self	Initiative culture	L	H

Note: H = High Importance   M = Moderate Importance   L = Low Importance
Source: *Survey of KFUPM students* and *U.S. college students conducted* during 2001/2002, *Lawrence Shatkin.*

The table of student perceptions basically reflects the current values and attitudes of Saudi society, with higher emphasis placed on prestige and social mobility rather than on professional mobility and adapting to knowledge-based economy (Wright et. al., 1996, Binzager, 2003).

The Saudi educational structure

In quantitative terms, the growth in educational levels of both males and females in Saudi Arabia has been impressive on all counts. According to the World Bank (Diwan and Girgis, 2002) and the Saudi Ministry of Planning (Ministry of Planning, 2002), during the last decade alone, the average education level increased 27% or by more than 1.5 years to 6.6 years on average. The implication for a rise in future productivity in the economy is positive, as World Bank research has tended to support the finding that a one-year rise in a nation's education level generates a 10% increase in GDP (Diwan and Girgis, 2002).

In comparison with other developing countries, Saudi Arabia does well, as seen from Figure 13.3.

Figure 13.3 Average year of education by region 1999

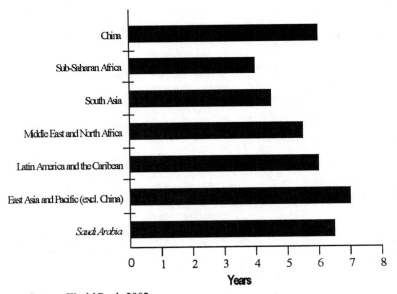

Source: *World Bank*, 2002.

Figure 13.3 shows that in 1999, only East Asia (excluding China) sharply exceeded Saudi Arabia for average years of education. The remarkable decline in the number of Saudis in lower levels of education occurred despite an increase in the Saudi population over the same period. In trying to provide quality education to all its citizens, Saudi Arabia is faced by one of the highest population growth rates, a youthful population profile, urbanization and high fertility rates, compared many other regions of the world. This is set out in Table 13.4.

Table 13.4 Projected comparative demographic and development trends: Saudi Arabia and other Arab countries, OECD, developing countries and world averages 1975-2015

Trend	Year	*Saudi Arabia*	Arab Countries	Developing Countries	OECD	World Average
Total population (million)	1975	*7.3*	126.0	2,908.0	925.0	4,066
	2000	*22.0*	246.0	4,695.0	1,129.0	6,057
	2015	*32.7*	333.0	5,773.0	1,209.0	7,207
Annual growth rates of population (%)	1975 – 2000	*4.1*	2.7	1.9	0.8	1.6
	2000 – 2015	*3.0*	2.0	1.4	0.5	1.2
Urbanization (ratio to total)	1975	*58.4*	40.3	26.1	70.4	37.9
	2000	*86.2*	52.8	40.0	76.9	47.2
	2015	*91.0*	59.0	48.5	80.4	53.7
Population below 15 years (ratio to total population)	2000	*42.9*	37.6	32.7	20.4	29.9
	2015	*38.6*	32.2	28.1	17.3	25.8
Fertility rate (infants per woman)	1970 – 1975	*7.3*	6.5	5.4	2.5	4.5
	1995 – 2000	*6.2*	4.1	3.1	1.8	2.8

Source: *SAMA*, 2003, p. 296, *UNDP Development Programme*, 2002.

Table 13.4 reveals that extremely rapid population growth has taken place, accompanied by substantial social changes, especially in the urbanization of Saudi Arabia. What was once a rural and isolated society has evolved into a largely urbanized one, exposed to a wide range of media, and dependent on an energy-based economy. The trend for urbanization has been matched by a major increase in the level of education.

According to the latest data, illiteracy rates are now very low in Saudi Arabia and compare favourably with many developing and other Arab countries. Figure 13.4 sets out the level of educational attainment for Saudis, male and female, over the age of ten, for the year 2000. We note that Saudi male illiteracy stood at around 20% and female at 28%. According to commentators, most illiterates were found in the older age groups (Wilson et. al., 2003) as adult literacy programs have only had a limited impact.

Figure 13.4 Breakdown of Saudi population (ten years old and above) by educational status in 2000

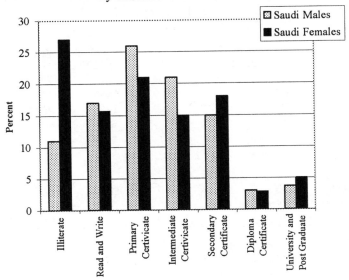

Source: *SAMA*, 2003, p. 311.

As of 2003, the number of all general education students enrolled was 4.29 million, of whom 2.24 million were male and 2.05 million were female (SAMA, 2002, p.290). These students were served by a total of 23,464 schools, of which 12,038 were for males and 11,426 were for females. The students were taught by 167,880 male and 179,172 female teachers. The pupil/teacher and pupil/school ratios for 2000 and 2001 and are given in Table 13.5.

Table 13.5 Saudi pupil/teacher and pupil/school ratios 2002/2003

	2000	*2001*	*2003*
Pupil/Teacher Ratio			
• Male	13.7	13.1	13.3
• Female	11.2	11.1	11.4
Pupil/School Ratio			
• Male	190.9	189.8	186.1
• Female	186.1	184.5	179.4

Source: *Ministry of Education*, 2002, *SAMA*, 2004.

The ratios for Saudi Arabia compare favourably with most developed countries, and are far superior to developing countries. They corroborate the significant budgetary allocations for educational development, which will be analyzed later in more detail. In spite of such impressive statistics, there is still much room for educational development. Reservations as to the quality of Saudi education are commonplace, and hence the figures mask the issue of qualitative education delivery and the state of the teaching profession at the general education level. According to surveys on this subject conducted for the Gulf Cooperation Council (GCC) countries, the following were the major problems relating to teachers (Arab News, 1 June 2003):

- Lack of expertise
- Poor commitment to the teaching profession
- Lack of teacher participation in setting curriculum, resulting in teacher apathy and low morale
- Low esteem of teachers in the eyes of society as a whole
- Teachers "moon-lighting" for additional income

As for the curriculum, one study (Dukhayil, 2002) made the following criticisms:

- Repetition and duplication of information from year to year
- Too much material, forcing memorization rather than absorbing contents intellectually
- Unrelated to the modern age
- Outdated information, often relying on the translation and copying of other sources
- No attention to special students – whether gifted, talented or those with disabilities
- Weak English language and science curriculum
- Students taught to obey authority and discouraged from showing initiative and creativity

While there are undoubtedly highly committed, dedicated and professional teachers at all levels in Saudi Arabia, yet, according to an employers' survey, there has been a noticeable decline in the quality of student graduates achievements especially in higher education. Saudi private sector employers are beginning to voice some concern (Binzager, 2003, Arab News, 2 June 2003, 27 May 2003).

A recent survey of 280 female college students in Dammam (Mishkhas, 2004) found that educational problems at colleges were still unresolved. Students cited "difficult curriculum, tough teachers, no choice in selecting their majors and lack of preparedness to handle research independently" as major factors. These issues, however, have not deterred Saudis from pursuing further education. Education is perceived as bringing economic and social advancement to those who continue to its higher levels. This became clear in a 2000 survey of average monthly compensation for Saudis and non-Saudis who had attained different levels of education, and is set out in Table 13.6.

Table 13.6 Average monthly compensation (Saudi Riyals) of Saudis and non-Saudis by educational levels in 2000

Educational level	Saudi	Non-Saudi
Illiterate	3,155	1,136
Read and Write	3,450	1,260
Primary School	4,600	1,378
Intermediate School	5,437	1,587
Secondary School	7,200	2,580
Intermediate School	6,810	2,880
University Graduate	10,893	10,856
Average (SR)	7,043	2,354

Source: *Central Department of Statistics*, 2000.

The survey also showed that compensation to Saudi males is, on average, twice that of Saudi females with the same education, and that compensation for Saudis is, on average, triple that of non-Saudis with the same level of education. The only exception is at the university and post-graduate levels, where it is twice the difference. The unequal compensation levels currently paid to Saudis and non-Saudis pose challenges for labour policy in the Kingdom, especially for the private sector, which is being forced into employing more Saudis under accelerated *Saudization* programs.

Pride in academic achievements, but inherent weaknesses

For sustainable economic development to take place in Saudi Arabia, the educational system's output has to be geared towards the economy's current and future needs. Figure 13.5 is a flow chart of education and training provided in Saudi Arabia under the government's auspices.

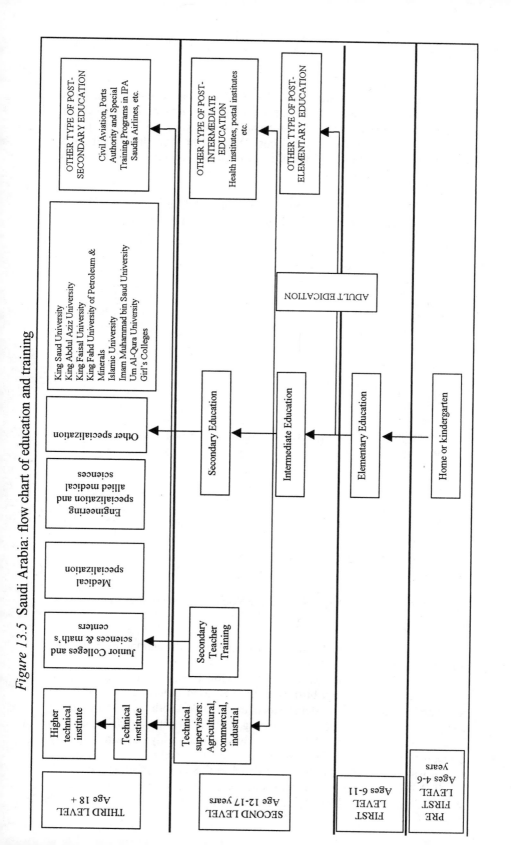

Figure 13.5 Saudi Arabia: flow chart of education and training

At first glance, it would seem that the Kingdom caters for different types of educational needs, right through from kindergarten to university, as well as specialized technical and vocational institutes. Girls' education is catered for, albeit on a segregated basis from elementary level, and today girls account for just under 50% of all students in general education, as we see in Table 13.7.

Table 13.7. Number of students, teaching staff and schools at the general education level in the Kingdom 1996-2002

	1996	1998	2000	2003	% Share in the total (2003)
Number of students					**% of female students**
Primary	2,248,122	2,243,613	2,285,328	2,342,214	47.9%
Intermediate	887,520	982,430	1,073,175	1,093,946	46.1%
Secondary	497,857	641,542	755,419	855,525	48.3%
Total	3,633,499	3,867,585	4,113,922	4,291,685	47.6%
Number of Teachers					**% of female teachers**
Primary	169,321	182,534	190,570	198,181	51.4%
Intermediate	69,310	80,547	86,686	97,131	49.5%
Secondary	35,746	47,723	55,277	68,392	52.4%
Total	274,377	310,804	332,533	363,704	51.1%
Number of Schools					**% of girls' schools**
Primary	11,217	11,858	12,415	12,880	50.4%
Intermediate	4,895	5,505	6,104	6,735	45.6%
Secondary	2,316	2,841	3,290	3,849	48.6%
Total	18,428	20,204	21,809	23,464	48.7%

Source: *Statistics Card for the Academic* Year 2002, *Ministry of Education, SAMA,* 2004, p. 290.

The growth in student numbers has been truly astounding over a short period of time.

However, to put the growth in educational enrolment in perspective given Saudi Arabia's high birth rate, in 1980 total general enrolment in the Kingdom's educational systems stood at 547,000, with girls representing 135,000 or 25% (Ministry of Planning, 2002). The first girls' school in Saudi Arabia opened in 1960. Girls' education has truly come a long way compared to the early days of the Kingdom's establishment, when the debate was on whether to allow female education at all (Al-Rasheed, 2002, Baadi, 1982). In term of numbers, girls seem to be more eager for higher education than boys, which we can see in Table 13.8.

Table 13.8 Saudi Arabia: statistical summary of higher education during the academic year 2003

Level	Number of enrolled students			Number of graduates			No. of institutions
	Male	Female	Total	Male	Female	Total	
Universities	142,465	68,943	*211,430*	20,520	6,541	*30,061*	108
Girl Colleges (Ministry of Education)	0	232,884	*232,884*	0	30,684	*30,684*	87
Teacher Colleges (Ministry of Education)	29,989	0	*29,989*	4,932	0	*4,932*	18
Medical Colleges and Institutions	4,711	2,682	*7,393*	10,025	540	*1,565*	38
Jubayl and Yanbu' Industrial Colleges	3,856	0	*3,856*	454	0	*454*	2
Technical Colleges	33,876	0	*33,876*	4,802	0	*4,802*	20
Private Colleges	745	797	*1,542*	2	0	*2*	6
Institute of Public Administration	3,714	470	*184*	953	154	*1,107*	1
Health Affairs in the National Guard	0	190	*190*	0	0	*0*	1
Total	*219,356*	*305,984*	*525,344*	*32,806*	*40,919*	*73,607*	*281*

Source: Information Centre General Department for Studies and Information, Ministry of Higher Education, SAMA 2004, p. 293.

Table 13.8's figures for the universities sector alone seem to indicate a low ratio for women, with a total of 211,000 students enrolled in 2003, of whom 32% were female. The disparity is partially explained by the fact that some 232,000 Saudi female students were enrolled in women-only colleges, lifting the overall share of Saudi females to 55% out of a total of 523,000 enrolled higher education students in 2003.

The phenomenon of higher enrolments for women's education is not particular to Saudi Arabia: the rest of the Gulf Cooperation Council (GCC) member states exhibit the same trends. It also seems to hold for other developed economies, as we can see in Table 13.9, which shows gross higher education enrolment for the period 1980-1998 and a breakdown by gender for 1998.

Table 13.9 Gross higher education enrolment rates (%) – selected years 1980-1998 and by gender 1998

Country	1980	1985	1990	1995	1998		
					Total	*Male*	*Female*
Middle East:							
Bahrain	5.0	12.8	17.7	20.0	*25.0*	*19.0*	*30.0*
Egypt	16.1	18.1	15.8	20.2	*21.0*	*24.2*	*15.9*
Jordan	13.4	13.1	16.1	16.0	*17.9*	*26.3*	*29.4*
Kuwait	11.3	16.6	12.5	19.2	*19.3*	*14.6*	*24.0*
Lebanon	30.0	27.8	28.9	27.0	*27.0*	*27.2*	*26.8*
Oman	0.5	0.8	4.1	5.3	*8.0*	*9.0*	*7.0*
Qatar	10.4	20.7	27.0	27.5	*26.6*	*13.6*	*40.9*
Saudi Arabia	*7.1*	*10.6*	*11.6*	*15.8*	*19.0*	*16.0*	*21.0*
UAE	3.1	6.8	9.2	11.0	*13.0*	*15.2*	*19.8*
Others:							
Belgium	26.0	32.2	40.2	56.3	*56.0*	*53.0*	*59.0*
Canada	57.1	69.6	94.7	87.8	*87.3*	*80.7*	*95.3*
Ireland	18.1	22.3	29.3	39.6	*48.0*	*44.0*	*52.0*
Norway	25.5	29.6	42.3	58.6	*65.0*	*55.0*	*77.0*
UK	19.1	21.7	30.2	49.6	*58.0*	*53.0*	*64.0*
USA	55.5	60.2	75.2	80.9	*81.0*	*70.6*	*91.8*

Source: *World Bank*, Salmi (2002), p. 149.

The level of female higher education enrolment in the USA and Canada of over 90% dwarfs other European countries, which range between 52-77%. Within the GCC and other selected Arab countries, Oman scores a low of 7% while Qatar is the highest at 41%.

Paying the price for education

Given a high population growth rate and the political will to provide education to as much of the Saudi population as possible, the Kingdom has raised the amounts allocated to human resource development as well as the relative allocation to this sector compared to other expenditures. This expenditure pattern is set out in Table 13.10.

Table 13.10 Saudi Arabia: Budget allocations for human resources development 1981-2004

	1981	1984	1994	1999	2002	2004
Human Resources Development (SR billion)	26.2	30.4	29.2	42.7	47.0	63.7
All Sectors (SR billion)	298.0	260.0	160.0	165.0	202.0	230.0
Human Resources Development as % to all sectors.	8.8	11.7	18.2	25.8	23.3	28

Source: *SAMA*, 2003, *Ministry of Finance*, 2003.

From around 9% in 1981, human resource development expenditure now accounts for 28%. The 2004 budgetary allocation has re-emphasized this aspect of public expenditure. While the figures might appear impressive on the surface, the Kingdom lags behind other Arab and GCC countries, as well as more developed economies, when we examine the overall share of higher education expenditure as a share of total public expenditure on education. Table 13.11 shows a declining trend for Saudi Arabia over the period 1980-1998.

Table 13.11 Current public expenditure on higher education as share of total current public expenditure on education for 1980-1998 (%)

Country	1980	1985	1990	1995	1998
Middle East:					
Egypt	30.9	28.8	36.0	35.4	32.6
Jordan	24.4	34.1	35.1	34.9	N/A
Kuwait	16.5	17.5	N/A	29.2	32.1
Lebanon	N/A	N/A	30.6	32.4	22.5
Oman	N/A	15.3	7.4	3.0	2.0
Qatar	N/A	N/A	16.3	22.5	26.7
Saudi Arabia	*27.9*	*27.1*	*21.2*	*17.8*	*17.0*
UAE	N/A	6.1	8.3	12.5	18.4
Others:					
Belgium	17.3	16.7	16.5	20.5	22.0
Canada	29.0	30.7	31.4	38.2	30.4
Ireland	17.6	17.7	20.4	22.6	26.0
Norway	13.6	13.5	15.2	27.1	26.0
UK	22.4	19.8	19.6	23.7	22.0
USA	N/A	25.1	24.1	25.2	26.3

Source: *World Bank*, Salmi (2002), p. 150.

The Saudi government is aware that expenditure on education must be allocated in an efficient manner in order to produce an output compatible with the economy's future needs. In the higher education sector alone, the Seventh Development Plan period (2000-2004) envisages a total of 668,000 new entrants to the different higher education institutes, while some 372,000 graduates are expected over the same period, as cited in Table 13.12. Once again, the impressive advances made in girls' higher education levels are noted.

To assess whether the massive investment in education has brought about the desired output of graduates, we look at the breakdown of graduates by specific specialization.

Table 13.12 Planned number of male and female students in the Seventh Development Plan 2002-2004

University	New Entrants			Graduates		
	Male	Female	Total	Male	Female	Total
King Saud University	47,700	22,300	70,000	32,300	15,700	48,000
King Abdul Aziz University	33,600	26,400	60,000	20,800	14,700	35,500
King Faisal University	10,800	7,200	18,000	5,700	5,500	11,200
King Fahd University (KFUPM)	9,000	-	9,000	4,300	-	4,300
Islamic University	6,000	-	6,000	4,500	-	4,500
Imam University	58,500	11,500	70,000	39,200	8,150	47,350
Umm Al-Qura University	24,400	15,600	40,000	8,600	8,700	17,300
King Khalid University	13,500	3,500	17,000	12,000	800	12,800
Girl's Colleges	-	200,000	200,000	-	92,500	92,500
Technical Colleges	95,636	-	95,636	46,924	-	46,924
Vocational Colleges	82,893	-	82,893	52,302	-	52,302
Total	**382,029**	**286,500**	**668,529**	**226,626**	**146,050**	**372,676**

Source: *Seventh Development Plan, Ministry of Planning*, 2000, pp. 264, 271.

Table 13.13 shows that, in general, most Saudi graduates still opt for non-science subjects. The figures reveal a very limited total output of Saudis relative to the needs of the private sector labour force.

Table 13.13 Saudi Arabia: New entrants to the labour force by level of education (1990-2000)

Highest level of Education Completed	1990 – 1995				1995 - 2000			
	Male	Female	Total	%	Male	Female	Total	%
University (Total)	**38,300**	**30,300**	**68,600**	**30.5%**	**73,800**	**40,900**	**114,700**	**32.9%**
➤ Engineering	4,700	0	4,700	2.0%	10,100	0	10,100	2.9%
➤ Natural Sciences	4,100	4,700	8,800	3.9%	10,000	5,500	15,500	4.4%
➤ Medical Sciences & Health	2,300	1,000	3,300	1.4%	5,500	2,600	8,100	2.3%
➤ Statistics, Math, Computer Sciences	3,000	2,100	5,100	2.3%	12,700	4,100	16,800	4.8%
➤ Economics and Business	3,700	1,600	5,300	2.4%	2,600	700	3,300	0.9%
➤ Social Sciences	8,600	10,400	19,000	8.5%	9,000	12,800	21,800	6.3%
➤ Teacher Education	5,400	5,200	10,600	4.7%	8,000	4,500	12,500	3.6%
➤ Religious Study	6,500	5,300	11,800	5.3%	15,900	10,700	26,600	7.6%
Junior Colleges: Technical (Total)	**7,400**	**0**	**7,400**	**3.3%**	**12,800**	**0**	**12,800**	**3.7%**
➤ Industrial	5,700	0	0		N/A			
➤ Commercial	1,700	0	0		N/A			
Secondary School (Total)	**139,500**	**9,000**	**148,500**	**66.2%**	**209,600**	**11,500**	**221,100**	**63.4%**
➤ General Education	103,100	7,500	110,600	49.1%	172,000	8,900	180,900	51.9%
➤ Technical and Vocational	36,400	1,500	37,900	17.1%	37,600	2,600	40,200	11.6%
Total	**185,200**	**39,300**	**224,500**	**100%**	**296,200**	**52,400**	**348,600**	**100%**

Source: *Ministry of Planning, Sixth Development Plan*, 1995.

Teacher education, social sciences and religious studies accounted for nearly 60% of total university graduates during the period 1990-1995, although this declined to around 53% by 2000. The largest change occurred for courses in the computer sciences; these saw their share of graduates double from 7.4% in the period between 1990-1995, to 14.6% in the years between 1995-2000. Engineering remained steady at around 9% of all university graduates.

The results of the past decades' educational transformation in the Kingdom have been impressive, at least on paper. The real question is whether the inherent structural imbalances in the output of graduates can be sustained, or whether a fundamental reform of the whole educational system is needed.

Restructuring the Saudi education system

The government of Saudi Arabia has sought advice from the World Bank and UNESCO in restructuring the education system of the Kingdom (Kibbi, 2002). Their aim is to ensure quality education that can meet the twin objectives of internal efficiency and desired learning outcomes. By internal efficiency we mean the ability of institutions to keep students enrolled and progressing in order to reduce dropout levels. By learning outcomes, we mean the extent to which systems produce graduates who possess the knowledge and skills required for effective participation in the economy. The desired outcome for both would be to link education with the world of work. How has Saudi Arabia performed?

Table 13.14 sets out the number of higher education students, both male and female, for all levels of education. It is interesting to note that females account for a larger number of students in higher education than males. Technical training is not yet open to females, while unaccompanied Saudi female students are not normally provided with state assistance for training abroad. Those that do so must enrol privately for their education.

Table 13.14 Saudi Arabia: summary of higher education students by level during the academic year 2001

Level	Number of new students			Number of enrolled students			Number of graduates		
	Male	Female	Total	Male	Female	Total	Male	Female	Total
Ph.d	161	123	284	975	369	1,344	71	82	154
Master's	907	639	1,546	3,676	2,403	6,079	480	333	813
Higher Diploma	470	60	530	969	317	1,286	455	102	557
Bachelor	30,137	57,177	87,314	142,450	195,196	337,646	16,273	23,178	39,451
Intermediate Diploma	14,141	10,960	25,101	32,294	19,055	51,349	6,455	8,195	12,850
Total	45,816	68,959	114,775	180,364	217,340	397,704	21,934	31,891	53,825
%	39.9%	60.1%	100.0%	45.3%	54.7%	100.0%	40.7%	59.3%	100.0%

Source: *Ministry of Education,* General Organization for Technical Education and Vocation Training, Ministry of Health and the Jubail and Yanbu industrial cities.

Saudi women pursue higher education because they feel that bachelors degrees are no longer enough to obtain a job; they hope higher degrees are the answer (Al Mana, 1981, Baadi, 1982). However, because the degree programs open for girls are slightly limited, many female students do not feel optimistic about entering the labour market. The World Bank estimated their labour participation in 2001 at only 6% (Diwan and Girgis, 2002). This compares with 18% for Europe and 23% for the USA.

With Saudi female students restricted to employment in just a few sectors, including teaching, administration or the social and health services, their participation in science or technical training is minimal. Table 13.15 shows that those enrolled in technical or vocational training are almost exclusively male students. In 2003, the Kingdom decided to open a new nursing college for Saudi women as a first step in widening the scope of their labour participation (Arab News, 31 December 2003). While this move is to be welcomed, data on women's education indicate that they are being trained largely for teaching and clerical jobs, severely restricting their access to the labour market. In a bold move however, one of Saudi Arabia's leading female colleges - Dar Al Hikma – has embarked on a program to offer its students engineering degrees in association with Duke University of USA.

Table 13.15 Technical education at institutions of the General Organization for Technical Education and Vocational Training 2002 (males only)

	Number of new enrolment	Number of total students	Number of graduates	Number of institutes
Technical colleges	13,939	30,060	4,784	17
Industrial secondary institutes	4,086	11,590	2,243	10
Commercial secondary institutes	3,175	7,794	1,782	16
Agricultural institutes	147	303	74	4
Technical inspectors' institutes	1,084	2,987	711	5
Vocational training centres	8,735	13,332	6,606	31
Total	31,166	66,066	16,200	83

Source: *General Organization for Technical Education and Vocational Training,* 2003.

With only 16,000 graduates in technical and vocational training, the system is far from meeting the private sector's requirements for such skills, given the size of the Saudi economy. It shows us that the present Saudi Arabian educational system is still geared towards arts, social and religious studies. The Saudi government, recognizing this need, has recently taken major steps to steer public expenditure towards vocational training. SR 3.7 billion (US $1 billion) was set aside for training 100,000 Saudis in technical skills. The government also increased the allocation for vocational training in the 2004 budget, from SR 1.5 billion to SR 2.9 billion (Arab News, 5 November 2003).

A growing emphasis on science and technology was also detected in the 2004 budget outlays, in which universities teaching these core subjects had their allocation increased, at the expense of the social sciences, arts and humanities-based universities (Al-Sheikh, 2003). This is set out in Table 13.16, which illustrates the budgetary appropriations for all the major Saudi government universities over the period 2001-2004.

Table 13.16 Saudi Arabia: budget allocation to higher education establishments 2001-2004

				SR million	
	2001	*2002*	*2003*	*2004*	*2004% Change*
Institute of Public Administration	222	224	203	202	-0.5%
General Organization for Technical Education	1,396	1,509	1,540	2,880	87.0%
King Saud University	2,257	2,268	2,403	2,420	0.7%
King Abdulaziz University	1,433	1,456	1,538	1,500	-2.5%
Imam Muhammed Bin Saud University	1,255	1,257	1,250	1,170	-6.4%
King Faisal University	356	407	422	469	11.1%
King Fahd University of Petroleum & Minerals	547	540	574	622	8.4%
Umm-Al-Qura University	743	711	745	673	-9.7%
Islamic University of Madinah	277	281	288	310	7.6%
Medinah University			-	178	-
Qasim University			-	309	-
Taif University			-	122	-

Source: *Ministry of Finance*, December 2003.

Because of the perception that the public educational system does not provide a wide career choice, there is now a thriving sector of private education in Saudi Arabia. The private delivery and finance of education provides a significant means through which the government can, in a cost-effective way, address the twin challenges of improving quality and expanding access. But in order to maximize the private sector's substantial potential for growth, the Saudi government needs to adopt a different approach to regulating the private pre-university educational sector. At the same time, it must safeguard the broader public interest in education.

The Saudi government has also approved the establishment of private sector universities to cope with increased student numbers currently at the elementary and intermediate public schools (Arab News, 22 June

2003). This experiment in private higher education will be watched with great interest to see if such universities will produce the kind of graduates that the labour market needs. They will also observe how the private institutions will affect existing state universities. In the meantime, Saudi parents are placing their children in even larger numbers in private schools, as we can see in Figure 13.6 and the next set of data.

Figure 13.6 Percent change in enrolment, public and private secondary schools 1996/1997-1999/2000

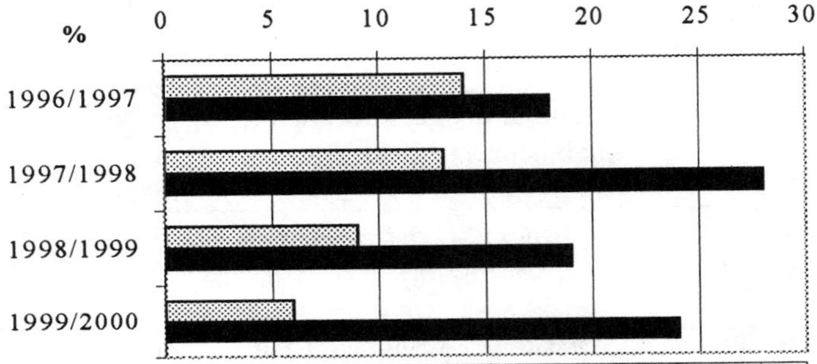

	1999/2000	1998/1999	1997/1998	1996/1997
▓ Public	6	9	13	14
■ Private	24	19	28	18

Source: *Saudi Arabia Yearbook* (2001).

Private school enrolment grew from 25% to 50% of the kindergarten school market between the periods 1996/1997 and 2000/2001, and grew approximately 6-7% for elementary, intermediate and secondary schools. A total of nearly 300,000 students were enrolled at private schools in 2000/2001. The declining enrolment growth rates in public schools compared with private schools stand out for the period.

Table 13.17 (A) Private school enrolments by year and education level, 1996/1997-2000/2001

Year	Kindergarten	Elementary	Intermediate	Secondary	Total
1996/1997	43,207	134,354	36,689	23,875	238,125
1997/1998	43,058	137,520	40,706	28,237	249,521
1998/1999	45,474	139,677	44,881	36,189	487,646
1999/2000	47,118	136,113	45,448	43,136	271,815
2000/2001	46,936	146,731	50,605	53,440	297,712
Growth 1996/1997 to 2000/2001	*Kindergarten*	*Elementary*	*Intermediate*	*Secondary*	*Total*
Number	3,729	12,377	13,916	29,565	59,587
Percent (%)	8.6	9.2	37.9	123.8	25.0

Table 13.17 (B) Private school market share by year and education
level 1996/1997-2000/2001

Year	Kindergarten	Elementary	Intermediate	Secondary	Total
1996/1997	50.0	6.0	4.1	4.8	6.4
1997/1998	49.2	6.1	4.4	5.0	6.5
1998/1999	49.8	6.2	4.6	5.6	12.3
1999/2000	50.2	6.0	4.4	6.1	6.6
2000/2001	49.9	6.4	4.7	7.1	7.1
Change in Market Share 1996/1997 to 2000/2001 (%)	-0.1	0.4	0.6	2.3	0.7

Source: *Saudi Arabia Yearbook* (2001).

The Saudi government has initiated some internal reform of the educational structure, especially at the elementary and intermediate levels. Their goal is to make the system more responsive to current world standards and to parents' demand for change. For example, the Saudi government has now approved English language instruction from an earlier age at schools, following internal debate on the subject. English will now be taught from sixth grade (12 years) rather than seventh grade (13 years) starting in 2003/2004 (Abdulgafour, 2003).

The Saudi Cabinet decision in August, 2003, to introduce English at an earlier age also included the commitment to "improve the teaching of English at intermediate and secondary levels by updating curricula, enhancing the competence of teachers and using modern technologies" (Adbulgafour, Arab News, 26 August 2003). Another major change followed the 2003 Saudi Cabinet reshuffle, when the Minister of Education took responsibility for girls' education under a separate Deputy Minister for Girls Education, having removed it from the previously autonomous Presidency of Girls Education (Qusti, R. May, 2003).

Saudi education and employment

Changes in any educational system cannot be quick-fix solutions, as they must be responsive to social, economic and international labour pressures. Saudi Arabia cannot long ignore the need for a transformation from a state-led employment path to one that is driven by the labour market. In the current development phase, the absence of a unified labour market, where relative wages are set freely for both Saudis and non-Saudis, undermines a key signal about the real value of acquired skills. This can cause people to have less incentive to gain a market-responsive education (Schawb, K. 2003).

A new regulatory approach for the Saudi school system is needed to cope with the demands of the market place. Table 13.18 summarizes key areas where current government educational control needs to be either loosened or tightened, and is based on a comprehensive World Bank study of the Saudi educational system.

Table 13.18 A new regulatory approach for Saudi school education

Issue	Current approach to regulating education	Degree of control by government	Proposed approach to regulating education
Stakeholders expectation	• Few expectation from stakeholders • Limited performance specifications	From loose to tight	• High expectations from stakeholders • Clear sector performance specifications
Teaching autonomy	• Prescriptive and input-based • Minimal autonomy for private schools	From tight to loose	• Output-based and freedom to innovate • Greater institutional autonomy
Accountability and performance assessment	• Weak accountability for results • Little performance measurement • Few sanctions for failures	From loose to tight	• Strong accountability for results • Information on academic results disclosed • Annual national assessment performance for all schools/students

Source: Based on a *World Bank Study for Saudi Arabia*, 2000.

Change must also occur at the higher education level. The transformation of domestic economics and international education flows are powerful forces for change in Saudi Arabia. Higher education will face the necessity to competitively deliver competent and relevant educational programs that meet society's needs and achieve international accreditation. Figure 13.7 sets out some of these major forces for change that impact on the higher education sector. Given rising student numbers and budgetary constraints, there will be a growing need for higher education to forge links with industry and external independent financing.

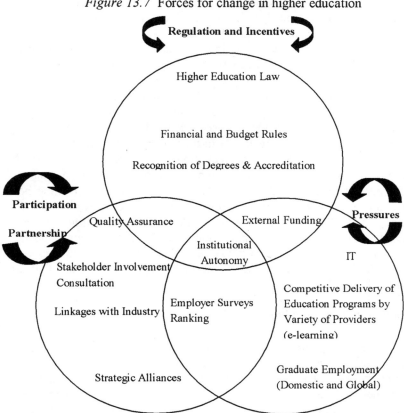

Figure 13.7 Forces for change in higher education

Adapted from the *World Bank* 2000.

Most universities in developing countries seem to function at the periphery of the international scientific community, unable to participate in the production and adaptation of knowledge necessary to confront their countries' most important economic and social problems (Larocque, 2002). One growing issue is their lack of access to the global knowledge pool and the international academic environment . This situation is often compounded by cumbersome administrative rules and bureaucratic procedures. In many countries, the ministries of higher education determine staffing policies, budgetary allocations and the number of student admissions; the universities have little say about the number of positions, level of salaries and promotion of their staff.

Such total government control is the most extreme scenario. For Saudi Arabia, the truth lies somewhat more in the middle. The Ministry of Higher Education still has a powerful influence, but the Saudi universities are gaining a larger degree of independence concerning educational and staff issues (Dukhayil, 2003). The 2003 Cabinet reshuffle granted greater autonomy to the Saudi University Rectors. But until universities acquire further institutional autonomy, they will be hampered by a cumbersome government bureaucracy that is slow to react to the competition that Saudi universities face from private sector higher education colleges and universities.

Recognizing a potential niche in this area, the GCC state of Bahrain (population 700,000) authorized the establishment of eight new private sector universities. Their obvious target market is Saudi Arabia. All new private universities in Bahrain and United Arab Emirates (UAE) have established strong strategic alliances and supra-national links with worldwide centres of academic excellence. This makes their degrees more recognizable and attractive than those from Saudi universities. The issues of degree credibility, accreditation and degree equivalency will become major concerns if private universities proliferate, as a result of both altruistic and profit motives. The focus of teaching in these new Gulf universities is on computer sciences, natural sciences and business management. The fact that they are also co-educational, with both sexes taught together, expands opportunities for Saudi female students, especially those who wish to pursue a broader range of disciplines than Saudi Arabia offers, while still living and studying in societies that are culturally compatible to the Kingdom.

Looking towards the future

The interplay among a variety of elements – erratic oil revenues, demographic trends, a rigid educational system and low labour productivity – has deeply affected the direction of development outcomes in Saudi Arabia in the past few decades (Abdelkarim, 1999, Bourland, 2002). Saudi Arabia's real per capita income has fallen considerably from SR 61,177 in 1981 to SR 30,203 in 2002. Population has grown faster than oil revenue and labour productivity has not kept pace with private sector market forces (SAMA, 2003). In order to compensate for this "oil drag", labour productivity, and hence educational standards will have to rise significantly in the next decade. The educational levels of both males and females in Saudi Arabia have demonstrated impressive improvement by world standards, but the 20-year boom of current education patterns and job creation is now under strain. Government financial flexibility is more restricted and the public sector has reached an unsustainable size: the wage bill is now around 50% of total government expenditures (Al-Sheikh, 2003).

Because of these factors, Saudi Arabia is opening up, especially in the education sector, where a revised curriculum and educational approach are needed to ensure Saudi Arabia can compete in the global environment. Saudi Arabia has set the right general priorities in education, but its goals and means are not yet adequate to solving the problem. A mismatch remains between educational output, quality and the needs of the Saudi labour market. Some have argued that the Kingdom is giving undue attention to "education push" rather than "job pull" in the private sector (Cordesman, 2003). This criticism ignores to some extent the recognition by Saudi planners for the need for fundamental reforms to education, to align its output with private sector needs. Some of the government's recommendations, as set out in the Seventh Development Plan (2000-2004), illustrate its priorities. These are summarized in Table 13.19.

Table 13.19 Saudi government education development plan recommendations and outcomes

Recommendations	Outcomes
• Establishing new channels and patterns of higher education such as Open Universities and distance learning.	• Achieved in both areas
• Improving the internal efficiency of the universities by reducing number of years for students to graduation	• Process is underway with universities reporting on achievements to the Ministry of Higher Education.
• Encouraging the private sector to establish private universities and colleges.	• Achieved - new colleges and universities opened such as Prince Sultan University, Prince Mohammed University, Institute of College of Business Administration, Dar Al-Faisal University.
• Establishing more effective co-ordination between research centres and development centres, so that the producers and users of national technological solutions are linked.	• Several initiatives to establish Technology Cities and Science Parks e.g Jeddah Bio-Technology, Prince Abdullah bin Abdulaziz Science Park at KFUPM.

There are a range of plans in place: to include private sector participants in the continuous review of curricula to ensure that proposed academic trends are commensurate with the actual needs of the market; to improve training in advanced technology; and to develop a national plan for the use of information technology and of information sources, including databases.

Curriculum development plans in the Kingdom were accelerated after the events of 11 September 2001, and the violence within Saudi Arabia following the Riyadh bombings of May, 2003. In addition, the GCC countries publicly endorsed such educational reforms at their GCC summit meeting in Kuwait in December, 2003 (Arab News, December, 2003). Education and other reform issues took centre stage at national dialogue forums held in Riyadh and Makkah in 2003 and early 2004 under the auspices of Crown Prince Abdullah, who was presented with the *Makkah* forum's recommendation to "root out extremism, immediate reform of academic curricula, and more freedom of media" (Abdulghafour, 15 January 2004).

Conclusion

The emphasis on qualitative education is now recognized by Saudi intellectuals and others but it will be a hard transition for the younger generation to make. Without change, Saudi youth will be competing in a highly sophisticated market with underdeveloped skills, causing frustration and resentment (Birks et. al., 1980, World Bank, 1995, Yamani, 2000). Their inherited deference to patriarchal authority means the young blame employers and turn to the government for solutions. They definitely prefer government employment, when available. There are encouraging signs of more realistic attitudes towards job searches and the educational needs of the market (Ghamdi, 2003), but the task is still an uphill one. However, the Government of Saudi Arabia is tackling other major internal reform issues, in addition to education, with a new realism and openness. This sense of increased candour and decisive action gives rise to genuine optimism.

Summary of key points:

- *Financial resources have enabled Saudi Arabia to build a large educational infrastructure for both males and females in a short period of time. Expenditure on education is now a major item in budgetary expenditures and rising. The government is aware that education plays a crucial role in economic development and in meeting the demands of the globalization age.*
- *Saudi Arabia faces several challenges in its education policies, namely providing relevant education to meet the needs of a modern society, as well as providing quality education that is adaptable to worldwide education changes.*
- *In terms of the quantity of education output, the Kingdom has done well in comparison with other developing countries in pupil/teacher and pupil/school ratios. There are inherent weaknesses in terms of low output of higher education science and vocational and technical graduates.*
- *Female higher level education has grown rapidly. Currently females outnumber males at the undergraduate and postgraduate levels. Saudi females can now take science based subjects which previously were only available to male students, but technical education is still restricted to males.*
- *To meet enrollment shortages in government owned schools, the Kingdom has encouraged the provision of education through privately owned education institutions which have seen a remarkable growth in the number of students enrolled.*
- *The issue of Saudi education and meeting the employment requirements of the private sector is one of immediate concern.*

The Saudi education system is being pressed to deliver a varied educational program that is of high quality, relevant to societies' needs and internationally recognized.

- *The interplay between erratic oil revenues, high demographic trends, a rigid educational system and low Saudi labor productivity has affected the direction of development outcomes in Saudi Arabia. Education was driven by "education push" rather than "jobs-pull" in the private sector. This is changing, as recent government budgetary allocations for different higher education establishments indicates that new priorities are now being set out.*

Critical thinking

1. "We need to have more private sector education and less from the government to meet the future needs of Saudi labor force". Is this a fair statement? Can the private sector alone meet the future needs of the labor market?

2. Why does a society such as Saudi Arabia need education? What type of education do you think is necessary for a well rounded citizen?

3. "Globalization requires a different approach to education". Discuss the constraints facing Saudi education today in meeting globalization challenges.

4. Discuss the significance of increasing numbers of females entering the higher education system on Saudi society in (a) the economic sphere, and (b) the social and demographic sphere.

5. "Let market forces determine the type of education output of a country". Discuss the pros and cons of such a move for Saudi education. What type of quality safeguards are necessary?

Chapter 14
SAUDI ARABIA AND THE GULF
COOPERATION COUNCIL (GCC)

When your neighbour's house is on fire, your own property is at stake.

Horace

Learning outcomes

By the end of this section, you should understand:

- *The objectives for establishing the GCC*
- *The different settings of the GCC member states*
- *Facing up to economic diversification and integration*
- *The importance of oil and gas to the GCC*
- *The lack of progress on industrial diversification*
- *The GCC financial sector and regulatory framework*
- *The evolving banking structure*
- *The GCC capital markets*
- *GCC trade patterns*
- *Demographics and the GCC labour markets, the issue of expatriate labour*

Introduction

On 25 May 1981, in Abu Dhabi, the Charter creating the Gulf Cooperation Council (GCC) was signed by the Heads of State of these Arab Gulf countries: Bahrain, Oman, Kuwait, Saudi Arabia, Qatar and United Arab Emirates. The objectives of the GCC, as stated in its founding Charter, are to effect coordination and interconnection between member states in all fields, so as to achieve unity between them, and to deepen and strengthen relations and cooperation between their peoples in various fields. The GCC is further charged with formulating similar regulations in most areas of national concern. The comprehensive list includes economic and financial affairs, agriculture, industry, commerce, customs, communications, education, culture, social and health affairs, information and tourism. In addition, the GCC aims to encourage cooperation by the private sector (Nakleh, 1986, Ramazani, 1988).

Since 1981, the GCC has managed to assemble a few joint efforts in various fields. In defence, a joint military force called "Peninsular Shield" was established with headquarters in *Hafr Al Batin* in Saudi Arabia (Ramazani, 1988). On the economic front, on 1 January 2003, a common customs and tariffs policy was agreed that set tariffs at 5% among all member states. This had been preceded in 1982 by a Unified Economic Agreement, and in 1984 by the establishment of the Gulf Investment Corporation (GIC). In the same year, the Gulf Standards Organization was created when the Saudi Arabian Standards Organization was transformed into a regional body serving all the GCC countries. The GCC Commercial Arbitration Centre was created in December, 1993, to settle trade disputes between GCC citizens, or between GCC citizens and foreigners.

Administratively, the GCC is managed through the Secretariat General, headquartered in Riyadh, and headed by a Secretary-General who is appointed by the Supreme Council for a three-year term, renewable only once. The Supreme Council is the GCC's highest authority and is composed of the member states.

The GCC has evolved into a powerful economic bloc in its own right, with strong negotiating authority with other economic blocs, such as the European Union. (Devlin, 1996). As we will see in this chapter, while they share many interests, there are also differences between individual member countries in many fields, despite the hopes of those who signed the original establishment Charter.

States of the GCC: the setting

Any analysis of the GCC must take into consideration the member states themselves. Half a century ago, all of the six countries that make up the present GCC were poor; some were very thinly populated and had a loose central government (Bebawi, 1984, Niblock, 1980). All were pushed into modernity by oil and they were left scrambling to find their own way to manage their sudden riches. Each country has had to cope with more extreme social upheavals and dramatic changes than anywhere in living memory. They had no blueprints or common guidance on which to fall back (Fahim, 1995, Netton, 1986). They now face the fastest population growth rates in the world and the most rapid urbanization; at the same time they are dealing with some of the effects of the biggest tide of *managed* worker immigration in recent history.

First and foremost, the majority of the GCC States are fairly small. Their total area is under one million square miles, ranging from the smallest, Bahrain (260 square miles) to the largest, Saudi Arabia (approximately 865,000 square miles). The six states are primarily desert with minimal rainfall, so they are not self-sufficient in agriculture. Food security is a real issue and one major challenge is to secure future food independence.

In terms of population, the GCC states face significant problems, including for some, the small size of their native population, their large foreign workforce, a shortage of trained national workers and dependency on a narrow source of income and economic base. Economic diversification is now an imperative, but different countries of the GCC have achieved different degrees of success (Devlin, 1996, El Arian, et. al., 1997).

The GCC in a "snapshot"

According to other researchers on the GCC (El Arian, et. al., 1997), the GCC economies passed through several distinct phases, which can be summarized as follows:

i. *Extending the Expansion Phase 1981-1985*
This phase focussed on expanding the physical and social infrastructure and on diversifying the economic base, given the historically high oil prices. There was expenditure on development projects, especially petrochemical projects. Sizeable foreign reserves and budget surpluses were built up during this period.

ii. *Consolidation Phase 1986-1989*
This period witnessed lower oil prices, which contributed to imbalances in the budgets. There were reductions in some capital project expenditures, but current expenditures remained high. Budget deficits increased as did draw-downs on external reserves. Fiscal consolidation differed significantly across GCC states, reflecting the varied successes of economic diversification measures.

iii. *The First Gulf Crisis 1990-1991*
The Iraqi invasion of Kuwait in August, 1990, put pressure on government budgets and external reserves, despite higher oil prices. This period was characterized by an erosion of investment income, sharp declines in oil exports and the high costs of restructuring and rebuilding Kuwait after the liberation.

iv. *Rehabilitation Period 1992-1994*
GCC countries emerged financially weaker from the first Gulf crisis and Kuwait suffered from human and economic dislocation. The period was characterized by oil market weakness and a slowdown in world economies. Budget deficits increased in most GCC countries, to reach over 10% of GDP despite lower capital expenditures and foreign borrowing for some GCC countries.

v. *Adjustment and Reforms 1995 -*
GCC financial imbalances were reduced, helped by increased oil prices and economic diversification. Non-oil revenues increased, employment policies were geared towards private sector needs and inflation remained modest. Despite the second Gulf crisis of 2003 and the Iraq War, the GCC countries continued their internal

economic and social reforms in the fields of education, administration and politics.

This period also witnessed further concrete efforts at inter-GCC economic consolidation with reduction in custom duties to 5% and some progress made on joint defence issues. The groundwork for full monetary union by 2010 was laid. The movement of citizens between GCC countries was streamlined, as well as the granting of inter-GCC banking licenses.

Tables 14.1 and 14.2 offer a snapshot view of the main social, demographic and economic indicators of the six GCC member states. Table 14.1 sets out the social indicators; one is immediately struck by the relatively young population profile in all the GCC countries, with a large percentage under 14 years of age. Oman and Saudi Arabia have the highest percentage in this age group, and the UAE has the lowest at 29%, but this still outstrips other developed countries (World Bank, Global Development Prospects, 2001).

Table 14.1 also shows that the region as a whole has one of the highest population growth rates. Qatar and the UAE lead the way at 6.4% and 5.7% respectively. Bahrain, with relatively higher literacy, education enrolment and labour participation rates, registered the lowest population growth rate of the GCC at 2.6% p.a.

According to Table 14.1 all GCC countries have an imbalance of males to females; Oman has a 53:47 ratio, but the UAE shows the most imbalance at 63:37, highlighting the recent trend amongst UAE nationals to marry from outside. All GCC countries are largely urbanized – the GCC average is around 75%.

Oman is the exception at 28% urbanization, reflecting the relative importance of agriculture in that more geographically diverse country. Most members of the labour force are male, but both Kuwait and Bahrain show high female participation rates of 27% and 23% respectively, reflecting the relatively more advanced status of female labour participation in these two countries from early independence days.

While school enrolment is high for all the GCC countries, Kuwait, Qatar and Bahrain have the highest ratios at all levels of education. Bahrain leads the way with 85% adult literacy. Saudi Arabia reached 70% level adult literacy by 2001, up from 63% in 1995.

Table 14.1. GCC Countries: Population, Labour Force, and Social Indicators *(1997 or most recent year)*

	Bahrain	Kuwait	Oman	Qatar	Saudi Arabia	U.A.E
Demographic indicators						
Population (million)	0.7	2.40	2.50	0.7	22.7	3.60
Aged 0-14 (percent of total)	35	35	46	30	44	29
Aged 15 and over (percent of total)	65	65	54	70	56	71
Population growth (percent, 1993-1999 average)	2.6	3.4	5.0	6.4	3.8	5.7
Population gender ratio (men: women)	57:43	56:44	53:47	63:37	55:45	63:37
Age dependency ratio (1)	0.6	0.6	1.0	0.5	0.9	0.5
Urban population (percent of total)	90	97	28	92	79	89
Labour force indicators						
Total labour force (millions)	0.25	0.82	0.55	0.33	6.26	1.14
Male (percent of total)	82	73	85	88	88	89
Female (percent of total)	23	27	15	12	12	11
Labour force growth (percent, 1993-1999 average)	2.3	-1.6	5.2	3.9	3.3	3.9
Participation rate (percent)	54	49	25	52	33	46
Unemployment %	4.0	0.7	8.0	—	13.0	2.3
Social indicators						
School enrolment (percent)						
Primary (1997)	100	100	85	90	75	100
Secondary (1997)	99	99	55	84	45	49
Tertiary (1997)	30	30	15	29	18	16
Adult literacy rate (percent, 1997)	85	79	35	79	70	79
Population per physician (1997)	760	650	1200	667	749	1208
Access to safe water (percent of population, 1997)	100	100	85	100	93	98
Life expectancy at birth (years)	75	78	70	74	71	78
Infant mortality rate (per 1,000 live births)	19	11	18	18	21	16

Sources: *World Bank, Social Indicators of Development,* 1999, *UNDP, Human Development Report,* 1998, *Arab World Competitiveness Report,* 2003.

(1) Population under the age of 15 and over the age of 65 as a share of the total working-age population

In terms of life expectancy, Saudi Arabia was the lowest at 70 years, and Kuwait and UAE were the highest, a reflection of the evolution of widespread national health programs in these countries. This has resulted in a lower infant mortality rate for both countries, in contrast with Saudi Arabia, which had the highest at 21 deaths per 1,000 live births.

Table 14.2: GCC countries: economic indicators 2002

	Bahrain	Kuwait	Oman	Qatar	Saudi Arabia	UAE
GDP ($ million)	8,328	35,900	20,180	17,466	188,240	71,021
Real GDP Growth 2002 (%)	5.5	2.3	1.9	2.0	2.1	1.2
Population 2001 (million)	0.7	2.4	2.5	0.7	22.7	3.6
GDP per capita ($)	11,614	14,958	8,073	26,920	8,465	19,728
Total Government Expenditure (% of GDP)	34.3%	45.9%	36.1%	37.7%	37.1%	33.3%
Gross National Savings (% of GDP)	22.9%	34.7%	26.3%	45.3%	24.6%	34.8%
Gross Capital Formation (% of GDP)	16.8%	19.3%	21.6%	29.7%	16.3%	22.4%
Government Revenue (% of GDP)	28.3%	68.6%	32.8%	47.6%	33.5%	27.1%
Foreign Direct Investment ($ Million)	5,908	527	2,517	N/A	28,845	2,642
Imports ($ million)	5,542	7,091	5,867	4,325	32,267	35,000
Exports ($ million)	6,773	15,366	11,205	11,030	71,583	47,900
Trade Balance ($ million)	1,231	8,257	5,338	6,705	39,316	12,900
Current Account ($ million)	(412)	4,162	2,315	4,300	15,000	4,100
Budget Surplus/Deficit ($ million)	(490)	4,860	(843)	500	(5,730)	(6,300)
Surplus/Deficit % of GDP	(5.8)	13.5	(4.2)	2.0	(3.0)	(8.9)
Inflation (%)	0.2	1.4	1.5	1.0	(0.4)	3.0
External Debt ($ million)	3,588	9,219	5,700	16,000	36,215	18,513
Foreign Currency Reserves ($ million)	1,736	8,860	3,257	1,720	23,106	14,897
Sovereign Rating (S&P)	A-	A+	BBB	A+	A	A2 *

Source: *MEED*, 2003, *Arab Competitiveness Report*, 2003.

* UAE Sovereign Rating is by Moody's. There is no rating by S&P

S+P ratings are for long term foreign currency.

- Table 14.2 sets out selected major GCC economic indicators that reveal some interesting country differences. While dwarfing other GCC countries in terms of GDP, Saudi Arabia is at the lower end of the GDP per capita league at $8,465 for 2002. This can be compared with $26,920 for Qatar and $19,728 for UAE, both of which had lower GDP growth rates for the same year.

According to Table 14.2, all GCC countries show positive trade balances and current account surpluses for 2002; the largest trade surpluses were registered for Saudi Arabia, Kuwait and Qatar. Kuwait and Qatar also registered budget surpluses, while the remaining GCC members had budget deficits for 2002.

Inflationary trends seem to be under control for all GCC countries. Saudi Arabia and Bahrain registered the lowest rates and the UAE had the highest at 3%. This could be a reflection of the more open economy of the UAE. It has a larger volume of trade with the world compared to its population size, as demonstrated by a total import figure of $35.0 billion for 2002. This compared favourably with Saudi Arabia's $32.3 billion for a population 6.3 times that of the UAE.

Saudi Arabia had the largest foreign currency reserves, closely followed by the UAE and Kuwait. These represent local currency cover – not the total amount of foreign liquid investments held by the GCC countries.

In terms of sovereign country credit rating, the highest rating was A+ for Kuwait and Qatar by Standard & Poor with A for Saudi Arabia. Oman had the lowest credit rating at BBB, while Bahrain stood at A-. The Standard & Poor rating for Saudi Arabia was the first from that agency, and was granted due to the Kingdom's improved macroeconomic indicators during 2002/2003.

In terms of external debt, all the GCC countries showed varying degrees of external debt levels. Saudi Arabia had the highest ($36.2 billion), followed by Qatar ($16.0 billion) and the UAE ($18.5 billion). Bahrain was the lowest at $3.6 billion. Qatar's external debt resulted from its international borrowing for massive gas-related projects, while the UAE's debt includes borrowing by the smaller Emirates of *Sharjah* and *Dubai* for their construction and energy-related projects. The Saudi external debt is not officially classified as direct sovereign borrowing by the state, but rather non-recourse borrowing by semi-governmental organizations, without guarantees from the Kingdom of Saudi Arabia.

Table 14.2 illustrates the relatively lower level of gross national savings and gross capital formation for Saudi Arabia, compared to the other GCC states. Qatar led the way in gross national savings with 45.3%, helped by rising gas-related income and low population. Qatar also took the lead in gross capital formation at nearly 30%. The UAE was a respectable second in both categories.

Saudi Arabia, by virtue of its size and market potential, took the lion's share of foreign direct investment (FDI), with total FDI standing at $28.8 billion. Despite its small size, Bahrain received just under $6 billion, which is a tribute to its economic reforms and "investor-friendly" legislation (Bisisu, 1984, Azzam, 1988).

In all the GCC countries, the government plays an important role in the economic fortunes of the member states through its expenditure. Total government expenditure as % of GDP stood at nearly 46% for Kuwait and 32% for the UAE; this indicated that Kuwait had not diversified its economy from a one-resource economic base. This is confirmed by the fact that Kuwait had the GCC's highest ratio of government revenue as % of GDP (47.6%), compared to the more diversified economies of Bahrain (28%) and the UAE (27%) (Eltony, 2000).

Social and economic indicators confirm that the GCC countries experienced an enviable boom from the mid-1970s to mid-1980s; economic prosperity touched every facet of life in these countries, fuelled by a rise in oil prices and revenues. A whole infrastructure for social and public services, industrial development and education was created within a few years. However, fluctuating oil revenues from the mid-1980s, energy competition from other oil producers, and uneven world economic growth began to affect the GCC countries. Doubts crept in about the general soundness of certain economic policies they were following. The crash of the unofficial Kuwaiti stock market (*Souk Al Manakh*) in 1984, was a great shock to both Kuwait and the other Gulf states, and involved close to $100 billion. This triggered a search for a sounder financial and economic footing for the GCC member states (Jumail, 1986).

Economic diversification and economic integration

The aspiration to achieve economic productivity in order to reduce an overwhelming dependence on oil revenues was one of the main driving forces behind the concept of GCC economic integration in 1981 (Askari, et. al., 1997, Abdulkerim, 1999). Some have argued that a collapse of the oil boom may slow down the process of economic integration.

All of the GCC States, except Bahrain, have large oil reserves and therefore a longer time to develop their non-oil productive capacity before oil runs out. This fact does not, however, affect their determination to reduce their dependence on oil as soon as possible (Askari, et. al., 1997, Erian, 1997).

The economies of the GCC hold 44% of known world oil reserves, 15.5% of gas reserves and produce 20% of world crude output (Oweiss, 2000). However, despite an extremely positive economic performance in 2003 and 2004, when it was estimated that the combined GCC countries earned $35 billion more than in 2002 due to strong oil prices (Gulf News, 7 January 2004), the Gulf states need to increase their efforts to lower budget deficits and diversify non-oil revenues.

Tables 14.3 and 14.4 illustrate the enormous global importance of the GCC countries' energy reserves in both oil and gas.

Table 14.3.   Proven oil reserves of GCC countries
(in billions of barrels / year-end figures)

Country	1978	1988	1998	Global Shares
Bahrain	-----	-----	0.2	-----
Kuwait	69.4	94.5	96.5	9.2%
Oman	2.5	4.1	5.3	0.5%
Qatar	4.0	3.2	3.7	0.4%
Saudi Arabia	168.9	172.6	261.5	24.8%
UAE	31.3	98.1	97.8	9.3%
Total	276.1	372.5	465.0	44.2%

Source: *British Petroleum, BP Amoco Statistical Review of World Energy, June,* 1999.

Table 14.4 Proven natural gas reserves of GCC countries
(in trillion cubic meters)

Country	1978	1988	1998	Global Shares
Bahrain	0.20	0.19	0.12	0.1%
Kuwait	0.96	1.38	1.49	1.0%
Oman	0.06	0.26	0.80	0.5%
Qatar	1.13	4.44	8.49	5.8%
Saudi Arabia	2.73	4.30	5.79	4.0%
UAE	0.61	5.71	6.00	4.1
Total	**5.69**	**16.28**	**22.69**	**15.5%**

Source: *British Petroleum, BP Amoco Statistical Review of World Energy*, June, 1999.

Saudi Arabia has the largest oil reserves (56% of the total) in the GCC, as well as the third largest gas reserves at around 25%. The Qatari gas reserves are the third largest in the world, after Russia and Iran, and account for 37% of total GCC gas reserves. Unlike Saudi gas production, which is associated gas (produced as a by-product of oil production), Qatar gas production is mostly non-associated (Mabro, 2002).

Qatar oil reserves have been depleting and today Qatar exports around 450,000-500,000 barrels per day or nearly 4% of total GCC exports. For Qatar, gas is now the driving force of the economy.

While Bahrain has some oil reserves, the level is negligible. Bahrain was one of the first oil exporters of the GCC in the 1920s, but now depends mainly on services as the main support of its economy. The UAE and Kuwait have approximately the same oil reserves, but the UAE's gas reserves are the second largest in the GCC, slightly ahead of Saudi Arabia's.

The figures in the two previous Tables demonstrate that for both proven oil and gas reserves, the GCC countries have increased their share of the world's reserves over the past two decades. Decisions on the quantity of production, export levels and pricing have an impact, not only on the GCC countries themselves, but on the wider world.

The significance of GCC oil exports and their level of production in meeting world demand are explored in Tables 14.5 and 14.6.

Table 14.5 Exports of crude oil in GCC countries

1,000 barrels per day

	Bahrain	Kuwait	Oman	Qatar	Saudi Arabia	UAE	TOTAL
1988	-----	698.0	580.5	305.0	3030.1	1345.0	*5958.6*
1991	-----	85.0	694.8	336.6	6526.3	2195.0	*9837.7*
1992	-----	695.6	729.6	362.3	6581.9	2060.0	*10429.4*
1996	-----	1224.2	815.5	367.0	6126.3	1943.0	*10476.0*
2003*	-----	2300.0	860.0	460.0	8700.0	2380.0	*14800.0**

Source: *Annual Statistical Abstracts, OPEC and OAPEC, International Energy Authority*, * 2003 Forecast.

Saudi Arabian oil exports comprise around 60% of total GCC exports, with UAE and Kuwait coming second and third. Kuwait's oil exports built up rapidly after the 1990/1991 Iraq occupation, once the damaged Kuwaiti oil facilities were repaired, and total exports are now almost at the same level as those of Abu Dhabi, the major oil exporter in the United Arab Emirates federation.

Oil revenues fuel an erratic boom

Table 14.6 illustrates the dramatically fluctuating oil revenue fortunes of the individual GCC countries. It shows the volatile revenue patterns, especially during the mid-1980 period, and the unpredictable nature of such a revenue source.

Table 14.6 Oil revenues in the GCC countries 1974-1999
(Billions of U.S. dollars)

Year	Bahrain	Kuwait	Oman	Qatar	Saudi Arabia	UAE	GCC total
1974	0.99	10.03	0.82	1.98	31.06	6.33	*51.21*
1981	3.90	14.20	4.40	5.50	111.50	18.30	*157.80*
1986	1.80	6.00	2.50	1.00	20.00	7.00	*38.30*
1990	0.80	5.56	3.99	2.80	40.13	15.69	*68.97*
1995	1.10	11.80	4.75	2.60	42.70	13.35	*76.30*
1998	0.80	8.39	3.71	3.11	31.98	10.26	*58.25*
1999	1.16	10.50	5.22	4.16	42.34	13.13	*76.51*

Source: *ESCWA, Survey of Economic and Social Developments in the ESCWA Region.*

Table 14.6 shows that Saudi Arabia oil revenues dominate the GCC total, representing almost 55% of oil revenues in 1999, down from a peak of 70% in 1981. When oil prices fell sharply in the mid 1980s, other GCC states gradually built up their oil production capacity, while Saudi Arabia cut back on oil production. This explains the revenue flows. Saudi Arabia tried to help prop up oil prices by acting as a "swing producer" (Wilson, 2003). This was reversed during 2004, when Saudi Arabia was the major supplier of extra oil production, after prices rose to over $50 a barrel.

Given the importance of the hydrocarbon sector to the GCC, how successful have the countries concerned been in diversifying their economies away from dependency on energy revenue?

To some extent, the GCC has succeeded, as we can see in the next set of graphs and tables. The contribution of the oil sector to the GDPs of the respective countries has been diminishing from the mid-1970s to date, as Table 14.7 shows.

Table 14.7   Contribution of the oil sector to GDP 1977-1998

%

Country	1977	1981-1985	1986-1990	1991-1995	1996-1998
Bahrain	27	32.3	12.8	15.7	16.8
Kuwait	61	61.4	37.2	37.5	38.7
Oman	61	60.3	47.2	39.1	37.7
Qatar	68	64	34.7	33.9	38
Saudi Arabia	63	42.8	28.9	35.2	34.4
UAE	59	48.9	38.1	37.6	28.2

Sources: *ESCWA and the League of Arab States, Statistical Indicators of the Arab World for the Period* 1970-1979, *ESCWA, Statistical Abstract of the ESCWA Region,* 17th and 19th issues, 1999.

From around 60% in 1977, the contribution of the oil sector fell to about 30% by 1998. The UAE's 28% was the lowest, compared with the high of 39% for Kuwait. Bahrain's oil sector contribution fell to around 17% in 1998 from 27% in 1977, but, as explained earlier, the importance of oil to the Bahrain economy has been diminishing over the years. According to the Saudi Arabian Monetary Agency's (SAMA) latest reports, the oil sector contributed 31.2% to the GDP in 2002 (SAMA, 2003). Despite the fall in the oil sector's contribution to GDP, Saudi Arabia's GDP accounts for over 50% of the combined GCC Gross Domestic Product, with the UAE coming second at 21%. These percentages can be seen in Figure 14.1.

Figure 14.1 Country share of total GCC GDP: average 1999-2001

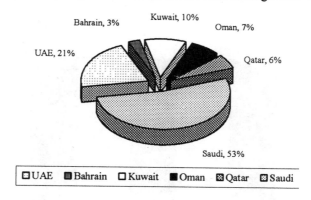

Source: Gulf Organization for Industrial Consulting, 2002.

In each of the GCC countries, the dependency on oil revenues as the main source of government revenues makes it difficult to chart a long-term economic policy, given oil price fluctuations and ever-changing trends (Oweiss, 2000).

Assuming stable government revenues against the GCC's high population growth rates, the per capita income could shrink for most member states and the standard of living could decline over time. For that reason, the economic diversification in their non-oil GDP is encouraging.

Population growth projections for the GCC countries over the period 1990-2005 indicate an expected increase of 55% over the 15-year period (World Bank Population Conference, April, 1999). Unless oil prices increase by the same ratio, per capita income will decline and budget deficits will increase. Per capita expenditures on health, education and general welfare must be reduced unless other measures are taken, and at the same time, labour productivity must be increased. Studies have shown that labour productivity in the GCC contributed 9-11% of overall growth, which contrasts with industrialized nations, where their levels are at 75% (Oweiss, 2000). The main source of growth, then, comes from natural resources.

But progress is being made on the manufacturing front in an effort to diversify and to create value-added economic growth.

The share of manufacturing in the GCC's GDP has been growing, albeit at a slow pace, and stood at 10% for 2001. Total investments reached nearly $90 billion for the same year, as seen in Figures 14.2 and 14.3. Given the pressure to find jobs for nationals, this sector employed nearly 623,000 workers in all the GCC countries in 1997, although a large proportion of this labour force is foreign, as we will soon discuss.

Figure 14.2 Share of manufacturing in GCC GDP 1999-2001

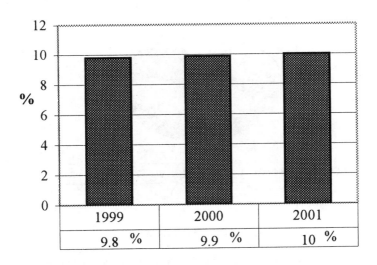

Source: *Gulf Organization for Industrial Consulting,* 2000.

Figure 14.3 Total GCC investment in manufacturing (US$ billion)
(1999-2001)

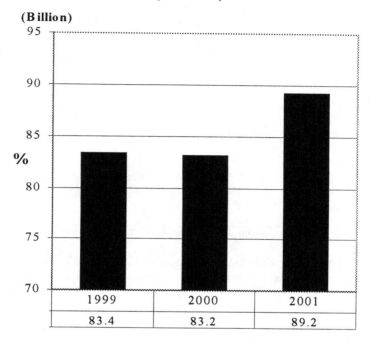

	1999	2000	2001
	83.4	83.2	89.2

Source: *Gulf Organization for Industrial Consulting*, 2000.

The individual country analysis in Table 14.8 presents interesting data revealing that the level of manufacturing's contribution to GDP is still relatively small, reaching a maximum of around 13% for Bahrain in 1998, slightly less for Kuwait, but around only 10% for Saudi Arabia. This figure has not changed much, for it stood at 10.4% in 2002 according to SAMA (SAMA, 2003, p. 221). For Qatar, the percentage has nearly fallen by half – down to 7.4% -- because the impact of the gas projects coming on-stream since 1997 began to dwarf Qatar's other domestic sectors. Oman's small ratio, 4.7%, reflects the more diversified economic base of that country, where agriculture at 8.5% is still a major contributing sector to GDP. This differs from the rest of the GCC, where agriculture's share ranges from 1% to 5%; Saudi Arabia's share was 5.3% in 2002 (SAMA, 2003).

What Table 14.8 does not reveal, however, is that the majority of the GCC's manufacturing industry is still dominated by petrochemical-related industries and refining, and that this component rose to 53% in 2001, from 48.8% in 2000 (Gulf Organization for Industrial Consulting, 2003, p. 21). Non-metal minerals, fabricated metals and food beverages were the next largest components at around 7% each.

Table 14.8 Value-added by the manufacturing industry in the GCC
countries 1980-1998
(Millions of U.S.$, current prices)

Country	1980	1985	1991	1995	1998
Bahrain	558	369	517	1,026	788
Kuwait	1,609	1,273	536	2,982	3,009
Oman	45	241	390	643	669
Qatar	410	486	852	683	718
Saudi Arabia	6,555	6,764	9,559	11,434	12,542
UAE	1,142	1,521	2,661	4,452	5,500
Bahrain	18.0	10.1	11.2	17.5	12.7
Kuwait	5.9	5.9	5.0	11.2	11.9
Oman	0.8	2.4	3.4	4.7	4.7
Qatar	5.2	7.9	12.4	8.4	7.4
Saudi Arabia	4.2	7.8	8.1	8.9	9.7
UAE	3.8	1.9	7.8	10.4	11.8

Source: *ESCWA, Statistical Abstract of the ESCWA Region, 19th issue,* 1999.

The emphasis on capital-intensive industries reveals a planning bias towards such kinds of development, dating from the early economic boom days of the GCC countries. This bias persists, despite the fact that smaller firms are the ones that employ a larger number of people, as illustrated in Figure 14.4.

Figure 14.4. Gulf Cooperation Council: % distribution of manufacturing firms according to size of work force 1997

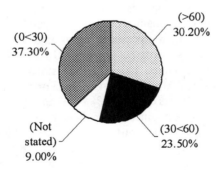

Source: *Gulf Organization for Industrial Consulting,* 2000.

The distribution of workers in these categories shows that nearly 61% of workers were employed in small-sized manufacturing firms of less than 60 employees, with nearly 40% working in companies having less than 30 employees. This reinforces the argument of those advocating small and medium-sized enterprises (SMEs) as an important employment mechanism for the GCC, especially in countries with high unemployment levels.

Emphasis on hydrocarbon projects continues

Declining costs and new techniques in mining engineering have contributed towards declining costs in upstream development (exploration and production) worldwide, which will help to boost non-OPEC and OPEC hydrocarbon production due to reduction in costs.

Table 14.9 Selected major upstream oil and gas projects in the GCC 2004

Country	Project	Cost ($ Million)	Scope of Work	Status
i. Saudi Arabia				
•Saudi Aramco	Khurais Field Development	3,000	Full Field Development	Gas project.
•Saudi Aramco	Eastern Province Straddle Plant	1,100	Construction of 800 million cu. ft./day plant to handle NGL	Jacobs Engineering is prime contractor
•Saudi Aramco	Haradh Gas Plant Expansion	400	Increasing capacity by 500,000 cu. ft/day	Tender to be issued
•Saudi Aramco	Hawiyah Gas Plant Expansion	400	Increasing capacity by 800,000 cu. ft/day	Jacobs Engineering is prime contractor
ii. Qatar				
• Qatargas II	Trains 4 & 5	12,000	Two trains of 7.8 million tons/year each	Chiyoda doing downstream feed, while McDermott upstream. First gas due in 2008
• Rasgas III	Trains 5 & 6	12,000	Two trains of 7.8 million tons/year each	Qatar Petroleum and Exxon Mobil. First gas 2008/2009
• QP/Royal Dutch/Shell	Ras Laffan GTL Plant	5,000	140,000 barrel/day	First production due 2008/2009
• QP/DEL	Dolphin Gas Pipeline.	3,500	120 km. Pipeline	Gas pipeline to Dubai
iii. UAE				
• GASCO/ ADCO	NGL feed gas	2,300	Additional volumes of NGL/Gas	Tenders submitted
• ADMA/OPCO	Umm Shaif Gas Re-injection	1,200	600 million cu. ft./day GAS	Company selection
• ADNOC	District gas grid	380	Construction of new LPG train on Das Island	Chiyoda
• GASCO	Habshan gas expansion	350	350 million cu. ft./day train	Fluor Daniel
iv. Kuwait				
• KPC	Project Kuwait	7,000	Doubling oil production from fields to 900,000 barrel/day	International Oil Companies
• KOC	Flowlines replacement	800	Replacement of flowlines	Tender issued
• KOC	Water Disposal	150	Western oil fields	Tender in 2004
v. Oman				
• PDO	Haweel Phase II gas injection	850	Construction of gas injection in seven fields	AMEC awarded contract
• PDO	48 inch loop	350	265 km. gas pipeline	Tender in 2004
• PDO	Kawther Field Development	250	Gas field development	New gas project – under tender

Source: *MEED*, 28 November to 4 December 2003, pp. 49-50.

The GCC countries will continue to benefit from technological improvements in upstream development. Also in their favour is their role as large reserve and low-cost producers, and a geographic location that is convenient for meeting the future growing energy demands of the world's fastest growing regions: South East Asia, China and India.

Each GCC country, to one extent or another, is embarking on either upgrading or expanding its upstream industry. Table 14.9 sets out the largest projects currently under way in this sector.

Table 14.9 shows that the bulk of projects are in gas-related developments, a result of GCC countries' attempts to expand their market share, with an eye to entering this environmentally friendly energy sector. Kuwait is the exception; its projects are mainly in oil development projects. We see that Qatar is by far the leader in planned new projects, with around $32.5 billion or 63% of total GCC planned mega-projects; Kuwait follows with 15.4%. Saudi Arabia's share of these mega-projects is just under 10%. Bahrain is missing altogether from this list of projects, for that island Kingdom diversifies its economy by concentrating on non-hydrocarbon industries and services .

The development of these upstream projects will enable the GCC countries to expand their downstream (by-product) operations and ensure diversification into end-user petrochemical industries. This will generate high-value jobs, skills for their citizens and a more stable revenue source compared to the unpredictable income from oil and gas.

The financial sector: A shining example

Over the past decade, the thriving GCC financial system is becoming integrated with international markets. Several countries, such as Bahrain and Dubai, have established themselves as world financial centres with numerous foreign financial institutions operating there. In one form or another, domestic bank intermediation has led to increased deposits and a large capital base. Their productivity has improved through the acquisition of new technology and their profits have been enhanced through developing consumer-based services. GCC Central Banks have strengthened domestic regulations and bank supervision, especially around the problem of money laundering.

With the exception of Bahrain and Dubai, competition in most countries has been relatively limited to domestic banks, by applying restrictions to bank licensing and foreign participation. In January, 2004, Kuwait reversed a long-standing policy and agreed to allow foreign banks to open branches there (Haddadin, 2004). There has been some success by banks originating in the GCC to establish branches in other GCC countries. For example, Saudi Arabia has already given three licenses to banks registered in Bahrain, Kuwait and UAE – Gulf International Bank (GIB), National Bank of Kuwait (NBK) and Emirates Bank respectively.

The domestic capital markets still lack depth and diversification. In a number of cases, equity investment and financing continue to face supply constraints, while listing and trading also experience restrictions (Azzam, 1998, Bakheet, 1999).

Like any other evolving financial sector worldwide, the GCC financial systems will face challenges in the future. There continue to be large government deficits and government borrowing from commercial banks – and these pose a long-term problem of "crowding out" private sector credit. At the same time, governments are exhorting the private sector to assume more responsibility through diversified economies (Seznec, 1995).

The pursuit of economic liberalization and privatization by many countries of the GCC will ensure that the GCC financial sector plays a role in mobilizing private financing for large investment projects in many infrastructure areas. In addition, external competition, a by-product of globalization, will push GCC banks to meet an increased demand for more varied financial services by a younger and more financially sophisticated population (Sheikh, 1999).

The regulatory framework

The six GCC countries have adopted open economic systems with free movement of capital and fixed exchange rate systems. Table 14.10 compares the exchange rate and capital restrictions of the individual member states. For exchange rate arrangements, all the GCC states are pegged to another currency – in this case to the U.S. dollar. They all have forward exchange markets with prices calculated on the premium or discount of such forward prices, based on the interest rate differentials between local and U.S. dollar interest rates. In nearly all cases, local currencies exhibit small interest premiums over comparable U.S. dollar rates.

The sharp fall in the value of the U.S. dollar in 2003 and 2004 is beginning to cause some concern amongst oil producers, as well as the GCC states themselves. Their cost of non-dollar imports rises, adding to current account pressure.

Table 14.10 shows that, with the exception of Oman, there were virtually no controls on current payments and transfers, and even in Oman's case these controls were on payments for "invisible" transactions on current transfers. Qatar and Bahrain, followed by the UAE, instituted the fewest controls on capital transactions. Saudi Arabia and Kuwait had the most controls. All GCC states avoided controls on liquidation of direct foreign investment, in a bid to create a more liberal and open economy. Liberalization of the financial services sector requires a reduction of direct financial market intervention, especially when they do not address market imperfections. An open and efficient financial market, will, *ceteris paribus*, positively affect the saving and investment environment, and improve the domestic allocation of resources.

Table 14.10 The Gulf Cooperation Council: exchange rate and capital restrictions

Index	Saudi Arabia	UAE	Bahrain	Qatar	Oman	Kuwait
Exchange Rate Arrangement						
Currency	Saudi Riyal	UAE Dirham	Bahrain Dinar	Qatar Riyal	Omani Riyal	Kuwait Dinar
Exchange Rate Structure	Unitary	Unitary	Unitary	Unitary	Unitary	Unitary
Classification	Conventional Pegged	Conventional Pegged	Conventional Pegged	Conventional Pegged	Conventional Pegged	Conventional Pegged
Exchange Tax	No	No	No	No	No	No
Exchange Subsidy	No	No	No	No	No	No
Forward Exchange Market	Yes	Yes	Yes	Yes	Yes	Yes
Controls on Current Payments and Transfers						
Arrangements for Payments and Receipts	No	No	No	No	No	No
Control on Payments for Invisible Transactions and Current transfers	No	No	No	No	Yes	No
Proceeds from Exports and/or Invisible Transactions	No	No	No	No	No	No
Capital Controls						
Capital Market Securities	Yes	Yes	Yes	No	Yes	Yes
Money Market Instruments	Yes	No	No	No	No	Yes
Collective Investment Securities	Yes	Yes	No	No	No	Yes
Derivatives and other instruments	Yes	No	No	No	No	Yes
Commercial Credit	Yes	No	No	No	No	No
Financial Credit	Yes	No	No	No	No	No
Direct Investment	Yes	Yes	Yes	Yes	Yes	Yes
Liquidation of Direct Investment	No	No	No	No	No	No
Real Estate Transactions	Yes	Yes	Yes	No	Yes	Yes
Personal Capital Movement	No	No	No	Yes	No	No
Provisions specific to commercial banks	Yes	Yes	Yes	No	Yes	Yes
Provision specific to institutional investors	No	No	No	No	No	No

Source: *World Economic Forum* "*Arab World Competitiveness Report 2002-2003*", 2003.

Central bank policies differ

Despite having roughly similar foreign exchange regimes and capital controls in place, not all the GCC Central banks have used similar monetary policies. Some have increased their reliance on open market instruments to try to control money supply and interest rates. Table 14.11 summarizes the main GCC central bank instruments.

Table 14.11 GCC central banks' main operating instruments

Bahrain:	Open market operations (purchase/sales of government securities, *repos* of government securities); open-market type operations (outright sales in the primary market); Central Bank lending operations (overdraft window, overnight lending)
UAE:	The UAE Central Bank relies mainly on purchases of foreign exchange and swap facility in Central Bank Certificates of Deposit
Qatar:	Same as UAE, plus a discount window facility
Saudi Arabia:	*Repo* operations in government and reverse *repos* for liquidity investments; foreign exchange swaps and government deposits with banks
Oman:	Mixture of FX purchase/sales and discount window
Kuwait:	Same as Bahrain; Central bank of Kuwait also has a "liquidity scheme" in the form of one month deposits with the Central Bank

Source: *Annual Reports, IMF*, 1997.

With the exception of the Saudi Arabia Monetary Agency (SAMA), all the other GCC Central Banks are in a position to support their commercial banks through overnight lending, discount window facilities or certificates of deposits. SAMA tries to overcome this lending and borrowing prohibition in its Charter of Establishment (Abdeen and Shook, 1984) through open market operations by using *repos* (with banks selling part of their securities to SAMA) and *reverse repos* (banks placing liquidity with SAMA).

The GCC regulatory authorities, have, in general, tended to err on the side of prudence and conservatism in regulating the commercial banking and financial sectors. The outcome, other than the Kuwaiti *Souk Al Manakh* fiasco in the early 1980s and the more recent collapses of unregulated financial companies in Qatar (Al Medinah Investments) and Saudi Arabia (Eid, Juma'a Companies), has resulted in the emergence of a highly profitable, well capitalized and diversified GCC commercial banking sector.

The GCC banking structure

The banking sector is a vital one for the development of any economy, and the GCC banking sector is no exception. Figure 14.5 sets out major banking indicators for the GCC countries. An analysis of these is quite revealing: In terms of the distribution of GCC bank assets, the Saudi banking industry dominates the other countries and accounts for around 42 % of total assets, followed by the UAE banking sector. Bahraini bank assets come third, but these include the so-called offshore banking units (OBUs), which distort the true picture for Bahrain; domestic Bahrain bank assets are 3% of total assets.

Figure 14.5. GCC countries distribution of GCC banks assets 1997:
banking sector indicator

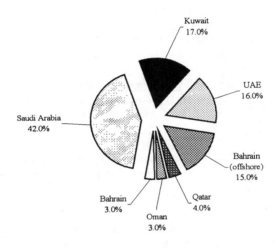

Source: *ESCWA, Statistical Abstract of the ESCWA Region*, 19th Issue, 1999.

In terms of the ratio of banking assets to GDP, Kuwait had the highest level at around 125% for 1997, with Oman the lowest at 44%. The Gulf average of 94% was down from 98% three years earlier. According to surveys, Japanese banks had a higher ratio at 167%, while UK banks excelled at 390%. U.S. banks were at 90% (Sheikh, 1999). Lower banking assets to GDP indicate the existence of larger informal financial economies, ones that are still outside the formal banking sector.

GCC banks' assets totalled around US$241 billion at the end of 1997, with the Saudi share at slightly over US$100 billion. However, in terms of return on assets, Bahraini, Omani and UAE banks outperformed Saudi, Qatari, and Kuwaiti banks. According to GOIC, Bahraini and Omani banks also showed the best return on equity, while Saudi, Kuwaiti and UAE banks followed next.

In terms of loans to deposit ratios, Omani banks were the highest at nearly 100%; Qatari and UAE banks followed behind them, and Saudi banks had the most conservative ratio at around 50%. This is due to

SAMA's policy of restricting Saudi bank lending to a maximum of 60% of loans to deposit ratio (Dukheil, 1995). During the same period, Japanese banks had an average ration of loans to deposit of approximately 88%, German banks had 83% and UK banks were at 65% (Sheikh, 1999).

By 1997, shareholder equity rose to around US$26.4 billion, with the Saudi shareholder equity bank share at just under US$11 billion. This capitalization provided a capital adequacy ratio for all the GCC banks that was more than acceptable, far surpassing the 7% Basle (Bank of International Settlements) requirement. The highest capital adequacy ratio was for UAE banks, at around 21% for 2000; Saudi banks followed, at just under 18% for 2002; Bahrain and Oman registered approximately 10%.

Using a three-bank concentration ratio, the GCC banking sector demonstrates a high level of concentration. Kuwait's three-bank concentrations for 1999 were nearly 78%, while for Qatar it was around 82%. Studies of Saudi Arabia indicate approximately 50% for the top three banks, which were the National Commercial Bank (NCB), Samba and Riyad Bank. NCB accounted for 20% of total bank assets of SR 508 billion at year-end 2002 (SAMA, 2003).

The most extreme case of bank asset concentration was in Qatar, where the largest bank (Qatar National Bank) accounted for slightly less than 70% of total Qatari bank assets.

Development of offshore and Islamic banking

In the GCC, Bahrain has since 1975 been the pioneer in the development of Offshore Banking Units (OBUs) (Bisisu, 1984). The principal condition imposed on OBUs was a prohibition from engaging in any individual or corporate business with Bahrain residents, without the specific permission of the Bahrain Monetary Agency. The reason for this was simple: Bahrain wanted to diversify its economy and take advantage of the increased flow of oil revenues that needed fast access to banks in the main financial markets. Besides Bahrain, both Dubai and Abu Dhabi have attempted to create rival financial centres, but the Bahrain Monetary Agency has acquired a reputation as one of the most solid supervising bodies in the GCC.

Dubai, however, seems to be the more energetic and is planning to further develop its economy with a series of "free zones" that it is now extending to the services sector. These include Dubai Internet City and Dubai Media City, but in 2004 it is set to launch the biggest of them all: Dubai International Financial Center (DIFC). The DIFC will be a major competitor to Bahrain's financial industry, although it will be based on western financial concepts and not on *Islamic Shariah*. Bahrain is not standing still either, for it is planning to launch its "Bahrain Financial Harbour" by 2005.

The OBU industry however, is also subject to unstable economic conditions in the GCC. Its growth potential has been reduced significantly by increasing competition from domestic banks in the region, especially in Saudi Arabia, as well as the greater ease by which international banks have been able to access the GCC markets from their head offices without having a physical presence in the OBUs. As such, Bahrain, especially, has concentrated on trying to create a niche financial market for itself in the Islamic banking sector.

Islamic banking is gradually gaining more acceptance and credibility in the various Gulf countries. Since its origins in the mid-1960s, it has grown, not just in the Gulf, but worldwide (Archer et al., 2002, Abdeen and Shook, 1984, MEED, 2001). According to these sources, the Islamic banking community is worth some US$100 billion and growing by 10-15% per annum. With rising demand for Islamic products, conventional banks in the GCC have begun to offer products that are compatible with Islam. Bahrain sees itself as a pioneer in this field, both in terms of a strong and respected regulatory and supervisory authority (the Bahrain Monetary Agency) and also in Islamic accounting practices. No other GCC state has as many Islamic banks and financial institutions as those registered to operate in Bahrain, with 26 institutions at the last count. These include four full commercial banks, three OBUs, 16 investment banks, one representative office and two other financial services providers (BMA, 17 June 2003).

With Saudi Arabia's impending membership in the World Trade Organization (WTO), all GCC states will have become members of that organization. Potentially, this presents both opportunities and threats to existing banks. Less efficient banks with high operating costs are likely to suffer international competition. There is some fear that the entry of foreign banks, such as those contemplated for Saudi Arabia, as well as the new banking law in Kuwait authorizing foreign banks, will lead to foreign banks dominating the GCC banking industry. Some have welcomed this, especially in Kuwait, which unlike other GCC states, did not have a foreign bank presence. It is felt that the presence of "foreign banks in Kuwait, with their expert administration, abilities and resources, will improve the performance and the patterns of spending by local banks" (Haddadin, 2004). One way forward is for GCC banks to merge, creating institutions with large capital bases, which, combined with their better knowledge of local markets, could help them to effectively compete with foreign banks.

The GCC capital markets

Equity markets in the GCC are expanding, as scope for private enterprise is increasing and demand for equity investment is rising (Azzam, 1998). Figure 14.6 shows that Saudi Arabia's equity market is by far the largest in the GCC in terms of capitalization, and, indeed, the largest in the Arab world. This Figure shows that by the end of 2002, Saudi stock market capitalization had reached around US$73 billion dollars, just behind Turkey's, to which with the rest of the Arab World and the GCC were compared. Egypt had the second largest Arab stock market, and UAE and Kuwait followed. The smallest was Oman's.

Figure 14.6 Market capitalization: GCC Countries, Arab World and Turkey 2002 (US$ million)

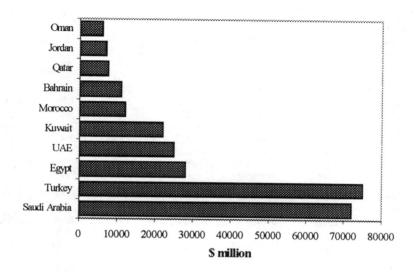

Source: *GCC Stock Market Reports, IMF*, 2003.

Earlier in this chapter, we considered how the GCC countries adopted policies to ensure that their markets were open to investors, at least from within the GCC region, as some – such as Saudi Arabia, Kuwait and UAE – do not allow foreign non-resident investors. The GCC markets are small, compared to other developing regions. The Asian Newly Industrialized Economies (ANIE's) of South East Asia are larger than Saudi Arabia's, but the Kuwaiti and Bahraini markets show a higher percentage of GDP. The Kuwaiti Stock Exchange is the most active in the GCC and Arab world in terms of volume of trading, while stock exchanges in Oman, Qatar and the UAE are relatively new (Naggar, 1994).

However, in common with Saudi Arabia, GCC equity markets exhibit few traded companies and low turnover ratios when compared with stock markets in industrial countries and other rapidly growing emerging markets. Table 14.12 also shows that the GCC equity markets face a number of constraints: there are insufficient brokers and market makers, and foreign access is generally restricted to GCC nationals. Only Oman and Bahrain markets are free to foreign entry, but these are restricted to GCC residents and foreign residents in their countries. UAE and Kuwait are restricted and Saudi Arabia is closed to foreign investors.

Table 14.12 Turkey and Arab Stock markets performance comparison
2001

Regional Comparison	No. of Listed	Market Capitalization $ million	Value Traded $ million	Price/ Earning	Price/ Book	Div. Yield
Saudi Arabia	75	*67171*	*17313*	*17.17*	*2.41*	*3.15*
Turkey	315	69659	179209	15.39	3.11	1.11
Egypt	1076	28741	11120	7.56	1.72	5.3
UAE	54	23262	118	15.1	na	na
Kuwait	77	20772	4210	9.3	na	na
Morocco	53	10899	1094	11.89	2.2	3.24
Bahrain	42	6624	247	12.94	1.04	4.03
Qatar	22	5152	239	9.5	na	na
Jordan	163	4943	416	13.9	1.16	3.39
Oman	131	3463	553	23.86	2.41	7.52
	Average Company Size ($ million)	*Entry to Foreign Investors*	*Stock Market Performance 2000*	*Turnover Ratio 2000*	*Gross National Income*	*Market Cap/GNI*
Saudi Arabia	895.5	Closed	12.1	27.1	173	39%
Turkey	221.1	Free	-51.7	196.5	186.49	37%
Egypt	26.7	Free	-44.3	36.1	86.54	33%
UAE	na	Restricted	-17.7	0.5	60.74	38%
Kuwait	269.8	Restricted	-6.5	21.3	32.5	64%
Morocco	205.6	Free	-20.1	8.9	33.71	32%
Bahrain	157.7	Free	-20.7	3.6	6.8	97%
Qatar	234.2	Free	-8	4.5	14.83	35%
Jordan	30.3	Free	-20.8	7.7	7.7	64%
Oman	26.4	Free	-16	14.2	17.83	19%

Source: *CCFI Database and Emerging Fact book*, 2001.

There is substantial scope in most GCC countries for further development of capital markets, including securities, money markets and stock exchanges. The range of instruments available to borrowers and savers could be expanded further, as borrowers switch from traditional banking instruments to equity and marketable securities. Ultimately, all the GCC countries are aiming to open up their markets to foreign investors, for the amount of foreign direct investment (FDI) to the region has been small relative to their economies. The GCC capital markets are indeed at a crossroad (Seznec, 1995). Qatar announced in 2004 that foreigners, both individuals and companies, could deal in its stock market as long as they did not hold more than 25% of a firm's issued capital (Zawya, 4 August 2004).

Several countries have implemented capital market reforms and introduced new regulations to ensure that capital markets are better served through independent authorities. Some examples are Saudi Arabia's new Capital Market Law of 2003, and those of the UAE, Bahrain and Oman the same year. These regulatory changes will take time to bear fruit, as reforms are also needed in legal and commercial laws to ensure foreign participation on an equal footing (Seznec 1995, Azzam, 1998).

Despite obvious advances in the financial and capital markets of the region over the past 30 years, there are those who advocate for further GCC financial reforms in order to create a "financial deepening" of existing capital markets. They reason that underdeveloped financial markets have limitations, whereby commercial bank activity tends to be restricted to deposit and loan activities. Regulations inhibit the rise of specialized financial institutions (such as savings and loans, real estate mortgage banks), and the supply of equity and debt instruments tends to be limited (Azzam, 1997).

The following is advocated:

First, there is a greater need for effective disclosure. Information and analysis on local companies and stock markets would provide investors with a reliable database, through which companies listed on the Gulf stock markets would maintain a higher level of public disclosure than present. This would comply with international accounting standards.

Second, an independent regulatory body needs to be established. While there are presently GCC regulations to prohibit price manipulation, monitoring and enforcement mechanisms in these markets are not very effective. The stock price movements are often turbulent, but with no apparent specific economic cause. Insider trading penalties should be enforced; family or affiliated group share holdings should be restricted.

Third, it is essential to deepen current stock markets by listing privately held, family-owned companies, which seem to be the mainstay and backbone of the Gulf economies (Field, 1992, Fahim, 1995). Given their economic significance in terms of investment, employment and GDP contribution, it is essential that the more successful family-owned businesses go public, on the assumption that the founding family retains some stake. This will increase the size of the market and provide liquidity and depth.

Fourth, the GCC stock markets should be linked. Some positive steps have already been taken, such as the UAE-based Arab Monetary Fund (AMF) linking six Arab stock markets in a database that can facilitate inter-Arab and GCC investment. Stock markets in Kuwait, Jordan, Bahrain, Tunisia, Oman and Morocco are linked into this AMF Arab markets database, which lists 377 companies. In 1995, the Bahrain and Oman stock markets were linked, making cross-buying and selling possible. Kuwait, Jordan and Qatar have all expressed an interest to join. This linking can facilitate government sales of sovereign securities in such cross-linked markets, increasing the amounts that can be borrowed and helping to deepen the capital markets.

Fifth, there is a need for specialist investment banks in the GCC. Such financial institutions would provide stronger financial analysis, underwriting of shares' issue, flotation of shares to the public and market making functions. They could advise GCC companies on the optimum mix of debt and equity borrowing, on pricing levels and on the timing for coming into the market. They could inform Gulf corporations about how to obtain international credit ratings from institutions such as Moody's and Standard & Poor.

Sixth, the GCC countries must not slow their efforts at economic and financial integration, if they are to have a powerful voice in international affairs. Debate surrounds the issue of the adoption of a common or unified currency for the region by 2010. Article 22 of the GCC Council Summit Unified Agreements states that, "Member States shall seek to coordinate their financial, monetary and banking policies and enhance cooperation between monetary agencies and central banks, including the endeavor to establish a joint currency in order to further their desired economies" (GCC Secretariat, 2001). The unified Gulf currency, whatever it may be called – *riyal, dirham or dinar* – will emerge as one of the major currencies of the Arab world and should help ease remittances between one country and another, and boost the development of the GCC capital markets.

The new currency will be fixed or pegged against major international currencies, such as the dollar, the Euro and the yen, to reflect the region's international trading partners (Oweiss, 2000). Much needs to be done beforehand, however, especially in achieving harmony and agreement between the GCC member states on acceptable levels of budget deficits, inflation, monetary and fiscal policies. These are matters that the European Union member states also had to deal with before establishing their single currency, the Euro. The first step towards monetary integration was taken when it was announced in 2004 that UAE would host the proposed GCC Central Bank (AFP, October 2004).

GCC trade patterns

The trade composition of GCC countries can best be described as "asymmetrical": exports are concentrated largely in crude oil and petroleum products, while imports are more diversified. This situation means that GCC countries are vulnerable to pricing developments in international commodity markets – oil in particular, over which the GCC countries have limited control. According to the World Trade Organization, Saudi Arabia accounted for some 5.4% of world exports in 1980 but this had fallen to 1.1% by 2001. Imports fell from 1.45% in 1980 to 0.50% in 2001 (WTO, 2001). Some have argued that in the face of this erosion of its global trading position, Saudi Arabia tended to adopt protectionist, import-substitution policies, in contrast to more outward-looking economic policies, such as those of the UAE and Bahrain (Wilson et. al., 2003).

The GCC economies are amongst the most open in the world, with no foreign exchange controls and relatively low tariff and quota protection. Figure 14.7 illustrates the geographical distribution of GCC foreign trade for 2001, and it demonstrates that the major export markets are Japan, South East Asia, European Union (EU) and U.S.A., in that order. The EU tended to dominate imports, with around 30% of total, while South East Asia, U.S.A. and Japan followed in importance.

Figure 14.7 Geographical distribution of GCC foreign trade in 2001 (%)

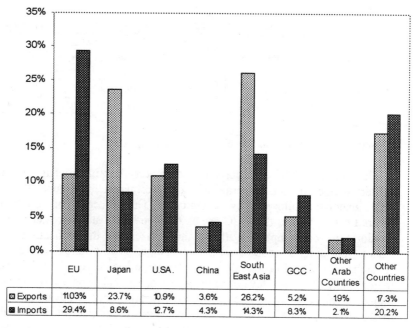

	EU	Japan	U.SA.	China	South East Asia	GCC	Other Arab Countries	Other Countries
Exports	11.03%	23.7%	10.9%	3.6%	26.2%	5.2%	1.9%	17.3%
Imports	29.4%	8.6%	12.7%	4.3%	14.3%	8.3%	2.1%	20.2%

Source: *Gulf Organization for Industrial Consulting,* 2002.

The GCC faces a very different world economy than only 20 years ago. Trade with South East Asia and Europe has now become much more significant, while trade with the U.S.A. is declining. International exchange rate adjustments have had a major impact on import sourcing, and the fixed exchange rate policies of the GCC, closely tied to the U.S. dollar, have affected the value of imports due to the sharp fall in the U.S. dollar during 2002/2003.

Even more striking is the lack of meaningful diversity in the pattern of GCC exports. This is illustrated by Figure 14.8.

*Figure 14.*8 GCC commodity exports by major commodities (%)

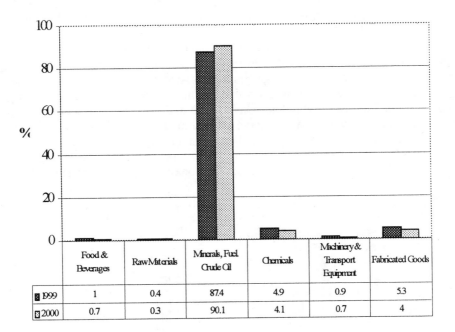

	Food & Beverages	Raw Materials	Minerals, Fuel Crude Oil	Chemicals	Machinery & Transport Equipment	Fabricated Goods
1999	1	0.4	87.4	4.9	0.9	5.3
2000	0.7	0.3	90.1	4.1	0.7	4

Source: *Gulf Organization for Industrial Consulting,* 2002.

The picture of GCC exports by commodity confirms what we said earlier: that crude oil, minerals and fuel accounted for around 90% of total exports, followed by chemicals. The process of economic diversification within the GCC seems to have had a much greater impact on domestic consumption patterns than on export diversification. The reason is simple: comparative advantage. The policy of export specialization based on comparative advantage has served the GCC well in the short-run. The development of petrochemicals and energy-related industries made economic sense in terms of comparative advantage. But in the long-term, GCC companies that aspire to compete internationally must establish cost control, effective marketing and product differentiation to help them to open up export markets.

Trade between GCC countries

Gulf economic specialists often comment on how little inter-GCC trade takes place in comparison with non-GCC countries (Wilson, 1998, Erian et. al., 1997, Wilson, 2003). The overwhelming amount of Saudi Arabian trade is with Asia, Europe and the U.S.A. but as Table 14.13 indicates, inter-GCC trade has began to rise steadily to reach around SR 14.8 billion in imports and SR 6.7 billion in exports for 2001.

Table 14.13 Saudi non-oil trade with GCC countries
(Million Riyals)

	(1999)			(2000)			(2001)		
	Imports from	*Exports to*	*The difference*	*Imports from*	*Exports to*	*The difference*	*Imports from*	*Exports to*	*The difference*
UAE	6,422	3,082	-3,340	8,289	3,261	-5,028	9,757	3,401	-6,356
Bahrain	2,043	995	-1,048	1,948	910	-1,038	2,744	503	-2,241
Kuwait	776	1,769	993	881	1,749	868	978	1,549	571
Qatar	399	671	272	594	709	115	757	740	-17
Oman	353	505	152	494	412	-82	563	548	-15
Total	9,993	7,022	-2,971	12,206	7,041	-5,165	14,799	6,741	-8,058

Source: *SAMA*, 2003.

Saudi Arabia runs a trade deficit with the GCC as a whole, especially with the UAE and Bahrain. The reduction of tariffs to 5% between the GCC countries from 1 January 2003 will give a further boost to trade, especially between Saudi Arabia and the UAE. The GCC was founded with the signing of the Unified Economic Agreement in 1981, which stipulated free trade between the member states (GCC Secretariat, 1981), but it is Dubai that has taken advantage of trade liberalization to boost its exports to Saudi Arabia.

Import figures for some GCC states, notably the UAE, are greater than local demand would indicate, due to significant re-exporting. Although there is some re-exporting from Bahrain and Kuwait to other GCC states, it is Dubai that is the major re-exporting hub of the GCC, as evidenced in Table 14.14. Dubai is the UAE's trading centre. The GCC's largest duty-free area, the *Jabal Ali* Duty-Free Zone in Dubai, now serves over 600 international companies. As the Table indicates, there has been almost a trebling of re-exports over the period 1986-1995, and this is expected to rise with the reduction of inter-GCC tariffs.

Table 14.14 Re-exports & exports from Dubai 1986-1995

	Re-exports Million Kilos	*Re-exports US$ million*	*Exports US$ million*	*Re-exports/exports Percentage(%)*
1986	562	943	351	268
1987	961	1,427	359	397
1988	594	1,385	469	295
1989	941	1,774	567	312
1990	950	2,070	625	331
1991	851	2,049	758	270
1992	1,050	2,451	899	272
1993	1,178	2,799	964	290
1994	1,185	2,906	891	326
1995	1,485	3,560	1,276	278

Source: *Dubai Chamber of Commerce External Trade Figures*, 1997.

As we have already mentioned in this chapter, the level of imports to the UAE have risen sharply, reaching US$35 billion for 2002. Most of this was re-exports through Dubai, with the ratio of re-exports to exports averaging at around 300%. Dubai's success stems from a combination of factors, ranging from an open economic system, minimal bureaucracy, ideal location for bulk imports and trans-shipment in smaller consignments after modification for the GCC markets. Dubai also offers the availability of bonded warehouses and logistics support. The government of Dubai has made no secret of its intention to be seen as the "Singapore" of the Middle East.

The opening up of the Iraqi market following the war in 2003, will only add to Dubai's pre-eminence as a major trading centre. Reports from the Saudi local press indicate that Saudi companies are seeking to capitalize on Dubai's strengths and there are unofficial estimates that as many as 2,500 Saudi companies have shifted their operations to Dubai over the past three years alone (Abdul Ghafour, P.K., 2003). If this exodus of Saudi companies to Dubai continues in the next few years, eventually it will be difficult to distinguish between Saudi and non-Saudi re-exports from Dubai to the Kingdom. The policy of "enforced" Saudization in the Kingdom might accelerate this trend.

GCC demographics and the labour market

The GCC countries have one of the highest population growth rates in the world. The growth rates of the UAE, Kuwait and Oman are even higher than Saudi Arabia, as illustrated in the next set of tables and graphs. Saudi Arabia's population dwarfs the combined GCC States. The large percentage of expatriates in virtually all the GCC countries is striking. The average is nearly 40% for all the GCC, with the highest rate of 77% for the UAE and the lowest of 25% for Oman for 2000. This is set out in Table 14.15.

Table 14.15 GCC: Percentage of expatriates in populations 1975-2000

	1975	*1985*	*1997*	*2000*
Bahrain	20.7	35.0	39.0	33.0
Kuwait	51.6	72.1	65.5	69.0
Oman	16.9	21.8	27.2	25.3
Qatar	58.8	60.0	67.3	70.0
KSA	25.4	23.2	30.8	25.0
UAE	69.5	78.7	75.6	77.0
GCC Average	**31.2**	**32.9**	**38.5**	**40.1**

Sources: *GCC Fact book*, 2001, National Plans.

During the past three decades, GCC governments have launched massive programs aimed at improving the living and educational standards of their native population. This has resulted in a reduction of infant mortality, in a longer life span and in higher birth rates. In fact, some GCC countries, such as Oman and Bahrain, have seen lower national birth rates recently, as seen from Table 14.16.

Table 14.16 Population growth rates, 1950-2000
(average annual percentages)

	1950-1960	1960-1970	1970-1980	1980-1990	1990-1997	1996-1997	1997-2000
Bahrain	3.0	3.5	4.7	3.8	3.0	3.6	2.5
Kuwait	6.2	10.4	6.3	4.5	1.0	6.8	5.3
Oman	2.0	2.7	4.2	4.4	5.8	3.7	2.8
Qatar	6.1	9.5	7.5	7.9	1.1	2.7	3.5
Saudi Arabia	2.4	3.5	5.0	5.4	3.3	3.8	3.6
UAE	2.6	9.5	16.4	4.6	6.3	5.6	5.4

Sources: *World Health Organization, GCC Fact Books*, (various years).

Rates of population growth ranging from 2.5 to 5.4% are high by international standards. A large majority are under-30s, as noted earlier in this chapter.

GCC population statistics and national labour participation rates are notoriously difficult to obtain for several reasons: the differing estimates provided by national governments, the irregularity of population censuses and of the breakdown by nationals and expatriates. Table 14.17 sets out the most recent population estimates for all the GCC countries and the figures indicate that nationals were approximately 20.6 million or 65% of a total population of 31.1 million in 2000.

Saudi Arabia's population – both national and expatriate – dwarfed all the other GCC countries. What is important in the long-term, is job creation for nationals of the GCC and labour participation for both males and females. The combined forces of population growth, rapid demand for education and the desire for the GCC states to economically diversify, have affected overall national labour participation levels and the direction of employment.

Table 14.17 Populations of nationals and expatriates 2000

	Nationals	Expatriates	Total
Bahrain	455,600	224,400	680,000
Kuwait	780,000	1,621,000	2,401,000
Oman	1,785,000	595,000	2,380,000
Qatar	195,000	455,000	650,000
KSA	16,725,000	5,575,000	22,300,000
UAE	664,700	2,255,300	2,890,000
GCC	20,605,300	10,705,700	31,311,000

Source: *World Bank, ESCWA*, 2001.

As Table 14.18 below illustrates, there are great challenges to overcome in meeting the labour participation aspirations of GCC nationals. The labour participation rate of nationals to foreigners is rather low for the GCC as a whole, at around 28% for 2000, but with marked country differences.

Table 14.18 Percentage of nationals in the workforce 1975-2000

	1975	1985	1997	2000
Bahrain	61.0	41.9	38.1	43.3
Kuwait	30.2	18.4	16.0	15.1
Oman	62.8	48.7	35.2	44.6
Qatar	18.2	18.4	18.4	17.2
KSA	57.0	28.3	35.7	39.0
UAE	15.2	9.2	9.6	8.2
GCC	40.2	27.6	25.5	27.9

Sources: *World Bank, ESCWA* (Various years).

Table 14.18 shows us that the highest national participation rates were in Oman and Bahrain at around 44%, while the lowest were for the UAE at 8.2% and Kuwait at 17.2%. The reason for these relatively low national labour participation rates is that from their boom days GCC countries have followed a common economic development strategy that was characterized by high labour imports.

As in Saudi Arabia, the labour markets in the GCC countries are segmented along several dimensions: between public and private sectors, national and non-nationals, and skilled and unskilled labour. In some GCC countries, unemployment is also beginning to rise, but for some countries it is still a relatively recent phenomenon of a largely frictional (in-between jobs) and voluntary nature. However, in the years ahead, labour market conditions are expected to tighten as the number of nationals entering the labour force grows. This is coupled with a situation in which some GCC governments can no longer act as employers of first and last resort because of budgetary considerations.

Limiting the number of expatriate workers

Given the preference for nationals to work in the government sector in the GCC, foreign workers tend to be employed in the private sector in manufacturing, construction and services. Policies such as the *Kafala* or sponsorship system in the GCC have heightened structural dependence on foreign labour, in fact insulating foreign labour from economic downswings in the national economies. This phenomenon of *Kafala* has been commented upon (Longva, 1997, Qudsi, 1997) and is one cause of the unusual occurrence of recurring foreign labour unemployment at the same time as labour shortages for the same skills. This is due to the inability of free "non-Kafala" labour market demand and supply forces to operate effectively.

One aspect of foreign labour in the GCC states that attracts most attention is the size of workers remittances, which local commentators argue is detrimental to the GCC economies. In terms of volume, the figures for remittances are substantial. Figure 14.9 shows that the outflow of workers remittances has been rising over the period 1975-1995, with some slight falls in various years due to economic downturn (Birks et. al., 1992). The total amount of remittances now accounts for around 22-25% of the combined GDP of the GCC countries (Chadhury, 1989, 1997, Sinclair, 1988).

Figure 14.9 GCC: Outflow of workers' remittances 1975-1995

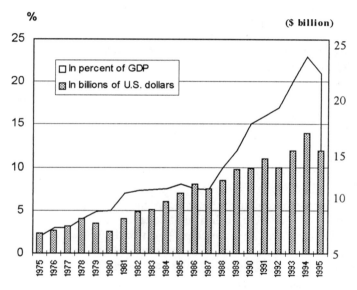

Source: *IMF*, 1997.

As unemployment is virtually non-existent in Qatar, there is no formal labour market strategy, while Saudi Arabia, Bahrain and Oman have implemented *Saudization, Bahrainization and Omanization* plans to replace foreigners with nationals. Kuwait has policies to achieve the creation of a specific number of jobs for their nationals; these include raising the cost of expatriate labour and upgrading the skills of nationals. As for the UAE, there are no formal plans covering all the Federation, but the Dubai Strategic Development Plan aims to increase the share of nationals in Dubai's labour force from 7% to 10% by raising labour force participation and facilitating the employment of nationals in the private sector.

The relatively limited amount of inter-GCC labour migration seems surprising 23 years after the GCC's establishment. With the exception of Bahraini skilled and semi-skilled labour working in Saudi Arabia's Eastern Province, and some Omani labour working in the UAE, there is little evidence to date of inter-GCC labour mobility. Such inter-GCC labour flows could overcome some of the perceived negative social aspects of non-Gulf labour (Attiyah, 1996, Girgis et. al., 2002, ESCWA, 1993).

Labour market issues are one of the key policy challenges for the GCC countries. They all recognize that such issues are closely linked to other structural policies related to economic efficiency and to the role of the private and public sectors. As such, policies to increase the flexibility of the labour market are now being defined in a broader framework that includes structural budget reforms and privatization to shoulder the burden of national job creation. These are all long-term structural policies. To create jobs for nationals in the short-run, GCC countries, to various degrees, will apply employment quotas, percentage restrictions on foreign labour, and administrative directives. None of the above measures can substitute for human resource development that aims to match the skill profile of national labour with the present and future requirements of the private sector. Dubai and Bahrain, and, to a lesser extent, Oman, have shown that it can be done and other GCC states are now embarking on upgrading their educational systems to cope with a knowledge-based economic future.

Conclusion

Half a century ago, all six of the countries that make up the modern day Gulf Cooperation Council were poor, mostly thinly populated and loosely governed. All were pushed into modernity by oil wealth and left trying to find their way in a fast changing world. All had to cope with some of the most radical social changes the world had ever seen in such a condensed period of time, including the world's fastest population growth rates, the most rapid urbanization and the biggest tide of managed labour migration. The consequences are still being felt today. Political events in the region, including the turmoil of wars and the problems of domestic terrorism, have affected the GCC. But with small but concrete steps, the GCC has steadily solidified the 1981 Union. The 24th GCC Summit held in Kuwait in December, 2003, boldly addressed domestic and international issues, ranging from cooperation on terrorism to reaffirming their commitment to a monetary union and single currency in 2005 and 2010 respectively (Arab News, 23 December 2003). Economic issues were high on the summit agenda, as were educational reforms aimed at reformulating school curricula to promote moderation and critical thinking among the young.

Undoubtedly, the GCC countries and citizens face many challenges in this new millennium. While there is some discussion about enlarging the GCC to include some other countries, this seems premature. In fact, the possibility of expansion was categorically denied by GCC Secretary General Al-Attiyah at the Kuwait Summit (Arab News, 20 December 2003). The success of the GCC to date has been based on the social, economic and cultural similarities of the member states. Diversity in membership might bring divisiveness.

However, it is more important to ensure that the GCC becomes open and accessible to the ordinary citizens of the member states so that they understand the objectives of the GCC and how it affects their lives. More co-ordination is needed to get this message across to those in the fields of economics, finance, commerce, education, communication and education. To date, the ordinary GCC citizen is not fully informed about the GCC and its structure, or about transnational opportunities for all its citizens in terms of jobs, mobility and economic opportunities.

At the same time the governments of the GCC are embarking on internal economic, political and social reforms with far-reaching consequences for their citizens.

Each state of the GCC is moving ahead at its own pace of reform and change. Inaction is no longer an option. It is a measure of statesmanship to balance change with taking care not to alienate those who are feeling most threatened. Such a balance will ensure that the GCC family survives as a stronger political and economic entity in the twenty-first Century.

Summary of Key points

- *The GCC was established to effect co-ordination and interconnection between its 6 founding member states in 1981 in the economic, social and political fields.*
- *The GCC economies face similar structural problems and are dependent on few revenue sources. The period since 1981 saw the GCC go through several phases including a consolidation phase, several crises phases relating to the Gulf wars, and the current adjustment and reform phase.*
- *The GCC countries adopt open, free market economic philosophies and are committed to economic and social reforms to meet the aspirations of their largely young population.*
- *Economic diversification and economic integration have now assumed great importance for all GCC countries in various degrees of success, as oil and gas revenue dependency is still high. Bahrain and Dubai have achieved some measurable degree of diversification into non-oil services.*
- *The diversification of the GCC manufacturing base has been erratic due to the size of the domestic national markets. There is continued emphasis on hydrocarbon projects in the major GCC energy producers.*
- *The GCC financial sector witnessed rapid development and integration with international markets and both Bahrain and*

Dubai have established themselves as world financial centers. Capital markets are being developed to tap national private sector capital back into GCC projects. The GCC central banks, recognizing that full monetary union is planned by 2010, are slowly integrating and harmonizing their policies.

- *GCC countries' international trade is still "asymmetrical", with exports highly concentrated largely in crude oil and petroleum products while imports are more diversified. This means that the GCC economies are vulnerable to pricing developments in international commodities. Trade between the GCC countries is still limited, except between Saudi Arabia and Dubai and Bahrain, with the latter countries enjoying a surplus trade balance due to re-exports to Saudi Arabia.*

- *Internal demographics and composition of the population of the GCC countries is causing some concern due to the imbalance between nationals and expatriates in some GCC countries. The UAE has the highest percentage of foreign workers at 77% of total population, followed by Qatar and Kuwait. The lowest is for Saudi Arabia at 25%. All GCC countries are currently re-examining their foreign labour force policies. Some have adopted "localization" as a means of employing nationals, with Saudization, Omanization, Bahrainization being the most prominent.*

Critical thinking

1. What have been the major benefits of the establishment of the GCC on (a) the ordinary citizen of the GCC, and (b) GCC international bargaining power?

2. "All the GCC countries need to harmonize their economic, monetary and fiscal policies before full monetary integration can occur in 2010". Discuss the   prospects for full monetary integration.

3. "Free movement of national labor between labor surplus and labor deficit countries of the GCC will solve regional unemployment". Is this necessarily true? What type of skills will be required for labor mobility to occur?

4. "The future of the region lies in non-oil diversification. Bahrain and Dubai have shown the way". What type of inter-GCC policies can be adopted to pursue this objective?

5. Discuss how an integrated GCC capital market can aid the economic development of the GCC countries. What measures need to be adopted to establish an inter-GCC capital market?

Chapter 15

CONCLUSION: THE CHALLENGES AHEAD

Reforms should begin at home and stay there.

Anonymous

So rich and yet so poor

For the last 30 years, modern economic history has seen few national changes as rapid and turbulent as those that have affected Saudi Arabia. They have transformed the desert Kingdom beyond recognition. For better or for worse, the Kingdom and its citizens have to live with the consequences of decisions taken in earlier days, and press on to meet the growing list of challenges facing the country in the new millennium. Sitting on top of a quarter of the world's proven oil reserves, Saudi Arabia attracts both envy and fear of its economic potential. However, no other country, some analysts would argue, is so rich and yet so poor. Despite massive oil reserves, its per capita income is declining; the country is beset by a rising tide of population growth and the spectre of growing unemployment. Despite many discussions about diversification and public exhortations to the private sector, the Kingdom is still reliant on two main exports: crude oil and energy-related petrochemical products.

Given its undoubted potential and world economic power, what are the major obstacles to Saudi Arabia assuming a more rightful position among the league of economic nations? Saudi Arabia's power was aptly demonstrated during 2004, when oil prices rose so sharply. The Kingdom, once again, played a significant moderating role on world oil prices by expanding output, thus confirming its position as the premier oil producer in times of global crises.

However, domestic issues are now paramount, including much-needed economic and social reforms, along with better management of citizens' expectations. In mid-January, 2003, Crown Prince Abdullah, who by all accounts is the main driving force behind current reforms, unveiled a "Charter to Reform the Arab Stand". This Charter is designed to strengthen the Arab position in the wider world, and it envisages substantial reforms across the region in the political, social and economic spheres. One such change would be greater political participation. Only through such changes, the Crown Prince believes, can the Arab nations develop and grow, including Saudi Arabia. The events following the third Gulf War in April, 2003, and the bombings in the Saudi capital of Riyadh in May, 2003, make this plea ever more urgent.

The external initiative of the Crown Prince has been matched by the need for internal reforms. A new Saudi Cabinet was announced in early May, 2003, representing the third Saudi Cabinet reshuffle: the first was in 1995 and the second in 1999. Most Ministers who had served two four-year terms were replaced by other people. The new Ministers were generally drawn from the nascent Saudi Parliament – the *Majlis Al Shoura*, or Consultative Council. One significant exception to this was oil Minister Naimi, whose term was extended to provide continuity in this strategic sector. The most visible changes were the separation of the Ministry of Finance and National Economy into two Ministries. A separate Ministry of Finance was created. The function of Economy was   rolled into the Ministry of Planning, resulting in a new Ministry of Economy and Planning.

Previous Ministries were amalgamated to create synergies and internal efficiencies. As such, new Ministries of Commerce and Industry, Communications and Information Technology, as well as Water and Electricity were created as "Super Ministries" to take the Saudi economy forward. The creation of the Communication and Information Technology portfolio underlined the urgency to position the Kingdom in the new technological era. The appointment of the President of the Jeddah Chamber of Commerce as a Minster of State was a welcome sign that the viewpoint of the private sector would be adequately represented.

There was some disappointment that a new independent Ministry of External Trade was not created, given the importance the Kingdom attaches to joining the WTO. Such a Ministry would also provide a boost for Saudi export markets.

Neither the Cabinet reshuffle nor the establishment of the new Ministries is a mere cosmetic change. The Saudi government is very much aware that the Kingdom has grown too rapidly in a short period of time and is now too complex an economy and society for only a small group of people, no matter how skilled, to manage. No small group can make all the decisions. Just as there is a call for diversification of the economy, so too there needs to be diversification in decision-making and responsibility; otherwise the Saudi administrative process might be overwhelmed by the sheer weight and speed of change.

It can be   argued that the Kingdom will not change, and that the decision-making process is slow and cumbersome, which sometimes makes it too late to be effective. However one can point to the enormous changes that have taken place over the last three decades. As stated earlier, there are probably few countries in the world today that have changed as dramatically as Saudi Arabia in such a short period.

The sequencing of reforms and changes is also important, so that it is not seen as competition between external and domestic reform. As the experiences of the newly emerging countries of the former Soviet bloc showed us, it can be destabilizing to move forward too quickly on the external agenda, leaving domestic reforms lagging behind. Both need to progress at a comparable pace. The events in Riyadh underscored this. At the same time, there were voices outside Saudi Arabia pressing for much faster changes and reforms within the Kingdom, especially on female issues, but they realized that this could not be externally driven and agreed that the pace of change had to come from within.

Physical infrastructural changes are not a key issue. Visitors to the Kingdom are often astonished at just how developed Saudi Arabia is, with all the trappings and luxuries of a modern consumer society. Rather, the issue is about changing people's attitudes, behaviours and expectations. The pace of change can be quickened or slowed to suit a particular country's social, religious and political evolution. It must maintain a harmonious relationship with the above factors, for otherwise there will be a widening gap between actual changes and reforms and the expectations of the citizens.

Managing expectations

While some sections of society might feel aggrieved that they have not shared in the prosperity that their elder brothers and fathers enjoyed during the boom years of the 1970s and early 1980s, there is a new dawn of realism within Saudi society that times have indeed changed. Crown Prince Abdullah has given a clear message about the end of the welfare state system. Young Saudis have began to lower their expectations of high salaries, automatic government tenure and minimal education levels in order to obtain jobs.

The spectre of unemployment, coupled with the younger generation's higher education levels, especially amongst females, has also brought about a change in social attitudes towards having large families. Younger, more educated Saudi females are no longer shy about discussing their preferred family size, the way their mothers and grandmothers were. It is not impossible to forecast a reduced Saudi population growth rate of under 2.5% p.a. within the next decade, as well as lower fertility rates than the current high levels. Birth control will eventually be taught at schools, bearing in mind social taboos on the subject.

But taboos of all sorts are being broken in Saudi Arabia at a quickening pace over the past few years, confounding critics who claim that Saudi Arabians do not willingly change. These challenges to taboos range from accepting women as factory workers to admonishing those institutions or gatherings that invite senior government officials , and then plant pre-screened questions for them with attendees. As the local media succinctly put it, "let the people speak their mind." It is crucial to the current ruling Saudi system for government officials to know directly and in person how the public feels and how they view their performance, not to hear it through intermediaries. It is still astonishing to note how accessible the current rulers of Saudi Arabia are to their citizens through face-to-face meetings, carried out in open receptions where citizens can personally meet the highest ranked Princes to air their grievances.

While some semblance of this practice might remain in the near future, eventually there will unfortunately be a more impersonal bureaucracy to handle such grievances, as we see in the developed world. While many might view this practice as a romantic idiosyncrasy, would not most people feel closer to their government or ruler if they had a comparable "Saudi system" in place?

The degree of success in generating sustainable levels of new employment will be the central measure by which any future Saudi administrative and economic reforms will be judged. *Saudization* can be a two-edged sword. The government's natural desire to replace foreigners with Saudis to resolve a growing unemployment problem needs to be a tempered with the long-term consequences to the private sector. These might include reduced efficiency, lower productivity, higher costs and economic slowdown should *Saudization* be unwillingly enforced. The model has to be more of a "partnership", exemplified by the commendable results of the Saudi banks' *Saudization* experience. Both foreign bank partners and the Saudi community benefited in terms of profitability, skill transfer, productivity and product innovation.

Saudis now occupy a diverse range of senior management positions in this key sector, for which they receive relatively high salaries due to productivity returns The Saudi banks' *Saudization* experiment has been the envy of other countries in the GCC, who had much earlier decided either to allow a dual national/foreign banking sector to emerge side-by-side (UAE, Bahrain), or forbade foreign banks completely (Kuwait). In 2004, interestingly enough, Kuwait reversed this policy and started to allow foreign banks to return.

Foreign workers

The issue of foreign workers and how they are treated and replaced must be approached with care and caution. This could become one of the most contentious issues in the years ahead. Most books on the economy of Saudi Arabia have tended to discuss this matter in purely statistical terms. They have neglected to delve more deeply, beyond the numbers, to assess the potential economic implications should the policy of *Saudization* be mishandled. A rushed policy of *Saudization* could bring about a reduction in both actual and potential Gross Domestic Product. If expatriate workers feel threatened and begin to voluntarily "withdraw" part of their labor input, they could create economic inefficiencies.

As we have pointed out in this book, it is difficult to speak of a Saudi Arabian labor market, in the sense of a unified, open market where a single price is paid for a specific amount of labor. Instead, the Saudi Arabian labour market is characterized by segmentation into nationalities. Within such groups, pay scales are determined relative to labor markets in their country of origin. As such, unrestricted labor mobility is a necessary prerequisite for a free labor market that eliminates pools of unemployed expatriates in the Kingdom. At the same time, the labor market experiences market price distortions because of the arrival of further expatriate workers, under the current sponsorship *kafeel* system.

Saudi Arabia has never accepted as permanent the immigrant communities in their midst; they have always planned that labour imports would be a temporary phenomenon. Saudi Arabia hopes, eventually, to repatriate all foreign nationals, although the Kingdom accepts the inevitability of some selective immigration and naturalization. Both options were discussed in 2004, when the *Majlis Al Shoura* debated granting Saudi citizenship to expatriates who met certain stringent religious, language, moral and other residency requirements. They also discussed a more invigorated attempt by the new Saudi Minister of Labor to curtail labour entry by screening visa applications submitted by the private sector. The Saudi authorities do not seem to have been caught off balance by the large numbers of foreign workers present in the country, and the Kingdom has shown a remarkable capability in managing this large flow that sets them apart from any nation in the world that utilizes migrant labour.

Foreign workers were meant to fulfil their obligations, receive their payment and return to their homeland. At no point, over the past three decades, did Saudi Arabia feel totally overwhelmed by the expatriates, or feel that they had lost control of the management and administration of this mass of people. Instead they have focused on the refinement of the sponsorship *iqama* (residency) system. Because the Kingdom is intensely concerned to preserve its unique cultural identity, they have also stressed the social aspects of the immigrants' presence.

This relationship sometimes puts a strain on the expatriate workforce. Most of them are in a temporary situation. They feel like they are in a hotel; they can never entertain the illusion of being at home. This feeling of isolation is magnified by the security threats faced by some western communities following domestic bombings and acts of terrorism. National groups stick together, even though, with some exceptions, they did not know each other before. Together they are a collection of solitudes.

The eventual entry of Saudi Arabia into the World Trade Organization and stricter adherence to International Labour Office (ILO) regulations will bring about some changes to current labour policies. Until then, the expatriate labour market will be open to abuse and some exploitation. It is not surprising that some sections of the Saudi private sector are reluctant to replace foreign workers with nationals on various pretexts.

And what of the expatriates who return after a "stint" of duty in the Kingdom – ranging from the shortest possible contract of two years to several decades for many workers? They often face problems when they return to reclaim their place in the societies they left. They find that their friends and associates back home don't understand or appreciate the things they have experienced. For those that do settle, their expanded experiences, the higher degree of responsibility they had assumed and the new technologies they learned, make expatriate labour more valuable to the home country.

Saudi Arabia has undoubtedly contributed to the human "capital transfer" process that has benefited labour exporting countries. For others that do not settle, there are a host of problems. They are forced to forget a whole area of their lives or to meet with other former expatriates, like veterans of campaigns. Some cannot make the adjustments and return overseas to become *defacto* career expatriates, moving from job to job around the world like nomads, maintaining contact with friends they have made along the way.

The presence of these expatriates has undoubtedly brought about all of Saudi Arabia's material benefits. Many voices, including from the government, have argued that expatriate workers are valued guests and will be protected as such. This was especially expressed during the tense period of the third Gulf War and domestic terror acts. This spirit needs to be nourished, if a successful and willing handover of responsibilities and technical skills to Saudi labour is to occur as part of the *"Saudization"* process. At the same time, any significant exodus of skilled expatriate labour will bring forward the day when qualified Saudis take responsibility in their own country, either through skill transfer or "learning by doing".

Regional events

While the official ending in April, 2003, of the third Gulf War in Iraq was welcomed by many, in the hope that it would ease the suffering and plight of ordinary Iraqis, others, including many Saudi economists, wondered about the immediate and long-term implications to the Kingdom.

With the prevailing "wait-and-see" attitude, pre-war economic activity slackened, and the Saudi private sector noted reduced consumption expenditure for non-essentials and other consumer durable goods. The stock market wavered during the earlier part of the conflict and shed nearly 6% of its 2003 gains. With the end of the war, the Saudi stock market index rallied to new highs, registering a record 70% gain for 2003, and 40% for the first half of 2004. This compares with falls or minimal gains by all major stock markets worldwide over the same period.

The new Saudi Capital Market Law was approved and implemented during 2004. It aims to sustain and deepen the Saudi stock market, which is now the second largest after Malaysia in the Islamic world. SAMA announced that there had been little sign of capital outflow during this conflict, compared to the 1990-1991 second Gulf War period. Saudi banks continued to report a rise in their deposits, reaching SR 397 billion in August, 2004, compared with SR 328.2 billion in December, 2002. Saudi bank assets rose to SR 608 billion by August, 2004, up by 19% over the December, 2002 figure of SR 508.2 billion.

Oil again

Oil prices and how they will perform over the medium to long-term are the main unknown factors for Saudi economic prospects. Some pessimistic predictions were made earlier in the war period for a fall of 5.22% in Saudi GDP for the year 2003, based on the assumption of a sharp reduction in oil prices for the period April-December, 2003 (CCFI, 2003). A later study prepared by the Saudi American Bank (SAMBA, 2003) was more positive. This revised real GDP growth upward from 3.8% to 6% for the year 2003, on the strength of sharply higher oil production and oil prices for 2003's first quarter. Oil revenues averaged $7.7 billion per month in the quarter compared with an average of $5.5 billion per month for 2002.

Even these revised figures proved to be an underestimation; 2003 registered the second budget surplus since 1982. The forecast is for 2004 to be the best year ever, with a predicted surplus of around SR 112 billion or nearly $30 billion according to SAMBA. Real GDP, which had remained sluggish, was forecasted to grow by 3% and nominal GDP by 7.4% for 2004. Even these forecasts are on the conservative side, as the nominal GDP registered a 13% growth rate for 2003 according to SAMA.

Despite the "bonus" of these short-term oil prices and the extra production, the forecast is for lower oil prices in the long-term, based on an assumption of increased world oil supplies. As Russian and Iraqi oil comes onto the market in greater volume, it will result in downward oil prices. To meet this challenge, OPEC will need to reconfigure production quotas. This downward spiral is offset by a forecast of stronger world economic growth from 2005 onwards, resulting in higher oil demand, primarily from China. Saudi oil revenues for 2005-2010 are forecasted to average at around the same level as 2002-2003. That was patently insufficient to meet Saudi budgetary requirements.

It is precisely the shortfall gain nature of temporary higher oil prices that painfully highlights the urgent need for a fundamental restructuring of the Saudi economy away from oil. Higher oil revenues such as those of 2003 and 2004 reduce some of the internal pressure to continue with the program of initiated reforms. They provide an artificial "feel good" factor that rapidly evaporates with the next reverse of the oil cycle. The end of the third Gulf War has provided a chance for Saudi decision-makers to take a longer-term view on Saudi Arabia's position within OPEC as a swing producer, and to review the need to re-adjust the economy on a sounder and sustained footing.

The sharp fall in oil prices to $23 per barrel at the end of April, 2003, from nearly $40 only a few months earlier, underscores the need for adjustment. This swing seems to have been overshadowed when oil prices again rose to over $50 per barrel in 2004. The OPEC "assumption" of Iraq's pre-war OPEC quota has not dispelled Saudi fear and uncertainty about the eventual shaping of the oil markets after the Iraq conflict. Iraq, to all intents and purposes, might remain outside the official OPEC quota and production ceilings, and Iraq's need to produce as much as that country can bear in the shortest possible time will have an unpredictable, but most likely downward effect on future oil prices. The lower average cost of production in Iraq of 0.75 cents per barrel, compared to the world low of $1.5 per barrel for Saudi oil, will only add to Iraq's attraction for key energy players.

The trend for non-OPEC oil production to take up more of OPEC's market share is due to new exploration in the Russian fields and to strategic diversification decisions by the USA. This has caused Saudi Arabia to assume an even a greater degree of responsibility to support the OPEC price range levels of $22-28 per barrel by once again acting as the key swing producer. Given increased budgetary expenditure requirements, a large domestic public debt, and the need to meet bare minimum public expectations about job creation for its citizens, Saudi Arabia might not so easily adopt the role of swing producer in the future.

This could herald a period of tense inter-OPEC quota bargaining, short-term compromises, ineffective monitoring and controls. At the same time, the Kingdom has to maintain a wary eye on oil exports to China and the Far East by other non-OPEC countries, especially Russia, thus eroding the oil price premium that Saudi oil exports have to those regions compared to oil price discounts to the European and U.S. markets. Non-oil revenue diversification and a sustainable export-led growth by the private sector will become more important than ever.

Counting the cost of the Gulf War

The last Gulf War's fallout, including its costs, will be counted in economic, political and social terms, and will affect all the Middle East. Saudi Arabia is no exception. The Economic and Social Commission made estimations of the costs of the war for Western Asia (ESCWA), during a regional conference in Beirut in April, 2003. They concluded that the actual cost of the war to Arab economies as a whole was over $100 billion for 2003, over $400 billion in lost productivity and two million lost job opportunities. No time period for the estimated $400 billion productivity losses was specified, but according to ESCWA, the region suffered GDP losses to the tune of U.S. $600 billion in the 10 years since the previous 1999 second Gulf War (ESCWA, 2003).

These are staggering figures for a region characterized by high actual and disguised unemployment, low productivity, high population growth and low levels of foreign direct investment. According to ESCWA, "the region needed a period of reflection" to reconsider its direction and agenda. That is why a period of domestic social and economic stability in Saudi Arabia is crucial for long-term investment and planning.

Whatever the level of costs estimated, some economists seem to agree that the biggest losers in the short-term will be the private sectors in these Arab economies. Loss of production, delayed strategic investment decisions and decreased foreign direct investment will lead to a period of uncertainty. Saudi Arabia emerged relatively unscathed in financial terms during the third Gulf War. This was in contrast to the second Gulf War, when all economic data pointed towards a sharp reduction in government official reserves, increased military spending and rising budgetary deficits.

While it hasn't been necessary to dip into official financial reserves, the worrying consequences for the Saudi private sector due to political and regional uncertainties could be more damaging, given the importance the government has placed on this sector to diversify the national economic base. Any sustained shrinkage or minimal growth in the private sector will deal a severe blow to this important government policy objective. The Saudi private sector has shown its resilience, though, as evidenced by capital repatriation and strong stock market performance, as well as enthusiasm for Initial Public Offerings (IPOs) and privatization purchases. World record IPO subscriptions were registered during 2004, especially for the Sahara and Ettihad Ettisalat IPO's, with the latter IPO taking in SR 51 billion for a SR 1 billion subscription. These augur well for long-term capital infrastructure project funding by the government.

Saudi Arabia is confident that its proximity to Iraq, as well as its long experience in participating in the U.N. Iraq oil-for-food program, will give it the opportunity to participate in the longer-term reconstruction of Iraq, as Saudi companies tend to be bigger than others in the GCC countries and can mobilize for larger projects..

Political and social fallout

All Middle East countries suffered a degree of political and social fallout following the conclusion of the third Gulf War. While the political structure and make-up of the Kingdom of Saudi Arabia is outside the scope of this book, the war did accelerate the pace of an ongoing domestic reform program in the Kingdom, independent of the war and regional disturbances. The Consultative Council or *Majlis Al Shoura* came of age during 2003 and 2004 and freely debated many economic and social matters affecting the Kingdom. They overturned Ministerial recommendations on some issues. One example was the proposed expatriate income tax, which might have proved "electorally" popular; the *Majlis Al Shoura*, however, took a broader view.

The trend for more devolution of power to the legislative arm of the Saudi government will continue in the foreseeable future, until the balance between appointed and elected *Shoura* Council membership reflects the different social, tribal and regional strata of the Kingdom. This has already been carried out by the Gulf Cooperation Council State of Qatar, which held a referendum in April, 2003, to approve a new National Constitution. Evolution and consensus-building, the hallmark of Saudi government, are key to allowing for economic planning and stability.

It is within this tradition for consensual change that the proposed Municipal elections will take place in Saudi Arabia with half of the candidates elected by eligible Saudi males, and half appointed by the Government. It is a first important step in the commitment for change and reform by the Saudi government. It will be interesting to observe which economic powers are devolved to the regional Municipal Councils, especially in the allocation of expenditures and the increase of future service tariffs and rates. After all, each region will try to attract domestic and international inward investment based on the region's perceived economic strengths and comparative advantages. The *Majlis Al Shoura* and the Minister of Finance have already debated the devolution of government budgetary allocations to the regions as a means of allocative efficiency.

Women's issues will be important

Women's issues will continue to become more prominent in the foreseeable future, a sign of which are the government-sponsored forums on the issue during 2003 and 2004. The Crown Prince has made a personal point of openly meeting and greeting female Saudi professionals during his various tours of private and public corporations. The message is clear: female participation in all aspects of Saudi working life is encouraged, within the confines of Saudi social customs and norms. These symbolic gestures have helped to speed up Saudi society's acceptance of women's participation in more activities and areas than hitherto allowed. The idea of women members of the *Majlis Al Shoura* or of women in cabinet positions is no longer inconceivable. Qatar has shown the way, with the appointment of its first female cabinet Minister in 2003, followed by Oman, Bahrain and the UAE during 2004. Meanwhile, in Saudi Arabia there was open discussion of the King appointing the country's first female Deputy Minister for Girls Education (Sharq Awsat, 2003).

The participation of relatively educated women will have an economic impact on productivity, consumption and reduction in foreign workers' remittances, for women could replace some expatriate workers in assembly lines, clerical, administrative, IT and customer support areas. This would have been inconceivable only 20 years ago. Female participation in the national economy is now a major factor in terms of investment, diversity and scope of employment, with females playing a prominent role in the various Chambers of Commerce and Industry. Fuller female participation in society, while respecting religion social customs, and traditions, will be a positive economic force in the future of the Kingdom.

More openness

Also inconceivable 20, or even ten, years earlier are the establishment of a private Human Rights Group. And yet, the Government of Saudi Arabia announced in May, 2003, that the Kingdom would soon have its first-ever Human Rights Group, operating independently of the government with its independence guaranteed (Saudi Press Agency, 2003). The Saudi Human Rights Group has embraced its responsibility with enthusiasm and, to its credit, is tackling both national and foreign workers' issues with equal commitment. It enjoys the Government's full support and backing.

The Riyadh bombings in May, 2003, and the domestic terrorism that followed, came as a shock to major sections of Saudi society, with some commentators likening it to Saudi Arabia's own "September 11th". The effect was to galvanize the on-going reform process. King Fahd openly addressed these issues during his speech for the inauguration of the new *Majlis Al Shoura*, only a few days after the bombings in May, 2003. He stressed the need for political and administrative reforms, tightening control on the performance of the government sector, educational reform, and broadening the scope of women's participation (Saudi Press Agency, 2003).

The challenges ahead

The Kingdom is evolving. The announcement of the privatization of 20 of the country's economic sectors in November, 2002, is probably the most high-profile example of upcoming changes, but it is also happening quietly, which is the typical Saudi way of doing things. Despite outside pressure, they will not be forced to compromise this approach, simply for the sake of change, as openly stated by the King in the inaugural *Majlis* speech (Saudi Press Agency, 2003). However, neither Government nor society is blind to the challenges that lay ahead.

In the financial sector, the Government needs to more energetically pursue the proposed reforms in the capital market, in order to create a more attractive climate for Foreign Direct Investment. The corporate bond markets in the Gulf region, and Saudi Arabia in particular, are likely to gain added depth and versatility in the coming years, as the need increases for long-term capital, borrowed at fixed rates. The first tentative steps to issue a Saudi corporate bond took place during 2003, but the amount involved, SR 50 million, is a tiny percentage of the forecasted capital expenditure needs of the next 20 years. These will reach over \$400 billion in key economic sectors.

The returns generated in the Saudi stock market, despite regional uncertainties in 2003 and 2004, will encourage capital inflows and provide a fresh source of financing for private and public projects. The implementation of the new Capital Market Law should go a long way in devolving market regulatory power and responsibilities. This will allow SAMA to concentrate on fine-tuning monetary policy and on overseeing the Saudi commercial banking system, as well as other emergent financial intermediaries and players, such as the insurance, brokerage and investment banking sectors.

The latter is particularly important, because there are only a few Arab financial institutions with sufficient expertise to price, underwrite and sell corporate bonds. The ambitious Saudi privatization program requires these kinds of financial services. The alternative would be that foreign financial institutions fulfil the role, to the detriment of domestic players. Local bank *Saudization* came full circle during 2003. The exit of Citibank from managing its local joint venture, SAMBA, demonstrated the maturity of the Saudi banking system. The following year saw the entry of new foreign banks to the Saudi market, when heavyweights such as Deutche Bank, BNP Paribas and HSBC were granted licenses. The presence of these new banks was a vote of confidence in the long-term future of the Kingdom, especially in its financial and capital markets, where these foreign banks are expected to play a significant role.

Although we saw the presence of excess liquidity in the domestic banking sector during 2002-2003, this is not a reason to delay the development of a Saudi corporate bond market, since Saudi bank lending is still primarily short to medium-term. The shortage of medium to long-term funding at fixed interest rates is perceived to be an impediment for industrial growth, and even the Saudi government lending agencies' ability to lend large amounts is presently curtailed due to public deficit constraints.

For these new capital markets to flourish, the lack of financial transparency has to change. That culture needs to be replaced by strong corporate governance, transparency and full disclosure, as well as a viable legal system, contract enforcement and internationally recognized and accepted accounting standards.

The globalization of the world's economies ensures that Saudi Arabia competes for Foreign Direct Investment on equal, if not more attractive, terms compared with its competitors for foreign capital. The reduction in the foreign corporate profit tax rate to 20% from previous levels of 40% was a welcome move in the right direction, but it is only one step. According to the head of the Saudi Arabian General Investment Authority (SAGIA) in mid-2003, the issue of transparency in government operations was cited as a greater impediment to potential investors in the Kingdom than the reduction in tax rates. (Arab News, 2003). Of late however, SAGIA seems to be shifting its emphasis and encouraging domestic capital repatriation by ensuring that the local investment climate and regulatory framework is "investor friendly".

Employment generation will be paramount

Job creation is, and will continue to be, one of the major policy objectives of the Saudi government in the foreseeable future. More attention needs to be given to small and medium-sized enterprises (SMEs), for they are more attractive in terms of job creation on a Saudi Riyal–to-Saudi Riyal investment basis than larger corporations.

This will help diversify the economy, reduce dependence on oil price volatility and create a new breed of private sector entrepreneurs to drive the economy forward. A small step has been taken with the increased allocation for SME loans through the Saudi Credit Bank and Government guarantees through Saudi commercial banks. These are small steps, however, and more is needed. At the same time, it is important to avoid the problem of lending hazard raised by the provision of such loans and guarantees. In May, 2003, Finance Minister Assaf announced further measures to help the SMEs. He established a SR 200 million fund that is to be equally supported by the State and commercial banks, and he opened up the Saudi Industrial Development Fund (SIDF) to this sector (Saudi Press Agency, 2003).

High value job creation in the Saudi oil and petrochemical-related industries should not be ignored. The Kingdom has a natural advantage in energy-related, value-added industries and products. In essence, despite vigorous attempts at economic diversification, the future of the Kingdom is still largely tied to its petrochemical and energy-related production, such as aluminium. The Saudi Arabian Basic Industry or SABIC's market share of the world petrochemical market could rise to 15% by 2010, from current 8-9% levels. This may cause potential conflict with existing European, U.S. and Japanese petrochemical producers and possible delays in Saudi's WTO membership.

Despite some increase in gas energy feedstock costs by ARAMCO to SABIC, the Kingdom has the cheapest energy production cost in the world at between $1.20 to $1.50 per barrel, which will give it a relative competitive advantage over other petrochemical producers. The opening up of the Saudi gas sector to foreign partners in both upstream and downstream joint ventures is one indication of how Saudi energy could open up in the future, after many years of ARAMCO monopoly. The joint ventures with Chinese and Russian energy companies demonstrate a possible future pattern of commercial and trading links for Saudi Arabia in its effort to diversify its international linkages.

The planned privatization of the Saudi mining industry will also open up this hitherto neglected, but valuable, resource-based economic sector in Saudi Arabia. The mining industry will establish an integrated excavation, processing and manufacturing industrial base, leading to job creation and regional economic diversification. This economic sector is less volatile than the more regionally-concentrated oil industry.

Joining WTO would allow Saudi Arabia to successfully argue their cost advantage and to keep the markets open for its petrochemical production. But tough battles lay ahead. WTO accession also requires that local laws be fair to both domestics and foreigners. Laws must be transparent, as the Kingdom must agree to international arbitration and jurisdiction. To the closed judicial systems of some of the GCC countries, this could present a choice between acceptance or potential legal conflicts around international arbitration decisions. Once again, speedy reform of the current judicial system and commercial law is essential for Saudi Arabia's successful and smooth entry into WTO.

The 2003 third Gulf War could have the desired effect of pulling the GCC countries into closer economic and political cooperation. The impetus for "strength through unity" could translate into more effective economic integration through their planned full customs union by 2005 and monetary union by 2010. The latter entails a Unified Gulf Banking Law, a single currency and a Gulf Central Bank that sets monetary policy and interest rate policy. It has already been agreed by the GCC to host the proposed new GCC Central Bank in the UAE.

There is also a need for guidelines that control government expenditure and acceptable levels of member states' deficits, as well as other economic indicators, including inflation and unemployment target levels. By its sheer size in relation to the other GCC member states, Saudi Arabia will play both a dominant and dominating role.

This kind of monetary union will raise questions about both the economic and political implications for the Kingdom's relationship with competing political and economic blocs that emerged after the third Gulf War. Will a unified Gulf currency still shadow the U.S. dollar or will monetary union attempt to follow a more independent line? Our earlier analysis of current Saudi fixed exchange rate policy showed that as the dollar weakened from 2001 onwards, the real, effective purchasing power of the Saudi Riyal declined. This resulted in a poorer balance of trade with non-dollar trading partners. The decision by Kuwait to peg its Dinar against the U.S. dollar from 1 January 2003, as opposed to a broader mix of currencies was, to all intents and purposes, a political move in support of the beleaguered American currency.

This hints at possible internal disagreements amongst the GCC countries should any of the member states propose diversifying the currency pegging in a more balanced way. The USA might not favourably view this full or partial diversification away from the U.S. dollar and towards the Euro zone, despite the economic benefits it might bring to more diversified trading countries, such as Saudi Arabia, Bahrain and Oman. The proposed full GCC Customs Union in 2005 will be a crucial date for Saudi Arabia and the GCC in general. The success or failure of operating the Customs Union will be a crucial indicator of whether or not there is a future for monetary union, and whether the idea of a single currency will be quietly dropped.

Education: quality, not quantity

The Saudi government is beginning to recognize the need for qualitative educational policies leading to a knowledge-based economy. This will be the way to provide its citizens with the technical skills necessary to meet the challenges of a more competitive IT-driven world economy. The creation of the new Ministry of Communication and Information Technology points in the right direction.

In order to foster practical and industry-related applied research, Saudi universities must be encouraged to adopt policies that would facilitate industry secondment with international and Saudi enterprises. The cross-fertilization of ideas will provide a pool of talented Saudi educationalists who have had practical experience within industry and who can generate solutions that give such industries a competitive manufacturing edge. The envisaged large-scale privatization of many Saudi public sector organizations will require the services of pragmatic and capable "captains of industry" to manage them.

Such university/industry cross-placements can be the breeding ground for future technical managers. Under progressive Rectors, the King Fahd University of Petroleum and Minerals (KFUPM) actively sought to implement such policies by encouraging Faculty to seek industrial experience during their full-time sabbaticals. This experiment will be followed closely by other Saudi universities.

The establishment of Science Parks in collaboration with universities (such as KFUPM's Prince Abdullah Science Park), as well as the establishment of Industrial Cities and Technology Parks by the Government, indicates the seriousness with which research and development and their scientific applications are being taken. At the same time, the 2003 and 2004 budget allocations sent an unmistakable signal that science-based education and technical training would, from now on, be the focus of expenditure.

In order to ensure a match between educational sector output and private sector needs, the government and various private sector organizations have been having a closer dialogue on assessing future skill needs. Over the next few decades, it is expected that the private sector will take the lead and establish privately-owned universities and other specialized educational institutions. Their goals will be to meet the needs of the market and to compensate for the shortfall due to budgetary constraints in student placements in Saudi government universities. It is important for the Saudi government to implement an appropriate quality control system, along with a course and degree accreditation system. This will raise confidence among parents, students and employers regarding the output of such private institutions.

Stake in society

In the final analysis, as numerous models of economic development and growth illustrate around the world, self-sustained economic development and "take-off" can only come from within society; called the endogenous or internal factor, it can be sparked by education, innovation, productivity or social cohesion.

This was very clearly articulated by King Fahd when he told the Consultative Council that, "We have learned from the experiences of the East and West that real reform is the one that emerges from the nation's faith, determination and heritage" (Arab News, 2003).

For Saudi Arabia, one such element for ensuring private sector "take-off" is the re-emergence and strengthening of the "middle classes" and other professional elements in society. These groups have watched the gradual erosion of their standard of living in real terms compared to the boom days of 1975-1984. At the same time, the professional middle classes have acquired a wide range of specialist education and transferable skills, and it is not inconceivable that Saudi professionals will seek employment abroad as engineers, bankers, doctors and lawyers, thus reversing, in a small way, a cycle of labour import to Saudi Arabia.

This has already begun in the banking, media, medical and legal professions, and can be considered a natural evolution of economic development. It will bring the Kingdom valuable invisible exports and added international skills.

Like other countries, Saudi Arabia is painfully discovering that only through its own sweat, toil, exertions and nation-building will it find its rightful place in the world and dispel the unfounded label of the "Kingdom of Inertia". Many observers have been surprised by the pace, diversity and scale of change to date. The hope is that it will continue to do so in the future, as the well-being of the Saudi economy has implications reaching far beyond its shores.

Bibliography

Abalkhail, Mohammed. "The Role of Fiscal Policy in Realizing the Vision". Centre for Economic and Management Studies". *Future Vision of Saudi Arabia.* Riyadh, Oct. 2002.

Abdeen, Adnan and Shook, Dale. *"The Saudi Financial System in the Context of Western and Islamic Finance"* .John Wiley & Sons, 1984.

Abdelkarim, Abbas. *"Oil, Population Change and Social Development in the Gulf : Some Major Trends and Indicators".* St. Martin's Press. Inc. 1999.

Abdul Ghafour,P.K. "Universities to add seats, new courses". *Arab News.* 20 August 2004.

Abdul Ghafour, P.K. "Saudi Arabia: Al Bilad Bank to be Launched Next Year". *Arab News.* 18 August 2004.

Abdul Ghafour, P.K. "Cabinet OK's Anti-Money Laundering legislation". *Arab News.* 19 August 2003.

Abdul Ghafour, P.K. "GCC Weighs Sales Tax". *Arab News.* 23 October 2004.

Abdul Ghafour, P.K. "Women to take up Business Issues". *Arab News.* 4 June 2004.

Abdul Ghafour, P.K. "Government to sell 50% of its stake in NCB". *Arab News.* 12 May 2003.

Abdulaziz, Al Waleed Bin Talal, HRH. "We have to get rid of the mindless bureaucracy". *Arab News Interview,* 9 July 2003

Abdulaziz, Talal, Bin. HRH. *Reuters Interview,* 4 March 1998

Abdullatif, Ahmed. "Future Role of Banking Sector". Shoura Council. *Future Vision of Saudi Arabia.* Riyadh, Oct. 2002.

Abdulqadir, A. "Saudization in Civil Service". Vice Minister Civil Service. *Future Vision of Saudi Arabia,* Riyadh . Oct. 2002

Abir, Mordechai. *"Saudi Arabia in the Oil Era: Regime and Elites, Conflict and Collaboration".* London, Croom Helm. 1988

Abir, Mordechai. *"Saudi Arabia: Government, Society and the Gulf Crisis".* London: Routledge, 1993.

Ackert, Lucy, Bryan, C. and Deaves, R. "Emotion and Financial Markets". *Economic Review.* Second Quarter, 88, p.33. 2003

Adelman, M.A. *"The Genie out of the Bottle: World Oil Since 1970"* Cambridge, MA and London: MIT Press. 1995.

Agarwal, J.P. "Determinants of foreign direct investment: a Survey". *Weltwirtschaftliches Archieve,* Vol. 116. 1980.

Agence France Presse . "UAE to Host GCC Central Bank". *AFP.* 25 October 2004.

Agence France Presse. "Dollar's Fall Worries Oil Producers". *AFP*. 14 January 2004.

Agence France Presse. "Naimi defends OPEC price band". *AFP*. 4 June 2004.

Agence France Presse. "Saudi Cabinet endorses Islamic Insurance Law". *AFP*. 15 July 2003.

Ahmad, Mahmoud. "Move to Employ Women in Factories Welcomed". *Arab News*. 13 March 2003.

Akeel, Maha. "Saudi businesswomen go off beaten track". *Arab News*, 18 March 2003.

Akeel, Maha. "Dialogue Forum ends amid Heated Debate". *Arab News*. 15 June 2004.

Akeel, Maha. "Anguish and Anger Run Deep". *Arab News*. 14 April 2004.

Ali Sheikh, Rustum. *"Saudi Arabia and Oil Diplomac"*. New York: Praeger, 1976.

Ali, Abdulrahman Yousef, Al. "Saudi Arabian Export Strategy: a Micro-Level Analysis". in J. Wright, (ed), *"Business and Economic Development in Saudi Arabia"*..London: Macmillan, 152-169. 1996.

Almana, Aisha Mohamed. *"Economic Development and its Impact on the Status of Women in Saudi Arabia"*. (Ph.D. Dissertation). Boulder: University of Colorado, 1981.

Andersen, Norman. *"The Kingdom of Saudi Arabia"*. Stacey Int. 1996

Ann Smith, Pamela. "Saudi Arabia Woos Investors". *Zawya*, UAE. July 2003

Arab Banking Corporation. *"The Arab Economies"*. 4th Revised Edition. Bahrain: Arab Banking Corporation. 1994.

Arab News. "Top 100 Saudi Companies -2001: Ranked by Sales, Assets and Employees". *Jeddah* . 2002.

Arab News. "Saudi Economic Offset Company makes Breakthrough". *Arab News* 12 June , 2003.

Archer, Simon and Karim, Abdel-Rifaat. *"Islamic Finance, Innovation and Growth"*. Euromoney Books and AAOIFI. 2002.

Askari, Hossein, Vahid Nowshirvani and Mohamed Jaber. *"Economic Development in the GCC: The Blessing and the Curse of Oil"*. Greenwich, Connecticut, JAI Press, 1997.

Askari, Hossein. "Saudi Arabia's Economy: Oil and the Search for Economic Development". *Contemporary Studies in Economic and Financial Analysis. No. 67*. Greenwich, Connecticut: Jai Press, 1990

Atiyyah, H.S. "Expatriate Acculturation in Arab Gulf Countries". *Journal of Management Development*; 15:5 pp.37-47.1996.

Auty, R.M. *"Resource Abundances and Economic Development"*. Oxford University Press. 2001.

Auty, R.M. "The transition from rent-driven growth to skill-driven growth: recent experience of five mineral economies". In: Maier, J., Chambers, B., Farooq, A. (eds.) *"Development Policies in Natural Resource Economies"*. Edward Elgar, Cheltenham. 1999.

Awaji, Ibrahim, Al. "Bureaucracy and development in Saudi Arabia: The case of local adminstration". *Journal of Asian and African Studies,* 24 (1-2), 49-61. 1989.

Azzam H. *"The Emerging Arab Capital Markets"*. Kegan Paul Int. 1997.

Azzam, H, "Preparing for a global future". *The Banker*. Vol. 47 , pp. 72-76. 1997.

Azzam, H. *"Development of Capital Markets in the Gulf"*. Gulf International Bank B.S.C., Bahrain. 1988.

Azzam, H. *"The Arab World: Facing the Challenges of the New Millennium"*. IB Tauris .2002.

Azzam, H. "Saudi Arabian Economy: the Outlook for 1998". *Saudi Economic Survey*, April 8 and 15. 1998.

Baadi, Hamad, Al. *"Social Change, Education, and the Roles of Women in Arabia"*. (Ph.D. Dissertion) Palo Alto: Standford University. 1982.

Bahrain Monetary Agency (BMA). "List of Islamic Banks and Financial Institutions as of 17 June 2003". *www.bma.gov.bh*

Bailey, Robert. "How will Saudi Arabia handle low oil prices?". *Gulf Business*. Aug. 1998.

Bakheet, Beshir. "Developing GCC Stock Markets: The Private Sector Role". *Middle East Policy. Vol. 6, no. 3* . pp. 72-77.February 1999.

Baland, J.-M. and P. Francois. "Rent-seeking and resource booms". *Journal of Development Economics*. 61: 527-542. 2000.

Bashir, Abdulwahab. "Dr Al Gosaibi Targets Saudi Businesses Again for Saudization". *Arab News*. 9 July 2004.

Bashir,Abdulwahab. "Saudis told to learn new things, develop new habits". *Arab News*. 4 June 2004.

Bashir, Abdulwahab. "New body to oversee education". *Arab News*. 22 June 2004.

Bashir, F, Al. *"A Structural Econometric Model of the Saudi Arabian Economy, 1960-1970"*. Wiley, New York, 1977.

Batlay, Grais, W., and Sendan E. "Financial Sector Reforms: International Experience and Issues for Saudi Arabia". World Bank. *Future Vision of Saudi Arabia*. Riyadh. Oct. 2002.

Bazai, Hamad, Al. "Privatization - A Prelude to Government Projects Reform". Ministry of Finance and National Economy. *Future Vision of Saudi Arabia.*, Riyahd, 2002.

Beblawi, Hazem. *"The Arab Gulf Economy in a Turbulent Age"*. Croom Helm. 1984.

Beblawi, Hazem. "The Rentier State in the Arab world". *Arab Studies Quarterly*. 9 (4), (Fall), 383 – 98. 1987.

Bernstein, H. (ed). *"Underdevelopment and Development"*. Penguin Book. Harmondsworth.1973.

Binzagar, Wahib. "You can't have one without the other". *Arab News*. 2nd June 2003.

Birks J.S. and C.A. Sinclair. *"Arab Manpower: The Crisis of Development"*. New York: St. Martin's Press. 1980.

Birks J.S. and C.A. Sinclair. "Repatriation, remittances and reunions: What is really at stake for Arab countries supplying labor to the Gulf Cooperation Council States?" in Charles E. Davies (ed.), *Global Interests in the Arab Gulf.* New York, St. Martin's Press. 1992.

Bisisu, Adnan. *"Off-Shore Banking in Bahrain"*. Bahrain: Chamber of Commerce and Industry, Unpublished. 1984.

Blakely, James R. "The Oweiss Demand Curve". *Blakely's Commodity Review.* Vol. 1, no. 1 : 1-8 May 1983.

Blondal, S, and H. Christiansen . "The Recent Experience with Capital Flows to Emerging Markets Economies". *Economics Department Working Paper.* 211 OECD, Paris. 1999.

Boeing Industrial Technology Group. (BITG). "Peace Shield Investment Offset Program". Seattle, 1985.

Bolbol A. and Omran, M. "Arab Stock Markets and Capital Investment". *Arab Monetary Fund Papers. No. 8,* Feb. 2004

Borensztein, E. and J.W.Lee. "How does foreign direct investment affect economic growth ?".*NBER Working Paper* No. 5057. 1995.

Bourbakri, Narjess and Jean-Claude Cosset: "The Financial and Operating Performance of Newly Privatized Firms: Evidence from Developing Countries". Mimeo, Universite Laval. 1997.

Bourland, Brad. *"Saudi Arabia's 2004 Budget, 2003 Performance"*. Saudi American Bank, Riyadh. December 2003.

Bourland, Brad. *"The Saudi Arabian Economy in 2000"*. Saudi American Bank, Riyadh. February 2001.

Bourland, Brad. *"The Saudi Arabian Economy in 2001"*. Saudi American Bank, Riyadh. February 2002.

Bourland, Brad. *"The Saudi Economy under the changing global context"*. Saudi American Bank. *Future Vision of Saudi Arabia*, Riyadh, Oct. 2002.

Bourland, Brad. *"The Saudi Economy: 2001 Performance and Forecast"*. Saudi American Bank, Riyadh.2001,

Bourland, Brad. *"The Saudi Economy: Mid-year 2003"*. Saudi American Bank, Riyadh. August 2003.

British Offset Office. "British Offset - Opportunities through Economic Cooperation in Saudi Arabia". London, 2002.

British Aerospace. "British Aerospace Project Finance Initiative for the Al-Yamamah Economic Offset program". London, 2001.

British Offset Office. "British Offset - Supporting you in the new joint ventures in Saudi Arabia". London, 2001.

Buhulaiga, Ihsan. "Challenges and Prospects of the Saudi Labor Market". *Arab News.* 20 January, 2004.

Carter, J.R.L. *"Merchant Families of Saudi Arabia"*. London, Scorpio Books. 1984

Central Department of Statistics. " *Statistical Yearbook 2002 "*. Ministry of Planning. Riyadh, 2003.

Central Department of Statistics. *"National Accounts of Saudi Arabia, 2000 & 2001 Indicators"*. Ministry of Planning. Riyadh 2002.

Central Department of Statistics. *"Employment and Wages- 2000"*. Ministry of Planning. Riyadh. 2001.

Central Department of Statistics. *"Statistical Yearbook 1999"*. Ministry of Planning . Riyadh,2001.

Chadhury, Kiren Aziz. "The Price of Wealth: Business and State in Labor Remittance and Oil Economies". *International Organization.* 43, 101 - 45. Winter 1989.

Chadhury, Kiren Aziz. *"The Price of Wealth: Economies and Institutions in the Middle East".* Ithaca: Cornell University Press, N.Y. 1997.

Chalk, N., A., El-Erian, M.A., Fennel, S.J., Kireyev, A.P. and Wilson, J.F. "Kuwait: from reconstruction to accumulation for future generations". *IMF Occasional Paper,* 150, Washington, IMF. 1997.

Chalk, N., A., V. Treichel, and J. Wilson, *"Financial Structure and Reform".* Building on Progress: Reform and Growth in the Middle East and North Africa. 1996

Champion, Daryl. *"The Paradoxical Kingdom: Saudi Arabia and the Momentum of Reform".* C. Hurst and Co. UK. 2003.

Chenery, H. *"Structural Change and Development Policy".* London, Oxford University. 1979.

Cleron, Jean-Paul. *"Saudi Arabia 2000: A Strategy for Growth".* Croom Helm. 1978.

Consulting Centre for Finance & Investment. (CCFI) *"Saudi Gross Domestic Product Review 2002. Forecast 2003".* Riyadh. March 2003.

Cordesman, A.H. *"Saudi Arabia Enters the 21st Century".* Praeger. 2003.

Cordesman, A.H. "Saudi Arabia: *Guarding the Desert Kingdom".* Boulder, Colorado: Westview 1997.

Cordesman, A.H. *"After the Storm: The Changing Military Balance in the Middle East".* Boulder, Colorado, Westview. 1993.

Cornelius, Peter (ed). "The Arab World Competitiveness Report 2002 - 2003". *World Economic Forum.* Oxford University Press. 2003.

Council of Saudi Chambers of Commerce and Industry. "CSCCI Creates Office for SME's". *CSCCI.* Riyadh. 14 March 2004.

Dabbagh, A, Al. "Mining in the Kingdom and its Role in Economic Diversification". *MAADEN. Future Vision of Saudi Arabia,* Riyadh, Oct. 2002.

Daghsh,Muna". Family Companies have SR250 Billion in Investments". *Arab News.* 2 April 2004.

Deutsche Presse-Agentur. *"Kuwait Plans Income Tax Bill First Time".* DPA.7 March 2004.

Devlin, Julia (ed.). *"Gulf Economies: Strategies for Growth in the 21st Century".* Washington, DC, Georgetown University. 1996.

Diwan, Ishac and Girgis, Maurice. "Labour Force Issues and Employment Strategies: A Strategic Vision for Saudi Arabia". World Bank. *Future Vision of Saudi Arabia.* Riyadh, Oct. 2002.

Dosary, Adel S, Al. *"Localization of Jobs in the Saudi Labor Market (Saudization) Strategies: Implementation Mechanisms through a Multiple Track Approach".* 4th Annual Saudization Conference , Jeddah. 2002.

Doumato, Eleanor Abdella. "Education in Saudi Arabia: Gender, Jobs and the Price of Religion". in Doumato, E and Poususney, M. (ed). *"Women and Globalization in the Arab Middle East - Gender, Economy and Society".* Lynne Reinmer, Inc. New York. 2003.

Doumato, Eleanor Abdella, and Posusrey, Marsha. "Women and Globalization in the Arab Middle East," in *Gender, Economy and Society*. Lynn Reinmer, Inc. 2003.

Doumato, Eleanor Abdella. "Between Breadwinner and Domestic Icon?" in Souad ,Joseph and Susan Slyomovics (ed) *Women and Power in the Middle East*. University of Pennsylvania Press. *2001*.

Doumato, Eleanor Abdella. "Women and the Stability of Saudi Arabia". *Middle East Report*. No. 171, 34-37,July -August 1991.

D'Souza, Juliet and William Megginson. "The Financial and Operating Performance of Privatized Firms During the 1990's". Mimeo, Department of Finance, Terry College of Business, The University of Georgis, Athens, GA. 1998.

Dukhayil, Abdulaziz, A, Al. "Higher Education Outputs and their Compatibility with Future Development Requirements in the Kingdom". KFUPM. *Future Vision of Saudi Arabia*,Riyadh. Oct. 2002.

Dukheil,Abdulaziz M,Al. "Impact of Dollar Depreciation on Saudi Economy". *Saudi Commerce and Economic Review*. Dammam. No 118. pp. 12-14.Feb . 2004.

Dukheil, Abdulaziz, M. Al. "The Future Role of the Stock Market in Mobilizing Domestic Savings". CCFI. *Future Vision of Saudi Arabia*, Riyadh, Oct 2002.

Dukheil, Abdulaziz, M, Al. *"The Banking System and its Performance in Saudi Arabia,"* Saqi Books. 1995.

Eastern Province Chamber of Commerce and Industry. "One Industrial Unit Launched every Alternate Day". *Saudi Commerce and Economic Review*. Dammam. No 100. August 2002.

Economic Bureau, The. "The Saudi Economic Offset Program". *Japan Institute of Middle East Economics*. Spring 1998.

Economist Intelligence Unit. *"Country Profile: Saudi Arabia, 2001-2002"*. London: 2003

Economist, The. *"Gulf citizen, no qualifications, seeks well-paid job"*. Vol. 343, No. 8012, p. 41. 1997.

Edwards, Robert (ed.). *"The GCC Demographic Report 1998"*. Dubai, MERAC. 1998

EFG-Hermes. "Profitable Growth at a Price: Analysis of Saudi Banks". *EFG-Hermes*. Cairo.14 Aug.2003.

Ehteshami, A. "The politics of participation in the oil monarchies". in Najem, Tom, and Hetherington, Martin (ed)" *Good Governance in the Middle East Oil Monarchies"*. Routledge Curzon, London. 2003.

Eichengree, B. " International Lending in the Long Run: Motives and Management*"*, in Richard Levich (ed.) *"Emerging Market Capital Flows"*. Kluwer Academic Publishers, 1998.

Eltony, M, Nazy. *"Can an Oil Based Economy be Diversified? A Case study of Kuwait"*. Arab Planning Institute, Kuwait. 2000.

Emirates Centre for Strategic Studies and Research. "Privatization and Deregulation in the Gulf Energy Sector*"*. ECSSR. Abu Dhabi, UAE. 1999.

Erian, Mohamed A, El. and Cyrus Sassanpour. "GCC's Macroeconomic Strategies: Towards the 21st Century, in Devlin, Julia (ed) *Gulf Economies: Strategies for Growth in the 21st Century*. Washington D.C., Georgetown University, 1997.

ESCWA. *"Bi-Annual ESCWA Session"*. Beirut, Lebanon. United Nations Economic and Social Commission for Western Asia. (ESCWA). April 2003.

ESCWA. *"Arab Labor Migration to the Gulf: Size, Impact and Major Policy Issues"*. Amman, United Nations Economic and Social Commission for Western Asia (ESCWA), 1993.

Essayyad M, Ramady M., and Al Hejji M. " Determinants of Bank Profitability of Petroleum Economy: The Case of Saudi Arabia". *Petroleum Accounting and Financial Management Journal*. Vol. 22. No. 3. pp 69-101. Fall/Winter 2003.

Estimo, Rodolfo. *"SME's face problems in Kingdom"*. Arab News, Jeddah. 8 March, 2004.

Evans, R. "Indirect Offset in Saudi Arabia: An Analysis of the Al-Yamamah Offset Program". *Executive Congress on International Business Offset in the Arabian Gulf*. International Business Communications. Abu Dhabi, May 5 - 7, 1996.

Fadel, Fida, Al. "Technological Incubators". UNESCO. *Future Vision of Saudi Arabia*. Riyadh, Oct. 2002.

Fadhel, Mohammed. "Gulf Family Business Urged to Sell Shares". *Arab News*. 18 October 2004.

Fahim, Mohammed, Al. *"From Rags to Riches: A Story of Abu Dhabi"*. London, Center for Arab Studies, 1995.

Faroqui, Mahmoud. *"Islamic Banking and Investment."* Kegan Paul Int. 2002.

Farsi, Fouad, Al. "Saudi *Arabia"*. LBC Information Services. 2001.

Farsi, Fouad, Al. *"Saudi Arabia: A Case Study in Development"*. London: Routledge and Kegan Paul International . 1982.

Fayez, Khalid, Al. "Future role for Banks and Saudi Financial Markets under the Globalisation of the Economy". Gulf International Bank. *Future Vision of Saudi Arabia,* Riyadh, Oct. 2002.

Feheid, Abdullah, Al. "Obstacles Hampering Inflow of Foreign Investment Identified". *Arab News*. 16 April 2003

Field, Michael. *"The Merchants: The Big Business Families of Saudi Arabia and the Gulf States"*. Woodstock. New York. Overlook Press.1985.

Financial Times. *"Collapse of Saudi gas talks reveals gap in understanding"*. FT. London. 7 June, 2003.

Gelb, A.H. and Associates. *"Oil Windfalls: Blessing or Curse?"*. New York, Oxford University Press, 1998.

Gently, B. (ed). *"Private Capital Flows and the Environment: Lessons from Latin America"*, Cheltenham, Edward Elgar Publishing , 1998.

Ghamdi, Qeman. "Unemployment Numbers". *Arab News*. 25 August 2003.

Ghamdi, Saeed, Al. "The Saudi Arabian Offset Program". *Air Command and Staff College*. Air University, Maxwell Air Force Base, Alabama, USA, April 1999.

Ghantus, Elias T. *"Arab Industrial Integration: A Strategy of Development"*. London: Croom Helm, 1982.

Ghazanfar,Ali Khan". Kingdom promises dialogue for Oil price stability ". *Arab News*. 12 May 2003.

Ghazanfar,Ali Khan. "World's Largest Islamic Financing Deal Concluded". *Arab News*. 27 September 2004.

Ghazanfar, Ali Khan. "SAMA initiates action to curb illegal money transactions". *Arab News*. 30 June 2003.

Girgis, Maurice. "National Versus Migrant Workers in the GCC: Coping with Change", in Handoussa, Heba and Zafirris Tzannatos, *"Employment Creation & Social protection in the Middle East and North Africa"*. The American University in Cairo Press. 2002.

Graham, E.H. "Foreign Direct Investment in the World Economy". *IMF Working Paper*. WP/95/59.1995

Gulf Cooperation Council. (GCC). *"The Unified Economic Agreement"*. Riyadh, Saudi Arabia: *Gulf Cooperation Council Secretariat*, Riyadh. 1981.

Gulf News. "Gulf countries earn \$33 billion more on strong oil prices". *Zawya*. 7 January, 2004.

Gupta, A. "A vision for Export Promotion in Saudi Arabia". World Bank. *Future Vision of Saudi Arabia*, Riyadh, Oct. 2002.

Gupta, K.L. *"Financial and Economic Growth in Developing Countries"*. Croom Helm, London, 1984.

Gutierrez, Edwin G. "Evaluation of Offset Programs in the Arab Gulf: A Case of Business Economic Investment Policy". *Economic Horizon*. UAE. Volume 18, No. 72, 1997.

Gylfason, T., Herbertsson, T., and G. Zoega. "A mixed blessing: Natural resources and economic growth". *Macro Economic Dynamics*. 3: 204-225. 1999.

Haddadin, H. "Kuwait to Open Banking Sector". *Reuters*. 13 January, 2004.

Hafni, Zainals. "Involving Saudi Women in Nation Building". *Al-Sharq Al-Awsat*. 21 August 2003.

Haidar, Saeed. "Saudization: The Objective is Clear, the Means are Not". *Arab News*, 13 July 2003.

Hamed, Osama. "Foreign labour, currency substitution and economic stability in Gulf Cooperation Council countries". A*rab Economic Journal*, no. 9. 1997.

Hammond, G. *"Counter-trade, Offsets and Barter in International Political Economy"*. Linter Publishers, London 1990.

Hanware, K. "Etisalat IPO Fetches Record SR51 Billion". *Arab News*. 1 November 2004.

Harrison, Roger. "Al Sabban calls for more Oil cooperation". *Arab News*. 21 January 2004.

Hassan, Javid. "Saudi Women make Debut in New Professions". *Arab News*. 14 August 2004.

Hassan, Javid. "RCCI Women's Wing Opens Today". *Arab News*. 20 March 2004.

Hassan, Javid. "Kingdom Signs Mega Gas Deals ". Arab News. 8 march 2004.

Hegelan, A, Al, and Palmer, M. "Bureaucracy and Development in Saudi Arabia", in Niblock, T, and Wilson R. (ed). *"The Political Economy of the Middle East"*. Volume 5. pp.1-22, Cheltenham, Edward Elgar, 1999.

Hijab, Nadia. *"Woman Power: The Arab Debate on Women at Work"*. Cambridge University Press. 1988.

Hindley, Angus. "Dubai ports ready for regional tussle". *Middle East Economic Digest*. October 24, 1997.

Holayan, Eissa. A. "Bill Gates and our Philanthropists". *OKAZ* .20 December, 2003.

Holden, David, and Johns, Richard. *"The House of Saud"*. London: Sidgwick and Jackson, 1981.

Hollis , Rosemary. *"Oil and Regional Developments in the Gulf"*. The Royal Institute of International Affairs. 1998.

Humaid, Abdulwahid, Al. "Labour and Saudization Policies". Manpower Council. *Future Vision of Saudi Arabia* . Riyadh. Oct. 2002.

Hunter, Shireen. *"Gulf Cooperation Council: Problems and Prospects"*. Washington DC: Center for Strategic and International Studies. 1984

Husseini, Saleh, Al. "Diversification of Industrial Sector". Ministry of Industry and Electricity. *Future Vision of Saudi Arabia*. Riyadh. Oct. 2002.

Ibrahim, Y. Al. and Wazar, M. Al. "Offset Perspective in Kuwait". *Offset Forum - Joint Investment for Development.* Ministry of Finance, Kuwait, May 13-14, 1996.

Iktissad Wal-Aamal, Al. (Economics and Business). *"Special Issue on Saudization".* Riyadh, March 1997.

International Monetary Fund. "Improvements in global financial system hinge on transparency and management of risk". Survey, 5 September, 110. 1999.

International Monetary Fund. *"Financial Systems and Labor Markets in the Gulf Cooperation Council Countries"*. Washington, DC: Middle Eastern Dept., International Monetary Fund, 1997.

Islami, A. Reza, S. and Rostam Mehraban Kavoussi. *"The Political Economy of Saudi Arabia"*. Seattle, WA: Department of Near Eastern Languages and Civilization, University of Washington. 1984.

Jagannathan,V. "Saudi Banks are the Best in the Gulf". *Standard & Poor* . 4 April 2004.

Jalal, Mahsoun, B. *"The Industrialization Option and the Role of the National Industrialization Company in its Implementation"*. Riyadh: Middle East Press, 1985.

Jamal, Faiz. "Human Rights Commissions". *Al Madinah*, 16 July 2003

Janoubi, S., Al. "Level of Performance in the Saudi Public Sector". Institute of Public Adminsitration. *Future Vision of Saudi Arabia*. Riyadh. Oct. 2002.

Jasser, Sulaiman, Al, and Banafe, Ahmed. "Monetary Policy Investments and Procedures in Saudi Arabia". *Saudi Arabian Monetary Agency.*(SAMA). 2002. Riyadh.

Jasser, Sulaiman, Al. "Developing the Financial Sector for Better Economic Growth". SAMA. *Future Vision of Saudi Arabia*. Riyadh. Oct. 2002.

Johany, Ali D, Michel Berne and Wilson Mixon, Jr. *"The Saudi Arabian Economy"*. John Hopkins University Press.1986.

Johany, Ali, D. *"The Myth of the OPEC Cartel: The Role of Saudi Arabia"*. New York: John Wiley, 1982.

Joseph, Suad, and Slyomovics, Susan. " *Women and Power in the Middle East"*. University of Pennsylvania Press, Philadelphia. 2001.

Jumail, H. Al. *"The Kuwait Stock Market Crisis"*. Kuwait 1986.

Kanovsky, Eliyahu. "The Economy of Saudi Arabia: Troubled Present, Grim Future". *The Washington Institute for Near East Policy Papers.* 1994

Kapiszewski, Andrzej. *"Nationals and Expatriates, Population and Labor Dilemma of the Gulf Cooperation Council States"*. Garner Publishing Limited. 2001.

Karl, Terry Lynn. *"The Paradox of Plenty: Oil Booms and Petro-States"*. Berkeley and Los Angeles: University of California Press. 1997.

Khalaf , Moo'dhy. "Third National Dialogue Forum : Diary of a Woman". *Arab News.* 25 June 2004.

Khalaf, Moo'dhy. "Even women without 'wasta' deserve justice". *Arab News.* 27 Feb 2004

Khalaf, Moo'dhy. "My Forbidden Presence". *Arab News.* 12 September 2003.

Khazindar, Abid. "Combating Rising Crime". *OKAZ.* 30 December 2003.

Khemani, R. S. "Fostering Diversification and Competitiveness; Strategies and Options for the Kingdom of Saudi Arabia". World Bank. *Future Vision of Saudi Arabia,* Riyadh. Oct. 2002.

Khereiji, M, Al. "Final arrangements under way to join WTO". *Arab News.* 11 July 2003

Khoshhal, Khader. "Investment Behavioral Decision Making - A Case Study of the Saudi Stock Market". *Unpublished MBA Project Dissertation.* King Fahd University of Petroleum and Minerals. June 2004.

Khoury, Nabil and Moghadam, Valentine. *"Gender and Development in the Arab World: Women's Economic Participation Patterns and Policies"*. Zed Books, London. 1995.

Kibbi, Jamal, Al. "Using knowledge for Development in Saudi Arabia". World Bank. *Future Vision of Saudi Arabia.* Riyadh. Oct. 2002.

Kim, Y. "Causes of Capital Flows in Developing Countries". *Journal of International Money and Finance,* 19, pp.235-53. 2000.

King Fahd University of Petroleum & Minerals. *"GCC Main Economic Indicators 1994-95"*. Economic and Industrial Research Division, Research Institute,1995.

Kirdar, Nemir A. "The Role of MENA's Private Sector in Globalization". Arab Bankers Association of North America. *ABANA,* vol. XIII, no. 3 pp. 9-10. March 1999.

Knauerhase, Ramon. "Saudi Arabia: Fifty Years of Economic Change. *"Current History, 82, No. 480, 19-23. January 1983.*

Knauerhase, Ramon. "The Economic Development of Saudi Arabia: An Overview". *Current History:* 6-10, 32-34. January 1977.

Knight, M. "Developing Countries and the Globalization of Financial Markets" *World Development.* 26(7), pp. 1185-1200. 1998.

Kofman, Eleonore and Gillian Youngs. *"Globalization: Theory and Practice"*. London: Printer. 1996.

Krimly, Rayed. "The political economy of adjusted priorities: Declining oil revenues and Saudi fiscal policies". *Middle East Journal. Vol.53 (2),* (Spring), pp.254-267. 1999.

Kurdi, Usamah, Al. "A Future Vision for the Development of Small and Medium Enterprises". Council of Saudi Chambers of Commerce. *Future Vision of Saudi Arabia.* Riyadh. Oct. 2002.

Kuwait Ministry of Finance. "Guidelines for the Counter trade Offset Program". *Kuwait. 1995.*

Kuwaiz, Abdullah, El. "OPEC and the International Oil Market: The Age of Realism". *OPEC Review.* Oxford 10, No.4. Winter. 393-408. 1986.

Lackner, Helen. *"The House Built on Sand: A Political Economy of Saudi Arabia".* London. Ithaca Press. 1978.

Lall, S. and Streeten P. *"Foreign Investment, Transnational and Developing Countries".* Westview Press. 1977.

Larocque, Norman. "Future of Higher Education: International Trends". World Bank. *Future Vision of Saudi Arabia.* Riyadh, Oct. 2002.

Lathom, Michael". Education Reform: Trends and Lessons Learned". World Bank. *Future Vision of Saudi Arabia.* Riyadh. Oct. 2002.

Law, Peter. "Opportunities and Issues of the Domestic National Gas Sector". World Bank. *Future Vision of Saudi Arabia.* Riyadh, Oct. 2002.

Lee, Kuan Yue. *"The Singapore Story: The Memoirs of Lee Kuan Yeu".* Singapore, Times Edition Pte. 1988.

Longva, Anh Nga. *"Walls Built on Sand: Migration, Exclusion and Society in Kuwait : Keeping migrant workers in check: The Kafala sytem in the Gulf".* Boulder, Colorado, Westview Press . 1997.

Looney, Robert. *"Economic Development in Saudi Arabia: Consequences of the Oil Price Decline".* Greenwich, Connecticut: Jai Press.1990.

Looney, Robert. "Factors Affecting Employment in the Arabian Gulf Region, 1975-1985". *International Journal of Social Economics.* Vol. 19. pp. 72-86. 1992

Looney, Robert. *"Saudi Arabia's Development Potential".* Lexington, MA: Lexington Books, 1982.

Looney, Robert. "Saudi Arabia's Development Strategy: Comparative Advantage versus Sustainable Development," *Orient.* 75-96 . March 1989.

Lumsden, Philip. "Dealing with the problems of Localization, " *Middle East Economic Digest,* Vol. 37 No. 10, pp. 46-48. 1993.

Mabro, Robert. "Strategic Consideration for Gas Development in Saudi Arabia". Oxford Institute for Energy Studies. *Future Vision of Saudi Arabia.* Riyadh. Oct. 2002.

Maeena, Khaled. "Arab Women Rising". *Arab News.* 27 Feb. 2004.

Mahdi, Kamil A. "Aspects of higher education in the Arab Gulf", in K. E. Shaw (ed.), *Higher Education in the Gulf: Problems and Prospects.* Exeter University Press, 1997

Malik, Monica. "The Role of the Private Sector" ,in Wilson, Rodney, A. Salamah, M. Malik and A. Rajhi. *"Economic Development in Saudi Arabia".* Routledge Curzon. Pp. 126-138. 2004.

Mallakh, Ragaei, El and Mallakh, Dorothea, El. *"Saudi Arabia: Energy, Developmental Planning, and Industrialization"* Lexington Books, Lexington, Mass. 1982.

Mallakh, Ragaei, El. *"Saudi Arabia: Rush to Development".* Croom Helm, London, 1982.

Marboli, Leopold. "Strategic Consideration for Mining Sector Development in Saudi Arabia". World Bank. *Future Vision of Saudi Arabia,* Riyadh. Oct. 2002.

Marvel, K. "International Offsets: An International Trade Development Tool". *Contract Management,* pp. 4 - 10. October 1995.

Masmoudi, M. "The Arab World and the Information Age: Promises and Challenges". in *"The* Information Revolution and the Arab World: Its Impact on State and Society". *The Emirates Centre for Strategic Studies and Research.* Abu Dhabi . pp. 120-140. 1988.

Masood, Rashid. *"Economic Diversification and Development in Saudi Arabia".* Sargam. 1989.

McHale , Thomas. "Saudi Oil Policy and the Changing World Energy Balance". *International Research Center for Energy and Economic Development.* Colorado. Occasional Paper. Number One. 1986.

Medley Advisors Group. "Oil brief: Saudi Arabia Lost in Translation". New York. 28 September 2004.

Medley Advisors Group. "Oil brief: OPEC - Soft Bands and Softer Pressure". New York. 18 December 2003.

Meccawy,Mariam. "Young women say superficial issues dominated Forum discussions". *Arab News.* 22 June 2004.

MEED. "First Private Sector Debut Issue in Pipeline". P.21. 7 March 2003.

MEED. *"Special Report: Saudi Arabia: Banking Results" ,* 22 Feb 2002.

Merrell Foster, Leila. *"Saudi Arabia".* Scholastic Library Publishing. 1996.

Mettale, Thomas. *"Saudi Oil Policy and the Changing World Energy Balance".* Institute Research Centre for Energy and Economics. 1987.

Middle East Economic Digest. *Various editions. London.*

Middle East Economic Survey. *Various editions. Cyprus.*

Ministry of Industry and Electricity. "Industrial Statistical Report for 1996 and 1998". Riyadh.April 1998.

Ministry of Planning. *"Achievements of the Development Plans: 1970-2000, Facts and Figures".* Riyadh. 2002

Ministry of Planning. *"Seventh Development Plan, 2000-2004",* Riyadh. 2000.

Ministry of Planning. *"Private Establishments Survey, Volume I, Summary Report".* Riyadh, 2000.

Mishkhas, Abeer. "Failing Students". *Arab News.* 17 February 2004.

Mofleh, Ibrahim, Al. "Promoting Direct Foreign Investment Development and Export Promotion". Saudi Fund for Development. *Future Vision of Saudi Arabia,* Riyadh. Oct. 2002.

Molives, Donald. *"The Economy of Saudi Arabia".* Praeger. 2001.

Montague, Caroline. "Talk of Reform". *Middle East International.* No. 704, pp 18-19.11 July 2003.

Moody, B., Evans, D. "Kingdom's 2004 Growth Seen Close to 6.4 Percent: Assaf". *Reuters.* 13 May, 2004.

Moon, Chung In. "Korean Contractors in Saudi Arabia: Their Rise and Fall," *Middle East Journal.* 40, No. 4, Autumn, 1986.

Morris, M.H, Marks, A.S. Allen, N.S. Perry, J. "Modeling Ethical Attitudes and Behavior under Conditions of Environmental Turbulence". *Journal of Business Ethics.* 15: 1119-1130. 1996.

Mughni, Haya. *"Women in Kuwait: The Politics of Gender"*. Sagi Books. London. 2001.

Naggar, Said, El. *"Financial Policies and Capital Markets in Arab Countries"*. Washington: International Monetary Fund, 1994.

Najem, Tom and Hetherington, Martin (ed). *"Good Governance in the Middle East Oil Monarchies"*. Routledge Curzon.2003.

Najjar, Baquer Salman, Al. *"Population Policies in the Countries of the Gulf Cooperation Council"*. St. Martin's Press Inc.1998.

Nakhleh, Emile A. *"The Gulf Cooperation Council"*. Praeger Publishers. New York. 1986.

Nashashibi, Hikmat, "The Role of Arab Capital Markets in Investing the Financial Surpluses", *Middle East Banking Finance*. Arab Press Service, Vol. 3, pp. 195-208. 1983.

Nasir,Halla, Al. "Business Women Need More Investment Opportunities says Princess Hissa". *Arab News*. 1 May 2003.

National Commercial Bank (NCB). *"Saudi Economic Perspectives"*. 1st Quarter 2003. Issue No.1 Volume No.2, Jeddah 2003.

National Commercial Bank (NCB). "Performance of Saudi banks during the first nine months 2002". *Market Review and Outlook*. December 2002.

National Commercial Bank (NCB). "What is Monetary Policy and Fiscal Policy? How does it work in the U.S. and Saudi Arabia?". *Saudi Economic Review*. Third/Fourth Quarter, 2001.

National Commercial Bank (NCB). "The Evolving role of Financial Institutions in the New Decade". *NCB*. Jeddah. First Quarter 2001.

National Commercial Bank (NCB). "The Mutual Funds Market in Saudi Arabia". *The NCB Economist*. Second Quarter, 2000.

Nazir, H. "The Role of Public-Private Partnership in Realizing Vision". Nazer Group. *Future Vision of Saudi Arabia*, Riyadh. Oct. 2002.

Netton, Ian Richard . *"Arabia and the Gulf: From Traditional Society to Modern States"*. London, Croom Helm, 1986

Newberry, David. "Oil Prices, Cartels, and the Problem of Dynamic Inconsistency". *Economic Journal,* 91, 363.September 1981.

Niblock, Tim. *"Social and Economic Development in the Arab Gulf"*. London: Croom Helm, 1980.

Niblock, Tim, (ed). *"State, Society, and the Economy in Saudi Arabia"*. London: Croom Helm, 1982.

Nojaidi, A, Al. "Experience and Vision in Foreign Investment Development and Export Promotion". Saudi Fund for Development and Export Promotion - A SABIC Perspective". SABIC. *Future Vision of Saudi Arabia*. Riyadh. Oct. 2002.

Nowaiser, Khalid,Al. "Terrorism in Saudi Arabia: Causes and Solutions". *Arab News*. 10 January 2004.

Nur, Uthman. *"The Labor Force in GCC Countries: Present and Future,"* Secretariat-General of the Arab Gulf Cooperation Council, 1995.

Organization of Petroleum Exporting Countries (OPEC). *Annual Reports*. Various Years. Vienna.

Osama, Abdul Rahman. *"The Dilemma of Development in the Arabian Peninsula"*. London: Croom Helm. 1987.

Ostapski,S.A,Oliver, J., Gonzales,G.T. "The Legal and Ethical Components of Executive Decision Making : A Course for Business Managers". *Journal of Business Ethics*. 15:571-579. 1996.

O'Sullivan, Edmund. "Crisis talks end, calm descends' .MEED Special Report: Saudi Arabia. *Middle East Economic Digest.* 8 November 1996.

O'Sullivan, Edmund. "Economic Offset in the GCC States: Issues, Challenges and Opportunities". *Way Ahead Conference,* Manama, Bahrain, pp. 1 - 10, March 1995.

O'Sullivan, Edmund. "GCC banks and the Offset Factor". *MEED,* Volume 39, No. 14, pp. 4 - 6. 1987.

O'Sullivan, Edmund. *"Saudi Arabia"*. MEED, London, 1993

Oweiss, Ibrahim M. "Economics of Petrodollars," in Haleh Esfandiari and A. L. Udovitch (ed) *The Economic Dimensions of Middle Eastern History"*. pp.179-197. Princeton, NJ: Darwin Press, 1990.

Oweiss, Ibrahim M. "Recent Developments of Crude Oil Prices". *Arab Bankers Association of North America,* vol. XIII, no. 3. 1996.

Oweiss, Ibrahim M. "The Arab Gulf Economies: Challenges and Perspectives". *The Emirates Center for Strategic Studies and Research.* Abu Dhabi. 2000.

Owen, Roger, and Pamuk Sevket. "A History of Middle East Economies in the Twenty First Century". *IB Tauris.* 1998.

Parker, Mustak. "Kingdom is Gearing Up for New IPO's*". Arab News*. 23 August 2004.

Parker, Mushtak. "Liberalization poses challenges to Saudi Banking sector. " *Arab News.* 12 July 2004.

Parker, Mushtak. "Kuwait Islamic Banking Law Opens Doors for Others. " *Arab News.* 19 May 2003.

Parker, Mushtak. "Saudi Insurance Market set for Boost ". *Arab News.* 17 June 2002.

Parker, Mushtak. "GCC Markets Enjoy Boom in Initial Public Offerings". *Arab News.* 25 October 2004.

Parra, Franscisco. "Oil Politics: A Modern History of Petroleum". *IB Tauris.* 2004.

Patrick, H.T. "Financial Development and Economic Growth in Underdeveloped Countries". *Economic Development and Cultural Change.* Vol. 14. No. 2 pp.174-177. 1996.

PFC Energy. "Saudi Arabia: Another Year of Budget Stability". Washington DC. 30 December 2003.

Pike, D. "Saudi Offset Deals Get off the Ground". *MEED.* pp. 4 - 5. Sept. 1989.

Power, Colin. "Higher education: Future vision". Paper presented at the Riyadh Conference on Higher Education, 22-25 February 1998.

Presley, John. R. *"Guide to the Saudi Arabian Economy"*. London: Macmillan, 1989.

Qedaihy, Anees. "SR100 Million Needed for Insurance Companies". *Arab News.* 23 September 2002.

Qedaihy, Anees. "New Law to double Insurance Market. " *Arab News.* 31 October 2001.

Quandt, William B. "*Saudi Arabia in the 1980s: Foreign Policy, Security, and Oil*". Washington, DC: Brookings Institution, 1982.

Qudsi, Sulayman, Al. "Labor Market Policies and Development in GCC: Does International Policy Consistency Matter?", in Julia Devlin, (ed). *Gulf Economies: Strategies for Growth in the 21st Century* .Center for Contemporary Arab Studies. Washington: Georgetown University,1977.

Qusti, Raid. "Nothing But Talk". *Arab News.* 16 June 2004.

Qusti, Raid. "Time to Stand Up and be Counted". *Arab News.* 14 April 2004.

Qusti, Raid. "Al-Ikhbariya Makes Waves". *Arab News.* 13 January 2004.

Qusti, Raid. "Dictates of Tradition". *Arab News.* 9 July 2003.

Qusti, Raid. "Tax on Foreign Firms Slashed". *Arab News.* 29 April 2003.

Qusti, Raid. "Who Are We?" *Arab News.* 16 July 2003.

Radwan, Ismail. "Small and Medium Enterprise Development: A Vision for Action in Saudi Arabia". World Bank. *Future Vision of Saudi Arabia*, Riyadh. Oct. 2002.

Ramady, M, Sahlawi, M, Al. "Education as a Force for Economic Change in an Oil Based Economy: A case study of Saudi Arabia". *Journal of Energy and Development.* Volume 30. No.2. Spring 2005.

Ramady, M. "Components of Technology Transfer: A Comparative Analysis of Offset and Non-Offset Companies in Saudi Arabia". *World Review of Science, Technology and Sustainable Development.* Volume 1. No.3. 2004

Ramady, M. "Government Finances: A Case Study of Saudi Arabian Budgetary Reforms". *Business & Economics Society International* . Anthology 2004.

Ramazani, R.K. "*The Gulf Cooperation Council: Record and Analysis*", University Press of Virginia, 1988.

Rashid, Abdulrahman. "Compassion for Expatriate Labor". *Arab News.* 24 July 2004.

Rasheed, M, Al. "*A History of Saudi Arabia*". Cambridge University Press. 2002

Reuters. "Crude Oil Races to New $49 High". London. 21 August 2004.

Reuters. "Historic WTO Pact on the Cards". London 1 August 2004.

Reuters. "Saudi Cabinet approves insurance, mining sell-offs". London, 24 May 2004.

Reuters. "S&P Affirms Ratings on Saudi Arabia". London, 24 April 2004.

Reuters. "Saudi Arabia's debt rating upgraded". London, 17 June 2003.

Reuters. "Kingdom scraps $ 15 Billion Exxon-led Gas Deal". London. 6 June 2003.

Reuters. "Standard + Poor's Ratings to Saudi Arabia: Outlook Stable". London, 14 July 2003.

Reuters. "World Bank/IMF Meetings: Jobs Key to Middle East Growth". 19 September 2003.

Richard, Alan, and Waterbury, John. "*A Political Economy of the Middle East: State, Class, and Economic Development* ". Boulder, Colorado: Westview Press, 1990.

Richard, Frederick. "Future Strategy for the Industrial Sector 2020". UNIDO. *Future Vision of Saudi Arabia*, Riyadh. Oct. 2002.

Rofail, Maged. "The Economic Impact of Broadening and Deepening the Saudi Stock Market". *Unpublished MBA Dissertation*. King Fahd University of Petroleum and Minerals. June 2003.

Romer, Paul. "The Origins of Endogenous Growth "*.Journal of Economic Perspectives*. Pp 3-22. Winter, 1994.

Rostow, Walt, W. *"Economic Growth"*. Oxford University Press. 1970.

Rostow, Walt, W. *"The Stages of Economic Growth: A Non-Communist Manifesto"*. Cambridge University Press. 1960.

Rugh, William. "Emergence of a New Middle Class in Saudi Arabia". *The Middle East Journal*, 27 (1), 7-20. 1973.

Sachs, J.D. and A.M. Warner. "The Curse of Natural Resources". *European Economic Review*. 45: 827-838. 2001.

SAGIA (Saudi Arabian General Investment Authority). "Women Only Industrial City Planned in Riyadh". *SAGIA*. 13 June 2004.

SAGIA (Saudi Arabian General Investment Authority). "Jeddah to have First Industrial City for Women". *SAGIA*. 3 June 2004.

SAGIA (Saudi Arabian General Investment Authority). "Future of SME's". *SAGIA*. 8 March 2004.

SAGIA (Saudi Arabian General Investment Authority). "Jeddah Economic Forum Opens with Active Saudi Women Participation". *SAGIA*. 18 January 2004.

Sajini, Ismail. "Effects of WTO on Small and Medium Enterprises". *Arab News*. 19 January 2004.

Salah, Ahmed. "Economic Impact of joining WTO". Ministry of Planning. *Future Vision of Saudi Arabia*. Riyadh, Oct. 2002.

Salmi, Jamil. "Constructing Knowledge Societies: New Challenges for Tertiary Education". World Bank. *Future Vision of Saudi Arabia*. Riyadh. Oct. 2003.

SAMBA Financial Group. *"The Saudi Economy at Mid-year 2004"*. August 2004.

SAMBA Financial Group. *"The Saudi Economy: 2003 Performance, 2004 Forecast"*. Riyadh. February 2004.

Sanabary, Nagat, El. "Female education in Saudi Arabia and the reproduction of gender division". *Gender and Education*. No. 2, 1994.

Sandusky, M.U. "The Saudi Arabian Offset Program". *Executive Congress on International Business Offset in the Arabian Gulf*, International Business Communications. Abu Dhabi, May 5 - 7, 1996.

Sandwick, J.A. (ed.). *"The Gulf Cooperation Council: Moderation and Stability in an Interdependent World"*. Boulder, Colorado: Westview Press,1987

Saravia, Edgar. "Regulation and Competition". World Bank. *Future Vision of Saudi Arabia*. Riyadh, Oct. 2002.

Sassanpour, Cyrus, "Policy Challenges in the Gulf Cooperation Council Countries". *Washington: International Monetary Fund, 1996*

Saudi American Bank (SAMBA). *"The Saudi Arabia Economy"*. 3rd Quarter, 2003.

Saudi Arabia Ministry of Education. *"Education in the Kingdom of Saudi Arabia within the Last Hundred Years"*. Riyadh: Ministry of Education, 2001.

Saudi Arabian Monetary Agency (SAMA). *Annual Reports*. Various issues. Riyadh.

Saudi Arabian Monetary Agency (SAMA). *"A Case Study on Globalization and the Role of Institution building in the Financial Sector in Saudi Arabia"*. Riyadh. February 2004.

Saudi Arabian Monetary Agency (SAMA). *Thirty-Nine Annual Report*, 2003, *Fortieth Annual Report*, 2004.

Saudi Aramco. "Facts and Figures 2002". *Saudi Aramco.2003*.

Saudi Aramco. "Master Gas System". *Saudi Aramco*. 2003.

Saudi British Bank. "Special Report on Saudi Banks; 2003". Riyadh. May 2003.

Saudi British Bank. "The Al-Yamamah Economic Offset program". Jeddah, 2001.

Saudi Commerce and Economic Review. Dammam. *Various editions*.

Saudi Commerce and Economic Review. Volume No 118, Dammam, February 2004.

Saudi Economic Offset Committee. *"Offset Guidelines"*. Riyadh, 1985.

Saudi Embassy, London. www.saudiembassy.org.uk 2004.

Saudi Gazette. "Eight banks to merge within days". Jeddah . 7 June 2004.

Saudi Offset Economic Secretariat. "Seminar on the Offset Program". Riyadh. Undated.

Saudi Press Agency . "Saudis to Hold 65% Stake in Etisalaat Company". Riyadh. 11 August 2004.

Saudi Press Agency. "Kingdom Announces Regulations for Municipal Elections". Riyadh. 10 August 2004.

Saudi Press Agency. "Crown Prince Abdullah makes Historic Visit to Russia. " Riyadh. 2 September 2003.

Saudi Press Agency. "Offset Initiative provides Saudization Opportunities says Prince Sultan". Riyadh. May 16, 1997.

Saudi Press Agency. "Prince Fahd Bin Abdullah warns Offset Companies to speed up Saudization". Riyadh. February 26, 1997.

Sayigh, Yusif. *"The Arab Economy: Past Performance and Future Prospects"*. Oxford University Press, 1982.

Seznec, Jean-Francois. *"The Financial Markets of the Arabian Gulf"*. London Croom Helm. 1987.

Seznec, Jean-Francois. "WTO and the dangers to Privatization: An analysis of the Saudi Case". *SIPA*. Columbia University, 2002.

Seznec, Jean-Francois. "The Gulf Capital Markets at a Crossroads. *"Columbia Journal of World Business*, Vol.30 (Fall), pp. 6-14. 1995.

Shaban, A, R. Asaad, R., and Al-Qudsi, S. "The Challenges of Employment in the Arab Region". *International Labour Review*, Vol. 134, pp. 65-82. 1995.

Shaikh, Habib. "Saudis trained to control key SAMA Departments". *Arab News*. 9 June 2004.

Shaik, Said, Al. "Impact on oil prices on GCC Economies and Labor Markets". Unpublished presentation. Bahrain. July 2003.

Shaik, Said, Al. "Kingdom Budget: An Underlying Expansionary Stance". *Arab News*. 29 December 2003.

Sheikh, Said. "Structure of Gulf Banking and effects of Globalization and Financial Liberalization". *The NCB Economist*. Issue No. 2. Volume 9 March/April. 1999.

Sharif, Abdullah. "Shrouded in Secrecy". *Arab News*. 2nd July 2003.

Sharway, A. "In search of Better Performance in the Public Sector". Institute of Public Administration. *Future Vision of Saudi Arabia,* Riyadh. Oct. 2002.

Shatkin, Lawrence. "The world of work as viewed from Saudi Arabia". *Unpublished Research Mimeo.* Dec. 2002.

Sheikh, F, El and Abdelrahman, A, El. *"The Legal Regime for Foreign Private Investment in Saudi Arabia".* Cambridge University Press. 2003.

Sinclair, C.A. "Migrant workers' remittances in the Arab world: scale, significance and prediction", in B.R. Pridham (ed.), *The Arab Gulf and the Arab World,* London, Croom Helm, 1988.

Singh, H. and K. Jun. "Some New Evidence on Determinants of Foreign Direct Investment in Developing Countries". *Policy Research Working Paper.* 1531, World Bank, Washington DC. 1995.

Sirageldin, I and Y. Al-Ebraheem. "Budget deficit, resource gap and human resource development in oil economics", in Sirageldin, I (ed). *Population and Development in the Middle East and North Africa: Challenges for the Twenty-First Century.* Working Paper, Baltimore, John Hokins University, 1999.

Soufi, Wahib Abdulfattah and Mayer, Richard. *"Saudi Arabian Industrial Investment: An Analysis of Government-Business Relationship".* Quorum Books. 2002

Speakman, John. "Privatization and Private Sector Participation in Infrastructure: A Vision for Saudi Arabia". World Bank. *Future Vision of Saudi Arabia,* Riyadh. Oct. 2002.

Stevens, Paul John. *"The* Interaction between Oil Policy and Industrial Policy in Saudi Arabia", in Ragaei El Mallakh and Dorothea H. El Mallakh (ed) *Saudi Arabia: Energy, Development Planning, and Industrialization",* p.27-45. Lexington, Mass.Lexington Books, D.C. 1982.

Sugair, Ali, Al. "Saud Credit Bank and Small and Medium Sector Support Programmes". Saudi Credit Bank. *Future Vision of Saudi Arabia.* Riyadh. Oct. 2002.

Sugair, Hamad, Al. Secretary to Saudi Economic Offset Committee. *Correspondence.* Riyadh. 2003.

Sugair, Hamad, Al. "Indirect Offsets in Saudi Arabia: An Electronic Offset Company". *The Executive Congress on International Business and Offset in the Arabian Gulf.* International Business Communication, Abu Dhabi, May 5-7, 1996.

Suhaimi, Jammaz. "Consolidation , Competition, Foreign presence and systematic Stability in the Saudi Banking Industry". *SAMA.* Riyadh. 2002.

Sulaiman, Zaid, Al. "An Open Letter to All Foreigners". *Arab News.* 17 June 2004.

Taher, Nahed. "Saudi Arabian Budget and Challenges of Sustainable Growth". *Arab News.* 22 December 2003.

Thirwall, A.P. *"Growth and Development".* London. Macmillan, 1964.

Todaro, M. *"Economic Development".* London. Longmans. 1994.

Towajri H.A. Al. *"The labor market in Saudi Arabia: family effects, compensating wage differentials, and selective bias. "*Ph.D. Thesis, University of Oregon, 1992.

Trivedi, P. "In Search of Better Performance of Public Sector: Vision for improving Public Sector efficiency in the Kingdom of Saudi Arabia". World Bank. *Future Vision of Saudi Arabia*, Riyadh. Oct. 2002.

U.S. Department of Defense. "Proposed Foreign Military Sale to Saudi Arabia announced". *U.S. Department of Defense*. Washington.8 September 2002.

UAE Offset Group. "A Guide to Offsets in the United Arab Emirates". Abu Dhabi, 1994.

UNCTAD. *World Investment Report. 1999, 2000.*

United Nations Development Program (UNDP). *"Arab Human Development Report 2002".* New York: United Nations Development Program/Arab Fund for Economic and Social Development, 2002.

Whelan, John, (ed). *"Saudi Arabia".* London: MEED, 1981.

Wilson, J.S.G. *"Banking and Structure: A Comparative Analysis".* Croom Helm, London. 1986.

Wilson, Rodney and Malik, Monica, Al-Salamah, A, Al-Rajhi, A. *"Economic Development in Saudi Arabia".* Routledge Curzon, 2003.

Wilson, Rodney. *"Economic Development in the Middle East".* London Routledge, 1995.

Wilson, Rodney. "The Changing Composition and Direction of GCC Trade". *The Emirates Center for Strategic Studies and Research.* Abu Dhabi. 1998.

Wilson, Rodney. *"Banking and Finance in the Arab Middle East"* .London: Macmillan, 1983.

Wilson, Rodney. "Good International Governance: Implications for Saudi Arabia's Political Economy", in Najeim, T. *"Good Governance in the Middle East Oil Monarchies".* Routledge Curzon, 2003.

Wilson, Rodney, " Saudi Arabia: WTO Membership," *Oxford Analytica Daily Brief.* May 14, 1997.

Woodward, Peter. *"Oil and Labour in the Middle East-Saudi Arabia and the Oil Boom".* New York: Praeger, 1988.

World Bank. *"Global Development Finance".* Washington, 2001.

World Bank. *"A Population Perspective on Development in the Middle East and North Africa".* Washington, DC.: World bank, August 1994.

World Bank. *Global Development Prospects.* Various editions.

World Bank. *"Will Arab Workers Prosper or Be Left Out in the Twenty-First Century?"* Washington, DC: World Bank, 1995.

World Bank. *World Development Indicators.* Various editions.

World Bank. *"The East Asia Miracle: Economic Growth and Government Policies".* Washington. 1993.

World Economic Forum (ed) Schwals, Klaus. *"The Arab World Competitiveness Report 2002 - 2003".* New York, Oxford University Press, 2003.

World Trade Organization (WTO). *"World Trade in 2000: Overview".* www.wto.org

World Trade Organization (WTO). *"World Merchandise Exports by Region and Selected Economy. 1980,1985,1990,1995, and 1991-2001".* www.wto.org

World Trade Organization (WTO). *"World Merchandise Imports by Region and Selected Economy. 1980, 1985, 1990, 1995 and 1991-2001".* www.wto.org

Wright, Jr, J.W. with Hani Khashoggi and Christopher Vaughn. "Labor Constraints on Saudi Business Development" in J. W. Wright, Jr (ed), *Business Development in Saudi Arabia*. London, Macmillan .1996.

Wright, Jr. J.W. "*Business and Economic Development in Saudi Arabia*", Macmillan Press Ltd. 1996.

Yamamah Al, (magazine). "Al-Salaam Aircraft Company". No. 137, Year 52. December 28, 2002 .

Yamani, Mai. "*Changed Identities: The Challenge of the New Generation in Saudi Arabia*". London. The Royal Institute of International Affairs. 2000.

Yamani, Mai. "The New Generation in the GCC: the case of Saudi Arabia", in Rosemary Hollis (ed.), "*Oil and Regional Developments in the Gulf*". London, The Royal Institute of International Affairs, 1998.

Zamil , Abdullah . "Manufacturers Message : Saudization –Insight from Zamil Air Conditioners Experience". *First Contractors Saudization Forum*. Saudi Aramco. Dammam. 22 Dec. 2003.

Zamil, A, Al. "Petrochemicals Industry in the Kingdom: Past, Present and Future". Al Zamil Group. *Future Vision of Saudi Arabia*. Riyadh. Oct. 2002.

Zamil, Ahmed, Al. "Future of Labour Market in the Kingdom after a Generation". Ministry of Labour and Social Affairs. *Future Vision of Saudi Arabia*. Riyadh. Oct. 2002.

Zarouk, Jamal. "Prospects for Expansion of Trade in Services in the Saudi Economy". World Bank. *Future Vision of Saudi Arabia*. Riyadh, Oct. 2002.

Zulficar, M. "*Women in Development: A Legal Study*". UNICEF, New York. January 1995.

Index